Les voyelles anglaises / English vowels

[ɑː]	f*a*r	*â*me
[æ]	m*a*n	s*a*lle
[e]	g*e*t	s*e*c
		l*e*

... . / English ... phthongs

[aɪ]	t*i*me	a*ï*e
[aʊ]	cl*ou*d	c*ia*o
[eɪ]	n*a*me	n*e*z suivi d'un *y* court
[ɔɪ]	p*oi*nt	cow-b*oy*
[oʊ]	s*o*	*eau*

['] indique que la syllabe suivante est accentuée: *ability* [ə'bɪlɪtɪ]

Some French words starting with h have ' before the h. This ' is not part of the French word. It shows i) that a preceding vowel does not become an apostrophe and ii) that no elision takes place. (This is called an aspirated h).

'hanche	la hanche, les hanches [no z sound between *les* and *hanches*]
habit	l'habit, les habits [a z sound between *les* and *habits*]

Langenscheidt
Universal Dictionary

French

French – English
English – French

edited by the
Langenscheidt editorial staff

Langenscheidt
Munich · Vienna

Compiled by LEXUS with: / Réalisé par LEXUS:

Sandrine François · Jane Goldie
Claire Guerreau · Julie Le Boulanger
Peter Terrell

© 2017 Langenscheidt GmbH & Co. KG, Munich
Printed in Germany

17010

Contents / Table des matières

Abbreviations / Abréviations

and	&	et
see	→	voir
registered trademark	®	marque déposée
adjective	*adj*	adjectif
adverb	*adv*	adverbe
agriculture	AGR	agriculture
anatomy	ANAT	anatomie
architecture	ARCH	architecture
astronomy	ASTR	astronomie
astrology	ASTROL	astrologie
attributive	*atr*	devant le nom
motoring	AUTO	automobiles
aviation	AVIAT	aviation
biology	BIOL	biologie
botany	BOT	botanique
British English	*Br*	anglais britannique
chemistry	CHIM	chimie
commerce, business	COMM	commerce
computers, IT term	COMPUT	informatique
conjunction	*conj*	conjonction
cooking	CUIS	cuisine
economics	ÉCON	économie
education	EDU	éducation
education	ÉDU	éducation
electricity	ÉL	électricité
electricity	ELEC	électricité
especially	*esp*	surtout
euphemism	*euph*	euphémisme
familiar, colloquial	F	familier
feminine	*f*	féminin
figurative	*fig*	figuré

finance	FIN	finance
formal	*fml*	langage formel
feminine plural	*fpl*	féminin pluriel
geography	GEOG	géographie
geography	GÉOGR	géographie
geology	GÉOL	géologie
geometry	GÉOM	géométrie
grammar	GRAM	grammaire
historical	HIST	historique
IT term	INFORM	informatique
interjection	*int*	interjection
invariable	*inv*	invariable
law	JUR	juridique
law	LAW	juridique
linguistics	LING	linguistique
literary	*litt*	littéraire
masculine	*m*	masculin
nautical	MAR	marine
mathematics	MATH	mathématiques
medicine	MED	médecine
medicine	MÉD	médecine
masculine and feminine	*m/f*	masculin et féminin
military	MIL	militaire
motoring	MOT	automobiles
masculine plural	*mpl*	masculin pluriel
music	MUS	musique
noun	*n*	nom
nautical	NAUT	marine
plural noun	*npl*	nom pluriel
singular noun	*nsg*	nom singulier
oneself	o.s.	se, soi
popular, slang	P	populaire
pejorative	*pej*	péjoratif

pejorative	*péj*	péjoratif
pharmacy	PHARM	pharmacie
photography	PHOT	photographie
physics	PHYS	physique
plural	*pl*	pluriel
politics	POL	politique
preposition	*prep*	préposition
preposition	*prép*	préposition
pronoun	*pron*	pronom
psychology	PSYCH	psychologie
something	*qch*	quelque chose
someone	*qn*	quelqu'un
radio	RAD	radio
railroad	RAIL	chemin de fer
religion	REL	religion
singular	*sg*	singulier
someone	s.o.	quelqu'un
sports	SP	sport
something	*sth*	quelque chose
subjunctive	*subj*	subjonctif
noun	*subst*	substantif
theater	THEA	théâtre
theater	THÉÂT	théâtre
technology	TECH	technique
telecommunications	TÉL	télécommunications
telecommunications	TELEC	télécommunications
typography, typesetting	TYP	typographie
television	TV	télévision
vulgar	V	vulgaire
auxiliary verb	*v/aux*	verbe auxiliaire
intransitive verb	*v/i*	verbe intransitif
transitive verb	*v/t*	verbe transitif
zoology	ZO	zoologie

A

à *lieu* in; *direction* to; *au bout de la rue* at/to the end of the street; *~ 2 heures d'ici* 2 hours from here; *~ cinq heures* at five o'clock; *~ Noël* at Christmas; *~ demain* until tomorrow; *c'est ~ moi* it's mine, it belongs to me; *aux cheveux blonds* with blonde hair; *~ pied* on foot; *~ dix euros* at *ou* for ten euros

abaissement *m* lowering; *(humiliation)* abasement; **abaisser** lower; *fig (humilier)* humble; **s'~** drop; *(se confier)* open up; **s'~ à** give way to

abandonner abandon; *pouvoir* give up; SP withdraw from; **s'~** *(se confier)* open up; **s'~ à** give way to

abasourdi amazed

abat-jour *m* (lamp)shade

abattre *arbre* fell; AVIAT shoot down; *animal* slaughter; *péj (tuer)* kill; *fig (épuiser)* exhaust; *(décourager)* dishearten; **s'~** collapse

abbaye *f* abbey

abcès *m* abscess

abdomen *m* abdomen

abeille *f* bee

aberrant F absurd

abêtir make stupid

abîmer spoil, ruin; **s'~** be ruined; *d'aliments* spoil

aboiement *m* barking

abolir abolish; **abolition** *f* abolition

abominable appalling

abondance *f* abundance

abonné, -e *m/f* subscriber; **abonnement** *m* subscription; *de transport, de spectacles* season ticket; **abonner**: **s'~ à** subscribe to

abord *m*: **d'~** first; **au premier ~** at first sight; **~s** surroundings; **aborder 1** *v/t (prendre d'assaut)* board; *(heurter)* collide with; *fig: question* tackle; *personne* approach **2** *v/i* land *(à* at)

aboutir *d'un projet* succeed; **~ à** end at; *fig* lead to; **aboutissement** *m (résultat)* result

aboyer bark

abréger abridge

abréviation *f* abbreviation

abri *m* shelter; **être sans ~** be homeless

abricot *m* apricot; **abricotier** *m* apricot (tree)

abriter *(loger)* take in, shelter; ~ **de** (*protéger*) shelter from; **s'~** take shelter

abrupt abrupt; *pente* steep

abruti stupid; **abrutir:** ~ **qn** be bad for s.o.'s brain; (*surmener*) exhaust s.o.

absence *f* absence; **absent** absent; *air* absent-minded; **absenter:** **s'~** leave, go away

absolu absolute; **absolument** absolutely

absorber absorb; *nourriture* eat; *boisson* drink; **s'~ dans** be absorbed in

abstenir: **s'~** POL abstain; **s'~ de faire qc** refrain from doing sth; **abstention** *f* POL abstention

abstrait abstract

absurdité *f* absurdity; **~(s)** nonsense

abus *m* abuse; ~ **de confiance** breach of trust; **abuser** overstep the mark; ~ **de qc** misuse ou abuse sth; **s'~** be mistaken; **abusif, -ive** excessive; *emploi d'un mot* incorrect

académie *f* academy

acajou *m* mahogany

accabler: *être accablé* **de** weighed down by; ~ **qn de qc** heap sth on s.o.

accalmie *f aussi fig* lull

accaparer ÉCON, *fig* monopolize

accéder: ~ **à** reach, get to; IN-FORM access; *à l'indépendance, au pouvoir* gain; *d'un chemin* lead to

accélérateur *m* AUTO gas pedal, *Br* accelerator; **accélérer** *aussi* AUTO accelerate

accent *m* accent; (*intonation*) stress; **mettre l'~ sur qc** *fig* put the emphasis on sth; **accentuer** *syllabe* stress, accentuate

acceptable acceptable; **accepter** accept; (*reconnaître*) agree; ~ **de faire** agree to do

accès *m aussi* INFORM access; MÉD fit

accessoire 1 *adj* incidental **2** *m* detail; **~s** accessories; THÉÂT props

accident *m* accident; *événement fortuit* mishap; *par* ~ by accident, accidentally; **accidentel, ~le** accidental

acclamation *f* acclamation; **~s** cheers, cheering; **acclamer** cheer

acclimater: **s'~** become acclimatized

accolade *f* embrace; *signe* brace, *Br* curly bracket

accommodation *f* adaptation; **accommoder** adapt; CUIS prepare; **s'~ à** adapt to; **s'~ de** make do with

accompagnateur, -trice *m/f* guide; MUS accompanist; **accompagner** accompany

accomplir accomplish; *souhait* realize

accord *m* agreement; MUS chord; **d'~** OK, alright; *être d'~* agree; *tomber d'~* come to an agreement; **accordé:**

(*bien*) ~ in tune

accordéon accordion

accorder *crédit* grant; GRAM make agree; MUS tune; **s'~** get on; GRAM agree; **s'~** *qc* allow o.s. sth

accouchement *m* birth; **accoucher** give birth (*de* to)

accouder: **s'~** lean (one's elbows); **accoudoir** *m* armrest

accoupler connect; **s'~** BIOL mate

accourir come running

accoutumance *f* MÉD dependence; **accoutumer**: ~ *qn* à *qc* get s.o. used to sth; **s'~** à *qc* get used to sth

accrocher *manteau* hang up; AUTO collide with; **s'~** à hang on to; *fig* cling to

accroître increase; **s'~** grow

accroupir: **s'~** crouch, squat

accueil *m* reception, welcome; **accueillir** greet, welcome

accumulation *f* accumulation; **accumuler** accumulate; **s'~** accumulate

accusation *f* accusation; JUR prosecution; *plainte* charge; **accusé**, ~e *m/f* JUR: *l'~* the accused **2** COMM: **accusé** *m* **de réception** acknowledgement (of receipt); **accuser** (*incriminer*) accuse (*de* of); (*faire ressortir*) emphasize

acerbe caustic

acéré sharp

acharnement *m* grim deter-

mination; **acharner**: **s'~** à *faire qc* be bent on doing sth; **s'~** *sur ou* **contre** *qn* pick on s.o.

achat *m* purchase; *faire des* **~s** go shopping

acheter buy

achever finish; **s'~** finish

acide 1 *adj* sour; CHIM acidic **2** *m* CHIM acid

acier *m* steel

acné *f* acne

à-coup *m* jerk; *par* **~s** in fits and starts

acoustique acoustic

acquéreur *m* purchaser; **acquérir** acquire; *droit* win

acquiescer: ~ à agree to

acquis acquired; *résultats* achieved

acquisition *f* acquisition

acquitter *facture* pay; JUR acquit; **s'~** *de* carry out; *dette* pay

âcre acrid; *goût*, *fig* bitter; **âcreté** *f* bitterness

acrobate *m/f* acrobat; **acrobatie** *f* acrobatics *pl*

acte *m* (*action*) action, deed; (*document officiel*) deed; THÉÂT act; ~ **de mariage** marriage certificate

acteur, **-trice** *m/f* actor; actress

actif, **-ive 1** *adj* active **2** *m* COMM assets *pl*

action *f* action; COMM share; **~s** stock, shares *pl*; **actionnaire** *m/f* shareholder

actionner operate; *alarme etc*

activer   12

activate

activer (*accélérer*) speed up
activité *f* activity
actualiser update
actualité *f* current events *pl*;
~s TV news *sg*
actuel, **~le** current, present;
(*d'actualité*) topical; **actuellement** currently, at present
adaptation *f* adaptation;
adapter adapt; **s'~ à** adapt
to
addition *f* addition; *au restaurant* check, *Br* bill; **additionner** add
adéquat suitable; *montant*
adequate
adhérent, **~e** *m/f* member;
adhérer stick, adhere (*à* to)
adhésif, **-ive 1** *adj* sticky, adhesive **2** *m* adhesive
adieu *m* goodbye; **faire ses
~x** say one's goodbyes (*à
qn* to s.o.)
adjectif *m* GRAM adjective
adjoint, **~e** *m/f & adj* assistant, deputy
admettre (*autoriser*) allow;
(*accueillir*) admit, allow in;
(*reconnaître*) admit
administrateur, **-trice** *m/f*
administrator; **administratif**, **-ive** administrative; **administration** *f* administration; (*direction*) management, running
admirateur, **-trice 1** *adj* admiring **2** *m/f* admirer; **admiration** *f* admiration; **admirer**
admire

admissible *candidat* eligible;
ce n'est pas **~** that's unacceptable
admission *f* admission
adolescence *f* adolescence;
adolescent, **~e** *m/f* adolescent, teenager
adopter adopt; **adoption** *f*
adoption
adorable adorable; **adorer**
REL worship; *fig* (*aimer*)
adore
adosser lean; **s'~ contre** *ou à*
lean against ou on
adoucir soften; **s'~ du temps**
become milder
adrénaline *f* adrenalin
adresse *f* address; (*habileté*)
skill; **~ électronique** email
address
adresser *lettre* address (*à* to);
remarque direct (*à* at); **~ la
parole à** address, speak to;
s'~ à qn apply to s.o.; (*être
destiné à*) be aimed at s.o.
adroit skillful, *Br* skilful
adulte 1 *adj* adult; *plante* mature **2** *m/f* adult, grown-up
adultère 1 *adj* adulterous **2** *m*
adultery
adverbe *m* GRAM adverb
adversaire *m/f* opponent, adversary
adversité *f* adversity
aération *f* ventilation; **aérer**
ventilate; *literie*, *pièce* air
aérien, **~ne** air *atr*; *vue* aerial
aérobic *f* aerobics
aérodynamique aerodynamic

aéronautique aeronautical
aéroport *m* airport
aérosol *m* aerosol
affable affable
affaiblir weaken; **s'~** weaken
affaire *f* (*question*) matter, business; (*entreprise*) business; *marché* deal; (*bonne occasion*) bargain; JUR case; (*scandale*) affair, business; **~s biens personnels** things, belongings; **les ~s étrangères** foreign affairs; **affairer: s'~** busy o.s.
affaisser: s'~ *du terrain* subside; *d'une personne* collapse
affamé hungry (**de** for)
affectation *f d'une chose* allocation; *d'un employé* assignment; MIL posting; (*pose*) affectation; **affecter** (*destiner*) allocate; *employé* assign; MIL post; (*émouvoir*) affect
affectif, -ive emotional
affection *f* affection; MÉD complaint
affectueux, -euse affectionate
affermir strengthen
affichage *m* billposting; IN-FORM display; **affiche** *f* poster; **afficher** *affiche* stick up; *attitude*, INFORM display
affilier: s'~ à *club* join; **être affilié à** be a member of
affiner refine
affinité *f* affinity
affirmatif, -ive affirmative;

personne assertive; **affirmation** *f* statement; **affirmer** (*prétendre*) maintain; *autorité* assert
affligeant distressing, painful; **affliger** distress
affluence *f*: **heures fpl d'~** rush hour *sg*; **affluent** *m* tributary; **affluer** come together
affolement *m* panic; **affoler** (*bouleverser*) madden, drive to distraction; *d'une foule, d'un cheval* panic; **s'~** panic
affranchir free; *lettre* meter, *Br* frank
affreux, -euse horrible; *peur, mal de tête* terrible
affront *m* insult, affront; **affronter** confront, face; SP meet; **s'~** confront ou face each other; SP meet
afin: **~ de faire** in order to do, so as to do; **~ que** (+ *subj*) so that
africain, ~e African; **Africain, ~e** *m/f* African; **Afrique** *f*: **l'~** Africa
agaçant annoying; **agacement** *m* annoyance; **agacer** annoy; (*taquiner*) tease
âge *m* age; **Moyen-Âge** Middle Ages *pl*; **personnes fpl du troisième ~** senior citizens; **quel ~ a-t-il?** how old is he?, what age is he?; **âgé** elderly; **~ de deux ans** aged two, two years old
agence *f* agency; *d'une banque* branch; **~ immobilière**

realtor's, *Br* estate agent's; **~ matrimoniale** marriage bureau

agenda *m* diary; **~ électronique** (personal) organizer

agenouiller: s'~ kneel (down)

agent *m* agent; **~ de change** stockbroker; **~ immobilier** realtor, *Br* real estate agent; **~ de police** police officer

agglomération *f* built-up area; *concentration de villes* conurbation

aggraver make worse; **s'~** worsen

agile agile; **~ité** *f* agility

agios *mpl* ÉCON bank charges

agir act; **~ sur qn** affect s.o.; *il s'agit de* it's about

agitation *f* hustle and bustle; POL unrest; *(nervosité)* agitation; **agiter** *bouteille* shake; *mouchoir, main* wave; *(préoccuper, énerver)* upset; **s'~** *d'un enfant* fidget; *(s'énerver)* get upset

agneau *m* lamb

agonie *f* death throes *pl*

agrafer *vêtements* fasten; *papier* staple; **agrafeuse** *f* stapler

agrandir enlarge; **agrandissement** *m* enlargement; *d'une ville* expansion

agréable pleasant (*à* to)

agrément *m* approval, consent; *les ~s (attraits)* the delights

agresser attack; **agresseur** *m* attacker; *pays* aggressor;

agressif, -ive aggressive; **agression** *f* attack; PSYCH stress

agriculteur *m* farmer; **agriculture** *f* agriculture, farming

agrumes *mpl* citrus fruit

ahuri astounded; **ahurissant** astounding

aide 1 *f* help, assistance; **à l'~ de qc** with the help of sth; **avec l'~ de qn** with s.o.'s help 2 *m/f (assistant)* assistant; **aider** 1 *v/t* help; **~ qn à faire qc** help s.o. to do sth; **aider qn à faire qc** use sth 2 *v/i* help; **~ à qc** contribute to sth

aïeul, ~e *m/f* ancestor; **aïeux** ancestors

aigle *m* eagle

aigre sour; *vent* bitter; *critique* sharp; *voix* shrill

aigu, ~ë sharp; *son* high-pitched; *conflit* bitter; *intelligence* keen; MÉD, GÉOM acute

aiguille *f* needle; *d'une montre* hand; *tour* spire

aiguiser sharpen; *fig: appétit* whet

ail *m* garlic

aile *f* wing; AUTO fender, *Br* wing

ailier *m* SP winger, winger

ailleurs somewhere else, elsewhere; **d'~** besides; **par ~** moreover

aimable kind

aimant *m* magnet

aimer like; *parent, enfant, mari etc* love; **~ mieux** prefer

aine f groin

aîné, **~e 1** adj elder; *de trois ou plus* eldest **2** m/f elder/ eldest; *il est mon ~ de deux ans* he is two years older than me

ainsi this way, thus *fml*; **~ que** and, as well as

air m air; *aspect* look; MUS tune; *se donner des ~s* give o.s. airs; **airbag** m airbag

aire f area; **~ de jeu** playground

aisance f ease; *(richesse)* wealth

aise f ease; *être à l'~* be comfortable; *être mal à l'~* be uncomfortable; *prendre ses ~s* make o.s. at home

aisselle f armpit

ajourner postpone *(de* for); JUR adjourn

ajouter add; *s'~* be added to

ajuster adjust; *vêtement* alter; *(viser)* aim at; *(joindre)* fit *(à to)*

alarme f alarm; *donner l'~* raise the alarm; **~** *antivol* burglar alarm; **alarmer** alarm; *s'~ de* be alarmed by

album m album

alcool m alcohol; **alcoolique** adj e m/f alcoholic; **alcoolisme** alcoholism; **alco(o)-test** m Breathalyzer®, *Br* Breathalyser®

aléatoire uncertain; INFORM, MATH random

alentour: **~s** *mpl* surroundings *pl*; *aux ~s de* in the vi-

cinity of; *(autour de)* about

alerte 1 adj alert **2** f alarm; **~** *à la bombe* bomb scare; **alerter** alert

algèbre f algebra

Algérie f: *l'~* Algeria; **algérien**, **~ne** Algerian; **Algérien**, **~ne** m/f Algerian

algue f BOT seaweed

aligner TECH align *(sur* with); *(mettre sur une ligne)* line up; *s'~* line up; *s'~ sur qc* align o.s. with sth

aliment m foodstuff; **~s** food; **alimentation** f food; *en eau, en électricité* supply; **~** *de base* staple diet; **alimenter** feed; *en eau, en électricité* supply *(en* with); *conversation* keep going

alinéa m paragraph

allaiter breast-feed

allécher tempt

allée f *(avenue)* path; **~s et venues** comings and goings

allégé *yaourt* low-fat; *confiture* low-sugar; **alléger** lighten; *impôt, tension* reduce

allègre cheerful

Allemagne f: *l'~* Germany; **allemand**, **~e 1** adj German **2** m *langue* German; **Allemand**, **~e** m/f German

aller 1 v/i go; **~** *en voiture* go by car; **~** *chercher* go for, fetch; *comment allez--vous?* how are you?; *je vais bien* I'm fine; *ça va?* is that OK?; *(comment te portes--tu?)* how are you?; *ça va*

bien merci fine, thanks; **~
bien avec** go well with; **on
y va!** F let's go!; **allez!** go
on!; **allons!** come on!; **allons donc!** come now!;
s'en~ leave; *d'une tâche* disappear; **cette couleur te va
bien** that color really suits
you **2** v/aux: **je vais partir
demain** I'm going to leave
tomorrow, I'm leaving to-
morrow **3** m: **~ et retour**
round trip, Br return trip;
billet ~ retour round-trip
ticket, Br return (ticket); **~
simple** one-way ticket, Br
single; **match** m **~** away game

allergie f allergy; **allergique**
allergic (**à** to)

alliance f **1** POL alliance; (*mariage*) marriage; (*anneau*)
wedding ring; **allié, ~e 1**
adj allied; *famille* related
by marriage **2** m/f ally; *famille* relative by marriage

allô hello

allocation f allowance; **~
chômage** workers' compensation, Br unemployment
benefit

allonger lengthen, make
longer; *jambes* stretch out;
s'~ get longer; (*s'étendre*)
lie down

allumage m AUTO ignition; **allumer 1** v/t light; *chauffage,
télévision etc* turn on **2** v/i
turn the lights on; **allumette**
f match

allure f (*démarche*) walk; (*vi-

tesse*) speed; (*air*) appearance; **avoir de l'~** have style

allusion f allusion

alors then; (*par conséquence*)
so; **~ que** temps when; *opposition* while

alouette f lark

alourdir make heavy

Alpes fpl: **les ~** the Alps

alphabet m alphabet

alpinisme m mountain-
eering; **alpiniste** m/f mountaineer

altercation f argument

altérer *denrées* spoil; *couleur*
fade; *vérité* distort; *texte* alter

alternance f alternation; *de
cultures* rotation; **alternative** f alternative; **alterner** alternate

altitude f altitude

alto m alto; *à cordes* viola

altruisme m altruism

aluminium m aluminum, Br
aluminium

amabilité f kindness

amadouer softsoap

amaigri thinner; **amaigrir: ~
qn** cause s.o. to lose weight;
s'~ lose weight, get thinner

amalgame m mixture, amal-
gamation

amande f almond

amant m lover

amarrer MAR moor

amas m pile; **amasser** amass

amateur m lover; *non professionnel* amateur; **en ~** as a
hobby

ambassade f embassy; **ambassadeur, -drice** m/f ambassador

ambiance f (atmosphère) atmosphere

ambigu, -ë ambiguous; **ambiguïté** f ambiguity

ambitieux, -euse 1 adj ambitious **2** m/f ambitious person; **ambition** f ambition

ambivalence f ambivalence

ambulance f ambulance; **ambulancier** m paramedic, Br ambulance man

ambulant traveling, Br travelling

âme f soul; **état** m **d'~** state of mind; **~ charitable** do-gooder

amélioration f improvement; **améliorer** improve; **s'~** improve, get better

aménager appartement arrange, lay out; terrain develop; vieille maison convert

amende f fine

amender improve; projet de loi amend

amener bring; (causer) cause; **s'~** turn up

amer, -ère bitter

américain, ~e 1 adj American **2** m LING American English; **Américain, ~e** m/f American; **américaniser** Americanize

amérindien, ~ne Native American; **Amérindien, ~ne** m/f Native American

Amérique f: **l'~** America; **l'~**

centrale Central America; **l'~ latine** Latin America; **l'~ du Nord** North America; **l'~ du Sud** South America

amertume f bitterness

ameublement m (meubles) furniture

ameuter rouse

ami, ~e 1 m/f friend; (amant) boyfriend; (maîtresse) girlfriend; **devenir ~ avec qn** make friends with s.o. **2** adj friendly; **amiable: à l'~** amicably; JUR out of court; arrangement amicable, friendly; JUR out-of-court

amical, ~e 1 adj friendly **2** f association

amincir 1 v/t make thinner; d'une robe make look thinner **2** v/i get thinner

amiral m admiral

amitié f friendship; **~s** best wishes

amnésie f amnesia

amnistie f amnesty

amoindrir diminish, lessen; **s'~** diminish

amollir soften

amonceler pile up

amont: en ~ upstream (de from)

amoral amoral

amorcer begin; INFORM boot up

amorphe sans énergie listless

amortir choc cushion; bruit muffle; douleur dull; dettes pay off; **amortisseur** m AUTO shock absorber

amour *m* love; **~s** love life; **faire l'~** make love; **amoureux, -euse** *regard* loving; *vie* love *atr*; *personne* in love (**de** with); **tomber ~** fall in love; **amour-propre** *m* pride

amphithéâtre *m* amphitheater, *Br* amphitheatre; *d'université* lecture hall

ample *vêtements* loose; *sujet* broad; *ressources* ample; **ampleur** *f d'un désastre* etc scale

amplification *f* TECH amplification; *fig* growth; **amplifier** TECH amplify; *fig: problème* magnify; *idée* expand

ampoule *f sur la peau* blister; *de médicament* ampoule; *lampe* bulb

amputer amputate; *fig* cut

amusant funny, amusing

amuse-gueule *m* appetizer

amuser amuse; **s'~** have a good time, enjoy o.s.; **s'~ à faire qc** have fun doing sth, enjoy doing sth; **faire qch pour s'~** do sth for fun

amygdale *f* ANAT tonsil; **amygdalite** *f* tonsillitis

an *m* year; **le jour ou le premier de l'~** New Year's Day; **elle a 15 ~s** she's 15 (years old)

analogie *f* analogy; **analogique** INFORM analog; **analogue** analogous (**à** with)

analphabète illiterate; **analphabétisme** *m* illiteracy

analyse *f* analysis; *de sang* test; **analyser** analyze, *Br* analyse; *sang* test; **analytique** analytical

ananas *m* BOT pineapple

anarchie *f* anarchy; **anarchiste** *m* anarchist

anatomie *f* anatomy

ancêtres *mpl* ancestors

anchois *m* anchovy

ancien, ~ne old; *de l'Antiquité* ancient; **anciennement** formerly

ancre *f* anchor

Andorre *f: l'~* Andorra

âne *m* donkey; *fig* ass

anéantir annihilate

anecdote *f* anecdote

anémie *f* MÉD anemia, *Br* anaemia

anesthésie *f* MÉD anesthesia, *Br* anaesthesia

ange *m* angel

angine *f* MÉD throat infection; **~ de poitrine** angina

anglais, ~e 1 *adj* English **2** *m langue* English; **Anglais, ~e** *m/f* Englishman; Englishwoman; **les ~** the English

angle *m* angle; *(coin)* corner; **~ mort** blind spot

Angleterre *f: l'~* England

anglophone English-speaking

angoisse *f* anguish; **angoisser** distress

anguille *f* eel

anguleux, -euse angular

animal 1 *m* animal; **~ domestique** pet **2** *adj* animal *atr*

animateur, -trice *m/f d'une*

émission host, presenter; *d'une discussion* moderator; *d'activités culturelles, d'une entreprise* leader; *de dessin animé* animator; **animation** *f (vivacité)* liveliness; *de mouvements* hustle and bustle; *de dessin animé* animation; **animé** *rue, quartier* busy; *conversation* lively, animated; **animer** *fête* liven up; *(stimuler)* animate; *discussion, émission* host; **s'~** come to life; *d'une personne, discussion* become animated

animosité *f* animosity

anneau *m* ring

année *f* year; **les ~s 90** the 90s; **bonne ~!** happy New Year!

annexe *f d'un bâtiment* annex; *d'un document* appendix; *d'une lettre* enclosure

anniversaire *m* birthday; *d'un événement* anniversary

annonce *f* announcement; *dans journal* ad (*vertisement*); *(présage)* sign; **petites ~s** classified ads; **annoncer** announce; **s'~ bien/mal** be off to a good/bad start

annotation *f* annotation

annuaire *m*: **~ du téléphone** phone book

annuel, ~le annual, yearly

annulaire *m* ring finger

annulation *f* cancellation; *d'un mariage* annulment; **annuler** cancel; *mariage* an-

nul

anodin harmless; *personne* insignificant; *blessure* slight

anomalie *f* anomaly

anonyme anonymous; **société** *f* **~** incorporated *ou Br* limited company

anorak *m* anorak

anorexie *f* anorexia; **anorexique** anorexic

anormal abnormal

anse *f d'un panier etc* handle; GÉOGR cove

antagonisme *m* antagonism

antarctique 1 *adj* Antarctic **2** *m* **l'Antarctique** Antarctica, the Antarctic

antécédents *mpl* history

antenne *f* ZO antenna, feeler; TV, *d'une radio* antenna, *Br* aerial

antérieur *(de devant)* front; *(d'avant)* previous, earlier; **~ à** prior to, before

anthropologie *f* anthropology

antibiotique *m* antibiotic

antibrouillard *m* fog lamp

anticipation *f* anticipation; **payer par ~** pay in advance; **d'~** *roman* science-fiction

anticiper anticipate; **~ un paiement** pay in advance

anticonstitutionnel, ~le unconstitutional

antidater backdate

antidérapant *m* AUTO non-skid tire *ou Br* tyre

antidote *m* MÉD antidote

antigel *m* antifreeze

antipathie

antipathie f antipathy
antipelliculaire: *shampoing* m ~ dandruff shampoo
antiquaire m antique dealer; **antique** ancient; *meuble antique*; *péj* antiquated; **antiquités** fpl antiques
antisémite 1 adj anti-Semitic **2** m/f anti-Semite
antiseptique m & adj antiseptic
antisocial antisocial
antiterroriste anti-terrorist
antivol m anti-theft device
anxiété f anxiety; **anxieux, -euse** anxious
août m August
apaiser *personne* calm down; *douleur* soothe; *soif, faim* satisfy
apathie f apathy
apercevoir see; *s'~ de qc* notice sth
apéritif m aperitif
à-peu-près m approximation
apitoyer: ~ *qn* move s.o. to pity; *s'~ sur qn* feel sorry for s.o.
aplanir flatten, level; *fig: différend* smooth over
aplatir flatten; *s'~* (*s'écraser*) be flattened; *s'~ devant* kowtow to
aplomb m self-confidence; (*audace*) nerve; *d'~* vertical, plumb; *je ne suis pas d'~ fig* I don't feel a hundred percent
apostrophe f (*interpellation*) rude remark; *signe apostro-phe*

apparaître appear; *faire ~* bring to light
appareil m device; AVIAT plane; *qui est à l'~?* TÉL who's speaking?; *~ ménager* household appliance; *~ photo* camera
apparemment apparently
apparence f appearance; *en ~* on the face of things; *sauver les ~s* save face; **apparent** visible; (*illusoire*) apparent
apparenté related (*à* to)
apparition f appearance
appartement m apartment, *Br* flat
appartenir belong (*à* to); *il ne m'appartient pas d'en décider* it's not up to me to decide
appauvrir impoverish; *s'~* become impoverished; **appauvrissement** m impoverishment
appel m call; MIL (*recrutement*) draft, *Br* call-up; JUR appeal; ÉDU roll-call; *faire ~ à qc* (*nécessiter*) require; *faire ~ à qn* appeal to s.o.; **appeler** call; (*nécessiter*) call for; *en ~ à qn* approach s.o.; *comment t'appelles-tu?* what's your name?, what are you called?
appendice m appendix; **appendicite** f MÉD appendicitis
appétissant appetizing; **appétit** m appetite; *bon ~!* en-

joy (your meal)!

applaudir applaud, clap; **applaudissements** *mpl* applause, clapping

applicateur *m* applicator

application *f* application; INFORM app; **appliquer** apply; **s'~** *personne* work hard; **~ Y sur X** smear X with Y

apport *m* contribution; **apporter** bring

appréciation *f* estimate; (*jugement*) opinion; COMM appreciation; **apprécier** estimate; *personne, musique, la bonne cuisine* appreciate

appréhender: ~ qc be apprehensive about sth; **~ qn** JUR arrest s.o.; **appréhension** *f* apprehension

apprendre learn; *nouvelle aussi* hear (*par qn* from s.o.); **~ qc à qn** (*enseigner*) teach s.o. sth; (*raconter*) tell s.o. sth

apprenti, ~e *m/f* apprentice; *fig* beginner; **apprentissage** *m* learning; *d'un métier* apprenticeship

apprivoiser tame

approbateur, -trice approving; **approbation** *f* approval

approcher 1 *v/t* bring closer (*de* to) **2** *v/i* approach; **s'~ de** approach

approfondir deepen; (*étudier*) go into in detail

approprié appropriate, suitable (*à* for); **approprier: s'~ qc** appropriate sth

approuver *loi* approve; *personne, manières* approve of

approvisionnement *m* supply (*en* of)

approximatif, -ive approximate; **approximation** *f* approximation

appui *m* support; *d'une fenêtre* sill; **prendre ~ sur** lean on; **appuyer 1** *v/t* lean on; (*tenir debout*) support; *fig candidat, idée* support, back **2** *v/i:* **~ sur** *bouton* press, push; *fig* stress; **s'~ sur** lean on; *fig* rely on

après 1 *prép* after; **d'~ les journaux** going by what the papers say **2** *adv* afterward **3** *conj:* **~ que** after

après-demain the day after tomorrow

après-midi *m ou f* afternoon

apr. J.-C. (= **après Jésus-Christ**) AD (= anno Domini)

aptitude *f* aptitude

aquarelle *f* watercolor, *Br* watercolour

aquarium *m* aquarium

arabe 1 *adj* Arab **2** *m langue* Arabic; **Arabe** *m/f* Arab; **Arabie** *f:* **l'~ Saoudite** Saudi (Arabia)

araignée *f* spider

arbitrage *m* arbitration

arbitre *m* referee; **libre ~** *m* free will; **arbitrer** arbitrate

arbre *m* tree; TECH shaft

arbuste *m* shrub

arc *m* ARCH arch; GÉOM arc

arc-en-ciel *m* rainbow

arche *f* arch; *Bible* Ark

archéologie *f* archeology, *Br* archaeology; **archéologue** *m/f* archeologist, *Br* archaeologist

archer *m* archer; MUS bow

archevêque *m* archbishop

architecte *m/f* architect; **architecture** *f* architecture

arctique 1 *adj* Arctic **2** *m* l'Arctique the Arctic

ardent *soleil* blazing; *désir* burning; *défenseur* fervent; **ardeur** *f fig* ardor, *Br* ardour

ardoise *f* slate

ardu arduous

arène *f* arena; ~**s** arena

arête *f d'un poisson* bone; *d'une montagne* ridge

argent *m* silver; *(monnaie)* money; ~ **liquide** *ou* **comptant** cash

argot *m* slang

argument *m* argument; **argumenter** argue

aride arid, dry

aristocrate *m/f* aristocrat; **aristocratie** *f* aristocracy

armateur *m* shipowner

arme *f* weapon *(aussi fig)*; ~ **à feu** firearm; **armée** *f* army; ~ **de l'air** airforce; **armement** *m* arming; ~**s** armaments; **armer** arm *(de* with); *fig* equip *(de* with)

armistice *m* armistice

armoire *f* cupboard; *pour les vêtements* closet, *Br* wardrobe

arnaque *f* F rip-off F; **arnaquer** F rip off F

aromate *m* herb; *(épice)* spice; **arome, arôme** *m* flavor, *Br* flavour; *(odeur)* aroma

arracher pull out; *pommes de terre* pull up; ~ **qc à qn** snatch sth from s.o.; **s'~ à** *ou* **de qc** free o.s. from sth; **s'~ qc** fight over sth

arrangement *m* arrangement; **arranger** arrange; *objet* fix; *différend* settle; *cela m'arrange* that suits me; **s'~ avec qn pour faire qch** come to an arrangement with s.o. about sth; **s'~ pour faire qch** manage to do sth

arrestation *f* arrest; *en état d'~* under arrest

arrêt *m (interruption)* stopping; *d'autobus* stop; JUR judgment; **sans ~** constantly; **arrêter 1** *v/i* stop **2** *v/t* stop; *moteur* turn off; *voleur* arrest; *jour, date* set; ~ **de faire qch** stop doing sth; **s'~** stop

arrière 1 *adv* back; *en* ~ backward; *regarder* back; *(à une certaine distance)* behind; *en ~ de* behind **2** *adj inv* rear **3** *m* AUTO, SP back; **à l'~** in back, at the back

arrière-goût *m* aftertaste; **arrière-grand-mère** *f* great-grandmother; **arrière-grand-père** *m* great-grandfather; **arrière-pensée** *f* ulterior motive; **arrière-petit- -fils** *m* great-grandson

arrivée *f* arrival; SP finish line; **arriver** arrive; *d'un événement* happen; ~ **à faire qch** manage to do sth; ~ **à qn** happen to s.o.; *j'arrive!* (I'm) coming!

arrogance *f* arrogance; **arrogant** arrogant

arrondir *vers le haut* round up; *vers le bas* round down; **arrondissement** *m d'une ville* district

arroser water; ~ **qch** *fig* have a drink to celebrate sth; **arrosoir** *m* watering can

art *m* art; **avoir l'~ de faire qch** have a knack for doing sth

artère *f* ANAT artery; *(route)* main road

arthrite *f* arthritis

artichaut *m* artichoke

article *m* article, item; JUR article, clause; *de presse*, GRAM article; ~**s de luxe** luxury goods

articulation *f* ANAT joint; *d'un son* articulation; **articuler** *son* articulate

artificiel, **~le** artificial

artisan *m* craftsman; **artisanal** hand-made; *fromage*, *pain* etc traditional

artiste 1 *m/f* artist; *comédien*, *chanteur* performer **2** *adj* artistic

as *m* ace

ascenseur *m* elevator, *Br* lift

ascension *f* ascent; *fig (progrès)* rise; **l'Ascension** REL Ascension

asiatique Asian; **Asiatique** *m/f* Asian; **Asie** *f:* **l'~** Asia

asile *m* shelter; POL asylum; ~ **de vieillards** old people's home; **demandeur** *m* **d'~** asylum seeker

aspect *m (vue)* look; *(point de vue)* angle, point of view; *d'un problème* aspect; *(air)* appearance; **à l'~ de** at the sight of

asperge *f* BOT stalk of asparagus; ~**s** asparagus

asperger sprinkle; ~ **qn de qch** spray s.o. with sth

asphyxie *f* asphyxiate

aspirateur *m* vacuum (cleaner); **aspirer** *de l'air* breathe in, inhale; *liquide* suck up; ~ **à (faire) qch** aspire to (doing) sth

aspirine *f* aspirin

assagir: **s'~** settle down

assaillir *vedette* mob; **être assailli de** be assailed by; *de coups de téléphone* be bombarded by

assainir *(nettoyer)* clean up; *eau* purify

assaisonnement *m* seasoning

assassin *m* murderer; *d'un président* assassin; **assassinat** *m* assassination; **assassiner** murder; *un président* assassinate

assemblée *f* gathering; *(réu-*

nion) meeting; **~ générale** annual general meeting; **assembler** assemble; **s'~** assemble, gather

asseoir: s'~ sit down

assez enough; (*plutôt*) quite; **~ d'argent** enough money; **~ grand** big enough

assidu *élève* hard-working

assiette *f* plate; **ne pas être dans son ~** *fig* be under the weather

assigner assign

assimiler (*comparer*) compare; *connaissances, étrangers* assimilate

assis: être ~ be sitting; **assise** *f* fig basis

assistance *f* (*public*) audience; (*aide*) assistance; **assistant, ~e** *m/f* assistant; **~e sociale** social worker; **assister 1** *v/i:* **~ à qc** attend sth, be (present) at sth **2** *v/t:* **~ qn** assist s.o

association *f* association; **associé, ~e** *m/f* partner; **associer** associate (**à** with); **s'~** join forces; COMM go into partnership; **s'~ à douleur** share in

assoiffé thirsty

assombrir: s'~ darken

assommant F deadly boring; **assommer** stun; F bore to death

Assomption *f* REL Assumption

assorti matching; **~ de** accompanied by; **assortiment** *m* assortment

assoupir send to sleep; *fig: douleur, sens* dull; **s'~** doze off; *fig* die down

assourdir deafen; *bruit* muffle

assumer take on, assume

assurance *f* assurance; (*contrat*) insurance

assuré, ~e 1 (*sûr*) confident **2** *m/f* insured party; **assurément** certainly; **assurer** *succès* ensure; *par une assurance* insure; **s'~** take out insurance; **s'~ de qc** (*vérifier*) make sure of sth, check sth

asthme *m* asthma

astiquer *meuble* polish; *casserole* scour

astre *m* star

astrologie *f* astrology

astronaute *m/f* astronaut

astronomie *f* astronomie; **astronomique** astronomical (*aussi fig*)

astuce *f* (*ingéniosité*) astuteness; (*truc*) trick; **astucieux, -euse** astute

atelier *m* workshop; *d'un artiste* studio

athée *m/f* atheist; **athéisme** *m* atheism

athlète *m/f* athlete; **athlétisme** *m* athletics *sg*

Atlantique m: **l'~** the Atlantic

atlas *m* atlas

atmosphère *f* atmosphere

atome *m* atom

atout *m* fig asset

atroce dreadful, atrocious;

atrocité f atrocity

attachant captivating

attaché-case m executive briefcase

attacher 1 v/t attach, fasten; *animal* tie up; *prisonnier* secure; *chaussures* do up **2** v/i cuis (*coller*) stick; **s'~ à** become attached to

attaquant, **~e** m/f sp striker; **attaque** f attack; **~ à la bombe** bomb attack; **attaquer** attack; *travail, sujet* tackle; **s'~ à** attack; *problème* tackle

attarder: s'~ linger

atteindre reach; *d'un projectile* strike, hit; *d'une maladie* affect

atteinte f fig attack; **porter ~ à qc** undermine sth; **hors d'~** out of reach

attendant: en ~ in the meantime; **en ~ qu'il arrive** (*subj*) while waiting for him to arrive; **attendre** wait; **~ qn** wait for s.o.; **s'~ à qc** expect sth; **~ un enfant** be expecting a baby

attendrir fig: *personne* move; *cœur* soften; **s'~** be moved (**sur** by); **attendrissement** m tenderness

attentat m attack; **~ à la bombe** bombing, bomb attack; **~ à la pudeur** indecent assault

attente f wait; (*espoir*) expectation

attentif, **-ive** attentive (**à** to); **attention** f attention; (**fais**) **~!** look out!, (be) careful!;

faire ~ à qc pay attention to sth

atténuer reduce; *propos, termes* tone down

atterrir aviat land; **~ en catastrophe** crash-land

attestation f certificate; **attester** certify; (*prouver*) confirm

attirance f attraction; **attirer** attract; **s'~ des critiques** come in for criticism

attitude f attitude; *d'un corps* pose

attraction f attraction

attrait m attraction

attraper catch; (*duper*) take in

attrayant attractive

attribuer attribute; *prix* award; *part, rôle* allot; *valeur* attach; **s'~** take; **attribution** f allocation; *d'un prix* award; **~s** (*compétence*) competence

attrister sadden

attroupement m crowd; **attrouper: s'~** gather

aube f dawn; **à l'~** at dawn

auberge f inn; **~ de jeunesse** youth hostel

aubergine f bot eggplant, Br aubergine

aucun, **~e 1** adj avec négatif no, not ...any; avec positif, interrogatif any **2** pron avec négatif none; **~ des deux** neither of the two; avec positif, interrogatif anyone, anybody

audace f daring, audacity; *péj* audacity; **audacieux, -euse** (*courageux*) daring, audacious; (*insolent*) insolent

au-delà beyond; ~ **de** above; **au-dessous**: ~ (**de**) below; **au-dessus**: ~ (**de**) above; **au-devant**: **aller** ~ **de** meet; désirs anticipate

audible audible

audience f d'un tribunal hearing

audiovisuel, ~**le** audiovisual

auditeur, **-trice** m/f listener; FIN auditor; **audition** f audition; (*ouïe*) hearing; de témoins examination

augmentation f increase; de salaire raise, Br rise; **augmenter 1** v/t increase; salarié give a raise ou Br rise to **2** v/i increase, rise

aujourd'hui today

auparavant beforehand; **deux mois** ~ two months earlier

auprès: ~ **de** beside, near

auquel → **lequel**

auriculaire m little finger

aurore f dawn

ausculter MÉD sound

aussi 1 adv too, also; **il est** ~ **grand que moi** he's as tall as me **2** conj therefore

aussitôt immediately; ~ **que** as soon as

austère austere

Australie f: **l'**~ Australia; **australien**, ~**ne** Australian; **Australien**, ~**ne** m/f Austral-ian

autant (*tant*) as much (*que* as); avec pluriel as many (*que* as); comparatif: ~ **de ... que** as much ... as ...; avec pluriel as many ... as ...; (*pour*) ~ **que je sache** (subj) as far as I know; **en faire** ~ do the same

auteur m/f author; d'un crime perpetrator

authenticité f authenticity; **authentique** authentic

autiste autistic

auto f car, automobile

autobiographie f autobiography

autocollant 1 adj adhesive **2** m sticker

autodéfense f self-defense, Br self-defence

autodidacte self-taught

auto-école f driving school

autographe m autograph

automatique adj & m automatic; **automatiquement** automatically; **automatiser** automate

automne m fall, Br autumn

automobile f car, automobile; **automobiliste** m/f driver

autonomie f independence; POL autonomy

autoradio m car radio

autorisation f authorization, permission; **autoriser** authorize, allow; **autoritaire** authoritarian; **autorité** f authority

aversion

autoroute f highway, Br motorway

auto-stop m: **faire de l'~** hitchhike

autour: ~ **(de)** around

autre 1 adj other; **un/une ~ ...** another ...; **nous ~s Américains** we Americans; **rien d'~** nothing else; ~ **part** somewhere else; **d'~ part** on the other hand 2 pron: **un/une ~** another (one); **l'~** the other (one); **les ~s** the others; *(autrui)* other people; **l'un l'~, les uns les ~** each other, one another

autrefois in the past

autrement *(différemment)* differently; *(sinon)* otherwise

Autriche f: **l'~** Austria; **autrichien, ~ne** Austrian; **Autrichien, ~ne** m/f Austrian

autrui other people pl, others pl

auxquelles, auxquels → **lequel**

av. (= avenue) Ave (= avenue)

aval 1 adv: **en ~** downstream *(de* from) 2 m FIN guarantee

avalanche f avalanche

avaler swallow

avance f advance; **d'une course** lead; **d'~** in advance; **en ~** ahead of time; **avancement** m progress; *(promotion)* promotion; **avancer** 1 v/t **chaise, date** bring forward; **main** put up; **argent**

advance; *thèse* put forward 2 v/i make progress; MIL advance; *d'une montre* be fast; **s'~ vers** come up to

avant 1 prép before; ~ **tout** above all; ~ **de faire qch** before doing sth 2 adv temps before; *espace* in front of; **en ~** forward 3 conj: ~ **que** (+ subj) before 4 adj: **roue** f ~ front wheel 5 m front; *d'un navire* bow; SP forward

avantage m advantage; **~s sociaux** fringe benefits; **avantager** suit; *(favoriser)* favor, Br favour

avant-dernier, -ère last but one

avant-hier the day before yesterday

avant-première f preview

avant-propos m foreword

avant-veille f: **l'~** two days before

avare adj miserly 2 m miser; **avarice** f miserliness

avarié *nourriture* bad

avec with

avenir m future; **à l'~** in future; **d'~** promising

Avent m Advent

aventure f adventure; *(liaison)* affair; **aventurer**: **s'~** venture *(dans* into)

avenue f avenue

avérer: **s'~** (+ adj) prove

averse f shower

aversion f aversion *(pour ou contre* to); **prendre qn en ~** take a dislike to s.o.

avertir inform (**de** of); (*mettre en garde*) warn (**de** of); avertissement *m* warning; avertisseur *m* AUTO horn

aveu *m* confession

aveuglant blinding; aveugle 1 *adj* blind 2 *m/f* blind man; blind woman; aveugler blind

aviateur, -trice *m/f* pilot; aviation *f* aviation, flying

avide greedy, avid (**de** for); avidité *f* greed

avilissant degrading

avion *m* (air)plane, *Br* (aero-)plane; (*réaction*)-plane; **par ~** (by) airmail

aviron *m* oar; SP rowing

avis *m* opinion; (*information*) notice; **à mon ~** in my opinion; **changer d'~** change one's mind; **sauf ~ contraire** unless otherwise stated

aviser: **~ qn de qc** advise *ou* inform s.o. of sth; **s'~ de qc** notice sth; **s'~ de faire qch** take it into one's head to do sth

av. J.-C. (= *avant Jésus-*-*Christ*) BC (= before Christ)

avocat, -e 1 *m/f* lawyer; (*défenseur*) advocate 2 *m* BOT avocado

avoir 1 *v/t* (*posséder*) have, have got; (*obtenir*) get; **j'ai froid/chaud** I am cold/hot; **~ 20 ans** be 20; **il y a** there is; *avec pluriel* there are; **qu'est-ce qu'il y a?** what's the matter?; **il y a un an a** year ago 2 *v/aux* have; **j'ai déjà parlé** I have *ou* I've already spoken; **je lui ai parlé hier** I spoke to him yesterday 3 *m* COMM credit; (*possessions*) possessions *pl*

avoisiner: **~ qc** border on sth

avortement *m* miscarriage; *provoqué* abortion; avorter 1 *v/t femme* terminate the pregnancy of; **se faire ~** have an abortion 2 *v/i* miscarry; *fig* fail

avouer: **~ (avoir fait qc)** confess (to having done sth)

avril *m* April

axe *m* axle; GÉOM axis; *fig* basis

B

babiller babble

bâbord *m* MAR: **à ~** to port

bac¹ *m bateau* ferry; *récipient* container

bac² *m* F, baccalauréat *m* exam that is a prerequisite for university entrance

bâche *f* tarpaulin

bâcler F botch F

badaud *m* onlooker

badiner joke

baffe *f* F slap

bafouiller 1 *v/t* stammer 2 *v/i* F talk nonsense

bagages *mpl* baggage, luggage; *fig (connaissances)* knowledge; **faire ses ~** pack

bagarre *f* fight; **bagarrer** F: **se ~** fight

bagnole *f* F car

bague *f* ring; **~ de fiançailles** engagement ring

baguette *f* stick; MUS baton; *pain* French stick; **~s pour manger** chopsticks

baie[1] *f* BOT berry

baie[2] *f (golfe)* bay; **Baie d'Hudson** Hudson Bay

baigner *enfant* bathe, Br bath; **se ~** go for a swim; **baignoire** *f* (bath) tub

bail *m* lease

bâiller yawn; *d'un trou* gape; *d'une porte* be ajar

bain *m* bath; **salle** *f* **de ~s** bathroom; **être dans le ~** *fig (au courant)* be up to speed; **~ de bouche** mouthwash; **bain-marie** *m* CUIS double boiler

baiser 1 *m* kiss **2** *v/t* V screw V

baisse *f* fall; **être en ~** be falling; **baisser 1** *v/t* lower; *radio, chauffage* turn down **2** *v/i de forces* fail; *de lumière* fade; *d'une température, d'un prix* drop, fall; *de vue* deteriorate; **se ~** bend down

bal *m* dance; *formel* ball

balade *f* walk, stroll; **balader** walk; **se ~** go for a walk *ou* stroll

baladeur *m* Walkman®

balai *m* broom; **donner un coup de ~ à qch** give sth a sweep

balance *f* scales *pl*; COMM balance; ASTROL **Balance** Libra; **balancer** *jambes* swing; F *(lancer)* chuck F; F *(jeter)* chuck out F; **se ~** swing; **balançoire** *f* swing

balayer sweep; *fig: gouvernement* sweep from power; *soucis* sweep away

balbutier stammer

balcon *m* balcony

baleine *f* whale

ballade *f* ballad

balle *f* ball; *d'un fusil* bullet; *de marchandises* bale

ballet *m* ballet

ballon *m* ball; *pour enfants,* AVIAT balloon

ballotter 1 *v/t* buffet **2** *v/i* bounce up and down

balnéaire: station *f* **~** seaside resort

balourd clumsy

balte Baltic; **Baltique: la (mer) ~** the Baltic (Sea)

balustrade *f* balustrade

bambou *m* bamboo

banal *(mpl* -als) banal; **banalité** *f* banality

banane *f* banana; **bananier** *m* banana tree

banc *m* bench, seat; **~ de sable** sandbank

bancaire bank *atr*

bancal *(mpl* -als) *table* wobbly

bandage *m* MÉD bandage

bande f de terrain, de tissu strip; MÉD bandage; (rayure) stripe; (groupe) group; péj gang, band; **bander** MÉD bandage; **~ les yeux à qn** blindfold s.o.

bandit m bandit; (escroc) crook

banlieue f suburbs pl; **de ~** suburban

bannière f banner

bannir banish

banque f bank; **~ du sang** blood bank

banquet m banquet

banquette f seat

banquier m banker

baptême m baptism; **baptiser** baptize

bar m bar; meuble cocktail cabinet

baraque f shack

barbant F boring

barbare 1 adj barbaric **2** m/f barbarian

barbe f beard; **~ à papa** cotton candy, Br candy floss

barbecue m barbecue

barber F bore rigid F

barbu bearded

barder F: **ça va~** there's going to be trouble

baromètre m barometer

barque f MAR boat

barrage m dam; (barrière) barrier

barre f bar; MAR helm; (trait) line; **~ des témoins** JUR witness stand

barreau m bar; d'échelle rung

barrer (obstruer) block, bar; mot cross out; **se ~** F leave

barrette f barrette, Br hairslide

barrière f barrier; (clôture) fence; **~s douanières** customs barriers

bar-tabac m bar-cum-tobacco store

bas, ~se 1 adj low; GÉOGR lower; instrument bass; voix deep **2** adv low; parler in a low voice, quietly; **en ~** downstairs; **là~** there **3** m bottom; (vêtement) stocking; **au ~ de** at the bottom of

basané weatherbeaten; naturellement swarthy

bas-côté m d'une route shoulder

basculer topple over

base f base; d'un édifice foundation; fig: d'une science basis; **de ~** basic; **à ~ de lait** milk-based

base f de données database

base-ball m baseball

baser base (sur) on; **se ~ sur** draw on; d'une idée be based on

basilic m BOT basil

basket(-ball) m basketball; **baskets** fpl sneakers, Br trainers

basque 1 adj Basque **2** m langue Basque; **Basque** m/f Basque

basse-cour f AGR farmyard; animaux poultry

bassine f bowl

bélier

bataille f battle; **livrer ~** give battle; **batailler** fig battle

bâtard m bastard; **chien** mongrel

bateau m boat; **faire du ~** go sailing; **mener qn en ~** fig put s.o. on, Br have s.o. on

bâti 1 adj built on; **bien ~** well-built **2** m frame

bâtiment m building; **secteur** construction industry; MAR ship

bâtir build

bâton m stick; **parler à ~s rompus** make small talk; **~ de rouge** lipstick; **~ de ski** ski pole ou stick

battant 1 adj **pluie** driving **2** m d'une **porte** leaf; **personne** fighter

batte f de base-ball bat

battement m de cœur beat; de **temps** interval

batterie f ÉL battery; MUS drums pl; dans un **orchestre** percussion; **batteur** m CUIS whisk; électrique mixer; MUS drummer; en base-ball batter; **battre 1** v/t beat; **cartes** shuffle **2** v/i beat; d'un **volet** bang; **se ~** fight

bavard, ~e 1 adj talkative **2** m/f chatterbox; **bavarder** chatter; (divulguer un secret) talk

baver drool, slobber; **bavure** f fig blunder, blooper F; **sans ~** impeccable

Bd (= **boulevard**) Blvd (= Boulevard)

B.D. f (= **bande dessinée**) comic strip

béant gaping

béat péj: **sourire** silly

beau, **bel**, **belle** (mpl **beaux**) beautiful, lovely; homme handsome; **il fait beau** (temps) it's lovely weather; **il a beau dire ...** it's no good him saying ...

beaucoup a lot; **~ de** lots of, a lot of; **~ de gens** lots ou a lot of people, many people; **je n'ai pas ~ d'argent** I don't have a lot of ou much money; **~ trop cher** much too expensive

beau-fils m son-in-law; d'un **remariage** stepson; **beau-frère** m brother-in-law; **beau-père** m father-in-law; d'un **remariage** stepfather

beauté f beauty

beaux-arts mpl: **les ~** fine art

beaux-parents mpl parents-in-law

bébé m baby

bec m d'un **oiseau** beak; d'un **récipient** spout; MUS mouthpiece; F mouth

bedaine f (beer) belly

bégayer stutter, stammer

béguin m fig F: **avoir le ~ pour** have a crush on

beige beige

beignet m CUIS fritter

belge Belgian; **Belge** m/f Belgian; **Belgique: la ~** Belgium

bélier m ZO ram; ASTROL **Bé-**

lier Aries

belle → **beau**

belle-famille *f* in-laws *pl*

belle-fille *f* daughter-in-law; *d'un remariage* stepdaughter; **belle-mère** *f* mother-in-law; *d'un remariage* stepmother; **belle-sœur** *f* sister-in-law

belliqueux, -euse warlike

bémol *m* MUS flat

bénédiction *f* blessing

bénéfice *m* benefit; COMM profit; **bénéficier** ~ **de** benefit from; **bénéfique** beneficial

Bénélux: *le* ~ the Benelux countries *pl*

bénévolat voluntary work; **bénévole 1** *adj travail* voluntary **2** *m/f* volunteer

bénin, -igne *tumeur* benign; *accident* minor

bénir bless; **bénit** consecrated; *eau f* ~*e* holy water

béquille *f* crutch; *d'une moto* stand

berceau *m* cradle; **bercer** rock; *se* ~ **d'illusions** delude o.s.

béret *m* beret

berger *m* shepherd; *chien* German shepherd, *Br aussi* Alsatian

berline *f* AUTO sedan, *Br* saloon

bermuda(s) *m (pl)* Bermuda shorts *pl*

berner fool

besogne *f* job, task

besoin *m* need; *avoir* ~ *de* *(faire) qch* need (to do) sth; *au* ~ if need be

bestial *m (sans pl)* livestock

bête 1 *adj* stupid **2** *f animal;* *(insecte)* insect; *chercher la petite* ~ nitpick; **bêtement** stupidly; **bêtise** *f* stupidity; *dire des* ~*s* talk nonsense; *une* ~ a stupid thing to do/ say

béton *m* concrete

betterave *f* beet, *Br* beetroot

beugler *de bœuf* low; F *d'une personne* scream

beurre *m* butter; ~ *de caca-huètes* peanut butter

bévue *f* blunder

biais 1 *adv*: *en* ~ diagonally; *de* ~ *regarder* sideways **2** *m fig (aspect)* angle; *par le* ~ *de* through

biberon *m* (baby's) bottle

Bible *f* bible

bibliothèque *f* library; *meuble* bookcase

bic® *m* ballpoint (pen)

bicentenaire *m* bicentennial, *Br* bicentenary

biceps *m* biceps

biche *f* ZO doe

bicyclette *f* bicycle; *aller en* ou *à* ~ cycle

bidon 1 *m* ~ *à essence* gas ou *Br* petrol can

bidonville *m* shanty town

bidule *m* F gizmo F

bien 1 *m* good; *(possession)* possession; *le* ~ *ce qui est* *juste* good; **faire le ~** do good; **faire du ~ à qn** do s.o. good; **~s** (*possessions*) property; (*produits*) goods **2** *adj* good; (*beau, belle*) good-looking; **être ~** feel well; (*à l'aise*) be comfortable; **ce sera très ~ comme ça** that will do very nicely; **se sentir ~** feel well; **avoir l'air ~** look good; **des gens ~ respectable** people **3** *adv* well; (*très*) very; **~ des fois** lots of times; **eh ~ !** well; **oui, je veux ~** yes please **4** *conj* **~ que** (+ *subj*) although

bien-être *m* welfare; *sensation agréable* well-being

bienfait *m* benefit

bien-fondé *m* legitimacy

bienheureux, -euse happy; REL blessed

bienséance *f* propriety

bientôt soon; **à ~!** see you (soon)!

bienveillance *f* benevolence

bienvenu, ~e1 *adj* welcome **2** *m/f* **être le/la ~(e)** be welcome **3** *f* **souhaiter la ~e à** welcome

bière *f* beer; **~ blanche** wheat beer; **~ brune** dark beer, Br bitter; **~ pression** draft (beer), Br draught (beer)

bifteck *m* steak

bifurquer: ~ (vers) fork (off onto); *fig* branch out (into)

bigame 1 *adj* bigamous **2** *m/f* bigamist; **bigamie** *f* bigamy

bijou *m* jewel; **~x** jewelry, Br

jewellery; **bijouterie** *f* jewelry store, Br jeweller's; **bijoutier, -ère** *m/f* jeweler, Br jeweller

bikini *m* bikini

bilan *m* balance sheet; *fig* (*résultat*) outcome; **faire le ~ de** take stock of

bilingue bilingual

billard *m* billiards *sg*; *table* billiard table; **~ américain** pool

bille *f* marble; *billard* (*billiard*) ball; **stylo** *m* (**à**) **~** ball-point (pen)

billet *m* ticket; (*petite lettre*) note; **~ (de banque)** note, Br (bank)note; **billeterie** *f* ticket office; *automatique* ticket machine; FIN ATM, Br *aussi* cash dispenser

biochimie *f* biochemistry

biodégradable biodegradable

biodiversité *f* biodiversity

biographie *f* biography

biologie *f* biology; **biologique** biological; *aliments* organic

biotechnologie *f* biotechnology

bis1 *adj*: **24~24A 2** *m* encore

biscornu *fig* weird

biscotte *f* rusk

biscuit *m* cookie, Br biscuit

bise *f*: **faire la ~ à** kiss

bisexuel, ~le bisexual

bisou *m* F kiss

bissextile: année *f* **~** leap year

bistro(t) *m* bistro

bit *m* INFORM bit

bitume *m* asphalt

bizarre strange, bizarre

blafard wan

blague *f* joke; *sans ~!* no kidding!; **blaguer** joke

blaireau *m* badger; *pour se raser* shaving brush

blâme *m* blame; (*sanction*) reprimand

blanc, blanche 1 *adj* white; *page* blank; *nuit f blanche* sleepless night **2** *m* white; *textile* (household) linen; *par opposé aux couleurs* whites *pl*; *dans un texte* blank **3** *m/f* **Blanc, Blanche** white, White

blancheur *f* whiteness; **blanchir 1** *v/t* whiten; *mur* whitewash; *linge* launder, wash; *du soleil* bleach; *fig: innocenter* clear **2** *v/i* go white

blasé blasé

blasphème *m* blasphemy; **blasphémer** blaspheme

blé *m* wheat, *Br* corn

blêmir turn pale

blesser hurt (*aussi fig*); *dans un accident* injure; *à la guerre* wound; *se~* injure *ou* hurt o.s.; **blessure** *f* *d'accident* injury; *d'arme* wound

bleu 1 *adj* blue; *viande* very rare **2** *m* blue; *fromage* blue cheese; *sur la peau* bruise; *fig* (*novice*) rookie F

blindage *m* armor, *Br* armour; **blinder** armor, *Br ar-*

mour; *fig* F harden

bloc *m* block; POL bloc; *de papier* pad; *faire ~* join forces

bloc-notes *m* notepad

blocus *m* blockade

blond, ~e 1 *adj* blonde; *tabac* Virginian; *sable* golden **2** *m/f* blonde **3** *f bière* beer, *Br aussi* lager

bloquer block; *mécanisme* jam; *roues* lock; *compte* freeze

blouson *m* jacket, blouson

bluff *m* bluff; **bluffer** bluff

bobard *m* F tall tale *ou Br* story

bocal *m* (glass) jar

bock *m: un ~* a (glass of) beer

bœuf *m* steer; *viande* beef

bohémien, ~ne *m/f* gipsy

boire drink; (*absorber*) soak up

bois *m* matière, forêt wood; *en ~* wooden

boisson *f* drink; *~s alcoolisées* alcohol

boîte *f* box; *en tôle* can, *Br aussi* tin; F (*entreprise*) company; *~ (de nuit)* nightclub; *en~* canned, *Br aussi* tinned; *~ à gants* glove compartment; *~ aux lettres* mailbox, *Br* letterbox

boiter limp; *fig: de raisonnement* be shaky; **boiteux, -euse** *table etc* wobbly; *fig: raisonnement* shaky; *être ~* *d'une personne* have a limp

boîtier *m* case, housing

bol *m* bowl

bouc

bombardement m bombing; *avec obus* bombardment; **bombarder** bomb; *avec obus, questions* bombard; **bombe** f bomb; (*atomiseur*) spray; *~ à retardement* time bomb; **bombé** bulging

bon, ~ne 1 *adj* good; *route, moment* right; *de ~ne foi personne* sincere; *être ~ en qch* be good at sth; *à quoi ~?* what's the use?; *witticism*; *~ anniversaire!* happy birthday!; *~ voyage!* have a good trip!, bon voyage!; *~ne chance!* good luck!; *~ne année!* Happy New Year!; *~ne nuit!* good night!; *ah ~* really **2** *adv*: *sentir ~* smell good; *tenir ~* not give in; *trouver ~ de faire qch* think it right to do sth **3** m COMM voucher; *avoir du ~* have its good points; *~ d'achat* gift voucher; *~ du Trésor* Treasury bond

bonbon m candy, Br sweet; *~s* candy, Br sweets

bond m leap; *d'une balle* bounce

bondé packed

bondir jump, leap (*de* with)

bonheur m happiness; (*chance*) luck; *par ~* luckily; *au petit ~* at random

bonhomme m F (*type*) guy F

boniment m *battage* spiel F, sales talk; F (*mensonge*) fairy story

bonjour m hello

bonne f maid

bonnet m hat; *gros ~ fig* F big shot F; *~ de douche* shower cap

bonsoir m hello, good evening

bonté f goodness

bonus m no-claims bonus

bord m edge; (*rive*) bank; *d'un verre* side; *du chapeau* brim; *au ~ de la mer* at the seaside; *être au ~ des larmes* be on the verge of tears; *monter à ~* go on board

bordel m F brothel; (*désordre*) mess F

bordélique F chaotic

border (*garnir*) edge (*de* with); (*être le long de*) border; *enfant* tuck in

bordure f border, edging; *en ~ de forêt, ville* on the edge of

borne f boundary marker; ÉL terminal; *~s fig* limits; *dépasser les ~s* go too far; **borné** narrow-minded; **borner**: *se ~ à (faire)* restrict o.s. to (doing)

bosse f (*enflure*) lump; *d'un bossu, d'un chameau* hump; *du sol* bump

bosser F work hard

bossu, ~e m/f hunchback

botanique 1 *adj* botanical **2** f botany

botte f *chaussure* boot

bouc m goat; *~ émissaire fig* scapegoat

bouche f mouth; *de métro* entrance; ~ *d'aération* vent; ~ *d'incendie* (fire) hydrant

bouché blocked; *temps* overcast

bouche-à-bouche m MÉD mouth-to-mouth resuscitation

bouchée f mouthful

boucher[1] v/t block; *trou* fill (in); **se** ~ *d'un évier* get blocked; **se** ~ **le nez** hold one's nose

boucher[2], **-ère** m/f butcher (*aussi fig*)

boucherie f *magasin* butcher's; *fig* slaughter

bouchon m top; *de liège* cork; *fig: trafic* hold-up

boucle f loop; *de ceinture* buckle; *de cheveux* curl; ~ *d'oreille* earring; **bouclé** *cheveux* curly; **boucler** *ceinture* fasten; *porte* lock; MIL surround; *en prison* lock away

bouddhisme m Buddhism; **bouddhiste** m Buddhist

bouder 1 v/i sulk 2 v/t: ~ *qn/qc* give s.o./sth the cold shoulder

boudin m: ~ **(noir)** blood sausage, Br black pudding

boue f mud

bouée f MAR buoy

bouffée f *de fumée, vent* puff; *de parfum* whiff

bouffer F eat

bouffi bloated

bouger move; *de prix* change

bougie f candle; AUTO spark plug

bouillie f baby food

bouillir boil; *fig* be boiling (with rage); **faire** ~ boil; **bouilloire** f kettle

bouillon m (*bulle*) bubble; CUIS stock; **bouillonner** bubble; *fig: d'idées* seethe

bouillotte f hot water bottle

boulanger, -ère m/f baker; **boulangerie** f bakery

boule f ball; *jeu* m *de* ~s bowls sg

bouleau m BOT birch (tree)

boulevard m boulevard

bouleversement m upheaval; **bouleverser** (*mettre en désordre*) turn upside down; *traditions* overturn; *émotionnellement* shatter

boulimie f bulimia

boulot m F work

bouquet m bouquet

bouquin m F book; **bouquiner** read

bourde f blunder, blooper F

bourdon m ZO bumblebee; **bourdonner** *d'insectes* buzz; *de moteur* hum; *d'oreilles* ring

bourgeois, ~e 1 adj middle-class 2 m/f member of the middle classes

bourgeoisie f middle classes pl

bourgeon m BOT bud

bourrasque f gust

bourratif, -ive stodgy

bourré crammed (*de* with); F

(*ivre*) drunk, sozzled F
bourrer *coussin* stuff; *pipe* fill; **se ~ de qc** F stuff o.s. with sth
bourru surly
bourse *f d'études* grant; (*porte-monnaie*) coin purse, *Br* purse; *Bourse (des valeurs)* Stock Exchange
boursouf(f)lé swollen
bousculer (*heurter*) jostle; (*presser*) rush; *fig: traditions* overturn
bousiller F *travail* screw F up; (*détruire*) wreck
boussole *f* compass
bout *m* end; (*morceau*) piece; **au ~ de** at the end; **d'un ~ à l'autre** right the way through; **être à ~** be at an end; **venir à ~ de** overcome
bouteille *f* bottle; *de butane* cylinder
boutique *f* store, *Br* shop; *de mode* boutique
bouton *m* button; *de porte* handle; ANAT spot, zit F; BOT bud; **bouton-d'or** *m* BOT buttercup; **boutonner** button; BOT bud; **boutonneux, -euse** spotty
bovin 1 *adj* attr 2 *mpl* **~s** cattle *pl*
bowling *m* bowling, *Br* tenpin bowling; *lieu* bowling alley
boxe *f* boxing; **boxer** box; **boxeur** *m* boxer
boycott *m* boycott; **boycotter** boycott

B.P. (= *boîte postale*) PO Box (= Post Office Box)
bracelet *m* bracelet
braconnier *m* poacher
braguette *f* fly
brailler bawl
braiser CUIS braise
brancard *m* (*civière*) stretcher
branche *f* branch; *de céleri* stick
brancher connect up (**sur** to); *à une prise* plug in; **branché** F (*informé*) clued up; (*en vogue*) trendy
brandir brandish
braquer 1 *v/t:* **~ sur** aim *ou* point at 2 *v/i* AUTO turn the wheel; **se ~ contre** *fig* turn against
bras *m* arm; **avoir le ~ long** *fig* have influence
brasse *f* stroke
brasser *bière* brew; **brasserie** *f* *usine* brewery; *établissement* restaurant
brave 1 *adj* brave; (*before the noun*) good 2 *m:* **un ~** a brave man; **braver** (*défier*) defy; **bravoure** *f* bravery
break *m* AUTO station wagon, *Br* estate (car)
brebis *f* ewe
bredouiller mumble
bref, -ève 1 *adj* brief, short 2 *adv* briefly, in short
Brésil: *le ~* Brazil; **brésilien,** **~ne** Brazilian; **Brésilien,** **~ne** *m/f* Brazilian
Bretagne: *la ~* Britanny
bretelle *f* *de lingerie* strap;

d'autoroute ramp, *Br* slip road; *~s de pantalon* suspenders, *Br* braces

brevet *m* diploma; *pour invention* patent; **breveter** patent

bric-à-brac *m inv* bric-a-brac

bricolage *m* do-it-yourself, DIY; **bricole** *f* little thing; **bricoler** do odd jobs

brièvement briefly; **brièveté** *f* briefness, brevity

brigade *f* MIL brigade; *de police* squad; *d'ouvriers* gang

brillamment brilliantly; **brillant** shiny; *couleur* bright; *fig* brilliant; **briller** shine (*aussi fig*); **faire ~ meuble** polish

brin *m d'herbe* blade; *de corde* strand

brindille *f* twig

brioche *f* CUIS brioche; F (*ventre*) paunch

brique *f* brick

briquet *m* lighter

brise *f* breeze

brisé broken

briser 1 *v/t* break; *vie, bonheur* destroy; (*fatiguer*) wear out **2** *v/i de la mer* break; **se ~ de verre etc** break; *des espoirs be* shattered

britannique British; **Britannique** *m/f* Briton, Britisher, Brit F; **les ~s** the British

broc *m* pitcher

brocante *f magasin* second--hand store

broche *f* CUIS spit; *bijou* brooch

brochet *m* pike

brochette *f* CUIS skewer; *plat* shish kebab

brochure *f* brochure

brocolis *mpl* broccoli *sg*

broncher: sans ~ without batting an eyelid

bronches *fpl* ANAT bronchial tubes

bronchite *f* MÉD bronchitis

bronze *m* bronze

bronzé tanned; **bronzer 1** *v/t peau* tan **2** *v/i* get a tan; **se ~** sunbathe

brosse *f* brush; *coiffure* crew-cut; **~ à dents/chevaux** toothbrush/hairbrush; **brosser** brush; **se ~ les dents** brush one's teeth

brouhaha *m* hubbub

brouillard *m* fog; **il y a du ~** it's foggy

brouille *f* quarrel; **brouiller** *œufs* scramble; *cartes* shuffle; *papiers* muddle; *radio* jam; *involontairement* cause interference to; *amis* cause to fall out; **se ~ du ciel** cloud over; *de vitres* mist up; *d'idées* get muddled; *d'amis* fall out

brouillon *m* draft; **papier** *m* **~** scratch paper, *Br* scrap paper

broussailles *fpl* undergrowth

broyer grind; **~ du noir** *fig* be down

bru f daughter-in-law

brugnon m BOT nectarine

bruine f drizzle

bruit m sound; *qui dérange* noise; *(rumeur)* rumor, Br rumour; *faire du ~* make a noise; *fig* cause a sensation

brûlant burning *(aussi fig)*; *(chaud)* burning hot; *liquide* scalding; **brûlé** burnt; **brûler 1** v/t burn; *d'eau bouillante* scald; *électricité* use; *~ un feu rouge* go through a red light **2** v/i burn; *se ~* burn o.s.; *d'eau bouillante* scald o.s.; **brûleur** m burner; **brûlure** f *sensation* burning, *lésion* burn; *~s d'estomac* heartburn

brume f mist

brun, *~e* **1** *adj* brown; *cheveux, peau* dark **2** m/f dark-haired man/woman; *une ~e* a brunette **3** m *couleur* brown

brushing® m blow-dry

brusque abrupt, brusque; *(soudain)* abrupt, sudden; **brusquement** abruptly, suddenly; **brusquer** rush

brut, *~e* **1** *adj* raw; *poids, revenu* gross; *pétrole* crude; *sucre* unrefined; *champagne* very dry **2** m crude (petroleum) **3** f brute; **brutal** brutal; **brutalement** brutally; **brutaliser** ill-treat; **brutalité** f brutality

Bruxelles Brussels

bruyant noisy

buanderie f laundry room

bûcher¹ m woodpile; *(échafaud)* stake

bûcher² v/i work hard; ÉDU F hit the books, Br swot

budget m budget

buée f steam, condensation

buffet m buffet; *meuble* sideboard

buisson m shrub, bush

bulbe m BOT bulb

bulgare 1 *adj* Bulgarian **2** m *langue* Bulgarian; **Bulgare** m/f Bulgarian; **Bulgarie**: *la ~* Bulgaria

bulle f bubble

bulletin m *(formulaire)* form; *(rapport)* bulletin; *à l'école* report card; *~ de vote* ballot *(paper)*; *~ de salaire* paystub; Br payslip

bureau m office; *meuble* desk; *~ de change* exchange office, Br bureau de change; *~ de poste* post office; *~ de tabac* tobacco store, Br tobacconist's; **bureaucratie** f bureaucracy; **bureautique** f office automation

bus m bus

buste m bust

but m *(cible)* target; *(objectif)* aim, goal; *d'un voyage* purpose; SP goal; *sans ~* aimlessly; **buteur** m goalscorer

buté stubborn

buter: *~ contre qch* bump into sth; *~ sur un problème* hit a problem; *se ~* fig dig

one's heels in
butin m booty; *de voleurs* haul
butte f (*colline*) hillock; **être**

en ~ à be exposed to
buvable drinkable; **buvette** f bar; **buveur, -euse** m/f drinker

C

c' → *ce*
ça that; *~ va?* how are things?; (*d'accord?*) ok?; *~ y est* that's it; *c'est ~!* that's right
cabale f (*intrigue*) plot
cabane f (*baraque*) hut
cabaret m (*boîte*) night club
cabine f cabin; *d'un camion* cab; *~ téléphonique* phone booth
cabinet m *petite pièce* small room; *d'avocat* office; *de médecin* office, Br surgery; (*clientèle*) practice; POL Cabinet
câble m cable
cabosser dent
cabrer: *se ~ d'un animal* rear
cabriolet m AUTO convertible
cacah(o)uète f BOT peanut
cacao m cocoa; BOT cocoa bean
cache-cache m: *jouer à ~* play hide-and-seek; **cache-nez** m scarf; **cacher** hide; *se ~ de* hide from
cachet m seal; *fig* (*caractère*) style; PHARM tablet; (*rétribution*) fee; *~ de la poste* postmark
cachette f hiding place; *en ~*

secretly
cachotterie f: *faire des ~s* be secretive; **cachottier, -ère** secretive
cactus m cactus
cadavre m (dead) body, corpse; *d'un animal* carcass
caddie® m cart, Br trolley
cadeau m present, gift; *faire un ~ à qn* give s.o. a present
cadenas m padlock
cadence f tempo rhythm; *de travail* rate
cadet, ~te m/f younger; *de plus de deux* youngest; *il est mon ~ de trois ans* he's three years younger than me
cadran m dial; *~ solaire* sundial
cadre m frame; *fig* framework; *d'une entreprise* executive; (*environnement*) surroundings *pl*
cafard m ZO cockroach; *avoir le ~* F be feeling down
café m coffee; *établissement* café; *~ crème* coffee with milk, Br white coffee
cafeteria f cafeteria
cafetière f coffee pot; *~ électrique* coffee maker

cage f cage

cagibi m F box room

cagneux, -euse knock-kneed

cagoule f hood; (*passe-montagne*) balaclava

cahier m notebook; ÉDU exercise book

cahoter jolt

cahoteux, -euse bumpy

caille f quail

cailler *du lait* curdle; *du sang* clot

caillou m pebble, stone

caisse f chest; *pour le transport* crate; *de champagne, vin* case; (*argent*) cash; (*guichet*) cashdesk; *dans un supermarché* checkout; **caissier, -ère** m/f cashier

cajoler (*câliner*) cuddle

calamité f disaster, calamity

calcium m calcium

calcul[1] m calculation

calcul[2] m MÉD stone; **~ rénal** kidney stone

calculatrice f: **~ (de poche)** (pocket) calculator; **calculer** calculate; **calculette** f pocket calculator

calé F: **être ~ en qch** be good at sth

caleçon m *d'homme* boxer shorts pl; *de femme* leggings pl

calembour m pun

calendrier m calendar; *emploi du temps* schedule, Br timetable

caler *moteur* stall; TECH wedge

califourchon: **à ~** astride

câlin 1 adj affectionate **2** m (*caresse*) cuddle

calmant 1 adj soothing; *contre douleur* painkilling **2** m tranquilizer, Br tranquillizer; *contre douleur* painkiller

calme 1 adj calm; *Bourse, vie* quiet **2** m calmness; MAR calm; (*silence*) peace and quiet; **calmement** calmly; **calmer** *personne* calm down; *douleur* relieve; **se ~** calm down

calomnie f slander; *écrite* libel; **calomnier** insult; *par écrit* libel

calorie f calorie

calquer trace

calvitie f baldness

camarade m/f friend; POL comrade

cambriolage m break-in, burglary; **cambrioler** burglarize, Br burgle

cambrioleur, -euse m/f house-breaker, burglar

camelote f F junk

caméra f camera

caméscope m camcorder

camion m truck, Br aussi lorry

camionnette f van

camomille f BOT camomile

camouflage m camouflage; *fig: intention* hide; *faute* cover up

camp m camp (*aussi* MIL, POL); **ficher le ~** F get lost F

campagne f country, countryside; MIL, *fig* campaign; **à la ~** in the country

camper camp; **se ~ devant** plant o.s. in front of; **campeur, -euse** *m/f* camper

camping *m:* (**terrain m de**) ~ campground, campsite; **faire du ~** go camping

Canada *le* ~ Canada; **canadien, ~ne** Canadian; **Canadien, ~ne** *m/f* Canadian

canal *m* channel; (*tuyau*) pipe; (*bras d'eau*) canal

canalisation *f* (*tuyauterie*) pipes *pl*, piping; **canaliser** *fig* channel

canapé *m* sofa; GASTR canapé

canapé-lit *m* sofa-bed

canard *m* duck; F newspaper

canari *m* canary

cancans *mpl* gossip

cancer *m* MÉD cancer; ASTROL **Cancer** Cancer

candeur *f* ingenuousness

candidat *m*, **~e** *m/f* candidate; **candidature** *f* candidacy; **à un poste** application

candide ingenuous

cane *f* (female) duck; **caneton** *m* duckling

canette *f* (*bouteille*) bottle

caniche *m* poodle

canicule *f* heatwave

canif *m* pocket knife

canin dog *atr*, canine

canine *f* canine

canne *f* cane, stick; **~ à pêche** fishing rod

cannelle *f* cinnamon

canoë *m* canoe; **activité** ca-

noeing

canon *m* MIL gun; HIST cannon; *de fusil* barrel

canot *m* small boat; **~ pneumatique** rubber dinghy; **~ de sauvetage** lifeboat

cantine *f* canteen

canular *m* hoax

caoutchouc *m* rubber; (*bande élastique*) rubber band

cap *m* GÉOGR cape; AVIAT, NAUT course

capable capable (**de faire** *de* doing)

capacité *f* (*compétence*) ability; (*contenance*) capacity

cape *f* cape

capitaine *m* captain

capital 1 *adj* essential **2** *m* capital; **capitaux** *pl* capital **3** *f* **ville** capital (city); **lettre** capital (letter)

capitalisme *m* capitalism

capituler capitulate

capot *m* AUTO hood, *Br* bonnet

capote *f* *vêtement* greatcoat; AUTO top, *Br* hood; **~** (**anglaise**) F condom

caprice *m* whim; **capricieux, -euse** capricious

Capricorne *m* ASTROL Capricorn

capter *regard* catch; RAD, TV pick up

capteur *m:* **~ solaire** solar panel

captif, -ive *m/f & adj* captive; **captivant** *personne* captivating; *lecture* gripping;

captiver *fig* captivate; **captivité** *f* captivity

capture *f* capture; *(proie)* catch; **capturer** capture

capuche *f* hood

car[1] *m* bus, *Br aussi* coach

car[2] *conj* for

carabine *f* rifle

carabiné F: **un ... carabiné** one hell of a ... F

caractère *m* character; **avoir bon ~** be good-natured; **caractériel troubles** emotional; *personne* emotionally disturbed

caractériser be characteristic of; **caractéristique** *f & adj* characteristic

carambolage *m* AUTO pile-up

caramel *m* caramel

caravane *f* AUTO trailer, *Br* caravan

carboniser burn

carburant *m* fuel

carburateur *m* TECH carburet(t)or

cardiaque MÉD 1 *adj* cardiac, heart *atr* 2 *m/f* heart patient

cardinal: les quatre points *mpl* **cardinaux** the four points of the compass

cardiologue *m/f* cardiologist, heart specialist

carême *m* REL Lent

carence *f (incompétence)* inadequacy; *(manque)* deficiency

caresse *f* caress; **caresser** caress; *idée* play with; *espoir* cherish

cargaison *f* cargo; *fig* load

caricature *f* caricature

carie *f* MÉD: **une ~** a cavity

carié *dent* bad

caritatif, **~ive** charitable

carnage *m* carnage

carnassier, **-ère** carnivorous

carnaval *m* carnival

carnet *m* notebook; *de tickets, timbres* book

carnivore 1 *adj* carnivorous **2** *m* carnivore

carotte *f* carrot; **poil de ~** ginger

carpe *f* ZO carp

carpette *f* rug

carré 1 *adj* square; *fig: réponse* straightforward **2** *m* square

carreau *m* de fenêtre pane; *cartes* diamonds; **à ~x** checked

carrefour *m* crossroads *sg (aussi fig)*

carrelage *m* (*carreaux*) tiles *pl*

carrément bluntly, straight out

carrière *f* quarry; *profession* career; **militaire m de ~** professional soldier

carrosserie *f* AUTO bodywork

carrure *f* build

cartable *m* schoolbag; *à bretelles* satchel

carte *f* card; *dans un restaurant* menu; GÉOGR map; NAUT, *du ciel* chart; **~ bancaire** debit card, banker's card; **~ de crédit** credit card;

~ d'embarquement boarding pass; **~ d'identité** identity card; **~ postale** postcard; **~ téléphonique** phonecard

carton *m* cardboard; *boîte* cardboard box; **~ jaune/rouge** *en football* yellow/red card

cartouche *f* cartridge; *de cigarettes* carton

cas *m* case; **en aucun ~** under no circumstances; **dans ce ~là** in that case; **en tout ~** in any case; **en ~ de** in the event of

casanier, -ère *m/f* stay-at-home

cascade *f* waterfall

case *f* (*hutte*) hut; (*compartiment*) compartment; *dans formulaire* box; *dans mots-croisés, échiquier* square

caser put; (*loger*) put up; **se ~** (*se marier*) settle down

caserne *f* barracks; **~ de pompiers** fire station

casier *m* *courrier* pigeonholes *pl*; *bouteilles, livres* rack; **~ judiciaire** criminal record

casino *m* casino

casque *m* helmet; *de radio* headphones *pl*; **casquette** *f* cap

cassable breakable

casse-cou *m inv* daredevil; **casse-croûte** *m* snack; **casse-noisettes** *m* nutcrackers *pl*; **casse-pieds** *m/f inv* F pain in the neck F

casser 1 *v/t* break; *noix* crack; JUR quash; **~ les pieds à qn** F (*embêter*) get on s.o.'s nerves F; **se ~** break **2** *v/i* break

casserole *f* (sauce)pan

casse-tête *m fig: problème* headache

cassette *f* cassette; **~ vidéo** video

cassis *m* BOT blackcurrant; (*crème f de*) **~** blackcurrant liqueur

castrer castrate

cataclysme *m* disaster

catalogue *m* catalog, *Br* catalogue; **cataloguer** catalog, *Br* catalogue; F *péj* label

catalytique AUTO: **pot** *m* **~** catalytic converter

cataracte *f* waterfall; MÉD cataract

catastrophe *f* disaster, catastrophe; **en ~** in a rush; **catastrophique** disastrous, catastrophic

catch *m* wrestling

catéchisme *m* catechism

catégorie *f* category; **catégorique** categorical

cathédrale *f* cathedral

catholique 1 *adj* (Roman) Catholic **2** *m/f* Roman Catholic

cauchemar *m* nightmare (*aussi fig*)

cause *f* cause; JUR case; **à ~ de** because of; **être en ~** d'honnêteté be in question

causer 1 *v/t* (*provoquer*) cause **2** *v/i* (*s'entretenir*) chat

censé

(*avec qn de* with s.o. about); **causette** *f* chat; **faire la ~** have a chat

caustique CHIM, *fig* caustic

caution *f* security; *pour logement* deposit; JUR bail; *fig* (*appui*) backing; **cautionner** stand surety for; JUR bail; *fig* (*se porter garant de*) vouch for; (*appuyer*) back

cavaler F: **~ après qn** chase after s.o.

cavalier, -ère 1 *m/f pour cheval* rider; *pour bal* partner **2** *m aux échecs* knight **3** *adj* offhand, cavalier

cave *f* cellar; **~ (à vin)** wine cellar

caverne *f* cave

caviar *m* caviar

cavité *f* cavity

CD *m* (= *compact disc*) CD; **CD-Rom** *m* CD-Rom

ce *m* (cet *m*, cette *f*, ces *pl*) **1** *adj* this, *pl* these; **~ livre-ci** this book; **~ livre-là** that book; **ces jours-ci** these days **2** *pron* **c'est pourquoi** that is *ou* that's why; **c'est triste** it's sad; **~ sont mes enfants** these are my children; **c'est un acteur** he is *ou* he's an actor; **c'est que tu as grandi!** how you've grown!; **ce que tu fais** what you're doing; **ce qui me plaît** what I like; **ce qu'il est gentil!** isn't he nice!; **sur ~** with that

ceci this

cécité *f* blindness

céder 1 *v/t* give up; **cédez le passage** AUTO yield, *Br* give way **2** *v/i* give in (**à** to); (*se casser*) give way

cédille *f* cedilla

cèdre *m* BOT cedar

ceinture *f* belt; ANAT waist; **~ de sécurité** seatbelt

cela that; **à ~ près** apart from that

célèbre famous

célébrer celebrate

célébrité *f* fame; *personne* celebrity

céleri *m* BOT: **~ (en branche)** celery; **~(-rave)** celeriac

célibat *m* single life; *d'un prêtre* celibacy; **célibataire 1** *adj* single, unmarried **2** *m* bachelor **3** *f* single woman

celle, celles → celui

cellophane *f* cellophane

cellule *f* cell

cellulose *f* cellulose

Celsius Celsius

celui *m* (celle *f*, ceux *mpl*, celles *fpl*) the one, *pl* those; **~ qui ...** *personne* he who ...; *chose* the one which; **celle de Claude** Claude's; **celui--ci** this one; **celui-là** that one

cendre *f* ash; **~s de cigarette** cigarette ash; **cendrier** *m* ashtray

cène *f* REL: **la ~** (Holy) Communion; **la Cène** *peinture* the Last Supper

censé: **il est ~ être malade** he's supposed to be sick

censure f censorship; *organe* board of censors; **censurer** censor

cent 1 adj hundred **2** m a hundred, one hundred; *monnaie* cent; *pour* ~ per cent; **centaine** f: *une* ~ *de* a hundred or so; *des* ~*s de* hundreds of

centenaire 1 adj hundred-year-old **2** m fête centennial, Br centenary

centième hundredth

centilitre m centiliter, Br centilitre; **centimètre** m centimeter, Br centimetre; *ruban* tape measure

central, ~**e 1** adj central **2** m TÉL telephone exchange **3** f power station; **centraliser** centralize

centre m center, Br centre; ~ *commercial* shopping center, mall; ~ *d'accueil* shelter; *for refugees* reception center; ~ *d'appels* call center; **centrer** center, Br centre

centre-ville m downtown area, Br town centre

cep m vine stock

cèpe m BOT cèpe, boletus

cependant yet, however

cercle m circle; ~ *vicieux* vicious circle

cercueil m casket, Br coffin

céréales fpl (breakfast) cereal

cérébral cerebral

cérémonie f ceremony; *sans* ~ *repas etc* informal; *se présenter etc* informally; *mettre*

à la porte unceremoniously

cerf m deer

cerf-volant m kite

cerise f cherry; **cerisier** m cherry (-tree)

cerne m: *avoir des* ~*s* have bags under one's eyes; **cerner** (*encercler*) surround; *fig: problème* define

certain 1 adj certain; *être* ~ *de qc* be certain of sth; *d'un* ~ *âge* middle-aged **2** pron: *certains*, *-aines* some (people)

certainement certainly; (*sûrement*) probably

certes certainly

certificat m certificate; ~ *de mariage* marriage certificate; **certifier** guarantee; ~ *qc à qn* assure s.o. of sth

certitude f certainty

cerveau m brain

cervelle f brains pl; *se brûler la* ~ fig blow one's brains out

ces → *ce*

cesser stop; ~ *de faire qch* stop doing sth; **cessez-le-feu** m ceasefire

cession f disposal

c'est-à-dire that is, that is to say

cet, cette → *ce*

ceux → *celui*

chacun, ~*e* each (one)

chagrin m grief; *faire du* ~ *à* upset

chahut m F racket, din; **chahuter** heckle

chaîne f chain; *radio*, TV

channel; **~s** AUTO snow chains; **~ hi-fi** hi-fi

chair *f* flesh; *avoir la ~ de poule* have goosebumps

chaise *f* chair; **~ longue** *(transatlantique)* deck chair

chalet *m* chalet

chaleur *f* heat; *plus modérée* warmth *(aussi fig)*; **chaleureusement** warmly

chamailler F: **se ~** bicker

chambre *f* (bed)room; JUR, POL chamber; **~ à air** de pneu inner tube; **~ à coucher** bedroom; **~ à un lit** single (room); **~ à deux lits** twin-bedded room; **~ d'amis** spare room

chambré *vin* at room temperature

chameau *m* camel

champ *m* field *(aussi fig)*; **~ de courses** racecourse

champagne *m* champagne

champêtre country *atr*

champignon *m* fungus; *nourriture* mushroom

champion, **-ne** *m/f* champion; **championnat** *m* championship

chance *f* luck; *(occasion)* chance; *bonne ~!* good luck!; *avoir de la ~* be lucky; *c'est une ~ que* (+ *subj*) it's lucky that

chanceler stagger; *d'un gouvernement* totter

chanceux, **-euse** lucky

chandail *m* sweater

change *m* exchange; *taux m*

de ~ exchange rate; *donner le ~ à qn* deceive s.o.; **changeant** changeable; **changement** *m* change; **~ de vitesse** AUTO gear shift; **changer 1** *v/t* change (**en** into); *(échanger)* exchange (**contre** for) **2** *v/i* change; **~ d'avis** change one's mind; **se ~** change

chanson *f* song

chant *m* song; *action de chanter* singing; *d'église* hymn

chantage *m* blackmail

chanter sing; *d'un coq* crow; *faire ~ qn* blackmail s.o.

chanteur, **-euse** *m/f* singer

chantier *m* building site; **~ naval** shipyard

chaos *m* chaos; **chaotique** chaotic

chaparder F pinch F

chapeau *m* hat; **chapeauter** *fig* head up

chapelet *m* REL rosary

chapelle *f* chapel

chapelure *f* CUIS breadcrumbs *pl*

chapitre *m* chapter; *division de budget* heading; *fig* subject

chaque each

charbon *m* coal; **~ de bois** charcoal

charcuterie *f* CUIS cold cuts *pl*, *Br* cold meat; *magasin* pork butcher's; **charcutier** *m* pork butcher

charge *f* load; *fig* burden; ÉL, JUR, MIL charge; *(responsa-*

bilité) responsibility; *avoir des enfants à* ~ have dependent children; *~s charges; (impôts)* costs; *~s fiscales* taxation

chargement *m* loading; *ce qui est chargé* load; **charger 1** *v/t navire, arme* load; *batterie,* JUR charge; *(exagérer)* exaggerate; *~ qn de qc* put s.o. in charge of sth; *se ~ de* look after **2** *v/i* charge

chariot *m pour bagages, achats* cart, *Br* trolley; *(charrette)* cart

charisme *m* charisma

charitable charitable; **charité** *f* charity; *faire la ~ à qn* give s.o. money

charmant charming, delightful; **charme** *m* charm; **charmer** charm

charnière *f* hinge

charnu fleshy

charognard *m* scavenger

charpente *f* framework; **charpentier** *m* carpenter

charte *f* charter

charter *m* charter

chasse[1] *f* hunting; *(poursuite)* chase; *prendre en ~* chase (after); *~ privée* private game reserve

chasse[2] *f*: *~ d'eau* flush

chasser *gibier* hunt; *(expulser)* drive away; *employé* dismiss; **chasseur** *m* hunter; AVIAT fighter; *dans un hôtel* bellhop, *Br* bellboy

châssis *m* frame; AUTO chassis

chaste chaste

chat[1] *m* cat

chat[2] *m* INFORM chatroom; *conversation* (online) chat

châtaigne *f* chestnut; **châtaignier** *m* chestnut (tree); **châtain** *inv* chestnut

château *m* castle; ~ *fort* (fortified) castle; ~ *d'eau* water tower

châtier punish; **châtiment** *m* punishment

chaton *m* kitten

chatouiller tickle

chatte *f* cat

chatter INFORM chat (online)

chaud 1 *adj* hot; *plus modéré* warm; *il fait* ~ it's hot/warm **2** *m* heat; *plus modéré* warmth; *j'ai* ~ I'm hot/warm; **chaudière** *f* boiler

chauffage *m* heating; ~ *central* central heating

chauffard *m* F roadhog

chauffer 1 *v/t* heat (up), warm (up); *maison* heat; *se* ~ warm o.s.; *d'un sportif* warm up **2** *v/i* warm *ou* heat up; *d'un moteur* overheat

chauffeur *m* driver; *privé aussi* chauffeur; ~ *de taxi* taxi *ou* cab driver

chaussée *f* pavement, *Br* roadway

chausser *bottes* put on; *se* ~ put one's shoes on; **chaussette** *f* sock; **chausson** *m* slipper; **chaussure** *f* shoe; *~s de marche* hiking boots;

~s de ski ski boots

chauve bald; **chauve-souris** *f* bat

chauvinisme *m* chauvinism

chef *m* (*meneur*), POL leader; (*patron*) boss; *d'une entreprise* head; *d'une tribu* chief; CUIS chef; *au premier* ~ first and foremost; *de propre mon* ~ on my own initiative

chef-d'œuvre *m* masterpiece

chemin *m* way; (*route*) road; (*allée*) path; ~ *de fer* railroad, *Br* railway

cheminée *f* chimney; (*âtre*) fireplace; (*encadrement*) mantelpiece; *de bateau* funnel

cheminot *m* rail worker

chemise *f* shirt; (*dossier*) folder; ~ *de nuit de femme* nightdress; **chemisier** *m* blouse

chêne *m* BOT oak (tree)

chenil *m* kennels *pl*

chenille *f* ZO caterpillar

chèque *m* COMM check, *Br* cheque; ~ *de voyage* traveler's check, *Br* traveller's cheque; **chéquier** *m* checkbook, *Br* chequebook

cher, **-ère 1** *adj* dear (*à qn* to s.o.); *coûteux* dear, expensive **2** *adv*: *payer qch* ~ pay a high price for sth **3** *m/f* **mon cher, ma chère** my dear

chercher look for; ~ *à faire qch* try to do sth; *aller* ~ fetch, go for; *venir* ~ collect,

come for; *envoyer* ~ send for

chéri darling

chétif, **-ive** puny

cheval *m* horse; AUTO horsepower; *aller à* ~ ride; *être à* ~ *sur qch* straddle sth; **chevalier** *m* HIST knight; **chevalière** *f* signet ring

chevelu *personne* long-haired; **chevelure** *f* hair

chevet *m* bedhead; *table f de* ~ nightstand, *Br aussi* bedside table

cheveu *m* hair; **~x** hair; *aux* **~x courts** short-haired

cheville *f* ANAT ankle; TECH peg

chèvre *f* goat

chevreau *m* kid

chevreuil *m* deer; CUIS venison

chez: ~ *lui* at his place; *direction* to his place; ~ *Marcel* at Marcel's; *quand nous sommes* ~ *nous* when we are at home; *rentrer* ~ *soi* go home; *aller* ~ *le coiffeur* go to the hairdresser *ou Br* hairdresser's; ~ *Molière* in Molière

chez-soi *m* home

chiant F boring

chic 1 *m* style **2** *adj* chic; (*sympathique*) decent

chicaner quibble (*sur* over)

chicorée *f* BOT chicory

chien *m* dog; *temps de* ~ *fig* F filthy weather; ~ *d'aveugle* seeing-eye dog, *Br* guide dog; chienne *f* dog; *le chien et la ~* the dog and the bitch

chier V shit; *ça me fait ~* P it pisses me off P

chiffon *m* rag; *~ (à poussière)* duster; chiffonner crumple; *fig* F bother

chiffre *m* number; *(code)* cipher

Chili: *le ~* Chili; chilien, *~ne* 1 *adj* Chilean; Chilien, *~ne* *m/f* Chilean

chimie *f* chemistry

chimiothérapie *f* chemotherapy

chimique chemical

Chine: *la ~* China; chinois, *~e* 1 *adj* Chinese 2 *m langue* Chinese; Chinois, *~e* *m/f* Chinese

chiot *m* pup

chips *mpl* chips, *Br* crisps

chirurgie *f* surgery; *~ esthétique* plastic surgery; chirurgien, *~ne* *m/f* surgeon; *~ dentiste* dental surgeon

choc *m* shock; *d'opinions, intérêts* clash

chocolat *m* chocolate

cœur *m* choir *en ~* in chorus

choisir choose; *~ de faire* decide to do; choix *m* choice; *(assortiment)* range; *de (premier) ~* choice

cholestérol *m* cholesterol

chômage *m* unemployment; *être au ~* be unemployed; *~ partiel* short time; chômeur, -euse *m/f* unemployed person; *les ~s* the

unemployed *pl*

chope *f* beer mug

choquant shocking; choquer: *~ qc* knock sth; *~ qn* shock s.o.

chorale *f* choir

chose *f* thing; *autre ~* something else; *c'est ~ faite* it's done

chou *m* BOT cabbage; *~x de Bruxelles* Brussels sprouts

chouette 1 *f* owl 2 *adj* F great

chou-fleur *m* cauliflower

chrétien, *~ne* *adj* & *m/f* Christian

christianisme *m* Christianity

chrome *m* chrome

chronique 1 *adj* chronic 2 *f d'un journal* column; *reportage* report; chroniqueur *m pour un journal* columnist

chronologique chronological, chronométrer time

chuchoter whisper

chut: *~!* hush

chute *f* fall; *~ des cheveux* hair loss

ci: *à cette heure~* at this time; *comme ~ comme ça* F so-so; *par~ par-là* here and there

cible *f* target; cibler target

ciboulette *f* BOT chives *pl*

cicatrice *f* scar *(aussi fig)*; cicatriser: *(se) ~* heal

ci-contre opposite; ci-dessous below; ci-dessus above

cidre *m* cider

ciel *m* sky; REL heaven

cigale *f* cicada
cigare *m* cigar
cigarette *f* cigarette; **~ électronique** e-cigarette
ci-inclus enclosed; **ci-joint** enclosed, attached
cil *m* eyelash
ciment *m* cement
cimetière *m* cemetery
ciné *m* F movie theater, *Br* cinema; **~ maison** *m* home theater, *Br* cinema; *art* cinema, movies *pl*
cinglé F mad, crazy
cinq five; **le ~ mai** May fifth, *Br* the fifth of May; **cinquantaine** *f* about fifty; **elle approche la ~** she's getting on for fifty; **cinquante** fifty; **cinquantième** fiftieth **cinquième** fifth
cintre *m* arch; *pour vêtements* coathanger
cirage *m* *pour parquet* wax, polish; *pour chaussures* polish
circonférence *f* circumference
circonspect circumspect
circonstance *f* circumstance
circuit *m* circuit; *de voyage* tour; *SP* track
circulaire *adj* & *f* circular
circulation *f* circulation; *voitures* traffic; **circuler** circulate; **faire ~ nouvelles** spread
cire *f* wax; **cirer** polish; *parquet aussi* wax
cirque *m* circus
cirrhose *f*: **~ du foie** cirrhosis

of the liver
ciseaux *mpl* scissors *pl*
citadin **~e 1** *adj* town *atr*, city *atr* **2** *m/f* town-dweller, city-dweller
citation *f* quotation; *JUR* summons *sg*
cité *f* city; **~ universitaire** fraternity house, *Br* hall of residence
citoyen **~ne** *m/f* citizen; **citoyenneté** *f* citizenship
citron *m* lemon; **~ vert** lime; **citronnier** *m* lemon (tree)
civière *f* stretcher
civil 1 *adj* civil; *non militaire* civilian; **état** *m* ~ marital status **2** *m* civilian; **en ~** in civilian clothes; *policier* in plain clothes; **civilisation** *f* civilization
civique civic
civisme *m* public-spiritedness
clair 1 *adj* clear; *couleur* light; *chambre* bright **2** *adv* *voir* clearly; *dire, parler* plainly **3** *m*: **~ de lune** moonlight
clairière *f* clearing
clairvoyant perceptive
clandestin secret, clandestine; **passager** *m* ~ stowaway
claque *f* slap; **claquer 1** *v/t* *porte* slam; *argent* F blow; **~ des doigts** snap one's fingers **2** *v/i* *d'un fouet* crack; *des dents* chatter; *d'un volet* slam
clarifier clarify

clarinette f clarinet

clarté f (lumière) brightness; (transparence) clarity

classe f class; **il a de la ~** he's got class; **~ économique** economy class

classement m position, place; BOT. zo classification; de lettres filing; **classer** classify; actes, dossiers file; **~ une affaire** consider a matter closed

classique 1 adj classical; (traditionnel) classic **2** m en littérature classical author; MUS classical music; film, livre classic

clause f clause; **~ pénale** penalty clause

clavicule f collarbone

clavier m keyboard

clé f key; TECH wrench; **~ de fa** MUS bass clef; **fermer à ~** lock; **sous ~** under lock and key

clef → **clé**

clément merciful

clergé m clergy

clic m bruit, INFORM click

client, **~e** m/f (acheteur) customer; d'un médecin patient; d'un avocat client; **clientèle** f customers pl, clientèle; d'un médecin patients pl; d'un avocat clients pl

cligner: **~ (des yeux)** blink; **~ de l'œil à qn** wink at s.o.

clignotant m turn signal, Br indicator; **clignoter** d'une lumière flicker

climat m climate (aussi fig)

climatisation f air conditioning; **climatisé** air conditioned

clin m: **~ d'œil** wink; **en un ~ d'œil** in a flash

clinique 1 adj clinical **2** f clinic

cliquer INFORM click (**sur** on)

clochard, **~e** m/f hobo, Br tramp

cloche f bell f; F (idiot) nitwit F; **clocher 1** m steeple F; **clocher 2** v/i F: **ça cloche** something's not right

cloison f partition

cloîtrer fig: **se ~** shut o.s. away

clonage m cloning; **clone** m clone; **cloner** clone

clope m ou f F cigarette, Br F fag; (mégot) cigarette end

cloque f blister

clôture f d'un débat closure; d'un compte closing; (barrière) fence

clou m nail; fig main attraction; MÉD boil; **clouer** nail; **être cloué au lit** to be confined to bed

clown m clown

club m club; **~ de gym** gym

coaguler du lait curdle; du sang coagulate

cobaye m zo, fig guinea pig

coca m Coke®

coccinelle f ladybug, Br ladybird; F AUTO Volkswagen® beetle

cocher sur une liste check, Br

collègue

aussi tick off

cochon 1 *m* ZO, *fig* pig **2** *adj* cochon; **~ne** F dirty; **cochonnerie** *f* F: **des ~s** filth; *nourriture* junk food

coco *m*: **noix** *f* **de ~** coconut

cocotte *f* CUIS casserole; F darling; *péj* tart; **~ minute** pressure cooker

code *m* code; **~ confidentiel** PIN number; **~ pénal** penal code; **se mettre en ~** switch to low beams; **~ postal** zip-code, *Br* postcode

cœur *m* heart; **de bon ~** gladly; **par ~** by heart; **j'ai mal au ~** I feel nauseous

coffre *m meuble* chest; FIN safe; AUTO trunk, *Br* boot; **coffre-fort** *m* safe

cogérer co-manage

cognac *m* brandy, cognac

cogner *v/t moteur* knock; **~ à** *ou* **contre qc** bang against sth; **se ~ à** *ou* **contre qc** bump into sth

cohabiter cohabit

cohérent *théorie* consistent, coherent

cohue *f* crowd, rabble

coiffer: **~ qn** do s.o.'s hair; **se ~** do one's hair; **coiffeur** *m* hairdresser, hair stylist; **coiffeuse** *f* hairdresser, hair stylist; *meuble* dressing table; **coiffure** *f* de cheveux hairstyle

coin *m* corner; *cale* wedge

coincer squeeze; *porte, tiroir* jam; **coincé dans un em-**

bouteillage stuck in a traffic jam

coïncidence *f* coincidence

col *m* collar; *d'une bouteille, d'un pull* neck; GÉOGR col; **~ blanc/bleu** white-collar/ /blue-collar worker

colère *f* anger; **se mettre en ~** get angry

colique *f* colic; *(diarrhée)* diarrhea, *Br* diarrhoea

colis *m* parcel, package

collaborateur, -trice *m/f* collaborator *((aussi* POL *péj)*; **collaboration** *f* collaboration, cooperation; POL *péj* collaboration; **collaborer** collaborate, cooperate (*avec* with; **à** on); POL *péj* collaborate

collant 1 *adj* sticky; *vêtement* close-fitting; F *personne* clingy **2** *m* pantyhose *pl*, *Br* tights *pl*

colle *f* glue; *fig* P *question* tough question; *(retenue)* detention

collecte *f* collection; **collectif, -ive** collective; **voyage** *m* **~** group tour

collection *f* collection; **collectionner** collect; **collectionneur, -euse** *m/f* collector

collège *m* école junior high, *Br* secondary school; **collégien, ~ne** *m/f* junior high student, *Br* secondary school pupil

collègue *m/f* colleague, co-worker

coller 1 *v/t* stick, glue **2** *v/i* stick (**à** to); **se ~ contre** *mur* press o.s against; *personne* cling to

collier *m bijou* necklace; *de chien* collar

colline *f* hill

collision *f* collision; **entrer en ~ avec** collide with

colocataire *m/f* roommate, *Br* flatmate

colombe *f* dove (*aussi fig*)

Colombie: la ~ Colombia; **colombien, ~ne** Colombian; **Colombien, ~ne** *m/f* Colombian

colonie *f* colony; **~ de vacances** summer camp

colonne *f* column

colorant 1 *adj shampoing* color *atr*, *Br* colour *atr* **2** *m* dye; *dans la nourriture* coloring, *Br* colouring; **colorer** color, *Br* colour

coma *m* coma

combat *m* fight; MIL *aussi* battle; **mettre hors de ~** put out of action; **combattant 1** *adj* fighting **2** *m* combatant; **combattre** fight

combien 1 *adv quantité* how much; *avec* **la** how many **2** *m*: **tous les ~** how often; **on est le ~ aujourd'hui?** what date is it today?

combinaison *f* combination; (*astuce*) scheme; *de mécanicien* coveralls *pl*, *Br* boiler suit; *lingerie* (full-length)

slip; **~ de plongée** wet suit

combiner combine; *voyage, projet* plan

comble 1 *m fig*: *sommet* height; **~s** *pl* attic; **de fond en ~** from top to bottom **2** *adj* full (to capacity); **combler** *trou* fill in; *déficit* make good; *personne* overwhelm; **~ qn de qch** shower s.o. with sth

combustible 1 *adj* combustible **2** *m* fuel

comédie *f* comedy; **~ musicale** musical; **comédien, ~ne** *m/f* actor; *qui joue le genre comique* comic actor

comestible 1 *adj* edible **2** *mpl* **~s** food

comique 1 *adj* THÉÂT comic; (*drôle*) funny, comical **2** *m* comedian; *acteur* comic (actor); *genre* comedy

comité *m* committee

commande *f* COMM order; TECH control; INFORM command; **commander 1** *v/t* COMM order; (*ordonner*) command, order; MIL be in command of; TECH control **2** *v/i* (*diriger*) be in charge; COMM order

comme 1 *adv* like; **noir ~ la nuit** as black as night; **~ ci ~ ça** F so-so; **~ vous voulez** as you like; **~ si** as if; **il travaillait ~** ... he was working as a ...; **moi, ~ les autres, je** ... like the others, I ... **2** *conj* as

commencement *m* beginning, start; **commencer** begin, start; **~ qc par qc** start sth with sth; **~ par faire qc** start by doing sth

comment *adv*; **~?** (*qu'avez-vous dit?*) pardon me?, *Br* sorry?; **~!** *surpris* what!

commentaire *m* comment; RAD, TV commentary; **commenter** comment on; RAD, TV commentate on

commerçant, **~e 1** *adj*: **rue f ~e** shopping street **2** *m/f* merchant, trader

commerce *m* trade, commerce; (*magasin*) store, *Br* shop; *fig* (*rapports*) dealings *pl*; **commercial** commercial; **commercialiser** market

commettre commit; *erreur* make

commis *m*: **~ voyageur** commercial traveler *ou Br* traveller

commissaire *m* commission member; *de l'UE* Commissioner; SP steward; **commissariat** *m* commissionership; **~ (de police)** police station

commission *f* commission; (*message*) message

commode 1 *adj* handy; *arrangement* convenient; *pas ~ personne* awkward **2** *f* chest of drawers; **commodité** *f* convenience

commotion *f* MÉD: **~ cérébrale** stroke

commun 1 *adj* common; *œu-*vre joint; **mettre en ~** *argent* pool **2** *m*: **hors du ~** out of the ordinary

communal (*de la commune*) local

communauté *f* community; *de hippies* commune

communication *f* communication; (*message*) message; **~ téléphonique** telephone call

communion *f* REL Communion

communiquer 1 *v/t* communicate; *maladie* pass on, give (**à qn** to s.o.) **2** *v/i* communicate

communisme *m* communism; **communiste** *m/f & adj* Communist

commutateur *m* switch

compact compact

compagne *f* companion; *dans couple* wife

compagnie *f* company; **~ aérienne** airline

compagnon *m* companion; *dans couple* husband; *employé* journeyman

comparaison *f* comparison; **par ~ à** compared with; **comparer** compare (**à** to, **avec** with)

compartiment *m* compartment; *de train* car, *Br* compartment

compas *m* compass

compassion *f* compassion

compatible compatible

compatir: **~ à** sympathize

with

compatriote *m/f* compatriot

compenser compensate for

compétence *f* (*connaissances*) ability, competence; JUR jurisdiction; **compétent** competent, skillful, *Br* skilful; JUR competent

compétitif, **-ive** competitive; **compétition** *f* competition

compiler compile

complaire: **se ~ dans/à faire** delight in/in doing

complet, **-ète1** *adj* complete; *hôtel*, *description*, *jeu de cartes* full; *pain* whole wheat, *Br* wholemeal **2** *m* suit; **complètement** completely; **compléter** complete; **se ~** complement each other

complexe *adj* & *m* complex

complication *f* complication

complice 1 *adj* JUR: **être ~** be an accessory to **2** *m/f* accomplice

compliment *m* compliment; **mes ~s** congratulations

compliqué complicated; **compliquer** complicate; **se ~** become complicated

comporter (*comprendre*) comprise; (*impliquer*) involve; **se ~** behave (o.s)

composer 1 *v/t* (*former*) make up; MUS compose; *livre*, *poème* write; *numéro* dial **2** *v/i* transiger come to terms (*avec* with); **se ~ de** consist of

compositeur, **-trice***m/f* com-

poser

composter *billet* punch

compote *f*: **~ de pommes** stewed apples

compréhension *f* understanding

comprendreunderstand; (*inclure*) include; (*comporter*) comprise

compresse*f* MÉD compress

comprimé *m* tablet

compris(*inclus*) included; **y ~** including

compromettre compromise

comptabilité *f* accountancy; (*comptes*) accounts *pl*; **comptable** *m/f* accountant

comptant: **au ~** cash

compte *m* account; (*calcul*) calculation; **~s** accounts; **en fin de ~** when all's said and done; **se rendre ~ de** realize; **tenir ~ de qc** take sth into account; **~ courant** checking account, *Br* current account; **~ rendu** report; *de réunion* minutes *pl*; (*prévoir*) allow; (*inclure*) include; **~ faire** plan on doing **2** *v/i* count; **~ sur** rely on; **à ~ de** starting (from); **compteur** *m* meter

comptoir *m* *d'un café* bar; *d'un magasin* counter

con, **~ne** P **1** *adj* damn stupid F **2** *m/f* damn idiot F

concentration *f* concentration; **concentrer** concentrate; **se ~** concentrate

(*sur* on)

concept *m* concept

conception *f* (*idée*) concept; (*planification*) design; BIOL conception

concernant concerning, about; **concerner** concern

concert *m* MUS concert; **de ~ avec** together with

concession *f* concession; AUTO dealership

concevable conceivable; **concevoir** (*comprendre*) understand, conceive; (*inventer*) design; BIOL, *plan*, *idée* conceive

concierge *m/f* superintendent, Br caretaker; *d'école* janitor, Br *aussi* caretaker; *d'un hôtel* concierge

concis concise

concitoyen, **~ne** *m/f* fellow citizen

conclure conclude; **~ de** conclude from; **conclusion** *f* conclusion

concombre *m* cucumber

concours *m* competition; (*assistance*) help

concret, **-ète** concrete

concurrence *f* competition; **faire ~ à** compete with; **concurrent**, **~e 1** *adj* rival **2** *m/f* competitor

condamnation *f* sentence; *action* sentencing; *fig* condemnation

condamner JUR sentence; *malade* give up; (*réprouver*) condemn; *porte* block up

condescendance *f* péj condescension

condition *f* condition; **~ préalable** prerequisite; **à** (**la**) **~ que** (+ *subj*) on condition that; **conditionner** (*emballer*) package; PSYCH condition

condoléances *fpl* condolences

conducteur, **-trice 1** *m/f* driver **2** *m* PHYS conductor

conduire 1 *v/t* take; (*mener*) lead; *voiture* drive; EL conduct; **se ~** behave **2** *v/i* AUTO drive; (*mener*) lead

conduit *m* d'eau, de gaz pipe; **~ d'aération** ventilation shaft

conduite *f* (*comportement*) behavior, Br behaviour; *direction* management; *d'eau, de gaz* pipe; AUTO driving

cône *m* cone

confection *f* making; *industrie* clothing industry

conférence *f* conference; (*exposé*) lecture; **être en ~** be in a meeting

confesser confess; **~ qn** REL hear s.o.'s confession; **se ~** REL go to confession; **confession** *f* confession; (*croyance*) faith

confiance *f* confidence; **faire ~ à** trust; **confiant** confident; (*crédule*) trusting

confidence *f* confidence; **faire une ~ à** confide in; **confident**, **~e** *m/f* confidant; confidentiel, **~le** confidential

confier: **~** *qc à qn* (*laisser*) entrust s.o. (with sth); **se ~ à** confide in

confirmation *f* confirmation (*aussi* REL); **confirmer** confirm (*aussi* REL)

confiserie *f* confectionery; *magasin* confectioner's; **~s** candy , *Br* sweets

confisquer confiscate (*à* from)

confiture *f* jelly, *Br* jam

conflit *m* conflict; (*d'idées*) clash

confondre confuse; (*déconcerter*) take aback; **se ~** (*se mêler*) merge

conforme: **~** *à* in accordance with; **conformiste** *m/f* conformist

confort *m* comfort; **confortable** comfortable; *somme* sizeable

confronter confront; (*comparer*) compare

confusion *f* confusion; (*embarras*) embarrassment

congé *m* vacation, *Br* holiday; MIL leave; *avis de départ* notice; **prendre ~ de** take one's leave of; **~** *de maladie* sick leave

congélateur *m* freezer; **congelé** *aliment* frozen; **congeler** freeze

congénital congenital

congestion *f* MÉD congestion; **~** *cérébrale* stroke; **congestionné** *visage* flushed

congrès *m* convention, conference; **Congrès** *aux États-Unis* Congress

conique conical

conjecture *f* conjecture

conjoint, **~e 1** *adj* joint **2** *m/f* spouse

conjonctivite *f* MÉD conjunctivitis

conjugaison *f* GRAM conjugation

conjugal conjugal; *vie* married

conjuguer *efforts* combine; GRAM conjugate

connaissance *f* knowledge; (*conscience*) consciousness; *personne connue* acquaintance; **~s** *d'un sujet* knowledge; **connaisseur** *m* connoisseur; **connaître** know; (*rencontrer*) meet; **s'y ~** **en** be an expert on

connecter TECH connect; **se ~** INFORM log on

connerie *f* V: *une* **~** a damn stupid thing to do/say

connexion *f* connection; *hors* **~** INFORM off-line

connu well-known

conquérir conquer

conquête *f* conquest

consacrer REL consecrate; (*dédier*) dedicate; *temps, argent* spend; **se ~ à** dedicate *ou* devote o.s. to

conscience *f moral* conscience; *physique,* PSYCH consciousness; **prendre ~**

de become aware of

consécutif, -ive consecutive; **~ à** resulting from

conseil *m* advice; *(conseiller)* adviser; *(assemblée)* council; **un ~** a piece of advice; **~ d'administration** board of directors

conseiller *personne* advise; **~ qc à qn** recommend sth to s.o.

consentir 1 *v/i* consent, agree (**à** to) **2** *v/t prêt, délai* agree

conséquence *f* consequence; **en ~** consequently

conservation *f* preservation; *des aliments* preserving

conserve *f* preserve; *en boîte* canned food, *Br aussi* tinned food; **conserver** keep; *aliments* preserve

considérable considerable; **considération** *f* consideration; **considérer** consider

consigne *f* orders *pl; d'une gare* baggage checkroom, *Br* left luggage office; *pour bouteilles* deposit; *ÉDU* detention

consistance *f* consistency; **consistant** *liquide, potage* thick; *mets* substantial; **consister: ~ en/dans** consist of; **~ à faire** consist in doing

consolation *f* consolation

console *f* console; **jouer à la ~** play computer games

consoler consolet; **se ~ de** get over

consolider consolidate

consommateur, -trice *m/f* consumer; *dans un café* customer; **consommation** *f* consumption; *dans un café* drink; **consommer 1** *v/t* consume, use **2** *v/i dans un café* drink

consonne *f* consonant

conspiration *f* conspiracy; **conspirer** conspire

constamment constantly

constance *f (persévérance)* perseverance; *en amour* constancy

constant constant; *ami* staunch; *efforts* persistent

constater observe

consternation *f* consternation; **consterner** fill with consternation, dismay

constipation *f* MÉD constipation

constituer constitute; *comité, société* form; *rente* settle (**à** on); **se ~** *fortune* build up

constitution *f (composition)* composition; ANAT, POL constitution; *d'un comité, d'une société* formation

construction *f* construction, building; **construire** construct, build; *théorie, roman* construct

consul *m* consul; **consulat** *m* consulate

consultation *f* consultation; **consulter 1** *v/t* consult **2** *v/i* be available for consultation

contact *m* contact; **se mettre**

en ~ avec contact; **mettre/couper le ~** AUTO switch the engine on/off

contagieux, -euse contagious; *rire* infectious

contaminer contaminate; MÉD *personne* infect

conte m story, tale

contempler contemplate

contemporain m & adj contemporary

contenir contain; *foule* control; *larmes* hold back; *peine* suppress; **se ~** contain o.s.

content pleased, content (**de** with)

contenu m content

contestation f discussion; *(opposition)* protest; **contester** challenge

contexte m context

continent m continent

contingent m *(part)* quota

continu continuous; ÉL *courant* direct; **continuer 1** v/t continue; *rue, ligne* extend **2** v/i continue, go on; *de route* extend; **~ à ou de faire** continue to do, go on doing; **continuité** f continuity; *d'une tradition* continuation

contorsion f contorsion

contour m contour; *d'une fenêtre, d'un visage* outline; **~s** *(courbes)* twists and turns

contourner get around

contraceptif, -ive contraceptive; **contraception** f contraception

contracter *dette* incur; *mala-*

die aussi contract; *obligation, engagement* enter into; *assurance* take out; *habitude* acquire

contradiction f contradiction

contraindre: ~ qn à faire qc force s.o. to do sth; **contrainte** f constraint; **sans ~** freely, without restraint

contraire 1 adj sens opposite; *principes* conflicting; *vent* contrary **2** m: **le ~ de** the opposite ou contrary of; **au ~** on the contrary

contrarier *personne* annoy; *projet* thwart

contraster contrast

contrat m contract

contravention f infringement; *(procès-verbal)* ticket

contre 1 prép against; *(en échange)* in (exchange) for; **tout ~ qch** right next to sth; **par ~** on the contrary; **quelque chose ~ la diarrhée** something for diarrhea **2** m: **le pour et le ~** the pros and the cons pl

contrebande f smuggling; *marchandises* contraband; **contrebandier** m smuggler

contrebasse f double bass

contrecœur: à ~ reluctantly

contrecoup m after-effect

contredire contradict

contrée f country

contrefaire counterfeit; *signature* forge; *personne, gestes* imitate; *voix* disguise

contre-nature unnatural

contrepartie f compensation; **en ~** in return

contre-plaqué m plywood

contrer counter

contresens m misinterpretation; **prendre une route à ~** go down a road the wrong way

contretemps m hitch

contribuable m taxpayer; **contribuer** contribute (**à** to); **~ à faire** help to do

contrôle m (vérification) check; (domination) control; (maîtrise de soi) self-control; **~ douanier** customs inspection; **~ radar** radar speed check; **contrôler** identité, billets etc check; (maîtriser, dominer) control; **se ~** control o.s.

controversé controversial

contusion f MÉD bruise

convaincre (persuader) convince; **~ qn de faire qch** persuade s.o. to do sth

convalescent, ~e m/f convalescent

convenable suitable; (correct) personne respectable; salaire adequate; **convenance** f: **les ~s** the proprieties

convenir: **~ à qn** suit s.o.; **~à qc** be suitable for sth; **~ de qc** (décider) agree on sth; **~ que** (reconnaître que) admit that; **comme convenu** as agreed

convention f convention

converger converge

conversation f conversation; **~ téléphonique** telephone conversation, phonecall

conversion f conversion

convertir convert

conviction f conviction

convive m/f guest; **convivialité** f conviviality, friendliness; INFORM user-friendliness

convocation f d'une assemblée convening; JUR summons sg

convoi m convoy

convoquer assemblée convene; JUR summons; candidat notify; employé, écolier call in

convoyer MIL escort

convulsion f convulsion

coopération f cooperation; **coopérer** cooperate (**à** in)

coordination f coordination

coordonnées fpl MATH coordinates pl; de personne contact details

copain m F pal

copie f copy; ÉDU paper; **copier** copy (**sur qn** from s.o.)

copieux, -euse copious

copine f F pal

copropriétaire m/f co-owner, part owner

coq m rooster

coquelicot m BOT poppy

coquetier m eggcup

coquetterie f flirtatiousness; (élégance) stylishness

coquillage m shell; **des ~s**

shellfish

coquille *f* shell; *erreur* misprint, typo

coquin, **~e 1** *adj enfant* naughty **2** *m/f* rascal

corbeau *m* ZO crow

corbeille *f* basket; *au théâtre* circle

corbillard *m* hearse

corde *f* rope; MUS, *de tennis* string

cordialité *f* cordiality

cordon *m* cord; **~** *littoral* offshore sand bar

cordonnier *m* shoe repairer

Corée: *la* **~** Korea; **coréen**, **~e 1** *adj* Korean **2** *m langue* Korean; **Coréen**, **~ne** *m/f* Korean

corne *f* horn

cornée *f* cornea

corneille *f* crow

corner *m en football* corner

cornet *m sachet* (paper) cone; MUS cornet

cornichon *m* gherkin

corporation *f* body; HIST guild

corporel, **~le** *hygiène* personal; *châtiment* corporal; *art* body *atr*

corps *m* body; *mort aussi* corpse; MIL corps; **prendre ~** take shape

corpulence *f* stoutness, corpulence

correct correct; *tenue* suitable; F *(convenable)* acceptable, ok F

correcteur *m:* **~** *orthographi-*

que spellchecker

correction *f qualité* correctness; *(modification)* correction; *(punition)* beating

correspondance *f* correspondence; *de train etc* connection; **correspondre** correspond with; **~** *à réalité* correspond with; *preuves* tally with; *idées* fit in with

corridor *m* corridor

corriger correct; *épreuve* proof-read; *(battre)* beat

corrompre corrupt; *(soudoyer)* bribe

corrosion *f* corrosion

corruption *f* corruption; *(pot-de-vin)* bribery

corsage *m* blouse

corse Corsican; **Corse 1** *m/f* Corsican **2** *f* **la Corse** Corsica

corsé *vin* full-bodied; *sauce* spicy; *café* strong; *facture* stiff; *problème* tough

cortège *m* cortège; *(défilé)* procession

cortisone *f* cortisone

corvée *f* chore; MIL fatigue

cosmétique *m & adj* cosmetic

cosmopolite *m & adj* cosmopolitan

costaud F sturdy

costume *m* costume; *pour homme* suit

cote *f en Bourse* quotation; *d'un document* identification code

63

côte f ANAT rib; (*pente*) slope; *à la mer* coast; *viande* chop; **~ à ~** side by side

côté m side; **à ~** (*près*) nearby; **à ~ de** next to; **de ~** aside; **de l'autre ~ de** on the other side of; **sur le ~** on one's/its side; **mettre de ~** put aside

côtelette f CUIS cutlet

cotisation f contribution; *à une organisation* subscription

coton m coton

côtoyer rub shoulders with; **~ qc** border sth

cottage m cottage

cou m neck

couchant 1 m west 2 adj: **soleil m ~** setting sun

couche f *layer*; *de peinture aussi* coat; *de bébé* diaper, Br nappy

coucher 1 v/t (*mettre au lit*) put to bed; (*héberger*) put up; (*étendre*) put ou lay down 2 v/i sleep; **se ~** go to bed; (*s'étendre*) lie down; *du soleil* set, go down 3 m: **~ du soleil** sunset

coucou m (*oiseau*) cuckoo; (*pendule*) cuckoo clock

coude m ANAT elbow; *d'une route* turn

coudre sew; *bouton* sew on; *plaie* sew up

couette f comforter, Br quilt

couler 1 v/i *flow*, run; *de l'eau de bain* run; *d'un bateau* sink 2 v/t *liquide* pour;

(*mouler*) cast; *bateau* sink

couleur f color, Br colour

coulisse f: **~s** THÉÂT wings; **dans les ~s** fig behind the scenes

couloir m passage, corridor; *d'un bus, avion* aisle

coup m blow; *dans jeu* move; **boire un ~** F have a drink; **du ~** and so; **après ~** after the event; **tout d'un ~, tout à ~** suddenly, all at once; **coup de couteau** stab; **coup de foudre**: *ce fut le ~* it was love at first sight; **coup de main**: **donner un ~ à qn** give s.o. a hand; **coup d'œil**: **au premier ~** at first glance; **coup de pied** kick; **coup de poing** punch; **donner un ~ à** punch; **coup de téléphone** (phone) call; **coup de soleil**: **avoir un ~** have sun stroke

coupable 1 adj guilty 2 m/f culprit, guilty party

coupe[1] f *de cheveux, d'une robe* cut

coupe[2] f (*verre*) glass; SP cup; *de fruits, glace* dish

coupe-ongles m inv nail clippers pl

couper 1 v/t *morceau, eau* cut off; *robe, chemise* cut out; *vin* dilute; *animal* castrate 2 v/i cut; **se ~** cut o.s.; (*se trahir*) give o.s. away

couple m couple

coupon m *de tissu* remnant; COMM coupon; (*ticket*) ticket

coupure f cut; de journal cutting; (billet de banque) bill, Br note; ~ **de courant** power outage, Br power cut

cour f court; ARCH courtyard; **Cour internationale de justice** International Court of Justice

courage m courage, bravery; **courageux, -euse** brave, courageous

couramment fluently

courant 1 adj current; eau running; langage everyday **2** m current (aussi ÉL); ~ **d'air** draught, Br draft; **au ~ de qch** know about sth

courbature f stiffness; **avoir des ~s** be stiff

courbe 1 adj curved **2** f curve; **courber** bend; **se ~** (se baisser) stoop, bend down

coureur m runner; péj skirt-chaser

courge f BOT squash, Br marrow

courgette f BOT zucchini, Br courgette

courir 1 v/i run (aussi d'eau); d'un bruit go around **2** v/t risque, danger run; ~ **les magasins** go around the stores

couronne f crown; **de fleurs** wreath; **couronnement** m coronation

courriel m e-mail

courrier m mail, Br aussi post; (messager) courier; ~ **électronique** e-mail

courroie f belt

cours m course; ÉCON price; de devises rate; (leçon) lesson; à l'université class, Br aussi lecture; **donner libre ~ à** give free rein to; **en ~ de route** on the way

course f à pied running; SP race; en taxi ride; (commission) errand; ~**s** (achats) shopping; **faire des ~s** go shopping

court[1] m (aussi ~ **de tennis**) (tennis) court

court[2] adj short; **à ~ de** short of

court-circuit m ÉL short circuit

courtier m broker

courtisane femme court

courtoisie f courtesy

cousin, ~e m/f cousin

coussin m cushion

coût m cost; **coûter 1** v/t cost; **combien ça coûte?** how much is it?, how much does it cost? **2** v/i cost; ~ **cher** be expensive

couteau m knife

coûteux, -euse expensive, costly

coutume f custom; **avoir ~ de faire** be in the habit of doing

couture f sewing; d'un vêtement, bas etc seam

couvée clutch; fig brood

couvent m convent

couver 1 v/t hatch; personne pamper **2** v/i d'un feu smolder, Br smoulder; d'une révolution be brewing

couvercle *m* cover

couvert 1 *adj ciel* overcast; **~ de** covered with *ou* in 2 **m à table** place setting; **~s** flatware, *Br* cutlery; **mettre le ~** set the table; **couverture** *f* cover; *sur un lit* blanket

couvrir cover (**de** with *ou* in); **~ qn** *fig* (*protéger*) cover (up) for s.o.; **se~** (*s'habiller*) cover o.s. up; *du ciel* cloud over

covoiturage *m* carpooling; **faire du ~** carpool

crabe *m* crab

cracher spit

crachin *m* drizzle

craie *f* chalk

craindre fear, be frightened of; **~ de faire** be afraid of doing; **~ que (ne)** (+ *subj*) be afraid that

crainte *f* fear; **de~ de** for fear of

craintif, -ive timid

cramoisi crimson

crampe *f* MÉD cramp

crampon *m* crampon

cran *m* notch; **il a du ~** F he's got guts F

crâne *m* skull

crâner F (*pavaner*) show off

crapaud *m* ZO toad

crapule *f* villain

craquelé cracked

craquement *m* crackle; **craquer** crack; *d'un parquet* creak; *de feuilles* crackle; *d'une couture* split; *d'une personne* (*s'effondrer*) crack up

crasse 1 *adj ignorance* crass 2 *f* dirt

cravate *f* necktie, *Br* tie

crayon *m* pencil; **~ à bille** ballpoint pen; **~ de couleur** crayon

créance *f* COMM debt; **créancier, -ère** *m/f* creditor

création *f* creation; *de mode, design* design; **créativité** *f* creativity

créature *f* creature

crèche *f* day nursery; *de Noël* crèche, *Br* crib

crédibilité *f* credibility; **crédit** *m* credit; (*prêt*) loan; (*influence*) influence; **acheter à ~** buy on credit; **faire ~ à qn** give s.o. credit

créditeur, -trice 1 *m/f* creditor **2** *adj solde* credit *atr*; **être ~** be in credit

crédule credulous

créer create; *institution* set up; COMM *produit* design

crématorium *m* crematorium

crème 1 *f* cream; **~ anglaise** custard; **~ dépilatoire** hair remover; **~ solaire** suntan cream **2** *m* coffee with milk, *Br* white coffee **3** *adj inv* cream

créneau *m* AUTO space; COMM niche

crêpe *f* CUIS pancake

crépiter crackle

crépu frizzy

crépuscule *m* twilight

crétin, ~e m/f idiot, cretin

creuser hollow out; *trou* dig; *fig* look into

creux, -euse 1 adj hollow; **assiette** f **creuse** soup plate **2** adv: **sonner ~** ring hollow **3** m hollow

crevaison f flat, Br puncture

crevant F (*épuisant*) exhausting; (*drôle*) hilarious

crevasser crack; **se ~** crack

crever 1 v/t ballon burst; pneu puncture **2** v/i burst; F (*mourir*) kick the bucket; F AUTO have a flat ou Br puncture

crevette f shrimp

cri m shout, cry; **c'est le dernier ~** fig it's all the rage

cribler sieve; **criblé de** fig riddled with

cric m jack

crier 1 v/i shout; **~ au scandale** protest **2** v/t shout

crime m crime; (*assassinat*) murder; **criminel, ~le 1** adj criminal **2** m/f criminal; (*assassin*) murderer

crinière f mane

criquet m ZO cricket

crise f crisis; MÉD attack; **~ cardiaque** heart attack

crisper muscles tense; visage contort; fig F irritate; **se ~** tense up

crisser squeak

cristal m crystal

critère m criterion

critique 1 adj/ critical **2** m critic **3** f criticism; d'un film etc review; **critiquer** criticize;

(*analyser*) look at critically

croc m (*dent*) fang; de boucherie hook

crochet m hook; ouvrage crochet; d'une route sharp turn; **~s** en typographie square brackets

crochu nez hooked

crocodile m crocodile

croire 1 v/t believe; (*penser*) think; **~ qc de qn** believe sth about s.o. **2** v/i: **~ à qc** believe in sth; **~ en Dieu** believe in God **3**: **il se croit intelligent** he thinks he's intelligent

croisade f crusade

croisement m crossing (aussi BIOL); animal cross; **croiser 1** v/t cross (aussi BIOL); **~ qn dans la rue** pass s.o. in the street **2** v/i MAR cruise; **se ~** de routes cross; de personnes meet

croisière f MAR cruise

croissance f growth

croissant m de lune crescent; CUIS croissant

croître grow

croix f cross; **mettre une ~ sur qc** fig give sth up

croquer 1 v/t crunch; (*dessiner*) sketch **2** v/i be crunchy

croquis m sketch

crotte f droppings pl

crouler collapse (aussi fig)

croupir stagnate (aussi fig)

croustillant crusty

croûte f de pain crust; de fromage rind; MÉD scab

croûton m crouton

croyance f belief; **croyant, ~e** m/f REL believer

cru 1 adj raw; lumière, verité harsh; paroles blunt **2** m (domaine) vineyard; de vin wine

cruauté f cruelty

cruche f pitcher

crucial crucial

crucifier crucify; **crucifix** m crucifix

crudité f crudeness; de paroles bluntness; de lumière harshness; de couleur garishness; **~s** CUIS raw vegetables

cruel, ~le cruel

crustacés mpl shellfish pl

Cuba f Cuba; **cubain, ~e** Cuban; **Cubain, ~e** m/f Cuban

cube MATH m 1 m cube 2 adj cubic; **cubisme** m ART cubism

cueillir pick

cuiller f, **cuillère** f spoon; **cuillerée** f spoonful

cuir m leather; **~ chevelu** scalp

cuirasse f armor, Br armour

cuire cook; au four bake; rôti roast

cuisine f cooking; pièce kitchen; **la ~ italienne** Italian cooking ou cuisine; **cuisiner** cook; **cuisinière** f cook; (fourneau) stove

cuisse f ANAT thigh; CUIS de poulet leg

cuisson f cooking; du pain baking; d'un rôti roasting

cuit cooked, done; rôti, pain done

cuivre m copper; **~ jaune** brass; **~s** brasses

cul m V ass P, Br arse P

cul-de-sac m blind alley; fig dead end

culminer fig peak

culotte f short pants pl, Br short trousers pl; de femme panties pl

culpabilité f guilt, culpability

culte m worship; (religion) religion; (service) church service; fig cult

cultivateur, -trice m/f farmer; **cultiver** cultivate (aussi fig); légumes, tabac grow; **se ~** improve one's mind

culture f culture; AGR cultivation; de légumes, fruits etc growing

culturel, ~le cultural

cumuler: ~ des fonctions have more than one position

cupidité f greed, cupidity

cure f MÉD course of treatment; **~ de repos** rest cure

curé m curate

cure-dent m tooth pick

curiosité f curiosity; objet rare curio

curry m curry

curseur m INFORM cursor

cuvée f de vin vatful; vin wine, vintage; **cuver 1** v/i mature **2** v/t: **~ son vin** fig sleep it off

cuvette f (bac) basin; de cabinet bowl

CV m (= curriculum vitae) ré-

sumé, *Br* CV (= curriculum vitae)
cybercafé *m* Internet café
cycle *m* cycle; **cyclisme** *m* cycling; **cycliste** *m/f* cyclist
cyclone *m* cyclone

cygne *m* swan
cylindre *m* cylinder
cynique 1 *adj* cynical **2** *m/f* cynic
cystite *f* MÉD cystitis

D

dactylo *f* typing; *personne* typist
daigner: ~ **faire qch** deign to do sth
daim *m* ZO deer; *peau suede*
dalle *f* flagstone
daltonien, **~ne** colorblind, *Br* colourblind
dame *f* lady; *aux échecs, cartes* queen; *jeu m de* ~**s** checkers *sg*, *Br* draughts *sg*
damner damn
Danemark: *le* ~ Denmark
danger *m* danger; *courir un* ~ be in danger
dangereux, **-euse** dangerous
danois, **~e 1** *adj* Danish **2** *m langue* Danish; **Danois**, **~e** *m/f* Dane
dans in; *boire* ~ *un verre* drink from a glass
danse *f* dance; *action* dancing; ~ *folklorique* folk dance; **danser** dance; **danseur**, **-euse** *m/f* dancer
dard *m d'une abeille* sting
date *f* date; *de longue* ~ *amitié* long-standing; ~ *limite* deadline; ~ *limite de conservation* use-by date; **da-**ter **1** *v/t* date **2** *v/i* ~ *de* date from; *à* ~ *de ce jour* from today
datte *f* date
davantage more
de 1 *prép origine* from; *possession* of; *il vient* ~ *Paris* he comes from Paris *la maison* ~ *mon père* my father's house; *un film* ~ *Godard* a movie by Godard; ~ *jour* by day; *trembler* ~ *peur* shake with fear; *cesser* ~ *travailler* stop working **2** *partitif*: *du pain* (some) bread; *des petits pains* (some) rolls; *je n'ai pas d'argent* I don't have any money, I have no money; *est-ce qu'il y a des disquettes?* are there any diskettes?
dé *m jeu* dice; ~ *(à coudre)* thimble
dealer *m* dealer
déambuler stroll
débâcle *f de troupes* rout; *d'une entreprise* collapse
déballer unpack
débandade *f* stampede
débarbouiller: ~ *un enfant*

wash a child's face

débardeur *m vêtement* tank top

débarquement *m de marchandises* unloading; *de passagers* landing, disembarkation; **débarquer 1** *v/t marchandises* unload; *passagers* land, disembark; **2** *v/i* land, disembark; **~ chez qn** *fig* F turn up at s.o.'s place

débarrasser *table etc* clear; **~ qn de qc** take sth off s.o.; **se ~ de qc** get rid of

débat *m* debate; (*polémique*) argument

débattre: ~ qc discuss *ou* debate sth; **se ~** struggle

débauche *f* debauchery; **débaucher** (*licencier*) lay off; F lead astray

débile 1 *adj* weak; F idiotic **2** *m*: **~ mental** mental defective

débit *m* (*vente*) sale; *d'un stock* turnover; *d'une usine* output; (*élocution*) delivery; FIN debit; **débiter** *marchandises* sell (retail); *péj: fadaises* talk; *texte étudié* deliver, *péj* recite; *d'une pompe* deliver; *d'une usine, de produits* output; *bois, viande* cut up; FIN debit (*de* with); **débiteur, -trice** *m/f* debtor **2** *adj compte* overdrawn; *solde de* debit

déblayer *endroit* clear; *débris* clear (away)

débloquer 1 *v/t* TECH release;

prix, compte unfreeze; *fonds* release **2** *v/i* F be crazy; **se ~ d'une situation** get sorted out

déboguer debug

déboires *mpl* disappointments

déboisement *m* deforestation

déboîter 1 *v/t* MÉD dislocate **2** *v/i* AUTO pull out; **se ~ l'épaule** dislocate one's shoulder

débonnaire kindly

débordé snowed under (*de* with); **~ par les événements** overwhelmed by events; **déborder** *d'une rivière* overflow its banks; *du lait, de l'eau* overflow

débouché *m d'une vallée* entrance; COMM outlet; **~s d'une profession** prospects; **déboucher 1** *v/t tuyau* unblock; *bouteille* uncork **2** *v/i:* **~ de** emerge from; **~ sur** lead to (*aussi fig*)

débourser (*dépenser*) spend

debout standing; *objet* upright, on end; **être ~** stand; (*levé*) be up, be out of bed; **se mettre ~** stand up, get up

déboutonner unbutton

débraillé untidy

débrancher ÉL unplug

débrayer AUTO declutch; *fig* down tools

débris *mpl* debris *sg*; *fig* remains

débrouillard resourceful; **débrouiller** disentangle; *fig: affaire* clear up; **se ~** cope

début *m* beginning, start; **~s** THÉÂT, POL debut; **débutant, ~e** *m/f* beginner

décacheter *lettre* open

décadent decadent

décaféiné: café *m* ~ decaffeinated coffee, decaff F

décalage *m* dans l'espace moving; (*différence*) difference; *fig* gap; **décaler** *rendez-vous* change the time of; *dans l'espace* move

décamper F clear out

décaper *surface* clean; *meuble vernis* strip

décapiter decapitate

décapotable *f* (*voiture* *f*) ~ convertible

décapsuleur *m* bottle opener

décarcasser: se ~ F busta a gut F

décéder die

déceler (*découvrir*) detect; (*montrer*) point to

décembre *m* December

décemment decently; (*raisonnablement*) reasonably

décennie *f* decade

décent decent,

décentralisation *f* decentralization

déception *f* disappointment

décerner *prix* award

décès *m* death

décevoir disappoint

déchaîner *fig* provoke; **se ~**

d'une tempête break; *d'une personne* fly into a rage

décharge *f* JUR acquittal; *dans fusillade* discharge; **~ électrique** electric shock; **décharger** unload; *batterie* discharge; *arme* fire; *accusé* acquit; *colère* vent (**contre** on); **~ qn de qch** relieve s.o. of sth

décharné skeletal

déchausser: se ~ take one's shoes off

déchéance *f* decline; JUR forfeiture

déchets *mpl* waste

déchiffrer decipher

déchiqueté *côte* jagged; **déchiqueter** *corps, papier* tear to pieces

déchirant heart-breaking; **déchirer** *tissu* tear; *papier* tear up; *fig: silence* pierce; **se ~** *d'une robe* tear; **~ un muscle** tear a muscle

décidé (*résolu*) determined (**à faire qc** to do sth); **décidément** really; **décider 1** *v/t* decide on; *question* settle, decide; **~ qn à faire qc** convince s.o. to do sth; **~ de faire qch** decide to do sth **2** *v/i* decide; **se ~** make one's mind up, decide (**à faire qch** to do sth)

décimal decimal

décimer decimate

décimètre *m*: **double ~** ruler

décisif, -ive decisive; **décision** *f* decision; (*fermeté*) determination

déclaration f declaration, statement; *d'une naissance* registration; *de vol, perte* report; déclarer declare; **naissance** register; **se ~** declare o.s.; *en amour* declare one's love; *d'un feu, d'une épidémie* break out

déclencher trigger; **se ~** be triggered

déclic m bruit click

déclin m decline

décliner 1 v/i *du soleil* go down; *du jour, des forces, du prestige* wane; *de la santé* decline **2** v/t *offre* decline

décoder decode; **décodeur** m decoder

décoiffer *cheveux* ruffle

décollage m AVIAT take-off; **décoller 1** v/t peel off **2** v/i AVIAT take off; **se ~** peel off

décolleté 1 adj *robe* low-cut **2** m neckline

décolorer *tissu, cheveux* bleach; **se ~** fade

décombres mpl rubble

décommander cancel; **se ~** cancel

décomposer *produit* break down (**en** into); CHIM decompose; **se ~** *d'un cadavre* decompose; *d'un visage* become contorted

décompresser F unwind, chill out F

décompte m deduction; *d'une facture* breakdown

déconcentrer: ~ *qn* make it

hard for s.o. to concentrate

déconcertant disconcerting

déconfit disheartened

déconfiture f collapse

décongeler *aliment* thaw out

décongestionner *route* decongest; *nez* clear

déconnecter unplug, disconnect; **se ~** INFORM log off, log out

déconner P *actions* fool around; *paroles* talk crap P

déconseiller advise against

décontenancer disconcert

décontracter relax; **se ~** relax

décor m decor; *fig* (*cadre*) setting; **~s** *de théâtre* sets, scenery; **décorateur, -trice** m/f decorator; THÉÂT set designer; **décorer** decorate (**de** with)

découler: ~ *de* arise from

découper cut up; *photo* cut out (**dans** from); **se ~ sur** *fig* stand out against

décourager discourage (**de faire qc** from doing sth); **se ~** lose heart, become discouraged

découvert, ~e 1 adj *tête, épaules* bare, uncovered; **à ~** FIN overdrawn **2** m overdraft **3** f discovery; **découvrir** uncover; (*trouver*) discover; *ses intentions* reveal; (*comprendre*) find (**que** that); **se ~** *d'une personne* take off a couple of layers; (*enlever son chapeau*) take off one's hat; *du ciel* clear

décret *m* decree

décrire describe; **~ une orbite autour de** orbit

décrocher *tableau* take down; *fig* F *prix, bonne situation* land F; **~ le téléphone** pick up the receiver; *pour ne pas être dérangé* take the phone off the hook

décroître decrease, decline

déçu disappointed

décupler increase tenfold

dédaigner 1 *v/t* scorn; *personne* treat with scorn **2** *v/i*: **~ de faire qch** disdain to do sth; **dédaigneux, -euse** disdainful; **dédain** *m* disdain

dedans inside

dédicace *f* dedication; **dédier** dedicate

dédommager compensate (**de** for)

dédouanement *m* customs clearance; **dédouaner: ~ qch** clear sth through customs; **~** *fig* clear s.o.

dédoublement *m*: **~ de personnalité** split personality; **dédoubler** split in two; **se ~** split

dédramatiser play down, downplay

déduction *f* deduction; **déduire** COMM deduct; (*conclure*) deduce (**de** from)

déesse *f* goddess

défaillance *f* weakness; *fig* shortcoming; *technique* fail-

ure; **défaillir** weaken; (*se trouver mal*) feel faint

défaire undo; (*démonter*) take down, dismantle; *valise* unpack; **se ~** come undone; **se ~ de qn/qc** get rid of s.o./ sth; **défait** *visage* drawn; *chemise, valise* undone; *armée, personne* defeated; **défaite** *f* defeat; **défaitisme** *m* defeatism

défaut *m* (*imperfection*) defect; *morale* shortcoming, failing; (*manque*) lack; JUR default; **faire ~** be lacking; **par ~** INFORM default *atr*

défavorable unfavorable, *Br* unfavourable; **défavorisé** disadvantaged; **les milieux ~s** the underprivileged classes

défectueux, -euse defective

défendre defend; **~ à qn de faire qc** forbid s.o. to do sth

défense *f* defense, *Br* defence *f*; *d'un éléphant* tusk; **~ de fumer** no smoking; **défenseur** *m* defender; *d'une cause* supporter; JUR defense attorney, *Br* counsel for the defence; **défensif, -ive** *adj* & *f* defensive

déférent deferential; **déférer: ~ qn à la justice** prosecute s.o.

défi *m* challenge; (*bravade*) defiance

défiance *f* distrust, mistrust

déficience *f* deficiency; **~ immunitaire** immune deficiency

déficit *m* deficit; **déficitaire** *balance* showing a deficit; *compte* in debit

défier (*provoquer*) challenge; (*braver*) defy; **~ qn de faire qch** dare s.o. to do sth

défigurer disfigure; *fig: réalité* misrepresent

défilé *m* parade; GÉOGR pass; **~ de mode** fashion show; **défiler** parade, march

défini definite; **bien ~** well defined; **définir** define; **définitif, -ive** definitive; **en définitive** in the end; **définition** definition; **définitivement** definitely; (*pour de bon*) for good

déflagration *f* explosion

défoncer *voiture* smash up, total; *porte* break down; *terrain* break up

déformer deform; *chaussures* stretch (out of shape); *visage, fait* distort; *idée* misrepresent; **se ~ de chaussures** lose their shape

défouler: se ~ give vent to one's feelings

défroisser *vêtement* crumple

défunt, ~e 1 *adj* late **2** *m/f*: **le ~** the deceased

dégagement *m d'une route* clearing; *de chaleur* release; **dégager** (*délivrer*) free; *route* clear; *odeur, chaleur* give off; **se ~** free o.s.; *d'une route, du ciel* clear

dégât *m* damage; **~s** damage

dégel *m* thaw (*aussi* POL)

dégeler 1 *v/t frigidaire* defrost; *crédits* unfreeze **2** *v/i d'un lac* thaw

dégénérer degenerate (**en** into)

dégivrer defrost; TECH de-ice

déglutir swallow

dégonfler let the air out of, deflate; **se ~** deflate; *fig* F lose one's nerve

dégourdi resourceful; **dégourdir** *membres* loosen up; **se ~ les jambes** stretch one's legs

dégoût *m* disgust; **dégoûtant** disgusting; **dégoûter** disgust; **~ qn de qch** put s.o. off sth; **se ~ de qc** take a dislike to sth

dégrader MIL demote; *édifice* damage; (*avilir*) degrade; **se ~** deteriorate; *d'un édifice* fall into disrepair

degré *m* degree; (*échelon*) level

dégressif, -ive *tarif* tapering

dégringoler fall

dégriser sober up

déguerpir clear off

dégueulasse P disgusting; **dégueuler** F vomit

déguisement *m* disguise; *pour bal masqué etc* costume; **déguiser** disguise; *enfant* dress up (**en** as); **se ~** disguise o.s.; *pour bal masqué etc* dress up

dégustation *f* tasting; **déguster** taste

dehors 1 *adv* outside **2** *prép:* **en ~ de** outside **3** *m* exterior

déjà already; *c'est qui déjà?* F who's he again?

déjeuner 1 *v/i midi* (have) lunch; (*date limite*) dead-lunch; *matin* (have) break-fast **2** *m* lunch; *petit ~* break-fast

déjouer thwart

DEL *f* (= *diode électrolumi-nescente*) LED (= light--emitting diode)

délabré dilapidated

délacer loosen, unlace

délai *m* (*temps imparti*) time allowed; (*date limite*) dead-line; (*prolongation*) exten-sion; *sans ~* without delay

délaisser (*abandonner*) leave; (*négliger*) neglect

délassement *m* relaxation; **délasser** relax; *se ~* relax

délateur, -trice *m/f* informer; **délation** *f* denunciation

délayer dilute, water down; *fig: discours* pad out

délecter: *se ~ de* take delight in

délégué, ~e *m/f* delegate; **dé-léguer** delegate

délibération *f* deliberation; (*décision*) resolution; **délibé-ré** deliberate; **délibérer** deliberate

délicat delicate; *problème* tricky; (*plein de tact*) tactful; **délicatesse** *f* delicacy; (*tact*) tact; **délicatement** deli-cately

délicieux, -euse delicious

délier loosen, untie; *~ la lan-gue à qn* loosen s.o.'s tongue

délimiter define

délinquance *f* crime, delin-quency

délire *m* delirium; *enthousias-me* frenzy; *foule en ~* ecstat-ic crowd; **délirer** be deliri-ous; F *être fou* be stark rav-ing mad

délit *m* offense, *Br* offence; *commettre un ~ de fuite* leave the scene of an acci-dent

délivrance *f* release; (*soula-gement*) relief; (*livraison*) delivery; *certificat* issue

délivrer release; (*livrer*) de-liver; *certificat* issue

délocaliser relocate

déloyal disloyal; *concurren-ce f ~* unfair competition

deltaplane *m* hang-glider; *faire du ~* go hang-gliding

déluge *m* flood

demain tomorrow; *à ~!* see you tomorrow!

demande *f* (*requête*) request; *écrite* application; ÉCON de-mand; *sur ou à la ~ de* at the request of; *demandé* popular, in demand; **de-mander** ask for; *somme d'argent* ask; (*nécessiter*) call for; *~ qch à qn* ask s.o. for sth; (*vouloir savoir*) ask s.o. sth; *~ à qn de faire qc* ask s.o. to do sth; *se ~ si* wonder if

démanger: *le dos me démange* my back itches; *ça me démange depuis longtemps* I've been itching to do it for ages

démanteler dismantle

démaquillant *m* cleanser; *lait m ~* cleansing milk; **démaquiller**: *se ~* take off one's make-up

démarcation *f* demarcation

démarchage *m* selling

démarche *f* step (*aussi fig*); *faire des ~s* take steps

démarquer: *se ~* stand out (*de* from)

démarrage *m* start; **démarrer** start (up)

démasquer unmask

démêlé *m* argument; *avoir des ~s avec la justice* have problems with the law; **démêler** disentangle; *fig* clear up

déménager move; **déménageurs** *mpl* movers, removal men

démence *f* dementia; **dément** demented; *c'est ~ fig* F it's unbelievable

démener: *se ~* struggle; (*s'efforcer*) make an effort

démenti *m* denial

démentir (*nier*) deny; (*infirmer*) belie

démerder: *se ~* F manage, sort things out

démesuré enormous; *orgueil* excessive

démettre *poignet* dislocate;

se ~ de ses fonctions resign one's office

demeure *f* residence; **demeurer** (*habiter*) live; (*rester*) stay, remain; **demeuré** retarded

demi 1 *adj* half; *une heure et ~e* an hour and a half; *il est quatre heures et ~e* it's four thirty, it's half past four **2** *adv* half; *à ~* half **3** *m* half; *bière* half a pint; *en football, rugby* halfback

demi-cercle *m* semi-circle

demi-finale *f* semi-final

demi-frère *m* half-brother

demi-heure *f* half-hour

démilitariser demilitarize

demi-litre *m* half liter *ou Br* litre

demi-mot: *il nous l'a dit à ~* he hinted at it to us

demi-pension *f* American plan, *Br* half board

demi-pression *f* half-pint of draft *ou Br* draught beer

demi-sel *m* slightly salted butter

demi-sœur *f* half-sister

démission *f* resignation; *fig* renunciation; **démissionner 1** *v/i* resign; *fig* give up **2** *v/t* sack

demi-tarif *m* half price

demi-tour *m* AUTO U-turn; *faire ~ fig* turn back

démocrate democrat; **démocratie** *f* democracy

démodé old-fashioned

démographique demographic; **poussée** f ~ population growth

demoiselle f (*jeune fille*) young lady; ~ **d'honneur** bridesmaid

démolir demolish (*aussi fig*); **démolition** f demolition

démon m demon

démonstration f demonstration

démonter dismantle; *fig* disconcert

démontrer demonstrate, prove; (*faire ressortir*) show

démoraliser demoralize

démordre: *il n'en démordra pas* he won't change his mind

démotiver demotivate

démuni penniless

dénaturer distort

dénicher find

dénier deny

dénigrer denigrate

dénivellation f difference in height

dénombrer count

dénomination f name

dénoncer denounce; *à la police* report; *contrat* terminate; *se* ~ *à la police* give o.s. up to the police; **dénonciateur, -trice** m/f informer; **dénonciation** f denunciation

dénoter indicate, denote

dénouement m ending; **dénouer** loosen; *se* ~ *fig d'une scène* end; *d'un mystère* be cleared up

denrée f: ~**s** (*alimentaires*) foodstuffs

dense dense; **densité** f density; *du brouillard*, *d'une forêt* denseness

dent f tooth; *j'ai mal aux* ~**s** I've got toothache; *avoir une* ~ *contre qn* have a grudge against s.o.; **dentaire** dental

dentelle f lace

dentier m false teeth *pl*; **dentifrice** m toothpaste; **dentiste** m/f dentist

dénuder strip

dénué: ~ *de qc* devoid of sth; ~ *de tout* deprived of everything; **dénuement** m destitution

déodorant m deodorant

dépannage m AUTO *etc* repairs *pl*; (*remorquage*) recovery; **dépanner** repair; (*remorquer*) recover; ~ *qn* *fig* F help s.o. out; **dépanneur** m repairman; *pour voitures* mechanic; **dépanneuse** f wrecker, *Br* tow truck

départ m departure; SP, *fig* start; *au* ~ at first

départager decide between

départemental departmental; *route* ~**e** secondary road

dépassé out of date, old-fashioned; **dépasser** *personne* pass; AUTO pass, *Br* overtake; *but etc* overshoot; *fig* exceed; *se* ~ surpass o.s.

dépaysement m disorientation; *changement agréable* change of scene

dépêcher dispatch; **se ~ de faire qch** hurry to do sth; **dépêche-toi!** hurry up!

dépendance *f* dependence; **~s bâtiments** outbuildings; **entraîner une (forte) ~** be (highly) addictive; **dépendre:** **~ de** depend on; *moralement* be dependent on

dépens *mpl:* **aux ~ de** at the expense of

dépense *f* expenditure; *d'essence, d'électricité* consumption, use; **dépenser** spend; *son énergie, ses forces* use up; *essence* consume, use; **se ~** exert o.s., be physically active; **dépensier, -ère 1** *adj* extravagant **2** *m/f* spendthrift

dépérir waste away; *fig d'une entreprise* go downhill

dépeuplement *m* depopulation

dépilatoire: crème *f* **~** hair remover, depilatory cream

dépistage *m* *d'un criminel* tracking down; MÉD screening

dépit *m* spite; **en ~ de** in spite of

dépité crestfallen

déplacé out of place; *(inconvenant)* uncalled for; POL displaced; **déplacer** move; *personnel* transfer; *problème* shift the focus of; **se ~** move; *(voyager)* travel

déplaire: ~ à qn *(fâcher)* offend s.o.; *cela lui déplaît de faire ...* he dislikes doing ...

déplaisant unpleasant

dépliant *m* leaflet; **déplier** unfold

déploiement *m* MIL deployment; *de forces, courage* display

déplorable deplorable

déporter POL deport; **se ~** *d'un véhicule* swing

déposer 1 *v/t* put down; *armes* lay down; *passager* drop; *roi* depose; *argent, boue* deposit; *projet de loi* table; *ordures* dump; *plainte* lodge **2** *v/i d'un liquide* settle; JUR testify; **se ~** *de la boue* settle; **dépôt** *m* deposit; *chez le notaire* lodging; *d'un projet de loi* tabling; *des ordures* dumping; *(entrepôt)* depot

dépouiller *animal* skin; *(voler)* rob *(de* of); *(examiner)* go through; **~ le scrutin** ou **les votes** count the votes

dépourvu **~ de** devoid of; **prendre qn au ~** take s.o. by surprise

dépoussiérer dust; *fig* modernize

dépraver deprave

déprécier *chose* decrease the value of; *personne* belittle; **se ~** depreciate, lose value; *d'une personne* belittle o.s.

dépression *f* depression; **fai-**

re une ~ be depressed

déprime *f* depression; **déprimer** depress

dépuceler deflower

depuis 1 *prép* since; *espace* from; **j'attends ~ une heure** I have been waiting for an hour; **~ quand permettent-ils que …?** since when do they allow …? **2** *adv* since **3** *conj*: **~ que** since

député *m* POL MP, Member of Parliament; **~ européen** *m* Euro MP

déraciner uproot; (*extirper*) root out, eradicate

dérailler go off the rails; *fig* F: *d'un mécanisme* go on the blink; (*déraisonner*) talk nonsense; **dérailleur** *m* *d'un vélo* derailleur

déraisonnable unreasonable

dérangement *m* disturbance; **déranger** disturb

déraper AUTO skid

déréglé *vie* wild

déréglementer deregulate

dérégler *mécanisme* upset

dérision *f* derision; **tourner en ~** deride

dérisoire derisory, laughable

dérivatif *m* diversion; **dériver 1** *v/t* MATH derive; *cours d'eau* divert **2** *v/i* MAR, AVIAT drift; **~ de** *d'un mot* be derived from

dermatologue *m/f* dermatologist

dernier, -ère last; (*le plus récent*) *mode, roman etc* latest;

extrême utmost; **ce ~** the latter; **dernièrement** recently, lately

dérobée: à la ~ furtively; **dérober** steal; **~ qch à qn** rob s.o. of sth, steal sth from s.o.; **se ~ à** *discussion* shy away from; *obligations* shirk

déroger JUR: **~ à** make an exception to, depart from

déroulement *m* unfolding; **le ~ du projet** the running of the project; **dérouler** unroll; *bobine, câble* unwind; **se ~** take place; *d'une cérémonie* go (off)

dérouter (*déconcerter*) disconcert

derrière 1 *adv* behind **2** *prép* behind **3** *m* back; ANAT bottom; **de ~** *patte etc* back *atr*

dès from, since; **~ lors** from then on; (*par conséquent*) consequently; **~ lundi** as of Monday; **~ que** as soon as

désabuser disillusion

désaccord *m* disagreement

désaffecté disused; *église* deconsecrated

désagréable unpleasant, disagreeable

désappointement *m* disappointment

désapprobateur, -trice disapproving

désapprouver disapprove of

désarmement *m* MIL disarmament; **désarmer** disarm (*aussi fig*)

désarroi *m* disarray

désastre *m* disaster

désavantage *m* disadvantage; **désavantager** put at a disadvantage

désaveu *m* disowning; *d'un propos* retraction; **désavouer** disown; *propos* retract

descendance *f* descendants *pl*; **descendant**, **~e** *m/f* descendant

descendre 1 *v/i* go/come down; *d'un bus* get off; *d'une voiture* get out; *de température, prix* go down; *d'un chemin* descend; AVIAT descend; **~ chez qn** stay with s.o.; **~ de qn** be descended from s.o. **2** *v/t* (*porter vers le bas*) bring down; (*emporter*) take down; *passager* drop off; F (*abattre*) shoot down; *vallée, rivière* descend; **~ les escaliers** come/go downstairs; **descente** *f* descent; (*pente*) slope; *en parachute* jump; **~ de lit** bedside rug

description *f* description

désemparé at a loss

déséquilibre PSYCH unbalanced

désert 1 *adj* deserted; *une île* **~e** a desert island **2** *m* desert; **déserter** desert; **déserteur** *m* MIL deserter

désertification *f* desertification

désertion *f* desertion

désespérant depressing

désespérer 1 *v/t* drive to despair **2** *v/i* despair

désespoir *m* despair; **en ~ de cause** in desperation

déshabillé *m* negligee; **déshabiller** undress; **se ~** get undressed

déshériter disinherit

déshonorer disgrace, bring dishonor *ou* Br dishonour on

déshydraté *aliments* dessicated; *personne* dehydrated; **déshydrater: se ~** become dehydrated

design *m*: **~ d'intérieurs** interior design

désigner (*montrer*) point to, point out; (*appeler*) call; (*nommer*) appoint (**pour** to), designate

désillusion *f* disillusionment

désinfectant *m* disinfectant

désintéressé disinterested, impartial; (*altruiste*) selfless; **désintéresser: se ~ de** lose interest in

désintoxication *f*: **faire une cure de ~** go into detox

désinvolture *f* casualness

désir *m* desire; (*souhait*) wish

désirer want; *sexuellement* desire; **~ faire qch** want to do sth; **désireux, -euse** eager (**de faire** to do)

désister POL: **se ~** withdraw, stand down

désobéir disobey; **~ à** disobey; **désobéissant** disobedient

désobligeant disagreeable

désodorisant *m* deodorant

désolé upset (*de* about, over); *je suis ~* I am so sorry

désopilant hilarious

désordre *m* untidiness; *en ~* untidy

désorganisé disorganized

désormais now; *à partir de maintenant* from now on

désosser remove the bones from

despote *m* despot; **despotique** despotic

dessécher dry out; *de fruits* dry

dessein *m* intention; *à ~* intentionally; *dans le ~ de faire qc* with the intention of doing sth

desserrer loosen

dessert *m* dessert

desservir *des transport publics* serve; (*s'arrêter à*) stop at; *table* clear; *~ qn* do s.o. a disservice

dessin *m* drawing; (*motif*) design; **dessiner** draw

dessoûler F sober up

dessous 1 *adv* underneath; *en ~* underneath **2** *m* underside; *ci-~* below; *les voisins du ~* the downstairs neighbors

dessous-de-plat *m inv* table mat

dessus 1 *adv* on top; *sens ~ dessous* upside down; *en ~* on top; *par~* over; *ci-~* above **2** *m* top; *les voisins*

du ~ the upstairs neighbors; *avoir le ~ fig* have the upper hand; **dessus-de-lit** *m inv* bedspread

déstabilisant unnerving; **déstabiliser** destabilize

destin *m* destiny, fate

destinataire *m* addressee; **destination** *f* destination; **destinée** *f* destiny; **destiner** mean, intend (*à* for)

destituer dismiss; MIL discharge

destructeur, -trice destructive; **destruction** *f* destruction

désuet, -ète obsolete; *mode* out of date

détachable detachable; **détacher** detach; *ceinture* undo; *chien* release; *employé* second; (*nettoyer*) clean; *se ~ sur* stand out against

détail *m* detail; COMM retail trade; *vendre au ~* sell retail; *prix* *m* *de ~* retail price; *en ~* detailed

détaillant *m* retailer

détartrage *m* descaling

détecteur *m* sensor

détective *m* detective

déteindre fade; *~ sur* come off on; *fig* rub off on

détendre slacken; *se ~ d'une corde* slacken; *fig* relax

détenir hold; *fig* detain, hold

détente *f d'une arme* trigger; *fig* relaxation; POL détente

détention *f* holding; JUR detention

détenu, **~e** *m/f* inmate

détergent *m* detergent

détériorer damage; **se ~** deteriorate

déterminant decisive; **déterminer** establish, determine

déterrer dig up

détester detest, hate

détonation *f* detonation

détour *m* detour; **d'un chemin, fleuve** bend; **sans ~** *fig*: **dire qch** straight out

détourné *fig* indirect; **détourner** *trafic* divert; *avion* hijack; *tête, yeux* turn away; *de l'argent* embezzle; **se ~** turn away

détresse *f* distress

détriment *m*: **au ~ de** to the detriment of

détritus *m* garbage, *Br* rubbish

détroit *m* strait

détromper put right

détruire destroy; *(tuer)* kill

dette *f* debt

deuil *m* mourning; **il y a eu un ~ dans sa famille** there's been a bereavement in his family

deux 1 *adj* two; **les ~** both; **nous ~** the two of us, both of us; **~ fois** twice **2** *m* two; **en ~** in two, in half; **~ à ou par ~** in twos, two by two; **deuxième** second; **étage** third, *Br* second; **deux-pièces** *m inv* bikini two-piece swimsuit; *appartement* two--room apartment; **deux-**

-points *m inv* colon

dévaliser *banque* rob, raid; *maison* burglarize, *Br* burgle; *personne* rob; *fig*: *frigo* raid

dévalorisant demeaning; **dévalorisation** *f* drop in value; *fig* belittlement; **dévaloriser** devalue; *fig* belittle

dévaluation *f* devaluation; **dévaluer** devalue

devancer be ahead of; *désir, objection* anticipate

devant 1 *adv* in front; **droit ~** straight ahead **2** *prép* in front of; **passer ~ l'église** go past the church; **~ Dieu** before God **3** *m* front

devanture *f* shop window

dévaster devastate

développement *m* development; **développer** develop; **se ~** develop

devenir become; **il devient vieux** he's getting old; **que va-t-il ~?** what's going to become of him?

dévergondé *sexuellement* promiscuous

déverser *ordures* dump; *passagers* disgorge

dévêtir undress

déviation *f* **d'une route** detour; *(écart)* deviation

dévier 1 *v/t* divert, reroute **2** *v/i* deviate (**de** from)

deviner guess

devis *m* estimate

dévisager stare at

devise *f* FIN currency; *(moto,*

règle de vie motto; **~s étrangères** foreign currency
dévisser unscrew
dévoiler unveil; *secret* reveal, disclose
devoir 1 *v/t de l'argent* owe **2** *v/aux*: **il doit le faire** he has to do it, he must do it; **il aurait dû me le dire** he should have told me; **tu devrais l'acheter** you should buy it; **ça doit être cuit** it should be done **3** *m* duty; **pour l'école** homework
dévorer devour
dévouement *m* devotion; **dévouer: se ~ pour** dedicate one's life to
dextérité *f* dexterity, skill
diabète *m* diabetes *sg*
diable *m* devil; **diabolique** diabolical
diagnostic *m* MÉD diagnosis; **diagnostiquer** MÉD diagnose
diagonal, ~e 1 *adj* diagonal **2** *f* diagonal (line); **en ~e** diagonally
diagramme *m* diagram
dialogue *m* dialog, *Br* dialogue
diamant *m* diamond
diamètre *m* diameter
diarrhée *f* diarrhea, *Br* diarrhoea
dictateur *m* dictator; **dictature** *f* dictatorship
dictée *f* dictation
dictionnaire *m* dictionary
dièse *m/adj* MUS sharp; IN-

FORM **(touche)** **~** hash key
diesel *m* diesel
diète *f* diet
Dieu *m* God; **~ merci!** thank God!
diffamer slander
différence *f* difference; **différencier** differentiate
différend *m* dispute
difficile difficult; *(exigeant)* hard to please; **difficulté** *f* difficulty
difformité *f* deformity
diffusion *f* spread; RAD, TV broadcast; *de chaleur etc* diffusion
digérer digest
digestion *f* digestion
digital digital; **empreinte** *f* **~e** fingerprint
digne *(plein de dignité)* dignified; **~ de** worthy of; **dignité** *f* dignity; *(charge)* office
digue *f* dyke
dilater expand; *pupille* dilate
dilemme *m* dilemma
diluer dilute
dimanche *m* Sunday
dimension *f* dimension; *(taille)* size; *d'une faute* magnitude
diminuer 1 *v/t nombre, prix* reduce; *joie, forces* diminish; *mérites* detract from; *souffrances* lessen, decrease **2** *v/i* decrease
diminutif *m* diminutive; **diminution** *f* decrease, decline; *d'un nombre, prix* reduction

disposer

dinde f turkey; **dindon** m turkey

dîner 1 v/i dine **2** m dinner

dingue F crazy, nuts F

diplomate m diplomat; **diplomatie** f diplomacy

diplôme m diploma; *universitaire* degree; **diplômé** diploma holder; *de l'université* graduate

dire say; (*informer, révéler, ordonner*) tell; **~ à qn de faire qch** tell s.o. to do sth; **à vrai ~** to tell the truth; **cela va sans ~** that goes without saying

direct direct; **en ~** *émission* live; **directement** directly; **directeur, -trice** f adj comité management **2** m/f manager; *plus haut dans la hiérarchie* director; ÉDU principal, Br head teacher; **direction** f (*sens*) direction; (*gestion, directeurs*) management; AUTO steering; **~ assistée** power steering; **directive** f instruction; *de l'UE* directive

dirigeant m leader; **diriger** manage, run; *pays* lead; *orchestre* conduct; *voiture* steer; *arme, critique* aim (*contre* at); *regard, yeux* turn (*vers* to); *personne* direct; **se ~ vers** head for

discerner make out; **~ le bon du mauvais** tell good from bad

discipline f discipline

disc-jockey m disc jockey,

DJ

discontinu *ligne* broken; *effort* intermittent

discorde f discord

discothèque f (*boîte*) discotheque, disco; *collection* record library

discours m speech

discréditer discredit

discret, -ète (*qui n'attire pas l'attention*) unobtrusive; *couleur* quiet; *robe* simple; (*qui garde le secret*) discreet; **discrétion** f discretion

discrimination f discrimination

disculper clear, exonerate; **se ~** clear o.s.

discussion f discussion; (*altercation*) argument; **discuter** discuss; (*contester*) question

disjoncter 1 v/t ÉL break **2** v/i F be crazy; **disjoncteur** m circuit breaker

disparaître disappear; (*mourir*) die; *d'une espèce* die out; **faire ~** get rid of

disparition f disappearance; (*mort*) death; **espèce en voie de ~** endangered species

dispenser ~ qn de (faire) qc excuse s.o. from (doing) sth

disperser disperse; **se ~** (*faire trop de choses*) spread o.s. too thin

disponibilité f availability; **disponible** available

disposer (*arranger*) arrange;

~ de qn/qc have s.o./sth at one's disposal; **se ~ à faire qc** get ready to do sth

dispositif m device

disposition f (arrangement) arrangement; d'une loi provision; (humeur) mood; (tendance) tendency; **être à la ~ de qn** be at s.o.'s disposal; **avoir des ~s pour qch** have an aptitude for sth

disputer match play; **~ qc à qn** compete with s.o for sth.; **se ~** quarrel, fight

disqualifier disqualify

disque m disk; SP discus; ~ **compact** compact disc; **disquette** f diskette, disk; ~ **de sauvegarde** backup disk

dissertation f ÉDU essay

dissimuler conceal, hide (à from)

dissiper dispel; brouillard disperse; fortune squander; **se ~ du brouillard** clear

dissoudre dissolve

dissuader: **~ qn de faire qc** dissuade s.o. from doing sth, persuade s.o. not to do sth; **dissuasion** f dissuasion

distance f distance; **prendre ses ~s avec qn** distance o.s. from s.o.; **distancer** outdistance

distiller distill; **distillerie** f distillery

distinct distinct; ~ **de** different from; **distinctif, -ive** distinctive; **distinguer** (percevoir) make out; (différen-

cier) distinguish (de from); **se ~** (être différent) stand out (de from)

distraction f (passe-temps) amusement; (inattention) distraction

distraire du travail, des soucis distract (de from); (divertir) amuse, entertain; **se ~** amuse o.s.; **distrait** absent-minded

distribuer distribute; courrier deliver; **distributeur** m distributor; ~ **automatique** vending machine

dit (surnommé) referred to as; (fixé) appointed

divaguer talk nonsense

divan m couch

diverger diverge; d'opinions differ

divers (différent) different, varied; au pl (plusieurs) various

diversifier diversify

diversion f diversion

diversité f diversity

divertir amuse, entertain; **divertissement** m amusement, entertainment

divin divine; **divinité** f divinity

diviser divide; **se ~** be divided (en into); **division** f division

divorce m divorce; **demander le ~** ask for a divorce; **divorcé, ~e** m/f divorcee; **divorcer** get a divorce (d'avec from)

dix ten; **dix-huit** eighteen; **dixième** tenth; **dix-neuf** nineteen; **dix-sept** seventeen; **dizaine** *f*: *une ~ de* about ten, ten or so

D.J. *m/f* (= **disc-jockey**) DJ, deejay (= disc jockey)

docile docile

docteur *m* doctor; **doctorat** *m* doctorate, PhD

doctrine *f* doctrine

document *m* document; **documentation** *f* documentation; **documenter**: *se ~* collect information

dodu chubby

dogmatique dogmatic

doigt *m* finger; *~ de pied* toe; *croiser les ~s* keep one's fingers crossed

dollar *m* dollar

domaine *m* estate; *fig* domain

dôme *m* dome

domestique 1 *adj* domestic **2** *m* servant

domicile *m* place of residence; **domicilié**: *~ à* resident at

domination *f* domination; **dominer 1** *v/t* dominate **2** *v/i* (*prédominer*) be predominant; *se ~* control o.s.

dommage *m*: *(quel) ~!* what a pity!; *c'est ~ que* (+ *subj*) it's a pity (that); *~s et intérêts* JUR damages

dompter *animal* tame; *rebelle* subdue; **dompteur** *m* trainer

DOM-TOM *mpl* (= **départe-** ments et territoires d'outre-mer) overseas departments and territories of France

don *m* donation; (*cadeau, aptitude*) gift; *~ du ciel* godsend; **donation** *f* donation

donc *conclusion* so; *écoutez ~!* do listen!; *comment ~?* how (so)?; *allons ~!* come on!

données *fpl* data *sg* (*aussi* IN-FORM), information; **donner 1** *v/t* give **2** *v/i*: *~ sur la mer* look onto the sea

dont whose; *le film ~ elle parlait* the movie she was talking about; *la manière ~ elle me regardait* the way (in which) she was looking at me

doré *bijou* gilded; *couleur* golden

dorénavant from now on

dorer gild

dormeur, -euse *m/f* sleeper; **dormir** sleep

dortoir *m* dormitory

dos *m* back; *~ d'âne* speed bump; *pont* hump-backed bridge

dose *f* MÉD dose; PHARM proportion; **doser** measure out

dossier *m* d'une chaise back *f*; *de documents* file, dossier; *~ médical* medical record(s)

douane *f* customs *pl*; **douanier, -ère 1** customs *atr* **2** *m/f* customs officer

double 1 *adj* double **2** *m*

doubler

deuxième exemplaire duplicate; *au tennis* doubles (match); *le* ~ double, twice as much; **doubler 1** *v/t* double; AUTO pass, *Br* overtake; *film* dub; *vêtement* line **2** *v/i* double; **doublure** *f d'un vêtement* lining

doucement gently; *(bas)* softly; *(lentement)* slowly; **douceur** *f d'une personne* gentleness; ~s *(jouissance)* pleasures; *(sucreries)* sweet things

douche *f* shower; **prendre une** ~ shower, take a shower

doué gifted; ~ **de qc** endowed with sth

douleur *f* pain

douloureux, -euse painful

doute *m* doubt; **sans** ~ without doubt; **sans aucun** ~ undoubtedly; **douter:** ~ **de qn/qch** doubt s.o./sth.; **se** ~ **de qc** suspect sth; **se** ~ **que** suspect that; **douteux, -euse** doubtful

doux, douce sweet; *temps* mild; *personne* gentle; *au toucher* soft

douzaine *f* dozen; **douze** twelve; **douzième** twelfth

dragée *f* sugared almond

draguer *rivière* dredge; F *femmes* try to pick up; **dragueur** *m* F ladies' man

dramatique dramatic; **dramatiser** dramatize; **drame** *m* drama

drap *m de lit* sheet

drapeau *m* flag

drap-housse *m* fitted sheet

dresser put up; *contrat* draw up; *animal* train; ~ **qn contre qn** set s.o. against s.o.; **se** ~ straighten up; *d'une tour* rise up; *d'un obstacle* arise

drogue *f* drug; ~ **douce** soft drug; ~ **récréative** recreational drug; **drogué,** ~**e** *m/f* drug addict; **droguer** drug; **se** ~ take drugs; MÉD *(traiter)* give medication to; **se** ~ take drugs; MÉD *péj* pop pills; **droguerie** *f* hardware store

droit 1 *adj côté* right; *ligne* straight; *(debout)* erect; *(honnête)* upright **2** *adv tout* ~ straight ahead **3** *m* right; *(taxe)* fee; JUR law; **être en** ~ **de faire qch** be entitled to do sth; ~**s d'auteur** royalties

droite *f* right; *côté* right-hand side; **à** ~ on the right(-hand side)

drôle funny; **une** ~ **d'idée** a funny idea

dubitatif, -ive doubtful

duc *m* duke

duchesse *f* duchess

duel *m* duel

dûment duly

dune *f* (sand) dune

Dunkerque Dunkirk

duper dupe

duplex *m* duplex

duquel → **lequel**

dur 1 *adj* hard; *climat* harsh; *viande* tough **2** *adv travailler,* échapper

frapper hard
durable durable, lasting; *croissance, utilisation de matières premières* sustainable
durant during; *des années* ~ for years
durcir 1 *v/t* harden **2** *v/i:* **se** ~ harden
durée *f* duration; ~ *de vie* life; *d'une personne* life expectancy

durement harshly; *être frappé* ~ *par* be hard hit by
durer last
duvet *m* down; *(sac de couchage)* sleeping bag
DVD *m* DVD (= digitally versatile disk)
dynamique 1 *adj* dynamic **2** *f* dynamics
dynamo *f* dynamo
dyslexique dyslexic

E

eau *f* water; *tomber à l'*~ fall in the water; *fig* fall through; ~ *courante* running water; ~ *gazeuse* carbonated water, *Br* fizzy water; ~ *de Javel* bleach
eau-de-vie *f* brandy
ébahi dumbfounded
ébaucher *tableau, roman* rough out; *texte* draft; ~ *un sourire* smile faintly
ébéniste *m* cabinetmaker
éblouir dazzle *(aussi fig)*
éboueur *m* garbageman, *Br* dustman
éboulement *m* landslide
ébouriffé tousled; **ébouriffer** *cheveux* ruffle
ébranler shake; **s'**~ move off
ébriété *f* inebriation
ébruiter *nouvelle* spread
ébullition *f* boiling point; *être en* ~ be boiling
écaille *f de coquillage, tortue* shell; *de poisson* scale; *de*

peinture, plâtre flake; *matière* tortoiseshell; **écailler** *poisson* scale; *huître* open; **s'**~ *de peinture* flake (off); *de vernis à ongles* chip
écart *m (intervalle)* gap; *(différence)* difference; *moral* indiscretion; *à l'*~ at a distance *(de* from)
écarter *jambes* spread; *fig: idée* reject; *danger* avert; **s'**~ *de (s'éloigner)* stray from
écervelé scatterbrained
échafaudage *m* scaffolding
échancré low-cut
échange *m* exchange; ~*s extérieurs* foreign trade; *en* ~ in exchange *(de* for); **échanger** exchange *(contre* for);
échangeur *m* interchange
échantillon *m* COMM sample
échappement *m* AUTO exhaust; *tuyau m d'*~ tail pipe; **échapper** *d'une personne* ~ *à qn* escape from s.o.; ~ *à*

qc escape sth; *l'~ belle* have a narrow escape; *s'~* escape

écharde *f* splinter

écharpe *f* scarf; *de maire* sash; *en ~* MÉD in a sling

échauffer heat; *s'~* SP warm up; *~ les esprits* get people excited

échéance *f d'un contrat* expiration date, *Br* expiry date; *de police* maturity

échec *m* failure; *essuyer un ~* meet with failure

échecs *mpl* chess; *jouer aux ~* play chess

échelle *f* ladder; *d'une carte, des salaires* scale; *à l'~ mondiale* on a global scale

échelonner space out; *paiements* spread, stagger (*sur un an* over a year)

échevelé disheveled, *Br* dishevelled

échiner F: *s'~ à faire qch* go to great lengths to do sth

échiquier *m* chessboard

écho *m* echo

échotier, -ère *m/f* gossip columnist

échouer fail; (*s'*)~ *d'un bateau* run aground

éclabousser spatter

éclair *m* flash of lightning; CUIS eclair; *comme un ~* in a flash; **éclairage** *m* lighting

éclaircie *f* clear spell; **éclaircir** lighten; *fig: mystère* clear up; *s'~ du ciel* clear

éclairer light; *~ qn* light the way for s.o.; *fig* enlighten

s.o.

éclat *m de verre* splinter; *de métal* gleam; *des yeux* sparkle; *de couleurs, fleurs* vividness; *~ de rire* peal of laughter; *un ~ d'obus* a piece of shrapnel; **éclatant** dazzling; *couleur* vivid; *rire* loud; **éclater** *d'une bombe* blow up, explode; *d'un ballon, pneu* burst; *d'un coup de feu* ring out; *d'une guerre, d'un incendie* break out; *fig: d'un groupe, parti* break up; *~ en sanglots* burst into tears

éclipser eclipse (*aussi fig*); *s'~* F vanish, disappear

éclore *d'un oiseau* hatch out; *de fleurs* open

écluse *f* lock

écœurement *m* disgust; (*découragement*) discouragement; **écœurer** disgust, sicken; (*décourager*) dishearten; *~ qn d'un aliment* make s.o. feel nauseous

école *f* school; *~ maternelle* nursery school; *~ primaire* elementary school, *Br* primary school *~ publique* state school; **écolier** *m* schoolboy; **écolière** *f* schoolgirl

écologie *f* ecology; **écologique** ecological

économe economical, thrifty

économie *f economy; science* economics *sg*; *~ souterraine* black economy; *~s* savings;

économiser save; ~ **sur qc** save on sth; **économiseur** *m* **d'écran** INFORM screen saver

écorce *f* *d'un arbre* bark; *d'un fruit* rind

écorcher *animal* skin; *(égratigner)* scrape; *fig*: *nom, mot* murder

écossais, ~e Scottish; **Écossais, ~e** *m/f* Scot; **Écosse** *f*: **l'~** Scotland

écoulement *m* flow; COMM sale; **écouler** COMM sell; **s'~** flow; *du temps* pass; COMM sell

écourter shorten; *vacances* cut short

écoute *f*: **être à l'~** be always listening out; *aux heures de grande* ~ RAD at peak listening times; TV at peak viewing times; **écouter 1** *v/t* listen to **2** *v/i* listen; **écouteur** *m* TÉL receiver; **~s** RAD headphones

écran *m* screen; **porter à l'~** TV adapt for television; ~ **plat** flat screen; ~ **tactile** touch screen; ~ **total** sunblock

écrasant overwhelming; **écraser** crush; *cigarette* stub out; *(renverser)* run over; **s'~ au sol** *d'un avion* crash

écrémé: **lait** *m* ~ skimmed milk

écrevisse *f* crayfish

écrier: **s'~** cry out

écrire write; *comment est-ce que ça s'écrit?* how do you

spell it?; **écrit** *m* document; **l'~** *examen* the written exam; **par** ~ in writing; **écriteau** *m* notice; **écriture** *f* writing, COMM entry; **les (Saintes) Écritures** Holy Scripture

écrivain *m* writer

écrou *m* nut

écrouler: **s'~** collapse

écru *couleur* natural

écueil *m* reef; *fig* pitfall

éculé *chaussure* worn-out; *fig* hackneyed

écume *f* foam

écureuil *m* squirrel

écurie *f* stable

édenté toothless

édifice *m* building; **édifier** erect; *fig* build up

éditer *livre* publish; *texte* edit; **éditeur, -trice** *m/f* publisher; *(commentateur)* editor; **édition** *f* publishing; *action de commenter* editing; *(tirage)* edition; **maison** *f* **d'~** publishing house; **éditorial** *m* editorial

édredon *m* eiderdown

éducatif, -ive educational; **éducation** *f* education; *(culture)* upbringing

éduquer educate; *(élever)* bring up

effacer erase; **s'~** *d'une inscription* wear away; *d'une personne* fade into the background

effarement *m* fear; **effarer** frighten

effectif, -ive 1 *adj* effective **2**

m manpower, personnel; **effectivement** true enough

effectuer carry out

efféminé *péj* effeminate

effervescent effervescent; *fig: foule* excited

effet *m* effect; COMM bill; **en ~** sure enough; **faire de l'~** have an effect; **~s** (personal) effects

efficace *remède* effective; *personne* efficient; **efficacité** *f* effectiveness; *d'une personne* efficiency

effleurer brush against; *(aborder)* **s'~** touch on

effondrement *m* collapse; **effondrer: s'~** collapse

efforcer: s'~ de faire qch try very hard to do sth

effort *m* effort; **faire un ~** make an effort, try a bit harder

effraction *f* JUR breaking and entering

effrayant frightening; **effrayer** frighten; **s'~** be frightened (**de** at)

effroi *m* fear

effronterie *f* impertinence, effrontery

effroyable terrible, dreadful

égal 1 *adj* equal; *surface* even; *vitesse* steady; **ça lui est ~** it's all the same to him **2** *m* equal; **sans ~** unequalled; *Br* unequalled; **également** *(pareillement)* equally; *(aussi)* as well, too; **égaler** equal; **égaliser 1** *v/t haies, cheveux*

even up; *sol* level **2** *v/i* SP tie the game, *Br* equalize; **égalité** *f* equality; *en tennis* deuce; **être à ~** be level; *en tennis* be at deuce

égard *m*: **à cet ~** in that respect; **à l'~ de qn** to(ward) s.o.; **par ~ pour** out of consideration for; **~s** respect

égarer *personne* lead astray; *chose* lose; **s'~** get lost; *du sujet* stray from the point

égayer cheer up

église *f* church

égocentrique egocentric

égoïsme *m* selfishness, egoism; **égoïste 1** *adj* selfish **2** *m/f* egoist

égorger: ~ qn cut s.o.'s throat

égout *m* sewer

égoutter drain

égratignure *f* scratch

Égypte *f: l'~* Egypt; **égyptien**, **~ne** Egyptian; **Égyptien**, **~ne** *m/f* Egyptian

éjecter eject; *F personne* kick out

élaborer *projet* draw up

élan *m* momentum; SP run-up; *de tendresse* upsurge; *de générosité* fit; *(vivacité)* enthusiasm

élancer *v/i*: **ma jambe m'élance** I've got shooting pains in my leg; **s'~** dash; SP take a run-up

élargir widen, broaden; *vêtement* let out; *(libérer)* release

élastique 1 *adj* elastic **2** *m* elastic; *de bureau* rubber band

électeur, -trice *m/f* voter; **élection** *f* election; **électorat** *m* droit franchise; *personnes* electorate

électricien, ~ne *m/f* electrician; **électricité** *f* electricity; **~ statique** static (electricity); **électrique** electric; **électriser** electrify

électrocuter electrocute

électroménager: *appareils mpl* **~s** household appliances

électronique 1 *adj* electronic; *livre* ~ e-book, electronic book **2** *f* electronics

élégance *f* elegance; **élégant** elegant

élément *m* element; *(composante)* component; *d'un puzzle* piece; **~s** *(rudiments)* rudiments; **élémentaire** elementary

éléphant *m* elephant

élevage *m* breeding; **~ (du bétail)** cattle farming

élève *m/f* pupil

élevé high; *esprit* noble; *style* elevated; **bien/mal ~** well/ badly brought up; **élever** raise; *prix, température* raise, increase; *statue* put up, erect; *enfants* bring up, raise; *animaux* breed; **s'~** rise; *d'une tour* rise up; *d'un cri* go up; **s'~ contre** rise up against; **s'~ à** amount to; **éleveur, -euse** *m/f* breeder

élimination *f* elimination; *des déchets* disposal; **éliminatoire** *f* qualifying round; **éliminer** eliminate; *difficultés* get rid of

élire elect

elle *f* she; *après prép* her; *chose* it

elle-même herself; *chose* itself

elles *fpl* they; *après prép* them

elles-mêmes themselves

éloigné remote

éloigner move away; *soupçon* remove; **s'~** move away *(de* from); **s'~ de qn** distance o.s. from s.o.

éloquence *f* eloquence; **éloquent** eloquent

élu, ~e 1 *adj:* **le président ~** the President elect **2** *m/f* POL *(député)* representative

élucider *mystère* clear up; *question* clarify

émacié emaciated

e-mail *m* e-mail

émanciper emancipate; **s'~** become emancipated

emballage *m* packaging; **emballer** package; *fig* F thrill; **s'~ d'un moteur* race; *fig* F get excited; **emballé sous vide** vacuum packed

embargo *m* embargo

embarquer 1 *v/t* load **2** *v/i ou* **s'~** embark; **s'~ dans** F get involved in

embarras *m* difficulty; *(gêne)* embarrassment; **être dans**

embarrassant

92

l'~ be in an embarrassing position; *sans argent* be short of money; **embarrassant** embarrassing; *(encombrant)* cumbersome; **embarrasser** embarrass; *(encombrer)* escaliers clutter up

embaucher take on, hire

embellir 1 *v/t* make more attractive; *fig* embellish **2** *v/i* become more attractive

embêtant F annoying; **embêter** F *(ennuyer)* bore; *(contrarier)* annoy; *s'~* be bored

emblème *m* emblem

emboîter insert; *~ le pas à qn* fall into step with s.o. *(aussi fig)*; *s'~* fit together

embolie *f* embolism

embonpoint *m* stoutness

embouchure *f* GÉOGR mouth; MUS mouthpiece

embouteillage *m* traffic jam

emboutir crash into

embranchement *m* branch; *(carrefour)* intersection, *Br* junction

embrasser kiss; *période, thème* take in, embrace; *métier* take up; *~ du regard* take in at a glance

embrayage *m* AUTO clutch; *action* letting in the clutch

embrouiller muddle; *s'~* get muddled

embryon *m* embryo

éméché F tipsy

émeraude *f & adj* emerald

émerger emerge

émerveiller amaze; *s'~* be

amazed *(de* by)

émetteur *m* RAD, TV transmitter

émettre *radiations etc* give off, emit; RAD, TV broadcast, transmit; *opinion* voice; *action, nouveau billet* issue; *emprunt* float

émeute *f* riot

émietter crumble

émigration *f* emigration; **émigré, ~e** *m/f* émigré; **émigrer** emigrate

émincer cut into thin slices

éminent eminent

émission *f* emission; RAD, TV program, *Br* programme; COMM, FIN issue

emmagasiner store

emmêler *fils* tangle; *fig* muddle

emménager: *~ dans* move into

emmener take

emmerder F: *~ qn* get on s.o.'s nerves; *s'~* be bored rigid

emmitoufler wrap up; *s'~* wrap up

émotion *f* emotion; F *(frayeur)* fright

émouvant moving; **émouvoir** *(toucher)* move; *s'~* be moved

emparer: *s'~ de* seize; *clés, héritage* grab; *des doutes, de la peur* overcome

empâter: *s'~* thicken

empêchement *m*: *j'ai eu un ~* something has come up; **em-**

pêcher prevent; **~ qn de faire qc** prevent *ou* stop s.o. doing sth; (*il*) **n'empêche que** nevertheless

empereur *m* emperor

empiéter: ~ sur encroach on

empiffrer F: **s'~** stuff o.s.

empiler pile (up)

empire *m* empire; *fig* (*maîtrise*) control

empirer get worse, deteriorate

emplacement *m* site

emplette *f* purchase; **faire des ~s** go shopping

emplir fill; **s'~** fill (**de** with)

emploi *m* (*utilisation*) use; ÉCON employment; **~ du temps** schedule, *Br* timetable; **chercher un ~** be looking for work ou for a job

employé, ~e *m/f* employee; **employer** use; *personnel* employ; **s'~ à faire qc** strive to do sth; **employeur, -euse** *m/f* employer

empocher pocket

empoigner grab, seize

empoisonner poison

emporter take; *prisonnier* take away; (*entraîner, arracher*) carry away; *du courant* sweep away; *d'une maladie* carry off; **l'~ sur qn/qc** get the better of s.o./sth; **s'~** fly into a rage

empreinte *f* impression; *fig* stamp; **~ génétique** genetic fingerprint

empresser: s'~ de faire qc rush to do sth; **s'~ auprès de qn** be attentive to s.o.

emprise *f* hold

emprisonnement *m* imprisonment; **emprisonner** imprison

emprunt *m* loan; **emprunter** borrow (**à** from); *chemin, escalier* take

ému moved, touched

en¹ *prép* in; *direction* to; **agir ~ ami** act as a friend; **~ voiture** by car; **~ or** of gold; **en même temps** while; when; **~ mode** by

en² *pron*: **qu'~ pensez-vous?** what do you think about it?; **il y ~ a deux** there are two (of them); **j'~ ai** I have some; **j'~ ai cinq** I have five; **je n'~ ai pas** I don't have any; **il ~ est mort** he died of it

encadrer *tableau* frame; **encadré de deux gendarmes** *fig* flanked by gendarmes

encaisser COMM take; *chèque* cash; *fig* take

en-cas *m* CUIS snack

encastrer build in

enceinte¹ *adj* pregnant

enceinte² *f* enclosure; **~ (acoustique)** speaker

encens *m* incense

encercler encircle

enchaîner chain up; *fig*: *pensées, faits* link (up)

enchanté enchanted; **~!** how do you do?; **enchanter** (*ravir*) delight; (*ensorceler*) enchant

enchère f bid; **vente** f **aux ~s** auction

enchevêtrer tangle; *fig:* situation confuse; **s'~** *de fils* get tangled up; *d'une situation* get muddled

enclin: **être ~ à faire** **qch** be inclined to do sth

encoche f notch

encolure f neck; *tour de cou* neck (size)

encombrant cumbersome; **être ~** *d'une personne* be in the way; **encombrer** *maison* clutter up; *rue, passage* block; **s'~ de** load o.s. down with

encore *de nouveau* again; *(toujours)* still; **pas ~** not yet; **~ une bière?** another beer?; **~ plus rapide** even faster

encourageant encouraging; **encourager** encourage; *projet, entreprise* foster

encrasser dirty; **s'~** get dirty

encre f ink

encyclopédie f encyclopedia

endetter: s'~ get into debt

endeuillé bereaved

endive f chicory

endolori painful

endommager damage

endormi asleep; *fig* sleepy; **endormir** send to sleep; *douleur* dull; **s'~** fall asleep

endosser *vêtement* put on; *responsabilité* shoulder; *chèque* endorse

endroit m *(lieu)* place; *d'une*

étoffe right side

enduire: ~ de cover with; **enduit** m *de peinture* coat

endurance f endurance

endurcir harden

endurer endure

énergie f energy; **énergique** energetic; *protestation* strenuous

énervant irritating; **énerver:** **~ qn** *(agacer)* get on s.o.'s nerves; *(agiter)* make s.o. edgy; **s'~** get excited

enfance f childhood

enfant m ou f child

enfer m hell *(aussi fig)*

enfermer shut *ou* lock up; *champ* enclose; **s'~** shut o.s. up

enfiler *aiguille* thread; *perles* string; *vêtement* slip on; *rue* turn into

enfin *(finalement)* at last; *(en dernier lieu)* lastly, last; *(bref)* in a word

enflammer set light to; *allumette* strike; MÉD inflame; *fig: imagination* fire; **s'~** catch; MÉD become inflamed; *fig: de l'imagination* take flight

enfler swell; **enflure** f swelling

enfoncer 1 *v/t clou, pieu* drive in; *couteau* thrust, plunge *(dans* into); *porte* break down **2** *v/i dans sable etc* sink *(dans* into); **s'~** sink

enfreindre infringe

enfuir: s'~ run away

engagement *m* (*obligation*) commitment; *personnel* recruitment; THÉÂT booking; (*mise en gage*) pawning

engager (*lier*) commit (**à** to); *personnel* hire; TECH (*faire entrer*) insert; *discussion* begin; (*entraîner*) involve (**dans** in); THÉÂT book; (*mettre en gage*) pawn; **s'~** (*se lier*) commit o.s. (**à doing qc** to doing sth); (*commencer*) begin; MIL enlist

engelure *f* chillblain

engendrer *fig* engender

engin *m* machine; MIL missile; F *péj* thing

englober include

engloutir (*dévorer*) devour, wolf down; *fig* engulf

engouffrer devour, wolf down; **s'~ dans** *de l'eau* pour in; *fig: dans un bâtiment* rush into; *dans une foule* be swallowed up by

engourdir numb; **s'~** go numb

engraisser fatten

engrenage *m* gear

engueuler F bawl out; **s'~** have an argument

énigme *f* enigma; (*devinette*) riddle

enivrer intoxicate; *fig* exhilarate

enjamber step across; *d'un pont* span

enjeu *m* stake

enjoliveur *m* AUTO wheel trim, hub cap

enjoué cheerful, good humored, *Br* good-humoured

enlèvement *m* (*rapt*) abduction, kidnap; **enlever** take away, remove; *vêtement* take off, remove; (*kidnapper*) abduct, kidnap; **~ qc à qn** take sth away from s.o.

enneigé *route* blocked by snow; *sommet* snow-capped

ennemi, **~e 1** *m/f* enemy **2** *adj* enemy *atr*

ennui *m* boredom; **~s** problems; **ennuyer** (*contrarier*, *agacer*) annoy; (*lasser*) bore; **s'~** be bored; **ennuyeux**, **-euse** (*contrariant*) annoying; (*lassant*) boring

énoncé *m* statement; *d'une question* wording; **énoncer** state; **~ des vérités** state the obvious

énorme enormous; **énormément** enormously; **~ de** F an enormous amount of

énormité *f* enormity

enquête *f* inquiry; *policière aussi* investigation; (*sondage d'opinion*) survey; **enquêter**: **~ sur** investigate

enraciné deep-rooted

enregistrement *m* registration; *de disques* recording; AVIAT check-in; **enregistrer** register; *disques* record; *bagages* check in

enrhumer: **s'~** catch (a) cold

enrichir enrich; **s'~** get richer

enrouer: **s'~** get hoarse

enrouler *tapis* roll up; **~ qc**

autour de qch wind sth
around sth
enseignant, **~e** *m/f* teacher
enseignement *m* education;
d'un sujet teaching; **ensei-**
gner teach (*qc à qn* s.o. sth)
ensemble 1 *adv* (*simultané-*
ment) together **2** *m* (*totalité*)
whole; (*groupe*) group, set;
MUS, *vêtement* ensemble;
MATH set; *dans l'~* on the
whole
ensevelir bury
ensoleillé sunny
ensommeillé sleepy
ensuite then; (*plus tard*) after
entacher smear
entaille *f* cut; (*encoche*)
notch; **entailler** notch; **s'~**
la main cut one's hand
entamer start; *économies*
make
entasser *choses* pile up; *per-*
sonnes cram
entendre hear; (*comprendre*)
understand; (*vouloir dire*)
mean; *~ faire qc* intend to
do sth; *~ dire que* hear that;
s'~ (avec qn) get on (with
s.o.); (*se mettre d'accord*)
come to an agreement (with
s.o.); *entendu regard* knowing; *bien ~* of course; **enten-**
te *f* agreement
enterrement *m* burial; *céré-*
monie funeral; **enterrer**
bury
en-tête *m* heading; INFORM
header; COMM letterhead;
d'un journal headline

entêtement *m* stubbornness;
entêter: **s'~** persist (*dans*
in; *à faire qc* in doing sth)
enthousiasme *m* enthusiasm; **enthousiasmer**: **s'~**
pour be enthusiastic about
enticher: **s'~ de** *personne* become infatuated with; *acti-*
vité develop a craze for
entier, **-ère** whole, entire; (*in-*
tégral) intact; *confiance, sa-*
tisfaction full
entonnoir *m* funnel
entorse *f* MÉD sprain
entortiller (*envelopper*) wrap
entourage *m* entourage;
(*bordure*) surround; **entou-**
rer: *~ de* surround with;
s'~ de surround o.s. with
entraide *f* mutual assistance;
entraider: **s'~** help each other
entrailles *fpl* intestines
entrain *m* liveliness; **entraî-**
nement *m* SP training; TECH
drive; **entraîner** (*charrier,*
emporter) sweep along; SP
train; *fig* result in; *frais en-*
tail; *personne* drag; TECH
drive; **s'~** train
entrave *f* *fig* hindrance; **en-**
traver hinder
entre between; *le meilleur d'~*
nous the best of us; *~ autres*
among other things
entrebâiller half open
entrechoquer: **s'~** knock
against one another
entrecôte *f* rib steak
entrée *f* entrance, way in; *ac-*

cès *au théâtre*, *cinéma* admission; (*billet*) ticket; (*vestibule*) entry(way); CUIS starter; INFORM *touche* enter (key); *de données* input; **~ interdite** no admittance

entrejambe *m* crotch

entrelacer interlace

entremets *m* CUIS dessert

entremise f: **par l'~ de** through (the good offices of)

entreposer store; **entrepôt** *m* warehouse

entreprenant enterprising; **entreprendre** undertake; **entrepreneur, -euse** *m/f* entrepreneur; **entreprise** f enterprise; (*firme*) company, business

entrer 1 *v/i* come/go in, enter; **~ dans** come/go into, enter; *voiture* get into; *enter*; *catégorie* fall into; *l'armée*, *le parti etc* join 2 *v/t* bring in; INFORM input, enter

entre-temps in the meantime

entretenir *maison*, *machine etc* maintain; *famille* keep, support; *amitié* keep up; **s'~ de qc** talk to each other about sth

entretien *m* maintenance, upkeep; (*conversation*) conversation

entrevoir glimpse; *fig* foresee

entrevue f interview

entrouvrir half open

énumérer list, enumerate

envahir invade; *d'un sentiment* overwhelm; **envahissant** *personne* intrusive; *sentiments* overwhelming

enveloppe f *d'une lettre* envelope; **envelopper** wrap; **enveloppé de brume**, *mystère* enveloped in

envenimer poison (*aussi fig*)

envergure f *d'un oiseau*, *avion* wingspan; *fig* scope; *d'une personne* caliber, *Br* calibre

envers 1 *prép* toward, *Br* towards 2 *m d'une feuille* reverse; *d'une étoffe*: wrong side; **à l'~** pull inside out; (*en désordre*) upside down

envie f (*convoitise*) envy; (*désir*) desire (*de* of); **avoir ~ de (faire) qc** want (to do) sth; **envier** envy; **~ qc à qn** envy s.o. sth

environ 1 *adv* about 2 *mpl*: **~s** surrounding area; **dans les ~s** in the vicinity

environnement *m* environment

envisager (*considérer*) think about; (*imaginer*) envisage

envoi *m* shipment; *d'un fax* sending

envoler: **s'~** fly away; *d'un avion* take off; *fig*: *du temps* fly

envoyé *m* envoy; *d'un journal* correspondent; **envoyer** send; *gifle* give

éolienne f wind turbine

épais, ~se thick; *foule* dense;

épaisseur f thickness; **épaissir** thicken

épancher: s'~ pour out one's heart (**auprès de** to)

épanouir: s'~ blossom

épargne f saving; **~s** (*économies*) savings; **épargner 1** v/t save; *personne* spare; **~ qc à qn** spare s.o. sth **2** v/i save

éparpiller scatter

épars sparse

épatant F great, terrific; **épater** astonish

épaule f shoulder

épave f wreck (*aussi fig*)

épée f sword

épeler spell

éperdu *besoin* desperate; **~ de** beside o.s. with

épi m ear

épice f spice; **épicer** spice; **épicerie** f grocery store, *Br* grocer's; **épicier, -ère** m/f grocer

épidémie f epidemic

épier spy on; *occasion* watch for

épilepsie f epilepsy; **crise** f **d'~** epileptic fit

épiler remove the hair from

épinards mpl spinach

épine f d'une rose thorn; d'un hérisson spine, prickle; **épineux, -euse** *problème* thorny

épingle f pin; **~ de sûreté** safety pin; **tiré à quatre ~s** fig well turned-out

Épiphanie f Epiphany

épisode m episode

éploré tearful

éplucher peel; *fig* scrutinize; **épluchures** fpl peelings

éponge f sponge; **éponger** sponge down; *flaque* sponge up; *déficit* mop up

époque f age, epoch; **meubles** mpl **d'~** period *ou* antique furniture

époumoner: s'~ F shout o.s. hoarse

épouse f wife; **épouser** marry; *principe etc* espouse

épousseter dust

époustouflant F breathtaking

épouvantable dreadful

épouvantail m scarecrow

épouvanter horrify; *fig* terrify

époux m husband; **les ~** the married couple

éprendre: s'~ de fall in love with

épreuve f trial; SP event; *imprimerie* proof; *photographie* print; **à toute ~** confiance etc never-failing; **à l'~ du feu** fireproof

éprouver test, try out; (*ressentir*) experience

épuisé exhausted; *livre* out of print; **épuiser** exhaust; **~ les ressources** be a drain on resources; **s'~** tire o.s. out (**à faire qch** doing sth); *d'une source* dry up

épurer purify

équateur m equator

équilibre *m* balance, equilibrium; **équilibrer** balance

équipage *m* crew

équipe *f* team; *d'ouvriers* gang; **~ de nuit** night shift; **~ de secours** rescue party; **équipement** *m* equipment; **équiper** equip (**de** with)

équitable just, equitable

équitation *f* riding

équivalent 1 *adj* equivalent (**à** to) **2** *m* equivalent

équivoque 1 *adj* equivocal, ambiguous **2** *f* ambiguity; (*malentendu*) misunderstanding

érable *m* BOT maple

érafler scratch; **éraflure** *f* scratch

ère *f* era

érection *f* erection

éreinter exhaust; **s'~** exhaust o.s. (**à faire qch** doing sth)

ériger erect; **s'~** set o.s. up as

érosion *f* erosion

érotisme *m* eroticism

errer roam; *des pensées* stray

erreur *f* mistake, error; **~ de calcul** miscalculation

érudit erudite; **érudition** *f* erudition

éruption *f* eruption; MÉD rash

escabeau *m* (*tabouret*) stool; (*marchepied*) stepladder

escalade *f* climbing; **~ de violence etc** escalation in; **escalader** climb

escalator *m* escalator

escale *f* stopover; **faire ~ à**

MAR call at; AVIAT stop over in

escalier *m* stairs *pl*, staircase; **dans l'~** on the stairs; **~ de secours** fire escape

escalope *f* escalope

escamoter (*dérober*) make disappear; *antenne* retract; *fig: difficulté* get around

escapade *f*: **faire une ~** get away from it all

escargot *m* snail

escarpement *m* slope

esclaffer: **s'~** guffaw, laugh out loud

esclavage *m* slavery; **esclave** *m/f* slave

escompte *m* discount; **escompter** discount; *fig* expect

escorter escort

escrime *f* fencing; **escrimer**: **s'~** fight, struggle (**à** to)

escroc *m* crook

espace *m* space; **espacer** space out; **s'~** become more and more infrequent

Espagne *f* Spain; **espagnol, ~e 1** *adj* Spanish **2** *m langue* Spanish; **Espagnol, ~e** *m/f* Spaniard

espèce *f* kind, sort (**de** of); BIOL species; **~ d'abruti!** *péj* idiot!; **en ~s** COMM cash

espérer 1 *v/t* hope for; **~ que** hope that; **~ faire qch** hope to do sth **2** *v/i* hope; **~ en** trust in

espiègle mischievous

espion, ~ne *m/f* spy; **espionnage** *m* espionage, spying;

espionner spy on

espoir *m* hope

esprit *m* spirit; (*intellect*) mind; (*humour*) wit

esquisse *f* sketch; *fig: d'un roman* outline; **esquisser** sketch; *fig: projet* outline

esquiver dodge; **s'~** slip away

essai *m* (*test*) test, trial; (*tentative*) attempt, try; *en rugby* try; *en littérature* essay; **à l'~** on trial

essaim *m* swarm

essayage *m*: **cabine** *f* **d'~** changing cubicle; **essayer** try; (*mettre à l'épreuve, évaluer*) test; *vêtement* try on; ~ **de faire qc** try to do sth; **s'~ à qc** try one's hand at sth

essence *f* essence; *carburant* gas, *Br* petrol; *Bot* species *sg*

essentiel, **~le1** *adj* essential **2** *m*: **l'~** the main thing; *de sa vie* the main part

essieu *m* axle

essor *m* *fig* expansion

essorer wring out; *d'une machine à laver* spin

essoufflé out of breath

essuie-glace *m* (windshield) wiper, *Br* (windscreen) wiper; **essuie-mains** *m* hand-towel; **essuyer** wipe; *fig* suffer

est **1** *m* east **à l'~ de** (to the) east of **2** *adj* east, eastern

est-ce que: ~ **c'est vrai?** is it true?; **est-ce qu'ils se portent bien?** are they well?

esthéticienne *f* beautician

esthétique esthetic, *Br* aesthetic

estimatif, **-ive** estimated; **devis** ~ estimate; **estimation** *f* estimation; *des coûts* estimate

estime *f* esteem; **estimer** *valeur* estimate; (*respecter*) have esteem for; (*croire*) feel, think; **s'~ heureux** consider o.s. lucky

estival summer *atr*

estomac *m* stomach

Estonie *f* Estonia

estrade *f* podium

estropier cripple

estuaire *m* estuary

et and; ~ ... ~ ... both ... and ...

étable *f* cowshed

établi *m* workbench

établir *entreprise* establish, set up; , *contact, ordre* establish; *salaires, prix* set, fix; *facture, liste* draw up; *record* set; *culpabilité* establish, prove; *raisonnement, réputation* base (*sur* on); **s'~** (*s'installer*) settle; **établissement** *m* establishment; *de salaires, prix* setting; *d'une facture, liste* drawing up; *d'un record* setting; *d'une loi, d'un impôt* introduction

étage *m* floor, story, *Br* storey; *d'une fusée* stage

étagère *f meuble* bookcase, shelves *pl*; *planche* shelf

étain *m* pewter

étalage m display; **faire ~ de qch** show sth off; **étaler** carte spread out; peinture, paiements spread (**sur** over); vacances stagger; marchandises display; fig (exhiber) show off; **s'~ de peinture** spread; de paiements be spread out (**sur**); (se vautrer) sprawl; par terre fall flat

étanche watertight; **étancher** make watertight

étang m pond

étape f lieu stopover, stopping place; d'un parcours stage, leg; fig stage

état m state; (liste) statement, list; **en tout ~ de cause** in any case, anyway; **hors d'~** out of order

États-Unis mpl: **les ~ the** United States

été m summer

éteindre incendie, cigarette put out; électricité, radio, chauffage turn off; **s'~ de feu**, lumière go out; de télé etc go off; euph (mourir) pass away

étendre malade, enfant lay (down); beurre, enduit spread; peinture apply; bras stretch out; linge hang up; vin dilute; sauce thin; influence extend; **s'~** extend, stretch (**jusqu'à** as far as, to); d'une personne lie down; d'un incendie, d'une maladie spread; d'un tissu

stretch; **étendue** f extent; d'eau expanse; de connaissances, d'une catastrophe extent

éternel, ~le eternal; **éternité** f eternity

éternuer sneeze

éthique 1 adj ethical **2** f ethics

étinceler sparkle; **étincelle** f spark

étiqueter label (aussi fig)

étiquette f label; (protocole) etiquette

étirer: **s'~** stretch

étoffe f material; **étoffer** fig flesh out

étoile f star (aussi fig); **~ filante** falling star, Br shooting star; **~ de mer** starfish

étonnement m astonishment, surprise; **étonner** astonish, surprise; **s'~ de be** astonished ou surprised at; **s'~ que** (+ subj) be surprised that

étouffant stifling, suffocating; **étouffée** CUIS: **à l'~** braised; **étouffer** suffocate; avec un oreiller smother, suffocate; fig: bruit quash; révolte put down, suppress; cri smother; scandale hush up

étourderie f foolishness; action foolish thing to do

étourdi foolish, thoughtless; **étourdir** daze; **~ qn** d'alcool, de succès go to s.o.'s head; **étourdissement** m (vertige) dizziness, giddiness

étrange strange

étranger, -ère 1 *adj* strange; *de l'étranger* foreign **2** *m/f* stranger; *de l'étranger* foreigner **3** *m*: *à l'~* abroad; *investissement* foreign, outward

étrangler strangle; *fig: critique, liberté* stifle

être 1 *v/i* be; *nous sommes lundi* it's Monday; *nous avons été éliminé* we were eliminated; *~ à qn appartenir* à belong to s.o. **2** *v/aux* have; *elle n'est pas encore arrivée* she hasn't arrived yet; *elle est arrivée hier* she arrived yesterday **3** *m* being; *personne* person

étreindre grasp; *ami* embrace, hug; *de sentiments* grip; **étreinte** *f* hug, embrace; *de la main* grip

étrenner use for the first time

étrennes *fpl* New Year's gift

étroit narrow; *tricot* tight, small; *amitié* close; *être ~ d'esprit* be narrow-minded

étroitesse *f* narrowness

étude *f* study; *salle à l'école* study room; *de notaire* office; *activité* practice; *faire des ~s* study; *~ de marché* market research; *étudiant, ~e m/f* student; **étudier** study

étui *m* case

étuvée CUIS: *à l'~* braised

euphorique euphoric

euro *m* euro

Europe *f*: *l'~* Europe; **européen, ~ne** European; **européen, ~ne m/f** European

eux *mpl* they; *après prép* them

eux-mêmes *mpl* themselves

évacuation *f* evacuation

évadé *m* escaped prisoner, escapee; **évader**: *s'~* escape

évaluer *(estimer)* evaluate; *tableau, meuble* value; *coût, nombre* estimate

évanouir: *s'~* faint; *fig* vanish, disappear

évaporer: *s'~* evaporate

évasif, -ive evasive; **évasion** *f* escape

éveil *m* awakening; *en ~* alert; **éveiller** wake up; *fig* arouse; *s'~* wake up; *fig* be aroused

événement *m* event

éventail *m* fan; *fig: de marchandises* range

éventé boisson flat; **éventer** fan; *fig: secret* reveal

éventualité *f* eventuality, possibility; **éventuel, ~le** possible

évêque *m* bishop

évertuer: *s'~ à faire qc* try one's hardest to do sth

évident obvious

évier *m* sink

éviter avoid; *~ qc à qn* spare s.o. sth; *~ de faire qc* avoid doing sth

évoluer develop, evolve; **évolution** *f* development; BIOL evolution

évoquer *esprits* conjure up; *~*

un **problème** bring up a problem

exact *nombre, poids* exact, precise; *reportage* accurate; *calcul, date, solution* right, correct; *personne* punctual; **exactitude** *f* accuracy; *(ponctualité)* punctuality

ex æquo: *être ~* tie, draw

exagération *f* exaggeration; **exagérer** exaggerate

exalter excite; *(vanter)* exalt

examen *m* exam; MÉD examination; *passer un ~* take an exam; *être reçu à un ~* pass an exam; **examiner** examine

exaspérer exasperate

excédent *m* excess; *budgétaire, de trésorerie* surplus; *~ de bagages* excess baggage; **excéder** exceed; *(énerver)* irritate

excellence *f* excellence; *Excellence* Excellency; **excellent** excellent; **exceller** excel (*dans* in; *en* in; *à faire qch* at doing sth)

excepté 1 *adj:* **la Chine ~** except for China **2** *prép* except; *~ que* except for the fact that; *~ si* unless, except if; **excepter** exclude, except; **exception** *f* exception; *à l'~ de* with the exception of; **exceptionnel, ~le** exceptional

excès *m* excess; *à l'~* to excess, excessively; *~ de vitesse* speeding; **excessif, -ive** excessive

excitation *f* excitement; *(pro-*

vocation) incitement (*à* to); *sexuelle* arousal; **exciter** excite; *(provoquer)* incite (*à* to); *sexuellement* arouse; *appétit* whet; *imagination* stir

exclamation *f* exclamation; **exclamer:** *s'~* exclaim

exclure exclude

exclusion *f* expulsion; *à l'~ de* to the exclusion of; *(à l'exception de)* with the exception of

exclusivité *f* COMM exclusivity, sole rights *pl;* *en ~* exclusively

excursion *f* trip, excursion

excuse *f* excuse; *~s* apology; **excuser** excuse; *s'~* apologize (*de* for); *excusez-moi* excuse me

exécuter *ordre, projet* carry out; MUS perform; *loi, jugement* enforce; *condamné* execute; **exécution** *f d'un ordre, projet* carrying out; MUS performance; *d'une loi, un jugement* enforcement; *d'un condamné* execution

exemplaire 1 *adj* exemplary **2** *m* copy; *(échantillon)* sample; *en deux ~s* in duplicate

exemple *m* example; *par ~* for example; *donner l'~* set a good example

exempt exempt (*de* from); *souci* free (*de* from); **exempter** exempt (*de* from); **exemption** *f* exemption

exercer *corps* exercise; *in-*

fluence exert, use; *pouvoir* use; *profession* practise, Br practise; *mémoire* train; MIL drill; **s'~** (*s'entraîner*) practice, Br practise; **exercice** *m* exercise (*aussi* ÉDU); *d'une profession* practice; COMM fiscal year, Br financial year; MIL drill

exhiber exhibit; *document* produce; **s'~** make an exhibition of o.s.; **exhibitionniste** *m* exhibitionist

exigeant demanding; **exigence** *f* demand; **exiger** demand

exigu, -ë tiny

exil *m* exile; **exilé, -e** *m/f* exile; **exiler** exile; **s'~** go into exile

existence *f* existence; **exister** exist

exonérer exempt

exorbitant exorbitant

exotique exotic

expansion *f* expansion

expatrier *argent* move abroad *ou* out of the country; **s'~** settle abroad

expédier send; COMM ship, send; *travail* do quickly

expéditeur, -trice *m/f* sender; COMM shipper, sender; **expédition** *f* sending; COMM shipment; (*voyage*) expedition

expérience *f* experience; *scientifique* experiment

expérimenté experienced; **expérimenter** (*tester*) test

expert, -e *adj & m/f* expert;

expertise *f* (*estimation*) valuation; JUR expert testimony

expier expiate

expiration *f d'un délai* expiration, Br expiry; *de souffle* exhalation; **expirer** *d'un contrat, délai* expire; (*respirer*) exhale; (*mourir*) die, expire *fml*

explication *f* explanation; **expliquer** explain; **s'~** explain o.s.; **s'~ avec qn** talk things over with s.o.

exploit *m sportif, médical* feat; *amoureux* exploit

exploitant, -e *m/f agricole* farmer

exploitation *f d'une ferme, ligne aérienne* running; *du sol* farming; *de richesses naturelles péj*: *des ouvriers* exploitation; (*entreprise*) operation

exploiter *ferme, ligne aérienne* run; *sol* farm; *richesses naturelles* exploit (*aussi péj*)

explorateur, -trice *m/f* explorer; **explorer** explore

exploser explode (*aussi fig*); **~ de rire** F crack up F; **explosif, -ive** *adj & m* explosive; **explosion** *f* explosion (*aussi fig*)

exportateur, -trice 1 *adj* exporting **2** *m* exporter; **exportation** *f* export; **exporter** export

exposé *m* account, report; ÉDU presentation; **exposer**

art, *marchandise* exhibit, show; *problème, programme* explain; *à l'air, à la chaleur* expose (*aussi* PHOT); **exposition** *f d'art, de marchandise* exhibition; *d'un problème* explanation; *au soleil* exposure (*aussi* PHOT)

exprès[1] *adv* (*intentionnellement*) deliberately, on purpose; (*spécialement*) expressly

exprès[2], **-esse 1** *adj* express **2** *adj inv* **lettre** *f* **exprès** express letter

express[1] *adj inv* express **2** *m train* express; *café* espresso

expressément expressly

expression *f* expression

exprimer express; **s'~** express o.s.

expulser expel; *d'un pays* deport; **expulsion** *f* expulsion; *d'un pays* deportation

exquis exquisite

extase *f* ecstasy

extension *f des bras, jambes* stretching; (*prolongement*) extension; *d'une épidémie* spread; INFORM expansion

exténuer exhaust

extérieur 1 *adj* external; *mur aussi* outside **2** *m* (*partie externe*) outside, exterior; **à l'~ de** outside; **extérioriser** express, let out; **s'~** *d'un sentiment* find expression; *d'une*

personne express one's emotions

exterminer exterminate

externaliser COM outsource

externe external

extincteur *m* extinguisher

extinction *f* extinction (*aussi fig*)

extirper *mauvaise herbe* pull up; MÉD remove; *fig renseignement* drag out

extorquer extort

extorsion *f* extortion

extraction *f* extraction

extrader extradite

extraire extract

extrait *m* extract

extraordinaire extraordinary

extraterrestre *m/f* extraterrestrial, alien

extravagance *f* extravagance; *d'une personne, d'une idée* eccentricity

extraverti extrovert

extrême 1 *adj* extreme **2** *m* extreme; **à l'~** to extremes

Extrême-Orient *m*: **l'~** the Far East

extrémiste *m/f* POL extremist; **extrémité** *f d'une rue* (very) end; *d'un doigt* tip; (*situation désespérée*) extremity; **~s** ANAT extremities

exubérant exuberant

exulter exult

eye-liner *m* eyeliner

F

fable *f* fable

fabricant, **~e** *m/f* manufacturer, maker; **fabrication** *f* making; *industrielle* manufacture; **fabriquer** make; *industriellement aussi* manufacture; *histoire* fabricate

fabuleux, **-euse** fabulous

fac *f* (= **faculté**) uni, university

façade *f* façade

face *f* face; *d'une pièce* head; **en ~ (de)** opposite; **faire ~ à** face up to; **face-à-face** *m inv* face-to-face (debate)

fâché annoyed; **fâcher** annoy; **se ~** get annoyed; **~ avec qn** fall out with s.o.; **fâcheux, -euse** annoying; (*déplorable*) unfortunate

facile easy; *personne* easy-going; **facilement** easily; **facilité** *f* easiness; **à faire qch** ease; **~s de paiement** easy terms; **faciliter** make easier, facilitate

façon *f* (*manière*) way, method; **de ~ (à ce) que** (+*subj*) so that; **de toute ~** anyway, anyhow; **de cette ~** (in) that way; **à la ~ de** like, in the style of

facteur *m* mailman, *Br* postman; MATH, *fig* factor

factrice *f* mailwoman, *Br*

postwoman

facture *f* bill; COMM invoice; **facturer** invoice

facultatif, **-ive** optional

faculté *f* faculty

fade insipid

faible 1 *adj* weak; *bruit, lumière, espoir* faint; *avantage* slight **2** *m pour personne* soft spot; *pour chocolat etc* weakness; **faiblesse** *f* weakness; **faiblir** weaken

faille *f* GÉOL fault; *dans théorie* flaw

faillible fallible; **faillir**: **il a failli gagner** he almost won

faim *f* hunger; **avoir ~** be hungry; **mourir de ~** starve (*aussi fig*)

fainéant, **~e 1** *adj* idle, lazy **2** *m/f* idler

faire 1 *v/t* do; *robe, meuble, repas, liste* make; **~ de la natation/du ski** swim/ski, go swimming/skiing; **cinq plus cinq font dix** five and five are *ou* make ten; **ça ne fait rien** it doesn't matter; **~ rire qn** make s.o. laugh; **~ peindre la salle de bain** have the bathroom painted **2** *v/i*: **~ vite** hurry up, be quick **3** *impersonnel*: **il fait chaud/froid** it is *ou* it's warm/cold **4**: **ça ne se fait pas** it's not done; **se ~ rare** become rarer; **se ~ à qc** get used to sth; **je ne m'en fais pas** I'm not worried

faisable feasible

faisan *m* pheasant

faisceau *m* bundle; *de lumière* beam

fait[1] *m* fact; *(action)* act; *(événement)* development; **au ~** by the way; **de ce ~** consequently; **en ~** in fact; **tout à ~** absolutely; **un ~ divers** a brief news item

fait[2] *adj*: **être ~ pour qn/qch** be made for s.o./sth; **c'est bien ~ pour lui** serves him right!

falaise *f* cliff

falloir: **il faut un visa** you need a visa, you must have a visa; **il faut l'avertir** we have to warn him; **il me faut sortir, il faut que je sorte** (*subj*) I have to go out, I must go out; **s'il le faut** if necessary; **il aurait fallu prendre le train** we should have taken the train; **comme il faut** respectable; **il ne faut pas que je sorte** (*subj*) I mustn't go out

falsifier *argent* forge; *document* falsify; *vérité* misrepresent

famélique starving

fameux, -euse (*célèbre*) famous; (*excellent*) wonderful

familiariser familiarize; **familiarité** *f* familiarity; **familier, -ère** familiar

famille *f* family

famine *f* famine

fanatique 1 *adj* fanatical **2** *m/f* fanatic; **fanatisme** *m* fanaticism

faner: **se ~** fade

fanfare *f* (*orchestre*) brass band; (*musique*) fanfare; **fanfaron, -ne 1** *adj* boastful **2** *m* boaster

fantaisie *f* imagination; (*caprice*) whim

fantasme *m* fantasy; **fantasmer** fantasize

fantasque strange, weird

fantastique 1 *adj* fantastic; (*imaginaire*) imaginary **2** *m*: **le ~** fantasy

fantôme *m* ghost

farce *f* au théâtre farce; (*tour*) joke; cuis stuffing; **farceur, -euse** *m/f* joker; **farcir** cuis stuff; *fig* cram

fard *m* make-up; **~ à paupières** eye shadow

fardeau *m* burden (*aussi fig*)

farder: **se ~** make up

farine *f* flour; **~ de maïs** corn starch; *Br* cornflour

farouche (*timide*) shy; *volonté, haine* fierce

fascination *f* fascination; **fasciner** fascinate

faste *m* pomp

fast-food *m* fast food restaurant

fastidieux, -euse tedious

fastueux, -euse lavish

fatal fatal; (*inévitable*) inevitable; **fatalisme** *m* fatalism;

fataliste 1 *adj* fatalistic **2** *m/f* fatalist; **fatalité** *f* fate

fatigant tiring; (*agaçant*) tiresome; **fatigue** *f* tiredness; **fatiguer** tire; (*importuner*) annoy; **se ~** get tired

faubourg *m* (working-class) suburb

fauché F broke F; **faucher** *fig* mow down; F (*voler*) pinch F

faufiler: **se ~ dans une pièce** slip into a room

faune *f* wildlife, fauna

faussaire *m* forger; **fausser** *calcul*, *vérité* distort; *clef* bend

faute *f* mistake; (*responsabilité*) fault; **par sa ~** because of him; **~ de** for lack of; **sans ~** without fail

fauteuil *m* armchair; **~ roulant** wheelchair

fauve 1 *adj* tawny **2** *m* **félin** big cat

faux, fausse 1 *adj* false; *incorrect aussi* wrong; *bijoux* imitation, fake; **fausse couche** *f* miscarriage; **~ témoignage** perjury **2** *adv*: *chanter* **~** sing out of tune **3** *m* *copie* forgery, fake

faux-filet *m* CUIS sirloin

faux-monnayeur *m* counterfeiter, forger

faux-semblant *m* pretense, *Br* pretence

faveur *f* favor, *Br* favour; **de ~** *traitement* preferential; *prix* special; **en ~ de** in favor of

favorable favorable, *Br* fa-

vourable; **favori, ~te** *m/f* & *adj* favorite, *Br* favourite; **favoriser** favor, *Br* favour; *faciliter*, *avantager* promote; **favoritisme** *m* favoritism, *Br* favouritism

fax *m* fax; **faxer** fax

féconder fertilize; **fécondité** *f* fertility

fécule *f* starch

fédéral federal; **fédération** *f* federation

fée *f* fairy

feeling *m* feeling; **avoir un bon ~ pour qc** have a good feeling about sth

feindre: **~ l'étonnement** pretend to be astonished, feign astonishment; **~ de faire qch** pretend to do sth; **feinte** *f* feint

fêler: **se ~** crack

félicitations *fpl* congratulations; **féliciter** congratulate (**de** on)

fêlure *f* crack

femelle *f* & *adj* female

féminin 1 *adj* feminine; *sexe* female; *problèmes*, *magazines*, *mode* women's **2** *m* GRAM feminine; **féministe** *m/f* & *adj* feminist; **féminité** *f* femininity

femme *f* woman; (*épouse*) wife; **~ battue** battered wife; **~ au foyer** homemaker, *Br* housewife

fendre split; (*fissurer*) crack; *cœur* break; **se ~** split; (*se fissurer*) crack

fenêtre f window

fenouil m BOT fennel

fente f crack; *d'une boîte à lettres, jupe* slit; *pour pièces de monnaie* slot

fer m iron; **~ à cheval** horseshoe; **~ à repasser** iron

férié: jour m **~** (public) holiday

ferme[1] **1** *adj* firm; **terre f ~** dry land, terra firma **2** *adv* *travailler* hard; **s'ennuyer ~** be bored stiff

ferme[2] f farm

fermé closed, shut; *robinet* off; *club* exclusive

fermenter ferment

fermer 1 *v/t* close, shut; *eau, gaz, robinet* turn off; *manteau* fasten; **ferme-la!** shut up! **2** *v/i* close, shut; *d'un manteau* fasten; **se ~** close, shut

fermeté f firmness

fermeture f closing; *définitive* closure; *mécanisme* fastener; **~ éclair** zipper, *Br* zip (fastener)

fermier 1 *adj œufs, poulet* free-range **2** m farmer

féroce fierce, ferocious; **férocité** f fierceness, ferocity

ferré, ~e: voie f **~e** (railroad *ou Br* railway) track

ferroviaire railroad *atr*, *Br* railway *atr*

fertile fertile; **~ en** full of; **fertilité** f fertility

fervent fervent

fesse f buttock; **~s** butt, *Br*

bottom; **fessée** f spanking

festin m feast

festival m festival

festivités *fpl* festivities

fêtard m F reveler; *Br* reveller; **fête** f festival; *(soirée)* party; *publique* holiday; REL feast (day), festival; *jour d'un saint* name day; **les ~s (de fin d'année)** the holidays, Christmas and New Year; **faire la ~** party; **~ foraine** fun fair; **Fête des mères** Mother's Day; **Fête nationale** Bastille Day; **fêter** celebrate; *(accueillir)* fête

feu m fire; AUTO, MAR light; *de circulation* (traffic) light, *Br* (traffic) lights *pl*; *d'une cuisinière* burner; *fig* (enthousiasme) passion; **coup** m **de ~** shot; **prendre ~** catch fire; **vous avez du ~?** got a light?; **~ arrière** AUTO taillight

feuillage m foliage; **feuille** f leaf; *de papier* sheet; **~ d'impôt** tax return; **~ de paie** payslip; **feuilleter** *livre etc* leaf through

feuilleton m serial; TV soap opera

feutre m felt; *stylo* felt-tipped pen; *chapeau* fedora

février m February

fiable reliable

fiançailles *fpl* engagement; **fiancé, ~e** *m/f* fiancé; **fiancer: se ~ avec** get engaged to

fibre   110

fibre f fiber, Br fibre; *avoir la ~ paternelle* fig be a born father; *la ~ patriotique* patriotic feelings

ficeler tie up; **ficelle** f string; *pain* fine French stick

fiche f *pour classement* index card; *formulaire* form; ÉL plug

ficher F (*faire*) do; (*donner*) give; (*mettre*) stick; *fiche--moi la paix!* leave me alone!; *je m'en fiche* I don't give a damn

fichier m INFORM file; *~ joint* attachment

fichu F (*inutilisable*) kaput F; (*sale*) filthy; *être mal ~ santé* be feeling rotten

fictif, -ive fictitious; **fiction** f fiction

fidèle 1 *adj* faithful **2** *m/f* REL, *fig*: *les fidèles* the faithful *pl*; **fidélité** f faithfulness

fier¹: *se ~ à* trust

fier², -ère *adj* proud (*de* of); **fierté** f pride

fièvre f fever; *avoir de la ~* have a fever; **fiévreux, -euse** feverish

figer congeal; *se ~ fig*: *d'un sourire* become fixed

figue f fig; **figuier** m fig tree

figurant, ~e m/f *de théâtre* walk-on; *de cinéma* extra; **figure** f figure; (*visage*) face; **figuré** figurative; **figurer** figure; *se ~ qc* imagine sth

fil m thread; *de métal*, ÉL, TÉL wire; *coup* m *de ~* TÉL

(phone) call

filature f spinning; *usine* mill; *prendre qn en ~ fig* tail s.o.

file f line; *d'une route* lane; *~* (*d'attente*) line, Br queue

filer 1 *v/t* spin; F (*donner*) give; (*épier*) tail F **2** *v/i* F (*partir vite*) race off; *du temps* fly past

filet m *d'eau* trickle; *de pêche*, *tennis* net; CUIS fillet

filial, ~e 1 *adj* filial **2** f COMM subsidiary

fille f girl; *parenté* daughter; *vieille ~* old maid; **fillette** f little girl

filleul m godson; **filleule** f goddaughter

film m movie, Br *aussi* film; *couche* film; *~ policier* detective movie *ou* Br *aussi* film; **filmer** film

fils m son; *~ à papa* (spoilt) rich kid

filtre m filter; **filtrer 1** *v/t* filter; *fig* screen **2** *v/i* filter through; *fig* leak

fin¹ f end; *à la ~* in the end; *mettre ~ à qc* put an end to sth; *sans ~* endless; *parler* endlessly

fin² 1 *adj* fine; (*mince*) thin; *taille*, *cheville* slender; *esprit* refined; (*rusé*, *malin*) sharp **2** *adv* fine(ly)

final, ~e 1 *adj* final **2** m: *~e* MUS finale Br finial; **finale 1** m MUS finale **2** f SP final; **finaliser** finalize; **finaliste** m/f finalist

flottant

finance f finance; **financer** fund, finance; **financier, -ère 1** adj financial **2** m financier

finesse f (délicatesse) fineness

fini 1 adj finished **2** m finish; **finir 1** v/t finish **2** v/i finish; ~ **de faire qc** finish doing sth; ~ **par faire qc** finish up doing sth

finlandais, ~e 1 adj Finnish **2** m langue Finnish; **Finlandais, ~e** m/f Finn; **Finlande** f: **la ~** Finland

firme f firm

fisc m tax authorities pl

fissure f crack

fixe 1 adj fixed; adresse, personnel permanent **2** m basic salary; **fixer** fasten; (déterminer) fix, set; PHOT fix; (regarder) stare at; **se ~** (s'établir) settle down

flageolet m flageolet bean

flagrant flagrant; **en ~ délit** red-handed

flair m sense of smell; fig intuition; **flairer** smell (aussi fig)

flambant: ~ neuf brand new; **flamber 1** v/i blaze **2** v/t CUIS flambé

flamme f flame; fig fervor, Br fervour

flan m flan

flancher quail

flâner stroll

flanquer flank; F (jeter) fling; coup give

flaque f puddle

flasque flabby

flatter flatter; **se ~ de qc** congratulate o.s. on sth; **flatterie** f flattery; **flatteur, -euse 1** adj flattering **2** m/f flatterer

flèche f arrow; d'un clocher spire; **monter en ~** de prix skyrocket

fléchir 1 v/t bend; (faire céder) sway **2** v/i d'une poutre bend; fig (céder) give in; (faiblir) weaken; d'un prix, de ventes fall

flegmatique phlegmatic

flemme f laziness; **j'ai la ~ de le faire** I can't be bothered

flétrir: se ~ wither

fleur f flower; d'un arbre blossom; **fleurir** flower, bloom; fig flourish; **fleuriste** m/f florist

fleuve m river

flexibilité f flexibility; **flexible** flexible

flic m F cop F

flinguer f gun down

flipper 1 m pinball machine; **jeu pinball 2** v/i F freak out F

flirter flirt

flocon m flake; ~ **de neige** snowflake

Floride f Florida

florissant fig flourishing

flot m flood (aussi fig); **~s** waves; **remettre à ~** refloat (aussi fig)

flottant floating; vêtements baggy

flotte

flotte f fleet; F *(eau)* water; F *(pluie)* rain; **flotter** *d'un bateau* float; *d'un drapeau* flutter; *d'un sourire, air* hover; *fig* waver

flou blurred, fuzzy; *robe* loose-fitting

fluctuation f fluctuation; **fluctuer** COMM fluctuate

fluide 1 adj fluid; *circulation* moving freely **2** m PHYS fluid; **fluidité** f fluidity

fluorescent fluorescent

flûte f MUS, *verre* flute; *pain* thin French stick

fluvial river atr

flux m MAR flow

fœtus m fetus, Br foetus

foi f faith; **être de bonne/ mauvaise ~** be sincere/insincere

foie m liver; **une crise de ~** a stomach upset

foire f fair

fois f time; **une ~** once; **deux ~** twice; **trois ~** three times; **il était une ~ ...** once upon a time there was; **quatre ~ six** four times six; **à la ~** at the same time

foisonner be abundant

folie f madness; **faire des ~s** *achats* go on a spending spree

folk m folk (music)

folklore folklore

follement madly

fomenter foment

foncé *couleur* dark; **foncer** *de couleurs* darken; AUTO speed

along; **~ sur** rush at

foncier, -ère land

foncièrement fundamentally

fonction f function; *(poste)* office; **faire ~ de** act as; **en ~ de** according to; **prendre ses ~s** take up office

fonctionnaire m/f public servant

fonctionnement m functioning; **fonctionner** work; *du système* function

fond m bottom; *d'une salle, armoire* back; *d'une peinture* background; *(contenu)* content; *d'un problème* heart; *d'un pantalon* seat; **à ~** thoroughly; **au ~, dans le ~** basically

fondamental fundamental

fondateur, -trice m/f founder; **fondation** f foundation; **fondé** adj well-founded **2** m: **~ de pouvoir** authorized representative; **fondement** m fig basis; **sans ~** groundless; **fonder** found; **~ qch sur** base sth on; **se ~ sur** *d'une personne* base o.s. on; *d'une idée* be based on; **fondre 1** v/t neige melt; *dans l'eau* dissolve; *métal* melt down **2** v/i *de la neige* melt; *dans l'eau* dissolve; **~ sur** *proie* pounce on

fonds m **1** sg fund; *d'une bibliothèque* collection; **~ de commerce** business **2** pl (argent) funds

fondu melted

fondue f CUIS fondue; ~ **bourguignonne** beef fondue

fontaine f fountain; (source) spring

fonte f métal cast iron; ~ **des neiges** spring thaw

football m soccer, Br aussi football; ~ **américain** football, Br American football; **footballeur, -euse** m/f soccer player, Br aussi footballer

footing m jogging; **faire du** ~ jog, go jogging

force f strength; (violence) force; **à** ~ **de travailler** by working; **de** ~ by force; ~**s armées** armed forces

forcené, ~e m/f maniac

forcer force; **se** ~ force o.s.

forestier, -ère 1 adj forest atr **2** m ranger, Br forest warden

forêt f forest

forfait m COMM package; (prix) all-in price; **déclarer** ~ withdraw

formaliser: se ~ **de** take offense ou Br offence at; **formalité** f formality

format m format; **formater** format

formation f formation; (éducation) training; ~ **continue** continuing education

forme f form; **en** ~ **de** in the shape of; **être en** ~ be in form, be in good shape; **formel, ~le** formal; (explicite) categorical; **formellement** adv: ~ **interdit** strictly for-

bidden; **former** form; (instruire) train; **se** ~ form

formidable enormous; F great F

formulaire m form

formulation f wording

formule f formula; **formuler** formulate; vœux, jugement express

fort 1 adj strong; (gros) stout; coup, pluie heavy; somme big; **être** ~ **en qch** be good at sth **2** adv parler loudly; pousser, frapper hard; (très) extremely; (beaucoup) a lot **3** m strong point; MIL fort; **fortement** pousser hard; (beaucoup) greatly

fortifier strengthen

fortuit chance

fortune f luck; **de** ~ makeshift

fosse f pit; (tombe) grave; **fossé** m ditch; fig gulf; **fossette** f dimple

fossile m & adj fossil

fou, folle 1 adj mad; (incroyable) incredible; **être** ~ **de qn/qc** be mad ou crazy about s.o./sth; ~ **de joie** etc beside o.s. with **2** m/f madman; madwoman

foudre f lightning; **coup** m **de** ~ fig love at first sight

foudroyer strike down; ~ **qn du regard** give s.o. a withering look

fouet m whip; CUIS whisk

fougueux, -euse fiery

fouiller 1 v/i dig; (chercher) search **2** v/t de police search;

en archéologie excavate
fouiner nose around
foulard *m* scarf
foule *f* crowd; **une ~ de** masses of
fouler trample; **sol** set foot on; **se ~ la cheville** twist one's ankle; **se ~ f** sprain
four *m* oven; TECH kiln; *fig* F **(insuccès)** flop F
fourchette *f* fork; *(éventail)* bracket; **fourchu** forked; **cheveux** *mpl* **~s** split ends
fourgon *m* baggage car, *Br* luggage van; **camion ~** van; **fourgonnette** *f* small van
fourmi *f* ant
fourmillements *mpl* pins and needles; **fourmiller** swarm **(de** with)
fournaise *f fig* oven; **fourneau** *m* furnace; **gaz** F stove
fourni: bien ~ well stocked; **fournir** supply **(de, en** with); *occasion* provide; *effort* make; **~ qc à qn** provide s.o. with sth; **fournisseur** *m* supplier; **~ d'accès (Internet)** Internet service provider, ISP; **fourniture** *f* supply; **~s scolaires** school stationery and books
fourré¹ *m* thicket
fourré² *adj* CUIS filled; *vêtement* lined
fourrer stick, shove; *(remplir)* fill; **se ~ dans** get into
fourrière *f* pound
fourrure *f* fur
fourvoyer: se ~ go astray

foutre F do; *(mettre)* stick; *coup* give; **se ~ de qn** make fun of s.o.; *indifférence* not give a damn about s.o.; **je m'en fous!** I don't give a damn!
foyer *m* fireplace; *d'une famille* home; *de jeunes* club; *(pension)* hostel; *d'un théâtre* foyer; *d'un incendie* seat; *d'une infection* source
fracas *m* crash; **fracasser** shatter
fractionner divide (up) **(en** into)
fracture *f* MÉD *m* fracture; **fracturer** *coffre* break open; *jambe* fracture
fragile fragile; *santé* frail; *cœur* weak; **fragiliser** weaken; **fragilité** *f* fragility
fragment *m* fragment
fraîcheur *f* freshness; *(froideur)* coolness *(aussi fig)*; **fraîchir** *du vent* freshen; *du temps* get cooler
frais¹, fraîche *1 adj* fresh; *(froid)* cool; *peinture* wet; *nouvelles* recent; **servir ~** serve chilled; **il fait ~** it's cool **2** *adv* freshly, newly **3** *m*: **prendre le ~** get a breath of fresh air
frais² *mpl* expenses *pl*; COMM costs *pl*; **faire des ~** incur costs; **à mes ~** at my (own) expense; **~ bancaires** bank charges; **~ généraux** overhead, *Br* overheads
fraise *f* strawberry

framboise f raspberry

franc[1], **franche** adj frank; *regard* open; COMM free

franc[2] m franc

français, **~e 1** adj French **2** m *langue* French; **Français**, **~e** m/f Frenchman; French-woman; **les ~** the French pl; **France** f: **la ~** France

franchir cross; *obstacle* negotiate

franchise f *caractère* frankness; (*exemption*) exemption; COMM franchise; *d'une assurance* deductible, Br excess

franco adv: **~ (de port)** carriage free; **y aller ~** fig F go right ahead

francophone 1 adj French-speaking **2** m/f French speaker

franc-parler m outspokenness

frange f bangs pl, Br fringe

frappant striking; **frappe** f IN-FORM keying; **faute** f **de ~** typo, typing error; **frapper 1** v/t hit, strike; (*impressionner*) strike **2** v/i (*agir*) strike; **à la porte** knock (**à** at); **~ dans ses mains** clap (one's hands)

fraternel, **~le** brotherly, fraternal; **fraternité** f brotherhood

fraude f fraud; ÉDU cheating; **passer en ~** smuggle; **frauduleux**, **-euse** fraudulent

frayer: **se ~** *chemin* clear

frayeur f fright

fredonner hum

frein m brake; **sans ~** fig unbridled; **~ à main** parking brake, Br hand brake; **freiner 1** v/i brake **2** v/t fig curb, check

frêle frail

frelon m hornet

frémir shake; *de feuilles* quiver; *de l'eau* simmer; **frémissement** m shiver; *de feuilles* quivering

frénésie f frenzy; **avec ~** frenetically

fréquemment frequently; **fréquence** f frequency; **quelle est la ~ des bus?** how often do the buses go?; **fréquent** frequent; *situation* common

fréquentation f *d'un théâtre etc* attendance; **tes ~s** (*amis*) the company you keep; **fréquenter** *endroit* go to regularly, frequent; *personne* see; *groupe* go around with

frère m brother

fret m freight

frétiller wriggle

friable crumbly

friand: **être ~ de qc** be fond of sth; **friandises** fpl sweet things

fric m F money, dosh F

friche f AGR: **en ~** (lying) fallow

friction f friction; *de la tête* scalp massage; **frictionner** massage

frigidaire m refrigerator

frigide frigid

frigo m F icebox, fridge; **fri-gorifier** refrigerate

frileux, -euse: être ~ feel the cold

frimer show off; **frimeur, -euse** show-off

fringues fpl F clothes, gear F

frire 1 v/i fry 2 v/t: **faire ~** fry

frisé curly; **friser** cheveux curl; fig: le ridicule verge on

frissonner shiver

frit fried; (**pommes**) **frites** fpl (French) fries, Br aussi chips; **friteuse** f deep fryer; **friture** f poissons Br white-bait, small fried fish; huile oil; à la radio, TÉL interference

frivole frivolous; **frivolité** f frivolity

froid 1 adj cold (aussi fig); **j'ai ~** I'm cold; **prendre ~** catch (a) cold 2 m cold; **humour** m **à ~** dry humor; **froidement** fig coldly; (calmement) coolly; **tuer** in cold blood; **froideur** f coldness

froissement m bruit rustle; **froisser** crumple; fig of-fend; **se ~** crumple; fig take offense ou Br offence

fromage m cheese; **~ blanc** fromage frais; **~ à tartiner** cheese spread

froncer gather; **~ les sourcils** frown

front m front; ANAT forehead; **de ~** front; fig

head-on; **marcher de ~** walk side by side

frontière f frontier, border

frotter 1 v/i rub 2 v/t rub (**de** with); **meuble** polish; **sol** scrub; **allumette** strike

frousse f F fear; **avoir la ~** be scared

fructifier BOT bear fruit; d'un placement yield a profit

fructueux, -euse fruitful

fruit m fruit; **~s** fruit; **~s de mer** seafood

frustrant frustrating; **frustra-tion** f frustration

fugitif, -ive 1 adj runaway; fig fleeting 2 m/f fugitive

fugue f d'un enfant escapade; MUS fugue; **faire une ~** run away

fuir 1 v/i flee; du temps fly; d'un tuyau leak; d'un robinet drip; d'un liquide leak out 2 v/t shun; question avoid; **fui-te** f flight (**devant** from); d'un tuyau etc leak; **prendre la ~** take flight

fulgurant dazzling; vitesse lightning

fumé smoked; verre tinted

fumée f smoke; **fumer** smoke; **fumeur, -euse** m/f smoker

funèbre funeral atr; (lugubre) gloomy

funérailles fpl funeral

funeste fatal

fur: **au ~ et à mesure** as I/you etc go along; **au ~ et à mesu-re que** as

fureter ferret around

fureur f fury; *faire ~* be all the rage

furie (*colère*) fury; *femme* shrew; **furieux, -euse** furious (*contre qn* with s.o.; *de qch* with ou at sth)

furtif, -ive furtive, stealthy

fuseau m: *~ horaire* time zone

fusée f rocket

fusible m ÉL fuse

fusil m rifle; *~ de chasse* shotgun; **fusiller** execute by firing squad

fusion f COMM merger; PHYS fusion; **fusionner** COMM merge

futé cunning, clever

futile futile; *personne* frivolous

futur m & adj future

fuyant *menton* receding; *regard* evasive

G

gabarit m size; TECH template

gâcher fig spoil; *travail* bungle; *temps, argent* waste

gâchis m (*désordre*) mess; (*gaspillage*) waste

gadget m gadget

gaffe f F blooper F, blunder; *faire ~ à* F be careful of

gaffer F make a gaffe ou blooper F

gage fig forfeit; (*preuve*) token; *tueur* m *à ~s* hitman; *mettre en ~* pawn

gagnant, ~e 1 adj winning 2 m/f winner

gagne-pain m livelihood

gagner win; *salaire, amitié etc* earn; *place, temps* gain; *endroit* reach; *de peur etc* overcome; *~ sa vie* earn one's living

gai cheerful; *un peu ivre* tipsy; **gaieté** f cheerfulness

gain m gain; (*avantage*) bene-

fit; *~s* profits; *d'un employé* earnings

gaine f sheath

galant galant; *homme ~* gentleman

galaxie f galaxy

galère f: *il est dans la ~* fig he's in a mess; **galérer** F sweat

galerie f gallery; AUTO roofrack; *~ d'art* art gallery; *~ marchande* mall

galet m pebble

Galles fpl: *le pays* m *de ~* Wales; **gallois, ~e** 1 adj Welsh; *~* m langue Welsh; **Gallois, ~e** m/f Welshman; Welsh woman

galop m gallop; **galoper** gallop

galopin m urchin

galvaniser galvanize

gambader gambol, leap

gamin, ~e 1 m/f kid 2 adj

childlike

gamme f MUS scale; fig range; **bas de ~** downscale, Br downmarket

gang m gang

gangster m gangster

gant m glove; **~ de toilette** washcloth, Br faceclloth

garage m garage; **garagiste** m auto mechanic; *propriétaire* garage owner

garant, ~e m/f guarantor; **garantie** f guarantee; **garantir** guarantee

garce f F bitch

garçon m boy; (*serveur*) waiter; **~ d'honneur** best man; **~ manqué** tomboy; **garçonnière** f bachelor apartment *ou* Br flat

garde[1] f care (*de* of); MIL guard; **prendre ~** be careful; **être de ~** be on duty; **mettre qn en ~** put s.o. on their guard; **~ à vue** police custody

garde[2] m guard; **~ forestier** (forest) ranger

garde-boue m AUTO fender, Br wing

garde-fou m railing

garde-malade m/f nurse

garder *objet* keep; *vêtement* keep on; (*surveiller*) guard; *malade, enfant* look after; **se ~ de faire qch** be careful not to do sth

garderie f daycare center, Br daycare centre

gardien, ~ne m/f *de prison*

guard, Br warder; *d'un musée* attendant; *d'immeuble*, *d'école* janitor; fig guardian; **~ (de but)** goalkeeper **~ de la paix** police officer

gare[1] f station; **~ routière** bus station

gare[2]: **~ à toi!** watch out!; *ça va mal se passer* you'll be for it!

garer park; **se ~** park; *pour laisser passer* move aside

gargariser: se ~ gargle

gargouiller gurgle; *de l'estomac* rumble

garnement m rascal

garnir (*fournir*) fit (**de** with); (*orner*) trim (**de** with); **garniture** f *légumes* vegetables pl

gars m F guy F

gasoil m gas oil, Br diesel

gaspillage m waste; **gaspiller** waste; **gaspilleur, -euse** 1 *adj* wasteful 2 m/f waster

gastroentérite f gastroenteritis

gastronome m/f gourmet; **gastronomie** f gastronomy

gâteau m cake; **~ sec** cookie, Br biscuit

gâter spoil; **se ~** *d'un aliment* spoil; *du temps* deteriorate

gauche 1 *adj* left; *manières* gauche 2 f left; **à ~** on the left (**de** of); **gaucher, -ère** 1 *adj* left-handed 2 m/f left-hander

gaufre f waffle; **gaufrette** f wafer

gaver *oie* force-feed; **~ qn de qch** *fig* stuff s.o. full of sth

gaz *m* gas; **mettre les ~** step on the gas; **à effet de serre** greenhouse gas

gaze *f* gauze

gazeux, -euse *boisson* carbonated, *Br* fizzy

gazinière *f* gas cooker

gazole *m* gas oil, *Br* diesel

gazon *m* grass

gazouiller twitter

géant, ~e 1 *adj* gigantic, giant *atr* **2** *m/f* giant

geindre groan

gel *m* frost; *fig: des prix* freeze; *cosmétique* gel

gélatine *f* gelatine

gelée *f* frost; *CUIS* aspic; *confiture* jelly; *Br* jam; **geler 1** *v/t* freeze **2** *v/i d'une personne* freeze; **il gèle** there's a frost

Gémeaux *mpl* ASTROL Gemini

gémir groan; **gémissement** *m* groan

gênant (*embarrassant*) embarrassing

gencive *f* gum

gendarme *m* policeman; **gendarmerie** *f* police force; *lieu* police station

gendre *m* son-in-law

gêne *f* (*embarras*) embarrassment; (*dérangement*) inconvenience; *physique* difficulty; **sans ~** shameless; **gêner** bother; (*embarrasser*) embarrass; (*encombrer*) be in

the way

général, ~e 1 *adj* general; **en ~** generally **2** *m* MIL general **3** *f* THÉAT dress rehearsal; **généraliser** generalize; **se ~** spread; **généraliste** *m* MÉD generalist; **généralités** *fpl* generalities

générateur *m* generator; **générer** generate

généreux, -euse generous; **générosité** *f* generosity

génétique genetic; **génétiquement** genetically; **~ modifié** genetically modified, GM

génétiquement genetically; **~ modifié** genetically modified, GM

Genève Geneva

génial of genius; (*formidable*) terrific; **génie** *m* genius; TECH engineering; **avoir du ~** be a genius; **~ civil** civil engineering

genou *m* knee; **à ~x** on one's knees

genre *m* kind, sort; GRAM gender; **bon chic, bon ~** preppie *atr*

gens *mpl* people *pl*

gentil, ~le nice; *enfant* good; **gentillesse** *f* (*amabilité*) kindness

géographie *f* geography

géologie *f* geology; **géologue** *m/f* geologist

géomètre *m/f* geometrician; **géométrie** *f* geometry

gérance *f* management; **gé-**

rant, **~e** m/f manager
gerbe f de blé sheaf
gercé lèvres chapped
gérer manage
gériatrie f geriatrics
germain: cousin m **~**, cousine f **~e** (first) cousin
germe m germ (aussi fig); **germer** germinate
gestation f gestation
geste m gesture; **gesticuler** gesticulate
gestion f **~** (d'entreprise) (business) management; **~ des risques** risk management; **~ de la qualité** quality management; **gestionnaire** m/f manager
ghetto m ghetto
gibier m game
giboulée f wintry shower
gicler spurt
gifle f slap (in the face); **gifler** slap (in the face)
gigantesque gigantic
gigaoctet m gigabyte
gigot m d'agneau leg
gigoter F fidget
gilet m vest, Br waistcoat; (chandail) cardigan; **~ de sauvetage** lifejacket
gin m gin; **~ tonic** gin and tonic
gingembre m BOT ginger
girafe f giraffe
giratoire: sens m **~** traffic circle, Br roundabout
gisement m GÉOL deposit; **~ pétrolifère** ou **de pétrole** oilfield

gitan, **~e** m/f gypsy
gîte m holiday home
givre m frost; **givré** covered with frost; avec du sucre frosted; F (fou) crazy
glace f ice; (miroir) mirror; AUTO window; (crème glacée) ice cream; d'un gâteau frosting, Br icing; d'une tarte glaze; **glacer** freeze; (intimider) petrify; gâteau frost, Br ice; tarte glaze; **se ~** freeze; du sang run cold; **glacial** icy (aussi fig); **glacière** f cool bag; fig icebox; **glaçon** m icicle; artificiel icecube
glaise f (aussi terre f **~**) clay
gland m acorn
glande f gland
glander F hang around F
glauque eau murky; couleur blue-green
glissade f slip; accidentelle slip; **glissant** slippery; **glissement** m **~** de terrain landslide; **glisser 1** v/t slip (dans into) **2** v/i slide; sur l'eau glide (**sur** over); (déraper) slip; être glissant be slippery; **se ~ dans** slip into
global; prix, somme total, overall; **globalisation** f globalization; **globe** m globe; **~ oculaire** eyeball
gloire f glory; **glorieux, -euse** glorious; **glorifier** glorify
glousser cluck; rire giggle
gluant sticky
glycine f wisteria
goal m goalkeeper

gobelet *m* tumbler; *en carton, plastique* cup

gober gobble; F *mensonge* swallow

godet *m récipient* pot; *de vêtements* flare

gogo F: *à ~* galore

goinfrer: *se ~* péj stuff o.s.

golf *m* SP golf; *terrain golf* course

golfe *m* GÉOGR gulf

gomme *f* gum; *pour effacer* eraser; **gommer** *(effacer)* erase

gond *m* hinge; *sortir de ses ~s* fly off the handle

gondole *f* gondola

gonflable inflatable; **gonfler 1** *v/i* swell **2** *v/t* blow up; *(exagérer)* exaggerate

gonzesse *f* F péj chick F

gorge *f* throat; *(poitrine)* bosom; GÉOGR gorge; *avoir mal à la ~* have a sore throat; **gorgée** *f* mouthful; **gorger**: *se ~* gorge o.s. *(de* with)

gosier *m* throat

gosse *m/f* F kid F

goudron *m* tar

gouffre *m* abyss; *fig* depths *pl*

goujat *m* boor

goulot *m* neck; *boire au ~* drink from the bottle

goulu greedy

gourd numb (with the cold)

gourde *f récipient* water bottle; *fig* F moron F

gourer F: *se ~* goof F, Br boob

gourmand, ~e 1 *adj* greedy **2** *m/f* gourmand; **gourmandi-**

se *f* greediness; *~s mets* delicacies; **gourmet** *m* gourmet

gourmette *f* chain

gourou *m* guru

gousse *f* pod; *~ d'ail* clove of garlic

goût *m* taste; *de bon ~* tasteful, in good taste; *de mauvais ~* tasteless, in bad taste; *avoir du ~* have taste; **goûter 1** *v/t* taste; *~ à* enjoy **2** *v/i* prendre un *goûter* have an afternoon snack **3** *m* afternoon snack

goutte *f* drop; *~ de pluie* raindrop; **goutte-à-goutte** *m* MÉD drip; **goutter** drip; **gouttière** *f* gutter

gouvernement *m* government; **gouverner** *pays* govern; *passions* master, control; MAR steer; **gouverneur** *m* governor

grâce *f* grace; *(bienveillance)* favor, Br favour; JUR pardon; *faire ~ à qn de qc* spare s.o. sth.; *~ à* thanks to; **gracier** reprieve; **gracieux, -euse** graceful; *à titre ~* free

grade *m* rank; **gradé** *m* MIL noncommissioned officer

gradins *mpl* SP bleachers, Br terraces

graduellement gradually

graduer *(augmenter)* gradually increase; *instrument* graduate

graffitis *mpl* graffiti *sg ou pl*

grain *m* grain; MAR squall; *~ de*

beauté mole, beauty spot; ~ **de raisin** grape

graine *f* seed

graissage *m* lubrication, greasing; **graisse** *f* fat; TECH grease; **graisser** grease, lubricate; (*salir*) get grease on; **graisseux, -euse** greasy

grammaire *f* grammar; **grammatical** grammatical

gramme *m* gram

grand 1 *adj* big; (*haut*) tall; (*adulte*) grown-up; (*long*) long; (*important, glorieux*) great; **il est ~ temps** it's high time; **~e surface** *f* supermarket; **les ~es vacances** *fpl* the summer vacation, *Br* the summer holidays; **~ ensemble** new development, *Br* (*housing*) estate **2** *adv* **ouvrir** wide **3** *m* giant, great man

grand-chose: pas ~ not much

Grande-Bretagne: la ~ Great Britain

grandeur *f* (*taille*) size; **~ nature** lifesize

grandiose magnificent

grandir 1 *v/i* grow **2** *v/t:* **~ qn** make s.o. look taller; *de l'expérience* strengthen s.o.

grand-mère *f* grandmother

grand-père *m* grandfather

grands-parents *mpl* grandparents *pl*

granit(e) *m* granite

granuleux, -euse granular

graphique 1 *adj* graphic **2** *m*

chart; MATH graph; INFORM graphic

grappe *f* cluster; **~ de raisin** bunch of grapes

grappin *m:* **mettre le ~ sur qn** get one's hands on s.o.

gras, ~se 1 *adj* fatty, fat; *personne* fat; *cheveux, peau* greasy; **faire la ~se matinée** sleep late **2** *m* CUIS fat

gratification *f* (*prime*) bonus; PSYCH gratification; **gratifier: ~ qn de qc** present s.o. with sth

gratiné CUIS with a sprinkling of cheese; *fig* F *addition* colossal

gratitude *f* gratitude

gratte-ciel *m* skyscraper; **gratter** scrape; (*griffer, piquer*) scratch; (*enlever*) scrape off; *mot* scratch out; **se ~** scratch; **grattoir** *m* scraper

gratuit free; *fig* gratuitous

gravats *mpl* rubble

grave serious; *son* deep; *ce n'est pas ~* it's not a problem

graver engrave; *disque* cut

gravier *m* gravel

gravillon *m* grit; **~s** gravel, *Br* loose chippings *pl*

gravir climb

gravité *f* seriousness; PHYS gravity

gravure *f* ART engraving; (*reproduction*) print

gré *m:* **bon ~, mal ~** like it or not; **contre mon ~** against my will; **de bon ~** willingly; **de son plein ~** of one's own free will

grec, ~que 1 *adj* Greek **2** *m* *langue* Greek; **Grec, ~que** *m/f* Greek; **Grèce: la ~** Greece

greffe *graft* MÉD heart transplant; **greffer** *graft*; *cœur, poumon* transplant

greffier *m* clerk of the court

grêle[1] *adj jambes* skinny; *voix* shrill

grêle[2] *f* hail; **grêler: il grêle** it's hailing; **grêlon** *m* hailstone

grelotter shiver

grenade *f* BOT pomegranate; MIL grenade

grenadine *f* grenadine, pomegranate syrup

grenier *m* attic

grenouille *f* frog

grès *m* sandstone; *poterie* stoneware

grésiller sizzle; RAD crackle

grève[1] *f* strike; **être en ~, faire ~** be on strike; **se mettre en ~** go on strike; **~ de la faim** hunger strike

grève[2] *f (plage)* shore

gréviste *m/f* striker

gribouillage *m* scribble; *(dessin)* doodle; **gribouiller** scribble; *(dessiner)* doodle

grief *m* grievance

grièvement *blessé* seriously

griffe *f* claw; COMM label; *fig (empreinte)* stamp; **griffer** scratch

griffonner scribble

grignoter 1 *v/t* nibble on; *économies* nibble away at **2** *v/i* nibble

grill *m* broiler, *Br* grill; **grillade** *f* broil, *Br* grill

grillage *m* wire mesh; *(clôture)* fence

grille *f d'une fenêtre* grille; *(clôture)* railings *pl*; *d'un four* rack; *(tableau)* grid; **grille-pain** *m* toaster; **griller 1** *v/t viande* broil, *Br* grill; *pain* toast; *café, marrons* roast **2** *v/i d'une ampoule* burn out; **~ un feu rouge** go through a red light

grillon *m* cricket

grimace *f* grimace; **faire des ~s** pull faces

grimper climb

grincement *m* *de porte* squeaking; **grincer** *d'une porte* squeak; **~ des dents** grind one's teeth

grincheux, -euse grouchy

grippe *f* MÉD flu; **prendre qn en ~** take a dislike to s.o.; **grippé** MÉD: **être ~** have flu

gris *m* gray, *Br* grey; *temps, vie* dull; *(ivre)* tipsy

grisant exhilarating

grisâtre grayish, *Br* greyish

griser: ~ qn go to s.o.'s head; **se laisser ~ par** get carried away by

grisonner go gray *ou Br* grey

grognement *m (plainte)*

grumbling; *d'un cochon etc* grunt; **grogner** (*se plaindre*) grumble; *d'un cochon* grunt; **grognon**, **∼e: être ∼** be grumpy

grommeler mutter

gronder 1 *v/i* growl; *du tonnerre* rumble; *d'une révolte* brew **2** *v/t* scold

gros, **∼se 1** *adj* big; (*corpulent*) fat; *lèvres* big; *rhume*, *souliers* heavy; *chaussettes* thick; *plaisanterie* coarse; *vin* rough; **∼ mots** *mpl* bad language **2** *adv*: **gagner ∼** win a lot; **en ∼** (*globalement*) on the whole; COMM wholesale **3** *m personne* fat man; COMM wholesale trade

groseille *f* BOT currant; **∼ à maquereau** gooseberry

grossesse *f* pregnancy

grosseur *f* (*corpulence*) fatness; (*volume*) size; (*tumeur*) growth

grossier, **-ère** (*rudimentaire*) crude; (*indélicat*) coarse; (*impoli*) rude; *erreur* bad

grossir 1 *v/t au microscope* magnify; *nombre*, *rivière* swell; (*exagérer*) exaggerate; **∼ qn** *d'une robe etc* make s.o. look fatter **2** *v/i d'une personne* put on weight

grotesque grotesque

grotte *f* cave

grouiller: **∼ de** be swarming with; **se ∼** F get a move on

groupe *m* group; **∼ sanguin** blood group; **grouper**

group; **se ∼ autour de qn** gather around s.o.

grue *f* ZO, TECH crane

grumeleux, **-euse** lumpy

gué *m* ford

guenilles *fpl* rags

guêpe *f* wasp

guère: **ne ... ∼** hardly

guéridon *m* round table

guérir 1 *v/t* cure (**de** of) **2** *v/i* heal; *d'un malade* get better; **guérison** *f* (*rétablissement*) recovery

guerre *f* war; **en ∼** at war; **faire la ∼** be at war (**à** with); **∼ civile** civil war; **∼ des gangs** gang warfare; **guerrier**, **-ère 2** *m* warrior

guet *m*: **faire le ∼** keep watch; **guet-apens** *m* ambush; **guetter** keep an eye open for; (*épier*) watch

gueule *f* mouth; (*visage*) face; **ta ∼!** F shut it! F; **∼ de bois** hangover; **gueuler** F yell

gueuleton *m* F enormous meal

guichet *m de banque*, *poste* wicket, Br window; *de théâtre* box office; **∼ automatique** ATM, Br aussi cash dispenser

guide 1 *m* guide **2** *f* girl scout, Br aussi **3**: **∼s** *fpl* guiding reins; **guider** guide

guidon *m de vélo* handlebars *pl*

guillemets *mpl* quote marks

guindé stiff

guirlande f garland; **~s de Noël** tinsel
guise f: **agir à sa ~** do as one likes; **en ~ de** as, by way of
guitare f guitar; **guitariste** m/f guitarist
guttural guttural
Guyane: **la ~** Guyana

gym f gym; **gymnase** m SP gym; **gymnaste** m/f gymnast; **gymnastique** f gymnastics sg; corrective, matinale exercises pl
gynécologue m/f MÉD gynecologist, Br gynaecologist
gyrophare m flashing light

H

habile skillful, Br skilful; **habileté** f skill; **habilité** JUR authorized
habillé (élégant) dressy; **habiller** dress; **s'~** get dressed, dress; **élégamment** get dressed up
habit m: **~s** clothes
habitable inhabitable; **habitant,** **~e** m/f inhabitant; **habitation** f living; (domicile) residence; **habiter 1** v/t live in **2** v/i live
habitude f habit, custom; **d'~** usually; **par ~** out of habit; **habitué,** **~e** m/f regular; **habituel,** **~le** usual; **habituer: ~ qn à qch** get s.o. used to sth; **s'~ à** get used to
hache f ax, Br axe; **hacher** chop; **viande** f **hachée** ground beef, Br mince
hachisch m hashish
hachoir m appareil meat grinder, Br mincer; couteau cleaver; planche chopping board
haddock m smoked haddock

haie f hedge; SP hurdle; pour chevaux fence, jump; **une ~ de policiers** fig a line of police
haillons mpl rags
haine f hatred; **haineux, -euse** full of hatred
haïr hate
hâle m (sun)tan
haleine f breath; **hors d'~** out of breath
haleter pant
hall m d'hôtel, immeuble foyer; de gare concourse
halle f market
halloween f Halloween
hallucination f hallucination
halogène m: (lampe f) **~** halogen light
halte f stop; **faire ~** halt, make a stop
haltère m dumbbell; **faire des ~s** do weightlifting
haltérophilie f weightlifting
hamac m hammock
hameau m hamlet
hameçon m hook
hamster m hamster

'hanche f hip

'handicap m handicap; **'handicapé, ~e 1** adj disabled, handicapped **2** m/f disabled ou handicapped person

'hangar m shed; AVIAT hangar

'hanter haunt

'hantise f fear, dread

'happer catch; fig: de train, bus hit

'haras m stud farm

'harassant travail exhausting

'harceler harass

'hard m hardcore; MUS hard rock

'hardi bold

'hareng m herring

'hargne f bad temper; **'hargneux, -euse** venomous; chien vicious

'haricot m BOT bean; **c'est la fin des ~s** F that's the end

harmonie f harmony; **harmoniser** match (up); MUS harmonize; **s'~** de couleurs go together; **s'~ avec** go with

'harpe f MUS harp

'harpon m harpoon

'hasard m chance; **au ~** at random; **par ~** by chance; **'hasarder** hazard; **se ~ à faire qc** venture to do sth

'hâte f hurry, haste; **en ~** in haste; **avoir ~ de faire qc** be eager to do sth; **'hâter** hasten; **se ~** hurry

'hausse f increase, rise; **'hausser** increase; **~ les épaules** shrug (one's shoulders)

'haut 1 adj high; immeuble tall, high; cri, voix loud; fonctionnaire high-level **2** adv high; **de ~** from above; **de ~ en bas** from top to bottom; regarder ~ up and down; **en ~** above; **en ~ de** at the top of; **du ~ de** from the top of; **des ~s et des bas** ups and downs

'hautain haughty

'hauteur f height; fig haughtiness; **être à la ~ de qc** be up to sth

hebdomadaire m & adj weekly

hébergement m accommodations pl, Br accommodation; **héberger**: **~ qn** put s.o. up; fig take s.o. in

hébreu m: l'~ Hebrew

hectare m hectare (approx 2.5 acres)

'hein F eh?; **c'est joli, ~?** it's pretty, isn't it?

'hélas alas

'héler hail

hélice f MAR, AVIAT propeller; **escalier** m **en ~** spiral staircase

hélicoptère m helicopter

hémisphère m hemisphere

hémorragie f hemorrhage, Br haemorrhage

'hennir neigh

hépatite f hepatitis

herbe f grass; CUIS herb; **mauvaise ~** weed; **fines ~s** herbs

héréditaire hereditary; **hérédité** f heredity

hérésie f heresy; **hérétique 1** adj heretical **2** m/f heretic

'hérissé ruffled

'hérisson m hedgehog

héritage m inheritance; **hériter 1** v/t inherit **2** v/i: ~ **de qc** inherit sth; ~ **de qn** receive an inheritance from s.o.; **héritier, -ère** m/f heir

'hernie f MÉD hernia; ~ **discale** slipped disc

héroïne¹ f drogue heroin

héroïne² f heroine

héroïque heroic

héroïsme m heroism

'héron m heron

'héros m hero

herpès m herpes

hésitation f hesitation; **hésiter** hesitate

hétérogène heterogeneous

hétérosexuel, ~le heterosexual

heure f hour; **arriver à l'~** arrive on time; **de bonne ~** early; **à tout à l'~!** see you soon!; **quelle ~ est-il?** what time is it?; **il est six ~s** it's six (o'clock); ~ **locale** local time; **~s d'ouverture** opening hours

heureusement luckily, fortunately; **heureux, -euse** happy; (chanceux) fortunate

'heurt m de deux véhicules collision; fig (friction) clash; **'heurter** collide with; fig offend; **se** ~ collide (**à** with); fig (s'affronter) clash (**sur** over)

hiberner hibernate

'hibou m owl

'hideux, -euse hideous

hier yesterday

'hiérarchie f hierarchy

high-tech inv high tech, hi-tech

hilare grinning

hippique SP equestrian; **concours** m ~ horse show; **hippodrome** m race course

hirondelle f swallow

hirsute hairy

hispanique Hispanic

'hisser drapeau, voile hoist; (monter) lift, raise; **se** ~ pull o.s. up

histoire f history; (récit, conte) story; **faire des ~s** make a fuss

historique 1 adj historic **2** m chronicle

hiver m winter

H.L.M. m ou f (= **habitation à loyer modéré**) low cost housing

'hocher: ~ **la tête** approbation nod (one's head); désapprobation shake one's head

'hockey m sur gazon field hockey, Br hockey; sur glace hockey, Br ice hockey

'holding m holding company

'hold-up m holdup

hollandais, ~e 1 adj Dutch **2** m langue Dutch; **'Hollandais, ~e** m/f Dutchman; Dutchwoman; **'Hollande: la** ~ Holland

'homard m lobster

homéopathie f homeopathy

homicide m homicide; ~ **involontaire** manslaughter; ~ **volontaire** murder

hommage m homage; **rendre ~ à** pay homage to

homme m man; ~ **d'affaires** businessman; ~ **1** d'État statesman

homologue m counterpart, opposite number; **homologuer** record ratify; tarif authorize

homophobe homophobic

homosexuel, ~le m/f & adj homosexual

'Hongrie f: **la ~** Hungary; **'hongrois, ~e 1** adj Hungarian **2** m langue Hungarian; **Hongrois, ~e** m/f Hungarian

honnête honest; (convenable) decent; (passable) reasonable; **honnêteté** honesty

honneur m honor, Br honour; **en l'~ de** in honor of; **faire ~ à qc** honor sth; **honorable** honorable, Br honourable; **honoraire 1** adj honorary **2 ~s** mpl fees; honor honor, Br honour; **honorifique** honorific

honte f shame; **avoir ~ de** be ashamed of; **honteux, -euse** (déshonorant) shameful; (déconfit) ashamed

'hooligan m hooligan

hôpital m hospital; **à l'~** in the hospital, Br in hospital

'hoquet m hiccup; **avoir le ~** have (the) hiccups

horaire 1 adj hourly **2** m emploi du temps timetable, schedule; des avions, trains etc schedule, Br timetable

horizon m horizon

horizontal horizontal

horloge f clock

'hormis but

hormonal hormonal; **hormone** f hormone

horodateur m dans parking pay and display machine

horoscope m horoscope

horreur f horror; (monstruosité) monstrosity; **avoir ~ de qc** detest sth; (quelle) ~! how awful!

horrible horrible

horrifiant horrifying

'hors: ~ de (à l'extérieur de) outside; ~ **de danger** out of danger; ~ **sujet** beside the point; **être ~ de soi** be beside o.s.

'hors-bord m outboard

'hors-d'œuvre m CUIS appetizer, starter

'hors-jeu offside

horticulteur f horticulture

hospice m REL hospice; (asile) home

hospitalier, -ère hospitable; MÉD hospital atr

hospitaliser hospitalize

hospitalité f hospitality

hostile hostile; **hostilité** f hostility

'hot-dog m hot dog

hôte m host; (invité) guest

hôtel *m* hotel; **~ de ville** town hall

hôtellerie *f*: **l'~** the hotel business

hôtesse *f* hostess; **~ de l'air** air hostess

'houblon *m* BOT hop

'houille *f* coal

'houle *f* MAR swell; **'houleux, -euse** *fig* stormy

'housse *f* protective cover

'houx *m* BOT holly

'hublot *m* NAUT porthole; AVIAT window

'huer boo, jeer

huile *f* oil; **~ solaire** suntan oil; **huiler** oil

'huis *m*: **à ~ clos** behind closed doors; JUR in camera; **huissier** *m* JUR bailiff

'huit eight; **~ jours** a week; **demain en ~** a week tomorrow; **'huitaine** *f*: **une ~** about eight, eight or so; **une ~ (de jours)** a week; **'huitième** eighth

huître *f* oyster

humain human; *traitement* humane; **humaniser** humanize; **humanitaire** humanitarian; **humanité** *f* humanity

humble humble

humecter moisten

'humer breathe in

humeur *f* mood; (*tempérament*) temperament; **être de bonne/mauvaise ~** be in a good/bad mood

humide damp; (*chaud et ~*)

humid; **humidifier** moisten; *atmosphère* humidify; **humidité** *f* dampness; humidity

humiliation *f* humiliation; **humiliant** humiliating; **humilier** humiliate

humour *m* humor, *Br* humour; **avoir de l'~** have a (good) sense of humor

'huppé exclusive

'hurlement *m* *d'un loup* howl; *d'une personne* scream; **'hurler** *d'un loup* howl; *d'une personne* scream; **~ de rire** roar with laughter

hydratant *cosmétique* moisturizing

hydraulique hydraulic

hydroélectrique hydroelectric

hydrogène *m* CHIM hydrogen

hydroglisseur *m* jetfoil

hygiène *f* hygiene; **avoir une bonne ~ de vie** have a healthy lifestyle; **hygiénique** hygienic; **papier ~** toilet paper; **serviette ~** sanitary napkin, *Br* sanitary towel

hymne *m* hymn; **~ national** national anthem

hyperactif, -ive hyperactive

hypersensible hypersensitive

hypertension *f* MÉD high blood pressure

hypertexte: **lien** *m* **~** hypertext link

hypnotiser hypnotize

hypocrisie *f* hypocrisy; **hy-**

pocrite **1** *adj* hypocritical **2** *m/f* hypocrite

hypothèque *f* COMM mortgage

hypothèse *f* hypothesis; **hypothétique** hypothetical

hystérie *f* hysteria; **hystérique** hysterical

I

ici here; *jusqu'~* to here; *(jusqu'à maintenant)* so far; *par ~* this way; *(dans le coin)* around about here; *d'~ là* by then, by that time

icône *f* icon

idéal *m* & *adj* ideal; **idéaliser** idealize; **idéalisme** *m* idealism; **idéaliste 1** *adj* idealistic **2** *m/f* idealist

idée *f* idea; *(opinion)* view; *avoir dans l'~ de faire qch* be thinking of doing sth; *tu te fais des ~s (tu te trompes)* you're imagining things; *~ fixe* obsession

identifiant *m* identifier, ID

identifier identify *(avec, à* with); *s'~ avec ou à* identify with

identique identical *(à* to)

identité *f* identity; *pièce f d'~* identity, ID

idéologie *f* ideology

idiomatique idiomatic

idiot, ~e 1 *adj* idiotic **2** *m/f* idiot; **idiotie** *f* idiocy; *dire des ~s* talk nonsense

idole *f* idol

idylle *f* romance

ignare *péj* **1** *adj* ignorant **2** *m/f* ignoramus

ignoble vile

ignorance *f* ignorance; **ignorant** ignorant; **ignorer** not know; *personne, talent* ignore

il he; *chose* it; *impersonnel* it; *~ va pleuvoir* it is *ou* it's going to rain

île *f* island; *les ~s britanniques* the British Isles

illégal illegal

illégitime *enfant* illegitimate

illicite illicit

illimité unlimited

illisible illegible; *mauvaise littérature* unreadable

illogique illogical

illuminer light up, illuminate; *par projecteur* floodlight

illusion *f* illusion; *se faire des ~s* delude o.s.; **illusoire** illusory

illustration *f* illustration; **illustrer** illustrate; *s'~* distinguish o.s. *(par* by)

îlot *m* (small) island; *de maisons* block

ils *mpl* they

image *f* picture; *dans un miroir* reflection, image; *(ressemblance)* image

imaginaire imaginary; **ima-**

gination f imagination; **imaginer** imagine; (*inventer*) devise; **s'~ que** imagine that

imbattable unbeatable

imbécile 1 *adj* idiotic **2** *m*/f idiot, imbecile

imbiber soak (*de* with)

imbu: **~ de** *fig* full of

imitation f imitation; THÉÂT impersonation; **imiter** imitate; THÉÂT impersonate

immaculé immaculate

immangeable inedible

immatriculation f registration; **plaque** f **d'~** AUTO license plate, Br number plate; **immatriculer** register

immature immature

immédiat 1 *adj* immediate **2** *m*: **dans l'~** for the moment; **immédiatement** immediately

immense immense

immerger immerse; **s'~ d'un sous-marin** submerge

immeuble *m* building

immigrant, **~e** *m*/f immigrant; **immigration** f immigration; **immigrer** immigrate

imminent imminent

immiscer: **s'~ dans qc** interfere in sth

immobile immobile

immobilier, **-ère 1** *adj*: **biens** *mpl* **~s** real estate **2** *m* property

immobiliser immobilize; *train*, *circulation* bring to a standstill; *capital* tie up; **s'~**

(*s'arrêter*) come to a standstill

immonde foul

immoral immoral; **immoralité** f immorality

immortaliser immortalize; **immortalité** f immortality; **immortel**, **~le** immortal

immuniser immunize; **immunisé contre** *fig* immune to; **immunité** f JUR, MÉD immunity

impact *m* impact

impair 1 *adj* odd **2** *m* blunder

impardonnable unforgiveable

imparfait imperfect

impartial impartial

impasse f dead end; *fig* deadlock, impasse

impassible impassive

impatience f impatience; **impatient** impatient; **impatienter**: **s'~** get impatient

impayé unpaid

impeccable impeccable

impénétrable impenetrable

impératif, **-ive 1** *adj* imperative **2** *m* (*exigence*) requirement; GRAM imperative

impératrice f empress

imperceptible imperceptible

imperfection f imperfection

impérieux, **-euse** *personne* imperious; *besoin* urgent

impérissable immortal; *souvenir* unforgettable

imperméabiliser waterproof; **imperméable 1** *adj* *tissu* waterproof **2** *m* raincoat

impersonnel, **-le** impersonal

impertinence f impertinence; **impertinent** impertinent

imperturbable imperturbable

impétueux, **-euse** impetuous

impitoyable pitiless

implacable implacable

implanter fig introduce; usine set up; **s'~** become established; d'une industrie set up

implicite implicit

impliquer personne implicate; (entraîner) mean, involve; (supposer) imply

implorer beg for; **~ qn de faire qch** implore ou beg s.o. to do sth

impoli rude, impolite

impopulaire unpopular

importance f importance; d'une ville size; d'une somme, catastrophe magnitude; **important 1** adj important; ville, somme large, sizeable **2** m: **l'~**, **c'est que ...** the important thing is that ...

importateur, **-trice 1** adj importing **2** m importer; **importation** f import; **importer 1** v/t import; mode, musique introduce **2** v/i matter, be important (**à** to); **n'importe quand** any time; **n'importe quoi!** nonsense! **importun** troublesome; **importuner** bother

imposable taxable

imposant imposing; **imposer** impose; marchandise tax; **s'~** (être nécessaire) be essential; (se faire admettre) gain recognition

impossible 1 adj impossible **2** m: **faire l'~ pour faire qch** do one's utmost to do sth

imposteur m imposter

impôt m tax; **déclaration** f **d'~s** tax return

impotent crippled

impraticable projet impractical; rue impassable

imprécis vague, imprecise

imprégner impregnate (**de** with); **imprégné de** fig full of

impression f impression; **imprimerie** f printing; **impressionnant** impressive; (troublant) upsetting; **impressionner** impress; (troubler) upset; **impressionniste** m/f & adj impressionist

imprévisible unpredictable

imprévu 1 adj unexpected **2** m: **sauf ~** all being well

imprimante f INFORM printer; **~ laser** laser printer; **~ à jet d'encre** ink-jet (printer); **imprimé** m (formulaire) form; tissu print; **poste ~s** printed matter; **imprimer** print; INFORM print out; édition publish

improbable unlikely, improbable

improductif, **-ive** unproductive

impropre *mot, outil* inappropriate; ~ **à la consommation** unfit for human consumption

improviste: à l'~ unexpectedly

imprudence *f* imprudence; **imprudent** imprudent

impudence *f* impudence; **impudent** impudent

impudique shameless

impuissance *f* powerlessness; MÉD impotence; **impuissant** powerless; MÉD impotent

impulsif, -ive impulsive; **impulsion** *f* impulse; *à l'économie* boost

impuni unpunished

impur *eau* dirty, polluted; (*impudique*) impure

imputer attribute (**à** to); FIN charge (**sur** to)

inabordable *prix* unaffordable

inacceptable unacceptable

inaccessible inaccessible; *personne* unapproachable; *objectif* unattainable

inachevé unfinished

inactif, -ive idle; *population* non-working; *remède, méthode* ineffective; *marché* slack

inadéquat inadequate; *méthode* unsuitable

inadmissible unacceptable

inadvertance *f*: **par** ~ inadvertently

inanimé inanimate; (*mort*) lifeless; (*inconscient*) unconscious

inaperçu: *passer* ~ pass unnoticed

inapproprié inappropriate

inapte: ~ **à** unsuited to; MÉD, MIL unfit for

inattendu unexpected

inattention *f* inattentiveness; *erreur d'*~ careless mistake

inaudible inaudible

inaugurer inaugurate

inavouable shameful

incapable incapable (*de faire* of doing)

incapacité *f* (*inaptitude*) incompetence; *de faire qch* inability

incarcérer imprison

incassable unbreakable

incendiaire incendiary; *discours* inflammatory; **incendie** *m* fire; ~ **criminel** arson; **incendier** set fire to

incertain uncertain; *temps* unsettled; (*hésitant*) indecisive; **incertitude** *f* uncertainty

incessamment any minute now

inchangé unchanged

incident *m* incident; ~ **de parcours** mishap

incinérer incinerate; *cadavre* cremate

incisif, -ive incisive; **incision** *f* incision

inciter encourage (**à faire qch** to do sth); *péj* egg on, incite

inclinable tilting; **inclinaison** f slope

inclination f fig inclination (**pour** for); **~ de tête** (salut) nod; **incliner** tilt; **s'~** bend; pour saluer bow; **s'~ devant qc** (céder) yield to sth; **s'~ devant qn** aussi fig bow to s.o.

inclure include; dans une lettre include: **ci-inclus** enclose; **jusqu'au 30 juin ~** to 30th June inclusive

incohérence f de comportement inconsistency; de discours incoherence

incolore colorless, Br colourless

incomber: **il vous incombe de le lui dire** it is your duty to tell him

incommoder bother

incomparable incomparable

incompatibilité f incompatibility; **incompatible** incompatible

incompétence f incompetence; **incompétent** incompetent

incomplet, **-ète** incomplete

incompréhensible incomprehensible; **incompréhension** f lack of understanding

incompris misunderstood (**de** by)

inconcevable inconceivable

inconditionnel, **~le 1** adj unconditional **2** m/f fan, fanatic

inconfortable uncomfortable

inconnu, **~e 1** adj (ignoré) unknown; (étranger) strange **2** m/f stranger

inconscient unconscious; (irréfléchi) irresponsible

inconsidéré rash, thoughtless

inconsistant inconsistent; fig: raisonnement flimsy

inconsolable inconsolable

incontestable indisputable

incontesté outright

incontournable: **être ~** be a must

inconvénient m disadvantage m; **si vous n'y voyez aucun ~** if you have no objection

incorporer incorporate (**à** with, into); MIL draft

incorrect wrong, incorrect; tenue, langage improper

incorrigible incorrigible

incrédule (sceptique) incredulous; **incrédulité** f incredulity

incriminer personne blame; JUR accuse; paroles, actions condemn

incroyable incredible, unbelievable

inculpé, **~e** m/f: **l'~** the accused, the defendant; **inculper** JUR charge, indict (**de**, **pour** with)

inculquer: **~ qc à qn** instill ou Br instil sth into s.o.

inculte terre waste atr, uncultivated; (ignorant) uneducated

incurable incurable

incursion f MIL raid, incursion; fig: dans la politique etc venture (**dans** into)

Inde f: **l'~** India

indécent indecent; (incorrect) inappropriate, improper

indécis undecided; personne, caractère indecisive

indéfini indefinite; (imprécis) undefined

indéfinissable indefinable

indélicat personne, action tactless

indemne unhurt; **indemniser** compensate (**de** for); **indemnité** f (dédommagement) compensation; (allocation) allowance

indéniable undeniable

indépendance f independence; **indépendant** independent (**de** of); travailleur freelance; **indépendantiste** (pro-)independence atr

indescriptible indescribable

indésirable undesirable

indéterminé unspecified

index m index; doigt index finger

indicateur, -trice m (espion) informer; TECH gauge, indicator

indicatif m TÉL code

indication f (information) piece of information; **~s** instructions

indice m (signe) sign, indication; JUR clue

indien, ~ne Indian; d'Amérique aussi native American; **Indien** m/f Indian; d'Amérique aussi native American

indifférence f indifference; **indifférent** indifferent

indigène adj & m/f native

indigeste indigestible; **indigestion** f MÉD indigestion

indignation f indignation

indigne unworthy; parents unfit

indigner make indignant; **s'~ de qc/contre qn** be indignant about sth/with s.o.

indiqué appropriate; **ce n'est pas ~** it's not advisable; **indiquer** indicate, show; d'une pendule show; (recommander) recommend

indirect indirect

indiscipline f indiscipline; **indiscipliné** undisciplined; cheveux unmanageable

indiscret, -ète indiscreet; **indiscrétion** indiscretion

indispensable indispensable

indistinct indistinct

individu m individual; **individualisme** m individualism; **individuel, ~le** individual; secrétaire private, personal; liberté personal; chambre single; maison detached

indivisible indivisible

indolent lazy, indolent

indolore painless

indomptable fig indomitable

indu: à une heure ~e at some

ungodly hour

indubitable indisputable

induire: ~ **qn en erreur** mislead s.o.

indulgence f indulgence; *d'un juge* leniency; **indulgent** indulgent; *juge* lenient

industrialisé industrialized; **industrialiser** industrialize; **industrie** f industry; **industriel, ~le 1** adj industrial **2** m industrialist

inébranlable solid (as a rock)

inédit *(pas édité)* unpublished; *(nouveau)* original, unique

inégal unequal; *surface* uneven; *rythme* irregular; **inégalité** f inequality; *d'une surface* unevenness

inepte inept; **ineptie** f ineptitude; **~s** nonsense

inépuisable inexhaustible

inerte *corps* lifeless, inert; PHYS inert; **inertie** f inertia

inespéré unexpected, unhoped-for

inestimable *tableau* priceless; *aide* invaluable

inévitable inevitable; *accident* unavoidable

inexact inaccurate

inexcusable inexcusable, unforgivable

inexistant non-existent

inexplicable inexplicable

inexprimable inexpressible

infaillible infallible

infantile *mortalité* infant atr; *péj* infantile; *maladie* children's

infarctus m MÉD: ~ **du myocarde** coronary (thrombosis)

infatigable tireless, indefatigable

infect disgusting; *temps* foul; **infecter** infect; *air, eau* pollute; **s'~** become infected; **infectieux, -euse** infectious; **infection** f infection

inférieur, ~e 1 adj lower; *qualité* inferior **2** m/f inferior; **infériorité** f inferiority

infernal infernal

infidèle unfaithful; REL pagan atr; **infidélité** f infidelity

infiltrer: s'~ dans get into; *fig* infiltrate

infime tiny, infinitesimal

infini 1 adj infinite **2** m infinity

infirme 1 adj disabled **2** m/f disabled person; **infirmerie** f infirmary; ÉDU sickbay; **infirmier, -ère** m/f nurse; **infirmité** f disability

inflammation f MÉD inflammation

inflation f inflation

inflexible inflexible

infliger *peine* inflict (**à** on); *défaite* impose

influence f influence; **influencer** influence; **influent** influential

influer: ~ **sur** affect

info f F RAD, TV news item; **les ~s** the news sg

informaticien, ~ne m/f computer scientist

information f information; JUR inquiry; **une ~** a piece of information; **les ~s** RAD, TV the news sg; **traitement** m **de l'~** data processing

informatique 1 adj computer atr **2** f information technology, IT; **informatiser** computerize

informe shapeless

informer inform; **s'~** find out (**de qc auprès de qn** about sth from s.o.)

infraction f infringement (**à** of)

infranchissable impossible to cross; obstacle insurmountable

infrarouge infrared

infrastructure f infrastructure

infroissable crease-resistant

infructueux, -euse unsuccessful

infusion f herb tea

ingénierie f engineering; **ingénieur** m engineer

ingéniosité f ingeniousness

ingrat ungrateful; tâche thankless; **ingratitude** f ingratitude

ingrédient m ingredient

ingurgiter gulp down

inhabitable uninhabitable; **inhabité** uninhabited

inhalateur m MÉD inhaler; **inhaler** inhale

inhérent inherent (**à** in)

inhibé inhibited; **inhibition** f

PSYCH inhibition

inhospitalier, -ère inhospitable

inhumain inhuman

ininflammable non-flammable

ininterrompu uninterrupted; pluie, musique non-stop

initial, ~e 1 adj initial **2** f initial (letter)

initiation f initiation; **~ à** fig introduction to

inimitié f enmity

initiative f initiative

initié, ~e m/f insider; **initier** initiate (**à** in); fig introduce (**à** to)

injecté: ~ (de sang) bloodshot; **injecter** inject; **injection** f injection

injoignable unreachable, uncontactable

injure f insult; **~s** abuse; **injurier** insult, abuse

injuste unfair, unjust; **injustice** f injustice; d'une décision aussi unfairness

inlassable tireless

inné innate

innocence f innocence; **innocent** innocent; **innocenter** clear

innombrable countless; auditoire, foule vast

innovant innovative; **innovation** f innovation

inoccupé personne idle; maison unoccupied

inodore odorless, Br odourless

inoffensif, -ive harmless; *humour* inoffensive
inondation f flood; **inonder** flood; ~ *de fig* inundate with
inopiné unexpected
inopportun ill-timed
inorganique inorganic
inoubliable unforgettable
inouï unheard-of
inoxydable stainless
inquiet, -ète anxious, worried (*de* about); **inquiéter** worry; **s'~** worry (*de* about); **inquiétude** f anxiety
insaisissable elusive; *différence* imperceptible
insatiable insatiable
insatisfaisant unsatisfactory; **insatisfait** unsatisfied; *mécontent* dissatisfied
inscription f inscription; (*immatriculation*) registration; **inscrire** (*noter*) write down, note; *dans registre* enter; *à examen* register; (*graver*) inscribe; **s'~** put one's name down; *à l'université* register; *à un cours* enroll, *Br* enrol (*à* for)
insecte m insect; **insecticide** m insecticide
insécurité f insecurity; POL security problem
insensé mad, insane
insensibiliser numb; **insensible** ANAT numb; *personne* insensitive (*à* to)
insérer insert; *annonce* put; **insertion** f insertion
insigne m (*emblème*) insig-

nia; (*badge*) badge
insignifiant insignificant
insinuer insinuate; **s'~ dans** worm one's way into
insipide insipid
insistance f insistence; **insistant** insistent; **insister** insist; F (*persévérer*) persevere; ~ *pour faire qch* insist on doing sth; ~ *sur qc* (*souligner*) stress sth
insolation f sunstroke
insolence f insolence; **insolent** insolent
insolite unusual
insolvable insolvent
insomnie f insomnia
insonoriser soundproof
insouciant carefree
insoumis rebellious
insoutenable (*insupportable*) unbearable; *argument* untenable
inspecter inspect; **inspecteur, -trice** m/f inspector; **inspection** f inspection
inspiration f fig inspiration; **inspirer** 1 v/i breathe in, inhale 2 v/t inspire; **s'~ de** be inspired by
installation f installation; ~ **électrique** wiring; **~s** facilities; **installer** install; *appartement*: fit out; (*loger, placer*) put; **s'~** (*s'établir*) settle down; *à la campagne etc* settle; *d'un médecin, dentiste* set up
instant m instant, moment; **à l'~** just this minute; **dans un**

~ in a minute; **pour l'**~ for the moment; **instantané 1** *adj* immediate; *café* instant; *mort* instantaneous **2** *m* PHOT snap(shot)
instaurer establish
instinct *m* instinct; **instinctif, -ive** instinctive
instituer introduce; **institut** *m* institute; ~ **de beauté** beauty salon; **instituteur, -trice** *m/f* (primary) school teacher; **institution** *f* institution
instructeur *m* MIL instructor; **instructif, -ive** instructive; **instruction** *f* (*enseignement, culture*) education; MIL training; JUR preliminary investigation; INFORM instruction; ~**s** instructions; **instruire** ÉDU educate, teach; MIL train; JUR investigate; **instruit** (well-)educated
instrument *m* instrument
insu: **à l'**~ **de** unbeknownst to
insubordination *f* insubordination
insuffisance *f* deficiency; ~ *respiratoire* respiratory problem; **insuffisant** *quantité* insufficient; *qualité* inadequate
insulaire 1 *adj* island *atr* **2** *m/f* islander
insuline *f* insulin
insulte *f* insult; **insulter** insult
insupportable unbearable
insurger: **s'**~ **contre** rise up

against
insurrection *f* insurrection
intact intact
intégral full, complete; *texte* unabridged
intégration *f* (*assimilation*) integration
intègre of integrity
intégrer (*assimiler*) integrate; (*incorporer*) incorporate; **intégriste** *m/f* & *adj* fundamentalist
intégrité *f* (*honnêteté*) integrity
intellectuel, ~le *m/f* & *adj* intellectual
intelligence *f* intelligence; **intelligent** intelligent
intempéries *fpl* bad weather
intempestif, -ive untimely
intenable *situation, froid* unbearable
intense intense; **intensif, -ive** intensive; **intensification** *f* intensification; *d'un conflit* escalation; **intensifier** intensify; **s'**~ intensify; *d'un conflit* escalate; **intensité** *f* intensity
intenter: ~ *un procès contre* start proceedings against
intention *f* intention; **avoir l'**~ **de faire qch** intend to do sth; **à l'**~ **de** for; **intentionné**: *bien* ~ well-meaning; *mal* ~ ill-intentioned; **intentionnel, ~le** intentional
interactif, -ive interactive
intercéder: ~ *pour qn* intercede for s.o.

intercepter intercept; *soleil* shut out

interchangeable interchangeable

interdiction *f* ban; **interdire** ban; **~ à qn de faire qc** forbid s.o. to do sth; **interdit** forbidden; *(très étonné)* taken aback

intéressant interesting; *(avide)* selfish; *prix* good; *situation* well-paid; **intéressé** interested; *(concerné)* concerned; **intéresser** interest; *(concerner)* concern; **s'~ à** be interested in; **intérêt** *m* interest; *(égoïsme)* self-interest; **~s** COMM interest

interface *f* interface

intérieur 1 *adj poche* inside; *porte, vie* inner; *politique, vol* domestic; *mer* inland **2** *m* inside; *d'une auto etc* interior; **à l'~ (de)** inside

intérim *m* interim; *travail temporary work;* **intérimaire 1** *adj travail* temporary **2** *m/f* temp

interlocuteur, -trice *m/f*: **mon/son ~** the person I/ she was talking to

intermédiaire 1 *adj* intermediate **2** *m/f* intermediary; COMM middleman

interminable interminable

intermittence *f*: **par ~** intermittently

international, ~e *m/f* & *adj* international

internaute *m/f* web surfer

interne 1 *adj* internal; *oreille* inner; *d'une société* in-house **2** *m/f* *élève* boarder; *médecin* intern, *Br* houseman; **internet** intern

Internet *m* Internet; **sur ~** on the Internet

interpeller call out to; *de la police,* POL question

interphone *m* intercom; *d'un immeuble* entry phone

interposer: s'~ *(intervenir)* intervene

interprète *m/f*; *(porte-parole)* spokesperson; **interpréter** interpret; *rôle,* MUS play

interrogation *f* question; *d'un suspect* questioning, interrogation; **interrogatoire** *m* *par police* questioning; *par juge* cross-examination; **interroger** question; *de la police* question, interrogate; *d'un juge* cross-examine

interrompre interrupt; **s'~** break off

interrupteur *m* switch; **interruption** *f* interruption; **sans ~** without stopping

intervalle *m* space, gap; *de temps* interval

intervenir intervene; *d'une rencontre* take place; **intervention** *f* intervention; MÉD operation; *(discours)* speech

interview *f* interview; **interviewer** interview

intestin 1 *adj* internal **2** *m* intestin

intime 1 adj intimate; ami close; pièce cozy, Br cosy; vie private **2** m/f close friend
intimider intimidate
intimité f intimacy; vie privée privacy
intituler call; **s'~** be called
intolérable intolerable; **intolérance** f intolerance; **intolérant** intolerant
intoxication f poisoning; **~ alimentaire** food poisoning; **intoxiquer** poison; fig brainwash
intransigeant intransigent
intrépide intrepid
intrigue f plot; **~s** scheming, plotting; **intriguer 1** v/i scheme, plot **2** v/t intrigue
introduction f introduction; **introduire** introduce; visiteur show in; (engager) insert; **s'~ dans** gain entry to
introuvable impossible to find
introverti, ~e m/f introvert
intrus, ~e m/f intruder
intuitif, -ive intuitive; **intuition** f intuition; (pressentiment) premonition
inusable hard-wearing
inutile qui ne sert pas useless; (superflu) pointless, unnecessary; **inutilisable** unuseable
invalide 1 adj (infirme) disabled **2** m/f disabled person; **invalider** JUR, POL invalidate; **invalidité** f disability
invariable invariable

invasion f invasion
invendable unsellable
inventaire m inventory; COMM opération stocktaking
inventer invent; histoire make up; **inventeur, -trice** m/f inventor; **invention** f invention
inverse 1 adj MATH inverse; sens opposite; **dans l'ordre ~** in reverse order **2** m opposite, reverse; **inverser** invert; rôles reverse
investigation f investigation
investir FIN invest; (cerner) surround; **investissement** m FIN investment
invétéré inveterate
investisseur, -euse m investor
invincible invincible; obstacle insuperable
invisible invisible
invitation f invitation; **invité, ~e** m/f guest; **inviter** invite; **~ qn à faire qch** urge s.o. to do sth
invivable unbearable
involontaire unintentional; témoin unwilling; mouvement involuntary
invoquer Dieu call on, invoke; aide call on; texte, loi refer to; solution put forward
invraisemblable unlikely, improbable
Iran m: **l'~** Iran; **iranien, ~ne** Iranian; **Iranien, ~ne** m/f Iranian

Iraq *m*: *l'~* Iraq; **iraquien, ~ne**
Iraqi; **Iraquien, ~ne** *m/f* Iraqi

irascible irascible

irlandais, ~e 1 *adj* Irish **2** *m*
langue Irish (Gaelic); **Irlandais, ~e** *m/f* Irishman; **Irish-
woman; Irlande** *f*: *l'~* Ireland

ironie *f* irony; **ironiser** be
ironic

irraisonné irrational

irrationnel, ~le irrational

irréalisable *projet* impracti-
cable; *rêve* unrealizable

irréaliste unrealistic

irréconciliable irreconcilable

irrécupérable beyond repair;
personne beyond redemp-
tion; *données* irretrievable

irréductible indomitable; *ennemi* implacable

irréel, ~le unreal

irréfléchi thoughtless, reckless

irréfutable irrefutable

irrégulier, -ère irregular; *surface, terrain* uneven; *étudiant, sportif* erratic

irrémédiable *maladie* incurable; *erreur* irreparable

irremplaçable irreplaceable

irréparable *faute, perte* irreparable; *vélo* beyond repair

irréprochable irreproacha-
ble

irrésistible irresistible

irrésolu *personne* indecisive;
problème unresolved

irrespirable unbreathable

irresponsable irresponsible

irrigation *f* AGR irrigation

irritable irritable; **irritation** *f*
irritation; **irriter** irritate;
s'~ get irritated

islam, Islam *m* REL Islam;
islamique Islamic; **islamis-
te** Islamic fundamentalist

islandais, ~e 1 *adj* Icelandic
2 *m langue* Islandic; **Islandais, ~e** *m/f* Icelander; **Is-
lande** *f*: *l'~* Iceland

isolation *f* insulation; *contre
le bruit* soundproofing; **isolé** isolated; TECH insulated;
isolement *m* isolation; **isoler** isolate; *prisonnier* place
in solitary confinement; ÉL
insulate

Israël *m* Israel; **israélien, ~ne**
Israeli; **Israélien, ~ne** *m/f* Israeli

issu: *être ~ de parenté* come
from; *résultat* stem from

issue *f* way out (*aussi fig*), exit; (*fin*) outcome; *à l'~ de* at
the end of

Italie *f* Italy; **italien, ~ne 1**
adj Italian **2** *m langue* Italian; **Italien, ~ne** *m/f* Italian

itinéraire *m* itinerary

itinérance *f* TEL roaming

IVG *f* (= *interruption volontaire de grossesse*) termination, abortion

ivoire *m* ivory

ivre drunk; *~ de joie, colère*
wild with; **ivresse** *f* drunk-
enness; **ivrogne** *m/f* drunk

J

jacasser chatter
jacinthe *f* BOT hyacinth
jade *m* jade
jaillir shoot out (*de* from)
jalousie *f* jealousy; (*store*) Venetian blind; **jaloux, -ouse** jealous
jamais ◇ *positif* ever; **à ~** for ever, for good; ◇ *négatif* never; **ne ... ~** never; **je ne lui ai ~ parlé** I've never spoken to him
jambe *f* leg
jambon *m* ham
jante *f* rim
janvier *m* January
Japon: **le ~** Japan; **japonais, ~e 1** *adj* Japanese **2** *m langue* Japanese; **Japonais, ~e** *m/f* Japanese
jappement *m* yap
jaquette *f* d'un livre dust jacket
jardin *m* garden; **~ botanique** botanical gardens *pl*; **~ public** park; **jardinage** *m* gardening; **jardinier** garden; **jardinier** *m* gardener; **jardinière** *f* à fleurs window box; *femme* gardener
jargon *m* jargon; *péj* (*charabia*) gibberish
jarret *m* back of the knee; CUIS shin
jaser gossip
jatte *f* bowl

jauge *f* gauge; **jauger** gauge
jaunâtre yellowish; **jaune 1** *adj* yellow **2** *m*: **~ d'œuf** egg yolk; **jaunir** go yellow; **jaunisse** *f* MÉD jaundice
jazz *m* jazz; **jazzman** *m* jazz musician
je I
jean *m* jeans *pl*; **veste** *m* **en ~** denim jacket
jeep *f* jeep
Jésus-Christ Jesus (Christ)
jet *m* (*lancer*) throw; (*jaillissement*) jet; *de sang* spurt; **~ d'eau** fountain
jetable disposable
jetée *f* MAR jetty
jeter throw; (*se défaire de*) throw away; **~ un coup d'œil à qch** glance at sth
jeton *m* token; *de jeu* chip
jeu *m* play (*aussi* TECH); *activité, en tennis* game; (*série, ensemble*) set; *de cartes* deck, *Br* pack; MUS playing; THÉÂT acting; **le ~** gambling; **être en ~** be at stake; **~ de mots** play on words
jeudi *m* Thursday
jeun: **à ~** on an empty stomach
jeune 1 *adj* young; **~s mariés** newly-weds **2** *m/f*: **un ~** a young man; **les ~s** young people *pl*, the young *pl*
jeûne *m* fast; **jeûner** fast

jeunesse f youth; *caractère jeune* youthfulness

J.O. *mpl* (= *Jeux Olympiques*) Olympic Games

joaillerie f *magasin* jewelry store, Br jeweller's; *articles* jewelry, Br jewellery; **joaillier, -ère** m/f jeweler, Br jeweller

jogging m jogging; (*survêtement*) sweats pl, Br tracksuit; **faire du ~** go jogging

joie f joy; **débordant de ~** jubilant

joindre join; *efforts* combine; *à un courrier* enclose (*à* with); *personne* contact, get in touch with; *mains* clasp; **se ~ à qn pour faire qch** join s.o. in doing sth

joint m joint; *d'étanchéité* seal, gasket; *de robinet* washer

joli pretty

joncher strew (*de* with)

jonction f junction

jongler juggle; **jongleur** m juggler

joue f cheek

jouer 1 v/t play; *argent, réputation* gamble; THÉÂT *pièce* perform; *film* show; **~ la comédie** put on an act **2** v/i play; *d'un acteur* act; *parier* gamble; **~ au football** play football; **~ d'un instrument** play an instrument; **~ sur cheval etc** put money on

jouet m toy

joueur, -euse m/f player; de

jeux d'argent gambler; **être beau/mauvais ~** be a good/bad loser

jouir have an orgasm, come; **~ de qc** enjoy sth; (*posséder*) have sth; **jouissance** f enjoyment; JUR possession

jour m day; (*lumière*) daylight; (*ouverture*) opening; **au grand ~** in broad daylight; **de nos ~s** these days; **du ~ au lendemain** overnight; **être à ~** be up to date; **se faire ~** de problèmes come to light; **deux ans ~ pour ~** two years to the day; **il fait ~** it's (getting) light; **au petit ~** at first light

journal m (news)paper; *intime* diary; TV, à la radio news sg; **journalisme** m journalism; **journaliste** m/f journalist

journée f day

jovial jovial

joyeux, -euse joyful; **~ Noël!** Merry Christmas!

jubilation f jubilation; **jubiler** be jubilant; *péj* gloat

jucher perch

judiciaire legal

judicieux, -euse sensible, judicious

judo m judo

juge m judge; **~ d'instruction** examining magistrate; **~ de touche** SP linesman; **jugement** m judg(e)ment; *en matière criminelle* sentence; **porter un ~ sur** pass judg(e)-

ment on; **juger 1** *v/t* JUR try; (*évaluer*) judge; **~ qc/qn intéressant** consider sth/s.o. interesting; **~ que** think that; **~ de qn/qc** judge s.o./sth **2** *v/i* judge

juif, -ive *adj* Jewish; **Juif, -ive** *m/f* Jew

juillet *m* July

juin *m* June

jumeau, jumelle *m/f & adj* twin; **jumeler** *villes* twin; **jumelles** *fpl* binoculars

jument *f* mare

jungle *f* jungle

jupe *f* skirt

juré *m* JUR juror; **jurer** swear (**de qch** to sth)

juridiction *f* jurisdiction

juridique legal

juron *m* curse

jury *m* JUR jury; *d'un concours* panel, judges *pl*; ÉDU board of examiners

jus *m* juice

jusque 1 *prép:* **jusqu'à lieu** as far as, up to; *temps* until; **jusqu'où vous allez?** how far are you going? **2** *adv* even, including **3** *conj:* **jusqu'à ce qu'il s'endorme** (*subj*) until he falls asleep

juste 1 *adj* fair, just; *salaire, récompense* fair; (*précis*) right, correct; *vêtement* tight **2** *adv* just; *viser, tirer* accurately; **chanter ~** sing in tune; **justesse** *f* accuracy; **de ~** only just; **justice** *f* fairness, JUR justice; **la ~** the law; **faire ~ à qn** do s.o. justice

justification *f* justification; **justifier** justify; **~ de qc** prove sth

juteux, -euse juicy

juvénile youthful; **délinquance ~** juvenile delinquency

juxtaposer juxtapose

K

kaki khaki

kamikaze *m/f* suicide bomber

kangourou *m* kangaroo

kébab *m* kabob, *Br* kebab

kermesse *f* fair

kérosène *m* kerosene

ketchup *m* ketchup

kg (= *kilogramme*) kg (= kilogram)

kidnapping *m* kidnapping; **kidnapper** kidnap

kilo(gramme) *m* kilo(gram); **kilométrage** *m* mileage; **kilomètre** *m* kilometer, *Br* kilometre; **kilo-octet** *m* kilobyte, k

kinésithérapeute *m/f* physiotherapist

kiosque *m* pavilion; COMM kiosk; **~ à journaux** newsstand

kit *m*: **en ~** kit

klaxon m AUTO horn; **klaxonner** sound one's horn, hoot
km (= *kilomètre*) km (= kilometer)

knock-out m knockout
K-O m (= *knock-out*) KO
Ko m (= *kilo-octet* m) k (= kil-
obyte)

L

la¹ → *le*
la² *pron personnel* her; *chose*
it
là here; *dans un autre lieu
qu'ici* there; *causal* hence;
par~ that way; **là-bas** (over)
there
laboratoire m laboratory, lab
laborieux, -euse laborious;
personne hardworking
labourer plow, Br plough
labyrinthe m labyrinth, maze
lac m lake
lacer tie
lacet m *de chaussures* lace; *de
la route* sharp turn
lâche 1 *adj* loose; *personne*
cowardly **2** m coward
lâcher 1 *v/t* let go of; (*laisser
tomber*) drop; (*libérer*) release; *ceinture* loosen; *juron,
vérité* let out; SP leave behind **2** *v/i de freins* fail;
d'une corde break
lâcheté f cowardice
lacrymogène *gaz* tear *atr*;
grenade tear-gas *atr*
lactose m lactose
lacune f gap
là-dedans inside; **là-des-
sous** underneath; *derrière*
behind it; **là-dessus** on it,

on top; *à ce moment* at that
instant; *sur ce point* about it;
là-haut up there
laid ugly; **laideur** f ugliness;
(*bassesse*) meanness
lainage m *étoffe* woolen *ou*
Br woollen fabric; *vêtement*
woolen, Br woollen; **laine** f
wool; **laineux, -euse** fleecy
laïque 1 *adj* REL secular; (*sans
confession*) State *atr* **2** m/f
lay person
laisse f leash
laisser leave; (*permettre*) let;
se ~ aller let o.s. go
laisser-aller m casualness
laissez-passer m pass
lait m milk; **laitage** m dairy
product; **laitier, -ère** dairy
atr
laiton m brass
laitue f BOT lettuce
lambin, ~e m/f F slowpoke F,
Br slowcoach F
lambris m paneling, Br panelling
lame f blade; (*plaque*) strip;
(*vague*) wave
lamentable deplorable; **la-
menter: se ~** complain
lampadaire m floor lamp;
dans la rue street light

lampe f lamp; **~ de poche** flashlight, *Br* torch

lancé established; **lancement** m launch; **lancer** throw; *avec force* hurl; *injure* shout, hurl (**à** at); *cri* give; *fusée,* COMM launch; INFORM *programme* run; *moteur* start; **se ~ sur** marché enter; *piste de danse* step out onto; **se ~ dans** *des activités* take up; *des explications* launch into; *des discussions* get involved in

langage m language

langouste f spiny lobster

langue f tongue; LING language; **mauvaise ~** gossip; **~ maternelle** mother tongue

languette f *d'une chaussure* tongue

languir languish; *d'une conversation* flag

lanière f strap

laper lap up

lapider stone

lapin m rabbit

laps m: **~ de temps** period of time

laque f lacquer

larcin m petty theft

lard m bacon

lardon m lardon, diced bacon

large **1** *adj* wide; *épaules, hanches* broad; *mesure, rôle* large; *(généreux)* generous **2** *adv*: *voir* ~ think big **3** m MAR open sea; *prendre le* ~ *fig* take off; **largesse** f generosity; **largeur** f width; **~ d'es-**

prit broad-mindedness

larme f tear; **une ~ de** a drop of; **larmoyer** *des yeux* water; *(se plaindre)* complain

laryngite f laryngitis

las, ~se weary

laser m laser

lasser weary, tire; **se ~ de** tire *ou* weary of

latent latent

latéral lateral, side *pl*

latitude f latitude

latte f lath; *de plancher* board

lauréat, ~e m/f prizewinner

laurier m laurel; **feuille** f **de ~** CUIS bayleaf

lavabo m (wash)basin; **~s** toilets

lavage m washing

lavande f lavender

laver wash; *tâche* wash away; **laverie** f: **~ automatique** laundromat, *Br* laundrette; **lavette** f dishcloth; *fig péj* spineless individual

lave-vaisselle m dishwasher

laxatif, -ive *adj & m* laxative

laxisme m laxness

le *complément d'objet direct* him; *chose* it; **oui, je ~ sais** yes, I know

le, f la, *pl* les *article défini* the; **le garçon/les garçons** the boy/the boys; **je me suis cassé la jambe** I broke my leg; **j'aime le vin** I like wine; **les dinosaures avaient ...** dinosaurs had ...; **le premier mai** May first, *Br* the first of May; **ouvert le samedi**

open (on) Saturdays; **10 euros les 5** 10 euros for 5; **tu
connais la France?** do you
know France; **le printemps
est là** spring is here; **je ne
parle pas l'italien** I don't
speak Italian

leader m POL leader

lécher lick

leçon f lesson

lecteur, -trice 1 m/f reader; *à
l'université* foreign language
assistant **2** m INFORM drive; ~
de CDs CD player; **lecture** f
reading

ledit, ladite the said

légal legal; **légaliser** *signature* authenticate; *(rendre légal)* legalize; **légalité** f legality

légende f legend; *sous image*
caption; *d'une carte* key

léger, -ère 1 light; *erreur, retard*
slight; *mœurs* loose; *(frivo-
le, irréfléchi)* thoughtless; **à
la légère** lightly; **légèrement** lightly; *(un peu)*
slightly; **légèreté** f lightness;
(frivolité, irréflexion)
thoughtlessness

légion f legion; ~ **étrangère**
Foreign Legion; **légionnai-
re** m legionnaire

législation f legislation

légitime legitimate

legs m legacy

léguer bequeath

légume m vegetable

lendemain m: **le ~** the next *ou*
following day; **le ~ de son**

élection the day after he
was elected

lent slow; **lentement** slowly;
lenteur f slowness

lentille f TECH lens; *légume sec*
lentil

léopard m leopard

lequel, laquelle (*pl* **lesquels,
lesquelles**) *interrogatif*
which (one); *relatif, avec personne* who; *avec chose* which

les¹ → le

les² *pron personnel* them

lesbien, ~ne *adj* & f lesbian

léser injure; *intérêts* damage;
droits infringe

lésiner skimp (**sur** on)

lésion f MÉD lesion

lessive f *produit* laundry detergent, Br washing powder;
liquide detergent; *linge*
laundry; **faire la ~** do the
laundry

leste agile; *propos* crude

léthargie f lethargy

lettre f letter; **à la ~, au pied
de la ~** literally; **en toutes
~s** in full; *fig* in black and
white; ~ **s** literature; *études*
arts; **lettré** well-read

leucémie f MÉD leukemia, Br
leukaemia

leur 1 *adj possessif* their **2**
pron personnel **le/la ~, les
~s** theirs **3** *complément
d'objet indirect* (to) them

leurrer *fig* deceive

levé: être ~ be up; **levée** f lifting; *d'une séance* adjourn-
ment; *du courrier* collec-

tion; *aux cartes* trick; **lever 1**
v/t raise, lift; *poids, interdiction* lift; *impôts* collect **2** *v/i*
de la pâte rise; *se ~* get up;
du soleil rise; *du jour* break
3 *m:* **~ du jour** daybreak; **~**
du soleil sunrise

levier *m* lever; **~ de vitesse**
gear shift, *surtout Br* gear lever

lèvre *f* lip

levure *f* yeast; **~ chimique**
baking powder

lézard *m* lizard

lézarde *f* crack

liaison *f* connection; *amoureuse* affair; *de train* link;
LING liaison

liant sociable

libellule *f* dragonfly

libéral liberal; *profession f*
~e profession; **libéralisme**
m liberalism

libérateur, -trice 1 *adj* liberating **2** *m/f* liberator; **libération** *f* liberation; *d'un prisonnier* release; **~ conditionnelle** parole; **libérer** liberate; *prisonnier* release,
free (*de* from); *gaz, d'un engagement* release

liberté *f* freedom, liberty;
mettre en ~ set free, release

librairie *f* bookstore, *Br*
bookshop

libre free (*de faire* to do); **libre-service** *m* self-service;
magasin self-service store

Libye *f* Libya; **libyen, ~ne** Libyan; **Libyen, ~ne** *m/f* Libyan

licence *f* license, *Br* licence;
diplôme degree

licenciement *m* layoff; (*renvoi*) dismissal; **licencier** lay
off; (*renvoyer*) dismiss

lié: être ~ par be bound by;
être très ~ avec qn be very
close to s.o.

lien *m* tie, bond; (*rapport*)
connection; **avoir un ~ de**
parenté be related

lier tie (up); *d'un contrat* be
binding on; CUIS thicken;
pensées, personnes connect;
~ amitié avec qn make
friends with s.o.

lierre *m* BOT ivy

lieu *m* place; **~x** premises; JUR
scene; **au ~ de (faire)** *qch* instead of (doing) sth; **avoir ~**
take place; **donner ~ à** give
rise to; **en premier ~** in the
first place; **s'il y a ~** if necessary

lièvre *m* hare

ligne *f* line; *d'autobus* number; **garder la ~** keep one's
figure; **être pris en ~ de compte** be taken into consideration; **pêcher à la ~** go angling; **en ~** INFORM on line;
achats en ~ on-line shopping

liguer: se ~ join forces (*pour*
faire to do)

lilas *m & adj inv* lilac

limace *f* slug

lime *f* file; **~ à ongles** nail file;
limer file

limitation *f* limitation; **~ de**

limite

vitesse speed limit; **limite** f limit; *(frontière)* boundary; **à la ~** if absolutely necessary; **date** f **~** deadline; **vitesse** f **~** speed limit; **limiter** limit **(à** to)

limoger POL dismiss

limonade f lemonade

limousine f limousine

lin m BOT flax; **toile** linen

linéaire linear

linge m linen; *(lessive)* washing

lingerie f lingerie

linguiste m/f linguist

lion m lion; ASTROL **Lion** Leo; **lionne** f lioness

liposuccion f liposuction

liqueur f liqueur

liquidation f liquidation; *vente au rabais* sale

liquide 1 *adj* liquid; **argent** m **~** cash **2** m liquid; **~ de freins** brake fluid; **liquider** liquidate; *stock* sell off; *problème* dispose of

lire read

lis m BOT lily

lisible legible

lisse smooth; **lisser** smooth

liste f list; **~ d'attente** waiting list; **~ de commissions** shopping list; **lister** list; **listing** m printout

lit m bed; **aller au ~** go to bed; **~ de camp** cot, *Br* camp bed; **literie** f bedding

litige m dispute

litre m liter, *Br* litre

littéraire literary; **littérature** f literature

littoral 1 *adj* coastal **2** m coastline

livraison f delivery

livre[1] m book; **~ de poche** paperback

livre[2] f *poids, monnaie* pound

livrer *marchandises* deliver; *prisonnier* hand over; *secret* divulge; **se ~** *(se confier)* open up; *(se soumettre)* give o.s. up; **se ~ à** *(se confier)* confide in; *activité* indulge in; *l'abattement* give way to

livret m booklet; *d'opéra* libretto

livreur m delivery man; **~ de journaux** paper boy

lobby m lobby

lobe m: **~ de l'oreille** earlobe

local 1 *adj* local **2** m *(salle)* premises pl; **locaux** premises; **localisation** f location; *de software etc* localization; **localiser** locate; *(limiter)*; *de software* localize

locataire m/f tenant; **location** f *par propriétaire* renting out; *par locataire* renting; *(loyer)* rent; *au théâtre* reservation

logement m accommodations, *Br* accommodation, pl; *(appartement)* apartment, *Br aussi* flat; **loger 1** v/t accommodate **2** v/i live; **logeur** m landlord; **logeuse** f landlady

logiciel m INFORM software

logique 1 *adj* logical **2** f logic

loi *f* law

loin far (*de* from); *dans le passé* long ago; *dans l'avenir* a long way off; *au ~* in the distance

lointain 1 *adj* distant **2** *m* distance

loisir *m* leisure; *~s* leisure activities

Londres London

long, longue 1 *adj* long; *à ~ terme* in the long term; *à la longue* in time; *être ~ (à faire qch)* take a long time (doing sth) **2** *adv*: *en dire ~* speak volumes **3** *m*: *de deux mètres de ~* two meters long; *le ~ de* along

longer follow

longitude *f* longitude

longtemps a long time

longuement for a long time; *parler* at length

longueur *f* length; *sur la même ~ d'onde* on the same wavelength

loquace talkative

loque *f* rag

loquet *m* latch

lorgner eye; *héritage, poste* have one's eye on

lors: *dès ~* from then on; *~ de* during

lorsque when

lot *m* (*destin*) fate; *à la loterie* prize; (*portion*) share; COMM batch

loterie *f* lottery

loti: *bien/mal ~* well/badly off

lotion *f* lotion

lotissement *m* (*parcelle*) plot; *terrain loti* housing development

louable praiseworthy; **louange** *f* praise

louche[1] *adj* sleazy

louche[2] *f* ladle

loucher squint

louer[1] rent

louer[2] (*vanter*) praise (*de, pour* for)

loup *m* wolf

loupe *f* magnifying glass

louper F *travail* botch; *bus* miss

lourd heavy; *plaisanterie* clumsy; *temps* oppressive; **lourdaud, ~e 1** *adj* clumsy **2** *m/f* oaf; **lourdement** heavily

loyal honest; *adversaire* fair-minded; *ami* loyal

loyer *m* rent

lubie *f* whim

lubrifiant *m* lubricant; **lubrifier** lubricate

lucarne *f* skylight

lucide lucid; (*conscient*) conscious; **lucidité** *f* lucidity

lucratif, -ive lucrative

lueur *f* faint light; *une ~ d'espoir* a glimmer of hope

luge *f* toboggan; *faire de la ~* go tobogganing

lugubre gloomy, lugubrious

lui *complément d'objet indirect, masculin* (to) him; *féminin* (to) her; *chose, animal* (to) it; *après prép, masculin* him; *animal* it

lui-même himself; *de chose* itself
luire glint, glisten
lumière f light; *à la ~ de* in the light of
lumineux, -euse luminous; *ciel, couleur* bright; *affiche* illuminated; *idée* brilliant
lunaire lunar
lunatique lunatic
lundi m Monday
lune f moon; *~ de miel* honeymoon
lunette f: *~s* glasses; *~s de soleil* sunglasses; *~s de ski* ski goggles
lustre m (*lampe*) chandelier; *fig* luster, *Br* lustre; **lustrer** polish

lutte f fight, struggle; SP wrestling; **lutter** fight, struggle; SP wrestle
luxe m luxury; *de ~* luxury *atr*
Luxembourg: *le ~* Luxemburg; **luxembourgeois, ~e** of/from Luxemburg, Luxemburg *atr*; **Luxembourgeois, ~e** m/f Luxemburger
luxer: *se ~ l'épaule* dislocate one's shoulder
luxueux, -euse luxurious
luxuriant luxuriant
lycée m senior high, *Br* grammar school; **lycéen, ~ne** m/f student (at a lycée)
lyophilisé freeze-dried
lyrique lyric; *qui a du lyrisme* lyrical; *artiste ~* opera singer

M

M. (= *monsieur*) Mr
ma → *mon*
macabre macabre
macédoine f: *~ de légumes* mixed vegetables *pl*; *~ de fruits* fruit salad
macérer CUIS: *faire ~* marinate
mâcher chew
machin m F thing
machinal mechanical
machine f machine; NAUT engine; *fig* machinery; *~ à laver* washing machine; *~ à sous* slot machine
machisme m machismo; **macho 1** *adj* male chauvinist **2**

m macho type
mâchoire f jaw; **mâchonner** chew (on); (*marmonner*) mutter
maçon m bricklayer; *avec des pierres* mason; **maçonnerie** f masonry
maculer spatter
madame f: *Madame Durand* Mrs Durand; *mesdames et messieurs* ladies and gentlemen
mademoiselle f: *Mademoiselle Durand* Miss Durand
madone f Madonna
magasin m (*boutique*) store, *surtout Br* shop; (*dépôt*)

store room; *grand* ~ department store; **magasinier** *m* storeman

magazine *f* magazine

mage *m*: *les Rois* ~*s* the Three Wise Men, the Magi

magicien, ~**ne** *m/f* magician; **magie** *f* magic; **magique** magic, magical

magistral *ton* magisterial; *fig* masterly; *cours* ~ lecture

magistrat *m* JUR magistrate

magnanime magnanimous

magner: *se* ~ F move it F

magnétique magnetic

magnétophone *m* tape recorder

magnétoscope *m* video (recorder)

magnifique magnificent

magouille *f* F scheming; ~*s* **électorales** election shenanigans F

mai *m* May

maigre thin; *résultat, salaire* meager, *Br* meagre; **maigrir** get thin, lose weight

mailing *m* mailshot

maille *f* stitch

maillet *m* mallet

maillot *m* SP shirt, jersey; *de coureur* vest; ~ (*de bain*) swimsuit

main *f* hand; *fait à la* ~ handmade; *prendre qc en* ~ take sth in hand; *perdre la* ~ *fig* lose one's touch; *sous la* ~ to hand, within reach

main-d'œuvre *f inv* manpower, labor, *Br* labour

maint *fml* many; *à* ~*es reprises* time and again

maintenance *f* maintenance

maintenant now; ~ *que* now that

maintenir keep; *tradition* uphold; (*tenir fermement*) hold; *d'une poutre* hold up; (*soutenir*) maintain; *se* ~ *d'un prix* hold steady; *d'une tradition, d'une fête* last; *se* ~ *au pouvoir* stay in power; **maintien** *m* maintenance; ~ *de la paix* peace keeping

maire *m* mayor; **mairie** *f* town hall

mais 1 *conj* but **2** *adv*: ~ *bien sûr!* of course!; ~ *non!* no!

maïs *m* BOT corn, *Br aussi* maize; *en boîte* sweet corn

maison *f* house; (*chez-soi*) home; COMM company; *à la* ~ at home; *pâté* ~ *m* homemade pâté; ~ *de campagne* country house

maître *m* master; (*professeur*) school teacher; (*peintre, écrivain*) maestro; ~ *chanteur* blackmailer; ~ *d'hôtel* maitre d', *Br* head waiter; ~ *nageur* swimming instructor

maîtresse 1 *f* mistress (*aussi amante*); (*professeur*) schoolteacher **2** *adj*: *idée* ~ main idea

maîtrise *f* mastery; *diplôme* MA, master's (degree); ~ *de soi* self-control; **maîtri-**

ser master; *cheval* gain control of; *incendie* bring under control

majestueux, -euse majestic

majeur 1 *adj* major; *être* ~ JUR be of age **2** *m* middle finger; **majorité** *f* majority

majuscule *f & adj*: (*lettre f*) ~ capital (letter)

mal 1 *m* evil; (*maladie*) illness; (*difficulté*) difficulty; *faire* ~ hurt; *avoir* ~ *aux dents* have toothache; *se donner du* ~ go to a lot of trouble; *faire du* ~ *à qn* hurt s.o.; ~ *de mer* seasickness **2** *adv* badly; *pas* ~ not bad; *se sentir* ~ feel ill **3** *adj*: *faire/dire qc de* ~ do/say sth bad

malade ill, sick; *tomber* ~ fall ill; ~ *mental* mentally ill; **maladie** *f* illness

maladresse *f* clumsiness; **maladroit** clumsy

malaise *m* discomfort; POL malaise; *faire un* ~ faint

malavisé ill-advised

malchance *f* bad luck

mâle *m & adj* male

malédiction *f* curse

malencontreux, -euse unfortunate

malentendant hard of hearing

malfaiteur *m* malefactor

malgré in spite of

malheur *m* misfortune; (*malchance*) bad luck; *par* ~, unfortunately; **malheureusement** unfortunately;

malheureux, -euse unfortunate; (*triste*) unhappy; (*insignifiant*) silly little

malhonnête dishonest; **malhonnêteté** *f* dishonesty

malice *f* malice; (*espièglerie*) mischief; **malicieux, -euse** malicious; (*coquin*) mischievous

malin, -igne (*rusé*) crafty, cunning; (*méchant*) malicious; MÉD malignant

malle *f* trunk; **mallette** *f* little bag

malodorant foul-smelling

malpoli impolite

malpropre dirty

malsain unhealthy

malt *m* malt

Malte *f* Malta; **maltais, ~e** Maltese; **Maltais, ~e** *m/f* Maltese

maltraiter mistreat, maltreat

malveillant malevolent

malvoyant, ~e 1 *adj* visually impaired **2** *m/f* visually impaired person

maman *f* Mom, *Br* Mum

mamelle *f* de vache udder; *de chienne* teat

mamie *f* F granny

mammifère *m* mammal

manager *m* manager

manche[1] *m* d'outils handle; *d'un violon* neck

manche[2] *f* sleeve; SP round; **la Manche** the English Channel

manchette *f* cuff; *d'un journal* headline

mandarine *f* mandarin (orange)

mandat *m* POL term of office, mandate; (*procuration*) proxy; *de la poste* postal order; ~ *d'arrêt* arrest warrant; **mandataire** *m/f* à *une réunion* proxy

manège *m* riding school; (*carrousel*) carousel, *Br* roundabout; *fig* game

mangeable edible, eatable

mangeoire *f* manger

manger eat; *argent, temps* eat up; *mots* swallow

maniable *voiture* easy to handle

maniaque fussy; **manie** *f* mania

manier handle

manière *f* way, manner; ~**s** manners; *affectées* airs and graces; à la ~ *de* in the style of; *de cette* ~ (in) that way; *de toute* ~ anyway; *d'une* ~ **générale** generally speaking; *de* ~ à faire *qch* so as to do sth; **maniéré** affected

manifestant, -e *m/f* demonstrator; **manifestation** *f* *de joie etc* expression; POL demonstration; *culturelle, sportive* event

manifeste 1 *adj* obvious **2** *m* POL manifesto; **manifester 1** *v/t* show; *se* ~ *de maladie, problèmes* manifest itself/themselves **2** *v/i* demonstrate

manipulateur, -trice manipu-

lative; **manipulation** *f d'un appareil* handling; *d'une personne* manipulation; ~ **génétique** genetic engineering; **manipuler** handle; *personne* manipulate

mannequin *m dans magasin* dummy; *personne* model

manœuvre 1 *f* maneuver, *Br* manoeuvre; *d'un outil, une machine etc* operation **2** *m* unskilled laborer *ou Br* labourer; **manœuvrer** maneuver, *Br* manoeuvre

manoir *m* manor (house)

manque *m* lack; **par** ~ *de* for lack of; **manqué** unsuccessful; *rendez-vous* missed; **manquer 1** *v/i* (*être absent*) be missing; (*faire défaut*) be lacking; (*échouer*) fail; *tu me manques* I miss you; ~ à *promesse* fail to keep; *devoir* fail in **2** *v/t* (*être absent à*) miss; *examen* fail; *elle a manqué (de) se faire écraser* she was almost run over **3** *impersonnel il manque des preuves* there's a lack of evidence

manteau *m* coat; *de neige* blanket; ~ **de cheminée** mantelpiece

manucure *f* manicure

manuel, -le *adj* & *m* manual; ~ **d'utilisation** instruction manual

manufacturé: produits *mpl* ~**s** manufactured goods

manuscrit 1 *adj* handwritten

2 *m* manuscript

maquereau *m* ZO mackerel; F (*souteneur*) pimp

maquette *f* model

maquillage *m* make-up; **maquiller** make up; *crime, vérité* conceal; **se ~** put one's make-up on

marais *m* swamp

marathon *m* marathon

marbre *m* marble

marc *m*: **~ de café** coffee grounds *pl*

marchand, **~e 1** *adj valeur* market *atr*; *rue* shopping *atr*; *marine* merchant *atr* **2** *m/f* merchant, storekeeper, *Br* shopkeeper; **marchander** haggle, bargain; **marchandise** *f*: **~s** merchandise; **train** *m* **de ~s** freight train

marche *f* walking; *d'escalier* step; MUS, MIL march; *des événements* course; (*démarche*) walk; (*arrière* AUTO reverse; **mettre en ~** start (up)

marché *m* market; (*accord*) deal; (*à*) **bon ~** cheap; **par-dessus le ~** into the bargain; **~ boursier** stock market; **le Marché Commun** POL the Common Market; **~ noir** black market

marcher walk; MIL march; *d'une machine* run, work; F (*réussir*) work; *d'un bus, train* run; **faire ~ qn** pull s.o.'s leg

mardi *m* Tuesday; **Mardi gras** Mardi Gras, *Br* Shrove Tuesday

mare *f* pond; **~ de sang** pool of blood

marécage *m* swamp; **marécageux, -euse** swampy

marée *f* tide; **~ basse/haute** low/high tide; **~ noire** oil slick

margarine *f* margarine

marge *f* margin; **en ~ de** on the fringes of

marguerite *f* daisy

mari *m* husband

mariage *m* *fête* wedding; *état* marriage

marié 1 *adj* married **2** *m* (bride)groom; **mariée** *f* bride; **marier** marry; **se ~** get married; **se ~ avec** marry, get married to

marijuana *f* marijuana

marin 1 *adj air* sea *atr*; *animaux* marine **2** *m* sailor

marine *f* MIL navy; (*bleu*) **~** navy (blue)

marionnette *f* puppet; *avec des ficelles aussi* marionnette

marmelade *f* marmalade

marmite *f* (large) pot

marmonner mutter

maroquinerie *f* leather goods shop; *articles* leather goods *pl*

marquant remarkable

marque *f* mark; COMM brand; *de voiture* make; COMM (*signe*) trademark; **~ déposée** registered trademark; **de ~**

COMM branded; *fig: personne* distinguished; **marquer** mark; (*noter*) write down; *personnalité* leave its mark on; *d'un baromètre etc* show; (*accentuer*) taille emphasize; **~ un but** score (a goal); **marqueur** *m* marker pen

marraine *f* godmother

marrant F funny

marre F: *j'en ai* ~ I've had enough, **marrer** F: *se* ~ have a good laugh

marron 1 *m* chestnut 2 *adj inv* brown; **marronnier** *m* chestnut tree

mars *m* March

marteau *m* hammer; ~ **piqueur** *m* pneumatic drill; **marteler** hammer

martyr, ~e[1] *m/f* martyr; **martyre**[2] *m* martyrdom; **martyriser** abuse; *petit frère, camarade de classe* bully

masculin male; GRAM masculine

masque *m* mask; **masquer** mask

massacre *m* massacre; **massacrer** massacre

massage *m* massage

masse *f* masse; ÉL ground, Br earth; *en* ~ in large numbers, en masse; *manifestation* massive; *une* ~ *de choses à faire* masses *pl* (of things) to do

massif, -ive 1 *adj* massif; *or, chêne* solid 2 *m* massif; ~ *de fleurs* flowerbed

massue *f* club

mastiquer *nourriture* chew

mat[1] matt; *son* dull

mat[2] *inv* aux échecs checkmated

mât *m* mast

match *m* game, Br aussi match; ~ *nul* tied game, Br draw

matelas *m* mattress; ~ *pneumatique* air bed

matelot *m* sailor

matérialiser: *se* ~ materialize; **matériau** *m* material; **matériel**, ~**le** 1 *adj* material 2 *m de camping*, SP equipment; INFORM hardware

maternel, ~**le** 1 *adj* maternal; *langue f* ~**le** mother tongue 2 *f* nursery school; **maternité** *f* motherhood; *établissement* maternity hospital; (*enfantement*) pregnancy

mathématicien, ~**ne** *m/f* mathematician; **mathématique** 1 *adj* mathematical 2 *fpl*: ~**s** mathematics

matière *f* matter; PHYS, PHIL matter; (*sujet*) subject; *entrée en* ~ introduction; *en* ~ *de* when it comes to; ~ *première* raw material

matin *m* morning; *le* ~ in the morning; *tous les lundis* ~**s** every Monday morning; **matinal** morning *atr*; *être* ~ be an early riser; **matinée** *f* morning; (*spectacle*) matinée; *faire la grasse* ~ sleep late

matou

matou *m* tom cat

matricule *m* number

matrimonial matrimonial

maturité *f* maturity

maudire curse; **maudit** F damn F!

mauvais 1 *adj* bad; (*erroné*) wrong **2** *adv* bad; **il fait ~** the weather is bad

mauve mauve

maximum *adj & m* maximum; **au ~** at most, at the maximum

mayonnaise *f* mayonnaise, mayo F

mdr *abr* (*mort de rire*) lol (*laughing out loud*)

me *me*; *(complément d'objet indirect)* (to) me; **je ~ suis coupé** I've cut myself; **je ~ lève à …** I get up at …

mec *m* F guy F

mécanicien *m* mechanic; **mécanique 1** *adj* mechanical **2** *f* mechanics; **mécanisme** *m* mechanism

méchanceté *f* nastiness; *action, parole* nasty thing to do/say; **méchant, ~e 1** *adj* nasty; *enfant* naughty **2** *m/f* F: **les gentils et les ~s** the goodies and the baddies

mèche *f de bougie* wick; *d'explosif* fuse; *de perceuse* bit; *de cheveux* strand

méconnaissable unrecognizable

mécontent unhappy, displeased (**de** with); **mécontenter** displease

médaille *f* medal; **médaillon** *m* medallion

médecin *m* doctor

médecine *f* medicine; **les ~s douces** alternative medicines

média *m* media *pl*

médiateur, -trice *m/f* mediator

médiatique media *atr*

médical medical; **médicament** *m* medicine, drug

médiéval medieval, *Br* mediaeval

médiocre mediocre; **~ en** ÉDU poor at

médire: ~ de qn run s.o. down

méditation *f* meditation; **méditer 1** *v/t* think about, reflect on **2** *v/i* meditate (**sur** on)

Méditerranée: la ~ the Mediterranean; **méditerranéen, ~ne** Mediterranean; **Méditerranéen, ~ne** *m/f* Mediterranean *atr*

méduse *f* zo jellyfish

meeting *m* meeting

méfait *m* JUR misdemeanor, *Br* misdemeanour; **~s de la drogue** harmful effects

méfiance *f* mistrust, suspicion; **méfiant** suspicious; **méfier: se ~ de** mistrust, be suspicious of; (*se tenir en garde*) be wary of

mégaoctet *m* INFORM megabyte

mégarde *f*: **par ~** inadvertently

mention

mégot *m* cigarette butt

meilleur 1 *adj* better; **le ~ ...** the best ... **2** *m*: **le ~** the best

mél *m* email

mélancolie *f* gloom, melancholy

mélange *m* mixture; *de thés* blend; *action* mixing; *de thés* blending; **mélanger** mix; *thés* blend; *(brouiller)* jumble up, mix up

mêlée *f* fray, melee; *en rugby* scrum; **mêler** mix; *(réunir)* combine; *(brouiller)* jumble up, mix up; **~ qn à qc** *fig* involve s.o. in sth; **se ~ à qc** get involved in sth; **se ~ de qc** interfere in sth

mélodie *f* tune, melody; **mélodieux, -euse** tuneful, melodious; *voix* melodious

mélodramatique melodramatic; **mélodrame** *m* melodrama

melon *m* BOT melon

membre *m* ANAT limb; *fig* member

même 1 *adj*: **le/la ~**, **les ~s** the same; **la bonté ~** kindness itself **2** *pron*: **le/la ~** the same one; **les ~s** the same ones; **cela revient au ~** it comes to the same thing **3** *adv* even; **~ pas** not even; **faire de ~** do the same; **de ~!** likewise!; **être à ~ de faire** be able to do; **tout de ~** all the same; **quand ~** all the same; **moi de ~** me too

mémoire 1 *f* memory; **à la ~**

de in memory of **2** *m* *(exposé)* report; *(dissertation)* thesis; **~s** memoirs; **mémorable** memorable; **mémoriser** memorize

menace *f* threat; **menacer** threaten *(de* with; *de faire* to do)

ménage *m* *(famille)* household; *(couple)* (married) couple; **faire le ~** clean house; *Br* do the housework; **ménagement** *m* consideration; **ménager**[1] *v/t* treat with consideration; *temps, argent* use sparingly; *(arranger)* arrange; **ménager**[2], **-ère 1** *adj* household *atr* **2** *f* home-maker, housewife

mendiant, ~e *m/f* beggar; **mendier 1** *v/i* beg **2** *v/t* beg for

mener 1 *v/t* lead; *(amener, transporter)* take **2** *v/i*: **~ à d'un chemin** lead to; **ne ~ à rien des efforts** come to nothing; **meneur** *m* leader; *péj* ringleader

mensonge *m* lie; **mensonger, -ère** false

mensualité *f* somme à payer monthly payment; **mensuel, ~le** monthly

mental mental; **calcul** *m* **~** mental arithmetic; **mentalité** *f* mentality

menteur, -euse *m/f* liar

menthe *f* BOT mint

mention *f* mention; **à un examen** grade, *Br aussi* mark;

mentionner mention

mentir lie (**à** to)

menton *m* chin

menu **1** *adj* slight; *morceaux* small **2** *adv* finely, fine **3** *m* menu (*aussi* INFORM); (*repas*) set meal; **par le ~** in minute detail

menuisier *m* carpenter

méprendre: **se ~** be mistaken (**sur** about)

mépris *m* (*indifférence*) disdain; (*dégoût*) scorn; **méprisable** despicable; **méprisant** scornful; **mépriser** *argent, ennemi* despise; *conseil, danger* scorn

mer *f* sea; **en ~** at sea; **la Mer du Nord** the North Sea

mercenaire *m* mercenary

mercerie *f magasin* notions store, Br haberdashery; *articles* notions, Br haberdashery *pl*

merci **1** *int* thanks, thank you (**de, pour** for); **~ bien** thanks a lot, thank you very much **2** *f* mercy

mercredi *m* Wednesday

merde *f* P shit P; **merder** P screw up P

mère *f* mother

méridional southern

mérite *m* merit; **mériter** deserve; **~ le détour** be worth a visit

merle *m* blackbird

merveille *f* wonder, marvel; **à ~** wonderfully well; **merveilleux, -euse** wonderful

mes → **mon**

mésaventure *f* mishap

mesquin mean

message *m* message; **messager, -ère** *m/f* messenger, courier; **messagerie** *f* parcels service; *électronique* electronic mail; **~ vocale** voicemail

messe *f* REL mass

mesure *f* measurement; *disposition* measure, step; MUS (*rythme*) time; **à ~ que** as; **être en ~ de faire qch** be in a position to do sth; *outre* **~** excessive; **sur ~** *fig* tailor-made; **mesurer** measure; *risque, importance* gauge; *paroles* weigh; **se ~ avec qn** pit o.s. against s.o.

métal *m* metal; **métallique** metallic

métamorphoser: **se ~** metamorphose

météo *f* weather forecast

météore *m* meteor

météorologie *f* meteorology; *service* weather office

méthode *f* method

méticuleux, -euse meticulous

métier *m* profession; *manuel* trade; (*expérience*) experience; *machine* loom

métrage *m un film* footage; **court ~** short

mètre *m* meter, Br metre; (*règle*) tape measure

métrique metric

métro *m* subway, Br underground; *à Paris* metro

métropole *f* metropolis; *de colonie* mother country

mettre *m*: *vêtements, lunettes, chauffage* put on; *réveil* set; *argent dans entreprise* put in; ~ *deux heures à faire qc* take two hours to do sth; *se* ~ *à faire* start to

meuble *m* piece of furniture; ~s furniture; **meubler** furnish

meurtre *m* murder; **meurtrier, -ère** 1 *adj* deadly 2 *m/f* murderer

meurtrir bruise; **meurtrissure** *f* bruise

meute *f* pack; *fig* mob

mexicain, ~e Mexican; **Mexicain, ~e** *m/f* Mexican; **Mexique:** *le* ~ Mexico

mi-... half; *à mi-chemin* halfway; *(à la) mi-janvier* mid-January

mi-bas *mpl* knee-highs, pop socks

miche *f* large round loaf

micro *m* mike; INFORM computer, PC; *d'espionnage* bug

microbe *m* microbe

microfilm *m* microfilm

micro-ondes *m* microwave

microphone *m* microphone

microscope *m* microscope

midi *m* noon, twelve o'clock; *(sud)* south; *le Midi* the South of France

mie *f de pain* crumb

miel *m* honey

mien: *le mien, la mienne, les miens, les miennes* mine

miette *f* crumb

mieux 1 *adv comparatif de bien* better; *superlatif de bien* best; *le* ~ best; *de* ~ *en* ~ better and better; *tant* ~ so much the better; *vous feriez* ~ *de* ... you would *ou* you'd do best to ... 2 *m:* *(progrès)* progress; *j'ai fait de mon* ~ I did my best; *le* ~, *c'est de* ... the best thing is to ...

mièvre insipid

mignon, ~ne *(charmant)* cute; *(gentil)* nice

migraine *f* migraine

migration *f* migration; **migrer** migrate

mijoter CUIS simmer; *fig* hatch

milieu *m (centre)* middle; *biologique, social* environment; *au* ~ *de* in the middle of; *le* ~ the underworld

militaire 1 *adj* military 2 *m* soldier; *les* ~s the military *sg ou pl*

militant active

militer: ~ *dans* be an active member of; ~ *pour/contre* *fig* militate for/against

mille 1 (a) thousand 2 *m* *mesure* mile; ~ *marin* nautical mile

millénaire 1 *adj* thousand-year old 2 *m* millennium

milliard *m* billion; **milliardaire** *m* billionaire

millième thousandth

millier *m* thousand

milligramme *m* milligram

millimètre millimeter, *Br* millimetre

million *m* million; **millionnaire** *m/f* millionaire

minable mean, shabby; *un salaire* ~ a pittance

mince thin; *personne* slim; *espoir* slight; *somme, profit* small; *argument* flimsy

mine¹ *f* appearance, look; *avoir bonne/mauvaise* ~ look/not look well

mine² *f* mine (*aussi* MIL); *de crayon* lead; **miner** undermine; MIL mine

minéral *adj* & *m* mineral

minéralogique AUTO: *plaque f* ~ license plate, *Br* number plate

mineur¹ *adj* JUR, MUS minor

mineur² *m* (*ouvrier*) miner

miniature *f* miniature

minimal minimum; **minime** minimal; *salaire* tiny; **miniminiser** minimize; **minimum** *adj* & *m* minimum; *au* ~ at the very least; *un* ~ *de* the least little bit of

ministère *m* department; (*gouvernement*) government; REL ministry; **ministre** *m* minister; ~ *des Affaires étrangères* Secretary of State, *Br* Foreign Secretary; ~ *de l'Intérieur* Secretary of the Interior, *Br* Home Secretary

minitel *m* small home terminal connected to a number of data banks

minorité *f* JUR, POL minority

minuit *m* midnight

minuscule 1 *adj* tiny, minuscule; *lettre* small, lower case **2** *f* small *ou* lower-case letter

minute *f* minute

minuterie *f* time switch

minutie *f* meticulousness; **minutieux, -euse** meticulous

miracle *m* miracle; **miraculeux, -euse** miraculous

mirage *m* mirage; *fig* illusion

miroir *m* mirror

miroiter sparkle

mise *f au jeu* stake; *de* ~ acceptable; ~ *en bouteilles* bottling; ~ *en marche ou route* start-up; **miser** stake (*sur* on)

misérable wretched; **misère** *f* destitution; (*chose pénible*) misfortune

miséricordieux, -euse merciful

misogyne *m* misogynist

missile *m* MIL missile

mission *f* mission; (*tâche*) task

mite *f* ZO (clothes) moth

mi-temps 1 *f* SP half-time **2** *m* part-time job; *à* ~ *travail* part-time

mitigé moderate; *sentiments* mixed

mi-voix: *à* ~ under one's breath

mixer, mixeur *m* CUIS blender; **mixte** mixed; **mixture** *f* *péj* vile concoction

MM (= *Messieurs*) Messrs.

Mme (= *Madame*) Mrs

Mo (= *mégaoctet*) **Mb** (= megabyte)

mobile 1 *adj* mobile; (*amovible*) movable; *feuilles* loose; *ombres* moving **2** *m* motive; ART mobile

mobilier, -ère 1 *adj* JUR movable, personal **2** *m* furniture

mobilisation *f* mobilization; **mobilité** *f* mobility

mobylette® *f* moped

moche F ugly; (*méprisable*) mean

mode¹ *m* method; **~ d'emploi** instructions (for use); **~ de vie** life-style

mode² *f* fashion; **être à la ~** be fashionable, be in fashion

modèle *m* model; *tricot* pattern; **modeler** model

modem *m* INFORM modem

modération *f* moderation; **modéré** moderate; **modérer** moderate; **se ~** control o.s.

moderne modern; **modernisation** *f* modernization; **moderniser** modernize

modeste modest; **modestie** *f* modesty

modification *f* modification; **modifier** modify

modique modest

module *m* TECH module; **moduler** modulate

moelle *f* marrow; **~ épinière** spinal cord; **moelleux, -euse** *lit* soft; *chocolat, vin*

smooth

mœurs *fpl* morals; (*coutumes*) customs

moi me; *avec ~* with me

moi-même myself

moindre lesser; *prix* lower; *quantité* smaller; *le/la ~* the least

moine *m* monk

moineau *m* sparrow

moins **1** *adv* less; *au ou du ~* at least; *à ~ que ... ne* (+ *subj*) unless; *de ~ en ~* less and less; *20 euros de ~* 20 euros less **2** *m*: *le ~* the least **3** *prép* MATH minus; *dix heures ~ cinq* it's five of ten, *Br* it's five to ten; *il fait ~ deux* it's 2 below zero

mois *m* month

moisi 1 *adj* moldy, *Br* mouldy **2** *m* BOT mold, *Br* mould; **moisir** go moldy *ou Br* mouldy; **moisissure** *f* BOT mold, *Br* mould

moisson *f* harvest; **moissonner** harvest

moite damp, moist

moitié *f* half; *à ~ vide/endormi* half-empty/-asleep; *~ ~* fifty-fifty

molaire *f* molar

molécule *f* molecule

molester rough up

molette *f* de réglage knob

mollesse *f* softness; *d'une personne, d'actions* lethargy

mollet¹, **-te** *adj* soft; *œuf* soft--boiled

mollet² *m* calf

môme

môme *m/f* F kid F

moment *m* moment; **d'un ~ à l'autre** at any moment; **par ~ s** at times, sometimes; **pour le ~** for the moment

momentané temporary; momentanément for a short while

mon *m*, ma *f*, mes *pl* my

monarchie *f* monarchy; monarque *m* monarch

monastère *m* monastery

monceau *m* mound

mondain *vie* society *atr*; mondanités *fpl* social niceties

monde *m* world; *gens* people *pl*; **tout le ~** everybody, everyone; **mettre au ~** bring into the world

mondial world *atr*, global; mondialisation *f* globalization

monétaire monetary; *marché* money *atr*

moniteur, -trice *1 m/f* instructor *2 m* INFORM monitor

monnaie *f* money; (*pièces*) change; (*unité monétaire*) currency

monologue *m* monolog, *Br* monologue

monopole *m* monopoly; monopoliser monopolize

monospace *m* people carrier, MPV

monotone monotonous; monotonie *f* monotony

monsieur *m* (*pl* messieurs) *dans lettre* Dear Sir; Mon-

sieur Durand Mr Durand; bonjour ~ good morning

monstre 1 *m* monster 2 *adj* colossal

mont *m* mountain

montage *m* TECH assembly; *d'un film* editing; *d'une photographie* montage; ÉL connecting

montagnard, ~e 1 *adj* mountain *atr* 2 *m/f* mountain dweller; montagne *f* mountain; **à la ~** in the mountains; **~s russes** roller coaster; montagneux, -euse mountainous

montant 1 *adj robe* high-necked; *mouvement* upward 2 *m somme* amount

montée *f sur montagne* ascent; (*pente*) slope; *de prix, de température* rise; monter 1 *v/t* climb, go/come up; *valise* take/bring up; *machine* assemble; *tente* put up; THÉÂT put on; *film* edit; *entreprise* set up; *cheval* ride 2 *v/i* come/go upstairs; *d'avion, de route* climb; *des prix* rise, go up; *de baromètre, fleuve* rise; **~ dans** *avion, train* get on; *voiture* get in(to) 3: **se ~ à** *de frais* amount to

montre *f* (*wrist*)watch

montrer show; **~ qn/qc du doigt** point at s.o./sth

monture *f* (*cheval*) mount; *de lunettes* frame; *d'un diamant* setting

moucher

monument *m* monument; **monumental** monumental

moquer: se ~ de (*railler*) make fun of; (*dédaigner*) not care about; (*tromper*) fool; **moquerie** *f* mockery

moquette *f* wall-to-wall carpet

moqueur, -euse 1 *adj* mocking **2** *m/f* mocker

moral, ~e 1 *adj* moral; *souffrance, santé* spiritual **2** *m* morale **3** *f* morality, morals *pl; d'une histoire* moral

morbide morbid

morceau *m* piece; *d'un livre* passage

morceler divide up

mordant biting; **mordre** bite; *d'un acide* eat into

morfondre: se ~ mope; (*s'ennuyer*) be bored

morgue *f lieu* mortuary, morgue

moribond dying

morne gloomy

morose morose

mors *m* bit

morsure *f* bite

mort[1] *f* death

mort[2], **~e 1** *adj* dead; *eau* stagnant; *yeux* lifeless; *membre* numb; *ivre ~* dead drunk; *être ~ de rire* F die laughing **2** *m/f* dead man; dead woman; *les ~s* the dead *pl*

mortalité *f* mortality; *taux m de ~* death rate, mortality; **mortel, ~le** mortal; *blessure,*

dose, maladie fatal; *péché* deadly

morue *f* cod

morveux, -euse *m/f* F squirt F

mosaïque *f* mosaic

Moscou Moscow

mosquée *f* mosque

mot *m* word; (*court message*) note; *bon ~* witticism; **~ clé** key word; **~ de passe** password; *gros ~* rude word, swearword; **~ à ~** word for word

motard *m* motorcyclist, biker; *de la gendarmerie* motorcycle policeman

moteur, -trice 1 *m* engine, motor; *fig: personne* driving force (**de** behind) **2** *adj arbre* drive; *force* driving

motif *m* motive, reason; (*forme*) pattern; MUS theme, motif; *en prendre* motif

motion *f* POL motion

motivation *f* motivation; **motiver** motivate; (*expliquer*) be the reason for, prompt; (*justifier par des motifs*) give a reason for

moto *f* motorbike, motorcycle; *faire de la ~* ride one's motorbike; **motocycliste** *m/f* motorcyclist

motoriser mechanize; *je suis motorisé* F I have a car

mou, molle soft; *caractère, résistance* weak

mouche *f* fly

moucher: se ~ blow one's nose

moucheron

moucheron *m* gnat

mouchoir *m* handkerchief

moudre grind

moue *f* pout; **faire la ~** pout

mouette *f* seagull

moufle *f* mitten

mouillé wet; **mouiller 1** *v/t* wet; (*humecter*) dampen; *liquide* water down **2** *v/i* MAR anchor

moule 1 *m* mold, *Br* mould; CUIS tin **2** *f* ZO mussel

mouler mold, *Br* mould

moulin *m* mill; **~ (à vent)** windmill; **~ à café** coffee grinder

mourir die (**de** *of*); **~ de froid** freeze to death

mousse *f* foam; BOT moss; CUIS mousse; **mousser** lather; **mousseux, -euse 1** *adj* foamy **2** *m* sparkling wine

moustache *f* mustache, *Br* moustache

moustique *m* mosquito

moutarde *f* mustard

mouton *m* sheep; *viande* mutton; *fourrure* sheepskin

mouvement *m* movement; *trafic* traffic; **en ~** moving; **mouvementé** eventful; *débat* lively

mouvoir: **se ~** move

moyen, ~ne 1 *adj* average; *classe* middle; **Moyen Âge** *m* Middle Ages *pl*; **Moyen-Orient** *m* Middle East **2** *m* (*façon, méthode*) means *sg*; **~s** (*argent*) means *pl*; *intellectuelles* faculties; **au ~ de**,

par le ~ de by means of **3** *f* average; *statistique* mean; **en~ne** on average; **moyenâgeux, -euse** medieval

moyennant for

Mt (= **Mont**) Mt (= Mount)

muer *d'oiseau* molt, *Br* moult; *de voix* break

muet, ~te *adj* dumb; *fig* silent

mufle *m* muzzle; *fig* F boor

mugir moo; *du vent* moan

muguet *m* BOT lily of the valley

mule *f* mule

multicolore multicolored, *Br* multicoloured

multimédia *m* & *adj* multimedia

multinational, ~e 1 *adj* multinational **2** *f*: **multinationale** multinational

multiplication *f* multiplication; **la ~ de** (*augmentation*) the increase in the number of; **multiplier** multiply; **se ~** *d'une espèce* multiply

multitude *f*: **une ~ de** a host of; **la ~** *péj* the masses *pl*

multiusages versatile

municipal town *atr*, municipal; **municipalité** *f* (*commune*) municipality; **conseil ~** town council

munir: **~ de** fit with; *personne* provide with; **se ~ de qc** *d'un parapluie*, *de son passeport* take sth

mur *m* wall

mûr ripe

muraille *f* wall

mûre *f* BOT mulberry; *des ronces* blackberry

murer *enclos* wall in; *porte* wall up

mûrier *m* mulberry (tree)

mûrir ripen

murmure *m* murmur; **murmurer** murmur; *(médire)* talk

muscle *m* muscle; **musclé** muscular; **musculation** *f* body-building

museau *m* muzzle

musée *m* museum

museler muzzle *(aussi fig)*; **muselière** *f* muzzle

musical musical; **musicien, ~ne 1** *adj* musical **2** *m/f* musician; **musique** *f* music; **~ de fond** piped music

must *m* must

musulman, ~e *m/f & adj* Muslim

mutation *f* change; BIOL mutation; *de fonctionnaire* transfer

mutiler mutilate

mutuel, ~le mutual

myope shortsighted

myrtille *f* bilberry

mystère *m* mystery; **mystérieux, -euse** mysterious

mystifier fool, take in

mystique 1 *adj* mystical **2** *m/f* mystic **3** *f* mystique

mythe *m* myth; **mythologie** *f* mythology

mythomane *m/f* pathological liar

N

nabot *m péj* midget

nacre *f* mother-of-pearl

nage *f* swimming; *style* stroke; *être en ~ fig* be dripping with sweat

nageoire *f* fin

nager 1 *v/i* swim **2** *v/t*: *~ la brasse* do the breaststroke

naïf, naïve naive

nain, ~e *m/f & adj* dwarf

naissance *f* birth *(aussi fig)*

naître be born *(aussi fig)*; *faire ~ sentiment* give rise to

naïveté *f* naivety

nana *f* F chick F, girl

nantir provide *(de* with)

nappe *f* tablecloth; *de gaz, pétrole* layer

narcotique *m & adj* narcotic

narguer taunt

narine *f* nostril

narquois taunting

narrateur, -trice *m/f* narrator; **narration** *f* narration

nasal nasal

natal *pays etc* of one's birth, native; **natalité** *f*: *(taux m de) ~* birth rate

natation *f* swimming

natif, -ive native

nation *f* nation; **national, ~e 1** *adj* national **2** *mpl*: **natio-**

naux nationals **3** f highway;
nationaliser nationalize;
nationaliste 1 adj nationalist; péj nationalistic **2** m/f
nationalist; **nationalité** f nationality

natte f (tapis) mat; de cheveux braid, plait

naturalisation f naturaliza-
tion

nature 1 adj yaourt plain; thé,
café without milk or sugar;
personne natural **2** f nature;
~ **morte** ART still life; naturel, ~le **1** adj natural **2** m (caractère) nature; (spontanéi-
té) naturalness; **naturellement** naturally

naufrage m shipwreck; **faire
~** be shipwrecked

nausée f nausea; **j'ai la ~** I'm
nauseous, Br I feel sick;
nauséeux, -euse nauseating

nautique nautical; **ski** water
atr

nautisme m water sports and
sailing

naval naval; construction ship
atr

navet m rutabaga, Br swede;
fig turkey F, Br flop

navette f shuttle; **faire la ~** a
shuttle

navigable navigable; **navigation** f sailing; (pilotage) navigation; **~ aérienne** air travel; **~ spatiale** space travel;
naviguer d'un navire, marin
sail; d'un avion fly; (conduire), INFORM navigate; **~ sur**

Internet surf the Net

navire m ship

navrant upsetting; **navré: je
suis ~** I am so sorry

ne: je ... comprends pas I
don't understand, I do not
understand; **ne ... guère**
hardly; **ne ... jamais** never;
ne ... personne nobody; **ne
... plus** no longer; not any
more; **ne ... que** only; **ne
... rien** nothing, not anything; → aussi **guère, jamais**
etc

né born; **~e Lepic** nee Lepic
néanmoins nevertheless

néant m nothingness

nécessaire 1 adj necessary **2**
m necessary; **le strict ~** the
bare minimum; **~ de toilette**
toiletries pl; **nécessité** f necessity; **nécessiter** require,
necessitate

néerlandais, ~e 1 adj Dutch
2 m langue Dutch; **Néerlandais, ~e** m/f Dutchman;
Dutchwoman

néfaste harmful

négatif, -ive adj & m negative; **négation** f negation;
GRAM negative

négligé 1 adj travail careless;
tenue untidy; épouse, enfant
neglected **2** f negligee; **négligence** f negligence, care-
lessness; d'une épouse, d'un
enfant neglect; (nonchalan-
ce) casualness; **négligent**
careless, negligent; parent
negligent; geste casual; **né-**

gliger neglect; *occasion* miss; *avis* disregard; **~ de faire** fail to do

négoce *f* trade; **négociant** *m* merchant; **négociateur, -trice** *m/f* negotiator; **négociation** *f* negotiation; **négocier** negotiate

neige *f* snow; **neiger** snow

néon *m* neon

nerf *m* nerve; *(vigueur)* energy; **être à bout de ~s** be at the end of one's tether

nerveux, -euse nervous; *(vigoureux)* full of energy; AUTO responsive; **nervosité** *f* nervousness

n'est-ce pas: **il fait beau, ~?** it's a fine day, isn't it?; **tu la connais, ~?** you know her, don't you?

net, ~te 1 *adj (propre)* clean; *(clair)* clear; *différence* distinct; COMM net **2** *adv (aussi nettement)* tué outright; **~ refuser** flatly; **parler** plainly; **netteté** *f* cleanliness; *(clarté)* clarity

nettoyage *m* cleaning; **~ ethnique** ethnic cleansing; **~ à sec** dry cleaning; **nettoyer** clean; F *(ruiner)* clean out F; **~ à sec** dryclean

neuf[1] nine

neuf[2]**, neuve** *adj* new; **refaire à ~** *maison etc* renovate; *moteur* recondition

neutraliser neutralize; **neutralité** *f* neutrality; **neutre** neutral

neuvième ninth

neveu *m* nephew

névralgie *f* MÉD neuralgia

névrosé, ~e *m/f* neurotic

nez *m* nose

ni neither, nor; **je n'ai ~ intérêt ~ désir** I have neither interest nor inclination; **sans sucre ~ lait** without sugar or milk, with neither sugar nor milk; **~ moi non plus** neither *ou* nor do I, me neither

niais stupid; **niaiserie** *f* stupidity

niche *f dans un mur* niche; *d'un chien* kennel; **nicher** nest; *fig* F live

nicotine *f* nicotine

nid *m* nest; **~ de poule** *fig* pothole

nièce *f* niece

nier: **~ (avoir fait)** deny (doing)

nigaud 1 *adj* silly **2** *m* idiot, fool

niveau *m* level; ÉDU standard; *outil* spirit level; **~ de vie** standard of living; **niveler** *terrain* level; *fig: différences* even out

noble noble; **noblesse** *f* nobility

noce *f* wedding; **faire la ~** F paint the town red

nocif, -ive harmful, noxious

nocturne 1 *adj* night *attr*; ZO nocturnal **2** *f*: **un match joué en ~** an evening match

Noël *m* Christmas; **joyeux ~!**

nœud

Merry Christmas!; *le père* ~ Santa Claus, *Br aussi* Father Christmas

nœud *m* knot (*aussi* NAUT); *fig: d'un problème* nub; ~ *papillon* bow tie

noir 1 *adj* black; (*sombre*) dark; *il fait* ~ it's dark 2 *m* black; (*obscurité*) dark; *travail m au* ~ moonlighting

Noir *m* black man

noircir blacken

Noire *f* black woman

noisetier *m* hazel; **noisette** *f* & *adj inv* hazelnut

noix *f* walnut

nom *m* name; GRAM noun; *au* ~ *de qn* in *ou Br* on behalf of s.o.; ~ *de famille* surname, family name; ~ *de jeune fille* maiden name

nombre *m* number; *sans* ~ countless; **nombreux, -euse** numerous, many; *famille* large

nombril *m* navel

nomination *f* appointment; *à un prix* nomination

nommer name, call; *à une fonction* appoint; *se* ~ be called

non no; *j'espère que* ~ I hope not; *moi* ~ *plus* me neither; *c'est normal,* ~? that's normal, isn't it?

non-alcoolisé non-alcoholic

nonchalant nonchalant, casual

nonobstant notwithstanding

non-polluant environ-

mentally friendly, non-polluting

nord 1 *m* north; *au* ~ *de* (to the) north of 2 *adj* north; *hemisphère* northern

nord-américain, ~e North--American; **Nord-Américain**, ~e *m/f* North-American

nord-est *m* north-east

nord-ouest *m* north-west

normal, ~e 1 *adj* normal 2 *f*: *inférieur/supérieur à la* ~e above/below average; **normalement** normally; **normalisation** *f* normalization; TECH standardization; **normalité** *f* normality

norme *f* norm; TECH standard

Norvège *f*: *la* ~ Norway; **norvégien**, ~ne 1 *adj* Norwegian 2 *m langue* Norwegian; **Norvégien**, ~ne *m/f* Norwegian

nos → **notre**

nostalgie *f* nostalgia; *avoir la* ~ *de son pays* be homesick

notaire *m* notary

notamment particularly

note *f* note; *à l'école* grade, *Br* mark; (*facture*) check, *Br* bill; ~ *de frais* expense account; ~ *de service* memo; **noter** (*écrire*) write down; (*remarquer*) note

notice *f* note; (*mode d'emploi*) instructions *pl*

notifier *v/t*: ~ *qch à qn* notify s.o. of sth

notion *f* (*idée*) notion, concept; **~s** basics *pl*

notre, *pl* **nos** our

nôtre: le/la ~, les ~s ours

nouer *v/t*; *relations* establish

nougat *m* nougat

nouilles *fpl* noodles

nounou *f* F nanny

nounours *m* teddy bear

nourrice *f* child minder

nourrir feed; *fig*: *espoir* nurture

nourrisson *m* infant

nourriture *f* food

nous *sujet* we; *complément d'objet direct* us; *complément d'objet indirect* (to) us; **~ ~ sommes levés tôt** we got up early; **~ ~ aimons** we love each other

nouveau, nouvelle (*m nouvel before a vowel or silent h*; *mpl* **nouveaux**) **1** *adj* new; **de ou à ~** again; **Nouvel An** *m* New Year('s) **2** *m/f* new person

nouveau-né 1 *adj* newborn **2** *m* newborn baby

nouveauté *f* novelty

nouvelle *f* (*récit*) short story; **une ~** *dans les médias* a piece of news; **nouvelles** *fpl* news *sg*; **Nouvelle Zélande** *f* New Zealand

novembre *m* November

novice 1 *m/f* novice **2** *adj* inexperienced

noyade *f* drowning

noyau *m* pit, *Br* stone; PHYS nucleus; *fig* (small) group

noyer[1] *v/t* drown; AUTO flood;

se ~ drown; *se suicider* drown o.s.

noyer[2] *m* arbre, bois walnut

nu 1 *adj* naked; *arbre, bras, tête etc* bare **2** *m* ART nude

nuage *m* cloud; **nuageux, -euse** cloudy

nuance *f* shade; *fig* slight difference; (*subtilité*) nuance; **nuancé** subtle; **nuancer** qualify

nucléaire 1 *adj* nuclear **2** *m*: **le ~** nuclear power

nudiste *m/f & adj* nudist; **nudité** *f* nudity

nuée *f* *d'insectes* cloud; *de journalistes* horde

nuire: ~ à hurt, harm

nuit *f* night; **il fait ~** it's dark

nul, ~le 1 *adj* no; (*non valable*) invalid; (*sans valeur*) hopeless; (*inexistant*) nonexistent; **~le part** nowhere **2** *pron* no-one; **nullement** not in the least; **nullité** *f* JUR invalidity; *fig* hopelessness; *personne* loser

numérique numerical; INFORM digital

numéro *m* number; **~ vert** toll-free number, *Br* Freefone number; **numéroter 1** *v/t* number **2** *v/i* TÉL dial

nuque *f* nape of the neck

nurse *f* nanny

nutritif, -ive nutritional; *aliment* nutritious; **nutrition** *f* nutrition

nylon *m* nylon

O

obéir obey; **~ à** obey; **obéissance** f obedience; **obéissant** obedient

obèse obese; **obésité** f obesity

objecter: ~ qch pour ne pas faire qch give sth as a reason; **~ que** object that; **objectif, -ive 1** adj objective **2** m objective; PHOT lens; **objection** f objection; **objectivité** f objectivity

objet m object; **de réflexions, d'une lettre** subject

obligation f obligation; COMM bond; **obligatoire** compulsory, obligatory

obligeant obliging; **obliger** oblige; (forcer) force; **être obligé de faire qc** be obliged to do sth

oblique oblique

oblitérer timbre cancel

obscène obscene

obscur obscure; nuit, rue dark; **obscurcir** darken; **s'~** grow dark; **obscurité** f obscurity; **de la nuit, d'une rue** darkness

obséder obsess

obsèques fpl funeral

observateur, -trice m/f observer; **observation** f observation; d'une règle observance; **observatoire** m observatory; **observer** ob-

serve; changement notice; **faire ~ qc à qn** point sth out to s.o.

obsession f obsession

obstacle m obstacle; SP hurdle; pour cheval jump; **faire ~ à qc** stand in the way of sth

obstination f obstinacy; **obstiné** obstinate; **obstiner: s'~ à faire qc** persist in doing sth

obstruction f obstruction; dans tuyau blockage; **obstruer** obstruct, block

obtenir get, obtain

obturer seal; dent fill

obtus MATH, fig obtuse

obus m MIL shell

occasion f opportunity; marché bargain; **d'~** second-hand; **à l'~** when the opportunity arises; **occasionner** cause

Occident m: **l'~** the West; **occidental, ~e** western; Occidental, **~e** m/f Westerner

occulte occult

occupant 1 adj occupying **2** m occupant; **occupation** f occupation; **occupé** busy; pays, appartement occupied; chaise taken; TÉL busy; **occuper** occupy; personnel employ; **s'~ de politique** etc take an interest in; malade, organisation look after

occurrence f: **en l'~** as it hap-

pens
océan m ocean
octet m INFORM byte
octobre m October
oculaire eye atr
oculiste m/f eye specialist
odeur f smell; **~ corporelle**
BO
odieux, -euse hateful, odious
odorant scented
odorat m sense of smell
œil m (pl **yeux**) eye; **à vue d'~**
visibly
œillet m BOT carnation
œuf m egg; **~s brouillés**
scrambled eggs; **~ à la coque** soft-boiled egg; **~ sur
le plat** fried egg
œuvre 1 f work; **~ d'art** work
of art; **mettre en ~** (employer) use; (exécuter) carry
out **2** m ART, littérature works
of
offense f (insulte) insult; (péché) sin; **offenser** offend;
s'~ de take offense ou Br offence at
office m office; REL service;
d'~ automatically; **faire ~
de** act as
officiel, ~le official
officier m officer
officieux, -euse semi-official
officinal plante medicinal
offre f **d'emploi** job
offer; **offrir** offer; cadeau
give; **s'~ qc** treat o.s. to sth
offusquer offend
oie f goose
oignon m onion; BOT bulb

oiseau m bird; **à vol d'~** as the
crow flies
oiseux, -euse idle
oisif, -ive idle; **oisiveté** f idle-
ness
olive f olive; **olivier** m olive
(tree)
olympique Olympic
ombrage m shade; **ombragé**
shady; **ombrageux, -euse**
cheval skittish; personne
touchy; **ombre** f shade;
(silhouette) shadow; fig (anon-
nymat) obscurity; de regret
hint
ombrelle f sunshade
omelette f omelet, Br omelette
omettre leave out, omit; **~ de
faire** fail ou omit to do;
omission f omission
omnibus m: (**train m**) **~** slow
train
on (après que, et, où, qui, si
souvent **l'on**) (nous) we;
(tu, vous, indéterminé) you;
(quelqu'un) someone; (eux,
les gens) they, people; **~
m'a dit que...** I
was told that ...; **~ ne sait jamais** you never know, one
never knows fml
oncle m uncle
onction f REL unction; **onc-
tueux, -euse** smooth; fig
smarmy F, unctuous
onde f wave; **sur les ~s** RAD
on the air; **grandes ~s** long
wave
ondée f downpour

on-dit

on-dit *m* rumor, *Br* rumour

ondoyer *du blés* sway

ondulation *f de terrain* undulation; *de coiffure* wave; **onduler** *d'ondes* undulate; *de cheveux* be wavy

onéreux, -euse expensive

ONG *f abr (organisation non gouvernementale)* NGO *(non-governmental organisation)*

ongle *m* nail; *zo* claw

onguent *m* cream, salve

onze eleven; **le ~** the eleventh; **onzième** eleventh

opaque opaque

opéra *m* opera; *bâtiment* opera house

opérable MÉD operable; **opérateur, -trice** *m/f* operator; *en cinéma* cameraman; FIN trader; **opération** *f* operation; *action* working; FIN transaction; **opérer 1** *v/t* MÉD operate on; *(produire)* make; *(exécuter)* implement **2** *v/i* MÉD operate; *(avoir effet)* work; *(procéder)* proceed; **se faire ~** have an operation

opiner: *~ de la tête* nod in agreement

opiniâtre stubborn; **opiniâtreté** *f* stubbornness

opinion *f* opinion

opium *m* opium

opportun *ou* oportune; *moment* right; **opportuniste** *m/f* opportunist; **opportunité** *f* timeliness; *(occasion)* opportunity

opposant, ~e 1 *adj* opposing **2** *m/f* opponent; **les ~s** the opposition; **opposé 1** *adj* *pôles* opposite; *opinions* conflicting; **être ~ à qc** be opposed to sth **2** *m* opposite; **à l'~ de qn** unlike s.o.; **opposer** bring into conflict; *argument* put forward; **s'~ à qn/à qc** oppose s.o./sth; **opposition** *f* opposition; *(contraste)* contrast

oppresser oppress, weigh down; **oppression** *f* oppression

opprimer oppress

opter: *~ pour* opt for

opticien, ~ne *m/f* optician

optimisme *m* optimism; **optimiste 1** *adj* optimistic **2** *m/f* optimist

option *f* option

optique 1 *adj* *nerf* optic; *verre* optical **2** *f* *science* optics; *fig* viewpoint

or[1] *m* gold

or[2] *conj* now

orage *m* storm; **orageux, -euse** stormy

oraison *f* REL prayer

oral *adj & m* oral

orange *f & adj inv* orange; **oranger** *m* orange tree

orateur, -trice *m/f* orator

orbite *f* ANAT eyesocket; ASTR orbit *(aussi fig)*

orchestre *m* orchestra; *de théâtre* orchestra, *Br* stalls *pl*

orchidée *f* orchid

ordinaire 1 *adj* ordinary 2 *m* essence regular; **d'~** ordinarily

ordinateur *m* computer

ordonnance *f* arrangement, layout; *(ordre)* order *(aussi* JUR); MÉD prescription; ordonné tidy; ordonner organize; *(commander)* order; MÉD prescribe

ordre *m* order; **~ du jour** agenda; **de premier ~** first-rate; **mettre en ~** tidy

ordures *fpl (détritus)* garbage, *Br* rubbish; *fig* filth

oreille *f* ear; *d'un bol* handle; **dur d'~** hard of hearing

oreiller *m* pillow

oreillons *mpl* MÉD mumps *sg*

orfèvre *m* goldsmith

organe *m* organ; *(voix, porte-parole)* voice; *d'un mécanisme* part

organisation *f* organization; organiser organize; **s'~** *d'une personne* get organized; organiseur *m* INFORM personal organizer

organisme *m* organism; ANAT system; *(organisation)* organization, body

orgue *m* organ

orgueil *m* pride; orgueilleux, -euse proud

Orient *m*: **l'~** the East; *Asie* the East, the Orient; oriental, ~e east, eastern; *d'Asie* eastern, Oriental; Oriental, ~e *m/f* Oriental

orientation *f* direction; *d'une*

maison exposure; orienter orient, *Br* orientate; *(diriger)* direct; **s'~** get one's bearings; **s'~ vers** *fig* go in for

orifice *m* opening

originaire original; **être ~ de** come from; original 1 *adj* original; *péj* eccentric 2 *m* ouvrage original; *personne* eccentric; origine *f* origin; **à l'~** originally; originel, ~le original

ornement *m* ornament; ornementer ornament

orner decorate *(de* with)

orphelin, ~e *m/f* orphan; orphelinat *m* orphanage

orteil *m* toe

orthographe *f* spelling

ortie *f* BOT nettle

os *m* bone

osciller PHYS oscillate; *d'un pendule* swing; **~ entre** *fig* waver between

osé daring; oser: **~ faire** dare to do

osier *m* BOT osier; **en ~** wicker

ossements *mpl* bones; osseux, -euse ANAT bone *atr*; *visage, mains* bony

ostensible evident

otage *m* hostage

ôter remove; MATH take away

ou *or*; **~ bien** or (else); **~ ... ~ ...** either ... or

où *where*; **d'~ vient-il?** where does he come from?; **d'~ l'on peut déduire que ...** from which it can be deduced that

...; **le jour ~** ... the day when
...

ouate f absorbent cotton, Br
cotton wool; **ouater** pad,
quilt

oubli m forgetting; (omission)
oversight; **tomber dans l'~**
sink into oblivion; **oublier**
forget; **~ de faire** forget to do

ouest 1 m west; **à l'~ de** (to
the) west of **2** adj west, western

oui yes

ouï-dire: par ~ by hearsay

ouïe f hearing; **~s** zo gills

ouragan m hurricane

ourler hem; **ourlet** m hem

ours m bear; **ourse** f she-
-bear; **la Grande Ourse** ASTR
the Great Bear

oursin m zo sea urchin

outil m tool; **outillage** m tools
pl

outrage m insult; **outrager**
insult

outrance f excessively; **à ~**
excessively

outre 1 prép in addition to **2**
adv: **en ~** besides; **passer ~**
ignore

outré: être ~ de ou **par** be out-
raged by

outre-Atlantique on the other side of the Atlantic

outre-Manche on the other
side of the Channel

outre-mer: d'~ overseas atr

ouvert open; **ouverture** f
opening; MUS overture

ouvrable working; **jour** m **~**
workday; **ouvrage** m work;
ouvragé ornate

ouvre-boîtes m can opener,
Br aussi tin opener; **ouvre-
-bouteilles** m bottle opener

ouvrier, -ère 1 adj working-
-class **2** m/f worker

ouvrir 1 v/t open; radio, gaz
turn on **2** v/i d'un magasin
open; **s'~** open; fig open up

ovale m & adj oval

ovni m (= **objet volant non
identifié**) UFO (= unidenti-
fied flying object)

oxygène m oxygen

P

pacifier pacify; **pacifique 1**
adj personne peace-loving;
coexistence peaceful **2** m **le
Pacifique** the Pacific; **pacifiste** m/f & adj pacifist

pacte m pact; **~ avec** come to terms with

pagaie f paddle

pagaïe, pagaille f F mess

page f page; **~ d'accueil** IN-
FORM home page

paie, paye f pay; **paiement** m
payment

païen, -ne m/f & adj pagan

paillasson m doormat

paille f straw

pape

pain m bread; **~ au chocolat** chocolate croissant; **~ complet** whole wheat ou Br wholemeal bread; **~ d'épice** gingerbread; **petit ~** roll

pair 1 adj nombre even **2** m: **hors ~** unrivaled, Br unrivalled; **fille** f **au ~** au pair

paire f: **une ~ de** a pair of

paisible peaceful; personne quiet

paître graze

paix f peace; (calme) peace and quiet

Pakistan: **le ~** Pakistan; **pakistanais**, **~e** Pakistani; **Pakistanais**, **~e** m/f Pakistani

palais m **1** palace; **~ de justice** law courts pl **2** ANAT palate

pale f blade

pâle pale; fig: style colorless, Br colourless; imitation pale

Palestine: **la ~** Palestine; **palestinien**, **~ne** Palestinian; **Palestinien**, **~ne** m/f Palestinian

palette f de peinture palette

pâleur f paleness, pallor

palier m d'un escalier landing; TECH bearing; (phase) stage

pâlir go pale; de couleurs fade

palissade f fence

pallier alleviate; manque make up for

palme f BOT palm; de natation flipper; **palmier** m BOT palm tree

pâlot, **~te** pale

palper feel; MÉD palpate

palpitant fig exciting, thrilling; **palpitations** fpl palpitations; **palpiter** du cœur pound

pamplemousse m grapefruit

pan m de vêtement tail; de mur section

panache m plume; **avoir du ~** have panache; **panaché** m shandy-gaff, Br shandy

pancarte f sign; de manifestation placard

pané breaded

panier m basket

panique f panic; **paniquer** panic

panne f breakdown; **~ en panne** have a breakdown; **tomber en ~ sèche** run out of gas ou Br petrol; **~ d'électricité** power outage, Br power failure

panneau m board; TECH panel; **~ de signalisation** road-sign

panorama m panorama

pansement m dressing; **panser** blessure dress; cheval groom

pantalon m pants pl, Br trousers pl; **un ~** a pair of pants

pantelant panting

pantois inv: **rester ~** be speechless

pantoufle f slipper

paon m peacock

papa m dad

papal REL papal; **pape** m REL pope

paperasse f (souvent au pl ~s) péj papers pl

papeterie f magasin stationery store, Br stationer's

papi, papy m F grandpa

papier m paper; ~ (d')**aluminium** kitchen foil; ~ **hygiénique** toilet tissue; ~s **d'identité** identification, ID

papillon m butterfly; TECH wing nut; F (contravention) (parking) ticket

paquebot m liner

pâquerette f BOT daisy

Pâques msg ou fpl Easter; joyeuses ~! happy Easter

paquet m packet; de sucre, café bag; de la poste parcel

par lieu through; passif, moyen by; ~ **terre** on the ground; ~ **beau temps** in fine weather; ~ **curiosité** out of curiosity; ~ **hasard** by chance; **diviser** ~ **quatre** divide by four; ~ **an** a year; **finir** ~ **faire** finish by doing

parabolique: **antenne** f ~ satellite dish

paracétamol m paracetamol

parachute m parachute; **parachutiste** m/f parachutist; MIL para(trooper)

parade f parade; en escrime parry; à un argument counter

paradis m paradise

paradoxe m paradox

parages mpl: ; **dans les** ~ around; **dans les** ~ **de** in the vicinity of

paragraphe m paragraph

paraître appear; d'un livre come out, be published; **il paraît que** it seems that, it would appear that; **laisser** ~ show

parallèle 1 adj parallel (à to) **2** f MATH parallel (line) **3** m GÉOGR parallel (aussi fig)

paralyser paralyse; **paralysie** f paralysis

paramètre m parameter

paranoïaque m/f & adj paranoid

parapharmacie f (non-dispensing) pharmacy; **produits** toiletries pl

paraplégique m/f & adj paraplegic

parapluie m umbrella

parasite 1 adj parasitic **2** m parasite; ~s **radio** interference

parasol m parasol; de plage beach umbrella

paratonnerre m lightning rod, Br lightning conductor

paravent m windbreak

parc m park; **pour enfant** playpen

parcelle f de terrain parcel

parce que because

par-ci adv: ~, **par-là** espace here and there; temps now and then

parcimonie f: **avec** ~ parcimoniously

parcourir région travel through; distance cover; texte read quickly

parcours m route; *course d'automobiles* circuit

par-derrière from behind

par-dessous from underneath

pardessus m overcoat

par-dessus over

par-devant from the front

pardon m forgiveness; *~!* sorry!; *~?* excuse me?; **pardonner:** *~ qc à qn* forgive s.o. sth

pare-brise m windshield, *Br* windscreen

pare-chocs m bumper

pareil, ~le 1 adj similar (*à* to); (*tel*) such; *c'est toujours ~* it's always the same **2** adv: *habillés ~* similarly dressed, dressed the same way

parent, ~e 1 adj related **2** m/f relative; *~s* (*mère et père*) parents; **parenté** f relationship

parenthèse f parenthesis, *Br* (round) bracket; *entre ~s* fig by the way

parer *attaque* ward off; *en escrime* parry

paresse f laziness; **paresseux, -euse** lazy

parfait 1 adj perfect; *avant le substantif* complete **2** m GRAM perfect (tense)

parfois sometimes

parfum m perfume; *d'une glace* flavor, *Br* flavour

pari m bet; **parier** bet

parisien, ~ne Parisian, of/ from Paris; **Parisien, ~ne** m/f Parisian

parité f ÉCON parity

parking m parking lot, *Br* car park; *édifice* parking garage, *Br* car park

parlant *comparaison* striking; *preuves* decisive

Parlement m Parliament; **parlementaire 1** adj Parliamentary **2** m/f Parliamentarian

parler 1 v/i speak, talk; *sans ~ de* not to mention **2** v/t: *~ affaires* talk business; *~ anglais* speak English

parmi among

parodie f parody

paroi f partition

paroisse f REL parish

parole f word; *faculté* speech; *donner la ~ à qn* give s.o. the floor

parquer *bétail* pen; *réfugiés* dump

parquet m (parquet) floor; JUR public prosecutor's office

parrain m godfather; *dans un club* sponsor

parsemer sprinkle (*de* with)

part f share; (*fraction*) part; *faire ~ de qc à qn* inform s.o. of sth; *de la ~ de qn* on behalf of s.o.; *d'une ~ ... d'autre ~* on the one hand ... on the other hand; *autre ~* elsewhere; *nulle ~* nowhere; *quelque ~* somewhere; *à ~ traiter etc* separately; *à ~ cela* apart from that

partage m division; **partager**

partenaire m/f partner

parterre m de fleurs bed; au théâtre rear orchestra, Br rear stalls pl

parti[1] m side; POL party; **prendre ~ pour** side with; **tirer ~ de qc** turn sth to good use; **~ pris** preconceived idea

parti[2] adj F: **être ~** (ivre) be tight

partial biassed

participant, ~e m/f participant; **participer: ~ à** participate in, take part in; **bénéfices** share; **frais** contribute to; **douleur, succès** share in

particularité f special feature; **particulier, ~ère** 1 adj particular, special; **privé** private; **~ à** peculiar to 2 m (private) individual; **particulièrement** particularly

partie f part; d'un jeu game; JUR party; **lutte** struggle; **en ~** partly; **faire ~ de qch** be part of sth

partiel, ~le partial

partir leave (**à, pour** for); SP start; de la saleté come out; **~ de qc** (provenir de) come from sth; **à ~ de** (starting) from

partisan, ~e m/f supporter; MIL m partisan

partition f MUS score; POL partition

partout everywhere

parure f finery; de bijoux set

parvenir arrive; **faire ~ qc à qn** forward sth to s.o.; **~ à faire** manage to do

parvenu, ~e m/f upstart

pas[1] m step, pace; **faux ~** stumble; fig blunder, faux pas

pas[2] adv not; **ne ... ~** not; **il ne pleut ~** it's not raining; **il n'a ~ plu** it didn't rain

passable acceptable

passage m passage; fig (changement) changeover; **~ à niveau** grade crossing, Br level crossing; **de ~** passing

passager, ~ère 1 adj passing 2 m/f passenger

passant, ~e m/f passerby

passe f SP pass

passé[1] adj past 2 prép: **~ dix heures** after ten o'clock 3 m past; **~ composé** GRAM perfect

passe-partout m skeleton key

passe-passe m: **tour** m **de ~** conjuring trick

passeport m passport

passer 1 v/i pass, go past; d'un film show; **~ chez qn** drop by at s.o.'s place; **~ de mode** go out of fashion; **~ en seconde** AUTO shift into second; **~ pour qc** pass as sth; **faire ~** personne let past; **plat, journal** pass; **laisser ~ personne** let past; **lumière** let in; chance let slip 2 v/t

pauvre

frontière cross; *(omettre)* miss (out); *temps* spend; *examen* take; *vêtement* slip on; *film* show; *contrat* enter into; **~** *qc* **à** *qn* pass s.o. sth, pass sth to s.o. 3: **se ~** *(se produire)* happen; **se ~ de** *qc* do without sth

passerelle *f* footbridge; MAR gangway; AVIAT steps *pl*

passe-temps *m* hobby, pastime

passif, -ive 1 *adj* passive **2** *m* GRAM passive; COMM liabilities *pl*

passion *f* passion; **passionnant** *adj* exciting; **passionné, ~e 1** *adj* passionate **2** *m/f* enthusiast; **passionner** excite; **se ~ pour** have a passion for

passivité *f* passiveness, passivity

passoire *f* sieve

pastel *m* pastel

pastèque *f* BOT watermelon

pasteur *m* REL pastor

pasteuriser pasteurize

pastille *f* pastille

patate *f* F potato, spud F

patauger flounder

pâte *f* paste; CUIS: **à pain** dough; **à tarte** pastry; **~s** pasta *sg*

pâté *m* paté; **~ de maisons** block of houses

patère *f* coat peg

paternaliste paternalistic

paternel, ~le paternal

pâteux, -euse doughy; *bouche* dry

pathétique touching; F *(mauvais)* pathetic

pathologique pathological

patience *f* patience; **patient, ~e** *m/f* & *adj* patient; **patienter** wait

patin *m*: **faire du ~** go skating; **~ à roulettes** roller skate; **patinage** *m* skating; **patiner** skate; AUTO skid; *de roues* spin; **patineur, -euse** *m/f* skater; **patinoire** *f* skating rink

pâtisserie *f* cake shop; *gâteaux* cakes; **pâtissier, -ère** *m/f* pastrycook

patois *m* dialect

patrie *f* homeland

patrimoine *m* heritage

patriote 1 *adj* patriotic **2** *m/f* patriot

patron *m* boss; *(propriétaire)* owner; *d'une auberge* landlord; REL patron saint; *de couture* pattern

patronne *f* boss; *(propriétaire)* owner; *d'une auberge* landlady; REL patron saint

patronner sponsor

patrouille *f* patrol

patte *f* paw; *d'un oiseau* foot; *d'un insecte* leg; F hand, paw *péj*

paume *f* palm

paumer F lose

paupière *f* eyelid

pause *f* *(silence)* pause; *(interruption)* break; **~ café** coffee break

pauvre 1 *adj* poor **2** *m/f* poor

person; **les ~s** the poor *pl*;
pauvreté *f* poverty

pavé *m* paving; *(chaussée)*
pavement, *Br* road surface;
pierres rondes cobbles *pl*;
un ~ a paving stone; *rond*
a cobblestone; **paver** pave

pavillon *m* *(maisonnette)*
small house; *MAR* flag

pavot *m* BOT poppy

payable payable

payant *spectateur* paying;
parking which charges; *fig*
profitable

payer 1 *v/t* pay; **~ qc dix euros** pay ten euros for sth 2
v/i pay 3: **se ~ qc** treat o.s.
to sth

pays *m* country; **mal *m* du ~**
homesickness

paysage *m* landscape

paysan, **~ne 1** *m/f* small farmer; HIST peasant 2 *adj mœurs*
country *atr*

Pays-Bas *mpl*: **les ~** the
Netherlands

PC *m* (= *personal computer*)
PC

PDG *m* (= *président-direc-
teur général*) President,
CEO (= Chief Executive
Officer)

péage *m d'une autoroute* toll-
booth; **autoroute à ~** turnpike, toll road

peau *f* skin; *cuir* leather

pêche[1] *f* BOT peach

pêche[2] *f* fishing; *poissons*
catch

péché *m* sin; **pécher** sin

pêcher[1] *m* BOT peach tree

pêcher[2] 1 *v/t* fish for; *(attraper)* catch 2 *v/i* fish; **~ à la ligne** go angling

pêcheur, -eresse *m/f* sinner

pêcheur *m* fisherman; **~ à la
ligne** angler

pédagogie *f* education,
teaching; **pédagogique** educational; **méthode** teaching

pédale *f* pedal; **pédaler** *à vélo*
pedal

pédéraste *m* homosexual

pédestre: **sentier** *m* ~ footpath; **randonnée** *f* ~ hike

pédiatre *m/f* MÉD pediatrician

pédicure *m/f* podiatrist, *Br*
chiropodist

pègre *f* underworld

peigne *m* comb; **peigner**
comb; **se ~** comb one's hair

peignoir *m* robe, *Br* dressing
gown

peindre paint; *(décrire)* depict

peine *f* *(punition)* punishment; *(effort)* trouble; *(difficulté)* difficulty; *(chagrin)*
sorrow; **ce n'est pas la ~**
there's no point, it's not
worth it; **valoir la ~ de faire
qc** be worth doing sth; **à ~**
scarcely, hardly

peiner 1 *v/t* upset 2 *v/i* labor,
Br labour

peintre *m* painter

peinture *f* paint; *action, tableau* painting; *description*
depiction

péjoratif, -ive pejorative
pelage *m* coat
peler peel
pèlerin *m* pilgrim
pelle *f* spade
pellicule *f* film; **~s** dandruff
pelote *f* de fil ball
peloter F grope, feel up
peloton *m* ball; MIL platoon;
SP pack; **pelotonner** wind
into a ball; **se ~ contre qn**
snuggle up to s.o.
pelouse *f* lawn
peluche *f* jouet soft toy; **ours**
m **en ~** teddy bear
pelure *f* de fruit peel
pénaliser penalize; **pénalité** *f*
penalty
penchant *m* (*inclination*) liking, penchant
pencher 1 *v/t* put tilt; **penché**
écriture sloping; **~ la tête en
avant** bend *ou* lean forward
2 *v/i* lean; *d'un plateau* tilt;
d'un bateau list; **se ~ sur
un problème** fig examine a
problem
pendant¹ 1 *prép* during; *avec
chiffre* for **2** *conj:* **~ que**
while
**pendant² ** *adj* oreilles pendu-
lous; (*en instance*) pending
penderie *f* armoire, Br wardrobe
pendre hang; **se ~** hang o.s.
pendule 1 *m* pendulum **2** *f*
(*horloge*) clock
pénétrer 1 *v/t* penetrate; *pensées, personne* fathom out **2**
v/i: **~ dans** penetrate; *mai-*

son, bureaux get into
pénible *travail, vie* hard; *nouvelle* painful; *caractère* difficult
pénicilline *f* penicillin
péninsule *f* peninsula
pénis *m* penis
pénitence *f* REL penitence;
(*punition*) punishment; **pénitencier** *m* penitentiary,
Br prison
pénombre *f* semi-darkness
pense-bête *m* reminder
pensée *f* thought; BOT pansy;
penser think; **~ à** (*réfléchir
à*) think about; **faire ~
qn à faire qch** remind s.o.
to do sth; **~ faire qch** (*avoir
l'intention*) be thinking of
doing sth; **penseur** *m* think-
er; **pensif, -ive** thoughtful
pension *f* (*allocation*) allowance; *logement* rooming
house, Br boarding house;
école boarding school; **~
complète** American plan,
Br full board; **pensionnaire**
m/f d'un hôtel guest; *écolier*
boarder; **pensionnat** *m*
boarding school
pente *f* slope; **en ~** sloping
Pentecôte: **la ~** Pentecost
pénurie *f* shortage
pépin *m* de fruit seed
perçant *regard, froid* piercing
percée *f* breakthrough
percepteur *m* tax collector
perception *f* perception; *des
impôts* collection; *bureau*
tax office

percer 1 v/t make a hole in; *porte* make; (*transpercer*) pierce **2** v/i *du soleil* break through; **perceuse** f drill

percevoir perceive; *impôts* collect

perche f zo perch; *en bois, métal* pole

percher: (se) ~ *d'un oiseau* perch; F live; **perchoir** m perch

percolateur m percolator

percussion f mus percussion

percuter crash into

perdant, ~e **1** adj losing **2** m/f loser

perdre 1 v/t lose; *occasion* miss; *son temps* waste; **se** ~ *disparaître* disappear; *d'une personne* get lost **2** v/i: ~ *au change* lose out

perdrix f partridge

père m father (*aussi* REL)

perfection f perfection; **perfectionnement** m perfecting; **perfectionner** perfect; **se** ~ **en anglais** improve one's English

perfide treacherous

perforer perforate; *cuir* punch

performance f performance; **performant** high-performance

péril m peril; **périlleux, -euse** perilous

périmé out of date

périmètre m math perimeter

période f period; **en** ~ **de** in times of; **périodique 1** adj

periodic 2 m periodical

périphérie f *d'une ville* outskirts pl; **périphérique** m beltway, Br ringroad

périr perish; **périssable** *nourriture* perishable

péritel: prise f ~ scart

perle f pearl; (*boule percée*) bead; *fig: personne* gem; *de sang* drop; **perler: la sueur perlait sur son front** he had beads of sweat on his forehead

permanence f permanence; **être de** ~ be on duty; **en** ~ constantly; **permanent**, ~e **1** adj permanent **2** f *coiffure* perm

perméable permeable

permettre allow, permit; ~ **à qn de faire qch** allow s.o. to do sth; **se** ~ **qc** allow o.s. sth

permis m permit; **passer son** ~ sit one's driving test; ~ **de conduire** driver's license, Br driving licence; ~ **de séjour** residence permit

permission f permission; MIL leave

perpendiculaire perpendicular (**à** to)

perpétrer JUR perpetrate

perpétuel, ~le perpetual; **perpétuer** perpetuate; **perpétuité** f: **à** ~ in perpetuity; JUR *condamné* to life imprisonment

perplexe perplexed, puzzled

perron m steps pl

perroquet m parrot

perruque f wig

persécuter persecute

persévérance f perseverance; **persévérer** persevere (*dans* in)

persienne f shutter

persil m BOT parsley

persistance f persistence; **persister** persist (*à faire* in doing); *~ dans sa décision* stick to one's decision

personnage m character; (*dignitaire*) important person

personnalité f personality

personne¹ f person; *deux ~s* two people; *par ~* per person, each; *les ~s âgées* the old pl, old people pl

personne² pron no-one, nobody; *il n'y avait ~* no-one was there, there wasn't anyone there; *je ne vois jamais ~* I never see anyone; *qui que ce soit* anyone, anybody

personnel, ~le 1 adj personal; *conversation, courrier* private **2** m personnel pl, staff pl

perspective f perspective; *fig: pour l'avenir* prospect

perspicace shrewd; **perspicacité** f shrewdness

persuader persuade (*de faire* to do); *se ~* convince o.s.

perte f loss; *fig* (*destruction*) ruin; *à ~ de vue* as far as the eye can see; *une ~ de temps* a waste of time

pertinent relevant

perturbateur, -trice disruptive; **perturber** *personne* upset; *trafic* disrupt

pervers perverse; **pervertir** pervert

pesant heavy; **pesanteur** f PHYS gravity

pèse-personne f scales pl

peser weigh; *fig* weigh up; *mots* weigh

pessimisme m pessimism; **pessimiste 1** adj pessimistic **2** m/f pessimist

pétale f petal

pétard m firecracker; F (*bruit*) racket

péter F fart F

pétillant sparkling; **pétiller** *du feu* crackle; *d'une boisson, d'yeux* sparkle

petit, ~e 1 adj small, little; *~ à ~* gradually, little by little; *~ ami* m boyfriend; *~e amie* f girlfriend **2** m child; *une chatte et ses ~s* a cat and her young; *attendre des ~s* be pregnant

petite-fille f granddaughter

petit-fils m grandson

pétition f petition

pétrifier turn to stone; *fig* petrify

pétrin m fig F mess

pétrir knead

pétrole m oil, petroleum; *~ brut* crude (oil); **pétrolier, -ère 1** adj oil atr **2** m tanker

peu 1 adv: *~ gentil* not very nice; *~ après* a little after;

j'ai ~ dormi I didn't sleep much; **~ de pain** not much bread; **~ de choses à faire** not many things to do; **~ de gens** few people; *dans ~ de temps* in a little while; *un ~* a little, a bit; *un tout petit ~* just a very little, just a little bit; *un ~ de chocolat* a little chocolate, a bit of chocolate; *un ~ plus long* a bit *ou* little longer; *de ~ rater le bus* only just; **~ à ~** little by little; **à ~ près** (*plus ou moins*) more or less; (*presque*) almost

peuple *m* people; **peupler** *région* populate; *maison* live in

peuplier *m* BOT poplar

peur *f* fear (*de de*); *avoir ~* be frightened, be afraid (*de* of); *faire ~ à qn* frighten s.o. (*de ~ que* (+*subj*) in case; **peureux, -euse** fearful, timid

peut-être perhaps, maybe

phare *m* MAR lighthouse; AVIAT beacon; AUTO headlight; *se mettre en (pleins) ~s* switch to full beam

pharmacie *f* pharmacy, *Br aussi* chemist's; *science* pharmacy; *médicaments* pharmaceuticals *pl*; **pharmacien, -ne** *m/f* pharmacist

phénomène *m* phenomenon

philosophe *m* philosopher; **philosophie** *f* philosophy; **philosophique** philosophical

phobie *f* phobia

photo *f* photo; *l'art* photography; **prendre qn en ~** take a photo of s.o.

photocopie *f* photocopy; **photocopier** photocopy; **photocopieur** *m*, **photocopieuse** *f* photocopier

photographe *m/f* photographer; **photographie** *f* photograph; *l'art* photography; **photographier** photograph

phrase *f* GRAM sentence; MUS phrase; **sans ~s** straight out

physicien, ~ne *m/f* physicist

physique 1 *adj* physical **2** *m* physique **3** *f* physics

piailler *d'un oiseau* chirp; F *d'un enfant* scream

pianiste *m/f* pianist; **piano** *m* piano; **~ à queue** grand piano

pic *m* pick; *d'une montagne* peak; **à ~ tomber** steeply

pichet *m* pitcher, *Br* jug

pickpocket *m* pickpocket

pick-up *m* pick-up (truck)

pie *f* ZO magpie

pièce *f* piece; *de machine* part; (*chambre*) room; (*document*) document; *de monnaie* coin; *de théâtre* play; **cinq euros (la) ~** five euros each; **mettre en ~s** smash to smithereens; **~ jointe** enclosure

pied *m* foot; *d'un meuble* leg; *d'un champignon* stalk; **à ~** on foot; **~s nus** barefoot; **au ~ de** at the foot of; **mettre**

sur ~ set up

piège *m* trap; **piégé: voiture** *f*
~e car bomb; **piéger** trap;
voiture booby-trap

piercing *m* body piercing

pierre *f* stone; ~ **tombale**
gravestone; **pierreux, -euse**
sol stony

piétiner 1 *v/t* trample; *fig*
trample underfoot **2** *v/i fig*
(ne pas avancer) mark time

piéton, ~ne 1 *m/f* pedestrian **2**
adj: **zone** *f* ~**ne** pedestria-
nized zone, *Br* pedestrian
precinct

pieu *m* stake; F pit F

pieuvre *f* octopus

pieux, -euse *pious*

pigeon *m* pigeon

piger F understand, get F

pigment *m* pigment

pile¹ *f (tas)* pile; ÉL battery;
monnaie tails

pile² *adv:* **s'arrêter** ~ stop
dead; **à deux heures** ~ at
two o'clock on the dot

piler *ail* crush; *amandes* grind

pilier *m* pillar *(aussi fig)*

pillage *m* pillage, plunder;
piller pillage

pilote 1 *m* pilot; AUTO driver **2**
adj: **usine** *f* ~ pilot plant; **pi-**
loter pilot; AUTO drive

pilule *f* pill

piment *m* pimento; *fig* spice

pimenter spice up

pin *m* BOT pine

pinard *m* F wine

pince *f* pliers *pl*; *d'un crabe*
pincer; ~ **à épiler** tweezers

pl: ~ **à linge** clothespin, *Br*
clothespeg

pinceau *m* brush

pincer pinch; MUS pluck

ping-pong *m* ping-pong

pinson *m* chaffinch

pintade *f* guinea fowl

pioche *f* pickax, *Br* pickaxe;
piocher dig

pioncer F sleep, *Br* kip F

pipe *f* pipe

pipi *m* F pee F

pique *m aux cartes* spades

pique-nique *m* picnic

piquer *d'une abeille, des or-*
ties sting; *d'un moustique,*
serpent bite; *d'épine* prick;
fig: curiosité excite; ~ **qch**
(voler) pinch F; **se** ~ prick
o.s.; *se faire une piqûre* inject
o.s.

piquet *m* stake; ~ **de tente**
tent peg; ~ **de grève** picket
line

piquette *f* cheap wine

piqûre *f d'abeille* sting; *de*
moustique bite; MÉD injection

pirate *m* pirate; ~ **informati-**
que hacker; ~ **de l'air** hijacker; **pirater** pirate

pire worse; *le/la* ~ the worst

piscine *f* (swimming) pool; ~
couverte/en plein air in-
door/outdoor pool

pisser F pee F, piss F

piste *f* track; AVIAT runway; *ski*
alpin piste; *ski de fond* trail;
~ **cyclable** cycle path

pistolet *m* pistol

piston *m* piston; **pistonner** F pull strings for

pitié *f* pity; **avoir ~ de qn** take pity on s.o.

pitoyable pitiful

pittoresque picturesque

pivot *m* pivot

pizza *f* pizza

PJ (= **pièce(s) jointe(s)**) enclosure(s)

placard *m* (*armoire*) cabinet, Br cupboard; (*affiche*) poster; **placarder** *avis* stick up

place *f* de ville square; (*lieu*) place; (*siège*) seat; (*espace libre*) room, space; (*emploi*) position; **sur ~** on the spot; **à la ~ de** instead of; **~ de place avec** change places with

placement *m* (*emploi*) placement; FIN investment; **agence** *f* **de ~** employment agency; **placer** put, place; (*procurer emploi à*) find a job for; *argent* invest; *dans une famille etc* find a place for; **se ~** take one's place

plafond *m* ceiling

plage *f* beach; *lieu* seaside resort

plagiat *m* plagiarism

plaider *v/i* JUR plead **2** *v/t*: **~ la cause de qn** defend s.o.'s cause; *fig* plead s.o.'s cause

plaidoyer *m* JUR speech for the defense *ou* Br defence; *fig* plea

plaie *f* cut; *fig* wound

plaignant, **~e** *m/f* JUR plaintiff

plaindre pity; **se ~** complain

(**de** about; **à** to)

plaine *f* plain

plainte *f* complaint; (*lamentation*) moan

plaire: **s'il vous plaît, s'il te plaît** please; **Paris me plaît** I like Paris; **ça me plairait d'aller ...** I would like to go ...; **se ~ de personnes** be attracted to each other

plaisance *f*: **port** *m* **de ~** marina

plaisanter joke; **plaisanterie** *f* joke

plaisir *m* pleasure; **par ~, pour le ~** for pleasure; **faire ~ à** please

plan 1 *adj* flat, level **2** *m* (*surface*) surface; (*projet, relevé*) plan; **premier ~** foreground; **sur ce ~** in that respect; **sur le ~ économique** in economic terms

planche *f* plank; **~ à voile** sailboard

plancher *m* floor

planer hover; *fig* live in another world

planète *f* planet

planeur *m* glider

planifier plan

planning *m*: **~ familial** family planning

planquer F hide; **se ~** hide

plant *m* AGR seedling; (*plantation*) plantation

plante¹ *f* plant

plante² *f*: **~ du pied** sole of the foot

planter plant; *jardin* plant up

plus

poteau hammer in; *tente* put up

plaque *f* plate; *(inscription)* plaque; **~ électrique** hotplate; **~ tournante** turntable; *fig* hub

plaquer *argent, or* plate; *meuble* veneer; *fig* pin **(contre** to, against); F *(abandonner)* dump F; *au rugby* tackle

plastique *adj* & *m* plastic

plat 1 *adj* flat; *eau* still **2** *m* dish

plateau *m* tray; *de théâtre* stage; TV, *d'un film* set; GÉOGR plateau; **~ de fromages** cheeseboard

plate-bande *f* flower bed

plate-forme *f* platform; **~ de lancement** launch pad

platine 1 *m* CHIM platinum **2** *f*: **~ laser** *ou* **CD** CD player

platitude *f* dullness; *(lieu commun)* platitude

plâtre *m* plaster; **plâtrer** plaster

plausible plausible

plein 1 *adj* full **(de** of); **en ~ air** in the open (air); **en ~ Paris** in the middle of Paris; **en ~ jour** in broad daylight **2** *adv*: **~ de** F lots of, a whole bunch of F **3** *m*: **faire le ~** AUTO fill up

pleurer 1 *v/i* cry; **~ sur** complain about **2** *v/t (regretter)* mourn

pleurnicher F snivel

pleuvoir rain; *il pleut* it's raining

pli *m* fold; *d'une jupe* pleat; *d'un pantalon* crease; *(enveloppe)* envelope; *(lettre)* letter; **plier 1** *v/t (rabattre)* fold; *(courber, ployer)* bend **2** *v/i* bend; *fig (céder)* give in; **se ~ à** *(se soumettre)* submit to

plomb *m* lead; **sans ~** *essence* unleaded

plombage *m* filling

plomberie *f* plumbing; **plombier** *m* plumber

plongée *f* diving; **plonger 1** *v/i* dive **2** *v/t* plunge; **se ~ dans** bury o.s. in; **plongeur, -euse** *m/f* diver

pluie *f* rain; *fig* shower

plumage *m* plumage; **plume** *f* feather; **plumer** pluck; *fig* fleece

plupart: *la ~ d'entre nous* most of us; *pour la ~* mostly; *la ~ du temps* most of the time

pluriel, ~le *adj* & *m* plural

plus 1 *adv* more **(que, de** than); **~ grand** bigger; **~ efficace** more efficient; **le ~ grand** the biggest; **le ~ efficace** the most efficient; **~ il vieillit ~ il dort** the older he gets the more he sleeps; **le ~** the most; **tu en veux ~?** do you want some more?; **20 euros de ~** 20 euros more; **nous n'avons ~ d'argent** we have no more money, we don't have any more money; **elle n'y habite ~**

plusieurs

she doesn't live there any more, she no longer lives there; **je ne le reverrai - jamais** I won't see him ever again; **moi non -** me neither **2** *prép* MATH plus

plusieurs several

plutôt rather

pluvieux, -euse rainy

pneu *m* tire, *Br* tyre

pneumonie *f* pneumonia

poche *f* pocket; ZO pouch; **livre** *m* **de -** paperback; **argent de -** pocket money

pocher *œufs* poach

pochette *f* pour photos etc folder; *d'un disque, CD* sleeve; *(sac)* bag

poêle 1 *m* stove **2** *f* frypan, *Br* frying pan

poème *m* poem

poésie *f* poetry; *(poème)* poem

poète *m* poet; **poétique** poetic; *atmosphère* romantic

poids *m* weight; *fig (charge, fardeau)* burden; *(importance)* weight; **perdre/prendre du -** lose/gain weight

poignard *m* dagger; **poignarder** stab

poignée *f* petit nombre handful; *d'une valise etc* handle; **~ de main** handshake

poignet *m* wrist

poil *m* hair; **à ~** naked; **poilu** hairy

poinçonner *argent* hallmark; *billet* punch

poing *m* fist; **coup** *m* **de ~**

---

punch

point¹ *m* point; *de couture* stitch; **deux ~s** colon; **être sur le ~ de faire** be on the point of doing; **à ~** *viande* medium; **à ce ~** so much; **~ du jour** dawn; **~ de vue** point of view

point² *adv litt*: **il ne le fera ~** he will not do it

pointe *f* point; *d'asperge* tip; **en ~** pointed; **de ~** *technologie* leading-edge; *secteur* high-tech; **une ~ de** a touch of

pointer 1 *v/t sur liste* check, *Br* tick off **2** *v/i d'un employé* clock in

pointillé *m*: **les ~s** the dotted line

pointilleux, -euse fussy

pointu pointed; *voix* high-pitched

pointure *f* (shoe) size

point-virgule *m* GRAM semi-colon

poire *f* pear

poireau *m* BOT leek

poirier *m* BOT pear (tree)

pois *m* BOT pea; **petits ~** garden peas

poison 1 *m* poison **2** *m/f fig* F nuisance, pest

poisson *m* fish; **Poissons** *mpl* ASTROL Pisces

poissonnerie *f* fish shop, *Br* fishmonger's

poitrine *f* chest; *(seins)* bosom

poivre *m* pepper; **poivrer**

pepper

poivron *m* bell pepper, *Br* pepper

polaire polar; **pôle** *m* pole; *fig* center, *Br* centre; focus; **~ Nord** North Pole; **~ Sud** South Pole

poli (*courtois*) polite; *métal, caillou* polished

police *f* police; **~ d'assurance** insurance policy

policier, -ère 1 *adj* police *atr*; *film, roman* detective *atr* **2** *m* police officer

polir polish

politesse *f* politeness

politicien, ~ne *m/f* politician

politique 1 *adj* political; **homme** *m* ~ politician **2** *f* *d'un parti etc* policy; (*affaires publiques*) politics *sg*

pollen *m* pollen

polluer pollute; **pollution** *f* pollution; **~ atmosphérique** air pollution

Pologne: la ~ Poland; **polonais, ~e 1** *adj* Polish **2** *m langue* Polish; **Polonais, ~e** *m/f* Pole

poltron, ~ne *m/f* coward

polyclinique *f* (general) hospital

polycopié *m* (photocopied) handout

polystyrène *m* polystyrene

polyvalence *f* versatility; **polyvalent** multipurpose; *personne* versatile

pommade *f* MÉD ointment

pomme *f* apple; **~ de terre** po-

tato

pommette *f* ANAT cheekbone

pommier *m* BOT apple tree

pompe[1] *f faste* pomp; **~s funèbres** funeral director

pompe[2] *f* TECH pump; **à essence** gas pump, *Br* petrol pump; **pomper** pump; *fig* (*épuiser*) knock out

pompeux, -euse pompous

pompier *m* firefighter; **~s** fire department, *Br* fire brigade

pomponner F: **se ~** get dolled up F

poncer sand

ponctualité *f* punctuality; **ponctuel, ~le** *personne* punctual; *fig:* action one-off

ponctuer punctuate

pondération *f* *d'une personne* level-headedness; *de forces* balance; ÉCON weighting; **pondéré** *personne* level-headed; *forces* balanced; ÉCON weighted

pondre *œufs* lay; *fig* F come up with; *roman* churn out

poney *m* pony

pont *m* bridge; MAR deck; **faire le ~** make a long weekend of it

pontage *m*: **~ coronarien** (heart) bypass

pop *f* MUS pop

populaire popular; **populariser** popularize; **popularité** *f* popularity

population *f* population

porc *m* hog, pig; *fig* pig; *viande* de pork

porcelaine f porcelain

porcherie f hog ou pig farm

pore m pore; poreux, -euse porous

pornographique pornographic

port¹ m port; ~ de pêche fishing port

port² m d'armes carrying; courrier postage

portable 1 adj portable 2 m ordinateur laptop; téléphone cellphone, cell, Br mobile

portail m ARCH portal; d'un parc gate

portant mur load-bearing; à bout ~ at point-blank range; bien ~ well; mal ~ not well

portatif, -ive portable

porte f door; d'une ville gate; mettre qn à la ~ show s.o. the door

porte-bagages m AUTO roof rack; filet luggage rack; porte-bonheur m lucky charm; porte-clés m keyring; porte-documents m briefcase

portée f ZO litter; d'une arme range; (importance) significance; être à la ~ de qn fig be accessible to s.o.

portefeuille m portfolio (aussi POL, FIN); (porte-monnaie) billfold, Br wallet

portemanteau m coat rack; sur pied coatstand

porte-monnaie m coin purse, Br purse

porte-parole m spokesperson

porter 1 v/t carry; un vêtement, des lunettes etc wear; (apporter) take; bring; yeux, attention turn (sur to); toast drink; fruits, nom bear; ~ plainte make a complaint 2 v/i d'une voix carry; ~ sur (appuyer sur) rest on; (concerner) be about 3: il se porte bien/mal he's well/not well; se ~ candidat be a candidate, run

porteur m d'un message bearer

portier m doorman

portière f de train, voiture door

portion f portion

portrait m portrait

portugais, ~e 1 adj Portuguese 2 m langue Portuguese; Portugais, ~e m/f Portuguese; Portugal: le ~ Portugal

pose f d'un radiateur installation; de moquette fitting; de papier peint, rideaux hanging; (attitude) pose; posé poised, composed; poser 1 v/t (mettre) put (down); compteur, radiateur install, Br instal; moquette fit; papier peint, rideaux hang; problème pose; question ask; se ~ en set o.s. up as 2 v/i pose

positif, -ive positive

position f position

possédé possessed (de by); posséder own, possess;

pourboire

possesseur *m* owner; **possession** *f* possession, ownership

possibilité *f* possibility; **possible 1** *adj* possible; *le plus souvent* ~ as often as possible; *autant que* ~ as far as possible **2** *m*: *faire tout son* ~ do everything one can

poste¹ *f*, *Br aussi* face; *(bureau m de)* ~ post office; *mettre à la* ~ mail, *Br aussi* post

poste² *m* post; *(profession)* position; RAD, TV set; TÉL extension; ~ *de secours* first-aid post; ~ *de travail* INFORM work station

poster *soldat* post; *lettre* mail, *Br aussi* post

postérieur 1 *adj dans l'espace* back *atr*, rear *atr*; *dans le temps* later; ~ *à qch* after sth **2** *m* F posterior F

postérité *f* posterity

posthume posthumous

postier, **-ère** *m/f* post office employee

postillonner splutter

postuler apply for

posture *f* position, posture; *fig* position

pot *m* pot; ~ *à eau* water jug; *prendre un* ~ F have a drink; *avoir du* ~ F be lucky

potable fit to drink; *eau* ~ drinking water

potage *m* soup; **potager**, **-ère**: *jardin m* ~ kitchen garden

pot-au-feu *m* boiled beef dinner

pot-de-vin *m* F kickback F, bribe

poteau *m* post; ~ *indicateur* signpost

poterie *f* pottery; *objet* piece of pottery

potion *f* potion

potiron *m* BOT pumpkin

pou *m* louse

poubelle *f* trash can, *Br* dustbin

pouce *m* thumb

poudre *f* powder; *chocolat m en* ~ chocolate powder; **poudrier** *m* powder compact

pouffer: ~ *de rire* burst out laughing

poulailler *m* henhouse; *au théâtre* gallery, *Br* gods *pl*

poulain *m* zo foal

poule *f* hen; **poulet** *m* chicken

poulpe *m* octopus

pouls *m* pulse

poumon *m* lung

poupée *f* doll *(aussi fig)*

poupon *m* little baby

pour 1 *prép* for; ~ *20 euros de courses* 20 euros' worth of shopping; *je l'ai dit* ~ *te prévenir* I said that to warn you **2** *conj*: ~ *que* (+ *subj*) so that; *il parle trop vite* ~ *que je le comprenne* he speaks too fast for me to understand **3** *m*: *le* ~ *et le contre* the pros and the cons *pl*

pourboire *m* tip

pourcentage *m* percentage

pourparlers *mpl* talks

pourpre purple

pourquoi why

pourri rotten (*aussi fig*);
pourrir 1 *v/i* rot; *fig*: *d'une
situation* deteriorate **2** *v/t*
rot; *fig* (*corrompre*) corrupt;
(*gâter*) spoil; **pourriture** *f* rot
(*aussi fig*)

poursuite *f* chase, pursuit; *fig*
pursuit; **~s** JUR pursuits;
poursuivre pursue, chase;
fig: *bonheur* pursue; *de pensées* haunt; JUR sue; *malfaiteur* prosecute; (*continuer*)
carry on with

pourtant yet

pourvoir 1 *v/t emploi* fill; **~ de
voiture, maison** equip with **2**
v/i: **~ à besoins** provide for;
se ~ de provide o.s.

pourvu: ~ que (+ *subj*) provided that; *exprimant désir*
hopefully

pousse *f* AGR shoot; **poussée**
f thrust; MÉD outbreak; *de
fièvre* rise; *fig*: *de racisme
etc* upsurge; **pousser 1** *v/t*
push; *du vent* blow; *cri, soupir* give; *fig*: *recherches* pursue; **se ~ d'une foule** push
forward; *pour faire de la place* move over **2** *v/i* push; *de
cheveux, plantes* grow;
poussette *f pour enfants*
stroller, *Br* pushchair

poussière *f* dust; *particule*
speck of dust

poussin *m* chick

poutre *f* beam

pouvoir 1 *v/aux* be able to,
can; *je ne peux pas aider*
I can't *ou* cannot help; *je
ne pouvais pas accepter* I
couldn't accept, I wasn't
able to accept; *il se peut
que* (+ *subj*) it's possible
that; *tu aurais pu me prévenir!* you could have *ou* might
have warned me! **2** *m* power;
procuration power of attorney; *les ~s publics* the
authorities

prairie *f* meadow; *plaine* prairie

praline *f* praline

praticable *projet* feasible;
route passable

pratique 1 *adj* practical **2** *f*
practice; *expérience* practical experience; **pratiquement** (*presque*) practically;
dans la pratique in practice;
pratiquer practice, *Br* practise; *sports* play; *technique*
use; TECH *trou, passage*
make

pré *m* meadow

préado *m/f* pre-teen

préalable 1 *adj* (*antérieur*)
prior; (*préliminaire*) preliminary **2** *m* condition; *au ~* beforehand

préavis *m* notice

précaire precarious

précaution *f* caution; *mesure*
precaution; *par ~* as a precaution

précédent 1 *adj* previous **2** *m*

precedent; **précéder** precede

prêcher preach

précieux, -euse precious

précipice *m* precipice

précipitamment hastily, in a rush; **précipitation** *f* haste; **~s** *temps* precipitation; **précipiter** *(faire tomber)* plunge *(dans* into); *(pousser)* hurl; *(brusquer)* precipitate; *pas* hasten; **se ~** *(se jeter)* throw o.s.; *(se dépêcher)* rush

précis 1 *adj* precise **2** *m* precis, summary; **préciser** specify; **~ que** *(souligner)* make it clear that; **précision** *f* accuracy; *d'un geste* preciseness; *pour plus de* **~s** for further details

précoce early; *enfant* precocious; **précocité** *f* earliness; *d'un enfant* precociousness

préconçu preconceived

précurseur 1 *m* precursor **2** *adj*: *signe* **m ~** warning sign

prédateur, -trice 1 *adj* predatory **2** *m/f* predator

prédécesseur *m* predecessor

prédestiner predestine (**à qc** for sth; **à faire** to do)

prédiction *f* prediction

prédilection *f* predilection; **de ~** favorite, *Br* favourite

prédire predict

prédominer predominate

préfabriqué prefabricated

préface *f* preface

préférable preferable (**à** to);

préféré favorite, *Br* favourite; **préférence** *f* preference; **de ~** preferably; **préférer** prefer (**à** to); **~ faire qc** prefer to do sth; **je préfère que tu viennes** *(subj)* **demain** I would *ou* I'd prefer you to come tomorrow, I'd rather you came tomorrow

préfet *m* prefect; **~ de police** chief of police

préfixe *m* prefix

préjudice *m* harm; **porter ~ à** harm

préjugé *m* prejudice

prélever *échantillon* take; *montant* deduct (**sur** from)

préliminaire preliminary

préluder *fig*: **~ à** be the prelude to

prématuré premature

préméditer premeditate

premier, -ère 1 *adj* first; *rang* front; *objectif, cause* primary; *nombre* prime; **au ~ étage** on the second floor, *Br* on the first floor; ***Premier ministre*** Prime Minister; **le ~ août** August first, *Br* the first of August **2** *m/f*: *partir* **le ~** leave first **3** *m* second floor, *Br* first floor; **en ~** first **4** *f* THÉÂT first night; AUTO first (gear); *en train* first (class)

prémisse *f* premise

prémonition *f* premonition; **prémonitoire** *rêve* prophetic

prendre 1 *v/t* take; *(enlever)* take away; *froid* catch; *poids* put on; **~ qch à qn** take sth (away) from s.o. **2** v/i (*durcir*) set; *de mode* catch on; *d'un feu* take hold; **~ à droite** turn right **3**: **se ~** (*se laisser attraper*) get caught; **se ~ d'amitié pour qn** take a liking to s.o.

prénom *m* first name; **deuxième ~** middle name

préoccuper preoccupy; (*inquiéter*) worry; **se ~ de** worry about

préparatifs *mpl* preparations; **préparation** *f* preparation; **préparer** prepare; (*organiser*) arrange; **~ qn à qch** prepare s.o. for sth; **~ un examen** prepare for an exam; **se ~** get ready; *de dispute, d'orage* be brewing

prépondérant predominant

préposé *m* (*facteur*) mailman, *Br* postman; *au vestiaire* attendant; *des douanes* official; **préposée** *f* (*factrice*) mailwoman, *Br* postwoman

préretraite *f* early retirement

près 1 *adv* close, near; **de ~** closely **2** *prép*: **~ de qch** near sth, close to sth; **~ de 500** nearly 500

présage *m* omen

presbyte farsighted, *Br* longsighted

prescription *f* rule; MÉD prescription; **prescrire** stipulate; MÉD prescribe

présence *f* presence; **en ~ de** in the presence of; **présent 1** *adj* present **2** *m* present (*aussi* GRAM); **les ~s** those present; **à ~** at present; **à ~ que** now that; **jusqu'à ~** till now

présentateur, -trice *m/f* TV presenter; **~ météo** weatherman; **présentation** *f* presentation; **présenter** present; *chaise* offer; *personne* introduce; *pour un concours* put forward; *billet* show, present; *condoléances, félicitations* offer; *difficultés, dangers* involve; **se ~** introduce o.s.; *pour un poste, un emploi* apply; *aux élections* run; *de difficultés* come up

préservatif *m* condom

préserver protect (**de** from); *bois, patrimoine* preserve

présidence *f* chairmanship; POL presidency; **président, ~e** *m/f* *d'une réunion* chair; POL president; **présidentiel, ~le** presidential; **présider** *réunion* chair

présomption *f* presumption; **présomptueux, -euse** presumptuous

presque almost, nearly

presqu'île *f* peninsula

pressant *besoin* pressing, urgent; *personne* insistent

presse *f* press; **mise ~ sous ~** going to press

pressé *lettre, requête* urgent; *citron* fresh; **je suis ~** I'm in a hurry

pressentiment *m* foreboding, presentiment; **pressentir:** ~ **qch** have a premonition that sth is going to happen; ~ **qn pour un poste** approach s.o., sound s.o. out

presser 1 *v/t bouton* push, press; *fruit* squeeze; (*harceler*) press; *pas* quicken; *affaire* speed up; (*étreindre*) press, squeeze; **se** ~ **contre** press (o.s.) against **2** *v/i* be urgent; **se** ~ hurry up

pressing *m magasin* dry cleaner

pression *f* pressure; *bouton* snap fastener, *Br aussi* press-stud fastener; (*bière f*) ~ draft beer, *Br* draught beer; **faire** ~ **sur** pressure, put pressure on

prestance *f* presence

prestation *f* (*allocation*) allowance; ~**s familiales** child benefit

prestige *m* prestige

présumer 1 *v/t:* ~ **que** presume *ou* assume that **2** *v/i:* ~ **de** overrate

prêt[1] *adj* ready (**à** for; **à faire** to do)

prêt[2] *m* loan; ~ **immobilier** mortgage

prêt-à-porter *m* ready-to-wear clothes *pl*

prétendre 1 *v/t* maintain; ~ **faire qch** claim to do sth **2** *v/i:* ~ **à** lay claim to; **prétendu** so-called

prétentieux, -euse pretentious

prêter 1 *v/t* lend **2** *v/i:* ~ **à** give rise to; **se** ~ **à** *d'une chose* lend itself to; *d'une personne* be a party to

prétexte *m* pretext; **sous** ~ **de faire** on the pretext of doing

prêtre *m* priest; **prêtresse** *f* woman priest

preuve *f* proof, evidence; MATH proof; **faire** ~ **de courage** show courage

prévenance *f* consideration

prévenir (*avertir*) warn (**de** of); (*informer*) inform (**de** of); *besoin, question* anticipate; *crise, maladie* avert

préventif, -ive preventive; **prévention** *f* prevention; ~ **routière** road safety

prévision *f* forecast; ~**s météorologiques** weather forecast

prévoir (*pressentir*) foresee; (*planifier*) plan; **comme prévu** as expected; **prévoyance** *f* foresight; **prévoyant** farsighted

prier 1 *v/i* REL pray **2** *v/t* (*supplier*) beg; REL pray to; ~ **qn de faire qc** ask s.o. to do sth; **je vous en prie** don't mention it

prière *f* REL prayer; (*demande*) entreaty; **faire sa** ~ say one's prayers

primaire primary; *péj* narrow-minded

prime[1]: **de** ~ **abord** at first sight

prime² f d'assurance premium; de fin d'année bonus; (cadeau) free gift

primer 1 v/i take precedence **2** v/t take precedence over

primeur f: **avoir la ~ de** nouvelle be the first to hear objet have first use of; **~s** early fruit and vegetables

primitif, -ive primitive; couleur, sens original

primordial essential

prince m prince; **princesse** princess

principal, ~e 1 adj main, principal **2** m: **le ~** the main thing **3** m/f principal, Br head teacher

principe m principle; **par ~** on principle; **en ~** in principle

printemps m spring

priorité f priority (**sur** over); sur la route right of way

pris place taken; personne busy

prise f hold; d'un pion, une ville etc capture, taking; de poissons catch; ÉL outlet, Br socket; d'un film take; **être aux ~s avec** be struggling with; **~ de conscience** awareness; **~ de courant** outlet, Br socket

prison f prison; **prisonnier, -ère** m/f prisoner

privation f deprivation

privatisation f privatization; **privatiser** privatize

privé 1 adj private **2** m: **en ~** in private; **priver: ~ qn de** deprive s.o. of; **se ~ de** go without

privilège m privilege; **privilégier** favor, Br favour

prix m price; (valeur) value; (récompense) prize; **à tout ~** at all costs; **hors de ~** prohibitive; **au ~ de** at the cost of; **~ fort** full price; **~ de revient** cost price

probabilité f probability; **probable** probable

probant convincing

problème m problem

procédé m (méthode) method; TECH process; **~s** (comportement) behavior, Br behaviour

procéder proceed; **~ à qc** carry out sth

procès m JUR trial

processus m process

procès-verbal m minutes pl; (contravention) ticket

prochain, ~e 1 adj next **2** m/f: **son ~** one's neighbor ou Br neighbour

proche 1 adj close (**de** to), near; ami close; événement recent; **~ de** fig close to **2** mpl: **~s** family and friends

proclamer roi, république proclaim; résultats, innocence declare

procréer procreate

procuration f proxy, power of attorney; **procurer** get, procure; **se ~ qc** get, procure fml

prodigieux, -euse enormous,

tremendous

prodige extravagant; **prodiguer** lavish

producteur, -trice 1 adj producing **2** m/f producer; **productif, -ive** productive; **production** f production; **produire** produce; **se ~** happen; **produit** m product; d'un investissement yield; **~ d'entretien** cleaning product; **~ fini** end product

profane 1 adj art, musique secular **2** m/f fig lay person; **profaner** desecrate, profane

proférer menaces utter

professeur m teacher; d'université professor

profession f profession; **professionnel, ~le** m/f & adj professional

profil m profile

profit m COMM profit; (avantage) benefit; **profitable** beneficial; COMM profitable; **profiter: ~ de qc** take advantage of sth; **~ à qn** to be to s.o.'s advantage

profond deep; personne, pensées deep, profound; influence profound; **profondément** deeply, profoundly; **profondeur** f depth

programme m program, Br programme; INFORM program; **~ télé** TV program; **programmer** TV schedule; INFORM program; **programmeur, -euse** m/f programmer

progrès m progress; d'un incendie, d'une épidémie spread; **progresser** progress; d'une incendie, d'une épidémie spread; **progressif, -ive** progressive; **progression** f progress

prohiber ban, prohibit; **prohibition** f ban; **la Prohibition** HIST Prohibition

proie f prey (aussi fig); **en ~ à** prey to

projecteur m (spot) spotlight; au cinéma projector

projection f projection

projet m project; personnel plan; (ébauche) draft; **~ de loi** bill; **projeter** (jeter) throw; film screen; travail, voyage plan

proliférer proliferate

prologue m prologue

prolongation f extension; **~s** SP overtime, Br extra time; **prolonger** prolong; mur, route extend; **se ~** continue

promenade f walk; en voiture drive; **promener** take for a walk; **se ~** go for a walk; en voiture go for a drive; **promeneur, -euse** m/f stroller, walker

promesse f promise; **prometteur, -euse** promising; **promettre** promise (qc à qn s.o. sth, sth to s.o., **de faire** to do); **se ~ de faire qc** make up one's mind to do sth

promiscuité f overcrowding;

sexuelle promiscuity

promontoire *m* promontory

promoteur, -trice 1 *m/f (instigateur)* instigator **2** *m*: **~ immobilier** property developer; **promotion** *f* promotion; *sociale* advancement; ÉDU class, Br year; **en ~** on special offer; **promouvoir** promote

prompt swift

pronom *m* GRAM pronoun

prononcé *fig* marked, pronounced; *accent*, *traits* strong; **prononcer** *(dire)* say, utter; *(articuler)* pronounce; *discours* give; JUR *sentence* pass, pronounce; **se ~ d'un mot** be pronounced; *(se déterminer)* express an opinion; **se ~ pour/contre qch** come out in favor *ou* Br favour of/against sth; **prononciation** *f* pronunciation; JUR passing

propager *idée*, *nouvelle* spread; BIOL propagate; **se ~** spread; BIOL reproduce

propension *f* propensity (**à** for)

propice favorable, Br favourable; *moment* right

proportion *f* proportion; **toutes ~s gardées** on balance; **proportionnel**, **~le** proportional (**à** to)

propos 1 *mpl (paroles)* words **2** *m (intention)* intention; **à ~** at the right moment; **mal à ~**, **hors de ~** at the wrong

moment; **à ~!** by the way; **à ~ de** *(au sujet de)* about

proposer suggest, propose; *(offrir)* offer; **se ~ de faire** propose doing; **se ~** offer one's services; **proposition** *f (suggestion)* proposal, suggestion; *(offre)* offer; GRAM clause

propre 1 *adj* own; *(net)* clean; *(approprié)* suitable; **~ à** *(particulier à)* characteristic of **2** *m*: **mettre au ~** make a clean copy of; **propreté** *f* cleanliness

propriétaire *m/f* owner; *qui loue* landlord; *femme* landlady; **propriété** *f* ownership; *(caractéristique)* property

propulser propel; **propulsion** *f* propulsion

proscrire *(interdire)* ban; *(bannir)* banish

prospectus *m* brochure; FIN prospectus

prospère prosperous; **prospérer** prosper; **prospérité** *f* prosperity

prosterner: **se ~** prostrate o.s.

prostituée *f* prostitute; **prostitution** *f* prostitution

protecteur, -trice 1 *adj* protective; *péj*: *ton* patronizing **2** *m/f* protector; *(mécène)* sponsor, patron; **protection** *f* protection; **protéger** protect *(contre, de* from); *arts, artistes* be a patron of

protéine *f* protein

protestant, ~e REL *m/f* & *adj* Protestant

protestation *f* (*plainte*) protest; (*déclaration*) protestation; **protester** protest

prothèse *f* prosthesis

protocole *m* protocol

prototype *m* prototype

prouesse *f* prowess

prouver prove

provenance *f* origin; **en ~ de** avion, train from

provenir: ~ **de** come from

proverbe *m* proverb

providence *f* providence

province *f* province

proviseur *m* principal, *Br* head (teacher)

provision *f* supply; **~s** (*vivres*) provisions; (*achats*) shopping; *d'un chèque* funds *pl*; **chèque m sans ~** bad check *ou Br* cheque

provisoire provisional

provocant, provocateur, -trice provocative; **provoquer** provoke; *accident* cause

proximité *f* proximity; **à ~ de** near, in the vicinity of

prude prudish

prudence *f* caution, prudence; **prudent** cautious, prudent; *conducteur* careful

prune *f* BOT plum

pruneau *m* prune

prunier *m* plum (tree)

PS *m* (= **Parti socialiste**) Socialist Party; (= **Post Scriptum**) PS (= postscript)

psaume *m* psalm

pseudonyme *m* pseudonym

psychanalyser psychoanalyze; **psychanalyste** *m/f* psychoanalyst

psychiatre *m/f* psychiatrist

psychologie *f* psychology; **psychologique** psychological; **psychologue** *m/f* psychologist

psychopathe *m/f* psychopath

puant stinking; *fig* arrogant; **puanteur** *f* stink

pub *f*: **une ~** an ad; **faire de la ~** do some advertising

public, publique 1 *adj* public **2** *m* public; *d'un spectacle* audience

publication *f* publication

publicitaire advertising *atr*; **publicité** *f* publicity; COMM advertising; (*affiche*) ad

publier publish

publipostage *m* mailshot

puce *f* ZO flea; INFORM chip

pudeur *f* modesty; **pudique** modest; *discret* discreet

puer 1 *v/i* stink; **~ des pieds** have smelly feet **2** *v/t* stink of

puéril childish

puis then

puiser draw (**dans** from)

puisque since

puissance *f* power; *d'une armée* strength; **puissant** powerful; *musculature, médicament* strong

puits *m* well; *d'une mine* shaft; **~ de pétrole** oil well

pull(-over) *m* sweater, *Br*

aussi pullover
pulluler swarm
pulsation f beat, beating
pulsion f drive; **~s** fpl **de mort** death wish
pulvériser *solide* pulverize (*aussi fig*); *liquide* spray
punaise f ZO bug; (*clou*) thumbtack, *Br* drawing pin
punir punish; **punition** f punishment
pupille 1 m/f JUR ward **2** f ANAT pupil
pur pure; *whisky* straight
purée f puree; **~ de pommes de terre** mashed potatoes pl
pureté f purity

purge f purge; **purger** TECH bleed; POL purge; JUR *peine* serve
purification f purification; **purifier** purify
pur-sang m thoroughbred
pus m pus
pute f F slut
puzzle m jigsaw (puzzle)
P.-V. m (= *procès-verbal*) ticket
pyjama m pajamas pl, *Br* pyjamas pl
pyramide f pyramid
Pyrénées fpl Pyrenees
pyromane m pyromaniac; JUR arsonist

Q

quadragénaire m/f & adj forty-year old
quadrillé *papier* squared; **quadriller** fig: *région* put under surveillance
quadruple quadruple
quai m *d'un port* quay; *d'une gare* platform
qualification f qualification; (*appellation*) name; **qualifier** qualify; **~ qn d'idiot** describe s.o. as an idiot; **se ~** SP qualify
qualité f quality; **de ~** quality atr; **en ~ d'ambassadeur** as ambassador, in his capacity as ambassador
quand when; **~ je serai de retour** when I'm back

quant à as for
quantifier quantify
quantité f quantity; **une ~ de grand nombre** a great many; **abondance** a great deal of
quarantaine f MÉD quarantine; **une ~ de** about forty, forty or so; **avoir la ~** be in one's forties; **quarante** forty
quart m quarter; *de vin* quarter liter, *Br* quarter litre; **~ d'heure** quarter of an hour; **~ de finale** quarter-final
quartier m (*quart*) quarter; *d'orange* segment; *d'une ville* area; **~ général** MIL headquarters pl
quasiment virtually
quatorze fourteen

quatre four; quatre-vingt(s) eighty; quatre-vingt-dix ninety; quatrième fourth

quatuor *m* MUS quartet

que 1 *pron relatif personne* who, that; *chose, animal* which, that; *les étudiants ~ j'ai rencontrés* the students (who *ou* that) I met 2 *pron interrogatif* what; *qu'y a-t-il?* what's the matter?; *qu'est-ce que c'est?* what's that? 3 *adv dans exclamations:* ~ *c'est beau!* it's so beautiful!; ~ *de fleurs!* what a lot of flowers! 4 *conj* that; *je croyais ~ ...* I thought (that) ...; *plus grand ~ moi* bigger than me; *aussi petit ~ cela* as small as that; *ne ... ~* only

quel, ~le what, which; ~le femme! what a woman!

quelconque (*médiocre*) mediocre; *un travail ~* some sort of job

quelque some; ~**s** some, a few; ~ ... *que* (+ *subj*) whatever, whichever

quelque chose something; *avec interrogatif, conditionnel aussi* anything

quelquefois sometimes

quelques-uns, quelques--unes a few, some

quelqu'un someone, somebody; *avec interrogatif, conditionnel aussi* anyone, anybody

querelle *f* quarrel; quereller:

se ~ quarrel; querelleur, -euse quarrelsome

question *f* question; questionnaire *m* questionnaire; questionner question (*sur* about)

quête *f* search; (*collecte*) collection

queue *f* d'*un animal* tail; d'*un fruit* stalk; d'*une casserole* handle; d'*un train* rear; d'*une classe* bottom; d'*une file* line, *Br* queue; *faire la* ~ stand in line, *Br* queue (up); *à la* ~, *en* ~ at the rear

qui *interrogatif* who; *relatif, personne* who, that; *chose, animal* which, that

quiconque whoever; (*n'importe qui*) anyone, anybody

quincaillerie *f* hardware; *magasin* hardware store

quinquagénaire *m/f* & *adj* fifty-year old

quintal *m* hundred kilos *pl*

quinte *f:* ~ (*de toux*) coughing fit

quinzaine *f* de *jours* two weeks *pl*, *Br aussi* fortnight; *une* ~ de *personnes* about fifteen people *pl*; quinze fifteen; ~ *jours* two weeks, *Br aussi* fortnight

quitte: *être* ~ *envers qn* be quits with s.o.

quitter leave; *vêtement* take off; *se* ~ part; *ne quittez pas* TÉL hold the line please

quoi what; *après* ~, *il ...* after which he ...; *à* ~ *bon?* what's the point?; *il n'y a pas de ~!* don't mention it; *~ que* (+ *subj*) whatever

quoique (+ *subj*) although, though

quotidien, ~ne 1 *adj* daily; *de tous les jours* everyday **2** *m* daily

R

rabâcher keep on repeating
rabais *m* discount, reduction; **rabaisser** *prix* reduce; *mérites* belittle
rabattre 1 *v/t siège* pull down; *couvercle* shut; *col* turn down **2** *v/i fig*: *se ~ sur* fall back on; *d'une voiture* pull back into
râblé stocky
rabot *m* plane
rabougri stunted
rabrouer snub
racaille *f* rabble
raccommoder mend; *chaussettes* darn
raccompagner: *je vais vous ~ chez vous* à pied I'll take you home
raccord *m* join; *d'un film* splice; **raccorder** join
raccourci *m* shortcut; *en ~* briefly; **raccourcir 1** *v/t* shorten **2** *v/i* get shorter
raccrocher 1 *v/t* put back up; *~ le téléphone* hang up; *se ~ à* cling to **2** *v/i* TÉL hang up
race *f* race; (*ascendance*) descent; *zo* breed
rachat *m d'un otage* ransoming; *d'une société* buyout; **racheter** buy back; *otage*

ransom; *fig*: *faute* make up for; *se ~* make amends
racine *f* root
racisme *m* racism; **raciste** *m/f* & *adj* racist
racler scrape; *se ~ la gorge* clear one's throat
raconter tell
radar *m* radar
radeau *m* raft
radiateur *m* radiator
radiation *f* radiation; *d'une liste* deletion
radical *adj* & *m* radical
radier strike out
radieux, -euse radiant; *temps* glorious
radin F mean, tight
radio *f* radio; (*radiographie*) X-ray
radioactif, -ive radioactive
radiocassette *f* radio cassette player
radiographie *f procédé* radiography; *photo* X-ray
radioréveil radio alarm
radis *m* BOT radish
radoter ramble
radoucir make milder; *se ~ du temps* get milder
rafale *f de vent* gust; MIL burst
raffermir *chair* firm up; *auto-*

rité re-assert

raffinage m refining; **raffiné** refined; **raffiner** refine; **raffinerie** f refinery

raffoler: ~ **de** adore

rafraîchir 1 v/t cool down; *mémoire* refresh 2 v/i *du vin* chill; **se** ~ *de la température* get cooler; *d'une personne* have a drink (in order to cool down); **rafraîchissant** refreshing (*aussi* fig); **rafraîchissement** m de la température cooling; ~**s** (*boissons*) refreshments

rage f rage; MÉD rabies sg; **rageur, -euse** furious

ragoût m CUIS stew

raide *personne, membres* stiff; *pente* steep; *cheveux* straight; (*ivre, drogué*) stoned; **raideur** f stiffness; *d'une pente* steepness; **raidir**: **se** ~ *de membres* stiffen up

raie f (*rayure*) stripe; *des cheveux* part, *Br* parting; zo skate

rail m rail; ~ **de sécurité** crash barrier

railler mock; **raillerie** f mockery

raisin m grape; ~ **sec** raisin

raison f reason; *avoir* ~ be right; *avoir* ~ **de** get the better of; **à** ~ **de** at the rate of; **à plus forte** ~ all the more so; **en** ~ **de** (*à cause de*) because of; ~ **sociale** company name; **raisonnable** reasonable; **raisonnement** m reasoning; **raisonner** 1 v/i reason 2 v/t: ~ **qn** make s.o. see reason

rajeunir 1 v/t *thème* modernize; ~ **qn** make s.o. look (years) younger 2 v/i look younger

rajouter add

rajuster adjust; *coiffure* put straight

ralenti m AUTO idle; *dans un film* slow motion; **au** ~ fig at a snail's pace; **ralentir** slow down; **ralentissement** m slowing down; **ralentisseur** m de circulation speedbump

râler moan; F beef F; **râleur, -euse** F 1 *adj* grumbling 2 m/f grumbler

rallier rally; (*s'unir à*) join; **se** ~ **à** rally to

rallonger 1 v/t lengthen 2 v/i get longer

rallumer *télé, lumière* switch on again; fig revive

ramassage m collection; *de fruits* picking; **ramasser** collect; *ce qui est par terre* pick up; *fruits* pick; F *coup* get

rame f oar; *de métro* train

rameau m branch

ramener take back; (*rapporter*) bring back; *l'ordre* restore; **se** ~ **à** (*se réduire à*) come down to

ramer row; **rameur, -euse** m/f rower

ramification f ramification

ramollir soften; **se ~** soften; *fig* go soft

rampant crawling; BOT creeping; *fig: inflation* rampant

rampe *f* ramp; *d'escalier* bannisters *pl*; *au théâtre* footlights *pl*

ramper crawl; BOT creep

rance rancid

rancœur *f* resentment (**contre** toward)

rançon *f* ransom; **la ~ de** *fig* the price of

rancune *f* resentment; **rancunier, -ère** resentful

randonnée *f* walk; *en montagne* hill walk; **randonneur** *m* walker; *en montagne* hillwalker

rang *m* row; *(niveau)* rank; **être au premier ~** be in the forefront

rangée *f* row

ranger put away; *chambre* tidy up; *voiture* park; *(classer)* arrange; **se ~** *(s'écarter)* move aside; *fig (assagir)* settle down; **se ~ à une opinion** come around to a point of view

ranimer *personne* bring around; *fig:* force revive

rap *m* MUS rap

rapace 1 *adj animal* predatory; *personne* greedy **2** *m* bird of prey

rapatrier repatriate

râpe *f* grater; TECH rasp; **râper** CUIS grate; *bois* file; **râpé** CUIS grated; *manteau* threadbare

rapide 1 *adj* fast, rapid; *coup d'œil, décision* quick **2** *m dans l'eau* rapid; *train* fast train; **rapidité** *f* speed, rapidity

rapiécer patch

rappel *m* reminder; *d'un ambassadeur, produit* recall; THÉÂT curtain call; MÉD booster; **rappeler** call back; *ambassadeur* recall; **~ qc/qn à qn** remind s.o. of sth/s.o.; **se ~ qc** remember sth

rapport *m écrit, oral* report; *(lien)* connection; *(proportion)* proportion; COMM return; MIL briefing; **~s (sexuels)** sexual relations; **par ~ à** compared with; **être en ~ avec** be in touch with; **rapporter** return, bring/take back; *d'un chien* fetch; COMM bring in; *relater* report; **se ~ à** be connected with; **rapporteur** *m* reporter; *enfant* sneak

rapprochement *m fig* reconciliation; POL rapprochement; *analogie* connection; **rapprocher** bring closer (**de** to); *établir un lien* connect; **se ~** come closer

rapt *m* abduction

raquette *f* racket

rare rare; *marchandises* scarce; *(peu dense)* sparse; **raréfier: se ~** become rare; *de l'air* become rarefied; **rarement** rarely; **rareté** *f* rarity

ras short; *rempli à ~ bord* full to the brim; *faire table ~e* make a clean sweep

raser shave; *barbe* shave off; (*démolir*) raze to the ground; *murs* hug; F (*ennuyer*) bore

rasoir *m* razor; *~ électrique* electric shaver

rassasier satisfy

rassembler collect, assemble; *se ~* gather

rasseoir replace; *se ~* sit down again

rassis stale; *fig* sedate

rassurer reassure; *rassurez--vous* don't be concerned

rat *m* rat

ratatiner: *se ~* shrivel up

rate *f* ANAT spleen

raté, ~e 1 *adj* unsuccessful; *occasion* missed **2** *m/f personne* failure

râteau *m* rake

rater *v/t* miss; *examen* fail **2** *v/i d'une arme* misfire; *d'un projet* fail

ration *f* ration; *fig* (fair) share

rationaliser rationalize; **rationnel, ~le** rational; **rationner** ration

ratisser rake; (*fouiller*) search

rattacher *chien* tie up again; *cheveux* put up again; *lacets* do up again; *conduites d'eau* connect; *idées* connect; *se ~ à* be linked to

rattraper recapture; *objet qui tombe* catch; (*rejoindre*)

catch up (with); *retard* make up; *imprudence* make up for; *se ~* make up for it; (*se raccrocher*) get caught up

rature *f* deletion

rauque hoarse

ravages *mpl* devastation; *les ~ du temps* the ravages of time; **ravager** devastate

ravaler swallow; *façade* clean up

rave *f: céléri ~* celeriac

ravé *f* rave

ravi delighted (*de* with; *de faire* to do)

ravir (*enchanter*) delight

raviser: *se ~* change one's mind

ravissant delightful

ravisseur, -euse *m/f* abductor

ravitaillement *m* supplying; *en carburant* refueling, *Br* refuelling; **ravitailler** supply; *en carburant* refuel

raviver revive

rayé striped; *papier* lined; *verre, carrosserie* scratched; **rayer** scratch; *mot* score *ou* scratch out

rayon *m* ray; MATH radius; *d'une roue* spoke; (*étagère*) shelf; *de magasin* department; *~ laser* laser beam; **rayonner** *de chaleur* radiate; *d'un visage* shine; *~ de fig* radiate

rayure *f* stripe; *sur un meuble, du verre* scratch

raz *m: ~ de marée* tidal wave

réacteur m reactor; AVIAT jet engine; **réaction** f reaction; **avion m à ~** jet (aircraft); **réactionnaire** m/f & adj reactionary

réagir react (à to; contre against)

réalisable feasible; **réalisateur, -trice** m/f director; **réalisation** f d'un projet execution, realization; création, œuvre creation; d'un film direction; **réaliser** projet carry out; rêve fulfill, Br fulfil; vente make; film direct; bien, capital realize; (se rendre compte) realize; **se ~** d'un rêve come true; d'un projet be carried out

réalisme m realism; **réaliste 1** adj realistic **2** m/f realist; **réalité** f reality

réanimer resuscitate

rébarbatif, -ive off-putting, daunting

rebelle 1 adj rebellious **2** m/f rebel; **rebeller: se ~** rebel; **rébellion** f rebellion

rebondir bounce; (faire un ricochet) rebound; **faire ~ qch** fig get sth going again; **rebondissement** m fig unexpected development

rebord m edge; d'une fenêtre sill

rebours m: **compte m à ~** countdown

rebrousser: ~ chemin retrace one's footsteps

rebut m dregs pl; **mettre au ~** get rid of

rebuter (décourager) dishearten; (choquer) offend

récapituler recap

récemment recently

recenser population take a census of

récent recent

récépissé m receipt

récepteur m receiver

réception f reception; d'une lettre, de marchandises receipt; **réceptionniste** m/f receptionist, desk clerk

récession f ÉCON recession

recette f COMM takings pl; CUIS, fig recipe

recevoir receive; **être reçu à un examen** pass an exam

rechange m: **de ~** spare atr

rechargeable pile rechargeable; **recharger** camion, arme reload; accumulateur recharge; briquet refill

réchaud m stove

réchauffement m warming; **~ de la planète** global warming; **réchauffer** warm up

recherche f search (de for); scientifique research; **~s de la police** search; **rechercher** look for, search for; (prendre) fetch

rechute f MÉD relapse

récif m reef

récipient m container

réciproque reciprocal

récit m account; (histoire) story; **réciter** recite

réclamation f claim; (protes-

tation) complaint

réclame f advertisement

réclamer *secours, aumône* ask for; *son du* claim; (*nécessiter*) call for

réclusion f imprisonment

récolte f harvesting; *de produits* harvest, crop; *fig* crop; **récolter** harvest

recommander recommend; *lettre* register

recommencer start again

récompense f reward; **récompenser** reward (*de* for)

réconcilier reconcile

reconduire: ~ *qn chez lui* take s.o. home; *à la porte* see s.o. out

réconforter console, comfort

reconnaissance f recognition; *d'une faute* acknowledg(e)ment; (*gratitude*) gratitude; MIL reconnaissance; **reconnaissant** grateful (*de* for); **reconnaître** recognize; *faute* acknowledge; **se** ~ *de deux personnes* recognize each other; **se** ~ *à* be recognizable by; **reconnu** known

reconstituer reconstitute; *ville, maison* restore; *événement* reconstruct

reconstruire rebuild

reconvertir: **se** ~ retrain

recopier *notes* copy out

record m record; **recordman** m record holder; **recordwoman** f record holder

recourbé bent

recours m recourse, resort;

avoir ~ *à* resort to

recouvrer recover; *santé* regain

recouvrir recover; *enfant* cover up again; (*couvrir entièrement*) cover (*de* with); (*cacher, embrasser*) cover

récréation f relaxation; ÉDU recess, *Br* recreation

récriminations fpl recriminations

recrudescence f new outbreak

recrue f recruit; **recruter** recruit

rectangle m rectangle; **rectangulaire** rectangular

rectifier rectify; (*ajuster*) adjust; (*corriger*) correct

recto m *d'une feuille* front

reçu m receipt

recueil m collection; **recueillir** collect; *personne* take in; **se** ~ meditate

recul m *d'un fusil* recoil; *d'une armée* retreat; *de la production* drop; *fig* detachment; **reculer 1** v/t push back; *décision* postpone **2** v/i back away, recoil; MIL retreat; *d'une voiture* back, reverse; ~ *devant fig* back away from; **reculons:** *à* ~ backward, *Br* backwards

récupérer 1 v/t recover, retrieve; *ses forces* regain; *vieux matériel* salvage; *temps* make up **2** v/i recover

recyclable recyclable; **recyclage** m *du personnel* re-

training; TECH recycling; recycler retrain; TECH recycle

rédacteur, -trice *m/f* editor;
(*auteur*) writer; ~ **en chef**
editor-in-chief; rédaction *f*
editing; (*rédacteurs*) editorial team

redescendre 1 *v/i* come/go
down again; ~ **d'une voiture**
get out of a car again 2 *v/t*
bring/take down again;
montagne come down again

redevable: être ~ **de qc à qn**
owe s.o. sth; redevance *f*
d'un auteur royalty; TV licence fee

rédiger write

redire repeat, say again; (*rapporter*) repeat; **trouver à ~ à**
find fault with

redoubler 1 *v/t* double 2 *v/i*
ÉDU repeat a class; *d'une
tempête* intensify; ~ **d'efforts** redouble one's efforts

redoutable formidable; *hiver*
harsh; redouter dread (**de
faire** doing)

redresser *ce qui est courbe*
straighten; *ce qui est tombé*
set upright; **se ~** *d'un pays*
recover

réduction *f* reduction; MÉD
setting; réduire reduce; *personnel* cut back; **se ~ à**
amount to; *réduit* reduced;
possibilités limited

2 m small room

rééducation *f* MÉD rehabilita-
tion

réel, ~le real

refaire do again; *examen* re-
take; *erreur* repeat; *remettre
en état: maison* do up

réfectoire *m* refectory

référence *f* reference; ~**s** (*recommandation*) reference

référendum *m* referendum

référer: **en ~ à** consult; **se ~ à**
refer to

réfléchir 1 *v/t* reflect 2 *v/i*
think (**à, sur** about)

reflet *m* de lumière glint; *dans
miroir* reflection (*aussi fig*)

réflexe *m* reflex

réflexion *f* reflection; (*remarque*) remark

réforme *f* reform; **la Réforme**
REL the Reformation; réformer reform; MIL discharge

refouler push back; PSYCH repress

refrain *m* refrain, chorus

réfréner repress

réfrigérateur *m* refrigerator

refroidir cool down; *fig* cool;
se ~ *du temps* get colder;
MÉD catch a chill; refroidis-
sement *m* cooling; MÉD chill

refuge *m* refuge, shelter;
pour piétons traffic island;
en montagne (mountain)
hut; réfugié, ~e *m/f* refugee;
réfugier: **se ~** take shelter

refus *m* refusal; refuser refuse; ~ **de** ou **se ~ à faire** refuse to do

réfuter refute

regagner win back, regain;
endroit get back to

régal *m* treat; régaler regale

(de with)

regard m look; **regardant** *avec argent* careful with one's money; **ne pas être ~ sur** not to be too worried about; **regarder 1** v/t look at; *télé* watch; (concerner) regard, concern; **~ qn faire qch** watch s.o. doing sth **2** v/i look; **se ~** look at o.s.; *de plusieurs personnes* look at each other

régate f regatta

régime m POL government, régime; MÉD diet; *fiscal* system

région f region; **~ sinistrée** disaster area; **régional** regional

régir govern

régisseur m THÉÂT stage manager; *dans le film* assistant director

réglage m adjustment

règle f rule; *instrument* ruler; **en ~ générale** as a rule; **~s** (menstruation) period

réglé organisé settled; *vie* well-ordered; *papier* ruled

règlement m settlement; (règles) regulations pl; **réglementaire** in accordance with the rules; *tenue* regulation atr; **réglementer** control, regulate

régler affaire settle; TECH adjust; COMM pay, settle; *épicier etc* pay, settle up with

règne m reign; **régner** reign

régression f regression

regret m regret (de about); **à ~** with regret, reluctantly; **être au ~ de faire** regret to do; **regrettable** regrettable; **regretter** regret; *personne absente* miss; **~ d'avoir fait qc** regret doing sth, regret having done sth; **je ne regrette rien** I have no regrets; **je regrette mais ...** I'm sorry (but) ...

régulariser put in order; *situation* regularize; TECH regulate; **régularité** f regularity; *d'élections* legality; **régulier, -ère** regular; *allure, progrès* steady; *écriture* even; (réglementaire) lawful; (correct) honest; **régulièrement** regularly

réhabiliter rehabilitate; *quartier* renovate, redevelop

rehausser raise; fig (accentuer) emphasize

rein m ANAT kidney; **~s** lower back

reine f queen

réitérer reiterate

rejaillir spurt

rejeter reject; (relancer) throw back; (vomir) bring up; *responsabilité, faute* lay (sur on)

rejoindre personne join, meet; (rattraper) catch up with; MIL rejoin; *autoroute* get back onto; **se ~** meet

réjouir make happy, delight; **se ~ de** be delighted about; **réjouissance** f rejoicing

relâche

212

relâche *f:* **sans** ~ without a break, nonstop

relâcher *corde, emprise* loosen; *prisonnier* release; **se** ~ *d'un élève, de la discipline* become slack

relais *m* SP, EL relay; **prendre le** ~ **de** take over from

relancer *balle* throw back; *moteur* restart; *fig: économie* kickstart; *personne* contact again

relater relate

relatif, -ive relative; ~ **à** relating to; **relation** *f* relationship; *(connaissance)* acquaintance; **être en** ~ **avec qn** be in touch with s.o.; ~**s** relations; *(connaissances)* contacts; **relativement** relatively; ~ **à** compared with; *(en ce qui concerne)* relating to; **relativiser** look at in context

relaxer: se ~ relax

relayer take over from; TV, radio relay; **se** ~ take turns

reléguer relegate

relève *f* relief; **prendre la** ~ take over

relevé 1 *adj manche* turned up; *style* elevated; CUIS spicy **2** *m de compteur* reading; ~ **de compte** bank statement; **relever 1** *v/t raise*; *(remettre debout)* pick up; *col, chauffage* turn up; *manches* roll up; *siège* put up; *économie* improve; *(ramasser)* collect; *défi* take up; *faute* find;

adresse, date copy; *(relayer)* take over from; **se** ~ get up; *fig* recover **2** *v/i:* ~ **de** *(dépendre de)* be answerable to; *(ressortir de)* be the responsibility of

relief *m* relief; **mettre en** ~ *fig* highlight

relier connect (**à** to); *livre* bind

religieux, -euse 1 *adj* religious **2** *m* monk **3** *f* nun; **religion** *f* religion

reliure *f* binding

reluire shine

remanier *texte* re-work; POL reshuffle

remarquable remarkable

remarque *f* remark; **remarquer** notice; *(dire)* remark; **faire** ~ **qc à qn** point sth out to s.o.; **se faire** ~ *d'un acteur etc* get us. noticed; *d'un écolier* get into trouble; **se différencier** be conspicuous

rembourrer stuff

remboursement *m* refund; *de dettes* repayment; **rembourser** *frais* refund, reimburse; *dettes, emprunt* pay back

remède *m* remedy; **remédier:** ~ **à** remedy

remerciement *m:* ~**s** thanks; **remercier** thank (**de, pour** for); *(congédier)* dismiss

remettre put back; *vêtement* put on again; *peine* remit; *décision* postpone; *(ajouter)* add; ~ **qc à qn** give sth to s.o.; **se ~ à qc** take sth up again; **se ~ à faire qc** start doing sth again; **se ~ de qc** recover from sth; **s'en ~ à qn** rely on s.o.

remise f (hangar) shed; d'une lettre delivery; de peine remission; COMM discount; d'une décision postponement; **~ à neuf** reconditioning; **~ en question** questioning

rémission f MÉD remission

remonte-pente m ski lift

remonter 1 v/i come/go up again; dans une voiture get back in; de prix, température go up again; d'un avion, chemin climb, rise **2** v/t choses bring/take back up; rue, escalier come/go back up; montre wind; TECH reassemble; col turn up; stores raise

remords mpl remorse

remorque f véhicule trailer; câble towrope; **remorquer** voiture tow

remplaçant, ~e m/f replacement; **remplacement** m replacement; **remplacer** replace (par with)

remplir fill (de with); formulaire fill out; conditions fulfill, Br fulfil; tâche carry out; **remplissage** m filling

remporter take away; prix win

remue-ménage m (agitation) commotion

remuer 1 v/t move (aussi fig);

sauce stir; salade toss; terre turn over **2** v/i move; **se ~** move; fig F get a move-on F

rémunération f pay, remuneration; **rémunérer** pay

renaître REL be born again; fig be reborn

renard m fox

renchérir go up; **~ sur** outdo

rencontre f meeting; **aller à la ~ de** go and meet; **rencontrer** meet with; accueil meet with; difficulté encounter; amour find; (heurter) hit; **se ~** meet

rendement m AGR yield; d'un employé, d'une machine output; d'un placement return

rendez-vous m appointment; amoureux date; lieu meeting place; **prendre ~** make an appointment

rendre 1 v/t give back; salut, invitation return; (donner) give; (traduire) render; (vomir) bring up; MIL surrender; **~ visite à** visit **2** v/i de terre, d'un arbre yield; **se ~ à un endroit** go; MIL surrender; **se ~ malade** make o.s. sick

rêne f rein

renfermer (contenir) contain; **se ~ dans le silence** withdraw into silence

renforcer reinforce

renfort m reinforcements pl; **à grand ~ de** with copious amounts of

renier *qn* disown

renifler sniff

renne *m* reindeer

renom *m* (*célébrité*) fame, renown; (*réputation*) reputation; **renommée** *f* fame

renoncement *m* renunciation (**à** of); **renoncer**: **~ à qc** give sth up; **~ à faire** give up doing

renouer 1 *v/t amitié etc* renew **2** *v/i*: **~ avec** get back in touch with; *après brouille* get back together with

renouveler renew; *demande, promesse* repeat; **se ~** (*se reproduire*) happen again; **renouvellement** *m* renewal

rénovation *f* renovation; *fig* (*modernisation*) updating

renseignement *m* piece of information (**sur** about); **~s** information; MIL intelligence; **prendre des ~s sur** find out about; **renseigner**: **~ qn sur qc** tell *ou* inform s.o. about sth; **se ~** find out

rentabilité *f* profitability; **rentable** cost-effective; *entreprise* profitable; **ce n'est pas ~** there's no money in it

rente *f revenu d'un bien* private income; (*pension*) annuity; *versée à sa femme etc* allowance

rentrée *f* return; **~ des classes** beginning of the new school year; **~s** COMM takings

rentrer 1 *v/i* go/come in; *de nouveau* go/come back in; *chez soi* go/come home; *dans un récipient* go in, fit; *de l'argent* come in; **~ dans** (*heurter*) collide with; *serrure, sac* go into; *responsabilités* be part of **2** *v/t* bring/take in; *voiture* put away; *ventre* pull in

renversement *m d'un régime* overthrow; **renverser** reverse; (*mettre à l'envers*) upturn; (*faire tomber*) knock over; *liquide* spill; *gouvernement* overthrow

renvoi *m de personnel* dismissal; *d'un élève* expulsion; *d'une lettre* return; *dans un texte* cross-reference (**à** to); **renvoyer** (*faire retourner*) send back; *ballon* return; *personnel* dismiss; *élève* expel; *rencontre, décision* postpone

repaire *m* den

répandre spread; (*renverser*) spill; **se ~** spread; (*être renversé*) spill; **répandu** widespread

réparation *f* repair; (*compensation*) reparation; **en ~** being repaired; **réparer** repair; *fig* make up for

répartie *f* retort; **avoir de la ~** have a gift for repartee

repartir set off again; **~ de zéro** start again from scratch

répartir share out; *chargement* distribute; *en catégories* divide; **répartition** *f* distribution; *en catégories* division

repas *m* meal

repassage *m* ironing; **repasser 1** *v/t* come/go back again **2** *v/t linge* iron; *examen* take again

repentir 1: se ~ REL repent; **se** ~ **de** be sorry for **2** *m* penitence

répercussions *fpl* repercussions

repère *m* mark; (*point m de*) ~ landmark; **repérer** (*situer*) pinpoint; (*trouver*) find; (*marquer*) mark

répertoire *m* directory; THÉÂT repertoire

répéter repeat; THÉÂT rehearse; **répétition** *f* repetition; THÉÂT rehearsal

répit *m* respite

replacer put back, replace

repli *m* fold; *d'une rivière* bend; *replier* fold; *jambes* draw up; *journal* fold up; *manches* roll up; **se** ~ **sur soi-même** retreat into one's shell

répliquer retort; *d'un enfant* answer back

répondeur *m*: ~ **automatique** answering machine; **répondre 1** *v/t* answer, reply **2** *v/i* answer; (*réagir*) respond; ~ **à** answer, reply to; (*réagir à*) respond to; *besoin* meet; *attente* come up to; *signalement* match; **réponse** *f* answer; (*réaction*) response

reportage *m* report; **reporter** *m/f* reporter

repos *m* rest; **reposer 1** *v/t* (*remettre*) put back; *question* ask again; (*détendre*) rest; **se** ~ **rest 2** *v/i*: **sur** rest on

repoussant repulsive; **repousser 1** *v/t* (*dégoûter*) repel; (*différer*) postpone; *pousser en arrière*, MIL push back; (*rejeter*) reject **2** *v/i* grow again

reprendre 1 *v/t* take back; (*prendre davantage de*) take more; *ville* recapture; (*recommencer*) start again; (*corriger*) correct; *entreprise* take over (**à** *from*) **2** *v/i* (*recommencer*) start again; **se** ~ (*se corriger*) correct o.s.; (*se maîtriser*) pull o.s. together

représailles *fpl* reprisals

représentant, ~e *m/f* representative; **représentation** *f* representation; *au théâtre* performance; **représenter** represent; THÉÂT perform; **se** ~ **qc** imagine sth

répression *f* repression; **mesures** *fpl* **de** ~ crackdown (**contre** *on*)

réprimander reprimand

réprimer suppress

reprise *f de ville* recapture; *de marchandise* taking back; *de travail, de lutte* resumption; **à plusieurs** ~**s** on several occasions

repriser darn, mend

reproche *m* reproach; **reprocher** reproach; **~ qch à qn** reproach s.o. for sth

reproduction *f* reproduction; **reproduire** reproduce; **se ~** happen again; BIOL reproduce

républicain, ~e *m/f* & *adj* republican; **république** *f* republic

répugnant repugnant; **répugner: ~ à** be repelled by; **~ à faire** be reluctant to do

répulsion *f* repulsion

réputation *f* reputation

requérir require

requête *f* request

requin *m* shark

requis necessary

réseau *m* network

réservation *f* booking, reservation

réserve *f* reserve; (*entrepôt*) storeroom; **sans ~** unreservedly; **sous ~ de** subject to

réserver reserve; *dans hôtel, restaurant* book, reserve; (*mettre de côté*) put aside; **~ qc à qn** keep *ou* save sth for s.o.

réservoir *m* tank; *lac etc* reservoir

résidence *f* residence; **~ universitaire** dormitory, *Br* hall of residence; **résider** live; **~ dans** *fig* lie in

résidu *m* residue; MATH remainder

résigner resign; **se ~** resign o.s. (**à** to)

resilier *contrat* cancel

résistance *f* resistance; (*endurance*) stamina; *d'un matériau* strength; *la* **Résistance** HIST the Resistance; **résister** resist; **~ à** *tentation, personne* resist; *sécheresse* withstand

résolu determined (**à faire** to do); **résolution** *f* (*décision*) resolution; (*fermeté*) determination; *d'un problème* solving

résonner echo, resound

résoudre1 *v/t problème* solve **2** *v/i*: **~ de faire, se ~ à faire** decide to do

respect *m* respect; **respecter** respect; **~ le(s) délai(s)** meet the deadline; **se ~** have some self-respect; **mutuellement** respect each other; **se faire ~** command respect; **respectif, -ive** respective; **respectueux, -euse** respectful

respiration *f* breathing; **retenir sa ~** hold one's breath; **~ artificielle** MÉD artificial respiration; **respirer** breathe

resplendir glitter

responsabilité *f* responsibility (**de** for); JUR liability; **responsable** responsible (**de** for)

ressaisir: se ~ pull o.s. together

ressemblance *f* resemblance; **ressembler: ~ à** resemble, be like; **se ~** resem-

retomber

ble each other, be like each other

ressemeler resole

ressentiment *m* resentment

ressentir feel; *se* ~ *de* still feel the effects of

resserrer tighten; *fig: amitié* strengthen

ressort *m* TECH spring; *fig* motive; (*énergie*) energy; (*compétence*) province; JUR jurisdiction

ressortir 1 come/go out again **2** (*se détacher*) stand out; *faire* ~ bring out; ~ *à* JUR fall within the jurisdiction of

ressource *f* resource

restant 1 *adj* remaining **2** *m* remainder

restaurant *m* restaurant

restauration *f* catering; ART restoration; ~ *rapide* fast food; **restaurer** restore

reste *m* rest, remainder; ~*s* CUIS leftovers; *du* ~, *au* ~ moreover; **rester** (*subsister*) be left, remain; (*demeurer*) stay, remain; *on en reste là* we'll stop there; *il reste du vin* there's some wine left

restituer (*rendre*) return; (*reconstituer*) restore; **restitution** *f* restitution

restreindre restrict

restriction *f* restriction; *sans* ~ unreservedly

résultat *m* result; **résulter** result (*de* from)

résumé *m* summary

rétablir restore; *se* ~ recover

retard *m* lateness; *dans travail, paiement* delay; *avoir deux heures de* ~ be two hours late; *avoir du* ~ *sur qn* be behind s.o.; *être en* ~ be late; **retarder 1** *v/t* delay, hold up; *montre* put back **2** *v/i d'une montre* be slow; ~ *de cinq minutes* be five minutes slow; ~ *sur son temps fig* be behind the times

retenir *personne* keep; *argent* withhold; (*rappeler*) remember; *proposition* accept; (*réserver*) reserve; *se* ~ restrain o.s.

retentir sound; *du tonnerre* boom; ~ *sur* impact on; **retentissant** resounding (*aussi fig*)

retenu (*réservé*) reserved; (*empêché*) delayed

retenue *f sur salaire* deduction; *fig* (*modération*) restraint

réticence *f* (*omission*) omission; (*hésitation*) hesitation

retirer withdraw; *vêtement* take off; *promesse* take back; *profit* derive; ~ *qch de* remove sth from; *se* ~ withdraw; (*prendre sa retraite*) retire

retombées *fpl* fallout; **retomber** fall again; (*tomber*) land; *de cheveux, d'un rideau* fall; ~ *dans qc* sink back into sth

rétorsion POL: *mesure f de ~*
retaliatory measure

retoucher *texte, vêtement* alter; *photographie* retouch

retour *m* return; *être de ~* be
back; *bon ~!* have a good
trip home!; **retourner 1** *v/i*
return, go back; *~ sur ses
pas* backtrack **2** *v/t matelas,
tête* turn; *lettre* return; *vêtement* turn inside out; *~ au
lit* turn over (*aussi* AUTO);
(*tourner la tête*) turn
(around)

retrait *m* withdrawal; *en ~* set
back

retraite *f* retirement; (*pension*) retirement pension;
MIL retreat; *prendre sa ~* retire; **retraité**, *~e m/f* pen-
sioner, retired person

retrancher (*enlever*) remove,
cut (*de* from); (*déduire*) deduct

rétrécir 1 *v/t* shrink; *fig* narrow **2** *v/i de tissu* shrink; *se
~* narrow

rétrograder 1 *v/t* demote **2** *v/i*
retreat; AUTO downshift

rétrospectif, *-ive* **1** *adj* retrospective **2** *f*: *rétrospective*
retrospective

retrousser *manches* roll up

retrouver (*trouver*) find; *de
nouveau* find again; (*rejoindre*) meet; *santé* regain; *se ~*
meet; *se ~ seul* find o.s.
alone

rétroviseur *m* AUTO rear-view
mirror

réunion *f* meeting; POL reunion; **réunir** bring together;
pays reunite; *documents*
collect; *se ~* meet

réussi successful; **réussir 1**
v/i succeed; *~ à faire* manage
to do, succeed in doing **2** *v/t*
vie, projet make a success of;
examen be successful in;
réussite *f* success; *aux cartes*
solitaire, *Br* patience

revanche *f* revenge; *en ~* on
the other hand

rêve *m* dream

réveil *m* awakening; (*pendule*) alarm (clock); **réveiller**
wake up; *fig* revive; *se ~*
wake up

révélation *f* revelation; **révéler** reveal; *se ~ faux* prove to
be false

revenant *m* ghost

revendeur, *-euse m/f* retailer

revendication *f* claim, demand; **revendiquer** claim

revendre resell

revenir come back, return (*à*
to); *~ sur thème* go back to;
décision go back on; *~ à qn*
d'une part be due to s.o.; *~
de évanouissement* come
around from; *étonnement*
get over; *illusion* lose

revenu *m* income; *~s* revenue

rêver dream (*de*, *à* about)

réverbère *m* street lamp

rêverie *f* daydream

revers *m* back; *d'un pantalon*
cuff, *Br* turn-up; *fig* (*échec*)
reversal

revêtir *vêtement* put on; *forme, caractère* assume; *importance* take on

rêveur, -euse *adj* dreamy 2 *m/f* dreamer

revirement *m*: ~ *d'opinion* sudden change in the public's attitude

réviser *texte* revise; *machine* service; **révision** *f* revision; AUTO service

révocation *f* revocation; *d'un dirigeant etc* dismissal

revoir 1 *v/t* see again; *texte* review, ÉDU review, *Br* revise 2 *m*: *au* ~! goodbye!

révolte *f* revolt; **révolter** revolt; *se* ~ rebel, revolt

révolution *f* revolution; **révolutionner** revolutionize

revolver *m* revolver

révoquer *fonctionnaire* dismiss; *contrat* revoke

revue *f* review; *passer en* ~ *fig* review

rez-de-chaussée *m* first floor, *Br* ground floor

rhubarbe *f* rhubarb

rhum *m* rum

rhumatismes *mpl* rheumatism

rhume *m* cold; ~ *des foins* hay fever

ricaner sneer; *bêtement* snigger

riche rich; *sol* fertile; *décoration* elaborate; **richesse** *f* wealth; *du sol* fertility

rictus *m* grimace

ride *f* wrinkle, line

rideau *m* drape, *Br* curtain

rider *peau* wrinkle; *se* ~ become wrinkled

ridicule 1 *adj* ridiculous 2 *m* ridicule; (*absurdité*) ridiculousness; **ridiculiser** ridicule; *se* ~ make a fool of o.s.

rien 1 *pron* nothing; *quelque chose anything*; *de* ~ comme *réponse* you're welcome; *ne* ... ~ nothing, not anything 2 *m* trifle; *en un* ~ *de temps* in no time

rigide rigid

rigole *f* (*conduit*) channel

rigoler F (*plaisanter*) joke; (*rire*) laugh

rigolo, ~te F (*amusant*) funny

rigoureux, -euse rigorous; **rigueur** *f* rigor, *Br* rigour; *à la* ~ if absolutely necessary; *de* ~ compulsory

rincer rinse

riposte *f* riposte, response; *avec armes* return of fire; **riposter** reply, response; *avec armes* return fire

rire 1 *v/i* laugh (*de* about, at); (*s'amuser*) have fun; ~ *aux éclats* roar with laughter; ~ *de qn* laugh at s.o. 2 *m* laugh; ~s laughter

risque *m* risk; *à tes* ~s *et périls* at your own risk; **risqué** risky; *plaisanterie* risqué; **risquer** risk; ~ *de faire* risk doing; *se* ~ *dans* venture into

rituel, ~le *adj* & *m* ritual

rivage *m* shore

rival 220

rival, **~e** m/f & adj rival; **rivaliser** compete, vie; **rivalité** f rivalry

rive f d'un fleuve bank; d'une mer, d'un lac shore

riverain, **~e** m/f resident

rivet m TECH rivet

rivière f river

riz m BOT rice

robe f dress; d'un juge robe; **~ de chambre** robe, Br dressing gown

robinet m faucet, Br tap

robuste robust

roche f rock

rocher m rock; **rocheux**, **-euse** rocky

rôder prowl

rogne f: **être en ~** F be in a bad mood

rogner cut, trim

rognon m CUIS kidney

roi m king

rôle m role; (registre) roll; **à tour de ~** turn and turn about

roman m novel

romancier, **-ère** m/f novelist

romantique m/f & adj romantic; **romantisme** m romanticism

romarin m BOT rosemary

rompre 1 v/i break; **~ avec petit ami** break it off with; tradition break with; habitude break 2 v/t break; négociations, fiançailles break off

ronce f BOT: **~s** brambles

rond, **~e 1** adj round; joues, personne plump; F (ivre)

drunk **2** adv: **tourner ~** run smoothly **3** m figure circle m **4** f: **faire sa ronde** do one's rounds; de soldat, policier be on patrol; **à la ronde** around

rondelle f disk, Br disc; de saucisson slice; TECH washer

rondement (promptement) briskly; (carrément) frankly

rond-point m traffic circle, Br roundabout

ronflement m snoring; d'un moteur purr; **ronfler** snore; d'un moteur purr

ronger gnaw at; fig torment; **se ~ les ongles** bite one's nails; **rongeur** m ZO rodent

ronronner purr

rosbif m CUIS roast beef

rose 1 f BOT rose **2** m couleur pink **3** adj pink

rosé 1 m rosé **2** adj pinkish

roseau m BOT reed

rosée f dew

rosier m rose bush

rossignol m ZO nightingale

rot m F belch; **roter** F belch

rôti m roast; **rôtir** roast; **rôtisserie** f grill-room

rouage m cogwheel; **~s** d'une montre works; fig machinery

roue f wheel; **deux-~s** m two-wheeler; **quatre ~s motrices** all-wheel drive

roué crafty

rouer: **~ qn de coups** beat s.o. black and blue

rouge 1 adj red **2** adv fig: **voir ~** see red **3** m red; **~ à lèvres**

lipstick

rouge-gorge m robin (red-breast)

rougeole f MÉD measles sg

rougir go red; *d'une personne aussi* blush (*de* with); *de colère* flush (*de* with)

rouille f rust; **rouiller** rust; **se ~** rust; *fig* go rusty

rouleau m roller; *de pellicule etc* roll; CUIS rolling pin

rouler *v/i* roll; *d'une voiture* travel; **~ sur qc** *d'une conversation* be about sth 2 *v/t* roll; **~ qn** F cheat s.o.

roulette f *de meubles* caster; *jeu* roulette

roumain, ~e 1 adj Romanian **2** m *langue* Romanian; **Roumain, ~e** m/f Romanian; **Roumanie: la ~** Romania

rouspéter F complain

rousseur f: **taches** fpl **de ~** freckles

route f road; (*parcours*) route; *fig* (*chemin*) path; **en ~** on the way; **se mettre en ~** set off; *fig* get under way; **faire ~ vers** be heading for

routier, -ère 1 adj road **atr 2** m (*conducteur*) truck driver, Br long-distance lorry driver; *restaurant* truck stop, Br aussi transport café

routine f routine; **de ~** routine atr

roux, rousse personne red-haired; *cheveux* red

royal royal; *fig: pourboire, accueil* superb, right royal

royaume m kingdom; **le Royaume-Uni** the United Kingdom

R.-U. (= *Royaume-Uni*) UK (= United Kingdom)

ruban m ribbon; **~ adhésif** adhesive tape

rubéole f MÉD German measles sg

rubrique f heading

ruche f hive

rude *manières* uncouth; (*sévère*) harsh; *travail, lutte* hard

rudimentaire rudimentary; **rudiments** mpl rudiments

rue f street; **dans la ~** on the street

ruée f rush

ruelle f alley

rugby m rugby

rugir roar; *du vent* howl

rugueux, -euse rough

ruine f ruin; **ruiner** ruin

ruisseau m stream; (*caniveau*) gutter

ruisseler run

rumeur f hum; *de personnes* murmuring; (*nouvelle*) rumor, Br rumour

ruminer 1 *v/i* chew the cud, ruminate **2** *v/t* *fig*: **~ qch** mull sth over

rupture f breaking; *fig* split; *de négociations* breakdown; *de relations* breaking off; *de contrat* breach

rusé f ruse; **la ~** cunning; **rusé** crafty, cunning

russe 1 *adj* Russian **2** *m langue* Russian; **Russe** *m/f* Russian; **Russie:** *la* ~ Russia

rustique rustic

rustre *péj* **1** *adj* uncouth **2** *m* oaf

rythme *m* rhythm; (*vitesse*) pace; **rythmique** rhythmical

S

sa → **son**[1]

S.A. *f* (= **société anonyme**) Inc, *Br* plc

sable *m* sand; **sabler** sand; ~ *le champagne* break open the champagne

sablier *m* CUIS eggtimer

sabot *m* clog; *zo* hoof

sabotage *m* sabotage; **saboter** sabotage; F *travail* make a mess of

sac *m* bag; *de pommes de terre* sack; ~ *de couchage* sleeping bag; ~ *à dos* backpack; ~ *à main* purse, *Br* handbag

saccadé *mouvements* jerky; *voix* breathless

saccager (*piller*) sack; (*détruire*) destroy

saccharine *f* saccharine

sachet *m* sachet; ~ *de thé* teabag

sacoche *f* bag; *de vélo* saddlebag

sacré sacred; F damn F

sacrement *m* REL sacrament

sacrifice *m* sacrifice; **sacrifier** sacrifice; **se** ~ sacrifice o.s.

sacrilège 1 *adj* sacrilegious 2 *m* sacrilege

sadique 1 *adj* sadistic 2 *m/f* sadist

safran *m* saffron

sagace shrewd; **sagacité** *f* shrewdness

sage 1 *adj* wise; *enfant* good 2 *m* sage, wise man; **sage-femme** *f* midwife; **sagesse** *f* wisdom; *d'un enfant* goodness

Sagittaire *m* ASTROL Sagittarius

saignant bleeding; CUIS rare; **saigner** 1 *v/i* bleed 2 *v/t fig* bleed dry

saillant *pommettes* prominent; *fig* salient; **saillie** *f* ARCH projection; *fig* quip; **saillir** ARCH project

sain healthy; *poison* sound; ~ *d'esprit* sane

saint, ~e 1 *adj* holy 2 *m* saint; **sainteté** *f* holiness; **Saint-Sylvestre:** *la* ~ New Year's Eve

saisie *f* seizure; ~ *de données* INFORM data capture; **saisir** seize; *sens, intention* grasp; INFORM capture; **saisissant** striking; *froid* penetrating

saison *f* season; **saisonnier,**

-ère 1 *adj* seasonal **2** *m ouvrier* seasonal worker

salade *f* salad; **saladier** *m* salad bowl

salaire *m d'un ouvrier* wages *pl*; *d'un employé* salary; ~ **net** take-home pay

salarié, ~e 1 *adj travail* paid **2** *m/f ouvrier* wage-earner; *employé* salaried employee

salaud *m* P bastard *m*

sale *avant le substantif* dirty; *devant le substantif* nasty

salé *eau* salt; CUIS salted; *histoire* daring; *prix* steep; **saler** salt

saleté *f* dirtiness; **~s** *fig* (*grossièretés*) filthy remarks; F *choses sans valeur, mauvaise nourriture* junk

salière *f* salt cellar

salir: ~ *qch* get sth dirty

salive *f* saliva

salle *f* room; ~ *d'attente* waiting room; ~ *d'eau* shower room; ~ *à manger* dining room

salon *m* living room; *d'un hôtel* lounge; (*foire*) show; ~ *de l'automobile* auto show, Br motor show; ~ *de thé* tea room

salope *f* P bitch; **saloperie** *f* F *chose sans valeur* piece of junk; (*bassesse*) dirty trick

salopette *f* dungarees *pl*

salubre healthy

saluer greet; MIL salute; ~ *qn* (*de la main*) wave to s.o.

salut *m* greeting; MIL salute;

(*sauvegarde*) safety; REL salvation; ~! F hi!; (*au revoir*) bye!

salutaire salutary

samedi *m* Saturday

sanction *f* sanction

sanctuaire *m* sanctuary

sandale *f* sandal

sandwich *m* sandwich

sang *m* blood; **sang-froid** *m composure*; *garder son* ~ keep one's cool; *tuer qn de* ~ kill s.o. in cold blood; **sanglant** bloodstained; *combat, mort* bloody

sanglot *m* sob; **sangloter** sob

sanguin blood *atr*; *tempérament* sanguine; *groupe* *m* ~ blood group

sanitaire sanitary

sans without; ~ *manger* without eating; ~ *balcon* without a balcony

sans-abri *m/f*: *les* ~ the homeless *pl*

sans-emploi *m*: *les* ~ the unemployed *pl*

santé *f* health; *à votre* ~! cheers!, your very good health!

saper undermine

sapeur-pompier *m* firefighter

saphir *m* sapphire

sapin *m* BOT fir

sarcasme *m* sarcasm; **sarcastique** sarcastic

sardine *f* sardine

sardonique sardonic

S.A.R.L. *f* (= *société à res-*

ponsabilité limitée) Inc, *Br* Ltd

satellite *m* satellite

satin *m* satin

satirique satirical

satisfaction *f* satisfaction; **satisfaire 1** *v/i:* ~ **à 2** *v/t* satisfy; *attente* come up to; **satisfaisant** satisfactory; **satisfait** satisfied (**de** with)

saturer saturate

sauce *f* sauce

saucisse *f* sausage

saucisson *m* (dried) sausage

sauf [1] *prép* except; ~ **avis contraire** unless you/I / *etc* hear to the contrary

sauf [2], **sauve** *adj* safe

sauf-conduit *m* safe-conduct

saugrenu ridiculous

saule *m* BOT willow; ~ **pleureur** weeping willow

saumon *m* salmon

sauna *m* sauna

saupoudrer sprinkle (**de** with)

saut *m* jump; **faire un** ~ **chez qn** drop in briefly on s.o.; ~ **à l'élastique** bungee jumping; ~ **en longueur** broad jump, *Br* long jump; ~ **à la perche** pole vault

sauter 1 *v/i* jump; (*exploser*) blow up; *d'un fusible* blow; *d'un bouton* come off; ~ **sur** *personne* pounce on; *occasion*, *offre* jump at; *cela saute aux yeux* it's obvious **2** *v/t fossé* jump (over); *mot*, *repas* skip

sauterelle *f* grasshopper

sautiller hop

sauvage 1 *adj* wild; (*insociable*) unsociable; (*primitif*, *barbare*) savage; *pas autorisé* unauthorized **2** *m/f* savage; (*solitaire*) unsociable person

sauvegarde *f* safeguard; INFORM back-up

sauver save; *personne en danger* save, rescue; *navire* salvage; **se** ~ run away; F (*partir*) be off; (*déborder*) boil over

sauvetage *m* rescue; *de navire* salvaging; **sauveteur** *m* rescuer

sauveur *m* savior, *Br* saviour

savant 1 *adj* (*érudit*) learned; (*habile*) skillful, *Br* skilful **2** *m* scientist

saveur *f* taste

savoir 1 *v/t & v/i* know; *sais-tu nager?* can you swim?, do you know how to swim? **2** *m* knowledge

savoir-faire *m* expertise, knowhow

savoir-vivre *m* good manners *pl*

savon *m* soap

savourer savor, *Br* savour; **savoureux, -euse** tasty; *fig: récit* spicy

saxophone *m* saxophone, sax

scandale *m* scandal; **faire** ~ cause a scandal; **faire tout un** ~ make a scene; **scanda-**

liser scandalize; **se ~ de** be shocked by

scanner 1 *v/t* scan **2** *m* scanner

scaphandrier *m* diver

scarlatine *f* scarlet fever

sceau *m* seal; *fig (marque, signe)* stamp

scellé *m* official seal; **sceller** seal

scénario *m* scenario; *(script)* screenplay; **~ catastrophe** worst-case scenario

scène *f* scene *(aussi fig)*; *(plateau)* stage; **mettre en ~ pièce, film** direct; **présenter** stage; **~ de ménage** domestic argument

sceptique 1 *adj* skeptical, Br sceptical **2** *m* skeptic, Br sceptic

schéma *m* diagram; **schématiser** oversimplify

sciatique *f* sciatica

scie *f* saw; *fig* F bore

sciemment knowingly

science *f* science; *(connaissance)* knowledge; **scientifique 1** *adj* scientific **2** *m/f* scientist

scier saw; **branche** *etc* saw off

scinder *fig* split; **se ~** split up

scintiller sparkle

scission *f* split

scolaire *atr*; **succès, échec** academic; **scolarité** *f* education, schooling

scooter *m* (motor) scooter

score *m* SP score; POL share of the vote

scorpion *m* ZO scorpion; ASTROL **Scorpion** Scorpio

scotch® *m* Scotch tape®, Br sellotape®

scrupule *m* scruple; **scrupuleux, -euse** scrupulous

scruter scrutinize

scrutin *m* ballot; **~ majoritaire** majority vote system; **~ proportionnel** proportional representation

sculpter sculpt; **pierre** carve; **sculpteur** *m* sculptor; **sculpture** *f* sculpture

SDF *m/f* (= **sans domicile fixe**) homeless person

se *réfléchi masculin* himself; *féminin* herself; *chose, animal* itself; *pluriel* themselves; *avec 'one'* oneself; *réciproque* each other; **cela ne ~ fait pas** that isn't done; **ils ~ lèvent à ...** they get up at ...

séance *f* session; *de cinéma* show, performance; **~ tenante** *fig* immediately

seau *m* bucket

sec, sèche 1 *adj* dry; **fruits, légumes** dried; *(maigre)* thin; **réponse, ton** curt **2** *m*: **tenir au ~** keep in a dry place **3** *adv* **boire** neat, straight

sèche-cheveux *m* hair dryer; **sèche-linge** *m* clothes dryer; **sécher** dry; **d'un lac** dry up; **sécheresse** *f* dryness; **manque de pluie** drought; **de réponse, ton** curtness

second, ~e **1** *adj* second **2** *m* *étage* third floor, *Br* second floor; (*adjoint*) second in command **3** *f* second; *en train* second class; **secondaire** secondary; **seconder** *personne* assist

secouer shake; *poussière* shake off

secouriste *m/f* first-aider; **secours** *m* help; *matériel* aid; *au ~!* help!; **sortie** *f* **de ~** emergency exit; **premiers ~s** first aid

secousse *f* jolt; *électrique* shock; *tellurique* tremor

secret, -ète **1** *adj* secret **2** *m* secret; (*discrétion*) secrecy; **en ~** in secret

secrétaire 1 *m/f* secretary **2** *m* writing desk

secrétariat *m* secretariat; *profession* secretarial work

secte *f* REL sect

secteur *m* sector; (*zone*) area, district; ÉL *mains pl*

section *f* section; **sectionner** (*couper*) sever; *région etc* divide up

séculaire a hundred years old; *très ancien* centuries-old

séculier, -ère secular

sécurité *f* security; (*manque de danger*) safety; **Sécurité sociale** welfare, *Br* social security; **être en ~** be safe

sédatif *m* sedative

sédentaire sedentary; *population* settled

séduction *f* seduction; *fig* (*charme*) attraction; **séduire** seduce; *fig* (*charmer*) appeal to; *d'une personne* charm; **séduisant** appealing; *personne* attractive

ségrégation *f* segregation

seigle *m* AGR rye

seigneur *m* HIST the lord of the manor; REL: **le Seigneur** the Lord

sein *m* breast; *fig* bosom; **au ~ de** within

seize sixteen; **seizième** sixteenth

séjour *m* stay; (*salle f de*) ~ living room; **séjourner** stay

sel *m* salt

sélection *f* selection; **sélectionner** select

selle *f* saddle; MÉD stool

selon according to; **~ moi** in my opinion; **c'est ~** it all depends

semaine *f* week; **à la ~** by the week; **en ~** during the week, on weekdays

semblable 1 *adj* similar; *tel* such; **~ à** like, similar to **2** *m* (*être humain*) fellow human being

semblant *m* semblance; **faire ~ de faire** pretend to do

sembler seem

semelle *f* sole; *pièce intérieure* insole

semence *f* AGR seed

semer sow; *fig* (*répandre*) spread; **~ qn** F shake s.o. off

semestre *m* half-year

séminaire m seminar; REL seminary

semi-remorque m semi, Br articulated lorry

semonce f reproach

semoule f CUIS semolina

Sénat m POL Senate; **sénateur** m POL senator

sénile senile

sens m sense; (direction) direction; ~ **interdit** no entry; ~ **dessus dessous** upside down; ~ **de l'humour** sense of humor ou Br humour; (rue f à) ~ **unique** one-way street

sensation f feeling, sensation; effet de surprise sensation; **faire** ~ cause a sensation; **sensationnel,** ~le sensational

sensé sensible

sensibilité f sensitivity; sensible sensitive; (notable) appreciable; **sensiblement** appreciably; plus ou moins more or less

sensualité f sensuality; sensuel, ~le sensual

sentence f JUR sentence

sentier m path

sentiment m feeling; sentimental vie love atr; péj sentimental

sentinelle f MIL guard

sentir 1 v/t feel; (humer) smell; (dégager une odeur de) smell of; **se** ~ **bien** feel well 2 v/i: ~ **bon** smell good

séparable separable; sépa-

ration f separation; (cloison) partition; **séparatisme** m POL separatism; **séparé** separate; époux separated; **séparément** separately; **séparer** separate; **se** ~ separate

sept seven

septembre m September

septennat m term of office (of French President)

septentrional northern

septième seventh

septique septic

séquelles fpl MÉD after-effects; fig aftermath

séquence f sequence

serein calm

sérénité f serenity

série f series sg; de casseroles, timbres set; SP (épreuve) heat; **hors** ~ numéro special; **fabriquer en** ~ mass-produce

sérieux, -euse 1 adj serious; entreprise, employé professional; (consciencieux) conscientious **2** m seriousness; **prendre au** ~ take seriously

seringue f MÉD syringe

serment m oath; **prêter** ~ take the oath

sermon m sermon

séropositif, -ive HIV-positive

serpent m snake; **serpenter** wind, meander

serpillière f floor cloth

serre f greenhouse; ~**s** ZO talons

serré tight; pluie heavy; per-

sonnes closely packed; *café* strong

serrer 1 *v/t* (*tenir*) clasp; *ceinture* tighten; *d'un vêtement* be too tight for **2** *v/i*: *se ~* (*s'entasser*) squeeze up; *se ~ contre qn* press against s.o.

serrure *f* lock; **serrurier** *m* locksmith

serveur *m dans un café* bartender, *Br* barman; *dans un restaurant* waiter; INFORM server

serveuse *f dans un café* bartender, *Br* barmaid; *dans un restaurant* server, waitress

serviable helpful

service *m* service; (*faveur*) favor, *Br* favour; *au tennis* service, serve; *d'une entreprise, d'un hôpital* department; *être de ~* be on duty; *rendre ~ à qn* do s.o. a favor; *mettre en ~* put into service; *hors ~* out of order

serviette *f* serviette; *de toilette* towel; *pour documents* briefcase; *~ hygiénique* sanitary napkin

servile servile

servir serve; (*être utile*) be useful; *~ à qn* be of use to s.o.; *~ à qch/à faire qch* be used for sth/for doing sth; *~ de qc* act as sth; *se ~ à table* help o.s. (*en* to); *se ~ de* (*utiliser*) use

ses → **son¹**

seuil *m* doorstep; *fig* thresh-

old

seul 1 *adj* alone; (*solitaire*) lonely; *devant le subst* only, sole **2** *adv* alone; *faire qch tout ~* do sth all by o.s. *ou* all on one's own

seulement only; *non ~ ... mais encore ou mais aussi* not only ... but also

sévère severe; **sévérité** *f* severity

sévices *mpl* abuse

sévir *d'une épidémie* rage; *~ contre qn* come down hard on s.o.; *~ contre qc* clamp down on sth

sexagénaire *m/f & adj* sixty-year old

sexe *m* sex; *organes* genitals *pl*; **sexiste** *m/f & adj* sexist; **sexualité** *f* sexuality; **sexuel, ~le** sexual

shampo(o)ing *m* shampoo

short *m* shorts *pl*

si 1 *conj* (*s'il, s'ils*) if; *~ bien que* with the result that **2** *adv* (*tellement*) so; *après négation* yes; *de ~ bonnes vacances* such a good vacation; *~ riche qu'il soit* (*subj*) however rich he may be; *tu ne veux pas? - mais ~!* you don't want to? - oh yes, I do

sida *m* MÉD Aids

sidéré F thunderstruck

siècle *m* century; *fig* (*époque*) age

siège *m* seat; *d'une entreprise* headquarters *pl*; MIL siege; *~*

social COMM head office; **siéger** sit; **~ à** *d'une entreprise* be headquartered in

sien: *le sien, la sienne, les siens, les siennes d'homme* his; *de femme* hers; *de chose, d'animal* its; *avec 'one'* one's

sieste *f* siesta, nap

sifflement *m* whistle; **siffler** whistle; *d'un serpent* hiss; **sifflet** *m* whistle; **coup** *m* **de ~** blow on the whistle

signal *m* signal; **~ d'alarme** alarm (signal); **signalement** *m* description; **signaler** *par un signal* signal; *(faire remarquer)* point out; *(dénoncer)* report; **se ~ par** distinguish o.s. with

signature *f* signature

signe *m* sign; **faire ~ à** gesture *ou* signal to s; *(contacter)* get in touch with; **~ de ponctuation** punctuation mark; **signer** sign

signet *m* bookmark

signification *f* meaning; **signifier** mean; **~ qch à qn** *(faire savoir)* notify s.o. of sth

silence *m* silence; **silencieux, -euse 1** *adj* silent **2** *m d'une arme* muffler, *Br* silencer

silhouette *f* outline, silhouette; *(figure)* figure

sillage *m* wake *(aussi fig)*

sillon *m dans un champ* furrow; *d'un disque* groove; **sil-**

lonner *(parcourir)* criss-cross

similaire similar; **similitude** *f* similarity

simple 1 *adj* simple **2** *m au tennis* singles *pl;* **simplicité** *f* simplicity

simplifier simplify

simulateur, -trice 1 *m/f:* **c'est un ~** he's pretending **2** *m* TECH simulator; **simulation** *f* simulation; **simuler** simulate

simultané simultaneous

sincère sincere; **sincérité** *f* sincerity

singe *m* monkey; **singer** ape; **singerie** *f* imitation; **~s** F antics

singulier, -ère 1 *adj* odd, strange **2** *m* GRAM singular

sinistre 1 *adj* sinister; *(triste)* gloomy **2** *m* disaster; **sinistré 1** *adj* stricken **2** *m/f* disaster victim

sinon *(autrement)* or else, otherwise; *(sauf)* except; *(si ce n'est)* if not

sinueux, -euse *route* winding; *ligne* squiggly; *explication* complicated

sinus *m* sinus; **sinusite** *f* sinusitis

sirène *f* siren

sirop *m* syrup

siroter sip

sismique seismic

sitcom *m ou f* sitcom

site *m* site; *(paysage)* area; **~ Web** website

sitôt 1 *adv*: ~ *parti, il* ... as soon as he had left he ... **2** *conj*: ~ *que* as soon as

situation *f* situation; (*emplacement, profession*) position; situé situated

six six; **sixième** sixth

skateboard *m* skateboard; *activité* skateboarding

sketch *m* sketch

ski *m* ski; *activité* skiing; ~ *alpin* downhill (skiing); ~ *de fond* cross-country (skiing); ~ *nautique* water-skiing; **skier** ski; **skieur, -euse** *m/f* skier

slip *m de femme* panties *pl*; *d'homme* briefs; ~ *de bain* swimming trunks *pl*

slogan *m* slogan

slovaque *adj* Slovak(ian); **Slovaque** *m/f* Slovak(ian)

slovène *adj* Slovene, Slovenian; **Slovène** *m/f* Slovene, Slovenian

smoking *m* tuxedo, *Br* dinner jacket

SMS *m* text (message)

S.N.C.F. *f* (= *Société nationale des chemins de fer français*) French national railroad company

sobre sober; *style* restrained

sociable sociable

social social; *COMM company* atr; **socialiser** socialize; **socialisme** *m* socialism; **socialiste** *m/f adj* socialist

société *f* society; *firme* company; ~ *anonyme* corpora-

tion, *Br* public limited company, plc

sociologie *f* sociology

socquette *f* anklet, *Br* ankle sock

soda *m* soda, *Br* fizzy drink; *un whisky* ~ a whiskey and soda

sœur *f* sister; REL nun

sofa *m* sofa

soi oneself; *avec* ~ with one; *ça va de* ~ that goes without saying

soi-disant *inv* so-called

soie *f* silk

soif *f* thirst; *avoir* ~ be thirsty

soigné *personne* well-groomed; *travail* careful; **soigner** look after, take care of; *d'un médecin* treat; *se* ~ take care of o.s.; **soigneux, -euse** careful (*de* about)

soi-même oneself

soin *m* care; ~*s* care; MÉD care, treatment; *prendre* ~ *de* look after, take care of; *être sans* ~ be untidy

soir *m* evening; *le* ~ in the evening; **soirée** *f* evening; (*fête*) party

soit¹ *adv* very well, so be it

soit² *conj* ~ ..., ~ ... either ..., or ...; (*à savoir*) that is, ie

soixantaine *f* about sixty; **soixante** sixty; **soixante-dix** seventy

soja *m* BOT soy bean, *Br* soya

sol *m* ground; (*plancher*) floor; (*patrie*), GÉOL soil

solaire solar

sonner

soldat *m* soldier

solde[1] *f* MIL pay

solde[2] *m* COMM balance; **~s**
marchandises sale goods;
vente au rabais sale; *solder
compte* close, balance; *marchandises* sell off

sole *f* ZO sole

soleil *m* sun; *il y a du ~*
it's sunny; *coup m de ~* sunburn

solennel, *.le* solemn

solidaire: *être ~ de qn* suport
s.o.; **solidarité** *f* solidarity

solide 1 *adj* solid; *tissu*
strong; *argument* sound;
personne sturdy **2** *m* PHYS
solid; **solidité** *f* solidity;
d'un matériau strength;
d'un argument soundness

solitaire 1 *adj* solitary **2** *m*
loner **3** *m* *diamant* solitaire;
solitude *f* solitude

sollicitation *f* plea; **solliciter**
request; *attention* attract;
curiosité arouse; *~ un emploi* apply for a job; **sollicitude** *f* solicitude

solstice *m* ASTR solstice

soluble soluble; *café m ~* instant coffee

solution *f* solution

solvable solvent; *digne de
crédit* creditworthy

sombre *couleur, salle* dark;
temps overcast; *avenir, regard* somber, *Br* sombre

sommaire 1 *adj* brief; *exécution* summary **2** *m* summary

somme[1] *f* sum; *(quantité)*
amount; *en ~, ~ toute* in
short

somme[2] *m* nap, snooze

sommeil *m* sleep; *avoir ~* be
sleepy; **sommeiller** doze

sommelier *m* wine waiter

sommer: *~ qn de faire qc* order s.o. to do sth

sommet *m* *d'une montagne*
summit, top; *d'un arbre,
d'une tour* top; *fig* pinnacle;
POL summit

sommier *m* mattress

somnambule *m/f* sleepwalker

somnifère *m* sleeping tablet

somnolence *f* drowsiness,
sleepiness; **somnoler** doze

somptueux, -euse sumptuous; **somptuosité** *f* sumptuousness

son[1] *m*, *sa f*, *ses pl d'homme*
his; *de femme* her; *de chose,
d'animal* its; *avec 'one'* one's

son[2] *m* sound

sondage *m* probe; TECH drilling; *~ (d'opinion)* opinion
poll, survey

sonde *f* probe; **sonder** MÉD
probe; *personne, atmosphère* sound out

songe *m* litt dream; **songer:**
~ à (faire) qc think about
(doing) sth; **songeur, -euse**
thoughtful

sonner 1 *v/i de cloches, sonnette* ring; *d'un réveil* go
off; *d'un instrument, d'une
voix* sound; *d'une horloge*
strike; *midi a sonné* it has
struck noon; *~ creux/faux*

fig hollow/false **2** *v/t cloches* ring; **sonnerie** *f de cloches* ringing; (*sonnette*) bell; **sonnette** *f* bell

sonore *voix* loud; *rire* resounding; *cuivres* sonorous; *onde, film* sound *atr*; **sonorité** *f* sound, tone; *d'une salle* acoustics *pl*

sophistiqué sophisticated

soporifique sleep-inducing, soporific

soprano 1 *f* soprano **2** *m* treble

sorcellerie *f* sorcery, witchcraft

sorcier *m* sorcerer; **sorcière** *f* witch

sordide filthy; *fig* sordid

sort *m* fate; (*condition*) lot; *tirer au ~* draw lots; *jeter un ~ à fig* cast a spell on

sorte *f* (*manière*) way; (*espèce*) sort, kind; *en quelque ~* in a way; *de (telle) ~ que* and so

sortie *f* exit; (*promenade, excursion*) outing; *d'un livre* publication; *d'un disque* release; *d'une voiture* launch; TECH outlet; MIL sortie; ~ (*sur*) *imprimante* printout

sortir 1 *v/i* come/go out; *pour se distraire* go out (*avec* with); *d'un livre, un disque* come out; *au loto* come up; ~ *d'un endroit* leave; *accident, entretien* emerge from; (*provenir de*) come from **2** *v/t chose* bring/take out;

chien, personne take out; COMM bring out; F *bêtises* come out with **3**: *s'en ~ d'un malade* pull through

sot, ~**te 1** *adj* silly, foolish **2** *m/f* fool; **sottise** *f* foolishness; *action/remarque* foolish thing to do/say

sou *m* F penny; *être sans le ~* be penniless

souche *f d'un arbre* stump; *d'un carnet* stub

souci *m* worry, care; *sans ~* carefree; **soucier**: *se ~ de* worry about; **soucieux, -euse** anxious, concerned (*de* about)

soucoupe *f* saucer

soudain 1 *adj* sudden **2** *adv* suddenly

souder TECH weld; *fig* bring closer together

soudoyer bribe

souffle *m* breath; *d'une explosion* blast; *à bout de ~* breathless, out of breath; **souffler 1** *v/i du vent* blow; (*haleter*) puff; (*respirer*) breathe; (*reprendre son souffle*) get one's breath back **2** *v/t chandelle* blow out; ÉDU, *au théâtre* prompt; ~ *qc à qn* F (*enlever*) whisper sth to s.o.; (*enlever*) steal sth from s.o.

souffrance *f* suffering; **souffrant** unwell; **souffrir 1** *v/i* be in pain; ~ *de* suffer from **2** *v/t* suffer

soufre *m* CHIM sulfur, *Br* sulphur

souhait *m* wish; **à vos ~s!** bless you!; **souhaitable** desirable; **souhaiter** wish for; **~ que** (+ *subj*) hope that

souiller dirty, soil; *fig: réputation* tarnish

soûl drunk

soulagement *m* relief; **soulager** relieve; **~ qn au travail** help s.o. out

soûler F: **~ qn** get s.o. drunk; **se ~** get drunk

soulèvement *m* uprising; **soulever** raise; *enthousiasme* arouse; *protestations* generate; **se ~** raise o.s.; *(se révolter)* rise up

souligner underline

soumettre *pays, peuple* subdue; **à un examen** subject (**à** to); *(présenter)* submit; **se ~ à** submit to; *soumis peuple* subject; *(obéissant)* submissive; **soumission** *f* submission; COMM tender

soupçon *m* suspicion; **un ~ de** a hint of; **soupçonner** suspect; **soupçonneux, -euse** suspicious

soupe *f* CUIS (thick) soup

souper 1 *v/i* have dinner *ou* supper **2** *m* dinner, supper

soupir *m* sigh; **soupirer** sigh

souple flexible; **souplesse** *f* flexibility

source *f* spring; *fig* source

sourcil *m* eyebrow

sourd deaf; *voix* low; *douleur, bruit* dull; *colère* re-

pressed; **~-muet** deaf-and-dumb

souriant smiling

souricière *f* mousetrap; *fig* trap

sourire *v/i & m* smile

souris *f* mouse

sournois, ~e 1 *adj* underhanded **2** *m/f* underhanded person

sous under; **~ peu** soon; **~ la pluie** in the rain

souscription *f* subscription; **souscrire: ~ à** subscribe to *(aussi fig)*; *emprunt* approve

sous-entendre imply; **sous-entendu 1** *adj* implied **2** *m* implication

sous-estimer underestimate

sous-jacent underlying

sous-louer sublet

sous-marin 1 *adj* underwater **2** *m* submarine

sous-sol *m* *d'une maison* basement

sous-titre *m* subtitle

soustraire MATH subtract (**de** from); *fig: au regard de* remove; **à un danger** protect (**à** from)

sous-traitance *f* sub-contracting

sous-vêtements *mpl* underwear

soutane *f* REL cassock

soute *f* MAR, AVIAT hold

soutenir support; *pression* withstand; *conversation* keep going; *opinion* maintain; **~ que** maintain that;

se ~ support each other; **soutenu** *effort* sustained; *style* elevated

souterrain 1 *adj* underground, subterranean **2** *m* underground passage

soutien *m* support

soutien-gorge *m* brassiere, bra

souvenir 1: *se* ~ *de qn/qch* remember s.o./sth; *se* ~ *que* remember that **2** *m* memory; *objet* souvenir

souvent often; *le plus* ~ most of the time

souverain, -e *m/f* sovereign

soyeux, -euse silky

spacieux, -euse spacious

spaghetti *mpl* spaghetti *sg*

sparadrap *m* Band-Aid®, *Br* Elastoplast®

spasme *m* MÉD spasm; **spasmodique** spasmodic

spatial spatial; ASTR space *atr*

spécial special; **spécialiser:** *se* ~ specialize; **spécialiste** *m/f* specialist; **spécialité** *f* speciality

spécifier specify

spécifique specific

spécimen *m* specimen

spectacle *m* spectacle; *théâtre, cinéma* show, performance; **spectaculaire** spectacular

spectateur, -trice *m/f* (*témoin*) onlooker; SP spectator; *au théâtre* member of the audience

spectre *m* ghost; PHYS spec-

trum

spéculer speculate

spéléologie *f* caving

spermatozoïde *m* BIOL sperm

sperme *m* BIOL sperm

sphère *f* MATH sphere (*aussi fig*)

spirale *f* spiral

spirituel, ~le spiritual; (*amusant*) witty

spiritueux *mpl* spirits

splendeur *f* splendor, *Br* splendour, magnificence; **splendide** splendid

sponsor *m* sponsor; **sponsoriser** sponsor

spontané spontaneous

sport 1 *m* sport; *faire du* ~ do sport **2** *adj vêtements* casual *atr*

sportif, -ive **1** *adj résultats, association* sports *atr*; *allure* sporty; (*fair-play*) sporting **2** *m* sportsman **3** *f* sportswoman

square *m* public garden

squash *m* SP squash

squatter *m* squat; **squatteur**, -euse *m/f* squatter

squelette *m* skeleton

stabilisateur, -trice **1** *adj* stabilizing **2** *m* stabilizer; **stabiliser** stabilize; **stabilité** *f* stability; **stable** stable

stade *m* SP stadium; *d'un processus* stage

stage *m* training period; (*cours*) training course; *pour professeur* teaching practice; (*expérience professionnelle*) work placement; **stagiaire** *m/f* trainee

stagnant *eau* stagnant

stalle *f d'un cheval* box; **~** REL stalls

stand *m de foire* booth, *Br* stand; *de kermesse* stall

standard *eau* standard; TÉL switchboard

standardiser standardize

standardiste *m/f* TÉL (switchboard) operator

starter *m* AUTO choke

station *f* station; *de bus* stop; *de vacances* resort; **~ de taxis** cab stand, *Br* taxi rank; **~ thermale** spa

stationnement *m* parking; **stationner** park

station-service *f* gas station, *Br* petrol station

statistique 1 *adj* statistical **2** *f* statistic; *science* statistics *sg*

statue *f* statue

stature *f* stature

statut *m* status; **~s** *d'une société* statutes

stéréo *f* stereo

stéréotype *m* stereotype; **stéréotypé** stereotype

stérile sterile; **stériliser** sterilize; **stérilité** *f* sterility

steward *m* flight attendant, steward

stigmate *m* mark; **~s** REL stigmata

stimuler stimulate

stipulation *f* stipulation; **stipuler** stipulate

stock *m* stock; **stocker** stock; INFORM store

stoïque stoical

stop *m* stop; *écriteau* stop sign; *(feu m)* **~** AUTO brake light; *faire du* **~** F hitchhike; **stopper** stop

store *m d'une fenêtre* shade, *Br* blind; *d'un magasin, d'une terrasse* awning

strapontin *m* tip-up seat

stratagème *m* stratagem

stratégie *f* strategy

stress *m* stress; **stressant** stressful; **stressé** stressed-out

strict strict; *le* **~ nécessaire** the bare minimum

strident strident

strip-tease *m* strip(tease)

structure *f* structure

studieux, -euse studious

stupéfait stupefied; **stupéfiant 1** *adj* stupefying **2** *m* drug; **stupéfier** stupefy

stupeur *f* stupor

stupide stupid

style *m* style; **styliste** *m de mode, d'industrie* stylist

stylo *m* pen; **~ plume** fountain pen

suave *voix, goût* sweet

subalterne 1 *adj* junior **2** *m/f* junior, subordinate

subir (*endurer*) suffer; (*se soumettre volontairement à*) undergo

subit sudden

subjectif, -ive subjective

subjuguer *fig* captivate

sublime sublime

submerger submerge; *être submergé de* fig be buried in

subordonné, ~e adj & m/f subordinate; **subordonner** subordinate (à to)

subrepticement surreptitiously

subsidiaire subsidiary

subsistance f subsistence; **subsister** survive; *d'une personne aussi* live

substance f substance; **substantiel**, ~le substantial

substituer: ~ *X à Y* substitute X for Y

subterfuge m subterfuge

subtil subtle; **subtilité** f subtlety

subvenir: ~ *à* provide for

subvention f grant, subsidy; **subventionner** subsidize

subversif, -ive subversive

suc m: ~*s gastriques* gastric juices

succéder: ~ *à* follow; *personne* succeed; *se* ~ follow each other

succès m success

successeur m successor; **succession** f succession; JUR *(biens dévolus)* inheritance

succomber *(mourir)* die, succumb; ~ *à* succumb to

succulent succulent

succursale f COMM branch

sucer suck; **sucette** f bonbon lollipop; *de bébé* pacifier, Br dummy

sucre m sugar; **sucré** sweet; *au sucre* sugared; *péj* sugary; **sucrer** sweeten; *avec sucre* sugar; **sucreries** fpl sweet things

sud 1 m south; *au* ~ *de* (to the) south of 2 adj south; *hémisphère* southern

sud-américain, ~e South American; **Sud-Américain**, ~e m/f South American

sud-est m south-east

sud-ouest m south-west

Suède: *la* ~ Sweden; **suédois**, ~e 1 adj Swedish 2 m langue Swedish; **Suédois**, ~e m/f Swede

suer 1 v/i sweat 2 v/t sweat; fig *(dégager)* ooze; **sueur** f sweat

suffire be enough; *il suffit que tu le lui dises (subj)* all you have to do is tell her; *ça suffit!* that's enough!

suffisamment sufficiently, enough; ~ *intelligent* sufficiently intelligent, intelligent enough; ~ *de...* enough ..., sufficient ...; **suffisance** f arrogance; **suffisant** sufficient, enough; *(arrogant)* arrogant

suffocant suffocating; fig breath-taking; **suffocation** f suffocation; **suffoquer** suffocate

suffrage m vote; ~ *universel* universal suffrage

suggérer suggest (*à* to); **suggestion** *f* suggestion

suicide *m* suicide; **suicider:** *se* ~ commit suicide

suinter *d'un mur* ooze

suisse, Suisse 1 *m/f* Swiss **2 la Suisse** Switzerland

suite *f* pursuit; (*série*) series *sg*; (*continuation*) continuation; *d'un film, un livre* sequel; MUS, *appartement* suite; **la** ~ **de l'histoire** the rest of the story; ~**s** (*conséquences*) consequences; *d'un choc, d'une maladie* after-effects; **trois fois de** ~ three times in a row; **et ainsi de** ~ and so on; **par** ~ **de** as a result of; **tout de** ~ immediately

suivant, ~e 1 *adj* next, following **2** *m/f* next person; **au** ~! next! **3** *prép* (*selon*) according to **4** *conj:* ~ **que** depending on whether

suivi effort sustained; *relations* continuous; *argumentation* coherent

suivre 1 *v/t* follow; *cours* take **2** *v/i* follow; *à l'école* keep up; **faire** ~ *lettre* please forward; **à** ~ to be continued

sujet, ~te 1 *adj:* ~ **à** subject to **2** *m* subject; **au** ~ **de** on the subject of

sulfureux, -euse sultry

super 1 *adj* F great F, neat F **2** *m* essence premium

superbe superb

supercherie *f* hoax

superficie *f fig* surface; (*surface, étendue*) (surface) area; **superficiel, ~le** superficial

superflu 1 *adj* superfluous **2** *m* surplus

supérieur, ~e 1 *adj* higher; *étages, mâchoire* upper; (*meilleur, dans une hiérarchie*) superior (*aussi péj*) **2** *m/f* superior; **supériorité** *f* superiority

supermarché *m* supermarket

superposer stack; *couches* superimpose; **lits** *mpl* **superposés** bunk beds

superstitieux, -euse superstitious; **superstition** *f* superstition

superviser supervise

supplanter supplant

suppléant, ~e 1 *adj* acting **2** *m/f* stand-in, replacement; **suppléer:** ~ **à** make up for

supplément *m* supplement; **un** ~ **de ...** additional *ou* extra ...; **supplémentaire** additional

supplication *f* plea

supplice *m* torture; *fig* agony; **supplicier** torture

supplier: ~ **qn de faire** beg s.o. to do

support *m* support; **supportable** bearable; **supporter**[1] *v/t* TECH, ARCH support, hold up; *conséquences* take; *frais, douleur, personne* bear; *chaleur, alcool* tolerate; **sup-**

porter² m SP supporter, fan

supposer suppose; *(impliquer)* presuppose; **supposition** f supposition

suppression f suppression; **supprimer** *institution, impôt* abolish; *emplois* cut; *mot* delete; *concert* cancel

suprême supreme

sur on; **prendre qch ~ l'étagère** take sth off the shelf; **une fenêtre ~ la rue** a window looking onto the street; **tirer ~ qn** shoot at s.o.; **un film ~ ...** a movie on *ou* about ...; **un ~ dix** one out of ten

sûr sure; *(non dangereux)* safe; *(fiable)* reliable; **bien ~** of course; **à coup ~ il sera ...** he's bound to be ...

surcharge f overloading; *(poids excédentaire)* excess weight

surchauffer overheat

surclasser outclass

surcroît m: **un ~ de travail** extra work; **de ~, par ~** moreover

surdité f deafness

surdoué extremely gifted

surélever raise

sûrement surely

surenchère f *dans vente aux enchères* higher bid

surestimer overestimate

sûreté f safety; MIL security; *de jugement* soundness

surexciter overexcite

surexposer overexpose

surface f surface; **grande ~** COMM supermarket

surfait overrated

surfer surf; **~ sur Internet** surf the Net

surgelé 1 *adj* deep-frozen **2** *mpl*: **~s** frozen food

surgir suddenly appear; *d'un problème* crop up

sur-le-champ at once, straightaway

surlendemain m day after tomorrow

surligner highlight

surmener overwork; **se ~** overwork, overdo it F

surmonter dominate; *fig* overcome, surmount

surnaturel, ~le the supernatural

surnom m nickname; **surnommer** nickname

surpasser surpass

surpeuplé *pays* overpopulated; *endroit* overcrowded

surplomber overhang

surplus m surplus; **au ~** moreover

surprenant surprising; **surprendre** surprise; *voleur* catch (in the act); **se ~ à faire qch** catch o.s. doing sth; **surpris** surprised; **surprise** f surprise

sursaut m jump, start; **sursauter** jump

sursis m *fig* reprieve, stay of execution; **peine avec ~** JUR suspended sentence

surtaxe f surcharge

surtout especially; *(avant*

tout) above all; **~ que** F especially since

surveillance *f* supervision; *par la police etc* surveillance; **surveillant, ~e** *m/f* supervisor; *de prison* guard; **surveiller** watch; *élèves, employés* supervise; **se ~** *comportement* watch one's step; *poids* watch one's figure

survenir *d'une personne* arrive unexpectedly; *d'un événement* happen; *d'un problème* come up, arise

survêtement *m* sweats *pl*, *Br* tracksuit

survie *f* survival; REL afterlife; **survivant, ~e 1** *adj* surviving **2** *m/f* survivor; **survivre: ~ à** survive

susceptible sensitive, touchy; **~ de faire qch** likely to do sth

susciter arouse

suspect (*équivoque*) suspicious; (*d'une qualité douteuse*) suspect; **~ de qc** suspected of sth; **suspecter** suspect

suspendre suspend; (*accrocher*) hang up; **suspendu** suspended

suspens: en ~ *personne* in suspense; *affaire* outstand-ing

suspense *m* suspense

suspension *f* suspension

suspicion *f* suspicion

svelte trim, slender

sweat(-shirt) *m* sweatshirt

syllabe *f* syllable

symbole *m* symbol; **symboliser** symbolize

symétrie *f* symmetry

sympathie *f* sympathy; (*amitié, inclination*) liking; **sympathique** nice, friendly; **sympathiser** get on

symphonie *f* symphony

symptôme *m* symptom

synagogue *f* synagogue

synchroniser synchronize

syndical labor *atr*, *Br* (trade) union *atr*

syndicat *m* (labor) union, *Br* (trade) union; **~ d'initiative** tourist information office

syndiqué unionized

synonyme 1 *adj* synonymous (*de* with) **2** *m* synonym

synthèse *f* synthesis; **synthétiseur** *m* MUS synthesizer

systématique systematic; **système** *m* system; **~ antidémarrage** immobilizer; **~ d'exploitation** INFORM operating system

T

ta → **ton²**

tabac m tobacco; **bureau** m **de~** tobacco store, Br tobacconist's

table f table; **se mettre à~** sit down to eat

tableau m à l'école board; (peinture) painting; fig picture; (liste) list; (schéma) table; **~ de bord** AVIAT instrument panel

tablette f shelf; INFORM tablet; **~ de chocolat** chocolate bar

tablier m apron

tabouret m stool

tache f stain

tâche f task

tacher stain

tâcher: ~ de faire try to do

tacheté stained

tacite tacit

taciturne taciturn

tact m tact; **avoir du~** be tactful

tactique 1 adj tactical **2** f tactics pl

taie f: **~ (d'oreiller)** pillowslip

taille¹ f BOT pruning; de la pierre cutting

taille² f (hauteur) height; (dimension) size; ANAT waist

taille-crayon(s) m pencil sharpener

tailler BOT prune; vêtement cut out; crayon sharpen; pierre cut; **tailleur** m (couturier) tailor; vêtement (woman's) suit

taire: se ~ keep quiet (sur about); s'arrêter de parler stop talking; **tais-toi!** be quiet!, shut up!

talc m talc

talent m talent; **talentueux, -euse** talented

talon m heel; **talonner** (serrer de près) follow close behind; (harceler) harass

talus m bank

tambour m MUS, TECH drum; **tambouriner** drum

Tamise: la ~ the Thames

tamiser sieve; lumière filter

tampon m d'ouate pad; hygiène féminine tampon; (amortisseur) buffer; (cachet) stamp; **tamponnement** m AUTO collision; **tamponner** plaie clean; (cacheter) stamp; AUTO collide with

tandis que while

tangente f MATH tangent

tangible tangible

tango m tango

tanière f lair, den (aussi fig)

tanné tanned; peau weatherbeaten; **tanner** tan; fig F pester

tant 1 adv so much; **~ de vin** so much wine; **~ d'erreurs** so many errors; **~ mieux** so much the better; **~ pis** too bad, tough **2** conj: **~ que temps** as long as; **en ~ que Français** as a Frenchman; **~ ... que ...** both ... and ...

tante f aunt

tantôt this afternoon; **à ~** see you soon; **~ ... ~ ...** now ... now ...

taon m horsefly

tapage m racket; fig fuss; **tapageur, -euse** (voyant) flashy, loud; (bruyant) noisy

tape f pat

taper 1 v/t hit; table bang on; **~** (à l'ordinateur) F key, type **2** v/i hit; à l'ordinateur key; **~ sur les nerfs de qn** F get on s.o.'s nerves

tapir: se ~ crouch

tapis m carpet; SP mat; **~ roulant** TECH conveyor belt; pour personnes traveling ou Br travelling walkway; **~ de souris** mouse mat

tapisser avec du papier peint (wall)paper; **tapisserie** f tapestry; (papier peint) wallpaper

tapoter (qn; personne) pat

taquiner tease; **taquinerie** f teasing

tard 1 adv late; **plus ~** later (on); **au plus ~** at the latest **2** m: **sur le ~** late in life

tarder delay; **~ à faire** take a long time doing; **il me tarde de te revoir** I'm longing to see you again

tardif, -ive late

targuer: se ~ de qc litt pride o.s. on sth

tarif m rate; **~ unique** flat rate

tarir dry up (aussi fig); **se ~** dry up

tartan m tartan

tarte f tart; **tartelette** f tartlet

tartine f slice of bread; **~ de confiture** slice of bread and jam

tas m heap, pile; **un ~ de choses** heaps pl ou piles pl of things

tasse f cup; **une ~ de café** a cup of coffee; **une ~ à café** a coffee cup

tasser (bourrer) cram; **se ~** settle

tâter 1 v/t feel **2** v/i F: **~ de qc** try sth

tatillon, ~ne fussy

tâtons: avancer à ~ feel one's way forward

tatouage m action tattooing; signe tattoo

taudis m slum

taupe f zo mole

taureau m bull; ASTROL **Taureau** Taurus

taux m rate; **~ d'alcoolémie** blood alcohol level; **~ de change** exchange rate; **~ d'intérêt** interest rate

taxe f duty; (impôt) tax; **~ sur ou à la valeur ajoutée** sales tax, Br value added tax, VAT; **taxer** tax; **~ qn de qc** fig (accuser) tax s.o. with sth

taxi m taxi, cab

tchèque 1 adj Czech **2** m lan-

gue Czech; **Tchèque** m/f Czech

te you; _complément d'objet indirect_ (to) you; **tu t'es coupé** you've cut yourself; **si tu ~ lèves à …** if you get up at …

technicien, **~ne** m/f technician

technique 1 adj technical **2** f technique

technologie f technology; **~ informatique** computer technology; **~ de pointe** high-tech; **technologique** technological

tee-shirt m T-shirt

teindre dye

teint, **~e 1** adj dyed **2** m complexion; **fond m de ~** foundation (cream) **3** f tint; _fig_ tinge; **teinter** tinge; _bois_ stain; **teinture** f action dyeing; _produit_ dye; PHARM tincture

tel, **~le** such; **une ~le surprise** such a surprise; **de ce genre** a surprise like that; **~(s) ou ~le(s) que** such as, like

télé f TV, tube F, _Br_ telly F

télécharger INFORM download

télécommande f remote control

télécommunications f pl telecommunications

téléconférence f teleconference

téléguidage m remote control

téléobjectif m telephoto lens

télépathie f telepathy

téléphone m phone, telephone; **~ portable** cellphone, _Br_ mobile (phone); **coup m de ~** (phone) call; **~ avec appareil photo intégré** camera phone; **téléphoner 1** v/i phone, telephone; **à qn** call s.o., _Br aussi_ phone s.o. **2** v/t phone, telephone; **téléphonique** phone _atr_, telephone _atr_; **appel m ~** phone

téléréalité f reality TV

télescope m telescope; **télescoper** crash into; **se ~** crash

télésiège m chair lift

téléski m ski lift

téléspectateur, **-trice** m/f (TV) viewer

télévision f television; **~ câblée** cable (TV)

tellement so; _avec verbe_ so much; **pas ~** not really; **~ de chance** so much good luck; **~ de filles** so many girls

téméraire reckless; **témérité** f recklessness

témoignage m JUR testimony, evidence; _(rapport)_ account; _fig: d'estime_ token; **témoigner** JUR testify, give evidence; **~ de** (être le témoignage de) show; **témoin** m witness; **être (le) ~ de qch** witness sth

tempe f ANAT temple

tempérament m temperament; **à ~** in installments _ou Br_ instalments

température f temperature; *avoir de la ~* have a fever, *Br aussi* have a temperature

tempérer moderate

tempête f storm

temple m temple; *protestant* church

temporaire temporary

temporel, .le temporal

temporiser stall, play for time

temps m time; *atmosphérique* weather; TECH stroke; *à ~* in time; *de ~ en ~* from time to time; *il est ~ de partir* it's time to go; *il est ~ que tu t'en ailles* (*subj*) it's time you left; *en même ~* at the same time; *par beau ~* in good weather; *quel ~ fait-il?* what's the weather like?

tenace tenacious

tenailles fpl pincers

tendance f trend; (*disposition*) tendency; *avoir ~ à faire* have a tendency to do, tend to do

tendon m ANAT tendon

tendre¹ **1** v/t filet, ailes spread; *piège* set; *bras, main* hold out; *muscles* tense; *corde* tighten; *~ qch à qn* hold sth out to s.o.; *se ~ de rapports* become strained **2** v/i: *~ à qc* strive for sth; *~ à faire qc* tend to do sth

tendre² adj tender; *couleur* soft

tendresse f tenderness

tendu *corde* tight; *fig* tense;

relations strained

ténèbres fpl darkness; **ténébreux, -euse** dark

teneur f d'une lettre contents pl; (*concentration*) content

tenir 1 v/t hold; (*maintenir*) keep; *registre, promesse* keep; *caisse* be in charge of; *restaurant* run; *place* take up; *~ à qc/qn* (*donner de l'importance à*) value sth/ s.o.; *à un objet* be attached to sth; *~ à faire qc* really want to do sth; *cela ne tient qu'à toi* (*dépend de*) it's entirely up to you **2** v/i hold; *~ dans* fit into **3**: *se ~ d'un spectacle* be held; (*être, se trouver*) stand; *se ~ à qch* hold on to sth; *s'en ~ à* confine o.s. to

tennis m tennis; *terrain* tennis court; *~ pl* sneakers, *Br* trainers; SP tennis shoes

ténor m MUS tenor

tension f tension; MÉD blood pressure; *faire de la ~* F have high blood pressure

tentacule m tentacle

tentant tempting; **tentation** f temptation

tentative f attempt

tente f tent

tenter tempt; (*essayer*) attempt, try (*de faire* to do)

tenture f wallhanging

tenu: *être ~ de faire qc* be obliged to do sth; *bien ~* well looked after; *mal ~* badly kept; *enfant* neglected

ténu fine; *espoir* slim

tenue *f de comptes* keeping; *de ménage* running; (*conduite*) behavior; *Br* behaviour; *du corps* posture; (*vêtements*) clothes *pl*; **~ de soirée** evening wear

tergiverser hum and haw

terme *m* (*fin*) end; (*échéance*) time limit; (*expression*) term; **à court/long ~** in the short/long term; *emprunt, projet* short-/long-term

terminaison *f* GRAM ending; **terminer** finish; **se ~** end; **se ~ par** end with; *d'un mot* end in

terminus *m* terminus

ternir tarnish

terrain *m* ground; GÉOL, MIL terrain; SP field; **un ~** a piece of land; **sur le ~** *essai* field *atr*; *essayer* in the field; **~ d'aviation** airfield; **à bâtir** building lot; **~ de jeu** play park; **véhicule** *m* **tout ~** 4x4, off-road vehicle

terrasse *f* terrace; **terrasser** *adversaire* fell

terre *f* (*sol, surface*) ground; *matière* earth, soil; *opposé à mer, propriété* land; (*monde*) earth, world; *pays, région* land, country; ÉL ground; *Br* earth; **~ à ~ personne** down to earth; **à ou par ~** on the ground; **tomber par ~** fall down; **sur ~** on earth; **sur la ~** on the ground

terre-plein *m*: **~ central** median strip, *Br* central reservation

terrestre *animaux* land *atr*; REL earthly; TV terrestrial

terreur *f* terror

terrible terrible; F (*extraordinaire*) terrific; **c'est pas ~** it's not that good

terrien, **~ne 1** *adj*: **propriétaire** *m* **~** landowner **2** *m/f* (*habitant de la Terre*) earthling

terrier *m de renard* earth; ZO terrier

terrifier terrify

territoire *m* territory

terroir *m viticulture* soil; **du ~** (*régional*) local

terroriser terrorize; **terrorisme** *m* terrorism; **terroriste** *m/f & adj* terrorist

tertre *m* mound

tes → ton²

test *m* test; **~ de résistance** endurance test

testament *m* JUR will; **Ancien/Nouveau Testament** REL Old/New Testament

tester test

testicule *m* testicle

tête *f* head; (*cheveux*) hair; (*visage*) face; SP header; **de ~ calculer** in one's head; **répondre** without looking anything up; **avoir la ~ dure** be stubborn; **se casser la ~** *fig* rack one's brains; **n'en faire qu'à sa ~** do exactly as one likes; **tenir ~ à qn** stand up to s.o.; *péj* defy s.o.; **faire la ~** sulk; **il se paie ta ~** *fig* he's making a fool of you; **en ~** in the lead

tête-à-queue m AUTO spin; **tête-à-tête** m tête-à-tête; **en ~** in private

têtu obstinate

texte m text; **~s choisis** selected passages

textile m text; **le ~ industrie** the textile industry, textiles pl

texto m text (message); **envoyer un ~ à qn** send s.o. a text, text s.o.

texture f texture

T.G.V. m (= **train à grande vitesse**) high-speed train

thé m tea

théâtre m theater, Br theatre; fig: cadre scene

théière f teapot

thème m theme; ÉDU translation (into a foreign language)

théorie f theory; **théorique** theoretical

thérapeute m/f therapist; **thérapeutique 1** f (thérapie) therapy **2** adj therapeutic; **thérapie** f therapy

thermal thermal

thermomètre m thermometer

thermos f ou m thermos®

thèse f thesis

thon m tuna

thym m BOT thyme

tic m tic, twitch; fig habit

ticket m ticket; **~ de caisse** receipt

tiède warm; péj tepid, lukewarm (aussi fig); **tiédir** cool down; **devenir plus chaud** warm up

tien, ~ne: le tien, la tienne, les tiens, les tiennes yours

tiers, tierce 1 adj third; **le ~ monde** the Third World **2** m MATH third; JUR third party

tige f BOT stalk; TECH stem

tigre m tiger; **tigresse** f tigress

tilleul m BOT lime (tree); boisson lime-blossom tea

timbre m stamp; (sonnette) bell; (son) timbre; (tampon) stamp; **timbre-poste** m postage stamp

timide timid; en sociéte shy

timoré timid

tintement m tinkle; de clochettes ringing; **tinter** de verres clink; de clochettes ring; **~ à l'arc** archery

tir m fire; action, SP shooting; **~ à l'arc** archery

tirage m à la loterie draw; PHOT print; TYP printing; (exemplaires de journal) circulation; d'un livre print run; COMM d'un chèque drawing; F (difficultés) trouble; **par un ~ au sort** by drawing lots

tirailler pull; **tiraillé entre** fig torn between

tire f P AUTO car, jeep P; **vol m à la ~** pickpocketing

tiré traits drawn

tire-bouchon m corkscrew

tirelire f piggy bank

tirer 1 *v/t* pull; *chèque, ligne, conclusions* draw; *coup de fusil* fire; *oiseau, cible* fire at; PHOT, TYP print; *plaisir, satisfaction* derive **2** *v/i* pull (*sur* on); *avec arme* shoot (*sur* at); ~ **à sa fin** draw to a close **3**: **se** ~ **de** *situation difficile* get out of; **se** ~ F take off

tiret *m* dash; (*trait d'union*) hyphen

tiroir *m* drawer

tisane *f* herbal tea

tisser weave; *d'une araignée* spin; */fig* hatch

tissu *m* fabric, material; BIOL tissue

titre *m* title; *d'un journal* headline; FIN security; **à ce** ~ therefore; **à juste** ~ rightly; **à** ~ **d'essai** on a trial basis; **au même** ~ on the same basis

tituber stagger

titulaire *m/f* *d'un document, d'une charge* holder

toast *m* (*pain grillé*) piece of toast; *de bienvenue* toast

toboggan *m* slide; *rue* flyover

tocsin *m* alarm bell

toi *you*

toile *f* *de lin* linen; (*peinture*) canvas; ~ **d'araignée** spiderweb, Br spider's web; ~ **cirée** oilcloth; ~ **de fond** backcloth; *fig* backdrop

toilette *f* (*lavage*) washing; (*mise*) outfit; (*vêtements*) clothes *pl*; ~**s** toilet; **aller**

aux ~**s** go to the toilet; **faire sa** ~ get washed

toi-même yourself

toiser *fig*: ~ **qn** look s.o. up and down

toison *f* *de laine* fleece; (*cheveux*) mane of hair

toit *m* roof; ~ **ouvrant** AUTO sun roof; **toiture** *f* roof

tôle *f* sheet metal; ~ **ondulée** corrugated iron

tolérance *f* *aussi* TECH tolerance; **tolérant** tolerant; **tolérer** tolerate

tomate *f* tomato

tombe *f* grave

tombeau *m* tomb

tombée *f*: **à la** ~ **de la nuit** at nightfall

tomber fall; *de cheveux* fall out; *d'une colère* die down; *d'une fièvre, d'un prix, d'une demande* drop, fall; ~ **malade** fall sick; **laisser** ~ drop (*aussi fig*); ~ **sur** MIL attack; (*rencontrer*) bump into; ~ **d'accord** reach agreement

tome *m* volume

ton¹ *m* tone; MUS key; **il est de bon** ~ it's the done thing

ton² *m*, **ta** *f*, **tes** *pl* your

tondeuse *f* lawnmower; *de coiffeur* clippers *pl*; AGR shears *pl*; **tondre** *mouton* shear; *haie* clip; *herbe* mow, cut; *cheveux* shave off

tonifier tone up

tonique 1 *m* tonic **2** *adj climat* bracing

tourbillon

tonitruant thunderous

tonne f (metric) ton

tonneau m barrel; MAR ton

tonner thunder; fig rage

tonnerre m thunder

tonton m F uncle

tonus m d'un muscle tone; (dynamisme) dynamism

toqué F mad (de about)

torche f flashlight, Br torch

torchon m dishtowel

tordre twist; linge wring; se ~ twist; se ~ le pied twist one's ankle

tornade f tornado

torpille f torpedo; **torpiller** torpedo (aussi fig)

torrent m torrent; fig: de larmes flood; d'injures torrent

torse m torso

tort m fault; (préjudice) harm; à ~ wrongly; à ~ et à travers wildly; avoir ~ be wrong (de faire to do); donner ~ à qn prove s.o. wrong; (désapprouver) blame s.o.; faire du ~ à hurt, harm

torticolis m MÉD stiff neck

tortiller twist; se ~ wriggle

tortue f tortoise; ~ de mer turtle

tortueux, -euse winding; fig tortuous; esprit, manœuvres devious

torture f torture; **torturer** torture

tôt early; (bientôt) soon; le plus ~ possible as soon as possible; au plus ~ at the soonest ou earliest; ~ ou tard sooner or later

total 1 adj total **2** m total; au ~ in all; fig on the whole; **totalement** totally; **totaliser** total; **totalité** f: la ~ de all of; en ~ in full; **totalitaire** POL totalitarian

touchant touching

touche f touch; de clavier key; SP touchline; (remise en jeu) throw-in; pêche bite; être mis sur la ~ fig F be sidelined

toucher¹ v/t touch; but hit; (émouvoir) touch, move; (concerner) concern; (contacter) contact, get in touch with; argent get; réserves break into; d'une maison adjoin; ~ au but near one's goal; se ~ touch; de maisons, terrains adjoin

toucher² m touch

touffu dense, thick

toujours always; (encore) still; pour ~ for ever

toupet m F nerve

tour¹ f tower; (immeuble) high-rise

tour² m turn; (circonférence) circumference; (circuit) lap; (promenade) stroll, walk; (excursion, voyage) tour; (ruse) trick; TECH lathe; de potier wheel; à mon ~, c'est mon ~ it's my turn; en un ~ de main in no time at all

tourbe f matière peat

tourbillon m de vent whirlwind; *d'eau* whirlpool

tourelle *f* turret

tourisme *m* tourism; **~ écologique** ecotourism; **touriste** *m/f* tourist

tourment *m litt* torture, torment

tourmente *f litt* storm

tourmenter torment; **se ~** worry, torment o.s.

tournant 1 *adj* revolving **2** *m* turn; *fig* turning point

tournée *f* round; *d'un artiste* tour

tourner 1 *v/t* turn; *sauce* stir; *salade* toss; *difficulté* get around; *film* shoot; **bien tourné(e)** well-put **2** *v/i* turn; *du lait* turn; *j'ai la tête qui tourne* my head is spinning; **faire ~** *clé* turn; *entreprise* run **3**: **se ~** turn; **se ~ vers** *fig* turn to

tournesol *m* BOT sunflower

tournevis *m* screwdriver

tournoyer *d'oiseaux* wheel; *de feuilles* swirl

tournure *f (expression)* turn of phrase; *des événements* turn

tourterelle *f* turtledove

tous → tout

Toussaint: *la ~* All Saints' Day

tousser cough

toussoter have a slight cough

tout *m*, *pl* **tous**, *mpl*, **toutes** *fpl* **1** *adj* all; *(n'importe lequel)* any; **~ Français** every Frenchman, all French-

men; **tous les deux jours** every two days; **tous les ans** every year **2** *pron sg* **tout** everything; *pl* **tous, toutes** all of us/them; *après* **~** after all; *facile comme* **~** F as easy as anything; **nous tous** all of us; **3** *adv* **tout** very, quite; **c'est ~ un** ... it's just like a ...; **~ nu** completely naked; **c'est ~ près d'ici** it's just nearby; **je suis ~e seule** I'm all alone; **~ à fait** altogether; **oui, ~ à fait** yes, absolutely; **~ de suite** straight away; **~ pauvres qu'ils sont** (*ou* **soient** (*subj*)) however poor they are **4** *m* **tout** the whole lot, everything; **pas du ~** not at all

toutefois however

toux *f* cough **m ~**

toxique 1 *adj* toxic **2** *m* poison

trac *m* nervousness; *pour un acteur* stage fright

traçabilité *f* traceability

tracas *m*: *des* **~** worries; **tracasser**: **~ qn** *d'une chose* worry s.o.; *d'une personne* pester s.o.; **se ~** worry

trace *f (piste)* track, trail; *(marque)* mark; *fig* impression; **~s** *de sang*, *poison* traces; **des ~s de pas** footprints; **tracer** *plan* draw

trachée *f* windpipe, trachea

traction *f péj*: **~s** horsetrading

tracteur *m* tractor

tradition f tradition; **traditionaliste** m/f & adj traditionalist; **traditionnel, ~le** adj traditional

traducteur, -trice m/f translator; **traduction** f translation; **traduire** translate (**en** into); fig be indicative of; **se ~ par** result in

trafic m traffic; **trafiquant** m trafficker; **~ de drogue(s)** drug trafficker; **trafiquer** traffic in; moteur tinker with

tragédie f tragedy; **tragique 1** adj tragic **2** m tragedy

trahir betray; **trahison** f betrayal; crime treason

train m train; fig: de lois, décrets etc series sg; **être en ~ de faire qc** be doing sth; **mettre en ~** set in motion; **au ~ où vont les choses** at the rate things are going; **~ d'atterrissage** undercarriage, landing gear; **~ de vie** lifestyle

traîner 1 v/t drag; d'une voiture pull, tow **2** v/i de vêtements, livres lie around; d'une discussion drag on; **~ dans les rues** hang around street corners **3**: **se ~** drag o.s. along

train-train m F: **le ~ quotidien** the daily routine

traire milk

trait m (ligne) line; du visage feature; de caractère trait; d'une œuvre, époque feature, characteristic; **avoir ~**

à be about; **~ d'esprit** witticism; **~ d'union** hyphen

traite f COMM draft, bill of exchange; d'une vache milking; **d'une seule ~** in one go

traité m treaty

traitement m treatment; (salaire) pay; TECH, INFORM processing; **traiter 1** v/t treat; TECH, INFORM process; **~ qn de menteur** call s.o. a liar **2** v/i (négocier) negotiate; **~ de qc** deal with sth

traître, ~sse 1 m/f traitor **2** adj treacherous

trajet m (voyage) journey; (chemin) way

trame f fig: d'une histoire background; de la vie fabric

tramway m streetcar, Br tram

tranchant 1 adj cutting **2** m d'un couteau cutting edge

tranche f (morceau) slice; (bord) edge; **~ d'âge** age bracket

tranché fig clear-cut; couleur definite

tranchée f trench

trancher v/t cut; fig settle **2** v/i: **sur** stand out against

tranquille quiet; (sans inquiétude) easy in one's mind; **laisse-moi ~!** leave me alone!; **tranquillisant** m tranquilizer, Br tranquillizer; **tranquilliser: ~ qn** set s.o.'s mind at rest; **tranquillité** f quietness, tranquillity; du sommeil peacefulness; (stabilité morale) peace of mind

transaction f JUR compromise; COMM transaction

transatlantique 1 adj transatlantic **2** m bateau transatlantic liner; chaise deck chair

transcription f transcription; **transcrire** transcribe

transférer transfer; **transfert** m transfer; PSYCH transference

transformation f transformation; TECH processing; en rugby conversion; **transformer** transform; TECH process; appartement, en rugby convert

transfuge m defector

transfusion f: ~ (sanguine) (blood) transfusion

transgénique genetically modified

transgresser loi break, transgress

transi: ~ (de froid) frozen

transiger come to a compromise

transistor m transistor

transit m: en ~ in transit

transition f transition

transmettre transmit; message, talen, maladie pass on; tradition, titre hand down; **transmissible**: sexuellement ~ sexually transmitted; **transmission** f transmission; d'un message passing on; d'une tradition, d'un titre handing down; RAD, TV

broadcast

transparence f transparency; **transparent** transparent

transpercer pierce; de l'eau, de la pluie go right through

transpiration f perspiration; **transpirer** perspire

transplant m transplant; **transplantation** f transplanting; MÉD transplant; **transplanter** transplant

transport m transport; ~s publics mass transit, Br public transport; **transporter** transport, carry

transposer transpose

transversal cross atr

trapèze m trapeze

trappe f (ouverture) trapdoor

trapu stocky

traquer hunt

traumatiser PSYCH traumatize; **traumatisme** m MÉD, PSYCH trauma

travail m work; être sans ~ be out of work; **travaux** (construction) construction work; **travailler 1** v/i work **2** v/t work on; d'une pensée trouble; **travailleur, -euse 1** adj hard-working **2** m/f worker

travers 1 adv: de ~ crooked; marcher not straight; en ~ across **2** prép: à ~ qc, au ~ de qc through sth **3** m shortcoming

traversée f crossing; **traverser** rue, mer cross; forêt, crise go through; (percer) go right through

travesti 1 *adj pour fête* fancy-dress **2** *m* (*déguisement*) fancy dress; (*homosexuel*) transvestite; **travestir** *vérité* distort; **se ~** dress up (**en** as a)

trébucher trip (**sur** over)

trèfle *m* BOT clover; *aux cartes* clubs *pl*

treize thirteen; **treizième** thirteenth

tremblant trembling, quivering; **tremblement** *m* trembling; **~ de terre** earthquake; **trembler** tremble, shake (**de** with); *de la terre* shake

trémousser: se ~ wriggle

trempe *f* fig caliber, *Br* calibre

trempé soaked; *sol* saturated; **tremper** soak; *pain dans café etc* dunk; *pied dans l'eau* dip; *acier* harden; **~ dans** *fig* be involved in

tremplin *m* springboard; *pour ski* ski jump; *fig* stepping stone

trentaine *f*: **une ~ de personnes** about thirty people *pl*; **trente** thirty; **trentième** thirtieth

trépied *m* tripod

trépigner stamp (one's feet)

très very; **~ lu/visité** much read/visited

trésor *m* treasure; **Trésor** Treasury; **trésorier, -ère** *m/f* treasurer

tressaillir jump

tresse *f de cheveux* braid, *Br* plait

trêve *f* truce; **~ de ...** that's enough ...; **sans ~** without respite

tri *m* sort; **faire un ~ dans qc** sort sth out

triangle *m* triangle

tribord *m* MAR starboard

tribu *f* tribe

tribulations *fpl* tribulations

tribunal *m* court

tribune *f* platform; (*débat*) discussion; *dans stade* bleachers, *Br* stands

tributaire: **être ~ de** be dependent on

tricher cheat; **tricheur, -euse** *m/f* cheat

tricolore: **drapeau** *m* **~** tricolor *ou Br* tricolour

tricot *m* knitting; *vêtement* sweater; **tricoter** knit

trier (*choisir*) pick through; (*classer*) sort

trimballer *m* hump F, lug

trimer F work like a dog F

trimestre *m* quarter; ÉDU trimester, *Br* term

trinquer (*porter un toast*) clink glasses; **~ à** *fig* F toast, drink to

triomphe *m* triumph; **triompher** triumph (**de** over)

tripes *fpl* guts; CUIS tripe

triple triple; **triplés, -ées** *mpl, fpl* triplets

tripoter *objet* play around with; *femme* feel up

triste sad; *temps, paysage* dreary; **tristesse** *f* sadness

trivial vulgar; *litt* (*banal*) trite

troc *m* barter

trognon *m* *d'un fruit* core; *d'un chou* stump

trois 1 *adj* three; **le ~ mai** May third; *Br* the third of May **2** *m* three; **troisième** third

trombe *f*: **des ~s d'eau** sheets of water; **en ~** *fig* at top speed

trombone *m* MUS trombone; *pour papiers* paper clip

trompe *f* MUS horn; *d'un éléphant* trunk

tromper deceive; *époux* be unfaithful to; *confiance* abuse; **se ~** be mistaken; **se ~ de numéro** get the wrong number; **tromperie** *f* deception

trompette 1 *f* trumpet **2** *m* trumpet player

trompeur, -euse deceptive; (*traître*) deceitful

tronc *m* BOT, ANAT trunk; *à l'église* collection box

tronçon *m* section

trône *m* throne

trop too; *avec verbe* too much; *de lait/gens* too much milk/too many people

tropical tropical; **tropique** *m* tropic

trot *m* trot; **aller au ~** trot; **trotter** *d'un cheval* trot; *d'une personne* run around

trottiner scamper

trottinette *f* scooter

trottoir *m* sidewalk, *Br* pavement

trou *m* hole; **~ de mémoire** lapse of memory

trouble 1 *adj* *eau, liquide* cloudy; *explication* unclear; *situation* murky **2** *m* (*désarroi*) trouble; (*émoi*) excitement; MÉD disorder; **~s** POL unrest; **trouble-fête** *m* party-pooper F

troubler *liquide* make cloudy; *silence, sommeil* disturb; *réunion* disrupt; (*inquiéter*) bother; **se ~** get flustered *d'un liquide* go cloudy

trouée *f* gap; **trouer** make a hole in

troupe *f* troop; *de comédiens* troupe

troupeau *m* *de vaches* herd; *de moutons* flock

trousse *f* kit; **être aux ~s de qn** *fig* be on s.o.'s heels; **~ de toilette** toilet bag

trousseau *m* *d'une mariée* trousseau; **~ de clés** bunch of keys

trouver find; *plan* come up with; (*rencontrer*) meet; **~ que** think that; **se ~** (*être*) be; **il se trouve que** it turns out that

truc *m* F (*chose*) thing, thingamajig F; (*astuce*) trick

truffe *f* BOT truffle; *d'un chien* nose; **truffé** with truffles; **~ de** *fig*: *citations* peppered with

truie *f* sow

truite *f* trout

truquage *m* *dans film* special

effect; *d'une photo* faking; **truquer** *élections, cartes* rig
tu you
tuba *m* snorkel; MUS tuba
tube *m* tube; F (*chanson*) hit
tuberculose *f* MÉD tuberculosis, TB
tuer kill; *fig* (*épuiser*) exhaust; (*peiner*) bother; **se ~** (*se suicider*) kill o.s.; (*trouver la mort*) be killed; **tue-tête**: *à ~* at the top of one's voice; **tueur** *m* killer
tulipe *f* tulip
tumeur *f* MÉD tumor, *Br* tumour
tumulte *m* uproar; *fig* (*activité*) hustle and bustle; **tumultueux, -euse** noisy; *passion* tumultuous, stormy
tunique *f* tunic
Tunisie: *la ~* Tunisia; **tunisien, ~ne** Tunisian; **Tunisien, ~ne** *m/f* Tunisian
tunnel *m* tunnel
turbo-réacteur *m* AVIAT turbojet
turbulence *f* turbulence; *d'un élève* unruliness; **turbu-**

lent turbulent; *élève* unruly
turc, turque 1 *adj* Turkish **2** *m langue* Turkish; **Turc, Turque** *m/f* Turk
turf *m* SP horseracing; *terrain* racecourse
Turquie: *la ~* Turkey
tutelle *f* JUR guardianship; *d'un état, d'une société* supervision, control; *fig* protection
tuteur, -trice *m/f* JUR guardian **2** *m* BOT stake
tutoyer address as 'tu'
tuyau *m* pipe; *flexible* hose; F (*information*) tip; **~ d'arrosage** garden hose; **tuyauter** F: **~ qn** tip s.o. off
T.V.A. *f* (= **taxe sur** *ou* **à la valeur ajoutée**) sales tax, *Br* VAT (= value added tax)
type *m* type; F (*gars*) guy F; **contrat ~** standard contract
typhon *m* typhoon
typique typical (*de* of)
tyran *m* tyrant; **tyrannie** *f* tyranny; **tyranniser** tyrannize; *petit frère etc* bully

U

U.E. *f* (= **Union européenne**) EU (= European Union)
ulcère *m* MÉD ulcer; **ulcérer** *fig* aggrieve
ultérieur later, subsequent
ultimatum *m* ultimatum
ultime last

ultrason *m* PHYS ultrasound
ultraviolet, ~te *adj & m* ultraviolet
un, une 1 *article* a; *devant voyelle* an **2** *pron* one; *à la une* on the front page; *l'un des touristes* one of the

tourists; **les uns avaient ...** some (of them) had ...; **elles s'aident les unes les autres** they help each other; **l'un et l'autre** both of them **3 chiffre** one

unanime unanimous; **unanimité** f unanimity; **à l'~** unanimously

uni pays united; surface smooth; tissu solid(-colored), Br self-coloured; famille close-knit

unification f unification; **unifier** unite, unify

uniforme 1 adj uniform; existence unchanging **2** m uniform; **uniformité** f uniformity

unilatéral m unilateral

union f union; (cohésion) unity; **Union européenne** European Union

unique (seul) single; fils only; (extraordinaire) unique; **uniquement** only

unir POL unite; par moyen de communication link; couple marry; **s'~** unite; (se marier) marry

unité f unit

univers m universe; fig world; **universel, ~le** universal

universitaire 1 adj university atr **2** m/f academic; **université** f university

uranium m CHIM uranium

urbain urban; **urbaniser** urbanize; **urbanisme** m town planning

urgence f urgency; **une ~** an emergency; **d'~** emergency atr; **urgent** urgent

urine f urine; **uriner** urinate

urne f: **aller aux ~s** go to the polls

usage m use; (coutume) custom; linguistique usage; **hors d'~** out of use; **à l'~ de qn** for use by s.o.; **d'~** customary; **usager** m user

usé worn; vêtement, personne worn-out; **user** du gaz, de l'eau use, consume; vêtement wear out; yeux ruin; **s'~** wear out; personne wear o.s. out; **~ de qc** use sth

usine f plant, factory; **usiner** machine

usité mot common

ustensile m tool; **~ de cuisine** kitchen utensil

usuel, ~le usual; expression common

usure f (détérioration) wear; du sol erosion

utérus m ANAT womb, uterus

utile useful; **en temps ~** in due course

utilisateur, -trice m/f user; **~ final** end user; **utilisation** f use; **utiliser** use

utilitaire utilitarian

utilité f usefulness, utility; **ça n'a aucune ~** it's no use whatever

V

vacance f poste opening, Br vacancy; **~s** vacation, Br holiday(s); **vacancier, -ère** m/f vacationer, Br holiday-maker

vacarme m din, racket

vaccin m vaccine; **vaccination** f vaccination; **vacciner** vaccinate

vache 1 f cow **2** adj F mean

vachement F bon, content damn F, Br bloody F; changer, vieillir one helluva lot F

vaciller sur ses jambes sway; d'une flamme flicker; (hésiter) vacillate

vagabond, ~e 1 adj wandering **2** m/f hobo, Br tramp

vagin m vagina

vague[1] f wave (aussi fig); **~ de froid** cold snap

vague[2] **1** adj vague; regard faraway; **terrain** m ~ waste ground **2** m vagueness; **regarder dans le ~** stare into the middle distance

vaillant brave, valiant

vain vain; mots empty; **en ~** in vain

vaincre conquer; SP defeat; fig: angoisse overcome, conquer; obstacle overcome; **vaincu 1** adj conquered; SP defeated **2** m loser; **vainqueur** m winner, victor

vaisseau m ANAT, litt (bateau)

vessel; ~ **spatial** spaceship

vaisselle f dishes pl; **laver** ou **faire la ~** do ou wash the dishes

valable valid

valeur f value, worth; d'une personne worth; **~s** COMM securities; **sans ~** worthless; **mettre en ~** emphasize, highlight

valide (sain) fit; passeport, ticket valid; **valider** validate; ticket stamp; **validité** f validity

valise f bag, suitcase

vallée f valley

valoir be worth; (coûter) cost; ~ **mieux** be better (**que** than); **faire ~ droits** assert; **capital** make work; (mettre en valeur) emphasize

valoriser the value of; personne enhance the image of

valse f waltz

vandale m vandal; **vandaliser** vandalize

vanille f vanilla

vanité f (fatuité) vanity; (inutilité) futility; **vaniteux, -euse** vain

vanne f sluice gate; F dig F

vantard, ~e 1 adj boastful **2** m/f boaster; **vanter** praise; **se ~ de qch** pride o.s. on sth

vapeur f vapor, Br vapour; ~

vaporeux

(d'eau) steam; *cuire à la ~* steam

vaporeux, -euse *paysage* misty; *tissu* filmy

vaporisateur *m* spray; **vaporiser** spray

varappe *f* rock-climbing

variable variable; *temps, humeur* changeable; **variante** *f* variant; **variation** *f* (*changement*) change; (*écart*) variation

varice ANAT varicose vein

varicelle *f* MÉD chickenpox

varié varied; **varier** vary; **variété** *f* variety; **~s spectacle** vaudeville, Br variety show

variole *f* MÉD smallpox

vase¹ *m* vase

vase² *m* mud; **vaseux, -euse** muddy; F (*nauséeux*) off--color, Br off-colour; F *explication* muddled

vasistas *m* fanlight

vaurien, ~ne *m/f* good-for--nothing

vautour *m* vulture

veau *m* calf; *viande* veal

vedette *f* star; (*bateau*) launch; *mettre en ~* highlight

végétal 1 *adj* plant *atr*; *huile* vegetable **2** *m* plant; **végétalien, ~ne** *m/f & adj* vegan

végétarien, ~ne *m/f & adj* vegetarian

végétation *f* vegetation; **végéter** vegetate

véhémence *f* vehemence; **véhément** vehement

véhicule *m* vehicle (*aussi fig*)

veille *f* previous day; *absence de sommeil* wakefulness; *à la ~ de* on the eve of; **veiller** stay up late; *~ à faire qch* see to it that sth is done; *~ sur qn* watch over s.o.

veinard, ~e *m/f* F lucky devil F; **veine** *f* vein; F luck

vélo *m* bike; *~ électrique* e-bike; *faire du ~* go cycling; **vélomoteur** *m* moped

velours *m* velvet; *~ côtelé* corduroy; **velouté** velvety; (*soupe*) creamy

velu hairy

venaison *f* venison

vendable saleable

vendange *f* grape harvest

vendeur *m* sales clerk, Br shop assistant; **vendeuse** *f* sales clerk, Br shop assistant; **vendre** sell; *fig* betray; *à ~* for sale

vendredi *m* Friday; *Vendredi saint* Good Friday

vendu, ~e 1 *adj* sold **2** *m/f péj* traitor

vénéneux, -euse poisonous

vénérable venerable; **vénération** *f* veneration; **vénérer** revere

vénérien, ~ne: maladie *f* ~ne venereal disease

vengeance *f* vengeance; **venger** avenge (*qn de qc* s.o. for sth); *se ~ de qn* get one's revenge on s.o.; *se ~ de qc sur qn* get one's revenge for sth on s.o.

venimeux, -euse poisonous; **venin** *m* venom (*aussi fig*)

venir come; *à* ~ to come; *où veut-il en* ~? what's he getting at?; ~ *de* come from; *je viens de faire la vaisselle* I have just washed the dishes; *faire* ~ *médecin* send for

vent *m* wind; *coup m de* ~ gust of wind; *il y a du* ~ it's windy

vente *f* sale; *activité* selling; ~ *à crédit* installment plan, *Br* hire purchase

venteux, -euse windy

ventilateur *m* ventilator; *électrique* fan; **ventilation** *f* ventilation; **ventiler** *pièce* air; *montant* break down

ventre *m* stomach; ~ *à bière* beer belly

ventriloque *m* ventriloquist

venu *m* **1** *adj: bien/mal* ~ appropriate/inappropriate **2** *m/f: le premier* ~, *la première* ~*e* the first to arrive; *(n'importe qui)* anybody; **venue** *f* arrival

ver *m* worm; ~ *de terre* earthworm; ~ *à soie* silkworm

verbal verbal; **verbe** *m* verb

verdâtre greenish

verdict *m* verdict

verdir turn green

verdure *f* (*feuillages*) greenery; (*salade*) greens *pl*

verge *f* ANAT penis; (*baguette*) rod

verger *m* orchard

verglas *m* black ice

vergogne *f: sans* ~ shameless; *avec verbe* shamelessly

véridique truthful

vérification *f* check; **vérifier** check; *se* ~ turn out to be true

véritable real; *amour* true

vérité *f* truth; *en* ~ actually; *à la* ~ to tell the truth

vermeil, ~le bright red, vermillion

vermine *f* vermin

verni varnished; F lucky; **vernir** varnish; *céramique* glaze; **vernis** *m* varnish; *de céramique* glaze; ~ *à ongle* nail polish, *Br aussi* nail varnish

verre *m* glass; *prendre un* ~ have a drink; ~*s de contact* contact lenses

verrerie *f* glassmaking; *fabrique* glassworks *sg*; *objets* glassware

verrière *f* (*vitrail*) stained-glass window; *toit* glass roof

verrou *m* bolt; **verrouillage** *m*: ~ *central* AUTO central locking; **verrouiller** bolt; F lock up

verrue *f* wart

vers[1] *m* verse

vers[2] *prép* toward, *Br* towards; (*environ*) around

versant *m* slope

versatile changeable

Verseau *m* ASTROL Aquarius

versement *m* payment; **verser 1** *v/t* pour (out); *sang,* *larmes* shed; *argent à un compte* pay in; *intérêts, pension* pay **2** *v/i* (*basculer*) overturn

version *f* version; (*traduction*) translation

verso *m* d'une feuille back

vert 1 *adj* green; *fruit* unripe; *vin* too young; *fig: personne âgée* spry; *propos risqué* **2** *m* green; **les ~s** POL *mpl* the Greens

vertébral vertebral; **colonne** *f* **~e** spine, spinal column; **vertèbre** *f* vertebra

vertical, ~e 1 *adj* vertical **2** *f* vertical (line)

vertige *m* vertigo, dizziness; *fig* giddiness; *un* **~** a dizzy spell; *j'ai le* **~** I feel dizzy

vertu *f* virtue; (*pouvoir*) property; *en* **~ de** in accordance with; **vertueux, -euse** virtuous

verve *f* wit

vésicule *f* ANAT: **~ biliaire** gall bladder

vessie *f* ANAT bladder

veste *f* jacket

vestiaire *m* de théâtre checkroom, *Br* cloakroom; *d'un stade* locker room

vestibule *m* hall

vestiges *mpl* traces

veston *m* jacket, coat

vêtement *m* item of clothing, garment; **~s** clothes; (*industrie f du*) **~** clothing industry

vétérinaire 1 *adj* veterinary **2** *m/f* veterinarian, vet

vêtu dressed

vétuste *bâtiment* dilapidated, ramshackle

veuf 1 *adj* widowed **2** *m* widower

veuve 1 *adj* widowed **2** *f* widow

vexant humiliating; **vexation** *f* humiliation; **vexer:** **~ qn** hurt s.o.'s feelings; **se ~** get upset

viable *projet*, BIOL viable

viaduc *m* viaduct

viager, -ère: rente *f* **viagère** life annuity

viande *f* meat

vibration *f* vibration; **vibrer** vibrate

vice *m* (*défaut*) defect; (*péché*) vice

vice-président *m* COMM, POL vice-president; *Br* COMM vice-chairman

vicié *air* stale

vicieux, -euse lecherous; *cercle* vicious

victime *f* victim

victoire *f* victory; SP win, victory; **victorieux, -euse** victorious

vidange *f* emptying, draining; AUTO oil change

vide 1 *adj* empty **2** *m* (*néant*) emptiness; *physique* vacuum; (*espace non occupé*) (empty) space; *avoir peur du* **~** be afraid of heights

vidéo *adj & f* video **~ amateur** home movie; **vidéocassette** *f* video cassette

vingtaine

vide-ordures *m* rubbish chute

vider empty (out); F *personne* throw out; CUIS *volaille* draw; *siège* vacate, leave; *se* ~ empty; **videur** *m* F bouncer

vie *f* life; *moyens matériels* living; *à* ~ for life; *être en* ~ be alive; *coût de la* ~ cost of living; *gagner sa* ~ earn one's living

vieil → *vieux*

vieillard *m* old man; *les* ~**s** old people *pl*, the elderly *pl*

vieille → *vieux*

vieillesse *f* old age

vieillir 1 *v/t:* ~ *qn* age s.o. **2** *v/i* *d'une personne* get old, age; *d'un visage* age; *d'une théorie, d'un livre* become dated; *d'un vin* age, mature

viennoiseries *fpl* croissants and similar types of bread

vierge 1 *f* virgin; *Vierge* AS-TROL **Virgo 2** *adj* virgin; *feuille* blank

Viêt-nam: *le* ~ Vietnam; **vietnamien,** ~**ne 1** *adj* Vietnamese **2** *m langue* Vietnamese; **Vietnamien,** ~**ne** *m/f* Vietnamese

vieux, (*m vieil* before a vowel or silent h), **vieille** (*f*) **1** *adj* old **2** *m/f* old man/old woman; *les* ~ old people *pl*, the aged *pl*

vif, vive 1 *adj* lively; (*en vie*) alive; *plaisir, satisfaction* great; *critique, douleur*

sharp; *air* bracing; *froid* biting; *couleur* bright **2** *m* **à** ~ *plaie* open; *piqué au* ~ cut to the quick; *le* ~ *du sujet* the heart of the matter; *avoir les nerfs à* ~ be on edge

vigilance *f* vigilance; **vigilant** vigilant

vigile *m* (*gardien*) security man, guard

vigne *f* (*arbrisseau*) vine; (*plantation*) vineyard

vigneron, ~**ne** *m/f* wine grower

vignoble *m plantation* vineyard; *région* wine-growing area

vigoureux, -**euse** *adj* robust, vigorous; **vigueur** *f* vigor, *Br* vigour, robustness; *entrer en* ~ come into force

V.I.H. *m* (= *Virus de l'Immunodéficience Humaine*) HIV (= human immunodeficiency virus)

vilain nasty; *enfant* naughty; (*laid*) ugly

villa *f* villa

village *m* village; **villageois,** ~**e 1** *adj* village *atr* **2** *m/f* villager

ville *f* town; *grande* ~ city; *aller en* ~ go into town

vin *m* wine; ~ *d'honneur* reception; ~ *de pays* regional wine

vinaigre *m* vinegar

vinaigrette *f* salad dressing

vingt twenty; **vingtaine:** *une*

~ de personnes about twenty people *pl*; **vingtième** twentieth

viol *m* rape; *d'un lieu saint* violation; **violation** *f d'un traité* violation; *d'une église* desecration

violemment violently; *fig* intensely; **violence** *f* violence; *fig* intensity; **violent** violent; *fig* intense

violer *loi* break, *sexuellement* rape; *(profaner)* desecrate

violet, **~te** violet

violette *f* BOT violet

violon *m* violin; *musicien* violinist

violoncelle *m* cello

virage *m de la route* curve, corner; *d'un véhicule* turn; *fig* change of direction; **virement** *m* COMM transfer; **virer 1** *v/i (changer de couleur)* change color *ou Br* colour; *d'un véhicule* corner **2** *v/t: ~ argent* transfer; **~ qn** kick s.o. out

virginité *f* virginity

virgule *f* comma

viril male; *(courageux)* manly; **virilité** *f* manhood; *(vigueur sexuelle)* virility

virtuel, **~le** virtual; *(possible)* potential

virulent virulent

virus *m* MÉD, INFORM virus

vis *f* screw; *escalier m à ~* spiral staircase

visa *m* visa

visage *m* face

vis-à-vis 1 *prép: ~ de* opposite; *(envers)* toward, *Br* towards; *(en comparaison de)* compared with **2** *m* person sitting opposite; *(rencontre)* face-to-face meeting

viser 1 *v/t* aim at; *(s'adresser à)* be aimed at **2** *v/i* aim *(à* at); **~ à faire** aim to do

viseur *m d'une arme* sights *pl*; PHOT viewfinder

visibilité *f* visibility; **visible** visible; *(évident)* clear

vision *f* sight; *(conception, apparition)* vision; **visionnaire** *m/f & adj* visionary

visite *f* visit; *d'une ville* tour; **rendre ~ à qn** visit s.o.; **avoir droit de ~** *d'un parent divorcé* have access; **~ de douane** customs inspection; **~ médicale** medical (examination); **visiter** visit; *(faire le tour de)* tour; *bagages* inspect; **visiteur**, **-euse** *m/f* visitor

vison *m* mink

visqueux, **-euse** viscous; *péj* slimy

visser screw

visuel, **~le** visual; **champ m ~** field of vision

vital vital; **vitalité** *f* vitality

vitamine *f* vitamin

vite fast, quick; *(sous peu, bientôt)* soon; **~!** quick!; **vitesse** *f* speed; AUTO gear; **à toute ~** at top speed

viticulture *f* wine-growing

vitrage *m cloison* glass partition; *action* glazing; **ensem-**

ble de vitres windows *pl*
vitrail *m* stained-glass window
vitre *f* window (pane); *de voiture* window; **vitrer** glaze; **vitrier** *m* glazier
vitrine *f* (*étalage*) (store) window; *meuble* display cabinet
vivace hardy; *haine, amour* lasting; **vivacité** *f* liveliness, vivacity
vivant **1** *adj* alive; (*plein de vie*) lively; (*doué de vie*) living; *langue* modern **2** *m* living person; **de son** ~ in his lifetime
vivement (*d'un ton vif*) sharply; (*vite*) briskly; *ému, touché* deeply
vivoter just get by
vivre **1** *v/i* live **2** *v/t* experience **3** *mpl*: **~s** supplies
vocabulaire *m* vocabulary
vociférer shout
vodka *f* vodka
vœu *m* REL vow; (*souhait*) wish; **tous mes ~x!** best wishes!
voici here is *sg*, here are *pl*; **me ~!** here I am!; **le livre que ~** this book
voie *f* way; *de chemin de fer* track; *d'autoroute* lane; **en ~ de développement** developing; **être en ~ de guérison** be on the mend; **par ~ aérienne** by air; **par la ~ hiérarchique** through channels; **~ d'eau** leak; **~ express** expressway

voilà there is *sg*, there are *pl*; (*et*) **~!** there you are!; **en ~ assez!** that's enough!; **~ tout** that's all
voile 1 *m* veil **2** *f* MAR sail; SP sailing
voiler[1] *v/t* veil; **se ~** *d'une femme* wear the veil; *du ciel* cloud over
voiler[2]: **se ~** *du bois* warp; *d'une roue* buckle
voir see; **faire ~** show; **se ~** see each other; **cela se voit** that's obvious; **je ne peux pas le ~** I can't stand him
voisin, ~e 1 *adj* neighboring, Br neighbouring; (*similaire*) similar **2** *m/f* neighbor, Br neighbour; **voisinage** *m* neighborhood, Br neighbourhood; (*proximité*) vicinity
voiture *f* car; *d'un train* car, Br carriage; **en ~** by car; **~ de fonction** company car
voix *f* voice (*aussi* GRAM); POL vote; **à haute ~** in a loud voice, aloud; **à ~ basse** in a low voice, quietly
vol[1] *m* theft; **~ à main armée** armed robbery
vol[2] *m* flight; **à ~ d'oiseau** as the crow flies; **au ~** in flight; **~ à voile** gliding
volaille *f* poultry; (*poulet etc*) bird
volant *m* AUTO (steering) wheel; SP shuttlecock; *d'un vêtement* flounce
volcan *m* volcano

volée f d'oiseaux flock; en tennis, de coups de feu volley; **à la ~** in mid-air

voler[1] v/t steal; **~ qch à qn** steal sth from s.o.

voler[2] v/i fly

volet m de fenêtre shutter; fig part; **trier sur le ~** fig hand-pick

voleur, -euse 1 adj thieving 2 m/f thief; **~ à l'étalage** shop-lifter

volontaire 1 adj voluntary; (délibéré) deliberate; (décidé) headstrong 2 m/f volunteer

volonté f will; (souhait) wish; (fermeté) willpower; **de l'eau à ~** as much water as you like; **faire preuve de bonne ~** show willing

volontiers willingly, with pleasure

volt m ÉL volt; **voltage** m ÉL voltage

volte-face f about-turn (aussi fig)

volubilité f volubility

volume m volume; **volumineux, -euse** bulky

voluptueux, -euse voluptuous

vomir 1 v/i vomit, throw up 2 v/t bring up; fig spew out; **vomissement** m vomiting

vorace voracious

vos → **votre**

vote m vote; action voting; **voter** 1 v/i vote 2 v/t loi pass

votre, pl vos your

vôtre: le/la ~, les ~s yours

vouer dedicate (à to); **se ~ à** fig dedicate o.s. to

vouloir want; **il veut que tu partes** (subj) he wants you to leave; **je voudrais** I would like, I'd like; **je veux bien** I'd like to; **veuillez ne pas fumer** please do not smoke; **~ dire** mean; **en ~ à qn** have something against s.o.; **veux-tu te taire!** will you shut up!

voulu requisite; délibéré deliberate

vous sg et pl you; complément d'objet indirect, sg et pl (to) you; avec verbe pronominal yourself; pl yourselves; **~ ~ êtes coupé** you've cut yourself; **si ~ ~ levez à ...** if you get up at ...

vous-même, pl vous-mêmes yourself; pl yourselves

voûte f ARCH vault; **voûté** personne hunched; dos bent; ARCH vaulted

vouvoyer adress as 'vous'

voyage m trip, journey; en paquebot voyage; **~ d'affaires** business trip; **~ de noces** honeymoon; **~ organisé** package holiday; **voyager** travel; **voyageur, -euse** m/f traveler, Br traveller; par train, avion passenger; **~ de commerce** traveling ou Br travelling salesman

voyant, ~e 1 adj couleur garish 2 m (signal) light 3 m/f

(devin) clairvoyant
voyelle *f* GRAM vowel
voyou *m jeune* lout
vrac *m*: **en ~** COMM loose; *fig* jumbled together
vrai 1 *adj (après le subst)* true; *(devant le subst)* real, genuine; *ami* true **2** *m*: **à ~ dire, à dire ~** to tell the truth; **vraiment** really
vraisemblable likely, probable; **vraisemblance** *f* likelihood, probability
vrombir throb

VTT *m* (= *vélo tout terrain*) mountain bike
vu in view of
vue *f* view; *sens, faculté* sight; **à première ~** at first sight; **connaître qn de ~** know s.o. by sight; **avoir la ~ basse** be shortsighted; **point m de ~** viewpoint, point of view; **en ~ de faire** with a view to doing
vulgaire *(banal)* common; *(grossier)* common, vulgar
vulnérable vulnerable

W

wagon *m* car, *Br* carriage; *de marchandises* car, *Br* wagon; **wagon-lit** *m* sleeping car; **wagon-restaurant** *m* dining car
walkman *m* Walkman®

watt *m* ÉL watt
W.-C. *mpl* WC *sg*
week-end *m* weekend; **ce ~** on the weekend
whisky *m* whiskey, *Br* whisky

X, Y

xénophobe xenophobic; **xénophobie** *f* xenophobia
xérès *m* sherry
y there; **on ~ va!** let's go!; **ça ~ est!** that's it!; **j'~ suis** *(je comprends)* now I get it; **~**

compris including; **j'~ travaille** I'm working on it
yacht *m* yacht; **yachting** *m* yachting
yaourt *m* yoghurt
yeux *pl* → **œil**

Z

zapper channel-hop, *Br aussi* zap

zèbre *m* zebra

zèle *m* zeal; *faire du* ~ be overzealous; **zélé** zealous

zéro 1 *m* zero, *Br aussi* nought; *sp Br* nil; *fig* nonentity **2** *adj*: ~ *faute* no mistakes; *partir de* ~ start from nothing

zeste *m* peel, zest

zézayer lisp

zigouiller F bump off F

zigzag *m* zigzag; **zigzaguer** zigzag

zinc *m* zinc

zona *m* shingles *sg*

zone *f* area, zone; *péj* slums *pl*; ~ *euro* euro zone; ~ *industrielle* industrial park, *Br* industrial estate; ~ *interdite* prohibited area

zoo *m* zoo

zoologie *f* zoology; **zoologiste** *m/f* zoologist

zut! F blast!

A

a [ə] un(e)
abandon [ə'bændən] abandonner
abbreviate [ə'briːvɪeɪt] abréger; **abbreviation** abréviation *f*
abduct [əb'dʌkt] enlever
ability [ə'bɪlətɪ] capacité *f*; *skill* faculté *f*
able ['eɪbl] (*skillful*) compétent; **be ~ to do** pouvoir faire
abnormal [æb'nɔːrml] anormal
aboard [ə'bɔːrd] à bord
abolish [ə'bɑːlɪʃ] abolir; **abolition** abolition *f*
abort [ə'bɔːrt] suspendre; **abortion** MED avortement *m*; **have an ~** se faire avorter; **abortive** avorté
about [ə'baʊt] **1** *prep* (*concerning*) à propos de; *a book ~* un livre sur; *talk ~* parler de; *what's it ~?* *of book, movie* de quoi ça parle? **2** *adv* (*roughly*) à peu près; *~ noon* aux alentours de midi; *be ~ to do* (*be going to*) être sur le point de faire
above [ə'bʌv] au-dessus de; *on the floor ~* à l'étage du dessus

abrasive [ə'breɪsɪv] *personality* abrupt
abreast [ə'brest]: *three ~* les trois l'un à côté de l'autre; *keep ~ of* se tenir au courant de
abridge [ə'brɪdʒ] abréger
abroad [ə'brɔːd] à l'étranger
abrupt [ə'brʌpt] brusque
abscess ['æbsɪs] abcès *m*
absence ['æbsəns] absence *f*; absent absent; **absentee** absent(e) *m(f)*; **absenteeism** absentéisme *m*; **absent-minded** distrait
absolute ['æbsəluːt] absolu; **absolution** REL absolution *f*; **absolve** absoudre
absorb [əb'sɔːrb] absorber; **absorbent** absorbant; **absorbent cotton** coton *m* hydrophile; **absorbing** absorbant
abstain [əb'steɪn] *in vote* s'abstenir; **abstention** *in vote* abstention *f*
abstract ['æbstrækt] abstrait
absurd [əb'sɜːrd] absurde; **absurdity** absurdité *f*
abundance [ə'bʌndəns] abondance *f*; **abundant** abondant

abuse¹ [ə'bjuːs] n verbal insultes fpl; physical violences fpl; sexual sévices mpl sexuels; of power etc abus m

abuse² [ə'bjuːz] v/t verbally insulter; physically maltraiter; sexually faire subir des sévices sexuels à; power etc abuser de

abysmal [ə'bɪzml] (very bad) lamentable

academic [ækə'demɪk] **1** n universitaire m/f **2** adj year: at school scolaire; at university universitaire; interests intellectuel; **academy** académie f

accelerate [ək'seləreɪt] accélérer; **acceleration** accélération f; **accelerator** accélérateur m

accent ['æksənt] accent m; **accentuate** accentuer

accept [ək'sept] accepter; **acceptable** acceptable; **acceptance** acceptation f

access ['ækses] **1** n accès m **2** v/t also COMPUT accéder à; **accessible** accessible

accessory [ək'sesərɪ] for wearing accessoire m; LAW complice m/f

accident ['æksɪdənt] accident m; **by ~** par hasard; **accidental** accidentel; **accidentally** accidentellement

acclimate, acclimatize [ə'klaɪmət, ə'klaɪmətaɪz] s'acclimater

accommodate [ə'kɒmədeɪt] loger; needs s'adapter à; **accommodations** logement m

accompaniment [ə'kʌmpənimənt] MUS accompagnement m; **accompany** also MUS accompagner

accomplice [ə'kʌmplɪs] complice m/f

accomplished [ə'kʌmplɪʃt] accompli; **accomplishment** of task accomplissement m; (achievement) réussite f; (talent) talent m

accord [ə'kɔːrd] accord m; **of one's own ~** de son plein gré

accordance [ə'kɔːrdəns] **in ~ with** conformément à

according [ə'kɔːrdɪŋ]: **~ to** selon; **accordingly** (consequently) par conséquent; (appropriately) en conséquence

account [ə'kaʊnt] financial compte m; (report) récit m; **give an ~ of** faire le récit de; **on no ~** en aucun cas; **on ~ of** en raison de; **take ... into ~** tenir compte de; **accountable: be held ~** être tenu responsable; **accountant** comptable m/f; **accounts** comptabilité f

accumulate [ə'kjuːmjʊleɪt] **1** v/t accumuler **2** v/i s'accumuler; **accumulation** accumulation f

accuracy ['ækjʊrəsɪ] justesse f; **accurate** juste; **accurately** avec justesse

accusation [ækjuːˈzeɪʃn] accusation *f*; **accuse:** ~ *s.o. of doing sth* accuser qn de faire qch; **accused** LAW accusé(e) *m(f)*; **accusing** accusateur

accustom [əˈkʌstəm]: *get ~ed to* s'accoutumer à

ace [eɪs] *in cards* as *m*; *tennis* shot ace *m*

ache [eɪk] **1** *n* douleur *f* **2** *v/i: my arm ~s* j'ai mal au bras

achieve [əˈtʃiːv] accomplir; **achievement** (*thing achieved*) accomplissement *m*; *of ambition* réalisation *f*

acid [ˈæsɪd] acide *m*

acknowledge [əkˈnɒlɪdʒ] reconnaître; ~ *receipt of* accuser réception de; **acknowledg(e)ment** reconnaissance *f*; *of a letter* accusé *m* de réception

acoustics [əˈkuːstɪks] acoustique *f*

acquaint [əˈkweɪnt]: *be ~ed with* connaître; **acquaintance** *person* connaissance *f*

acquire [əˈkwaɪr] acquérir; **acquisition** acquisition *f*

acquit [əˈkwɪt] LAW acquitter; **acquittal** LAW acquittement *m*

acre [ˈeɪkər] acre *m* (4.047m²)

across [əˈkrɒs] **1** *prep* de l'autre côté de; *walk* ~ *the street* traverser la rue; ~ *Europe* all over dans toute l'Europe; ~ *from* en face de **2** *adv: swim* ~ traverser à la na-

ge; *10m* ~ 10 m de large

act [ækt] **1** *v/i* (*take action*) agir; THEA faire du théâtre **2** *n* (*deed*) fait *m*; *of play* acte *m*; *in vaudeville* numéro *m*; (*law*) loi *f*

action [ˈækʃn] action *f*; **take** ~ prendre des mesures

active [ˈæktɪv] actif; **activist** POL activiste *m/f*; **activity** activité *f*

actor [ˈæktər] acteur *m*

actress [ˈæktrɪs] actrice *f*

actual [ˈæktʃuəl] véritable; **actually** [ˈæktʃuəlɪ] en fait; *expressing surprise* vraiment

acute [əˈkjuːt] *pain* intense; *sense* très développé

AD [eɪˈdiː] (= *anno domini*) apr. J.-C. (= après Jésus Christ)

ad [æd] → *advertisement*

adamant [ˈædəmənt]: *be ~ that ...* soutenir catégoriquement que ...

adapt [əˈdæpt] **1** *v/t* adapter **2** *v/i of person* s'adapter; **adaptability** faculté *f* d'adaptation; **adaptable** adaptable; **adaptation** *of play etc* adaptation *f*; **adapter** ELEC adaptateur *m*

add [æd] **1** *v/t* ajouter; MATH additionner **2** *v/i of person* faire des additions

♦ **add on** *15% etc* ajouter

♦ **add up 1** *v/t* additionner **2** *v/i* avoir du sens

addict [ˈædɪkt] (*drug* ~) drogué(e) *m(f)*; *of TV program* *etc* accro *m/f*; **addicted** *to drugs* drogué; *to TV program etc* accro f; **addiction** *to drugs* dépendance f (**to** de); **addictive**: **be ~** entraîner une dépendance

addition [əˈdɪʃn] MATH addition *f*; *to list* ajout *m*; *to company* recrue *f*; **in ~ to** en plus de; **additional** supplémentaire; **additive** additif *m*; **add-on** accessoire *m*

address [əˈdres] **1** *n* adresse *f* **2** *v/t letter* adresser; *audience* s'adresser à; **addressee** destinataire *m/f*

adequate [ˈædɪkwət] (*sufficient*) suffisant; (*satisfactory*) satisfaisant; **adequately** suffisamment

◆ **adhere to** [ədˈhɪr] adhérer à

adhesive [ədˈhiːsɪv] adhésif *m*

adjacent [əˈdʒeɪsnt] adjacent

adjective [ˈædʒɪktɪv] adjectif *m*

adjoining [əˈdʒɔɪnɪŋ] attenant

adjourn [əˈdʒɜːrn] ajourner; **adjournment** ajournement *m*

adjust [əˈdʒʌst] ajuster; **adjustable** ajustable; **adjustment** ajustement *m*

ad lib [ædˈlɪb] **1** *adj* improvisé **2** *v/i* improviser

administer [ədˈmɪnɪstər] *country* administrer; **administration** administration *f*;

(*administrative work*) tâches *fpl* administratives; **administrative** administratif; **administrator** administrateur(-trice) *m(f)*

admirable [ˈædmərəbl] admirable; **admiration** admiration *f*; **admire** admirer; **admirer** admirateur(-trice) *m(f)*; **admiring** admiratif; **admiringly** admirativement

admissible [ədˈmɪsəbl] admis; **admission** (*confession*) aveu *m*; **~ free** entrée *f* gratuite; **admit** *to a place*, (*accept*) admettre; (*confess*) avouer; **admittance**: **no ~** entrée *f* interdite

adolescence [ædəˈlesns] adolescence *f*; **adolescent 1** *adj* adolescent **2** *n* adolescent(e) *m(f)*

adopt [əˈdɑːpt] adopter; **adoption** adoption *f*

adorable [əˈdɔːrəbl] adorable; **adoration** adoration *f*; **adore** adorer

adrenalin [əˈdrenəlɪn] adrénaline *f*

adult [ˈædʌlt] **1** *adj* adulte **2** *n* adulte *m/f*; **adultery** adultère *m*

advance [ədˈvæns] **1** *n money* avance *f*; *in science etc* avancée *f*; MIL progression *f*; **in ~** à l'avance; **payment in ~** paiement *m* anticipé; **make ~s** (*progress*) faire des progrès; *sexually* faire des avances **2** *v/i* MIL, (*make progress*) avancer **3** *v/t theory, sum of money* avancer; *human knowledge, cause* faire avancer; **advanced** avancé

advantage [əd'væntɪdʒ] avantage *m*; *take* ~ *of opportunity* profiter de; **advantageous** avantageux

adventure [əd'ventʃər] aventure *f*; **adventurous** aventureux

adverb ['ædvɜːrb] adverbe *m*

adversary ['ædvərsərɪ] adversaire *m/f*

adverse ['ædvɜːrs] adverse

advertise ['ædvərtaɪz] *product* faire de la publicité pour; *job* mettre une annonce pour; **advertisement** *for product* publicité *f*, pub *f*; *for job* annonce *f*; **advertiser** annoncer(-euse) *m(f)*; **advertising** publicité *f*

advice [əd'vaɪs] conseils *mpl*; *a bit of* ~ un conseil; **advisable** conseillé; **advise** conseiller

advocate ['ædvəkeɪt] recommander

aerial ['erɪəl] *Br* antenne *f*; **aerial photograph** photographie *f* aérienne

aerobics [e'roʊbɪks] aérobic *m*

aerodynamic [eroʊdaɪ'næmɪk] aérodynamique

aeroplane ['eroʊpleɪn] avion *m*

aerosol ['erəsɑːl] aérosol *m*

aesthetic *etc* → **esthetic** *etc*

affair [ə'fer] *(matter)* affaire *f*; *(love* ~) liaison *f*

affection [ə'fekʃn] affection *f*; **affectionate** affectueux; **affectionately** affectueusement

affirmative [ə'fɜːrmətɪv] affirmatif

affluence ['æfluəns] richesse *f*; **affluent** riche

afford [ə'fɔːrd]: *be able to* ~ *sth financially* pouvoir se permettre d'acheter qch

afloat [ə'floʊt] *boat* sur l'eau

afraid [ə'freɪd]: *be* ~ avoir peur *(of* de); *I'm* ~ *expressing regret* je crains

afresh [ə'freʃ]: *start* ~ recommencer

Africa ['æfrɪkə] Afrique *f*

African ['æfrɪkən] **1** *adj* africain **2** *n* Africain(e) *m(f)*; **African-American 1** *adj* afro-américain(e) **2** *n* Afro-Américain(e) *m(f)*

after ['æftər] **1** *prep* après; *it's ten* ~ *two* il est deux heures dix **2** *adv (afterward)* après; *the day* ~ le lendemain

afternoon [æftər'nuːn] après-midi *m*; *in the* ~ l'après-midi; *this* ~ cet après-midi; *good* ~ bonjour

'after sales service service *m* après-vente; **aftershave** lotion *f* après-rasage; **afterward** ensuite

again [ə'geɪn] encore; *I never saw him* ~ je ne l'ai jamais revu

against [ə'genst] contre

age [eɪdʒ] âge *m*; *she's five years of ~* elle a cinq ans; **aged**: *~ 16* âgé de 16 ans; **age group** catégorie *f* d'âge; **age limit** limite *f* d'âge

agency ['eɪdʒənsɪ] agence *f*

agenda [ə'dʒendə] ordre *m* du jour

agent ['eɪdʒənt] COM agent *m*

aggravate ['ægrəveɪt] faire empirer; *(annoy)* agacer

aggression [ə'greʃn] agression *f*; **aggressive** agressif; **aggressively** agressivement

aghast [ə'gæst] horrifié

agile ['ædʒaɪl] agile; **agility** agilité *f*

agitated ['ædʒɪteɪtɪd] agité; **agitation** agitation *f*; **agitator** agitateur(-trice) *m(f)*

agnostic [æg'nɒstɪk] agnostique *m/f*

ago [ə'gəʊ]: *two days ~* il y a deux jours; *long ~* il y a longtemps

agonize ['ægənaɪz] se tourmenter (*over* sur); **agonizing** terrible; **agony** ['ægənɪ] *mental* tourment *m*; *physical* grande douleur *f*

agree [ə'griː] 1 *v/i* être d'accord; *of figures* s'accorder; *(reach agreement)* s'entendre 2 *v/t price* s'entendre sur; **agreeable** *(pleasant)* agréable; **agreement** accord *m*

agricultural [ægrɪ'kʌltʃərəl] agricole; **agriculture** agriculture *f*

ahead [ə'hed] devant; *plan/think ~* prévoir/penser à l'avance

aid [eɪd] 1 *n* aide *f* 2 *v/t* aider

aide [eɪd] aide *m/f*

Aids [eɪdz] sida *m*

ailing ['eɪlɪŋ] *economy* mal en point

ailment ['eɪlmənt] mal *m*

aim [eɪm] 1 *n (objective)* but *m* 2 *v/i in shooting* viser; *~ to do sth* essayer de faire qch 3 *v/t*: *be ~ed at of remark* viser; *of gun* être pointé sur; **aimless** ['eɪmlɪs] sans but

air [er] 1 *n* air *m*; *by ~* par avion; *in the open ~* en plein air 2 *v/t room* aérer; *views* exprimer; **airbag** airbag *m*; **air-conditioned** climatisé; **air-conditioning** climatisation *f*; **aircraft** avion *m*; **aircraft carrier** porte-avions *m inv*; **air force** armée *f* de l'air; **air hostess** hôtesse *f* de l'air; **airline** compagnie *f* aérienne; **airliner** avion *m* de ligne; **airmail**: *by ~* par avion; **airplane** avion *m*; **airport** aéroport *m*; **air terminal** aérogare *f*; **air-traffic controller** contrôleur(-euse) aérien(ne) *m(f)*

aisle [aɪl] *in airplane* couloir *m*; *in theater* allée *f*

ajar [ə'dʒɑːr]: *be ~* être entrouvert

alarm [ə'lɑːrm] 1 *n (fear)* inquiétude *f*; *device* alarme *f*;

(~ *clock*) réveil *m* **2** *v/t* alarmer; **alarming** alarmant; **alarmingly** de manière alarmante

album ['ælbəm] album *m*

alcohol ['ælkəhɒːl] alcool *m*; **alcoholic 1** *adj drink* alcoolisé **2** *n* alcoolique *m/f*

alert [ə'lɜːrt] **1** *adj* vigilant **2** *n* signal alerte *f* **3** *v/t* alerter

alibi ['ælɪbaɪ] alibi *m*

alien ['eɪlɪən] **1** *adj* étranger (**to** à) **2** *n* étranger-(-ère) *m(f)*; *from space* extra-terrestre *m/f*; **alienate** s'aliéner

align [ə'laɪn] aligner

alike [ə'laɪk] **1** *adj*: *be ~* se ressembler **2** *adv*: *old and young ~* les vieux comme les jeunes

alimony ['ælɪmənɪ] pension alimentaire

alive [ə'laɪv]: *be ~* être en vie

all [ɒːl] **1** *adj* tout **2** *pron* tout; *~ of us/them* nous/eux tous; *he ate ~ of it* il l'a mangé en entier; *for ~ I know* pour autant que je sache; *~ but him (except)* tous sauf lui **3** *adv*: *~ at once (suddenly)* tout d'un coup; *(at the same time)* tous ensemble; *~ the better* encore mieux; *they're not at ~ alike* ils ne se ressemblent pas du tout; *not at ~!* pas du tout!; *two ~* SP deux à deux

allegation [ælɪ'geɪʃn] allégation *f*; **allege** alléguer; **alleged** supposé; **allegedly**:

he ~ killed two women il aurait assassiné deux femmes

allegiance [ə'liːdʒəns] loyauté *f* (**to** à)

allergic [ə'lɜːrdʒɪk] allergique (**to** à)

alleviate [ə'liːvɪeɪt] soulager

alley ['ælɪ] ruelle *f*

alliance [ə'laɪəns] alliance *f*

allocate ['æləkeɪt] assigner; **allocation** [æləʊ'keɪʃn] action assignation *f*; *amount allocated* part *f*

allot [ə'lɒt] assigner

allow [ə'laʊ] *(permit)* permettre; *(calculate for)* compter
◆ **allow for** prendre en compte

allowance [ə'laʊəns] *money* allocation *f*; *(pocket money)* argent *m* de poche

alloy ['ælɔɪ] alliage *m*

'all-purpose universel; *vehicle* tous usages; **all-round** général; *athlete* complet;
◆ **allude to** [ə'luːd] faire allusion à

alluring [ə'lʊrɪŋ] alléchant

all-wheel 'drive quatre roues motrices *fpl*; *vehicle* 4x4 *m*

ally ['ælaɪ] allié(e) *m(f)*

almond ['ɑːmənd] amande *f*

almost ['ɒːlməʊst] presque

alone [ə'ləʊn] seul

along [ə'lɒŋ] **1** *prep* le long de; *walk ~ this path* prenez ce chemin **2** *adv*: *bring ~* amener; *~ with in addition to* ainsi que

alongside [əlɒŋ'saɪd] paral-

lel to à côté de; *in cooperation with* aux côtés de
aloof [ə'luːf] distant
aloud [ə'laʊd] à haute voix
alphabet ['ælfəbet] alphabet *m*; **alphabetical** alphabétique
already [ɒːl'redɪ] déjà
alright [ɒːl'raɪt] (*permitted*) permis; (*acceptable*) convenable; **be ~** (*in working order*) fonctionner; **she's ~ not hurt** elle n'est pas blessée; **everything is ~** tout va bien
altar ['ɒːltər] autel *m*
alter ['ɒːltər] modifier; *person* changer; **alteration** modification *f*
alternate 1 ['ɒːltərneɪt] *v/i* alterner **2** ['ɒːltərnət] *adj*: **on ~ Mondays** un lundi sur deux
alternative [ɒːl'tɜːrnətɪv] **1** *adj* alternatif **2** *n* alternative *f*; **alternatively** sinon; **or ~** ou bien
although [ɒːl'ðəʊ] bien que (+*subj*), quoique (+*subj*)
altitude ['æltɪtuːd] altitude *f*
altogether [ɒːltə'geðər] (*completely*) totalement; (*in all*) en tout
altruism ['æltruːɪzm] altruisme *m*; **altruistic** altruiste
aluminum [ə'luːmənəm] **aluminium** [ælju'mɪnɪəm] aluminium *m*
always ['ɒːlweɪz] toujours
a.m. ['eɪem] (= *ante meridiem*) du matin

amass [ə'mæs] amasser
amateur ['æmətʃʊr] *SP* amateur *m/f*; **amateurish** *attempt* d'amateur; *painter* sans talent
amaze [ə'meɪz] étonner; **amazed** étonné; **amazement** étonnement *m*; **amazing** étonnant; (*very good*) impressionnant; **amazingly** étonnamment
ambassador [æm'bæsədər] ambassadeur(-drice) *m(f)*
amber ['æmbər]: **at ~** à l'orange
ambience ['æmbɪəns] ambiance *f*
ambiguity [æmbɪ'gjuːətɪ] ambiguité *f*; **ambiguous** ambigu
ambition [æm'bɪʃn] ambition *f*; **ambitious** ambitieux
ambivalent [æm'bɪvələnt] ambivalent
amble ['æmbl] déambuler
ambulance ['æmbjuləns] ambulance *f*
ambush ['æmbʊʃ] **1** *n* embuscade *f* **2** *v/t* tendre une embuscade
amend [ə'mend] modifier; **amendment** modification *f*; **amends**: **make ~** se racheter
amenities [ə'miːnətɪz] facilités *fpl*
America [ə'merɪkə] (*United States*) États-Unis *mpl*; *continent* Amérique *f*; **American 1** *adj* américain **2** *n* Américain(e) *m(f)*

amicable ['æmɪkəbl] à l'amiable; **amicably** à l'amiable

ammunition [æmju'nɪʃn] munitions *fpl*

amnesia [æm'niːzɪə] amnésie *f*

amnesty ['æmnəstɪ] amnistie *f*

among(st) [ə'mʌŋ(st)] parmi

amoral [eɪ'mɔːrəl] amoral

amount [ə'maʊnt] quantité *f*; *(sum of money)* somme *f*
◆ **amount to** s'élever à; *(be equivalent to)* revenir à

amphibian [æm'fɪbɪən] amphibien *m*

ample ['æmpl] beaucoup de

amplifier ['æmplɪfaɪə] amplificateur *m*; **amplify** amplifier

amputate ['æmpjʊteɪt] amputer; **amputation** amputation *f*

amuse [ə'mjuːz] *(make laugh)* amuser; *(entertain)* distraire; **amusement** *(merriment)* amusement *m*; *(entertainment)* divertissement *m*; **amusement park** parc *m* d'attractions; **amusing** amusant

an [æn] → *a*

anaemia *etc* → **anemia** etc

anaesthetic *etc* → **anesthetic** etc

analog ['ænəlɒg] analogique; **analogy** analogie *f*

analysis [ə'næləsɪs] PSYCH analyse *f*; **analyst** PSYCH analyste *m/f*; **analytical** analytique; **analyze** *also* PSYCH analyser

anarchy ['ænəkɪ] anarchie *f*

ancestor ['ænsestər] ancêtre *m/f*

anchor ['æŋkər] **1** *n* NAUT ancre *f*; TV présentateur(-trice) principal(e) *m(f)* **2** *v/i* NAUT ancrer

ancient ['eɪnʃənt] ancien; *Rome etc* antique

and [ænd] et

anemia [ə'niːmɪə] anémie *f*; **anemic** anémique

anesthetic [ænəs'θetɪk] anesthésiant *m*

angel ['eɪndʒl] ange *m*

anger ['æŋgər] **1** *n* colère *f* **2** *v/t* mettre en colère

angle ['æŋgl] angle *m*

angry ['æŋgrɪ] *person* en colère; *mood, look* fâché

animal ['ænɪml] animal *m*

animated ['ænɪmeɪtɪd] animé; **animated cartoon** dessin *m* animé; **animation** animation *f*

animosity [ænɪ'mɒsətɪ] animosité *f*

ankle ['æŋkl] cheville *f*

annex ['æneks] **1** *n* annexe *f* **2** *v/t state* annexer

annihilate [ə'naɪəleɪt] anéantir; **annihilation** anéantissement *m*

anniversary [ænɪ'vɜːrsərɪ] anniversaire *m*

announce [ə'naʊns] annoncer; **announcement** annonce *f*; **announcer** [ə'naʊnsər] TV, RAD speaker *m*, speakerine

f

annoy [əˈnɔɪ] agacer; **annoyance** (*anger*) agacement *m*; (*nuisance*) désagrément *m*; **annoying** agaçant

annual [ˈænʊəl] annuel

annul [əˈnʌl] annuler; **annulment** annulation *f*

anonymous [əˈnɑːnɪməs] anonyme

anorexia [ænəˈreksɪə] anorexie *f*

another [əˈnʌðər] **1** *adj* autre **2** *pron* un(e) autre *m(f)*; **they know one ~** ils se connaissent

answer [ˈænsər] **1** *n* réponse *f*; (*solution*) solution *f* (**to** à) **2** *v/t* répondre à **3** *v/i* répondre; **answerphone** répondeur *m*

ant [ænt] fourmi *f*

antagonism [ænˈtægənɪzm] antagonisme *m*; **antagonistic** hostile

Antarctic [ænˈtɑːrktɪk]: **the ~** l'Antarctique *m*

antenatal [æntɪˈneɪtl] prénatal

antenna [ænˈtenə] antenne *f*

antibiotic [æntaɪbaɪˈɑːtɪk] antibiotique *m*

anticipate [ænˈtɪsɪpeɪt] prévoir; **anticipation** prévision *f*

antics [ˈæntɪks] singeries *fpl*

antidote [ˈæntɪdoʊt] antidote *m*

antifreeze [ˈæntɪfriːz] antigel *m*

antipathy [ænˈtɪpəθɪ] antipa-

thie *f*

antiquated [ˈæntɪkweɪtɪd] antique

antique [ænˈtiːk] antiquité *f*

antiseptic [æntərˈseptɪk] **1** *adj* antiseptique **2** *n* antiseptique *m*

antisocial [æntərˈsoʊʃl] asocial, antisocial

antivirus program [æntərˈvaɪrəs] COMPUT programme *m* antivirus

anxiety [æŋˈzaɪətɪ] inquiétude *f*; **anxious** inquiet; (*eager*) soucieux

any [ˈenɪ] **1** *adj*: **are there ~ glasses?** est-ce qu'il y a des verres?; **is there ~ bread/improvement?** est-ce qu'il y a du pain/une amélioration?; **there isn't/aren't ~** ... il n'y a pas de ...; **have you ~ idea at all?** est-ce que vous avez une idée? **2** *pron*: **do you have ~?** est-ce que vous en avez?; **there aren't/isn't ~ left** il n'y en a plus; **~ of them could be guilty** ils pourraient tous être coupables

anybody [ˈenɪbɑːdɪ] quelqu'un; *with negatives* personne; *no matter who* n'importe qui; **there wasn't ~ there** il n'y avait personne

anyhow [ˈenɪhaʊ] (*anyway*) enfin; (*in any way*) de quelque façon que ce soit

anyone [ˈenɪwʌn] → **anybody**

anything [ˈenɪθɪŋ] quelque

chose; *with negatives* rien; **I
didn't hear ~** je n'ai rien entendu **~ but ...** tout sauf ...

anyway ['enɪweɪ] → *anyhow*

anywhere ['enɪweə] quelque
part; *with negative* nulle
part; **I can't find it ~** je ne
le trouve nulle part

apart [ə'pɑːrt] séparé; **~ from**
(*except*) à l'exception de; (*in
addition to*) en plus de

apartment [ə'pɑːrtmənt] appartement *m*; **apartment
block** immeuble *m*

ape [eɪp] singe *m*

aperitif [ə'perɪtiːf] apéritif *m*

apologize [ə'pɑːlədʒaɪz] s'excuser (**to s.o.** auprès de qn);
apology excuses *fpl*

app [æp] COMPUT application *f*

appalling [ə'pɔːlɪŋ] scandaleux

apparatus [æpə'reɪtəs] appareils *mpl*

apparent [ə'pærənt] (*obvious*) évident; (*seeming*) apparent; **apparently** apparemment

appeal [ə'piːl] (*charm*) charme *m*; *for funds etc*, LAW appel *m*

◆ **appeal for** *calm etc* appeler
à; *funds* demander

◆ **appeal to** (*be attractive to*)
plaire à

appealing [ə'piːlɪŋ] séduisant

appear [ə'pɪr] apparaître; *in
court* comparaître; (*seem*)
paraître; **~ to be ...** avoir
l'air d'être ...; **appearance**

apparition *f*; *in court* comparution *f*; (*look*) apparence *f*

appendicitis [əpendɪˈsaɪtɪs]
appendicite *f*

appendix [ə'pendɪks] MED, *of
book etc* appendice *m*

appetite ['æpɪtaɪt] appétit *m*;
appetizer à *boire* apéritif
m; *to eat* amuse-gueule *m*;
appetizing appétissant

applaud [ə'plɔːd] applaudir;
applause applaudissements
mpl

apple ['æpl] pomme *f*

appliance [ə'plaɪəns] appareil *m*

applicable [ə'plɪkəbl] applicable; **applicant** *for job* candidat(e) *m(f)*; **application**
for job candidature *f*; *for
passport etc* demande *f*; **apply 1** *v/t* appliquer **2** *v/i* of
rule, law s'appliquer

◆ **apply for** *job* poser sa candidature pour; *passport etc*
faire une demande de

◆ **apply to** (*contact*) s'adresser à; *of rules etc* s'appliquer
à

appoint [ə'pɔɪnt] *to position*
nommer; **appointment** *to
position* nomination *f*;
(*meeting*) rendez-vous *m*

appraisal [ə'preɪzəl] évaluation *f*

appreciable [ə'priːʃəbl] considérable; **appreciate 1** *v/t*
apprécier; (*acknowledge*) reconnaître **2** *v/i* FIN s'apprécier; **appreciative** *grateful*

apprehensive

apprehensive [æprɪ'hensɪv] appréhensif

approach [ə'prəʊtʃ] **1** *n* approche *f*; (*proposal*) proposition *f* **2** *v/t* (*get near to*) approcher; (*contact*) faire des propositions à; *problem* aborder; **approachable** *person* d'un abord facile

appropriate [ə'prəʊprɪət] approprié

approval [ə'pruːvl] approbation *f*; **approve** **1** *v/i* être d'accord **2** *v/t plan* approuver

approximate [ə'prɒksɪmət] approximatif; **approximately** approximativement

apricot ['eɪprɪkɒt] abricot *m*

April ['eɪprəl] avril *m*

apt [æpt] *remark* pertinent; **aptitude** aptitude *f*

aquarium [ə'kweərɪəm] aquarium *m*

Arab ['ærəb] **1** *adj* arabe **2** *n* Arabe *m/f*; **Arabic 1** *adj* arabe **2** *n* arabe *m*

arbitrary ['ɑːbɪtrərɪ] arbitraire

arbitrate ['ɑːbɪtreɪt] arbitrer; **arbitration** arbitrage *m*

arch [ɑːtʃ] voûte *f*

archaeology *etc* → **archeology** *etc*

archaic [ɑː'keɪɪk] archaïque

archeological [ɑːkɪə'lɒdʒɪkl] archéologique; **archeologist** archéologue *m/f*; **ar-**cheology archéologie *f*

architect ['ɑːkɪtekt] architecte *m/f*; **architectural** architectural; **architecture** architecture *f*

archives ['ɑːkaɪvz] archives *fpl*

Arctic ['ɑːktɪk]: **the ~** l'Arctique *m*

ardent ['ɑːdənt] fervent

arduous ['ɑːdjʊəs] ardu

area ['eərɪə] *of city* quartier *m*; *of country* région *f*; *of research* domaine *m*; *of room* surface *f*; GEOM, *of land* superficie *f*; **area code** TELEC indicatif *m* régional

arena [ə'riːnə] SP arène *f*

Argentina [ɑːdʒən'tiːnə] Argentine *f*

Argentinian [ɑːdʒən'tɪnɪən] **1** *adj* argentin **2** *n* Argentin(e) *m(f)*

arguably ['ɑːgjʊəblɪ]: **it was ~ ...** on peut dire que ...; **argue** (*quarrel*) se disputer; (*reason*) argumenter; **argument** (*quarrel*) dispute *f*; (*discussion*) discussion *f*; (*reasoning*) argument *m*

arid ['ærɪd] *land* aride

arise [ə'raɪz] *of situation* survenir

arithmetic [ə'rɪθmətɪk] arithmétique *f*

arm¹ [ɑːm] *n* bras *m*

arm² [ɑːm] *v/t* armer

armaments ['ɑːməmənts] armes *fpl*

'armchair fauteuil *m*

armed [ɑːrmd] armé; **armed forces** forces *fpl* armées; **armed robbery** vol *m* à main armée

'**armpit** aisselle *f*

arms [ɑːrmz] (*weapons*) armes *fpl*

army ['ɑːrmɪ] armée *f*

around [ə'raʊnd] **1** *prep* (*encircling*) autour de; **it's ~ the corner** c'est juste à côté **2** *adv* (*in the area*) dans les parages; (*encircling*) autour; (*roughly*) à peu près; **with expressions of time** à environ

arouse [ə'raʊz] susciter; *sexually* exciter

arrange [ə'reɪndʒ] arranger; *furniture* disposer; *meeting etc* organiser; *time* fixer; *appointment* prendre; **I've ~d to meet her** j'ai prévu de la voir; **arrangement** (*agreement*), *music* arrangement *m*; *of furniture* disposition *f*; *flowers* composition *f*

arrears [ə'rɪərz] arriéré *m*

arrest [ə'rest] **1** *n* arrestation *f*; **be under ~** être en état d'arrestation **2** *v/t* arrêter

arrival [ə'raɪvl] arrivée *f*; **arrive** arriver

◆ **arrive at** arriver à

arrogance ['ærəgəns] arrogance *f*; **arrogant** arrogant

arrow ['ærəʊ] flèche *f*

arson ['ɑːrsn] incendie *m* criminel

art [ɑːrt] art *m*

artery ['ɑːrtərɪ] artère *f*

'**art gallery** galerie *f* d'art

arthritis [ɑːr'θraɪtɪs] arthrite *f*

artichoke ['ɑːrtɪtʃəʊk] artichaut *m*

article ['ɑːrtɪkl] article *m*

articulate [ɑːr'tɪkjʊlət] *person* qui s'exprime bien

artificial [ɑːrtɪ'fɪʃl] artificiel

artillery [ɑːr'tɪlərɪ] artillerie *f*

artist ['ɑːrtɪst] artiste *m/f*; **artistic** artistique

'**arts degree** licence *f* de lettres

as [æz] **1** *conj* (*while, when*) alors que; (*because*) comme; (*like*) comme; **~ if** comme si; **~ usual** comme d'habitude **2** *adv*: **~ high ~ ...** aussi haut que ...; **~ much ~ that?** autant que ça?; **~ soon ~ possible** aussi vite que possible **3** *prep* comme; **work ~ a teacher** travailler comme professeur; **~ for** quant à; **~ from** *or* **of Monday** à partir de lundi

ash [æʃ] cendres *fpl*

ashamed [ə'ʃeɪmd] honteux; **be ~ of** avoir honte de

'**ash can** poubelle *f*

ashore [ə'ʃɔːr] à terre; **go ~** débarquer

ashtray ['æʃtreɪ] cendrier *m*

Asia ['eɪʒə] Asie *f*; **Asian 1** *adj* asiatique **2** *n* Asiatique *m/f*; **Asian-American 1** *adj* américain(e) d'origine asiatique **2** *n* Américain(e) *m(f)* d'origine asiatique

aside [ə'saɪd] de côté; **move ~**

please poussez-vous, s'il vous plaît; **take s.o. ~** prendre qn à part; **~ from** à part

ask [æsk] demander; *question* poser; (*invite*) inviter; **~ s.o. for sth** demander qch à qn

◆ **ask after** *person* demander des nouvelles de

◆ **ask for** demander; *person* demander à parler à

◆ **ask out: he's asked me out** il m'a demandé de sortir avec lui

asleep [ə'sli:p]: **be (fast) ~** être (bien) endormi; **fall ~** s'endormir

asparagus [ə'spærəgəs] asperges *fpl*

aspect ['æspekt] aspect *m*

aspirations [æspə'reɪʃnz] aspirations *fpl*

aspirin ['æsprɪn] aspirine *f*

ass[1] [æs] (*idiot*) idiot(e) *m(f)*

ass[2] [æs] (*butt*) cul *m*

assassin [ə'sæsɪn] assassin *m*; **assassinate** assassiner

assassination assassinat *m*

assault [ə'sɔːlt] **1** *n* agression *f*; MIL attaque *f* (**on** contre) **2** *v/t* agresser

assemble [ə'sembl] **1** *v/t parts* assembler **2** *v/i of people* se rassembler; **assembly** POL assemblée *f*; *of parts* assemblage *m*; **assembly line** chaîne *f* de montage

assent [ə'sent] consentir

assertive [ə'sɜːrtɪv] *person* assuré

assess [ə'ses] *situation* éva-

luer; *value* estimer; **assessment** *of situation* évaluation *f*; *of value* estimation *f*

asset ['æset] FIN actif *m*; atout *m*

assign [ə'saɪn] assigner; **assignment** mission *f*; EDU devoir *m*

assimilate [ə'sɪmɪleɪt] assimiler

assist [ə'sɪst] aider; **assistance** aide *f*; **assistant** assistant(e) *m(f)*; **assistant manager** sous-directeur *m*, sous--directrice *f*; *of department* assistant(e) *m(f)* du/de la responsable

associate 1 *v/t* [ə'souʃɪeɪt] associer **2** *n* [ə'souʃɪət] (*colleague*) collègue *m/f*; **association** association *f*

assortment [ə'sɔːrtmənt] assortiment *m*

assume [ə'suːm] (*suppose*) supposer; **assumption** supposition *f*

assurance [ə'ʃurəns] (*reassurance, confidence*) assurance *f*; **assure** (*reassure*) assurer

asthma ['æsmə] asthme *m*

astonish [ə'stɑːnɪʃ] étonner; **astonishing** étonnant; **astonishment** étonnement *m*

astound [ə'staund] stupéfier

astride [ə'straɪd] à califourchon sur

astrology [ə'strɑːlədʒɪ] astrologie *f*

astronaut ['æstrənɔːt] astronaute *m/f*

astronomer [əˈstrɒnəmər]
astronome *m/f*; **astronomical** *price etc* astronomique;
astronomy astronomie *f*

astute [əˈstuːt] fin

asylum [əˈsaɪləm] *political,
(mental ~)* asile *m*

at [æt] *with places &* chez Joe; **~ 10 dollars** au prix
de 10 dollars; **~ the age of 18**
à l'âge de 18 ans; **~ 5 o'clock**
à 5 heures; **be good/bad ~ ...**
être bon/mauvais en ...

atheist [ˈeɪθɪɪst] athée *m/f*

athlete [ˈæθliːt] athlète *m/f*;
athletic d'athlétisme;
(strong, sporting) sportif;
athletics athlétisme *m*

Atlantic [ətˈlæntɪk]: **the ~**
l'Atlantique *m*

atlas [ˈætləs] atlas *m*

ATM [eɪtiːˈem](= **automatic
teller machine**) distributeur
m automatique (de billets)

atmosphere [ˈætməsfɪr] atmosphère *f*

atom [ˈætəm] atome *m*; **atomic** atomique

◆ **atone for** [əˈtoʊn] racheter

atrocious [əˈtroʊʃəs] atroce;
atrocity atrocité *f*

at-'seat TV télévision que l'on
regarde à sa place, par exemple en avion

attach [əˈtætʃ] attacher; **attachment** *to e-mail* fichier
m joint

attack [əˈtæk] **1** *n* attaque *f* **2**
v/t attaquer

attempt [əˈtempt] **1** *n* tentative *f* **2** *v/t* essayer

attend [əˈtend] assister à;
school aller à

◆ **attend to** s'occuper de

attendance [əˈtendəns] présence *f*; **attendant** *in museum etc* gardien(ne) *m(f)*

attention [əˈtenʃn] attention
f; **pay ~** faire attention; **attentive** attentif

attic [ˈætɪk] grenier *m*

attitude [ˈætɪtuːd] attitude *f*

attorney [əˈtɜːrni] avocat *m*

attract [əˈtrækt] attirer; **attraction** *of job, doing sth etc*
attrait *m*; *romantic* attirance *f*;
touristic attraction *f*; **attractive** *person* attirant; *idea, city*
attrayant

auction [ˈɔːkʃn] vente *f* aux
enchères

audacity [ɔːˈdæsəti] audace *f*

audible [ˈɔːdəbl] audible

audience [ˈɔːdɪəns] public *m*

audio [ˈɔːdioʊ] audio; **audiovisual** audiovisuel

audit [ˈɔːdɪt] **1** *n* audit *m* **2** *v/t*
contrôler; *course* suivre en
auditeur libre

audition [ɔːˈdɪʃn] **1** *n* audition
f **2** *v/i* passer une audition

auditor [ˈɔːdɪtər] FIN audi-
teur(-trice) *m(f)*

auditorium [ɔːdɪˈtɔːrɪəm] *of
theater etc* auditorium *m*

August [ˈɔːɡəst] août *m*

aunt [ænt] tante *f*

au pair [oʊˈper] jeune fille *f* au
pair

aura ['ɔːrə] aura *f*

auspicious [ɔː'spɪʃəs] favorable

austere [ɔː'stiːr] austère; **austerity** austérité *f*

Australia [ɔː'streɪliə] Australie *f*; **Australian 1** *adj* australien **2** *n* Australien(ne) *m(f)*

Austria ['ɒːstriə] Autriche *f*; **Austrian 1** *adj* autrichien **2** *n* Autrichien(ne) *m(f)*

authentic [ɔː'θentɪk] authentique; **authenticity** authenticité *f*

author ['ɔːtər] auteur *m*

authoritarian [əθɑːrɪ'teriən] autoritaire; **authoritative** *source* qui fait autorité; *person, manner* autoritaire; **authority** [ə'θɑːrəti] autorité *f*; (*permission*) autorisation *f*; **authorization** autorisation *f*; **authorize** autoriser

autistic [ɔː'tɪstɪk] autiste

autobiography [ɔːtəbaɪ'ɑːgrəfɪ] autobiographie *f*

autocratic [ɔːtə'krætɪk] autocratique

autograph ['ɔːtəgræf] autographe *m*

automate ['ɔːtəmeɪt] automatiser; **automatic 1** *adj* automatique **2** *n car* automatique *f*; *gun* automatique *m*; **automatically** automatiquement; **automation** automatisation *f*

automobile ['ɔːtəmoʊbiːl] automobile *f*; **automobile**

industry industrie *f* automobile

autonomous [ɔː'tɑːnəməs] autonome

autopilot ['ɔːtoʊpaɪlət] pilotage *m* automatique

autopsy ['ɔːtɑːpsi] autopsie *f*

autumn ['ɔːtəm] *Br* automne *m*

auxiliary [ɔːg'zɪljəri] auxiliaire

available [ə'veɪləbl] disponible

avalanche ['ævəlænʃ] avalanche *f*

avenue ['ævənuː] avenue *f*; **explore all ~s** explorer toutes les possibilités

average ['ævərɪdʒ] **1** *adj* moyen **2** *n* moyenne *f*; **on ~** en moyenne

◆ **average out at** faire une moyenne de

averse [ə'vɜːrs]: *not be ~ to* ne rien avoir contre; **aversion** aversion *f* (*to* pour)

avid ['ævɪd] avide

avocado [ævə'kɑːdoʊ] avocat *m*

avoid [ə'vɔɪd] éviter

await [ə'weɪt] attendre

awake [ə'weɪk] éveillé; *it's keeping me ~* ça m'empêche de dormir

award [ə'wɔːrd] **1** *n* (*prize*) prix *m* **2** *v/t* décerner; *damages* attribuer; **awards** ceremony cérémonie *f* de remise des prix; EDU cérémonie *f* de remise des diplômes

aware [ə'weɪ]: *be ~ of sth* avoir conscience de qch; *become ~ of sth* prendre conscience de qch; **awareness** conscience *f*

away [ə'weɪ]: *be ~* être absent, ne pas être là; *walk ~* s'en aller; *look ~* tourner la tête; *it's 2 miles ~* c'est à 2 miles d'ici; *take sth ~ from s.o.* enlever qch à qn; **away game** SP match *m* à l'extérieur

awesome ['ɔːsəm] F *(terrific)* super *inv*

awful ['ɔːfəl] affreux

awkward ['ɔːkwərd] *(clumsy)* maladroit; *(difficult)* difficile; *(embarrassing)* gênant; *feel ~* se sentir mal à l'aise

ax, *Br* **axe** [æks] **1** *n* hache *f* **2** *v/t project* abandonner; *budget* faire des coupures dans; *job* supprimer

axle ['æksl] essieu *m*

B

baby ['beɪbɪ] bébé *m*; **baby-sit** faire du baby-sitting

bachelor ['bætʃələr] célibataire *m*; UNIV *~'s degree* licence *f*

back [bæk] **1** *n of person, clothes* dos *m*; *of chair* dossier *m*; *of drawer* fond *m*; *of house* arrière *m*; SP arrière *m*; *in ~ (of the car)* à l'arrière (de la voiture); *at the ~ of the book* à la fin du livre; *~ to front* à l'envers **2** *adj door* de derrière; *wheels, legs* arrière *inv* **3** *adv: move ~* se reculer; *give sth ~ to s.o.* rendre qch à qn; *she'll be ~ tomorrow* elle sera de retour demain **4** *v/t (support)* soutenir; *car* faire reculer; *horse* miser sur

♦ **back down** faire marche arrière

♦ **back out** *of commitment* se dégager

♦ **back up 1** *v/t (support)* soutenir; *file* sauvegarder **2** *v/i in car* reculer

'backache mal *m* de dos; **backbone** colonne *f* vertébrale; **backdate** antidater; **backdoor** porte *f* arrière

background *of picture* arrière-plan *m*; *social* milieu *m*; *of crime* contexte *m*; *his work ~* son expérience professionnelle

backhand *in tennis* revers *m*; **backing** *(support)* soutien *m*; MUS accompagnement *m*; **backing group** groupe *m* d'accompagnement; **backlash** répercussion(s) *f*(pl); **backlog** retard *m* (*of* dans); **backpack** sac *m* à dos; **backpacker** randonneur(-euse) *m(f)*; **back seat** siège *m* arrière; **back streets** petites rues *fpl*; *poor area* quartiers *mpl* pauvres; **backstroke** SP dos *m* crawlé; **backtrack** retourner sur ses pas; **backup** (*support*) renfort *m*; COMPUT copie *f* de sauvegarde; **backyard** arrière-cour *f*

bacon ['beɪkn] bacon *m*

bacteria [bæk'tɪrɪə] bactéries *fpl*

bad [bæd] mauvais; *person* méchant; (*rotten*) avarié; **go ~** s'avarier; *it's not ~* c'est pas mal; *that's really too ~* (*shame*) c'est vraiment dommage

badge [bædʒ] insigne *f*

bad language grossièretés *fpl*; **badly** mal; *injured* grièvement; *damaged* sérieusement; *he ~ needs ...* il a grand besoin de ...

badminton ['bædmɪntən] badminton *m*

bad-tempered [bæd'tempərd] de mauvaise humeur

baffle ['bæfl] déconcerter; *be ~d* être perplexe

bag [bæg] sac *m*; (*piece of baggage*) bagage *m*

baggage ['bægɪdʒ] bagages *mpl*; **baggage check** contrôle *m* des bagages

baggy ['bægɪ] flottant; *fashionably* large

bail [beɪl] LAW caution *f*; *be*

out on ~ être en liberté provisoire sous caution

bait [beɪt] appât *m*

bake [beɪk] cuire au four; **baked potato** pomme *f* de terre au four; **baker** boulanger(-ère) *m(f)*; **bakery** boulangerie *f*

balance ['bæləns] **1** *n* équilibre *m*; (*remainder*) reste *m*; *of bank account* solde *m* **2** *v/t* mettre en équilibre **3** *v/i* rester en équilibre; *of accounts* équilibrer; **balanced** (*fair*) objectif; *diet, personality* équilibré; **balance sheet** bilan *m*

balcony ['bælkənɪ] balcon *m*

bald [bɔːld] chauve; **balding** qui commence à devenir chauve

ball [bɔːl] *for soccer etc* ballon *m*; *for tennis, golf* balle *f*

ballad ['bæləd] ballade *f*

ballet [bæ'leɪ] ballet *m*; **ballet dancer** danseur(-euse) *m(f)* de ballet

'ball game match *m* de baseball

ballistic missile [bə'lɪstɪk] missile *m* balistique

balloon [bə'luːn] *child's* ballon *m*; *for flight* montgolfière *f*

ballot ['bælət] **1** *n* vote *m* **2** *v/t members* consulter par vote; **ballot box** urne *f*

'ballpark terrain *m* de baseball; **ballpark figure** chiffre *m* en gros; **ballpoint (pen)**

stylo *m* bille

balls [bɔːlz] V couilles *fpl*

bamboo [bæm'buː] bambou *m*

ban [bæn] **1** *n* interdiction *f* **2** *v/t* interdire

banal [bə'næl] banal

banana [bə'nænə] banane *f*

band [bænd] *MUS* orchestre *m*; *pop* groupe *m*; *of material* bande *f*

bandage ['bændɪdʒ] **1** *n* bandage *m* **2** *v/t* faire un bandage à

'Band-Aid® sparadrap *m*

bandit ['bændɪt] bandit *m*

bandy ['bændɪ] *legs* arqué

bang [bæŋ] **1** *n* noise boum *m*; (*blow*) coup *m* **2** *v/t* door claquer; (*hit*) cogner

bangle ['bæŋgl] bracelet *m*

bangs [bæŋz] frange *f*

banisters ['bænɪstərz] rampe *f*

banjo ['bændʒoʊ] banjo *m*

bank¹ [bæŋk] *of river* bord *m*, rive *f*

bank² [bæŋk] FIN banque *f*

◆ **bank on** compter sur

'bank account compte *m* en banque; **banker** banquier (-ière) *m(f)*; **banker's card** carte *f* d'identité bancaire; **banking** banque *f*; **bank loan** emprunt *m* bancaire; **bank manager²** directeur (-trice) *m(f)* de banque; **bank rate** taux *m* bancaire; **bankroll** financer; **bankrupt** en faillite; **go ~** faire faillite;

bankruptcy faillite *f*

banner ['bænər] bannière *f*

banquet ['bæŋkwɪt] banquet *m*

baptism ['bæptɪzm] baptême *m*; **baptize** baptiser

bar¹ [bɑːr] *n of iron, chocolate* barre *f*; *for drinks, counter* bar *m*

bar² [bɑːr] *v/t* exclure

barbaric [bɑːr'bærɪk] barbare

barbecue ['bɑːrbɪkjuː] **1** *n* barbecue *m* **2** *v/t* cuire au barbecue

barbed 'wire [bɑːrbd] fil *m* barbelé

barber ['bɑːrbər] coiffeur *m*

'bar code code *m* barre

bare [ber] nu; *room, shelves* vide; **barefoot**: *be ~* être pieds nus; **bare-headed tête** nue; **barely** à peine

bargain ['bɑːrgɪn] **1** *n* (*deal*) marché *m*; (*good buy*) bonne affaire *f* **2** *v/i* marchander

barge [bɑːrdʒ] NAUT péniche *f*

◆ **barge into** se heurter contre; (*enter noisily*) faire irruption dans

baritone ['bærɪtoʊn] baryton *m*

bark¹ [bɑːrk] **1** *n of dog* aboiement *m* **2** *v/i* aboyer

bark² [bɑːrk] *of tree* écorce *f*

barn [bɑːrn] grange *f*

barometer [bə'rɑːmɪtər] *also fig* baromètre *m*

barracks ['bærəks] MIL caserne *f*

barrel ['bærəl] tonneau *m*

barren ['bærən] *land* stérile

barrette [bə'ret] barrette *f*

barricade [bæri'keid] barricade *f*

barrier ['bæriər] barrière *f*

'bar tender barman *m*, barmaid *f*

barter ['bɑːrtər] **1** *n* troc *m* **2** *v/t* troquer (**for** contre)

base [beis] **1** *n* base *f* **2** *v/t* baser (**on** sur); **baseball** baseball *m*; *ball* ballon *m* de baseball; **baseball cap** casquette *f* de baseball; **baseboard** plinthe *f*; **basement** sous-sol *m*

basic ['beisik] (*rudimentary*) rudimentaire; (*fundamental*), *salary* de base; **basically** au fond

basin ['beisn] *for washing dishes* bassine *f*; *in bathroom* lavabo *m*

basis ['beisis] base *f*; *of argument* fondement *m*

bask [bæsk] se dorer

basket ['bæskit] panier *m*; **basketball** *game* basket (-ball) *m*; *ball* ballon *m* de basket

bass [beis] basse *f*; **double ~** contrebasse *f*; **~ guitar** basse *f*

bastard ['bæstərd] salaud(e) *m(f)*

bat¹ [bæt] **1** *n for baseball* batte *f*; *for table tennis* raquette *f* **2** *v/i* baseball batter

bat² [bæt] *animal* chauve-souris *f*

batch [bætʃ] *of students, data* lot *m*; *of bread* fournée *f*

bath [bæθ] (*~tub*) baignoire *f*

bathe [beið] (*have a bath*) se baigner

'bathrobe peignoir *m*; **bathroom** salle *f* de bains; *toilet* toilettes *fpl*; **bath towel** serviette *f* de bain; **bathtub** baignoire *f*

batter ['bætər] *for cakes, pancakes etc* pâte *f* lisse; *in baseball* batteur *m*; **battered** *wife, children* battu

battery ['bætəri] pile *f*; MOT batterie *f*

battle ['bætl] **1** *n* bataille *f*; *fig* lutte *f* **2** *v/i against illness etc* se battre, lutter; **battleship** cuirassé *m*

bawl [bɔːl] (*shout, weep*) brailler

bay [bei] (*inlet*) baie *f*

BC [biː'siː] (= *before Christ*) av. J.-C.

be [biː] ◇ être; **~ 15** avoir 15 ans; *it's me* c'est moi; *how much is...?* combien coûte ...?; *there is/are* il y a; *how are you?* comment ça va?
◇ *has the mailman been?* est-ce que le facteur est passé?; *I've never been to Japan* je ne suis jamais allé au Japon
◇ *tags: that's right, isn't it?* c'est juste, n'est-ce pas?; *she's American, isn't she?* elle est américaine, n'est-ce pas?

◇ *passive: he was killed* il a été tué; *it hasn't been decided* on n'a encore rien décidé

beach [biːtʃ] *n* plage *f*; **beachwear** vêtements *mpl* de plage

beads [biːdz] collier *m* de perles

beak [biːk] bec *m*

beam [biːm] **1** *n in ceiling etc* poutre *f* **2** *v/i* (*smile*) rayonner

bean [biːn] haricot *m*; *of coffee* grain *m*

bear[1] [ber] *n animal* ours *m*

bear[2] [ber] **1** *v/t weight* porter; *costs* prendre en charge; (*tolerate*) supporter; **bearable** supportable

beard [bɪrd] barbe *f*

beat [biːt] **1** *n of heart* battement *m*; *of music* mesure *f* **2** *v/i of heart* battre; *of rain* s'abattre **3** *v/t in competition*, (*hit*) battre; (*pound*) frapper

◆ **beat up** tabasser

beaten ['biːtən]: *off the ~ track* à l'écart; *beating physical* raclée *f*; **beat-up** déglingué

beautiful ['bjuːtəfʊl] beau; **beautifully** admirablement; **beauty** beauté *f*

beaver ['biːvər] castor *m*

because [bɪ'kɑːz] parce que; *~ of* à cause de

become [bɪ'kʌm] devenir; *what's ~ of her?* qu'est-elle devenue?; **becoming** seyant

bed [bed] *also of sea* lit *m*; *of*

flowers parterre *m*; *go to ~* aller se coucher; **bedding** literie *f*; **bedridden** cloué au lit; **bedroom** chambre *f* (à coucher); **bedtime** heure *f* du coucher

bee [biː] abeille *f*

beech [biːtʃ] hêtre *m*

beef [biːf] bœuf *m*; **beefburger** steak *m* hâché

beep [biːp] **1** *n* bip *m* **2** *v/i* faire bip

beer [bɪr] bière *f*

beet [biːt] betterave *f*

beetle ['biːtl] coléoptère *m*, cafard *m*

before [bɪ'fɔːr] **1** *prep* avant; *~ signing it* avant de le signer; *~ a vowel* devant une voyelle **2** *adv* auparavant; (*already*) déjà; *the week/day ~* la semaine/le jour d'avant **3** *conj* avant que (*+subj*); *I had a coffee ~ I left* j'ai pris un café avant de partir; **beforehand** à l'avance

befriend [bɪ'frend] se lier d'amitié avec

beg [beg] **1** *v/i* mendier **2** *v/t: ~ s.o. to do sth* prier qn de faire qch; **beggar** mendiant (e) *m (f)*

begin [bɪ'gɪn] **1** *v/i* commencer; **beginner** débutant(e) *m(f)*; **beginning** début *m*

behalf [bɪ'hɑːf]: *in or on ~ of* de la part de

behave [bɪ'heɪv] se comporter; *~ (yourself)!* sois sage!; **behavior**, *Br* **behaviour**

comportement *m*

behind [bɪ'haɪnd] **1** *prep* derrière; *be ~ ...* (*responsible for, support*) être derrière ... **2** *adv* (*at the back*) à l'arrière; *leave, stay* derrière; *be ~ in match* être derrière

beige [beɪʒ] beige

being [biːŋ] (*creature*) être *m*; (*existence*) existence *f*

belated [bɪ'leɪtɪd] tardif

belch [beltʃ] **1** *n* éructation *f*, rot *m* **2** *v/i* éructer, roter

Belgian ['beldʒən] **1** *adj* belge **2** *n* Belge *m/f*; **Belgium** Belgique *f*

belief [bɪ'liːf] conviction *f*; REL *also* croyance *f*; *in person* foi *f* (*in* en); **believe** croire

◆ **believe in** *God, person* croire en; *sth* croire à; *to cacher la vérité aux gens*

believer [bɪ'liːvər] *in God* croyant(e) *m(f)*; *in sth* partisan(e) *m(f)* (*in* de)

bell [bel] *on bike, door* sonnette *f*; *in church* cloche *f*; *in school:* electric sonnerie *f*; **bellhop** groom *m*

belligerent [bɪ'lɪdʒərənt] belligérant

bellow ['beloʊ] brailler; *of bull* beugler

belly ['belɪ] *of person* ventre *m*; *fat* bedaine *f*; *of animal* panse *f*

◆ **belong to** *of object* appartenir à; *club, organization* faire partie de

belongings [bɪ'lɔːŋɪŋz] affaires *fpl*

beloved [bɪ'lʌvɪd] bien-aimé

below [bɪ'loʊ] **1** *prep* au-dessous de **2** *adv* au-dessous; *in text* en bas; **10 degrees ~** moins dix

belt [belt] ceinture *f*

'**benchmark** référence *f*

bend [bend] **1** *n* tournant *m* **2** *v/t head* baisser; *arm, knees* plier; *metal, plastic* tordre **3** *v/i of road* tourner; *of person* se pencher

◆ **bend down** se pencher

beneath [bɪ'niːθ] **1** *prep* sous **2** *adv* (au-)dessous

benefactor ['benɪfæktər] bienfaiteur(-trice) *m(f)*

beneficial [benɪ'fɪʃl] bénéfique

benefit ['benɪfɪt] **1** *n* bénéfice *m* **2** *v/t* bénéficier à **3** *v/i* bénéficier (*from* de)

benevolent [bɪ'nevələnt] bienveillant

benign [bɪ'naɪn] doux; MED bénin

bequeath [bɪ'kwiːð] léguer; **bequest** legs *m*

beret ['bereɪ] béret *m*

berry ['berɪ] baie *f*

berth [bɜːrθ] couchette *f*; *for ship* mouillage *m*

beside [bɪ'saɪd] à côté de; *be ~ o.s.* être hors de soi; *that's ~ the point* c'est hors de propos

besides [bɪ'saɪdz] **1** *adv* d'ailleurs **2** *prep* (*apart from*) à part

best [best] **1** *adj* meilleur **2** *adv* le mieux; *I like her ~* c'est elle que j'aime le plus **3** *n*: *do one's ~* faire de son mieux; *the ~* le mieux; *the ~* (*outstanding thing or person*) le (la) meilleur(e) *m(f)*; *all the ~!* meilleurs vœux!; **best before date** date *f* limite de consommation; **best man** *at wedding* garçon *m* d'honneur

bet [bet] **1** *n* pari *m* **2** *v/t & v/i* parier; *you ~!* évidemment!

betray [bɪ'treɪ] trahir; **betrayal** trahison *f*

better ['betər] **1** *adj* meilleur; *get ~* s'améliorer; *he's ~ in health* il va mieux **2** *adv* mieux; *I'd really ~not* je ne devrais vraiment pas; *I like her ~* je l'aime plus; **better-off** (*richer*) plus aisé

between [bɪ'twiːn] entre

beware [bɪ'wer]: *~ of* attention à

bewilder [bɪ'wɪldər] confondre; **bewilderment** confusion *f*

beyond [bɪ'jɑːnd] au-delà de

bias ['baɪəs] parti *m* pris, préjugé *m*; **bias(s)ed** partial, subjectif

Bible ['baɪbl] Bible *f*; **biblical** biblique

bicentennial [baɪsen'teniəl] bicentenaire *m*

bicker ['bɪkər] se chamailler

bicycle ['baɪsɪkl] bicyclette *f*

bid [bɪd] **1** *n at auction* enchè-re *m*; (*attempt*) tentative *f*; *in takeover* offre *f* **2** *v/i at auction* faire une enchère; **bidder** enchérisseur(-euse) *m(f)*

biennial [baɪ'eniəl] biennal

big [bɪg] **1** *adj* grand; *sum of money, mistake* gros; *my ~ brother/sister* mon grand frère/ma grande sœur **2** *adv*: *talk ~* se vanter

bigamist ['bɪgəmɪst] bigame *m/f*

bighead crâneur(-euse) *m(f)*

bigot ['bɪgət] fanatique *m/f*, sectaire *m/f*

bike [baɪk] vélo *m*; (*motorbike*) moto *f*; **biker** ['baɪkər] motard(e) *m(f)*

bikini [bɪ'kiːni] bikini *m*

bilingual [baɪ'lɪŋgwəl] bilingue

bill [bɪl] facture *f*; *money* billet *m* (de banque); POL projet *m* de loi; (*poster*) affiche *f*; **billboard** panneau *m* d'affichage; **billfold** portefeuille *m*

billion ['bɪljən] milliard *m*

bin [bɪn] *for storage* boîte *f*

bind [baɪnd] (*connect*) unir; (*tie*) attacher; LAW (*oblige*) obliger; **binding** *agreement* obligatoire

binoculars [bɪ'nɑːkjuːlərz] jumelles *fpl*

biodegradable [baɪoʊdɪ'greɪdəbl] biodégradable

biographer biographe *m/f*; **biography** biographie *f*

biological [baɪoʊ'lɑːdʒɪkl]

biologique; **biology** biologie
f

bird [bɜːrd] oiseau *m*

biro® ['baɪrəʊ] *B* stylo *m* bille

birth [bɜːrθ] naissance *f*; (*labor*) accouchement *m*; **give ~ to** *child* donner naissance à; **date of ~** date *f* de naissance; **birth certificate** acte *m* de naissance; **birth control** contrôle *m* des naissances; **birthday** anniversaire *m* **happy ~!** bon anniversaire!

biscuit ['bɪskɪt] biscuit *m*

bisexual ['baɪseksjʊəl] **1** *adj* bisexuel **2** *n* bisexuel(le) *m(f)*

bishop ['bɪʃəp] évêque *m*

bit [bɪt] **1** (*piece*) morceau *m*; (*part: of book*) passage *m*; (*part: of garden, road*) partie *f*; COMPUT bit *m*; **a ~ of** (*a little*) un peu de

bitch [bɪtʃ] **1** *n* dog chienne *f*; F: *woman* garce *f* **2** *v/i* F (*complain*) rouspéter

bite [baɪt] **1** of dog, snake morsure *f*; of flea, mosquito piqûre *f*; of food morceau *m* **2** *v/t & v/i* of dog, snake, person mordre; of flea, mosquito piquer

bitter ['bɪtər] *taste, person* amer

black [blæk] **1** *adj* noir; *tea* nature; *future* sombre **2** *n color* noir *m*; *person* Noir(e) *m(f)*
◆ **black out** (*faint*) s'évanouir

'blackboard tableau *m* noir;

black coffee café *m* noir;

black economy économie *f* souterraine; **black eye** œil *m* poché; **blacklist** liste *f* noire; **blackmail 1** *n* chantage *m* **2** *v/t* faire chanter; **black market** marché *m* noir; **blackness** noirceur *f*; **blackout** ELEC panne *f* d'électricité; MED évanouissement *m*

bladder ['blædər] vessie *f*

blade [bleɪd] of knife lame *f*; of propeller ailette *f*; of grass brin *m*

blame [bleɪm] **1** *n* responsabilité *f* **2** *v/t*: **~ s.o. for sth** reprocher qch à qn

bland [blænd] fade

blank [blæŋk] **1** *adj paper, tape* vierge; *look* vide **2** *n* (*empty space*) espace *m* vide; **blank check**, *Br* **blank cheque** chèque *m* en blanc

blanket ['blæŋkɪt] couverture *f*

blast [blæst] **1** *n* (*explosion*) explosion *f*; (*gust*) rafale *f* **2** *v/t* tunnel etc percer (à l'aide d'explosifs); **~!** mince!; **blast-off** lancement *m*

blatant ['bleɪtənt] flagrant; *person* éhonté

blaze [bleɪz] **1** *n* (*fire*) incendie *m* **2** *v/i* of fire flamber

blazer ['bleɪzər] blazer *m*

bleach [bliːtʃ] **1** *n* for clothes eau *f* de Javel; for hair décolorant *m* **2** *v/t hair* décolorer

bleak [bliːk] *countryside* désolé; *weather* morne; *future* sombre

bleary-eyed ['blɪəraɪd] aux yeux troubles

bleat [bliːt] *of sheep* bêler

bleed [bliːd] saigner; **bleeding** saignement *m*

bleep [bliːp] **1** *n* bip *m* **2** *v/i* faire re bip

blemish ['blemɪʃ] tache *f*

blend [blend] **1** *n* mélange *m* **2** *v/t* mélanger; **blender** *machine* mixeur *m*

bless [bles] bénir; ~ **you!** *in response to sneeze* à vos souhaits!; **blessing** bénédiction *f*

blind [blaɪnd] **1** *adj* aveugle; ~ **corner** *m* masqué **2** *v/t of sun* aveugler; **blind alley** impasse *f*; **blind date** rendez-vous *m* arrangé; **blindfold 1** *n* bandeau *m* sur les yeux **2** *v/t* bander les yeux à; **blinding light** aveuglant; *headache* terrible; **blindly** sans rien voir; *fig* aveuglément; **blind spot** *in road* angle *m* mort

blink [blɪŋk] *of person* cligner des yeux; *of light* clignoter

blizzard ['blɪzəd] tempête *f* de neige

bloc [blɒk] POL bloc *m*

block [blɒk] **1** *n* bloc *m*; *buildings* pâté *m* de maisons; *(blockage)* obstruction *f m*; **it's three ~s away** c'est à trois rues d'ici **2** *v/t* bloquer; **blockage** obstruction *f*; **blockbuster** *movie* film *m*

à grand succès; *novel* roman *m* à succès; **block letters** capitales *fpl*

blond [blɒnd] blond; **blonde** *woman* blonde *f*

blood [blʌd] sang *m*; **blood donor** donneur(-euse) *m(f)* de sang; **blood group** groupe *m* sanguin

'blood poisoning empoisonnement *m* du sang; **blood pressure** tension *f* (artérielle); **blood sample** prélèvement *m* sanguin; **bloodshed** massacre *m*; **without ~** sans effusion de sang; **bloodshot** injecté de sang; **bloodstained** taché de sang; **blood test** test *m* sanguin; **bloodthirsty** sanguinaire

bloom [bluːm] *also fig* fleurir

blossom ['blɒsəm] **1** *n* fleur *f* **2** *v/i* fleurir; *fig* s'épanouir

blot [blɒt] tache *f*

♦ **blot out** effacer

blouse [blauz] chemisier *m*

blow¹ [bləu] *n also fig* coup *m*

blow² [bləu] **1** *v/t* souffler; ~ **one's whistle** donner un coup de sifflet **2** *v/i of wind, person* souffler; *of whistle* retentir; *of fuse* sauter; *of tire* éclater

♦ **blow out 1** *v/t candle* souffler **2** *v/i of candle* s'éteindre

♦ **blow over 1** *v/t* renverser **2** *v/i* se renverser; *(pass)* passer

♦ **blow up 1** *v/t with explosives* faire sauter; *balloon* gonfler; *photograph* agrandir **2** *v/i* of boiler etc sauter, exploser

'**blow-dry** sécher (au sèche-cheveux); **blow-out** of tire éclatement *m*

blue [bluː] *adj*; *movie* porno; **blueberry** myrtille *f*; **blue chip** de premier ordre; **blues** MUS blues *m*; **have the ~** avoir le cafard

bluff [blʌf] **1** *n* (deception) bluff *m* **2** *v/i* bluffer

blunder ['blʌndər] **1** *n* gaffe *f* **2** *v/i* faire une gaffe

blunt [blʌnt] émoussé; *person* franc; **bluntly** franchement

blur [blɜːr] **1** *n* masse *f* confuse **2** *v/t* brouiller

♦ **blurt out** [blɜːrt] lâcher

blush [blʌʃ] **1** *n* rougissement *m* **2** *v/i* rougir; **blusher** *cosmetic* rouge *m*

blustery ['blʌstəri] à bourrasques

BO [biː'ou] (= *body odor*) odeur *f* corporelle

board [bɔːrd] **1** *n* of wood planche *f*; *cardboard* carton *m*; *for game* plateau *m* de jeu; *for notices* panneau *m*; **~** (*of directors*) conseil *m* d'administration; **on~** à bord **2** *v/t* plane, ship monter à bord de; *train, bus* monter dans **3** *v/i* of passengers embarquer; *on train, bus* monter ♦ **board up** windows condamner

boarder ['bɔːrdər] pension-naire *m/f*; EDU interne *m/f*; **board game** jeu *m* de société; **boarding card** carte *f* d'embarquement; **boarding school** internat *m*, pension-nat *m*; **board meeting** réunion *f* du conseil d'administration; **board room** salle *f* du conseil

boast [boust] se vanter (*about* de)

boat [bout] bateau *m*; *small, for leisure* canot *m*

bodily ['bɑːdɪlɪ] **1** *adj* corporel **2** *adv*: **they ~ ejected him** ils l'ont saisi à bras-le-corps et l'ont mis dehors **body** corps *m*; *dead* cadavre *m*; **body-guard** garde *m* du corps; **bodywork** MOT carrosserie *f*

bogus ['bougəs] faux

boil[1] [bɔɪl] *n* (swelling) furoncle *m*

boil[2] [bɔɪl] **1** *v/t* faire bouillir **2** *v/i* bouillir ♦ **boil down to** se ramener à

boiler ['bɔɪlər] chaudière *f*

boisterous ['bɔɪstərəs] bruyant

bold [bould] **1** *adj* courageux; *text* en caractères gras **2** *n* *print* caractères *mpl* gras

bolster ['boulstər] confidence soutenir

bolt [boult] **1** *n* (metal pin) boulon *m*; *on door* verrou *m* **2** *adv*: **~ upright** tout droit **3** *v/t* (fix with bolts) boulonner; *close* verrouiller **4** *v/i* (run off) décamper; *of horse* s'emballer

bomb [baːm] **1** *n* bombe *f* **2** *v/t*
MIL bombarder; *of terrorist*
faire sauter; **bombard**
[baːm'baːrd] *also fig* bombarder; **bomb attack** attaque
f à la bombe; **bomber** *air-
plane* bombardier *m*; *terrorist* bombeur *m(f)* de bombes;
bomb scare alerte *f* à la
bombe; **bombshell**: **come
as a ~** faire l'effet d'une
bombe

bond [baːnd] **1** *n (tie)* lien *m*;
FIN obligation *f* **2** *v/i of glue*
se coller

bone [boun] os *m*; *in fish* arête
f

bonnet ['baːnɪt] *Br of car* capot *m*

bonus ['bounəs] *money* prime *f*; *(something extra)* plus
m

boob [buːb] P *(breast)* nichon
m

booboo ['buːbuː] F bêtise *f*

book [buk] **1** *n* livre *m* **2** *v/t*
seat réserver; *ticket* prendre;
of policeman donner un P.V.
à; **bookcase** bibliothèque *f*;
booked up complet; *perso*
complètement pris; **bookie**
F bookmaker *m*; **booking** réservation *f*; **bookkeeper**
comptable *m*

'**bookkeeping** comptabilité *f*;
booklet livret *m*; **bookmaker** bookmaker *m*; **books** *(accounts)* comptes *mpl*; **book-
seller** libraire *m/f*; **book-**

store librairie *f*

boom[1] [buːm] **1** *n* boum *m* **2**
v/i of business aller très fort

boom[2] [buːm] *n noise* boum
m

boost [buːst] **1** *n*: **give sth a ~**
stimuler qc **2** *v/t* stimuler

boot [buːt] botte *f*; *for climbing, football* chaussure *f*

◆ **boot up** COMPUT **1** *v/i* démarrer **2** *v/t* faire démarrer

booth [buːð] *at market* tente *f*
(de marché); *at fair* baraque
f; *at trade fair* stand *m*; *in restaurant* alcôve *f*

booze [buːz] boisson *f* (alcoolique)

border ['bɔːrdər] **1** *n* frontière
f; *(edge)* bordure *f* **2** *v/t country* avoir une frontière avec

◆ **border on** avoir une frontière avec; *(be almost)* friser

bore[1] [bɔːr] *v/t hole* percer

bore[2] [bɔːr] **1** *n person* ra-
seur(-euse) *m(f)* **2** *v/t* ennuyer

bored [bɔːrd] ennuyé; **be ~**
s'ennuyer; **boredom** ennui
m; **boring** ennuyeux, chiant
m

born [bɔːrn]: **be ~** être né

borrow ['baːrou] emprunter

bosom ['buzm] poitrine *f*

boss [baːs] patron(-onne)
m(f)

◆ **boss around** donner des
ordres à

bossy ['baːsɪ] autoritaire

botanical [bə'tænɪkl] botanique

botch [baːtʃ] bâcler

both [bəʊθ] **1** *adj & pron* les deux; **~ of them** tous(-tes) *m(f)* les deux **2** *adv:* **~ ...** *and ...* à la fois ... et ...

bother ['bɒðər] **1** *n* problème *mpl* **2** *v/t (disturb)* déranger; *(worry)* ennuyer **3** *v/i* s'inquiéter (**with** de)

bottle ['bɒtl] bouteille *f; for medicines* flacon *m; for baby* biberon *m*

◆ **bottle up** *feelings* réprimer

'**bottle bank** conteneur *m* à verre; **bottled water** eau *f* en bouteille; **bottleneck** rétrécissement *m; in production* goulet *m* d'étranglement; **bottle-opener** ouvre-bouteilles *m inv*

bottom ['bɒtəm] **1** *adj* du bas **2** *n of drawer, pan, garden* fond *m; (underside)* dessous *m; (lowest part)* bas *m; of street* bout *m; (buttocks)* derrière *m*

◆ **bottom out** se stabiliser

bottom 'line *financial* résultat *m; (real issue)* la question principale

boulder ['bəʊldər] rocher *m*

bounce [baʊns] **1** *v/t ball* faire rebondir **2** *v/i of ball* rebondir; *on sofa etc* sauter; *of check* être refusé; **bouncer** videur *m*

bound[1] [baʊnd] *adj:* **be ~ to do sth** *(sure to)* aller forcément faire qch

bound[2] [baʊnd] *adj:* **be ~ for** *of ship* être à destination de

bound[3] [baʊnd] *n (jump)* bond *m*

boundary ['baʊndərɪ] frontière *f*

bouquet [buˈkeɪ] bouquet *m*

bourbon ['bɜːrbən] bourbon *m*

bout [baʊt] MED accès *m; in boxing* match *m*

bow[1] [baʊ] **1** *n as greeting* révérence *f* **2** *v/i* faire une révérence **3** *v/t head* baisser

bow[2] [bəʊ] *(knot)* nœud *m;* MUS archet *m; for archery* arc *m*

bow[3] [baʊ] *of ship* avant *m*

bowels ['baʊəlz] intestins *mpl*

bowl[1] [bəʊl] *n* bol *m; for soup etc* assiette *f; for serving salad etc* saladier *m; for washing dishes* cuvette *f*

bowl[2] [bəʊl] *v/i* jouer au bowling

bowling ['bəʊlɪŋ] bowling *m;* **bowling alley** bowling *m*

bow 'tie [bəʊ] *(nœud m)* papillon *m*

box[1] [bɒks] *n container* boîte *f; on form* case *f*

box[2] [bɒks] *v/i* boxer

boxer ['bɒksər] boxeur *m;* **boxing** boxe *f;* **boxing glove** gant *m* de boxe; **boxing match** match *m* de boxe

'**box number** boîte *f* postale; **box office** bureau *m* de location

boy [bɔɪ] garçon *m; (son)* fils *m*

boycott ['bɔɪkɑːt] **1** *n* boycott

m **2** *v/t* boycotter

'boyfriend petit ami *m*; *younger* copain *m*

bra [brɑː] soutien-gorge *m*

bracelet ['breɪslɪt] bracelet *m*

bracket ['brækɪt] *for shelf* support *m* (d'étagère)

brag [bræg] se vanter (*about* de)

braid [breɪd] *in hair* tresse *f*; *trimming* galon *m*

braille [breɪl] braille *m*

brain [breɪn] ANAT cerveau *m*; **brainless** écervelé *m*; **brains** cerveau *m*; **brain surgeon** neurochirurgien(ne) *m(f)*; **brain tumor**, *Br* **brain tumour** tumeur *f* au cerveau; **brainwash** conditionner

brake [breɪk] **1** *n* frein *m* **2** *v/i* freiner

branch [bræntʃ] *of tree, company* branche *f*

brand [brænd] **1** *n* marque *f* **2** *v/t*: **be ~ed a liar** être étiqueté comme voleur; **brand image** image *f* de marque

brandish ['brændɪʃ] brandir

brand 'leader marque *f* dominante; **brand name** nom *m* de marque; **brand-new** flambant neuf

brandy ['brændɪ] brandy *m*

brassière [brə'zɪr] soutien-gorge *m*

brat [bræt] garnement *m*

brave [breɪv] courageux; **bravery** courage *m*

brawl [brɔːl] **1** *n* bagarre *f* **2** *v/i* se bagarrer

Brazil [brə'zɪl] Brésil *m*; **Brazilian 1** *adj* brésilien **2** *n* Brésilien(ne) *m(f)*

breach [briːtʃ] (*violation*) violation *f*; *in party* désaccord *m*; **breach of contract** rupture *f* de contrat

bread [bred] pain *m*

breadth [bredθ] largeur *m*; *of knowledge* étendue *f*

'breadwinner soutien *m* de famille

break [breɪk] **1** *n* fracture *f*; (*rest*) repos *m*; *in relationship* séparation *f* **2** *v/t* casser; *rules, law, promise* violer; *news* annoncer; *record* battre **3** *v/i* se casser; *of news, storm* éclater

◆ **break down 1** *v/i of vehicle, machine* tomber en panne; *of talks* échouer; *in tears* s'effondrer; *mentally* faire une dépression **2** *v/t door* défoncer; *figures* détailler

◆ **break even** rentrer dans ses frais

◆ **break in** (*interrupt*) interrompre qn; *of burglar* s'introduire par effraction

◆ **break up 1** *v/t into parts* décomposer; *fight* interrompre **2** *v/i of ice* se briser; *of couple, band* se séparer; *of meeting* se dissoudre

breakable ['breɪkəbl] cassable; **breakage** casse *f*; **breakdown** *of talks* échec *m*; (*nervous* ~) dépression *f* (nerveuse); *of figures* détail *m*

breakfast ['brekfəst] petit déjeuner *m*; **have ~** prendre son petit déjeuner; **break-in** cambriolage *m*; **breakthrough** percée *f*; **breakup** *of partnership* échec *m*

breast [brest] *of woman* sein *m*; **breastfeed** allaiter; **breaststroke** brasse *f*

breath [breθ] souffle *m*; **out of ~** à bout de souffle

breathe ['bri:ð] respirer

◆ **breathe in** inspirer

◆ **breathe out** expirer

breathing ['bri:ðɪŋ] respiration *f*

breathtaking ['breθteɪkɪŋ] à vous couper le souffle

breed [bri:d] **1** *n* race *f* **2** *v/t animals* élever; *plants, also fig* cultiver **3** *v/i of animals* se reproduire; **breeding** *of animals* élevage *m*; *of person* éducation *f*

breeze [bri:z] brise *f*; **breezy** venteux

brew [bru:] **1** *v/t beer* brasser **2** *v/i* couver; **brewery** brasserie *f*

Brexit ['breksɪt] POL, EU Brexit *m*

bribe [braɪb] **1** *n* pot-de-vin *m* **2** *v/t* soudoyer; **bribery** corruption *f*

brick [brɪk] brique *m*

bride [braɪd] *about to be married* (future) mariée *f*; *married* jeune mariée *f*; **bridegroom** *about to be married*

(futur) marié *m*; *married* jeune marié *m*; **bridesmaid** demoiselle *f* d'honneur

bridge [brɪdʒ] **1** *n* pont *m*; *of ship* passerelle *f* **2** *v/t gap* combler

bridle ['braɪdl] bride *f*

brief[1] [bri:f] *adj* bref, court

brief[2] [bri:f] **1** *n* (*mission*) instructions *fpl* **2** *v/t*: **~ s.o. on sth** (*give information*) informer qn de qch

'**briefcase** serviette *f*; **briefing instructions** instructions *fpl*; **briefly** brièvement; (*to sum up*) en bref; **briefs** slip *m*

bright [braɪt] *color* vif; *smile* radieux; *future* brillant; (*sunny*) clair; (*intelligent*) intelligent; **brightly** *smile* d'un air radieux; *colored* vivement; **shine** ~ resplendir

brilliance ['brɪljəns] *of person* esprit *m* lumineux; *of color* vivacité *f*; **brilliant** *sunshine etc* resplendissant; (*very good*) génial; (*very intelligent*) brillant

brim [brɪm] *of container, hat* bord *m*

bring [brɪŋ] *object* apporter; *person, peace* amener; *hope, happiness* donner

◆ **bring back** (*return*) ramener; (*re-introduce*) réintroduire; *it brought back memories of … childhood* ça m'a rappelé …

◆ **bring down** *also fig: government* faire tomber; *air-*

plane abattre; *price* faire baisser

◆ **bring on** *illness* donner
◆ **bring out** *(produce)* sortir
◆ **bring up** *child* élever; *subject* soulever; *(vomit)* vomir

brink [brɪŋk] bord *m*

brisk [brɪsk] vif; *(businesslike)* énergique; *trade* florissant

bristles ['brɪslz] *on chin* poils *mpl* raides; *of brush* poils *mpl*

Britain ['brɪtn] Grande-Bretagne; **British 1** *adj* britannique **2** *npl*: **the ~** les Britanniques

brittle ['brɪtl] fragile

broad [brɔːd] **1** *adj* large; *smile* grand; *(general)* général; *in ~ daylight* en plein jour **2** *n* F gonzesse *f*; **broadcast 1** *n* émission *f* **2** *v/t* transmettre; **broadcaster** présentateur(-trice) *m(f)* (radio/télé); **broad jump** saut *m* en longueur; **broadly**: **~ speaking** en gros; **broadminded** large d'esprit

broccoli ['brɑːkəlɪ] brocoli(s) *m(pl)*

brochure ['brouʃər] brochure *f*

broil [brɔɪl] griller; **broiler** *on stove* grill *m*; *chicken* poulet *m* à rôtir

broke [brouk] fauché; **broken** cassé; *home* brisé; **broker** courtier *m*

bronchitis [brɑːŋ'kaɪtɪs] bronchite *f*

bronze [brɑːnz] bronze *m*

brooch [broutʃ] broche *f*

brothel ['brɑːθl] bordel *m*

brother ['brʌðər] frère *m*; **brother-in-law** beau-frère *m*; **brotherly** fraternel

brow [brau] *(forehead)* front *m*; *of hill* sommet *m*

brown [braun] **1** *adj* marron *inv*; *(tanned)* bronzé **2** *n* marron *m*; **brownie** brownie *m*

brown paper 'bag sac *m* en papier kraft

browse [brauz] *in store* flâner; COMPUT surfer; **~ through a book** feuilleter un livre; **browser** COMPUT navigateur *m*

bruise [bruːz] bleu *m*; *on fruit* meurtrissure *f*

brunette [bruː'net] brune *f*

brush [brʌʃ] **1** *n* brosse *f*; *(conflict)* accrochage *m* **2** *v/t* brosser; *(touch lightly)* effleurer

◆ **brush aside** *person* mépriser; *remark, criticism* écarter
◆ **brush up** réviser

brusque [brusk] brusque

brutal ['bruːtl] brutal; **brutality** brutalité *f*; **brutally** brutalement; **brute** brute *f*

bubble ['bʌbl] bulle *f*

buck[1] [bʌk] *n* F *(dollar)* dollar *m*

buck[2] [bʌk] *v/i of horse* ruer

bucket ['bʌkɪt] seau *m*

buckle[1] ['bʌkl] **1** *n* boucle *f* **2** *v/t belt* boucler

buckle[2] ['bʌkl] *v/i of metal* déformer

bud [bʌd] BOT bourgeon *m*

buddy ['bʌdɪ] copain *m*, copine *f; form of address* mec

budge [bʌdʒ] **1** *v/t (move)* déplacer *f* **2** *v/i (move)* bouger

budget ['bʌdʒɪt] budget *m*

buff [bʌf] passionné(e) *m(f)*

buffalo ['bʌfələʊ] buffle *m*

buffer ['bʌfər] RAIL, COMPUT, *fig* tampon *m*

buffet ['bʊfeɪ] *meal* buffet *m*

bug [bʌg] **1** *n (insect)* insecte *m; (virus)* virus *m*; COMPUT bogue *f; (spy device)* micro *m* **2** *v/t room, telephone* mettre sur écoute; F *(annoy)* énerver

buggy ['bʌgɪ] *for baby* poussette *f*

build [bɪld] **1** *n of person* carrure *f* **2** *v/t* construire

◆ **build up** **1** *v/t strength* développer; *relationship* construire **2** *v/i* s'accumuler; *fig* s'intensifier

builder ['bɪldər] constructeur(-trice) *m(f)*; **building** bâtiment *m; activity* construction *f*

'**building site** chantier *m*; **building society** *Br* caisse *f* d'épargne-logement; **building trade** (industrie *f* du) bâtiment *m*; **build-up** accumulation *f*; *give s.o./sth a big* ~ faire beaucoup de battage autour de qn/qch; **built-in** encastré; *flash* incorporé

bulb [bʌlb] BOT bulbe *m*; *(light*

~) ampoule *f*

bulge [bʌldʒ] **1** *n* gonflement *m*, saillie *f* **2** *v/i* être gonflé, faire saillie

'**bulky** ['bʌlkɪ] encombrant; *sweater* gros

bull [bʊl] *animal* taureau *m*; **bulldozer** ['bʊldəʊzər] bulldozer *m*

bullet ['bʊlɪt] balle *f*

bulletin ['bʊlɪtɪn] bulletin *m*

'**bulletin board** tableau *m* d'affichage; COMPUT serveur *m* télématique

'**bullet-proof** protégé contre les balles; *vest* pare-balles

'**bull's-eye** mille *m*; *hit the* ~ *also fig* mettre dans le mille; **bullshit** merde *f* V, conneries *fpl* P

bully ['bʊlɪ] **1** *n* brute *f* **2** *v/t* brimer; **bullying** harcèlement *m*

bum [bʌm] **1** *n* F *(worthless person)* bon à rien *m; (tramp)* clochard *m* **2** *v/t: can I* ~ *a cigarette?* est-ce que je peux vous taper une cigarette?

bump [bʌmp] **1** *n* bosse *f* **2** *v/t* se cogner; **bumper** MOT pare-chocs *mpl; bumpy road* cahoteux; *we had a* ~ *flight* nous avons été secoués pendant le vol

bunch [bʌntʃ] *of people* groupe *m; of keys* trousseau *m; of grapes* grappe *f; of flowers* bouquet *m; thanks a* ~ merci beaucoup

bungle ['bʌŋgl] bousiller
bunk [bʌŋk] couchette *f*
buoy [bɔɪ] NAUT bouée *f*; **buoyant** *mood* jovial; *economy* prospère
burden ['bɜːdn] 1 *n* fardeau *m* 2 *v/t*: ~ **s.o. with sth** accabler qn de qch
bureau ['bjʊrou] bureau *m*; **bureaucrat** bureaucrate *m/f*; **bureaucratic** bureaucratique
burger ['bɜːrgər] steak *m* haché; *in roll* hamburger *m*
burglar ['bɜːrglər] cambrioleur(-euse) *m(f)*; **burglar alarm** alarme *f* antivol; **burglarize** cambrioler; **burglary** cambriolage *m*
burial ['berɪəl] enterrement *m*
burn [bɜːrn] 1 *n* brûlure *f* 2 *v/t* & *v/i* brûler
◆ burn down 1 *v/t* incendier 2 *v/i* être réduit en cendres
burp [bɜːrp] 1 *n* rot *m* 2 *v/i* roter
burst [bɜːrst] 1 *n in pipe* trou *m* 2 *adj tire* crevé 3 *v/t* & *v/i* crever; *of pipe* éclater; ~ **into tears** fondre en larmes; ~ **out laughing** éclater de rire
bus [bʌs] (auto)bus *m*; *long distance* (auto)car *m*
bush [bʊʃ] *plant* buisson *m*
bushy ['bʊʃɪ] *beard* touffu
business ['bɪznɪs] commerce *m*; (*company*) entreprise *f*; (*work*) travail *m*; (*sector*) secteur *m*; (*matter*) affaire *f*; **on ~** en déplacement (profes-

sionnel); **mind your own ~!** occupe-toi de tes affaires!; **business card** carte *f* de visite; **business class** classe *f* affaires; **businesslike** sérieux; **businessman** homme *m* d'affaires; **business meeting** réunion *f* d'affaires; **business school** école *f* de commerce; **business studies** *course* études *fpl* de commerce; **business trip** voyage *m* d'affaires; **businesswoman** femme *f* d'affaires
'bus station gare *f* routière; **bus stop** arrêt *m* d'autobus
bust[1] [bʌst] *n of woman* poitrine *f*
bust[2] [bʌst] F (*broken*) cassé
'bust-up F brouille *f*; **busty** à la poitrine plantureuse
busy ['bɪzɪ] *person*, TELEC occupé; *day*, *life* bien rempli; *street*, *shop* plein de monde; **busybody** curieux(-se) *m(f)*
but [bʌt] 1 *conj* mais 2 *prep*: **all ~ him** tous sauf lui; **the last ~ one** l'avant-dernier; ~ **for you** si tu n'avais pas été là; **nothing ~ the best** rien que le meilleur
butcher ['bʊtʃər] boucher (-ère) *m(f)*
butt [bʌt] 1 *n of cigarette* mégot *m*; F (*backside*) cul *m* 2 *v/t* donner un coup de tête à
butter ['bʌtər] beurre *m*; **butterfly** *also swimming* papillon *m*
buttocks ['bʌtəks] fesses *fpl*

button ['bʌtn] bouton *m*; *(badge)* badge *m*
buy [baɪ] acheter
◆ **buy out** COM racheter la part de
buyer ['baɪr] acheteur(-euse) *m (f)*
buzz [bʌz] **1** *n* bourdonnement *m* **2** *v/i* of insect bourdonner; **buzzer** sonnerie *f*
by [baɪ] *to show agent* par; *(near, next to)* près de; *(no later than)* pour; *mode of transport* en; ~ **bus** en bus; ~ **day** le jour; ~ **my watch** selon ma montre; ~ **o.s.** tout seul
bye(-bye) [baɪ] au revoir
'bypass *road* déviation *f*; MED pontage *m* (coronarien); **by--product** sous-produit *m*; **by-stander** spectateur(-trice) *m(f)*

C

cab [kæb] taxi *m*; *of truck* cabine *f*; **cab driver** chauffeur *m* de taxi
cabin ['kæbɪn] *of plane, ship* cabine *f*; **cabin attendant** *male* steward *m*; *female* hôtesse *f* (de l'air); **cabin crew** équipage *m*
cabinet ['kæbɪnɪt] *furniture* meuble *m* (de rangement); POL cabinet *m*; **display** ~ vitrine *f*
cable ['keɪbl] câble *m*; **cable car** téléphérique *m*; *on rail* funiculaire *m*; **cable television** (télévision *f* par) câble *m*
'cab stand station *f* de taxis
cactus ['kæktəs] cactus *m*
cadaver [kə'dævər] cadavre *m*
caddie ['kædɪ] *in golf* caddie *m*
Caesarean *Br* → **Cesarean**

café ['kæfeɪ] café *m*; **cafeteria** cafétéria *f*
caffeine ['kæfiːn] caféine *f*
cage [keɪdʒ] cage *f*; **cagey** évasif
cake [keɪk] gâteau *m*
calculate ['kælkjuleɪt] *(work out)* évaluer; *in arithmetic* calculer; **calculating** calculateur; **calculation** calcul *m*; **calculator** calculatrice *f*
calendar ['kælɪndər] calendrier *m*
calf¹ [kæf] *(young cow)* veau *m*
calf² [kæf] *of leg* mollet *m*
caliber, *Br* **calibre** ['kælɪbər] *of gun* calibre *m*
call [kɔːl] **1** *n* appel *m*; *(phone* ~ *also)* coup *m* de téléphone **2** *v/t on phone* appeler; **be** ~**ed** ... s'appeler ... **3** *v/i on phone* appeler; *(visit)* passer
◆ **call back 1** *v/t* rappeler **2** *v/i*

on phone rappeler; (*make another visit*) repasser
◆ **call for** (*collect*) venir chercher; (*demand*) demander
◆ **call off** annuler
caller ['kɔːlər] *on phone* personne *f* qui appelle; (*visitor*) visiteur *m*
callous ['kæləs] dur
calm [kɑːm] **1** *adj* calme, tranquille **2** *n* calme *m*
◆ **calm down 1** *v/t* calmer **2** *v/i* se calmer
calmly ['kɑːmlɪ] calmement
calorie ['kælərɪ] calorie *f*
camcorder ['kæmkɔːrdər] caméscope *m*
camera ['kæmərə] *appareil m* photo; *TV* caméra *f*; **cameraman** cadreur *m*, caméraman *m*; **camera phone** téléphone *m* avec appareil photo intégré
camouflage ['kæməflɑːʒ] **1** *n* camouflage *m* **2** *v/t* camoufler
camp [kæmp] **1** *n* camp *m* **2** *v/i* camper
campaign [kæm'peɪn] **1** *n* campagne *f* **2** *v/i* faire campagne
camper ['kæmpər] *person* campeur *m*; *vehicle* camping-car *m*; **camping** camping *m*; **campsite** (terrain *m* de) camping *m*
campus ['kæmpəs] campus *m*
can¹ [kæn] *v/aux* pouvoir; ~ *you hear me?* tu m'entends?; ~ *she swim?* sait-elle

nager?; ~ *I help you?* est-ce que je peux t'aider?
can² [kæn] *n for food* boîte *f*; *for drinks* canette *f*; *of paint* bidon *m*
Canada ['kænədə] Canada *m*; **Canadian 1** *adj* canadien **2** *n* Canadien *m*
canal [kə'næl] canal *m*
cancel ['kænsl] annuler; **cancellation** annulation *f*
cancer ['kænsər] cancer *m*
candid ['kændɪd] franc
candidacy ['kændɪdəsɪ] candidature *f*; **candidate** candidat *m*
candle ['kændl] bougie *f*; *in church* cierge *m*
candor, *Br* **candour** ['kændər] franchise *f*
candy ['kændɪ] (*sweet*) bonbon *m*; (*sweets*) bonbons *mpl*
cane [keɪn] canne *f*
canister ['kænɪstər] boîte *f* (métallique); *for gas, spray* bombe *f*
canned [kænd] en conserve, en boîte; (*recorded*) enregistré
cannot ['kænɑːt] = *can not*
canny ['kænɪ] (*astute*) rusé
canoe [kə'nuː] canoë *m*
'can opener ouvre-boîte *m*
can't [kænt] = *can not*
canteen [kæn'tiːn] *in factory* cantine *f*
canvas ['kænvəs] toile *f*
canyon ['kænjən] canyon *m*
cap [kæp] *hat* bonnet *m*; *with peak* casquette *f*; *of soldier,*

policeman képi *m*

capability [keɪpə'bɪlətɪ] capacité *f*; **capable** capable

capacity [kə'pæsətɪ] capacité *f*

capital ['kæpɪtl] *of country* capitale *f*; *letter* majuscule *f*; *money* capital *m*; **capitalism** capitalisme *m*; **capitalist 1** *adj* capitaliste **2** *n* capitaliste *m/f*; **capital punishment** peine *f* capitale

capsize [kæp'saɪz] chavirer

capsule ['kæpsʊl] *of medicine* gélule *f*; *(space ~)* capsule *f* spatiale

captain ['kæptɪn] capitaine *m*; *of aircraft* commandant *m* de bord

caption ['kæpʃn] légende *f*

captivate ['kæptɪveɪt] captiver, fasciner; **captive** captif; **captivity** captivité *f*; **capture 1** *n of city* prise *f*; *of person, animal* capture *f* **2** *v/t person, animal* capturer; *city, building* prendre; *market share* conquérir

car [kɑːr] voiture *f*, automobile *f*; *of train* wagon *m*, voiture *f*; **by ~** en voiture

carbon monoxide [kɑːrbən-mən'ɑːksaɪd] monoxyde *m* de carbone

carbureter, carburetor [kɑːr-bʊ'retər] carburateur *m*

carcass ['kɑːrkəs] carcasse *f*

card [kɑːrd] carte *f*; **cardboard box** carton *m*

cardiac ['kɑːrdɪæk] cardiaque

cardinal ['kɑːrdɪnl] REL cardinal *m*

care [ker] **1** *n of baby, pet* garde *f*; *of the elderly, sick* soins *mpl*; *(medical ~)* soins *mpl* médicaux; *(worry)* souci *m*; **care of → c/o**; **take ~** *(be cautious)* faire attention; **take ~ of** s'occuper de **2** *v/i* se soucier; **I don't ~!** ça m'est égal!
◆ **care about** s'intéresser à
◆ **care for** *(look after)* s'occuper de

career [kə'rɪr] carrière *f*

careful ['kerfl] *(cautious)* prudent; *(thorough)* méticuleux; *(be) ~!* (fais) attention!; **carefully** *(with caution)* prudemment; *worded etc* soigneusement; **careless** négligent; *work* négligé; **carelessly** négligemment

caress [kə'res] caresser

'car ferry (car-)ferry *m*, transbordeur *m*

cargo ['kɑːrgoʊ] cargaison *f*

caricature ['kærɪkətʃər] caricature *f*

carnival ['kɑːrnɪvl] fête *f* foraine; *with processions etc* carnaval *m*

carpenter ['kɑːrpɪntər] charpentier *m*; *for smaller objects* menuisier *m*

carpet ['kɑːrpɪt] tapis *m*; *fitted* moquette *f*

'car phone téléphone *m* de voiture; **carpool** forme *du* co-voiturage; **car rental** location *f* de voitures

carrier ['kærɪər] *company* entreprise *f* de transport; *of disease* porteur*-euse*) *m(f)*

carrot ['kærət] carotte *f*

carry ['kærɪ] **1** *v/t* porter; *of ship, bus etc* transporter **2** *v/i of sound* porter

◆ **carry on 1** *v/i (continue)* continuer (**with sth** qch) **2** *v/t business* exercer

◆ **carry out** *survey etc* faire; *orders etc* exécuter

cart [kɑːrt] charrette *f*

carton ['kɑːrtn] carton *m*; *of cigarettes* cartouche *f*

cartoon [kɑːr'tuːn] dessin *m* humoristique; *on TV* dessin *m* animé; (*strip* ~) BD *f*, bande *f* dessinée

carve [kɑːrv] *meat* découper; *wood* sculpter

case¹ [keɪs] *for eyeglasses, camera* étui *m*; *for gadget* pochette *f*; *of wine etc* caisse *f*; *Br* (*suitcase*) valise *f*

case² [keɪs] (*instance*), MED cas *m*; *for police* affaire *f*; LAW procès *m*; **in ~.** au cas où ...; **in any ~** en tout cas

cash [kæʃ] **1** *n (money)* argent *m*; (*coins and notes*) (argent *m*) liquide *m* **2** *v/t check* toucher; **cash desk** caisse *f*; **cash flow** COM trésorerie *f*; **I've got ~ problems** j'ai des problèmes d'argent; **cashier** *in store etc* caissier*-ère*) *m(f)*; **cashpoint** *Br* distributeur *m* automatique (de billets); **cash register** caisse *f*

enregistreuse

casino [kə'siːnoʊ] casino *m*

casket ['kæskɪt] (*coffin*) cercueil *m*

casserole ['kæsəroʊl] *meal* ragoût *m*; *container* cocotte *f*

cassette [kə'set] cassette *f*; **cassette player** lecteur *m* de cassettes

cast [kæst] **1** *n of play* distribution *f*; (*mold*) moule *m* **2** *v/t doubt* jeter; *metal* couler

cast iron fonte *f*

castle ['kæsl] château *m*

casual ['kæʒuəl] (*chance*) fait au hasard; (*offhand*) désinvolte; (*not formal*) décontracté; **casually dressed** de manière décontractée; **say** de manière désinvolte; **casualty** victime *f*

cat [kæt] chat(te) *m(f)*

catalog, *Br* **catalogue** ['kætəlɔːg] catalogue *m*

catalyst ['kætəlɪst] catalyseur *m*

catastrophe [kə'tæstrəfɪ] catastrophe *f*; **catastrophic** catastrophique

catch [kætʃ] **1** *n* prise *f* (au vol); *of fish* pêche *f*; (*lock: on door*) loquet *m*; (*problem*) entourloupette *f* **2** *v/t ball, prisoner, bus, illness* attraper; (*get on: bus, train*) prendre; (*hear*) entendre; **catching** *also fig* contagieux; **catchy** facile à retenir

categoric [kætə'gɑːrɪk] catégorique; **category** catégorie *f*

caterer ['keɪtərər] traiteur *m*

cathedral [kə'θiːdrl] cathédrale *f*

Catholic ['kæθəlɪk] **1** *adj* catholique **2** *n* catholique *m/f*; **Catholicism** catholicisme *m*

catty ['kætɪ] méchant

cause [kɔːz] **1** *n* cause *f*; (*grounds*) raison *f* **2** *v/t* causer

caution ['kɔːʃn] **1** *n* (*carefulness*) prudence *f* **2** *v/t* (*warn*) avertir; **cautious** prudent; **cautiously** prudemment

cave [keɪv] caverne *f*, grotte *f*

cavity ['kævɪtɪ] cavité *f*

CD [siː'diː] (= *compact disc*) CD *m* (= compact-disc *m*, disque *m* compact)

C'D player lecteur *m* de CD; **CD-ROM** CD-ROM *m*

cease [siːs] cesser

'cease-fire cessez-le-feu *m*

ceiling ['siːlɪŋ] plafond *m*

celebrate ['selɪbreɪt] **1** *v/i* faire la fête **2** *v/t* fêter; *Christmas, event* célébrer; **celebrated** célèbre; **celebration** fête *f*; *of event, wedding* célébration *f*; **celebrity** célébrité *f*

cell [sel] *for prisoner, of spreadsheet*, BIO cellule *f*

cellar ['selər] cave *f*

cello ['tʃeləʊ] violoncelle *m*

cell phone, cellular phone ['seljular] (téléphone *m*) portable *m*

cement [sɪ'ment] ciment *m*

cemetery ['semətrɪ] cimetière *m*

censor ['sensər] censurer

census ['sensəs] recensement *m*

cent [sent] cent *m*

centenary [sen'tiːnərɪ] centenaire *m*

center ['sentər] **1** *n* centre *m* **2** *v/t* centrer

centigrade ['sentɪgreɪd] centigrade

centimeter, *Br* **centimetre** ['sentɪmiːtər] centimètre *m*

central ['sentrəl] central

central 'heating chauffage *m* central; **centralize** centraliser; **central locking** MOT verrouillage *m* centralisé

centre *Br* → **center**

century ['sentʃərɪ] siècle *m*

CEO [siːiː'əʊ] (= *Chief Executive Officer*) directeur *m* général

ceramic [sɪ'ræmɪk] en céramique

cereal ['sɪrɪəl] céréale *f*; (*breakfast* ~) céréales *fpl*

ceremonial [serɪ'məʊnɪəl] **1** *adj* de cérémonie **2** *n* cérémonial *m*; **ceremony** cérémonie *f*

certain ['sɜːrtn] (*sure*) certain, sûr; (*particular*) certain; **certainly** certainement; **certainty** certitude *f*

certificate [sər'tɪfɪkət] certificat *m*

certified public accountant ['sɜːrtɪfaɪd] expert *m* comptable; **certify** certifier

Cesarean [sɪ'zeːrɪən] césarienne f

CFO [siːef'oʊ] (= *chief financial officer*) directeur m financier

chain [tʃeɪn] **1** n also of stores etc chaîne f **2** v/t: ~ **sth. to sth** enchaîner qch à qch

chair [tʃer] **1** n chaise f; (arm~) fauteuil m; at university chaire f **2** v/t meeting présider; **chair lift** télésiège m; **chairman** président m; **chairperson** président(e) m(f)

chalk [tʃɔːk] craie f

challenge ['tʃælɪndʒ] **1** n défi m, challenge m **2** v/t (defy) défier; (call into question) mettre en doute; ~ **s.o. to a game** proposer à qn de faire une partie; **challenger** challenger m; **challenging** job, undertaking stimulant

Chamber of 'Commerce Chambre f de commerce

champagne [ʃæm'peɪn] champagne m

champion ['tʃæmpɪən] **1** n SP, of cause champion(ne) m(f) **2** v/t cause être le (la) champion(ne) m(f) de; **championship** event championnat m; title titre m de champion(ne)

chance [tʃɑːns] (possibility) chances fpl; (opportunity) occasion f; (luck) hasard m; **by ~** par hasard; **take a ~** prendre un risque

change [tʃeɪndʒ] **1** n changement m; (money) monnaie f; **for a ~** pour changer un peu **2** v/t changer; bankbill faire la monnaie sur **3** v/i changer; (put on different clothes) se changer; **change-over** changement m; **changing room** SP vestiaire m; in shop cabine f d'essayage

channel ['tʃænl] on TV, radio chaîne f; (water) chenal m

chant [tʃænt] **1** n slogans mpl scandés; REL chant m **2** v/i of crowds scander des slogans; REL psalmodier

chaos ['keɪɑːs] chaos m; **chaotic** chaotique

chapel ['tʃæpl] chapelle f

chapter ['tʃæptər] chapitre m

character ['kærɪktər] caractère m; (person) personne f; in book personnage m; **characteristic 1** n caractéristique f **2** adj caractéristique; **characterize** caractériser

charge [tʃɑːrdʒ] **1** n (fee) frais mpl; LAW accusation f; **free of ~** gratuit; **be in ~** être responsable **2** v/t sum of money faire payer; LAW inculper (**with** de); battery charger; **can you ~ it?** (put on account) pouvez-vous le mettre sur mon compte? **3** v/i (attack) charger; **charge account** compte m; **charge card** carte f de paiement; **charger** ['tʃɑːrdʒər] (battery), TEL chargeur m

charitable ['tʃærɪtəbl] charitable; **charity** charité f; (*organization*) organisation f caritative

charm [tʃɑːrm] **1** n also on bracelet charme m **2** v/t (delight) charmer; **charming** charmant

charred [tʃɑːrd] carbonisé

chart [tʃɑːrt] diagramme m; (map) carte f

'charter flight (vol m) charter m

chase [tʃeɪs] **1** n poursuite f **2** v/t poursuivre

◆ **chase away** v/t chasser

chassis ['ʃæsɪ] of car châssis m

chat [tʃæt] **1** n causette f **2** v/i causer; **chatline** chat m téléphonique; **chat room** chat m

chatter ['tʃætər] **1** n bavardage m **2** v/i (talk) bavarder; **my teeth were ~ing** je claquais des dents

chauffeur ['ʃoʊfər] chauffeur m

chauvinist ['ʃoʊvɪnɪst] (male ~) machiste m

cheap [tʃiːp] bon marché, pas cher; (nasty) méchant; (mean) pingre

cheat [tʃiːt] **1** n person tricheur(-euse) m(f) **2** v/t tromper **3** v/i tricher

check¹ [tʃek] **1** adj shirt à carreaux **2** n carreaux m

check² [tʃek] n FIN chèque m; in restaurant etc addition f

check³ [tʃek] n to verify sth contrôle m, vérification f **2** v/t vérifier; **with a ~mark** cocher; coat etc mettre au vestiaire **3** v/i vérifier

◆ **check in** v/i at airport se faire enregistrer; at hotel s'inscrire

◆ **check out 1** v/i of hotel régler sa note **2** v/t (look into) enquêter sur; club etc essayer

◆ **check up on** se renseigner sur

'checkbook carnet m de chèques; **checked** material à carreaux

checkered ['tʃekərd] pattern à carreaux; career varié

'check-in (counter) enregistrement m; **checking account** compte m courant; **checklist** liste f (de contrôle); **check mark: put a ~ against sth** cocher qch; **check-out** caisse f; **checkpoint** contrôle m; **checkroom** for coats vestiaire m; for baggage consigne f; **checkup** medical examen m médical; dental examen m dentaire

cheek [tʃiːk] on face joue f

cheer [tʃɪr] **1** n hourra m **2** v/t acclamer **3** v/t pousser des hourras

◆ **cheer up 1** v/i reprendre courage; **cheer up!** courage! **2** v/t remonter le moral à

cheerful ['tʃɪrfəl] gai, joyeux; **cheering** acclamations fpl; **cheerleader** meneuse f de ban

cheese [tʃiːz] fromage m

chef [ʃef] chef m (de cuisine)

chemical ['kemɪkl] **1** adj chimique **2** n produit m chimique; **chemist** in laboratory chimiste m/f; Br pharmacien(ne) m(f); **chemistry** chimie f

chemotherapy [kiːmou'θerəpɪ] chimiothérapie f

cheque [tʃek] Br → **check?**

chess [tʃes] (jeu m d'échecs mpl; **play~** jouer aux échecs

chest [tʃest] poitrine f; (box) coffre m, caisse f

chew [tʃuː] mâcher; of rat ronger; **chewing gum** chewing-gum m

chick [tʃɪk] poussin m; F girl nana

chicken ['tʃɪkɪn] poulet m

chief [tʃiːf] **1** n chef m **2** adj principal; **chiefly** principalement

child [tʃaɪld] enfant m/f; **childhood** enfance f; **childish** puéril; **childlike** enfantin

children ['tʃɪldrən] pl → **child**

Chile ['tʃɪlɪ] Chili m; **Chilean 1** adj chilien **2** n Chilien(ne) m(f)

◆ **chill out** se relaxer

chilly ['tʃɪlɪ] also fig froid

chimney ['tʃɪmnɪ] cheminée f

chin [tʃɪn] menton m

China ['tʃaɪnə] Chine f

china ['tʃaɪnə] **1** n porcelaine f **2** adj en porcelaine

Chinese [tʃaɪ'niːz] **1** adj chinois **2** n language chinois m; person Chinois(e) m(f)

chip [tʃɪp] **1** n damage brèche f; in gambling jeton m; COMPUT puce f; **~s** (potato ~s) chips mpl; Br pommes frites fpl **2** v/t damage ébrécher

chipmunk tamia m rayé

chisel ['tʃɪzl] ciseau m, burin m

chlorine ['klɔːriːn] chlore m

chocolate ['tʃɑːkələt] chocolat m

choice [tʃɔɪs] **1** n choix m; **I had no ~** je n'avais pas le choix **2** adj (top quality) de choix

choir ['kwaɪr] chœur m

choke [tʃouk] **1** v/i s'étrangler **2** v/t (strangle) étrangler

cholesterol [kə'lestəroul] cholestérol m

choose [tʃuːz] choisir; **choosey** difficile

chop [tʃɑːp] **1** n of meat côtelette f **2** v/t couper

◆ **chop down** tree abattre

chore [tʃɔːr] **~s** travaux mpl domestiques

choreography [kɔːrɪ'ɑːgrəfɪ] chorégraphie f

chorus ['kɔːrəs] singers chœur m; of song refrain m

Christ [kraɪst] Christ m; **~!** mon Dieu!

christen ['krɪsn] baptiser

Christian ['krɪstʃən] **1** n chrétien(ne) m(f) **2** adj chrétien; **Christianity** christianisme m

Christmas ['krɪsməs] Noël m;

Merry ~! Joyeux Noël!;
Christmas card carte f de
Noël; **Christmas Day** jour
m de Noël; **Christmas Eve**
veille f de Noël; **Christmas
present** cadeau m de Noël;
Christmas tree arbre m de
Noël

chronic ['krɑnɪk] chronique

chubby ['tʃʌbɪ] potelé

chuck [tʃʌk] lancer

chuckle ['tʃʌkl] **1** n petit rire
m **2** v/i rire tout bas

chunk [tʃʌŋk] gros morceau m

church [tʃɜːrtʃ] église f;
church service office m;
churchyard cimetière m (autour d'une église)

chute [ʃuːt] for garbage vide-
ordures m; for escape toboggan m

cigar [sɪ'gɑːr] cigare m

cigarette [sɪgə'ret] cigarette
f; **cigarette lighter** briquet m

cinema ['sɪnɪmə] Br cinéma
m

circle ['sɜːrkl] **1** n cercle m **2**
v/i of plane tournoyer

circuit ['sɜːrkɪt] circuit m;
(lap) tour m (de circuit); **circuit board** COMPUT plaquette
f; **circular** ['sɜːrkjʊlər] **1** n
circulaire f **2** adj circulaire;
circulate ['sɜːrkjʊleɪt] **1** v/i
circuler **2** v/t memo faire circuler; **circulation** [sɜːrkjʊ-
'leɪʃn] circulation f; of newspaper tirage m

circumstances ['sɜːrkəm-
stænsɪz] circonstances fpl;
financial situation f finan-

cière

circus ['sɜːrkəs] cirque m

cistern ['sɪstərn] réservoir m;
of WC réservoir m de chasse
d'eau

citizen ['sɪtɪzn] citoyen(ne)
m(f); **citizenship** citoyenneté f

city ['sɪtɪ] (grande) ville f

city 'center, Br **city 'centre**
centre-ville m; **city hall** hôtel
m de ville

civic ['sɪvɪk] municipal; pride,
responsibilities civique

civil ['sɪvl] civil; (polite) poli;
civil ceremony mariage m
civil; **civil engineer** ingénieur m des travaux publics

civilian [sɪ'vɪljən] civil(e)
m(f); **civilization** civilisation
f; **civilize** civiliser; **civil
rights** droits mpl civils; **civil
servant** fonctionnaire m/f;
civil service fonction f publique, administration f; **civil
war** guerre f civile

claim [kleɪm] **1** n (request) demande f; (assertion) affirmation f **2** v/t (ask for as a right)
demander, réclamer; (assert)
affirmer; lost property réclamer; **claimant** ['kleɪmənt]
demandeur(-euse) m(f)

clam [klæm] palourde f, clam
m

clammy ['klæmɪ] moite

clamp [klæmp] fastener pince
f, crampon m
◆ **clamp down on** sévir contre

clandestine [klæn'destɪn] clandestine

clap [klæp] (*applaud*) applaudir

clarification [klærɪfɪ'keɪʃn] clarification *f*; **clarify** clarifier; **clarity** clarté *f*

clash [klæʃ] **1** *n between people* affrontement *m* **2** *v/i* s'affronter; *of colors* détonner; *of events* tomber en même temps

clasp [klæsp] **1** *n* agrafe *f* **2** *v/t in hand* serrer

class [klæs] **1** *n* (*lesson*) cours *m*; (*group of people, category*) classe *f*; **the ~ of 2002** la promo(tion) 2002 **2** *v/t* classer

classic ['klæsɪk] **1** *adj* classique **2** *n* classique *m*; **classical music** classique; **classification** classification *f*; **classified information** secret; **classified ad(vertisement)** petite annonce *f*; **classify** classifier; **classroom** salle *f* de classe; **classy** F *restaurant etc* chic *inv*; *person* classe

clause [klɔːz] (*in agreement*) clause *f*; GRAM proposition *f*

claustrophobia [klɔːstrə-'fəʊbɪə] claustrophobie *f*

claw [klɔː] *of cat* griffe *f*; *of lobster* pince *f*

clay [kleɪ] argile *f*, glaise *f*

clean [kliːn] **1** *adj* propre **2** *adv* (*completely*) complètement **3** *v/t* nettoyer; **cleaner** *male* agent *m* de propreté;

female femme *f* de ménage; (*dry~*) teinturier(-ère) *m(f)*

cleanse [klenz] *skin* nettoyer; **cleanser** *for skin* démaquillant *m*

clear [klɪr] **1** *adj* voice, photo net; *to understand*, sky, water clair; *conscience* tranquille **2** *v/t* roads etc dégager; *place* (faire) évacuer; *table* débarrasser; *ball* dégager; (*acquit*) innocenter; (*authorize*) autoriser **3** *v/i* of sky se dégager; *of mist* se dissiper; *of face* s'éclairer

◆ **clear out 1** *v/t closet* vider **2** *v/i* ficher le camp

◆ **clear up 1** *v/i in room* ranger; *of weather* s'éclaircir; *of illness* disparaître **2** *v/t* (*tidy*) ranger; *problem* résoudre

clearance ['klɪrəns] (*space*) espace *m* (libre); (*authorization*) autorisation *f*; **clearance sale** liquidation *f*; **clearing** clairière *f*; **clearly** speak, see clairement; *hear* distinctement; (*evidently*) manifestement

cleavage ['kliːvɪdʒ] décolleté *m*

clench [klentʃ] serrer

clergy ['klɜːdʒɪ] clergé *m*; **clergyman** ecclésiastique *m*; *Protestant* pasteur *m*

clerk [klɜːrk] *administrative* employé(e) *m(f)* de bureau; *in store* vendeur(-euse) *m(f)*

clever ['klevər] intelligent;

gadget ingénieux; (skillful) habile

click [klɪk] **1** n COMPUT clic m **2** v/i cliqueter

◆ **click on** COMPUT cliquer sur

client ['klaɪənt] client(e) m(f); **clientele** clientèle f

climate ['klaɪmət] also fig climat m

climax ['klaɪmæks] point m culminant

climb [klaɪm] **1** n up mountain ascension f **2** v/t monter sur; mountain escalader **3** v/i monter; **climber** alpiniste m/f

clinch [klɪntʃ] deal conclure

cling [klɪŋ] of clothes coller

◆ **cling to** s'accrocher à

clingy ['klɪŋɪ] person collant

clinic ['klɪnɪk] clinique f; **clinical** clinique

clip[1] [klɪp] **1** n fastener pince f; for hair barrette f **2** v/t: ~ **sth to sth** attacher qch à qch

clip[2] [klɪp] **1** n (extract) extrait m **2** v/t hair, grass couper; **clipping** from press coupure f (de presse)

clock [klɑːk] horloge f; **clock radio** radio-réveil m; **clockwise** dans le sens des aiguilles d'une montre

clone [kloʊn] **1** n clone m **2** v/t cloner; **cloning** clonage m

close[1] [kloʊs] **1** adj family, friend proche **2** adv près; ~ **at hand**, ~ **by** tout près; ~ **to** près de

close[2] [kloʊz] v/t fermer

closed-circuit 'television télévision f en circuit fermé; **close-knit** très uni; **closely** listen attentivement; watch de près; cooperate étroitement

closet ['klɑːzɪt] armoire f, placard m

close-up ['kloʊsʌp] gros plan m

closing date ['kloʊzɪŋ] date f limite

closure ['kloʊʒər] fermeture f

clot [klɑːt] **1** n of blood caillot m **2** v/i of blood coaguler

cloth [klɑːθ] tissu m; for drying torchon m; for washing lavette f

clothes [kloʊðz] vêtements mpl; **clothing** vêtements mpl

cloud [klaʊd] nuage m; **cloudless** sans nuages; **cloudy** nuageux

clout [klaʊt] fig (influence) influence f

clove of 'garlic [kloʊv] gousse f d'ail

clown [klaʊn] also pej clown m

club [klʌb] club m; weapon massue f

clue [kluː] indice m

clumsiness ['klʌmzɪnɪs] maladresse f; **clumsy** maladroit

cluster ['klʌstər] groupe m

clutch [klʌtʃ] **1** n MOT embrayage m **2** v/t étreindre

◆ **clutch at** s'agripper à

c/o (= **care of**) chez

Co. (= **Company**) Cie (= Compagnie)

coach [koutʃ] **1** n (trainer) entraîneur(-euse) m(f); Br (bus) (auto)car m **2** v/t SP entraîner; **coaching** entraînement m

coagulate [kou'ægjuleɪt] of blood coaguler

coal [koul] charbon m

coalition [kouə'lɪʃn] coalition f

'coalmine mine f de charbon

coarse [kɔːrs] fabric rugueux; hair épais; (vulgar) grossier; **coarsely** (vulgarly), ground grossièrement

coast [koust] côte f; **coastal** côtier; **coastguard** gendarmerie f maritime; person gendarme m maritime; **coastline** littoral m

coat [kout] **1** n veston m; (over~) pardessus m; of animal pelage m; of paint etc couche f **2** v/t (cover) couvrir (**with** de); **coathanger** cintre m; **coating** couche f

coax [kouks] cajoler

cocaine [kə'keɪn] cocaïne f

cock [kɑːk] chicken coq m; any male bird (oiseau m) mâle m; **cockpit** of plane poste m de pilotage, cockpit m; **cockroach** cafard m; **cocktail** cocktail m

cocoa ['koukou] cacao m

coconut ['koukənʌt] noix f de coco; **coconut palm** cocotier m

code [koud] code m; **in ~** codé

coeducational [kouedu-'keɪʃnl] mixte

coerce [kou'ɜːrs] forcer

coexist [kouɪg'zɪst] coexister; **coexistence** coexistence f

coffee ['kɑːfɪ] café m; **coffee maker** machine f à café; **coffee pot** cafetière f; **coffee shop** café m

cohabit [kou'hæbɪt] cohabiter

coherent [kou'hɪrənt] cohérent

coil [kɔɪl] of rope rouleau m; of snake anneau m

coin [kɔɪn] pièce f (de monnaie)

coincide [kouɪn'saɪd] coïncider; **coincidence** coïncidence f

Coke® [kouk] coca® m

cold [kould] **1** adj froid; **I'm ~** j'ai froid; **it's ~** of weather il fait froid **2** n froid m; MED rhume m; **cold-blooded** à sang froid; murder commis de sang-froid; **coldly** froidement; **coldness** froideur f; **cold sore** bouton m de fièvre

collaborate [kə'læbəreɪt] collaborer; **collaboration** collaboration f; **collaborator** collaborateur(-trice) m(f)

collapse [kə'læps] s'effondrer; of building s'écrouler; **collapsible** pliant

collar ['kɑːlər] col m; for dog collier m

colleague ['kɑːliːg] collègue

m/f

collect [kə'lekt] **1** *v/t person,
cleaning etc* aller/venir chercher; *as hobby* collectionner;
(gather together) recueillir **2**
v/i (gather together) s'assembler; **collect call** communication *f* en PCV; **collection**
collection *f*; *in church* collecte *f*; **collective** collectif; **collector** collectionneur(-euse)
m(f)

college ['kɑːlɪdʒ] université *f*

collide [kə'laɪd] se heurter;
collision collision *f*

colon ['kəʊlən] *punctuation*
deux-points *mpl*

colonel ['kɜːrnl] colonel *m*

colonial [kə'ləʊnɪəl] colonial;
colonize coloniser; **colony**
colonie *f*

color ['kʌlər] couleur *f*; **color-
-blind** daltonien; **colored**
person de couleur; **colorful**
also fig coloré

colossal [kə'lɑːsl] colossal

colour *Br* → **color**

colt [kəʊlt] poulain *m*

column ['kɑːləm] *architectural, of text* colonne *f*; **columnist** chroniqueur(-euse)
m(f)

coma ['kəʊmə] coma *m*

comb [kəʊm] **1** *n* peigne *m* **2**
v/t peigner; *area* passer au
peigne fin

combat ['kɑːmbæt] **1** *n* combat *m* **2** *v/t* combattre

combination [kɑːmbɪ'neɪʃn]
also of safe combinaison *f*;

combine 1 *v/t* combiner; *in-
gredients* mélanger **2** *v/i* se
combiner

come [kʌm] venir; *of train,
bus* arriver

◆ **come across** *(find)* tomber sur

◆ **come along** *(come too)* venir (aussi); *(turn up)* arriver;
(progress) avancer

◆ **come back** revenir

◆ **come down** descendre; *in
price etc* baisser; *of rain,
snow* tomber

◆ **come for** *(attack)* attaquer;
(to collect) venir chercher

◆ **come forward** se présenter

◆ **come from** venir de

◆ **come in** entrer; *of train, in
race* arriver; *of tide* monter

◆ **come in for** *criticism* recevoir

◆ **come off** *of handle etc* se
détacher

◆ **come out** sortir; *of results*
être communiqué; *of sun,
product* apparaître; *of stain*
partir

◆ **come to 1** *v/t (reach)* arriver à; *that comes to $70* ça
fait 70 \$ **2** *v/i (regain con-
sciousness)* revenir à soi

◆ **come up** monter; *of sun* se
lever

'comeback retour *m*, come-
-back *m*

comedian [kə'miːdɪən] *(comic)* comique *m/f*; *pej* pitre
m/f; **comedy** comédie *f*

comfort ['kʌmfərt] **1** *n* confort *m*; *(consolation)* réconfort *m* **2** *v/t* réconforter; **comfortable** confortable; **be ~** *of person* être à l'aise

comic ['kɑːmɪk] **1** *n* to read bande *f* dessinée; *(comedian)* comique *m/f* **2** *adj* comique; **comical** comique; **comic book** bande *f* dessinée, BD *f*; **comics** bandes *fpl* dessinées; **comic strip** bande *f* dessinée

comma ['kɑːmə] virgule *f*

command [kə'mænd] **1** *n (order)* ordre *m*; MIL commandement *m* **2** *v/t* commander

commandeer [kɑːmən'dɪr] réquisitionner

commander [kə'mændər] commandant(e) *m(f)*; **commander-in-chief** commandant(e) *m(f)* en chef

commemorate [kə'meməreɪt] commémorer

commence [kə'mens] commencer

commendable [kə'mendəbl] louable; **commendation** *for bravery* éloge *m*

comment ['kɑːment] **1** *n* commentaire *m* **2** *v/i*: **~ on** commenter; **commentary** commentaire *m*; **commentator** commentateur(-trice) *m(f)*

commerce ['kɑːmɜːrs] commerce *m*; **commercial 1** *adj* commercial **commercial** *n (ad)* publicité *f*; **commercial break** page *f* de publicité; **commercialize** commercialiser

commission [kə'mɪʃn] *(payment, committee)* commission *f*; *(job)* commande *f*

commit [kə'mɪt] *crime* commettre; *money* engager; **commitment** *in relationship* engagement *m*; *(responsibility)* responsabilité *f*; **committee** comité *m*

commodity [kə'mɑːdəti] marchandise *f*

common ['kɑːmən] courant; *species etc* commun; *(shared)* commun; **have sth in ~ with s.o.** avoir qch en commun; **commonly** communément; **common sense** bon sens *m*

commotion [kə'moʊʃn] agitation *f*

communal [kəm'juːnl] en commun

communicate [kə'mjuːnɪkeɪt] communiquer; **communication** communication *f*; **communicative** communicatif

Communion [kə'mjuːnjən] REL communion *f*

Communism ['kɑːmjʊnɪzəm] communisme *m*; **Communist 1** *adj* communiste **2** *n* communiste *m/f*

community [kə'mjuːnəti] communauté *f*

commute [kə'mjuːt] **1** *v/i* faire la navette (pour aller travailler) **2** *v/t* LAW commuer

compact 1 *adj* [kəm'pækt] compact **2** *n* ['kɑːmpækt] MOT petite voiture *f*

companion [kəm'pænjən] compagnon *m*

company ['kʌmpəni] COM société *f*; *(companionship)* compagnie *f*; *(guests)* invités *mpl*

comparable ['kɑːmpərəbl] comparable; **comparative** comparativement; **compare** comparer; **comparison** comparaison *f*

compartment [kəm'pɑːrtmənt] compartiment *m*

compass ['kʌmpəs] compas *m*

compassion [kəm'pæʃn] compassion *f*; **compassionate** compatissant

compatibility [kəmpætə'bɪlətɪ] compatibilité *f*; **compatible** compatible

compel [kəm'pel] obliger

compensate ['kʌmpənseɪt] **1** *v/t* dédommager **2** *v/i*: ~ **for** compenser; **compensation** *(money)* dédommagement *m*; *(reward)* compensation *f*; *(comfort)* consolation *f*

compete [kəm'piːt] être en compétition; *(take part)* participer (*in* à)

competence ['kɑːmpɪtəns] compétence *f*; **competent** *person* compétent, capable; *piece of work* (très) satisfaisant

competition [kɑːmpə'tɪʃn] *(contest)* concours *m*; SP compétition *f*; *(competing,*

competitors) concurrence *f*; **competitive** compétitif; *price, offer* concurrentiel; **competitiveness** COM compétitivité *f*; *of person* esprit *m* de compétition; **competitor** concurrent *m*

complacent [kəm'pleɪsənt] complaisant, suffisant

complain [kəm'pleɪn] se plaindre; **complaint** plainte *f*; IN SHOP réclamation *f*; MED maladie *f*

complementary [kɑːmplɪ'mentərɪ] complémentaire

complete [kəm'pliːt] **1** *adj* complet; *(finished)* terminé **2** *v/t task, building etc* terminer, achever; *form* remplir; **completely** complètement; **completion** achèvement *m*

complex ['kɑːmpleks] **1** *adj* complexe **2** *n building,* PSYCH complexe *m*; **complexion** *facial* teint *m*; **complexity** complexité *f*

compliance [kəm'plaɪəns] conformité *f*

complicate ['kɑːmplɪkeɪt] compliquer; **complicated** compliqué; **complication** complication *f*

complimentary [kɑːmplɪ'mentərɪ] élogieux, flatteur; *(free)* gratuit

comply [kəm'plaɪ] obéir; ~ **with ...** se conformer à

component [kəm'pəʊnənt] composant *m*

compose [kəm'pəʊz] composer; **composed** (*calm*) calme; **composer** MUS compositeur *m*; **composition** composition *f*; **composure** calme *m*

compound ['kɑːmpaʊnd] CHEM composé *m*

comprehend [kɑːmprɪ'hend] comprendre; **comprehension** compréhension *f*; **comprehensive** complet

compress [kəm'pres] comprimer; *information* condenser

comprise [kəm'praɪz] comprendre; (*make up*) constituer; **be ~d of** se composer de

compromise ['kɑːmprəmaɪz] **1** *n* compromis *m* **2** *v/i* trouver un compromis **3** *v/t* compromettre

compulsion [kəm'pʌlʃn] PSYCH compulsion *f*; **compulsive** *behavior* compulsif; *reading* captivant; **compulsory** obligatoire

computer [kəm'pjuːtər] ordinateur *m*; **computer game** jeu *m* informatique; **computerize** informatiser; **computer science** informatique *f*; **computing** informatique *f*

comrade ['kɑːmreɪd] camarade *m/f*; **comradeship** camaraderie *f*

conceal [kən'siːl] cacher; **concealment** dissimulation *f*

conceit [kən'siːt] vanité *f*;

conceited vaniteux

conceivable [kən'siːvəbl] concevable; **conceive** *of woman* concevoir

concentrate ['kɑːnsəntreɪt] *v/i* se concentrer **2** *v/t energies* concentrer; **concentration** concentration *f*

concept ['kɑːnsept] concept *m*; **conception** *of child* conception *f*

concern [kən'sɜːrn] **1** *n* (*anxiety, care*) inquiétude *f*, souci *m*; (*business*) affaire *f*; (*company*) entreprise *f* **2** *v/t* (*involve*) concerner; (*worry*) préoccuper; **concerned** (*anxious*) inquiet; (*caring, involved*) concerné; **concerning** concernant, au sujet de

concert ['kɑːnsərt] concert *m*; **concerted** concerté

concession [kən'seʃn] concession *f*

concise [kən'saɪs] concis

conclude [kən'kluːd] conclure; **~ sth from sth** déduire qch de qch; **conclusion** conclusion *f*; **conclusive** concluant

concrete ['kɑːŋkriːt] **1** *n* béton *m* **2** *adj* concret

concussion [kən'kʌʃn] commotion *f* cérébrale

condemn [kən'dem] condamner; **condemnation** condamnation *f*

condescend [kɑːndɪ'send] daigner (*to do* faire); **conde-**

scending condescendant
condition [kən'dɪʃn] **1** *(state, requirement)* condition *f*; MED maladie *f* **2** *v/t* PSYCH conditionner; **conditioning** PSYCH conditionnement *m*
condo ['kɑːndoʊ] *building* immeuble *m* (en copropriété); *apartment* appart *m*
condolences [kən'doʊlənsɪz] condoléances *fpl*
condom ['kɑːndəm] préservatif *m*
condominium [kɑːndə'mɪnɪəm] → *condo*
condone [kən'doʊn] excuser
conduct ['kɑːndʌkt] **1** *n (behavior)* conduite *f* **2** *v/t* [kən'dʌkt] *(carry out)* mener; ELEC conduire; MUS diriger; **conducted tour** visite *f* guidée; **conductor** MUS chef *m* d'orchestre; *on train* chef *m* de train
cone [koʊn] cône *m*; *for ice cream* cornet *m*; *of pine tree* pomme *f* de pin
conference ['kɑːnfərəns] conférence *f*; *discussion* réunion *f*; **conference room** salle *f* de conférences
confess [kən'fes] **1** *v/t* avouer, confesser **2** *v/i also to police* avouer; REL se confesser; **confession** confession *f*
confide [kən'faɪd] **1** *v/t* confier **2** *v/i*: **~ in s.o.** *(trust)* faire confiance à qn; **confidence** confiance *f*; *(in self)* assuran-

ce *f*; **confident** *(self-assured)* sûr de soi; *(convinced)* confiant; **confidential** confidentiel; **confidently** avec assurance
confine [kən'faɪn] *(imprison)* enfermer; *(restrict)* limiter; **confined** *space* restreint
confirm [kən'fɜːrm] confirmer; **confirmation** confirmation *f*
confiscate ['kɑːnfɪskeɪt] confisquer
conflict ['kɑːnflɪkt] **1** *n* conflit *m* **2** *v/i* [kən'flɪkt] être en conflit; *of dates* coïncider
confront [kən'frʌnt] *(face)* affronter; *(tackle)* confronter; **confrontation** confrontation *f*; *(clash, dispute)* affrontement *m*
confuse [kən'fjuːz] *(muddle)* compliquer; *person* embrouiller; **~ s.o. with s.o.** confondre qn avec qn; **confused** *person* désorienté; *ideas, situation* confus; **confusing** déroutant; **confusion** confusion *f*
congestion [kən'dʒestʃn] *on roads* encombrement *m*
congratulate [kən'grætʊleɪt] féliciter (**on** pour); **congratulations** félicitations *fpl*
congregate ['kɑːngrɪgeɪt] se rassembler; **congregation** REL assemblée *f*
Congress ['kɑːngres] le Congrès; **Congressional** du Congrès; **Congressman**

membre *m* du Congrès; **Congresswoman** membre *m* du Congrès

conjecture [kən'dʒektʃər] conjecture *f*

con man ['kɑːmæn] escroc *m*, arnaqueur *m*

connect [kə'nekt] raccorder, relier; TELEC passer; (*link*) associer; *to power supply* brancher; **connected:** *be well~* avoir des relations; *be ~ with* être lié à; **connection** *in wiring* branchement *m*, connexion *f*; *causal etc* rapport *m*; *when traveling* correspondance *f*; (*personal contact*) relation *f*

connoisseur [kɑːnəˈsɜːr] connaisseur *m*, connaisseuse *f*

conquer ['kɑːŋkər] conquérir; *fear etc* vaincre; **conqueror** conquérant *m*; **conquest** conquête *f*

conscience ['kɑːnʃəns] conscience *f*; **conscientious** consciencieux; **conscientiousness** conscience *f*

conscious ['kɑːnʃəs] conscient; (*deliberate*) délibéré; **consciously** (*knowingly*) consciemment; (*deliberately*) délibérément; **consciousness** conscience *f*; *lose/regain ~* perdre/reprendre connaissance

consecutive [kənˈsekjʊtɪv] consécutif

consensus [kənˈsensəs] con-

sensus *m*

consent [kən'sent] **1** *n* consentement *m* **2** *v/i* consentir (*to* à)

consequence ['kɑːnsɪkwəns] conséquence *f*; **consequently** par conséquent

conservation [kɑːnsərˈveɪʃn] protection *f*; **conservationist** écologiste *m/f*; **conservative** conservateur; *clothes* classique; *estimate* prudent; **conserve 1** *n* (*jam*) confiture *f* **2** *v/t energy* économiser

consider [kənˈsɪdər] considérer; (*show regard for*) prendre en compte; **considerable** considérable; **considerably** considérablement; **considerate** attentionné; **considerately** gentiment; **consideration** (*thought*) réflexion *f*; (*factor*) facteur *m*; (*thoughtfulness, concern*) attention *f*; *take sth into ~* prendre qch en considération

♦ **consist of** [kənˈsɪst] consister en

consistency [kənˈsɪstənsɪ] (*texture*) consistance *f*; (*unchangingness*) constance *f*; (*logic*) cohérence *f*; **consistent** (*unchanging*) constant; *logically etc* cohérent

consolidate [kənˈsɑːlɪdeɪt] consolider

conspicuous [kənˈspɪkjʊəs] voyant; *look~* se faire remarquer

conspiracy [kən'spɪrəsɪ] conspiration f; **conspirator** conspirateur(-trice) m(f); **conspire** conspirer

constant ['kɑːnstənt] constant; **constantly** constamment

constipated ['kɑːstɪpeɪtɪd] constipé; **constipation** constipation f

constitute ['kɑːnstɪtuːt] constituer; **constitution** constitution f; **constitutional** POL constitutionnel

constraint [kən'streɪnt] (restriction) contrainte f

construct [kən'strʌkt] construire; **construction** construction f; (trade) bâtiment m; **constructive** constructif

consul ['kɑːnsl] consul m; **consulate** consulat m

consult [kən'sʌlt] consulter; **consultancy** company cabinet-conseil m; (advice) conseil m; **consultant** consultant m; **consultation** consultation f

consume [kən'suːm] consommer; **consumer** consommateur m; **consumption** consommation f

contact ['kɑːntækt] **1** n contact m **2** v/t contacter; **contact lens** lentille f de contact

contagious [kən'teɪdʒəs] contagieux

contain [kən'teɪn] contenir; **container** récipient m; COM

conteneur m, container m

contaminate [kən'tæmɪneɪt] contaminer; **contamination** contamination f

contemporary [kən'tempərerɪ] **1** adj contemporain **2** n contemporain m

contempt [kən'tempt] mépris m; **contemptible** méprisable; **contemptuous** méprisant

contender [kən'tendər] in sport prétendant m; in competition concurrent m; POL candidat m

content¹ ['kɑːntent] n contenu m

content² [kən'tent] **1** adj content **2** v/t: ~ o.s. with se contenter de

contented [kən'tentɪd] satisfait; **contentment** contentement m

contents ['kɑːntents] contenu m

contest¹ ['kɑːntest] n (competition) concours m; in sport compétition f; (struggle for power) lutte f

contest² [kən'test] leadership etc disputer; (oppose) contester; **~ an election** se présenter à une élection

contestant [kən'testənt] concurrent m

context ['kɑːntekst] contexte m

continent ['kɑːntɪnənt] continent m; **continental** continental

continual [kənˈtɪnjʊəl] continuel; **continually** continuellement; **continuation** continuation f; *of story* suite f; **continue** continuer; **continuous** continu; **continuously** continuellement

contort [kənˈtɔːrt] *face* tordre; *~ one's body* se contorsionner

contraception [kɑːntrəˈsepʃn] contraception f; **contraceptive** contraceptif m

contract[1] [ˈkɑːntrækt] n contrat m

contract[2] [kənˈtrækt] **1** v/i (*shrink*) se contracter **2** v/t *illness* contracter

contractor [kənˈtræktər] entrepreneur m

contractual [kənˈtræktʊəl] contractuel

contradict [kɑːntrəˈdɪkt] contredire; **contradiction** contradiction f; **contradictory** contradictoire

contrary[1] [ˈkɑːntrərɪ] **1** adj contraire; *~ to ...* contrairement à ... **2** n: *on the ~* au contraire

contrary[2] [kənˈtrerɪ] adj (*perverse*) contrariant

contrast [ˈkɑːntræst] **1** n contraste m **2** v/t mettre en contraste **3** v/i contraster; **contrasting** contrastant; *views* opposé

contravene [kɑːntrəˈviːn] enfreindre

contribute [kənˈtrɪbjuːt] **1**

contribuer (*to* à); *to magazine* collaborer (*to* à) **2** v/t *money, suggestion* donner, apporter; **contribution** contribution f; *to political party, church* don m; **contributor** *of money* donateur m; *to magazine* collaborateur(-trice) m(f)

control [kənˈtroul] **1** n contrôle m; *be in ~ of* contrôler **2** v/t contrôler; *company* diriger

controversial [kɑːntrəˈvɜːrʃl] controversé; **controversy** controverse f

convenience [kənˈviːnɪəns] commodité f; *at your ~* à votre convenance; **convenience store** magasin m de proximité; **convenient** commode, pratique

convent [ˈkɑːnvənt] couvent m

convention [kənˈvenʃn] (*tradition*) conventions fpl; (*conference*) convention f; **conventional** conventionnel; *person* conformiste

conversation [kɑːnvərˈseɪʃn] conversation f; **conversational** de conversation

conversion [kənˈvɜːrʃn] conversion f; *of building* aménagement m; **convert 1** n converti m **2** v/t convertir; *building* aménager; **convertible** *car* (voiture f) décapotable f

convey [kənˈveɪ] (*transmit*) transmettre; (*carry*) transporter; **conveyor belt** convoyeur *m*, tapis *m* roulant

convict ['kɑːnvɪkt] *n* détenu *m* 2 [kən'vɪkt] *v/t* LAW déclarer coupable; **conviction** LAW condamnation *f*; (*belief*) conviction *f*

convince [kən'vɪns] convaincre

convoy ['kɑːnvɔɪ] convoi *m*

cook [kʊk] **1** *n* cuisinier(-ière) *m(f)* **2** *v/t meal* préparer; *food* faire cuire **3** *v/i* faire la cuisine; *of food* cuire; **cookbook** livre *m* de cuisine; **cookery** cuisine *f*; **cookie** cookie *m*; **cooking** cuisine *f*

cool [kuːl] **1** *n*: **keep one's ~** garder son sang-froid **2** *adj* frais; *dress* léger; (*calm*) calme; (*unfriendly*) froid; P (*great*) cool **3** *v/i* refroidir; *of tempers* se calmer; *of interest* diminuer **4** *v/t*: **~ it** on se calme

◆ **cool down 1** *v/i* refroidir; : *of weather* se rafraîchir; : *of tempers* se calmer **2** *v/t food* (faire) refroidir; *fig* calmer

cooperate [koʊ'ɑːpəreɪt] coopérer; **cooperation** coopération *f*; **cooperative 1** *n* COM coopérative *f* **2** *adj* coopératif

coordinate [koʊ'ɔːrdɪneɪt] coordonner; **coordination** coordination *f*

cop [kɑːp] P flic *m* F

cope [koʊp] se débrouiller; **~ with ...** faire face à ...

copier ['kɑːpɪər] *machine* photocopieuse *f*

copper ['kɑːpər] cuivre *m*

copy ['kɑːpɪ] **1** *n* copie *f*; *of book* exemplaire *m* **2** *v/t* copier; (*photocopy*) photocopier

cord [kɔːrd] (*string*) corde *f*; (*cable*) fil *m*, cordon *m*

cordon ['kɔːrdn] cordon *m*

cords [kɔːrdz] *pants* pantalon *m* en velours (côtelé)

core [kɔːr] **1** *n* *of fruit, problem* cœur *m*; *of party* noyau *m* **2** *adj issue* fondamental

cork [kɔːrk] *in bottle* bouchon *m*; *material* liège *m*; **corkscrew** tire-bouchon *m*

corn [kɔːrn] *grain* maïs *m*

corner ['kɔːrnər] **1** *n* coin *m*; *in road* virage *m*, tournant *m*; *in soccer* corner *m*; **on the ~** *of street* au coin **2** *v/t person* coincer; **~ the market** accaparer le marché **3** *v/i of driver, car* prendre le/les virage(s)

coronary ['kɔːrəneri] **1** *adj* coronaire **2** *n* infarctus *m* (du myocarde)

coroner ['kɔːrənər] coroner *m*

corporal ['kɔːrpərəl] caporal *m*; **corporal punishment** châtiment *m* corporel

corporate ['kɔːrpərət] COM d'entreprise; **corporation** (*business*) société *f*, entreprise *f*

corpse [kɔːrps] cadavre *m*,

corps *m*

corral [kəˈræl] corral *m*

correct [kəˈrekt] **1** *adj* correct; **the ~ answer** la bonne réponse; **that's ~** c'est exact **2** *v/t* corriger; **correction** correction *f*; **correctly** correctement

correspond [kɒrɪˈspɒnd] correspondre (**to** à); **correspondence** correspondance *f*; **correspondent** correspondant(e) *m(f)*

corridor [ˈkɒrɪdɔː] couloir *m*

corroborate [kəˈrɒbəreɪt] corroborer

corrosion [kəˈrəʊʒn] corrosion *f*

corrupt [kəˈrʌpt] **1** *adj also* COMPUT corrompu; MORALS, YOUTH dépravé **2** *v/t* corrompre; **corruption** corruption *f*

cosmetic [kɑːzˈmetɪk] cosmétique; *fig* esthétique; **cosmetics** cosmétiques *mpl*; **cosmetic surgery** chirurgie *f* esthétique

cosmopolitan [kɑːzməˈpɑːlɪtən] cosmopolite

cost [kɑːst] **1** *n also fig* coût *m* **2** *v/t* coûter; **how much does it ~?** combien ça coûte?

'cost-effective rentable; **cost of living** coût *m* de la vie

costume [ˈkɑːstuːm] *for actor* costume *m*

cosy *Br* → **cozy**

cot [kɑːt] (*camp-bed*) lit *m* de camp; *Br for child* lit *m* d'enfant

cottage [ˈkɑːtɪdʒ] cottage *m*

cotton [ˈkɑːtn] **1** *n* coton *m* **2** *adj* en coton; **cotton candy** barbe *f* à papa; **cotton wool** *Br* coton *m* hydrophile, ouate *f*

couch [kaʊtʃ] canapé *m*; **couch potato** téléphage *m/f*

cough [kɑːf] **1** *n* toux *f* **2** *v/i* tousser; **cough medicine**, **cough syrup** sirop *m* contre la toux

could [kʊd]: **~ I have my key?** pourrais-je avoir ma clef?; **~ you help me?** pourrais-tu m'aider?; **you ~ be right** vous avez peut-être raison; **you ~ have warned me!** tu aurais pu me prévenir!

council [ˈkaʊnsl] (*assembly*) conseil *m*, assemblée *f*; **councilor** conseiller *m*

counsel [ˈkaʊnsl] **1** *n* (*advice*) conseil *m*; (*lawyer*) avocat *m* **2** *v/t* conseiller; **counseling**, *Br* **counselling** aide *f* (psychologique); **counselor**, *Br* **counsellor** (*adviser*) conseiller *m*; LAW maître *m*

count [kaʊnt] **1** *n* compte *m* **2** *v/t & v/i* compter

◆ **count on** compter sur

'countdown compte *m* à rebours

counter [ˈkaʊntər] *in shop, café* comptoir *m*; *in game* pion *m*

'counteract neutraliser, contrecarrer; **counter-attack 1** *n* contre-attaque *f* **2** *v/i* contre-attaquer; **counterclock-wise** dans le sens inverse des aiguilles d'une montre; **counterespionage** contre-espionnage *m*; **counterfeit 1** *v/t* contrefaire **2** *adj* faux; **counterpart** *person* homologue *m/f*; **counterproductive** contre-productif

countless ['kauntlıs] innombrable

country ['kʌntrı] pays *m*; *as opposed to town* campagne *f*

county ['kauntı] comté *m*

coup [ku:] POL coup d'État; *fig* beau coup *m*

couple ['kʌpl] (*two people*) couple *m*; *a ~ of* (*a pair*) deux; (*a few*) quelques

courage ['kʌrıdʒ] courage *m*; **courageous** courageux

courier ['kurıər] (*messenger*) coursier *m*; *with tourist party* guide *m/f*

course [kɔːrs] *of lessons* cours *m*(*pl*); *of meal* plat *m*; *of ship, plane* route *f*; *for sports* piste *f*; *for golf* terrain *m*; *of ~* bien sûr; *of ~ not* bien sûr que non

court [kɔːrt] LAW tribunal *m*, cour *f*; FOR TENNIS court *m*; *for basketball* terrain *m*; *take s.o. to ~* faire un procès à qn; **court case** affaire *f*, procès *m*

courtesy ['kɜːrtəsı] courtoisie *f*

'**courthouse** palais *m* de justice, tribunal *m*; **courtroom**

salle *f* d'audience; **courtyard** cour *f*

cousin ['kʌzn] cousin(e) *m(f)*

cover ['kʌvər] **1** *n protective* housse *f*; *of book, magazine* couverture *f*; (*shelter*) abri *m*; (*insurance*) couverture *f*, assurance *f* **2** *v/t* couvrir

♦ **cover up 1** *v/t* couvrir; *scandal* dissimuler **2** *v/i* cacher la vérité

coverage ['kʌvərıdʒ] *by media* couverture *f* (médiatique)

covert ['kouvɜːrt] secret, clandestin

'**cover-up** black-out *m inv*

cow [kau] vache *f*

coward ['kauərd] lâche *m/f*; **cowardice** lâcheté *f*

'**cowboy** cow-boy *m*

co-worker ['kouwɜːrkər] collègue *m/f*

cozy ['kouzı] confortable, douillet

crab [kræb] crabe *m*

crack [kræk] **1** *n* fissure *f*; *in cup, glass* fêlure *f*; (*joke*) vanne *f* **2** *v/t* cup, glass fêler; *nut* casser; (*solve*) résoudre; *code* décrypter **3** *v/i* se fêler; **crack (cocaine)** crack *m*; **cracked** *cup* fêlé; **cracker** *to eat* cracker *m*

cradle ['kreıdl] berceau *m*

craft[1] [kræft] NAUT embarcation *f*

craft[2] (*trade*) métier *m*; *weaving, pottery etc* artisanat *m*; (*craftsmanship*) art *m*;

craftsman (*artisan*) artisan *m*; **crafty** malin, rusé

crag [kræg] (*rock*) rocher *m* escarpé

cram [kræm] fourrer; *food* enfourner; *people* entasser

cramps [kræmps] crampe *f*

crane [kreɪn] **1** *n* (*machine*) grue *f* **2** *v/t*: **~ one's neck** tendre le cou

crank [kræŋk] *person* allumé *m*; **cranky** (*bad-tempered*) grognon

crash [kræʃ] **1** *n noise* fracas *m*; *accident* accident *m*; COM faillite *f*; *of stock exchange* krach *m*; COMPUT plantage *m* **2** *v/i* s'écraser; *of car* s'effondrer; *of market* s'effondrer; COMPUT se planter **3** *v/t car* avoir un accident avec; **crash course** cours *m* intensif; **crash diet** régime *m* intensif; **crash helmet** casque *m* f; **crash-land** atterrir en catastrophe

crate [kreɪt] caisse *f*

crater ['kreɪtər] cratère *m*

crave [kreɪv] avoir très envie de; **craving** envie *f* (*irrepressible*)

crawl [krɔːl] **1** *n in swimming* crawl *m* **2** *v/i on belly* ramper; *on hands and knees* marcher à quatre pattes; (*move slowly*) se traîner

crayon ['kreɪɑːn] crayon *m* de couleur

craze [kreɪz] engouement *m*; **the latest ~** la dernière mo-

de; **crazy** fou

creak [kriːk] craquer, grincer; **creaky** qui craque, grinçant

cream [kriːm] **1** *n* crème *f*; *color* crème *m* **2** *adj* crème *inv*

crease [kriːs] **1** *n* pli *m* **2** *v/t accidentally* froisser

create [kriː'eɪt] créer; **creation** création *f*; **creative** créatif; **creator** créateur(-trice) *m(f)*

creature ['kriːtʃər] animal *m*; (*person*) créature *f*

credibility [kredə'bɪlətɪ] crédibilité *f*; **credible** crédible

credit ['kredɪt] crédit *m*; (*honor*) honneur *m*, mérite *m*; **creditable** honorable; **credit card** carte *f* de crédit; **credit limit** limite *f* de crédit; **creditor** créancier *m*; **creditworthy** solvable

creep [kriːp] **1** *n pej* sale type *m* **2** *v/i* se glisser (*in-*); (*move slowly*) avancer lentement; **creepy** F flippant F

cremate [krɪ'meɪt] incinérer; **cremation** incinération *f*, crémation *f*

crest [krest] crête *f*

crevice ['krevɪs] fissure *f*

crew [kruː] *of ship, airplane* équipage *m*; **crew cut** cheveux *mpl* en brosse

crib [krɪb] *for baby* lit *m* d'enfant

crime [kraɪm] crime *m*; **criminal 1** *n* criminel *m* **2** *adj* criminel; (*shameful*) honteux crimson ['krɪmzn] cramoisi

cripple ['krɪpl] 1 n handicapé(e) m(f) 2 v/t person estropier; fig paralyser

crisis ['kraɪsɪs] crise f

crisp [krɪsp] weather vivifiant; lettuce, apple croquant; bacon, toast croustillant; crisps Br chips fpl

criterion [kraɪ'tɪrɪən] critère m

critic ['krɪtɪk] critique m; critical critique; criticism critique f; criticize critiquer

crocodile ['krɑːkədaɪl] crocodile m

crony ['krəʊnɪ] pote m , copain m

crook [krʊk] escroc m; crooked de travers; streets tortueux; (dishonest) malhonnête

crop [krɑːp] 1 n culture f; (harvest) récolte f 2 v/t hair, photo couper

♦ crop up surgir

cross [krɑːs] 1 adj (angry) fâché 2 n croix f 3 v/t (go across) traverser; ~ o.s. REL se signer 4 v/i (go across) traverser; of lines se croiser

♦ cross off, cross out rayer

'crosscheck 1 n recoupement m 2 v/t vérifier par recoupement; cross-examine LAW faire subir un contre-interrogatoire à; cross-eyed qui louche; crossing NAUT traversée f; crossroads also fig carrefour m; crosswalk

passage m (pour) piétons; crossword (puzzle) mots mpl croisés

crotch [krɑːtʃ] entrejambe m

crouch [kraʊtʃ] s'accroupir

crowd [kraʊd] foule f; at sports event public m; crowded bondé, plein (de monde)

crown [kraʊn] also on tooth couronne f

crucial ['kruːʃl] crucial

crucifix ['kruːsɪfɪks] crucifix m; crucifixion of Christ crucifixion f; crucify REL crucifier; fig assassiner

crude [kruːd] 1 adj (vulgar) grossier; (unsophisticated) rudimentaire 2 n: ~ (oil) pétrole m brut

cruel ['kruːəl] cruel; cruelty cruauté f

cruise [kruːz] 1 n croisière f 2 v/i of people faire une croisière; of car rouler (à une vitesse de croisière); of plane voler (à une vitesse de croisière)

crumb [krʌm] miette f

crumble ['krʌmbl] of bread s'émietter; of stonework s'effriter; fig: of opposition etc s'effondrer

crumple ['krʌmpl] 1 v/t (crease) froisser 2 v/i (collapse) s'écrouler

crush [krʌʃ] 1 n (crowd) foule f 2 v/t écraser; (crease) froisser

crust [krʌst] on bread croûte f

crutch [krʌtʃ] *for injured person* béquille *f*
cry [kraɪ] **1** *n (call)* cri *m* **2** *v/i (weep)* pleurer
♦ **cry out** crier
cryptic ['krɪptɪk] énigmatique
crystal ['krɪstl] cristal *m*
cube [kju:b] cube *m*; **cubic** ['kju:bɪk] *adj* cubique; ~ **meter** mètre cube
cubicle ['kju:bɪkl] *(changing room)* cabine *f*
cuddle ['kʌdl] câliner
cue [kju:] *for actor etc* signal *m*; *for pool* queue *f*
cuff [kʌf] *of shirt* poignet *m*; *of pants* revers *m*; *(blow)* gifle *f*
culminate ['kʌlmɪneɪt]: ~ **in** se terminer par; **culmination** [~'neɪʃn] apogée *f*
culprit ['kʌlprɪt] coupable *m/f*
cult [kʌlt] *(sect)* secte *f*
cultivate ['kʌltɪveɪt] *land, person* cultiver; **cultivated** *person* cultivé; **cultivation** *of land* culture *f*
cultural ['kʌltʃərəl] culturel; **culture** culture *f*; **cultured** cultivé
cumulative ['kju:mjʊlətɪv] cumulatif
cunning ['kʌnɪŋ] **1** *n* ruse *f* **2** *adj* rusé
cup [kʌp] tasse *f*; *(trophy)* coupe *f*
cupboard ['kʌbərd] placard *m*
curb [kɜːrb] **1** *n of street* bord *m* du trottoir; *on powers etc* frein *m* **2** *v/t* réfréner
cure [kjʊr] **1** *n* MED remède *m*

2 *v/t* MED guérir; *meat* saurer
curiosity [kjʊrɪ'ɑːsətɪ] curiosité *f*; **curious** curieux
curl [kɜːrl] **1** *n in hair* boucle *f*; *of smoke* volute *f* **2** *v/t hair* boucler; *(wind)* enrouler **3** *v/i of hair* boucler; *of leaf, paper etc* se gondoler
♦ **curl up** se pelotonner
curly ['kɜːrlɪ] *hair* bouclé; *tail* en tire-bouchon
currency ['kʌrənsɪ] monnaie *f*; **foreign** ~ devise *f* étrangère; **current 1** *n in sea*, ELEC courant *m* **2** *adj* actuel; **current affairs** actualité *f*
curse [kɜːrs] **1** *n (spell)* malédiction *f*; *(swearword)* juron *m* **2** *v/t* maudire **3** *v/i (swear)* jurer
cursor ['kɜːrsər] COMPUT curseur *m*
cursory ['kɜːrsərɪ] superficiel
curt [kɜːrt] abrupt
curtain ['kɜːrtn] *also* THEA rideau *m*
curve [kɜːrv] **1** *n* courbe *f* **2** *v/i (bend)* s'incurver; *of road* faire une courbe
cushion ['kʊʃn] **1** *n* coussin *m* **2** *v/t blow, fall* amortir
custody ['kʌstədɪ] *of children* garde *f*; **in** ~ LAW en détention
custom ['kʌstəm] coutume *f*; COM clientèle *f*; **customer** client *m*; **customer service** service *m* clientèle
customs ['kʌstəmz] douane *f*; **customs officer** douanier

cut *m*
cut [kʌt] **1** *n with knife, scissors* entaille *f*; *(injury)* coupure *f*; *(incision)* coupe *f*; *(reduction)* réduction *f* **2** *v/t* couper; *(reduce)* réduire; **get one's hair** ~ se faire couper les cheveux
◆ **cut down 1** *v/t tree* abattre **2** *v/i on smoking etc* réduire
◆ **cut off** couper; *(isolate)* isoler
◆ **cut up** *meat etc* découper
cutback réduction *f*
cute [kjuːt] *in appearance* mignon; *(clever)* malin
'cutoff date date *f* limite; **cut--price** à prix *m* réduit; **cut--throat** *competition* acharné;

cutting 1 *n from newspaper* coupure *f* **2** *adj remark* blessant
cyber... ['saɪbər] cyber...
cycle ['saɪkl] **1** *n* vélo *m*; *of events* cycle *m* **2** *v/i* aller en vélo; **cycling** cyclisme *m*; **cyclist** cycliste *m/f*
cylinder ['sɪlɪndər] *in engine* cylindre *m*; **cylindrical** cylindrique
cynic ['sɪnɪk] cynique *m/f*; **cynical** cynique; **cynicism** cynisme *m*
Czech [tʃek] **1** *adj* tchèque; **the ~ Republic** la République tchèque **2** *n person* Tchèque *m/f*; *language* tchèque *m*

D

DA [diː'eɪ] (= **district attorney**) procureur *m*
◆ **dabble in** toucher à
dad [dæd] papa *m*
daily ['deɪlɪ] **1** *n paper* quotidien *m* **2** *adj* quotidien
'dairy ['deərɪ] *(food)* ~ **products** produits *mpl* laitiers; ~ **free** sans produits laitiers
dam [dæm] barrage *m*
damage ['dæmɪdʒ] **1** *n* dommage(s) *m(pl)*; *to reputation* préjudice *m* **2** *v/t* endommager; *fig*: *reputation* nuire à; **damages** LAW dommages--intérêts *mpl*; **damaging** préjudiciable

damn [dæm] **F 1** *interj* zut **2** *adj* sacré **3** *adv (very)* vachement **F**; **damning** *evidence, report* accablant
damp [dæmp] humide
dance [dæns] **1** *n* danse *f*; *social event* bal *m* **2** *v/i* danser; **dancer** danseur(-euse) *m(f)*; **dancing** danse *f*
Dane [deɪn] Danois(e) *m(f)*
danger ['deɪndʒər] danger *m*; **dangerous** dangereux
dangle ['dæŋgl] **1** *v/t* balancer **2** *v/i* pendre
Danish ['deɪnɪʃ] **1** *adj* danois **2** *n language* danois *m*
Danish (pastry) feuilleté *m*

(sucré)

dare [der] **1** *v/i* oser; **~ to do sth** oser faire qch **2** *v/t*: **s.o. to do sth** défier qn de faire qch; **daring** audacieux

dark [dɑːrk] **1** *n* noir *m* **2** *adj room* sombre, noir; *hair* brun; *eyes, color, clothes* foncé; **dark glasses** lunettes *fpl* noires; **darkness** obscurité *f*

darling ['dɑːrlɪŋ] chéri(e) *m(f)*

dart [dɑːrt] **1** *n for game* fléchette *f* **2** *v/i* se précipiter

dash [dæʃ] **1** *n punctuation* tiret *m*; *a ~ of* un peu de **2** *v/i* se précipiter **3** *v/t hopes* anéantir; **dashboard** tableau *m* de bord

data ['deɪtə] données *fpl*; **database** base *f* de données

date¹ [deɪt] *fruit* datte *f*

date² [deɪt] *date f; meeting, person* rendez-vous *m*; *out of ~ clothes* démodé; *passport* périmé; *up to ~ information* à jour; *style* à la mode; **dated** démodé

daughter ['dɔːtər] fille *f*; **daughter-in-law** belle-fille *f*

dawn [dɔːn] *also fig* aube *f*

day [deɪ] jour *m*; *stressing duration* journée *f*; **the ~ after** le lendemain; **the ~ after tomorrow** après-demain; **the ~ before** la veille; **the ~ before yesterday** avant-hier; *in those ~s* en ce temps-là, à l'époque; **the other ~** *(recently)* l'autre jour; **day-**

break aube *f*, point *m* du jour; **daydream 1** *n* rêverie *f* **2** *v/i* rêvasser; **daylight** jour *m*; **day spa** spa *m* urbain

dazed [deɪzd] *by news* hébété; *by blow* étourdi

dazzle ['dæzl] éblouir

dead [ded] **1** *adj; battery* à plat; **a great ~ of** beaucoup de **2** *v/t cards* distribuer

dead [ded] **1** *adj; battery* à plat; *a great ~ of* beaucoup de **2** *adv* F *(very)* très; **~ beat, ~ tired** crevé **3** *npl*: **the ~** les morts *mpl*; **dead end** *street* impasse *f*; **dead heat** arrivée *f ex æquo*; **deadline** date *f* limite; heure *f* limite, délai *m*; *for newspaper* heure *f* de clôture; **meet the ~** respecter le(s) délai(s); **deadlock** *in talks* impasse *f*; **deadly** mortel

deaf [def] sourd; **deafening** assourdissant; **deafness** surdité *f*

deal [diːl] **1** *n* accord *m*, marché *m*; *a great ~ of* beaucoup de **2** *v/t cards* distribuer

◆ **deal in** COM être dans le commerce de; *drugs* dealer

◆ **deal with** *(handle)* s'occuper de; *(do business with)* traiter avec; *(be about)* traiter de

dealer ['diːlər] marchand *m*; *(drug ~)* dealer *m*, dealeuse *f*; *large-scale* trafiquant *m* de drogue; **dealing** *(drug ~)* trafic *m* de drogue; **dealings** *(business)* relations *fpl*

dear [dɪr] cher; *Dear Sir* Monsieur

death

death [deθ] mort *f*; **death toll** nombre *m* de morts

debatable [dɪ'beɪtəbl] discutable; **debate 1** *n* débat *m* **2** *v/i* débattre **3** *v/t* débattre de

debit ['debɪt] **1** *n* débit *m* **2** *v/t account* débiter; *amount* porter au débit; **debit card** carte *f* bancaire

debris [də'briː] débris *mpl*

debt [det] dette *f*; **be in ~** être endetté; **debtor** débiteur *m*

debug [diː'bʌg] COMPUT déboguer

decade ['dekeɪd] décennie *f*

decadent ['dekədənt] décadent

decaffeinated [diː'kæfɪneɪtɪd] décaféiné

decay [dɪ'keɪ] **1** *n* détérioration *f*; *in wood, plant* pourriture *f*; *in teeth* carie *f* **2** *v/i of wood, plant* pourrir; *of civilization* tomber en décadence; *of teeth* se carier

deceased [dɪ'siːst]: **the ~** le défunt/la défunte

deceit [dɪ'siːt] duplicité *f*; **deceitful** fourbe; **deceive** tromper

December [dɪ'sembər] décembre *m*

decency ['diːsənsɪ] décence *f*; **decent** *person* correct, honnête; *salary* correct, décent; *meal, sleep* bon

deception [dɪ'sepʃn] tromperie *f*; **deceptive** trompeur

decide [dɪ'saɪd] décider; de-cided (*definite*) décidé; *views* arrêté; *improvement* décidé

decimal ['desɪml] décimale *f*

decipher [dɪ'saɪfər] déchiffrer

decision [dɪ'sɪʒn] décision *f*; **decisive** *(crucial)* décisif

deck [dek] *of ship* pont *m*; *of cards* jeu *m* (de cartes)

declaration [deklə'reɪʃn] déclaration *f*; **declare** déclarer

decline [dɪ'klaɪn] **1** *n* baisse *f*; *of civilization, health* déclin *m* **2** *v/t invitation* décliner; **~ to comment** refuser de commenter **3** *v/i (refuse)* refuser; *(decrease)* baisser; *of health* décliner

decode [diː'koʊd] décoder

décor ['deɪkɔːr] décor *m*

decorate ['dekəreɪt] *room* refaire; *with paint* peindre; *with paper* tapisser; *(adorn), soldier* décorer; **decoration** décoration *f*; **decorator** *(interior ~)* décorateur *m* (d'intérieur)

decoy ['diːkɔɪ] appât *m*, leurre *m*

decrease [dɪ'kriːs] **1** *n* baisse *f*, diminution *f*; *in size* réduction *f* **2** *v/t & v/i* diminuer

dedicate ['dedɪkeɪt] *book etc* dédicacer; **dedicated** dévoué; **dedication** *in book* dédicace *f*; *to cause, work* dévouement *m*

deduce [dɪ'djuːs] déduire

deduct [dɪ'dʌkt] déduire

(*from* de); **deduction** *from salary* prélèvement *m*; (*conclusion*) déduction *f*

deed [di:d] (*act*) acte *m*; LAW acte *m* (notarié)

deep [di:p] profond; *voice* grave; *color* intense; **deepen 1** *v/t* creuser **2** *v/i* devenir plus profond; *of mystery* s'épaissir; **deep freeze** congélateur *m*

deer [dɪr] cerf *m*; *female* biche *f*

deface [dɪˈfeɪs] abîmer

defamation [defəˈmeɪʃn] diffamation *f*; **defamatory** diffamatoire

defeat [dɪˈfiːt] **1** *n* défaite *f* **2** *v/t* battre

defect [ˈdiːfekt] défaut *m*; **defective** défectueux

defence Br → **defense**

defend [dɪˈfend] défendre; *decision* justifier; **defendant** défendeur *m*, défenderesse *f*; *in criminal case* accusé(e) *m(f)*; **defense** défense *f*; **defenseless** sans défense; **Defense Secretary** POL ministre de la Défense; **defensive 1** *n*: *go on (to) the ~* se mettre sur la défensive **2** *adj* défensif

deference [ˈdefərəns] déférence *f*

defiance [dɪˈfaɪəns] défi *m*; **defiant** [dɪˈfaɪənt] provocant; *look* de défi

deficiency [dɪˈfɪʃənsɪ] manque *m*; MED carence *f*

deficit [ˈdefɪsɪt] déficit *m*

define [dɪˈfaɪn] définir

definite [ˈdefɪnɪt] définitif; *improvement* net; (*certain*) catégorique; **definitely** sans aucun doute; **definitely** *not* certainement pas!

definition [defɪˈnɪʃn] définition *f*

deformity [dɪˈfɔːmətɪ] difformité *f*

defrost [diːˈfrɒst] *food* décongeler; *fridge* dégivrer

defuse [diːˈfjuːz] *bomb, situation* désamorcer

defy [dɪˈfaɪ] défier; *superiors* braver

degrading [dɪˈgreɪdɪŋ] dégradant

degree [dɪˈgriː] degré *m*; *from university* diplôme *m*

dehydrated [diːhaɪˈdreɪtɪd] déshydraté

deign [deɪn]: *~ to* daigner

dejected [dɪˈdʒektɪd] déprimé

delay [dɪˈleɪ] **1** *n* retard *m* **2** *v/t* retarder; *be ~ed* être en retard **3** *v/i* tarder

delegate [ˈdelɪgət] **1** *n* délégué(e) *m(f)* **2** *v/t* déléguer; **delegation** délégation *f*

delete [dɪˈliːt] effacer; (*cross out*) rayer; **deletion** *act* effacement *m*; *that deleted* rature *f*

deliberate 1 [dɪˈlɪbərət] *adj* délibéré **2** [dɪˈlɪbəreɪt] *v/i* délibérer; (*reflect*) réfléchir; **deliberately** délibérément, exprès

delicate ['delɪkət] délicat

delicatessen [delɪkə'tesn] traiteur *m*, épicerie *f* fine

delicious [dɪ'lɪʃəs] délicieux

delight [dɪ'laɪt] joie *f*, plaisir *m*; **delighted** ravi; **delightful** charmant

deliver [dɪ'lɪvər] *letters* livrer; *parcel etc* remettre; *message* transmettre; *baby* mettre au monde; *speech* faire; **delivery** *of goods* livraison *f*; *of mail* distribution *f*; *of baby* accouchement *m*; *of speech* débit *m*; **delivery date** date *f* de livraison

de luxe [də'lʌks] de luxe; *model* haut de gamme *inv*

demand [dɪ'mænd] **1** *n also* COM demande *f*; *of terrorist, unions etc* revendication *f*; **in** ~ demandé **2** *v/t* exiger; *pay rise etc* réclamer; **demanding** *job* éprouvant; *person* exigeant

demo ['deməʊ] *(protest)* manif *f*; *of video etc* démo *f*

democracy [dɪ'mɑːkrəsɪ] démocratie *f*; **democrat** démocrate *m/f*; **democratic** démocratique

demolish [dɪ'mɑːlɪʃ] *building, argument* démolir; **demolition** démolition *f*

demonstrate ['demənstreɪt] **1** *v/t (prove)* démontrer; *machine etc* faire une démonstration de **2** *v/i politically* manifester; **demonstration**

démonstration *f*; *(protest)* manifestation *f*; **demonstrator** *(protester)* manifestant(e) *m(f)*

demoralized [dɪ'mɔːrəlaɪzd] démoralisé; **demoralizing** démoralisant

demote [diː'məʊt] rétrograder

den [den] *room* antre *f*

denial [dɪ'naɪəl] *of accusation* démenti *m*, dénégation *f*; *of request* refus *m*

denim ['denɪm] jean *m*

Denmark ['denmɑːrk] le Danemark

denomination [dɪnɑːmɪ'neɪʃn] *of money* coupure *f*; *religious* confession *f*

dense [dens] *(thick)* dense; **density** ['densɪtɪ] densité *f*

dent [dent] **1** *n* bosse *f* **2** *v/t* bosseler

dental ['dentl] dentaire

dented ['dentɪd] bosselé

dentist ['dentɪst] dentiste *m/f*; **dentures** dentier *m*

Denver boot ['denvər] sabot *m* de Denver

deny [dɪ'naɪ] *charge* nier; *right, request* refuser

deodorant [diː'əʊdərənt] déodorant *m*

department [dɪ'pɑːrtmənt] *of company* service *m*; *of university* département *m*; *of government* ministère *m*; *of store* rayon *m*; **Department of State** ministère *m* des Affaires étrangères; **depart-**

ment store grand magasin *m*

departure [dɪ'pɑ:tʃər] départ *m; from standard etc* entorse *f* (**from** à); **departure lounge** salle *f* d'embarquement; **departure time** heure *f* de départ

depend [dɪ'pend] dépendre; **that ~s** cela dépend; **dependence, dependency** dépendance *f*

depict [dɪ'pɪkt] représenter

deplorable [dɪ'plɔ:rəbl] déplorable; **deplore** déplorer

deploy [dɪ'plɔɪ] (*use*) faire usage de; (*position*) déployer

deport [dɪ'pɔ:rt] expulser; **deportation** expulsion *f*

deposit [dɪ'pɑ:zɪt] **1** *n in bank* dépôt *m; on purchase* acompte *m; security* caution *f; of mineral* gisement *m* **2** *v/t money, object* déposer; **deposition** LAW déposition *f*

depot ['depoʊ] *for storage* dépôt *m*, entrepôt *m*

depreciation [dɪpri:ʃɪ'eɪʃn] FIN dépréciation *f*

depress [dɪ'pres] *person* déprimer; **depressed** déprimé; **depressing** déprimant; **depression** MED, *meteorological* dépression *f; economic* crise *f*, récession *f*

deprivation [deprɪ'veɪʃn] privation(s) *f(pl)*; **deprive**: ~ **s.o. of sth** priver qn de qch; **deprived** défavorisé

depth [depθ] profondeur *f; of color* intensité *f; in* ~ en pro-

fondeur

deputy ['depjuti] adjoint(e) *m(f); of sheriff* shérif *m* adjoint

derail [dɪ'reɪl]: **be ~ed of train** dérailler

derelict ['derəlɪkt] délabré

deride [dɪ'raɪd] se moquer de; **derision** dérision *f*; **derisory** dérisoire

derivative [dɪ'rɪvətɪv] (*not original*) dérivé

derive [dɪ'raɪv] tirer (**from** de); **be ~d from** dériver de

dermatologist [dɜ:rmə'tɑ:lədʒɪst] dermatologue *m/f*

derogatory [dɪ'rɑ:gətɔ:rɪ] désobligeant; *term* péjoratif

descendant [dɪ'sendənt] descendant(e) *m(f)*; **descent** descente *f*; (*ancestry*) descendance *f*

describe [dɪ'skraɪb] décrire; **description** description *f; of criminal* signalement *m*

desegregate [diː'segrəgeɪt] supprimer la ségrégation dans

desert[1] ['dezərt] *n* désert *m*

desert[2] [dɪ'zɜ:rt] **1** *v/t* abandonner **2** *v/i of soldier* déserter; **deserted** désert; **deserter** MIL déserteur *m*; **desertion** abandon *m*, MIL désertion *f*

deserve [dɪ'zɜ:rv] mériter

design [dɪ'zaɪn] **1** *n* (*subject*) design *m*; (*style*) style *m*; (*drawing, pattern*) dessin *m*

2 v/t (draw) dessiner; building, car concevoir

designate ['dezIgneIt] person désigner

designer [dI'zaInər] designer m/f; of car, ship concepteur(-trice) m(f); of clothes styliste m/f; **designer clothes** vêtements mpl de marque

desirable [dI'zaIrəbl] souhaitable; sexually, change désirable; house beau; **desire** désir m

desk [desk] bureau m; in hotel réception f; **desk clerk** réceptionniste m/f; **desktop publishing** publication f assistée par ordinateur

desolate ['desələt] place désolé

despair [dI'sper] **1** n désespoir m; **in ~** désespéré (of de); **2** v/i désespérer (of de); **desperate** désespéré; **be ~ for sth** avoir très envie de qch; **desperation** désespoir m; **in ~** en désespoir de cause

despicable [dIs'pIkəbl] méprisable; **despise** mépriser

despite [dI'spaIt] malgré, en dépit de

dessert [dI'zɜːrt] dessert m

destination [destI'neIʃn] destination f

destroy [dI'strɔI] détruire; **destroyer** NAUT destroyer m; **destruction** destruction f; **destructive** power destructeur; **a ~ child** un enfant

qui casse tout

detach [dI'tætʃ] détacher; **detached** (objective) neutre; **detachment** (objectivity) neutralité f

detail ['diːteIl] détail m; **detailed** détaillé

detain [dI'teIn] (hold back) retenir; as prisoner détenir; **detainee** détenu(e) m(f); **political ~** prisonnier m politique

detect [dI'tekt] déceler; of device détecter; **detection** of criminal découverte f; of smoke etc détection f; **detective** inspecteur m de police; **detector** détecteur m

détente ['deItɑːnt] POL détente f

deter [dI'tɜːr] dissuader

detergent [dI'tɜːrdʒənt] détergent m

deteriorate [dI'tIrIəreIt] se détériorer

determination [dItɜːrmI'neIʃn] (resolution) détermination f; **determine** (establish) déterminer; **determined** déterminé, résolu; effort délibéré

detest [dI'test] détester; **detestable** détestable

detour ['diːtʊr] détour m; (diversion) déviation f

devaluation [diːvæljʊ'eIʃn] dévaluation f; **devalue** dévaluer

devastate ['devəsteIt] dévaster; fig: person anéantir

develop [dɪˈveləp] **1** *v/t film, business* développer; *site* aménager; *technique, vaccine* mettre au point; *illness* attraper **2** *v/i (grow)* se développer; **developing country** pays *m* en voie de développement; **development** *of film, business* développement *m*; *of site* aménagement *m*; *of technique, vaccine* mise *f* au point

device [dɪˈvaɪs] appareil *m*; *(tool)* outil *m*

devil [ˈdevl] diable *m*; *a little ~* un petit monstre

devise [dɪˈvaɪz] concevoir

devote [dɪˈvout] consacrer; **devoted** *son etc* dévoué (**to** à); **devotion** dévouement *m*

devour [dɪˈvauər] dévorer

devout [dɪˈvaut] pieux

diabetes [daɪəˈbiːtiːz] diabète *m*; **diabetic** diabétique *m/f*

diagnose [ˈdaɪəgnouz] diagnostiquer; **diagnosis** diagnostic *m*

diagonal [daɪˈægənl] diagonal; **diagonally** en diagonale

diagram [ˈdaɪəgræm] diagramme *m*

dial [ˈdaɪl] **1** *n* cadran *m* **2** *v/i* TELEC faire le numéro **3** *v/t* TELEC *number* composer

dialog, *Br* **dialogue** [ˈdaɪəlɔːg] dialogue *m*

dial tone tonalité *f*

diameter [daɪˈæmɪtər] diamètre *m*

diamond [ˈdaɪmənd] diamant *m*; *shape* losange *m*

diaper [ˈdaɪpər] couche *f*

diaphragm [ˈdaɪəfræm] diaphragme *m*

diarrhea, *Br* **diarrhoea** [daɪəˈriːə] diarrhée *f*

diary [ˈdaɪrɪ] journal *m*; *for appointments* agenda *m*

dice [daɪs] dé *m*; *pl* dés *mpl*

dictate [dɪkˈteɪt] dicter; **dictator** POL dictateur *m*; **dictatorship** dictature *f*

dictionary [ˈdɪkʃənrɪ] dictionnaire *m*

die [daɪ] mourir
◆ **die down** *of storm* se calmer; *of excitement* s'apaiser
◆ **die out** disparaître

diet [ˈdaɪət] **1** *n (regular food)* alimentation *f*; *to lose weight, for health* régime *m* **2** *v/i* faire un régime

differ [ˈdɪfər] différer; *(disagree)* différence *f*; **different** différent; **differently** différemment

difficult [ˈdɪfɪklt] difficile; **difficulty** difficulté *f*

dig [dɪg] creuser

digest [daɪˈdʒest] digérer; *information* assimiler; **digestion** digestion *f*

digit [ˈdɪdʒɪt] chiffre *m*; **digital** numérique; **digital camera** appareil *m* photo numérique; **digital photo** photo *f* numérique

dignified [ˈdɪgnɪfaɪd] digne; **dignity** dignité *f*

dilapidated

dilapidated [dɪˈlæpɪdeɪtɪd] délabré

dilemma [dɪˈlemə] dilemme m

dilute [daɪˈluːt] diluer

dim [dɪm] **1** adj room, prospects sombre; light faible; outline vague; (stupid) bête **2** v/i of lights baisser

dime [daɪm] (pièce f de) dix cents mpl

dimension [daɪˈmenʃn] dimension f

diminish [dɪˈmɪnɪʃ] diminuer

din [dɪn] brouhaha m

dine [daɪn] dîner

dinghy [ˈdɪŋgɪ] small yacht dériveur m; rubber boat canot m pneumatique

dining car [ˈdaɪnɪŋ] RAIL wagon-restaurant m; **dining room** salle f à manger; in hotel salle f de restaurant

dinner [ˈdɪnər] dîner m; at midday déjeuner m; repas m; **dinner party** dîner m, repas m

dip [dɪp] **1** n for food sauce f (dans laquelle on trempe des aliments); in road inclinaison f **2** v/i of road s'incliner

diploma [dɪˈpləʊmə] diplôme m

diplomacy [dɪˈpləʊməsɪ] also (tact) diplomatie f; **diplomat** diplomate m/f; **diplomatic** diplomatique; (tactful) diplomate

direct [daɪˈrekt] **1** adj direct **2**

v/t to a place indiquer (**to sth** qch); play mettre en scène; movie réaliser; attention diriger

direction [dɪˈrekʃn] direction f; of movie réalisation f; **~s** (instructions) indications fpl; for use mode m d'emploi; for medicine instructions fpl; **ask for ~s** to a place demander son chemin; **directly** (straight) directement; (soon) dans très peu de temps; (immediately) immédiatement; **director** of company directeur(-trice) m(f); of movie réalisateur(-trice) m(f); of play metteur(-euse) m(f) en scène; **directory** répertoire m (d'adresses); TELEC annuaire m (des téléphones)

dirt [dɜːrt] saleté f; **dirty 1** adj sale; (pornographic) cochon **2** v/t salir

disability [dɪsəˈbɪlətɪ] infirmité f; **disabled** handicapé

disadvantage [dɪsədˈvæntɪdʒ] désavantage m; **disadvantaged** défavorisé

disagree [dɪsəˈgriː] of person ne pas être d'accord; **disagreeable** désagréable

disagreement désaccord m; (argument) dispute f

disappear [dɪsəˈpɪr] disparaître; **disappearance** disparition f

disappoint [dɪsəˈpɔɪnt] décevoir; **disappointing** décevant; **disappointment** déception f

disapproval [dɪsə'pruːvl] désapprobation f; **disapprove** désapprouver; ~ **of** *actions* désapprouver; *s.o.* ne pas aimer; **disapproving** désapprobateur

disarm [dɪs'ɑːrm] désarmer; **disarmament** désarmement m

disaster [dɪ'zæstər] désastre m; **disastrous** désastreux

disband [dɪs'bænd] **1** v/t disperser **2** v/i se disperser

disbelief [dɪsbə'liːf] incrédulité f

disc [dɪsk] disque m; **CD** CD m

discard [dɪ'skɑːrd] *old clothes etc* se débarrasser de; *boyfriend* abandonner

disciplinary [dɪsɪ'plɪnərɪ] disciplinaire; **discipline** discipline f

'disc jockey disc-jockey m

disclaim [dɪs'kleɪm] nier

disclose [dɪs'kləʊz] révéler

disco ['dɪskəʊ] discothèque f; *type of dance, music* disco m

discomfort [dɪs'kʌmfərt] gêne f; **be in ~** être incommodé

disconcert [dɪskən'sɜːrt] déconcerter

disconnect [dɪskə'nekt] *hose* détacher; *electrical appliance* débrancher; *supply, phones* couper

discontent [dɪskən'tent] mécontentement m

discontinue [dɪskən'tɪnuː]

product arrêter; *bus service* supprimer

discotheque ['dɪskətek] discothèque f

discount ['dɪskaʊnt] remise f

discourage [dɪs'kʌrɪdʒ] décourager

discover [dɪs'kʌvər] découvrir; **discovery** découverte f

discredit [dɪs'kredɪt] discréditer

discreet [dɪ'skriːt] discret

discrepancy [dɪ'skrepənsɪ] divergence f

discretion [dɪ'skreʃn] discrétion f

discriminate [dɪ'skrɪmɪneɪt]: ~ **against** pratiquer une discrimination contre; **discriminating** avisé; **discrimination** *sexual etc* discrimination f

discuss [dɪs'kʌs] discuter de; *of article* traiter de; **discussion** discussion f

disease [dɪ'ziːz] maladie f

disembark [dɪsəm'bɑːrk] débarquer

disentangle [dɪsən'tæŋgl] démêler

disfigure [dɪs'fɪgər] défigurer

disgrace [dɪs'greɪs] **1** n honte f **2** v/t faire honte à; **disgraceful** honteux

disguise [dɪs'gaɪz] **1** n déguisement m **2** v/t déguiser; *fear, anxiety* dissimuler

disgust [dɪs'gʌst] **1** n dégoût m **2** v/t dégoûter; **disgusting** dégoûtant

dish [dɪʃ] plat *m*; **~es** vaisselle *f*

disheartening [dɪsˈhɑːrtnɪŋ] décourageant

dishonest [dɪsˈɑːnɪst] malhonnête; **dishonesty** malhonnêteté *f*

dishonor [dɪsˈɑːnər] déshonneur *m*; **dishonorable** déshonorant

dishonour *etc Br* → **dishonor** *etc*

disillusion [dɪsɪˈluːʒn] désillusionner; **disillusionment** désillusion *f*

disinfect [dɪsɪnˈfekt] désinfecter; **disinfectant** désinfectant *m*

disinherit [dɪsɪnˈherɪt] déshériter

disintegrate [dɪsˈɪntəgreɪt] se désintégrer; *of marriage* se désagréger

disjointed [dɪsˈdʒɔɪntɪd] décousu

disk [dɪsk] *also* COMPUT disque *m*; *floppy* disquette *f*; **disk drive** COMPUT lecteur *m* de disque/disquette; **diskette** disquette *f*

dislike [dɪsˈlaɪk] **1** *n* aversion *f* **2** *v/t* ne pas aimer

dislocate ['dɪsləkeɪt] disloquer

disloyalty [dɪsˈlɔɪltɪ] déloyauté *f*

dismal ['dɪzməl] *weather* morne; *prospect* sombre; *person (sad)* triste; *person (negative)* lugubre; *failure* lamentable

dismantle [dɪsˈmæntl] *object* démonter; *organization* démanteler

dismay [dɪsˈmeɪ] consternation *f*

dismiss [dɪsˈmɪs] *employee* renvoyer; *idea* écarter; **dismissal** *of employee* renvoi *m*

disobedience [dɪsəˈbiːdɪəns] désobéissance *f*; **disobedient** désobéissant; **disobey** désobéir à

disorganized [dɪsˈɔːrgənaɪzd] désorganisé

disoriented [dɪsˈɔːrɪəntɪd] désorienté

disparaging [dɪˈspærɪdʒɪŋ] désobligeant

disparity [dɪˈspærətɪ] disparité *f*

dispassionate [dɪˈspæʃənət] impartial, objectif

dispatch [dɪˈspætʃ] *(send)* envoyer

disperse [dɪˈspɜːrs] se disperser

display [dɪˈspleɪ] **1** *n of paintings etc* exposition *f*; *of emotion, in store window* étalage *m*; COMPUT affichage *m* **2** *v/t emotion* montrer; *at exhibition, for sale* exposer; COMPUT afficher

displease [dɪsˈpliːz] déplaire à; **displeasure** mécontentement *m*

disposable [dɪˈspouzəbl] jetable; **disposal** *of waste* élimination *f*; *(sale)* cession *f*;

put sth at s.o.'s ~ mettre qch
à la disposition de qn
◆ **dispose of** [dɪ'spəʊz] (*get
rid of*) se débarrasser de
disprove [dɪs'pruːv] *v/t* réfuter
dispute [dɪ'spjuːt] **1** *n* contestation *f*; *between two countries* conflit *m*; **industrial ~**
conflit *m* social **2** *v/t* contester; (*fight over*) se disputer
disqualify [dɪskwɒlɪ-
fɪ'keɪʃn] disqualification *f*;
disqualify disqualifier
disregard [dɪsrə'gɑːrd] **1** *n* indifférence *f* (*for* à l'égard de)
2 *v/t* ne tenir aucun compte
de
disreputable [dɪs'repjʊtəbl]
peu recommandable
disrespect [dɪsrə'spekt]
manque *m* de respect, irrespect *m*; **disrespectful** irrespectueux
disrupt [dɪs'rʌpt] perturber;
disruption perturbation *f*
dissatisfaction [dɪssæt-
ɪs'fækʃn] mécontentement
m; **dissatisfied** mécontent
dissident ['dɪsɪdənt] dissident(e) *m/f*
dissolve [dɪ'zɒlv] **1** *v/t* dissoudre **2** *v/i* se dissoudre
distance ['dɪstəns] distance *f*;
in the ~ au loin; *distant* éloigné; *fig* (*aloof*) distant
distaste [dɪs'teɪst] dégoût *m*;
distasteful désagréable
distinct [dɪ'stɪŋkt] (*clear*) net;
(*different*) distinct; **distinctive** distinctif; **distinctly** dis-

tinctement; (*decidedly*) vraiment
distinguish [dɪ'stɪŋgwɪʃ] distinguer; *~ between X and Y*
distinguer X de Y; **distinguished** distingué
distort [dɪ'stɔːrt] déformer
distract [dɪ'strækt] *person*
distraire; *attention* détourner; **distraught** [dɪ'strɔːt]
angoissé
distress [dɪ'stres] **1** *n* douleur
f **2** *v/t* (*upset*) affliger; **distressing** pénible
distribute [dɪ'strɪbjuːt] *also*
COM distribuer; **distribution**
also COM distribution *f*; *of
wealth* répartition *f*; **distributor** COM distributeur *m*
district ['dɪstrɪkt] *of town*
quartier *m*; *of country* région
f; **district attorney** procureur *m*
distrust [dɪs'trʌst] méfiance
f
disturb [dɪ'stɜːrb] (*interrupt*)
déranger; (*upset*) inquiéter;
disturbance (*interruption*)
dérangement *m*; *~s* (*civil unrest*) troubles *mpl*; **disturbed**
perturbé; *mentally* dérangé;
disturbing dérangeant
disused [dɪs'juːzd] désaffecté
ditch [dɪtʃ] **1** *n* fossé *m* **2** *v/t* F
(*get rid of*) se débarrasser
de; *boyfriend*, *plan* laisser
tomber
dive [daɪv] **1** *n* plongeon *m*;
underwater plongée *f*; *of*

plane (vol *m*) piqué *m*; F *bar etc* bouge *m* **2** *v/i* plonger; *underwater* faire de la plongée sous-marine; *of plane* descendre en piqué; **diver** plongeur(-euse) *m(f)*

diverge [daɪ'vɜːrdʒ] diverger

diversification [daɪvɜːrsɪfɪ-'keɪʃn] COM diversification *f*; **diversify** COM se diversifier

diversion [daɪ'vɜːrʃn] *for traffic* déviation *f*; *to distract attention* diversion *f*; **divert** *traffic* dévier; *attention* détourner

divide [dɪ'vaɪd] (*share*) partager; MATH, *country, family* diviser

dividend ['dɪvɪdend] FIN dividende *m*

diving ['daɪvɪŋ] *from water* plongeon *m*; *underwater* plongée *f* (*sous-marine*); **diving board** plongeoir *m*

division [dɪ'vɪʒn] division *f*

divorce [dɪ'vɔːrs] **1** *n* divorce *m* **2** *v/t* divorcer de **3** *v/i* divorcer; **divorced** divorcé; **divorcee** divorcé(e) *m(f)*

divulge [daɪ'vʌldʒ] divulguer

DIY [diːaɪ'waɪ] (= *do-it-yourself*) bricolage *m*

dizziness ['dɪzɪnɪs] vertige *m*; **dizzy: feel ~** avoir un vertige des vertiges

DJ ['diːdʒeɪ] (= *disc jockey*) D.J. *m/f* (= disc-jockey)

DNA [diːen'eɪ] (= *deoxyribonucleic acid*) AND *m* (= acide *m* désoxyribonucléique)

do [duː] **1** *v/t* faire; **~ one's hair** se coiffer **2** *v/i* (*be suitable, enough*) aller; *that will ~!* ça va!; **~ well** in health, of business aller bien; (*be successful*) réussir; **well done!** (*congratulations*) bien!; **how ~ you ~?** enchanté
◆ **do away with** supprimer
◆ **do up** *building* rénover; *street* refaire; (*fasten*), *coat etc* fermer; *laces* lacer
◆ **do with: I could do with ...** j'aurais bien besoin de ...
◆ **do without 1** *v/i* s'en passer **2** *v/t* se passer de

docile ['dousaɪl] docile

dock[1] [dɑːk] **1** *n* NAUT bassin *m* **2** *v/i of ship* entrer au bassin; *of spaceship* s'arrimer

dock[2] [dɑːk] *n* LAW banc *m* des accusés

doctor ['dɑːktər] MED docteur *m*, médecin *m*; *form of address* docteur; **doctorate** doctorat *m*

doctrine ['dɑːktrɪn] doctrine *f*

document ['dɑːkjumənt] document *m*; **documentary** documentaire *m*; **documentation** documentation *f*

dodge [dɑːdʒ] *blow, person* éviter; *question* éluder

dog [dɔːg] **1** *n* chien *m* **2** *v/t of bad luck* poursuivre

dogma ['dɔːgmə] dogme *m*; **dogmatic** dogmatique

'dog tag MIL plaque *f* d'identification; **dog-tired** F crevé

do-it-yourself [duːɪtjər'self]

337 **download**

bricolage *m*
doldrums ['dəʊldrəmz]: *be in the ~ of economy* être dans le marasme; *of person* avoir le cafard
doll [dɑːl] *also F woman* poupée *f*
dollar ['dɑːlər] dollar *m*
dolphin ['dɑːlfɪn] dauphin *m*
dome [dəʊm] *of building* dôme *m*
domestic [də'mestɪk] *chores* domestique; *news* national; *policy* intérieur; **domestic flight** vol *m* intérieur
dominant ['dɑːmɪnənt] dominant; **dominate** dominer; **domination** domination *f*; **domineering** dominateur
donate [dəʊ'neɪt] faire don de; **donation** don *m*
donkey ['dɑːŋkɪ] âne *m*
donor ['dəʊnər] *of money* donateur(-trice) *m(f)*; MED donneur(-euse) *m(f)*
donut ['dəʊnʌt] beignet *m*
doom [duːm] *(fate)* destin *m*; *(ruin)* ruine *f*; **doomed** *project* voué à l'échec
door [dɔːr] porte *f*; *of car* portière *f*; **doorbell** sonnette *f*; **doorman** portier *m*; **doorway** embrasure *f* de porte
dope [dəʊp] **1** *n (drugs)* drogue *f*; *(idiot)* idiot(e) *m(f)*
dormant ['dɔːrmənt]: *~ volcano* volcan *m* en repos
dormitory ['dɔːrmɪtɔːri] résidence *f* universitaire; *Br* dortoir *m*

dose [dəʊs] dose *f*
dot [dɑːt] point *m*
double ['dʌbl] **1** *n* double *m*; *of film star* double *f* **2** *adj* double **3** *adv* deux fois (plus); **~ the size** deux fois plus grand **4** *v/t & v/i* doubler; **double bed** grand lit *m*; **doublecheck** revérifier; **double-click** double-cliquer; **doublecross** trahir; **doublepark** stationner en double file; **double room** chambre *f* pour deux personnes; **doubles** *in tennis* double *m*
doubt [daʊt] **1** *n* doute *m*; *be in ~* être incertain; *no ~ (probably)* sans doute **2** *v/t* douter de; **doubtful** *look* douteux; *be ~ of person* avoir des doutes; **doubtless** sans aucun doute
dough [dəʊ] pâte *f*
dove [dʌv] colombe *f*
down [daʊn] **1** *adv (downward)* en bas, vers le bas; *~ there* là-bas; *$200 ~ (as deposit)* 200 dollars d'acompte; *~ south* dans le sud; *be ~ of price, numbers* être en baisse; *(not working)* être en panne; F *(depressed)* être déprimé **2** *prep (along)* le long de; *run ~ the stairs* descendre des escaliers en courant; *it's just ~ the street* c'est à deux pas; **down-and-out** clochard(e) *m(f)*; **download** COMPUT **1** *v/t* télécharger **2** *n* fichier *m* téléchargé;

downmarket *Br* bas de gamme; **down payment** paiement *m* au comptant; **downplay** minimiser; **downpour** averse *f*; **downscale** bas de gamme; **downside** (*disadvantage*) inconvénient *m*; **downsize** *car etc* réduire la taille de; *company* réduire les effectifs de; **downstairs** **1** *adj* neighbors *etc* d'en bas **2** *adv* en bas; **down-town 1** *adj* du centre-ville **2** *adv* en ville

doze [dəuz] sommeiller

dozen ['dʌzn] douzaine *f*

draft [dræft] **1** *n* of air courant *m* d'air; of document brouillon *m*; MIL conscription *f*; **~ beer** bière *f* à la pression **2** *v/t* document faire le brouillon de; MIL appeler; **draft dodger** réfractaire *m*; **draftsman** dessinateur(-trice) *m(f)*

drag [dræg] **1** *v/t* traîner, tirer; (*search*) draguer **2** *v/i* of time se traîner; of show, movie traîner en longueur

drain [dreɪn] **1** *n* pipe tuyau *m* d'écoulement; *under street* égout *m* **2** *v/t* oil vidanger; *vegetables* égoutter; *land* drainer; *glass, tank* vider; (*exhaust: person*) épuiser; **drainage** (*drains*) système *m* d'écoulement des eaux usées; *of water from soil* drainage *m*; **drainpipe** tuyau *m* d'écoulement

drama ['drɑ:mə] drame *m*; **dramatic** dramatique; *scenery* spectaculaire; **dramatist** dramaturge *m/f*; **dramatize** *story* adapter (**for** pour); *fig* dramatiser

drapes [dreɪps] rideaux *mpl*

drastic ['dræstɪk] radical; *measures also* drastique

draught [dræft] *Br* → **draft**

draw [drɔ:] **1** *n* in competition match *m* nul; *in lottery* tirage *m* (au sort); (*attraction*) attraction *f* **2** *v/t* picture dessiner; (*pull*), *in lottery, gun* tirer; (*attract*) attirer; (*lead*) emmener; *from bank account* retirer **3** *v/i* of artist dessiner; *in competition* faire match nul

♦ **draw back 1** *v/i* (*recoil*) reculer **2** *v/t* (*pull back*) retirer; *drapes* ouvrir

♦ **draw out** *wallet, from bank* retirer

♦ **draw up 1** *v/t* document rédiger; *chair* approcher **2** *v/i* of vehicle s'arrêter

'drawback désavantage *m*, inconvénient *m*

drawer [drɔ:r] *of desk* tiroir *m*

drawing ['drɔ:ɪŋ] dessin *m*

drawl [drɔ:l] voix *f* traînante

dread [dred]: **~ doing** redouter de faire; **dreadful** épouvantable

dream [dri:m] **1** *n* rêve *m* **2** *v/i* rêver (**about, of** de)

♦ **dream up** inventer

dreary ['drɪrɪ] morne

dress [dres] **1** *n for woman* robe *f*; *(clothing)* tenue *f* **2** *v/t person* habiller; *wound* panser; **get ~ed** s'habiller **3** *v/i* s'habiller

◆ **dress up** s'habiller chic; *(wear a disguise)* se déguiser (**as** en)

'**dress circle** premier balcon *m*; **dresser** *(dressing table)* coiffeuse *f*; *in kitchen* buffet *m*; **dressing** *for salad* assaisonnement *m*; *for wound* pansement *m*; **dress rehearsal** (répétition *f*) générale *f*

dribble ['drɪbl] *of person* baver; *of water* dégouliner; SP dribbler

dried [draɪd] *fruit etc* sec

drier ['draɪər] → **dryer**

drift [drɪft] *of snow* s'amonceler; *of ship* être à la dérive; *(go off course)* dériver; *of person* aller à la dérive; **drifter** personne qui vit au jour le jour

drill [drɪl] **1** *n tool* perceuse *f*; *exercise*, MIL exercice *m* **2** *v/t hole* percer **3** *v/i for oil* forer; MIL faire l'exercice

drily ['draɪlɪ] *say* d'un ton pince-sans-rire

drink [drɪŋk] **1** *n* boisson *f*; **can I have a ~ of water?** est-ce que je peux avoir de l'eau? **2** *v/t & v/i* boire; **I don't ~** je ne bois pas; **drinkable** buvable; *water* potable

drinker ['drɪŋkər] buveur(-eu-

se) *m(f)*; **drinking water** eau *f* potable

drip [drɪp] **1** *n liquid* goutte *f*; MED goutte-à-goutte *m*, perfusion *f* **2** *v/i* goutter

drive [draɪv] **1** *n outing* promenade *f* (en voiture); *(energy)* dynamisme *m*; COMPUT unité *f*, lecteur *m*; *(campaign)* campagne *f* **2** *v/t vehicle* conduire; *(be the owner of)* avoir; *(take in car)* amener; TECH actionner **3** *v/i* conduire; **~ to work** aller au travail en voiture; **drive-in** *movie theater* drive-in *m*

drivel ['drɪvl] bêtises *fpl*

driver ['draɪvər] conducteur (-trice) *m(f)*; *of truck* camionneur(-euse) *m(f)*; COMPUT pilote *m*; **driver's license** permis *m* de conduire

'**driveway** allée *f*; **drive-thru** drive-in *m inv*

drizzle ['drɪzl] **1** *n* bruine *f* **2** *v/i* bruiner

drop [drɑːp] **1** *n* goutte *f*; *in price, temperature* chute *f* **2** *v/t object* faire tomber; *bomb* lancer; *person from car* déposer; *person from team* écarter; *(stop seeing)*, charges, subject laisser tomber; *(give up)* arrêter **3** *v/i* tomber

◆ **drop in** *(visit)* passer

◆ **drop off** *v/t person, goods* déposer **2** *v/i (fall asleep)* s'endormir; *(decline)* diminuer

◆ **drop out** *(withdraw)* se retirer (**of** de); *of school* abandonner (**of sth** qch)

drought [draʊt] sécheresse *f*

drown [draʊn] se noyer

drug [drʌg] **1** *n* MED médicament *m*; *illegal* drogue *f* **2** *v/t* droguer; **drug addict** toxicomane *m/f*; **drug dealer** dealer *m*, dealeuse *f*; *large--scale* trafiquant(e) *m(f)* de drogue; **druggist** pharmacien(ne) *m(f)*; **drugstore** drugstore *m*; **drug trafficking** trafic *m* de drogue

drum [drʌm] MUS tambour *m*; *container* tonneau *m*; **~s** batterie *f*; **drumstick** MUS baguette *f* de tambour

drunk [drʌŋk] **1** *n* ivrogne *m/f*; *habitually* alcoolique *m/f* **2** *adj* v/i soûl; **get ~** se soûler; **drunk driving** conduite *f* en état d'ivresse

dry [draɪ] **1** *adj sec* **2** *v/t clothes* faire sécher; *dishes, eyes* essuyer **3** *v/i* sécher; **dryclean** nettoyer à sec; **dry cleaner** pressing *m*; **dryer** *machine* sèche-linge *m*

dual ['duːəl] double

dub [dʌb] *movie* doubler

dubious ['duːbɪəs] douteux; *I'm still ~ about ...* j'ai encore des doutes quant à ...

duck [dʌk] **1** *n* canard *m*; *female* cane *f* **2** *v/i* se baisser

dud [dʌd] F *(false bill)* faux *m*

due [duː] *(owed)* dû; *the rent is~* **tomorrow** il faut payer le loyer demain

dull [dʌl] *weather* sombre; *sound, pain* sourd; *(boring)* ennuyeux

duly ['duːlɪ] *(as expected)* comme prévu; *(properly)* dûment, comme il se doit

dumb [dʌm] *(mute)* muet; F *(stupid)* bête

dump [dʌmp] **1** *n for garbage* décharge *f*; *(unpleasant place)* trou *m*; *house, hotel* taudis *m* **2** *v/t (deposit)* déposer; *(throw away)* jeter; *(leave)* laisser; *waste* déverser

dune [duːn] dune *f*

duplex (**apartment**) ['duː-pleks] duplex *m*

duplicate ['duːplɪkət] double *m*

durable ['dʊrəbl] *material* résistant

during ['dʊrɪŋ] pendant

dusk [dʌsk] crépuscule *m*

dust [dʌst] **1** *n* poussière *f* **2** *v/t* épousseter; **duster** *chiffon m* (à poussière); **dustpan** pelle *f* à poussière; **dusty** poussiéreux

duty ['duːtɪ] devoir *m*; *(task)* fonction *f*; *on goods* droit(s) *m(pl)*; **be on ~** être de service; **dutyfree** hors taxe

DVD [diːviː'diː] (= **digital versatile disk**) DVD *m*; **DVD-ROM** DVD-ROM *m*

dwarf [dwɔːrf] **1** *n* nain(e) *m(f)* **2** *v/t* rapetisser

dwindle ['dwɪndl] diminuer

dye [daɪ] **1** *n* teinture *f* **2** *v/t*

teindre

dying ['daɪɪŋ] *person* mourant; *industry* moribond; *tradition* qui se perd

dynamic [daɪˈnæmɪk] dynamique; **dynamism** dynamis-

dynasty ['dɪnəstɪ] dynastie *f*

dyslexic [dɪsˈleksɪk] **1** *adj* dyslexique **2** *n* dyslexique *m/f*

E

each [iːtʃ] **1** *adj* chaque **2** *adv* chacun; *they're $1.50 ~* ils coûtent $1.50 chacun, ils sont 1,50 $ pièce **3** *pron* chacun(e) *m(f)*; *~ of them* chacun(e) d'entre eux(elles) *m(f)*; *we know ~ other* nous nous connaissons

eager ['iːgər] désireux; *look* avide; *be ~ to do sth* désirer vivement faire qch; **eagerly** avec empressement; *wait* impatiemment; **eagerness** empressement *m*

eagle ['iːgl] aigle *m*; **eagle-eyed**: *be ~* avoir des yeux d'aigle

ear¹ [ɪr] oreille *f*

ear² [ɪr] *of corn* épi *m*

'earache mal *m* d'oreilles

early ['ɜːrlɪ] **1** *adv* (*not late*) tôt; (*ahead of time*) en avance **2** *adj stages, Romans* premier; *arrival* en avance; *retirement* anticipé; *music* ancien; (*in the near future*) prochain; (*in*) *~ October* début octobre; *have an ~ supper* dîner tôt or de bonne heure; **early bird**: *be an ~* (*early ris-*

er) être matinal

earmark ['ɪrmɑːrk] réserver

earn [ɜːrn] gagner; *interest* rapporter

earnest ['ɜːrnɪst] sérieux

earnings ['ɜːrnɪŋz] salaire *m*; *of company* profits *mpl*

'earphones écouteurs *mpl*;
earring boucle *f* d'oreille

earth [ɜːrθ] terre *f*; **earthen-ware** poterie *f*; **earthly** terrestre; *it's no ~ use doing* ... F ça ne sert strictement à rien de faire cela; **earth-quake** tremblement *m* de terre; **earth-shattering** stupéfiant

ease [iːz] **1** *n* facilité *f*; *feel at ~* se sentir à l'aise **2** *v/t pain, mind* soulager; *suffering, shortage* diminuer **3** *v/i* of pain diminuer

easel ['iːzl] chevalet *m*

easily ['iːzəlɪ] facilement; (*by far*) de loin

east [iːst] **1** *n* est *m* **2** *adj* est *inv*; *wind* d'est **3** *adv travel* vers l'est

Easter ['iːstər] Pâques *fpl*;
Easter Day (jour *m* de) Pâ-

ques *m*; **Easter egg** œuf *m* de Pâques

easterly ['i:stəlɪ] *wind* de l'est; *direction* vers l'est

Easter Monday lundi *m* de Pâques

eastern ['i:stən] de l'est; (*oriental*) oriental; **easterner** habitant(e) *m(f)* de l'Est des États-Unis

Easter Sunday (jour *m* de) Pâques *m*

eastward ['i:stwəd] vers l'est

easy ['i:zɪ] facile; (*relaxed*) tranquille; **easy chair** fauteuil *m*; **easy-going** accommodant

eat [i:t] manger; **eat out** manger au restaurant

eatable ['i:təbl] mangeable

eavesdrop ['i:vzdrɑːp] écouter de façon indiscrète (**on s.o.** qn)

ebb [eb] *of tide* descendre

e-bike ['i:baɪk] vélo *m* électrique, VAE *m*; **e-book** ['i:bʊk] livre *m* électronique; **e-business** commerce *m* électronique

eccentric [ɪk'sentrɪk] **1** *adj* excentrique **2** *n* original(e) *m(f)*; **eccentricity** excentricité *f*

echo ['ekoʊ] **1** *n* écho *m* **2** *v/i* faire écho **3** *v/t* *words* répéter; *views* se faire l'écho de

eclipse [ɪ'klɪps] **1** *n* éclipse *f* **2** *v/t fig* éclipser

ecological [i:kə'lɑːdʒɪkl] écologique; **ecologically** écolo-

giquement; **ecologically friendly** écologique; **ecologist** écologiste *m/f*; **ecology** écologie *f*

economic [i:kə'nɑːmɪk] économique; **economical** (*cheap*) économique; (*thrifty*) économe; **economics** économie *f*; *financial aspects* aspects *mpl* économiques; **economist** économiste *m/f*; **economize** économiser

♦ **economize on** économiser

economy [ɪ'kɑːnəmɪ] économie *f*; **economy class** classe *f* économique

ecosystem ['i:koʊsɪstm] écosystème *m*; **ecotourism** tourisme *m* écologique

ecstasy ['ekstəsɪ] extase *f*; **ecstatic** extatique

eczema ['eksmə] eczéma *m*

edge [edʒ] **1** *n* bord *m*; *of knife* tranchant *m*; **on ~** énervé **2** *v/i* (*move slowly*) se faufiler; **edgewise**: ***I couldn't get a word in ~*** je n'ai pas pu en placer une **F**; **edgy** énervé

edible ['edɪbl] comestible

edit ['edɪt] *text* mettre au point; *book* préparer pour la publication; *newspaper* diriger; *TV program* réaliser; *film* monter; **edition** édition *f*; **editor** *of text, book* rédacteur(-trice) *m(f)*; *of newspaper* rédacteur(-trice) *m(f)* en chef; *of TV program* réalisateur(-trice) *m(f)*; *of film* monteur(-euse) *m(f)*; **edito-**

343　　　　　　　　　　　　　　　　　electrify

rial 1 *adj* de la rédaction 2 *n*
éditorial *m*

educate ['edʒəkeɪt] instruire
(**about** sur); **she was ~d in
France** elle a fait sa scolarité
en France; **educated** instruit; **education** éducation
f; *as subject* pédagogie f; **educational** scolaire; (*informative*) instructif

eerie ['ɪrɪ] inquiétant

effect [ɪ'fekt] effet *m*; **effective** (*efficient*) efficace;
(*striking*) frappant

effeminate [ɪ'femɪnət] efféminé

efficiency [ɪ'fɪʃənsɪ] efficacité f; *in motel* chambre f avec
coin-cuisine; **efficient** efficace; **efficiently** efficacement

effort ['efərt] effort *m*; **effortless** aisé, facile

e.g. [iː'dʒiː] ex; *spoken* par
example

egg [eg] œuf *m*; **eggcup** coquetier *m*; **egghead** F intello
m/f F; **eggplant** aubergine f

ego ['iːgəʊ] PSYCH ego *m*; **egocentric** égocentrique; **egoism** égoïsme *m*; **egoist**
égoïste *m/f*

eiderdown ['aɪdərdaʊn]
(*quilt*) édredon *m*

eight [eɪt] huit; **eighteen** dix-huit; **eighteenth** dix-huitième; **eighth** huitième; **eightieth** quatre-vingtième; **eighty**
quatre-vingts; **~-two/four** *etc*
quatre-vingt-deux/-quatre
etc

either ['iːðər] 1 *adj* l'un ou
l'autre; (*both*) chaque 2 *pron*
l'un(e) ou l'autre 3 *adv*: **I
won't go ~** je n'irai pas non
plus 4 *conj*: **~ ... or** soit
...; *with negative* ni ... ni ...

eject [ɪ'dʒekt] 1 *v/t* éjecter 2
v/i from plane s'éjecter

♦ eke out [iːk] suppléer à l'insuffisance de; **eke out a living** vivoter

el [el] métro *m* aérien

elaborate [ɪ'læbərət] 1 *adj*
compliqué 2 *v/i* [ɪ'læbəreɪt]
donner des détails (**on** sur)

elapse [ɪ'læps] (se) passer

elastic [ɪ'læstɪk] 1 *adj* élastique 2 *n* élastique *m*; **elasticated** élastique

elated [ɪ'leɪtɪd] transporté (de
joie); **elation** exultation f

elbow ['elbəʊ] coude *m*

elder ['eldər] 1 *adj* aîné 2 *n* aî-
né(e) *m(f)*; **elderly** 1 *adj* âgé
2 *npl*: **the ~** les personnes *fpl*
âgées; **eldest** 1 *adj* aîné 2 *n*:
the ~ l'aîné(e) *m(f)*

elect [ɪ'lekt] 1 *adj* élire; **elected** élu;
election élection f; **election
campaign** campagne f élec-
torale; **election day** jour *m*
des élections; **electorate**
électorat *m*

electric [ɪ'lektrɪk] *also fig*
électrique; **electrical** électrique; **electric chair** chaise f
électrique; **electrician** élec-
tricien(ne) *m(f)*; **electricity**
électricité f; **electrify** électri-
fier; *fig* électriser

electrocute [ɪ'lektrəkjuːt] électrocuter

electron [ɪ'lektrɑːn] électron *m*; **electronic** électronique; **electronics** électronique *f*

elegance ['elɪgəns] élégance *f*; **elegant** élégant

element ['elɪmənt] élément *m*; **elementary** élémentaire; **elementary schoo** école *f* primaire

elephant ['elɪfənt] éléphant *m*

elevate ['elɪveɪt] élever; **elevated railroad** métro *m* aérien; **elevation** (*altitude*) altitude *f*; **elevator** ascenseur *m*

eleven [ɪ'levn] onze; **eleventh** onzième

eligible ['elɪdʒəbl]: **be ~ to do sth** avoir le droit de faire qch

eliminate [ɪ'lɪmɪneɪt] éliminer; **elimination** élimination *f*

élite [eɪ'liːt] **1** *n* élite *f* **2** *adj* d'élite

eloquence ['eləkwəns] éloquence *f*; **eloquent** éloquent

else [els]: *anything ~?* autre chose?; *nothing ~* rien d'autre; *no one ~* personne d'autre; *everyone ~ is going* tous les autres y vont; *someone ~* quelqu'un d'autre; *something ~* autre chose; *let's go somewhere ~* allons autre part; *or ~* sinon; *elsewhere* ailleurs

elude [ɪ'luːd] (*escape from*) échapper à; (*avoid*) éviter;

elusive insaisissable

emaciated [ɪ'meɪsɪeɪtɪd] émacié

e-mail ['iːmeɪl] **1** *n* e-mail *m*, courrier *m* électronique **2** *v/t person* envoyer un e-mail à; **e-mail address** adresse *f* e-mail, adresse *f* électronique

emancipation [ɪmænsɪ'peɪʃn] émancipation *f*

embalm [ɪm'bɑːm] embaumer

embankment [ɪm'bæŋkmənt] *of river* berge *f*; RAIL remblai *m*

embargo [em'bɑːrgou] embargo *m*

embark [ɪm'bɑːrk] (s')embarquer

embarrass [ɪm'bærəs] gêner, embarrasser; **embarrassed** gêné, embarrassé; **embarrassing** gênant, embarrassant; **embarrassment** gêne *f*, embarras *m*

embassy ['embəsɪ] ambassade *f*

embezzle [ɪm'bezl] détourner; **embezzlement** détournement *m* de fonds

emblem ['embləm] emblème *m*

embodiment [ɪm'bɑːdɪmənt] personnification *f*; **embody** personnifier

embrace [ɪm'breɪs] **1** *n* étreinte *f* **2** *v/t* (*hug*) serrer dans ses bras, étreindre; (*take in*) embrasser **3** *v/i of two people* se serrer dans les bras, s'étreindre

embroider [ɪm'brɔɪdər] broder; *fig* enjoliver

embryo [ˈembrɪəʊ] embryon *m*; **embryonic** *fig* embryonnaire

emerald [ˈemərəld] émeraude *f*

emerge [ɪ'mɜːrdʒ] sortir; *from mist, of fruit* émerger

emergency [ɪ'mɜːrdʒənsɪ] urgence *f*; **emergency exit** sortie *f* de secours; **emergency landing** atterrissage *m* forcé; **emergency services** services *mpl* d'urgence

emigrate [ˈemɪɡreɪt] émigrer; **emigration** émigration *f*

Eminence [ˈemɪnəns] REL: **His ~** son Éminence; **eminent** éminent

emission [ɪ'mɪʃn] *of gases* émission *f*; **emit** émettre

emotion [ɪ'məʊʃn] émotion *f*; **emotional** *problems* émotionnel, affectif; *(full of emotion)* ému; *reunion* émouvant

emphasis [ˈemfəsɪs] accent *m*; **emphasize** *syllable* accentuer; *fig* souligner; **emphatic** catégorique

empire [ˈempaɪr] *also fig* empire *m*

employ [ɪm'plɔɪ] employer; **employee** employé(e) *m(f)*; **employer** employeur(-euse) *m(f)*; **employment** *(jobs)* emplois *mpl*; *(work)* emploi *m*

emptiness [ˈemptɪnɪs] vide *m*; **empty 1** *adj* vide; *promises* vain **2** *v/t* vider **3** *v/i of room, street* se vider

emulate [ˈemjʊleɪt] imiter

enable [ɪ'neɪbl] permettre

enchanting [ɪn'tʃæntɪŋ] ravissant

encircle [ɪn'sɜːrkl] encercler

enclose [ɪn'kləʊz] *in letter* joindre; *area* entourer; **enclosure** *with letter* pièce *f* jointe

encore [ˈɑːŋkɔːr] bis *m*

encounter [ɪn'kaʊntər] **1** *n* rencontre **2** *v/t person* rencontrer; *problem, resistance* affronter

encourage [ɪn'kʌrɪdʒ] encourager; **encouragement** encouragement *m*; **encouraging** encourageant

encyclopedia [ɪnsaɪklə'piːdɪə] encyclopédie *f*

end [end] **1** *n (conclusion, purpose)* fin *f*; *(extremity)* bout *m*; **in the ~** à la fin **2** *v/t* terminer, finir **3** *v/i* se terminer, finir

◆ end up finir

endanger [ɪn'deɪndʒər] mettre en danger; **endangered species** espèce *f* en voie de disparition

endeavor, *Br* **endeavour** [ɪn'devər] **1** *n* effort *m* **2** *v/t* essayer (**to do sth** de faire qch)

endemic [ɪn'demɪk] endémique

ending ['endɪŋ] fin *f*; GRAM terminaison *f*; **endless** sans fin

endorse [ɪn'dɔːrs] *candidacy* appuyer; *product* associer son image à; **endorsement** *of candidacy* appui *m*; *of product* association *f* de son image à

end 'product produit *m* fini

endurance [ɪn'durəns] *of person* endurance *f*; *of car* résistance *f*; **endure 1** *v/t* endurer **2** *v/i* (*last*) durer; **enduring** durable

enemy ['enəmɪ] ennemi(e) *m(f)*

energetic [enərdʒetɪk] *also fig* énergique; **energy** énergie *f*; **energy supply** alimentation *f* en énergie

enforce [ɪn'fɔːrs] mettre en vigueur

engage [ɪn'geɪdʒ] **1** *v/t* (*hire*) engager **2** *v/i of machine part* s'engrener; **engaged** *to be married* fiancé; *Br* TELEC occupé; **get ~** se fiancer; **engagement** *to be married* fiançailles *fpl*; MIL engagement *m*; **engagement ring** bague *f* de fiançailles

engine ['endʒɪn] moteur *m*; **engineer** ingénieur *m/f*; NAUT, RAIL mécanicien(ne) *m(f)*; **engineering** ingénierie *f*

England ['ɪŋglənd] Angleterre *f*; **English 1** *adj* anglais **2** *n language* anglais *m*; **the** **~** les Anglais *mpl*; **English-man** Anglais *m*; **English-woman** Anglaise *f*

engrave [ɪn'greɪv] graver; **engraving** gravure *f*

engrossed [ɪn'groust]: **~ in** absorbé dans

engulf [ɪn'gʌlf] engloutir

enhance [ɪn'hæns] *flavor* rehausser; *reputation* accroître; *performance* améliorer; *enjoyment* augmenter

enigma [ɪ'nɪgmə] énigme *f*

enjoy [ɪn'dʒɔɪ] aimer; **~ o.s.** s'amuser; **~!** *said to s.o. eating* bon appétit!; **enjoyable** agréable; **enjoyment** plaisir *m*

enlarge [ɪn'lɑːrdʒ] agrandir; **enlargement** agrandissement *m*

enlighten [ɪn'laɪtn] éclairer

enlist [ɪn'lɪst] MIL enrôler

enmity ['enmətɪ] inimitié *f*

enormous [ɪ'nɔːrməs] énorme

enough [ɪ'nʌf] **1** *adj* assez de **2** *pron* assez; **will $50 be ~?** est-ce que $50 suffiront?; **that's ~** ça suffit **3** *adv* assez; **big ~** assez grand

enquire *etc* [ɪn'kwaɪr] → **inquire** *etc*

enroll, *Br* **enrol** [ɪn'roul] s'inscrire

en suite (bathroom) ['ɑːnswiːt] salle *f* de bains attenante

ensure [ɪn'ʃuər] assurer; **~ that ...** s'assurer que ...

entail [ɪn'teɪl] entraîner

entangle [ɪn'tæŋgl] *in rope* empêtrer

enter ['entər] **1** *v/t room, house* entrer dans; *competition* entrer en; COMPUT entrer **2** *v/i* entrer; *in competition* s'inscrire **3** *n* COMPUT touche *f* entrée

enterprise ['entərpraɪz] *(initiative)* (esprit *m* d')initiative *f*; *(venture)* entreprise *f*; **enterprising** entreprenant

entertain [entər'teɪn] *(amuse)* amuser; *(consider: idea)* envisager; **entertainer** artiste *m/f* de variété; **entertaining** amusant, divertissant; **entertainment** divertissement *m*

enthusiasm [ɪn'θuːzɪæzəm] enthousiasme *m*; **enthusiast** enthousiaste *m/f*; **enthusiastic** enthousiaste; **enthusiastically** avec enthousiasme

entire [ɪn'taɪr] entier; **entirely** entièrement

entitle [ɪn'taɪtl]: ~ *s.o. to sth* donner à qn droit à qch; **be** ~*d to* avoir droit à

entrance ['entrəns] entrée *f*

entranced [ɪn'trænst] enchanté

'entrance exam(ination) examen *m* d'entrée

entrant ['entrənt] inscrit(e) *m(f)*

entrepreneur [ɑ:ntrəprə'nɜːr] entrepreneur(-euse) *m(f)*; entrepre-

neurial *skills* d'entrepreneur

entrust [ɪn'trʌst] confier

entry ['entrɪ] entrée *f; for competition: person* participant(e) *m(f)*; **entryphone** interphone *m*

envelop [ɪn'veləp] envelopper

envelope ['envəloup] enveloppe *f*

enviable ['envɪəbl] enviable; envious envieux; **be** ~ **of s.o.** envier qn

environment [ɪn'vaɪrənmənt] environnement *m*; **environmental** écologique; **environmentalist** écologiste *m/f*; **environmentally friendly** écologique; **environs** environs *mpl*

envisage [ɪn'vɪzɪdʒ] envisager

envoy ['envɔɪ] envoyé(e) *m(f)*

envy ['envɪ] **1** *n* envie *f* **2** *v/t*: ~ **s.o. sth** envier qch à qn

epic ['epɪk] **1** *n* épopée *f; movie* film *m* à grand spectacle **2** *adj journey* épique

epicenter, *Br* epicentre ['epɪsentər] épicentre *m*

epidemic [epɪ'demɪk] *also fig* épidémie *f*

episode ['epɪsoud] épisode *m*

epitaph ['epɪtæf] épitaphe *f*

equal ['iːkwl] **1** *adj* égal; **be** ~ **to task** être à la hauteur de **2** *n* égal *m* **3** *v/t* égaler; **equality** égalité *f*; **equalize 1** *v/t* égaliser **2** *v/i Br* SP égaliser; **equalizer** *Br* SP but *m* égalisateur; **equally** *divide* de manière égale; *qualified, intelligent* tout aussi; **equal rights** égalité *f* des droits

equation [ɪ'kweɪʒn] MATH équation *f*

equator [ɪ'kweɪtər] équateur *m*

equip [ɪ'kwɪp] équiper; **equipment** équipement *m*

equity ['ekwətɪ] FIN capitaux *mpl* propres

equivalent [ɪ'kwɪvələnt] **1** *adj* équivalent **2** *n* équivalent *m*

era ['ɪrə] ère *f*

eradicate [ɪ'rædɪkeɪt] éradiquer; **erase** [ɪ'reɪz] effacer

e-reader ['iːriːdər] liseuse *f*

erect [ɪ'rekt] **1** *adj* droit **2** *v/t* ériger, élever; **erection** *of building, penis* érection *f*

ergonomic [ɜːrɡoʊ'nɑːmɪk] ergonomique

erode [ɪ'roʊd] éroder; *fig: power* miner; *rights* supprimer progressivement; **erosion** érosion *f*; *fig: of rights* suppression *f* progressive

errand ['erənd] commission *f*

erratic [ɪ'rætɪk] *performance, course* irrégulier; *driving* capricieux; *behavior* changeant

error ['erər] erreur *f*

erupt [ɪ'rʌpt] *of volcano* entrer en éruption; *of violence* éclater; *of person* exploser F; **eruption** *of volcano* éruption *f*; *of violence* explosion *f*

escalate ['eskəleɪt] s'intensifier; **escalation** intensifica-

tion *f*; **escalator** escalier *m* mécanique, escalator *m*

escape [ɪ'skeɪp] **1** *n of prisoner* évasion *f*; *of animal, gas* fuite *f* **2** *v/i* s'échapper

escort ['eskɔːrt] **1** *n* cavalier (-ière) *m(f)*; *(guard)* escorte *f* **2** *v/t* [ɪ'skɔːrt] *socially* accompagner; *(act as guard to)* escorter

especially [ɪ'speʃlɪ] particulièrement

espionage ['espɪənɑːʒ] espionnage *m*

espresso (coffee) [es'presoʊ] expresso *m*

essay ['eseɪ] *at school* rédaction *f*; *at university* dissertation *f*; *by writer* essai *m*

essential [ɪ'senʃl] essentiel

establish [ɪ'stæblɪʃ] *company* fonder; *(create, determine)* établir; **establishment** *firm, shop etc* établissement *m*

estate [ɪ'steɪt] *land* propriété *f*; *of dead person* biens *mpl*

esthetic [ɪs'θetɪk] esthétique

estimate ['estɪmət] **1** *n* estimation *f*; *from builder etc* devis *m* **2** *v/t* estimer

estuary ['estʃʊwerɪ] estuaire *m*

etc [et'setrə] (= **et cetera**) etc.

eternal [ɪ'tɜːrnl] éternel; **eternity** éternité *f*

ethical ['eθɪkl] *problem* éthique; *(morally right)* moral; **ethics** éthique *f*

ethnic ['eθnɪk] ethnique

EU [iː'juː] (= **European Un-**

ion) U.E. *f* (= Union *f* européenne)

euphemism ['ju:fəmɪzm] euphémisme *m*

euro ['jʊərəʊ] FIN euro *m*

Europe ['jʊərəp] Europe *f*; **European 1** *adj* européen **2** *n* Européen(ne) *m(f)*

euthanasia [ju:θə'neɪzɪə] euthanasie *f*

evacuate [ɪ'vækjʊeɪt] (*clear people from*) faire évacuer; (*leave*) évacuer

evade [ɪ'veɪd] éviter; *question* éluder

evaluate [ɪ'væljʊeɪt] évaluer; **evaluation** évaluation *f*

evaporate [ɪ'væpəreɪt] *also fig* s'évaporer; **evaporation** évaporation *f*

evasion [ɪ'veɪʒn] fuite *f*; **evasive** évasif

eve [i:v] veille *f*

even ['i:vn] **1** *adj breathing* régulier; *distribution* égal; (*level*) plat; *surface* plan; *number* pair; **get ~ with ...** prendre sa revanche sur ... **2** *adv* même; **~ bigger** encore plus grand; **~ not** pas même; **~ so** quand même; **~ if** même si **3** *v/t*: **~ the score** égaliser

evening ['i:vnɪŋ] soir *m*; **in the ~** le soir; **this ~** ce soir; **good ~** bonsoir; **evening class** cours *m* du soir; **evening dress** for woman robe *f* du soir; for man tenue *f* de soirée

evenly ['i:vnlɪ] (*regularly*) de

manière égale; *breathe* régulièrement

event [ɪ'vent] événement *m*; SP épreuve *f*; **eventful** mouvementé

eventually [ɪ'ventʃʊəlɪ] finalement

ever ['evər] jamais; **have you ~ been to Japan?** est-ce que tu es déjà allé au Japon?; **for ~** pour toujours; **~ since** depuis lors; **~ since we ...** depuis le jour où nous ...; **everlasting** éternel

every ['evrɪ]: **~ day** tous les jours, chaque jour; **~ one of ...** chacun de ...; **everybody** → **everyone**; **everyday** de tous les jours; **everyone** tout le monde; **~ who ...** tous ceux qui ...; **everything** tout; **everywhere** partout; (*wherever*) partout où

evict [ɪ'vɪkt] expulser

evidence ['evɪdəns] preuve(s) *f(pl)*; LAW témoignage *m*; **give ~** témoigner; **evident** évident; **evidently** (*clearly*) à l'évidence; (*apparently*) de toute évidence

evil ['i:vl] **1** *adj* mauvais **2** *n* mal *m*

evolution [i:və'lu:ʃn] évolution *f*; **evolve** évoluer

ex [eks] F *wife, husband* ex *m/f*

exact [ɪg'zækt] exact; **exacting** exigeant; **exactly** exactement

exaggerate [ɪg'zædʒəreɪt]

exagérer; **exaggeration** exagération *f*

exam [ıg'zæm] examen *m*; **examination** examen *m*; **examine** examiner

example [ıg'zɑːmpl] exemple *m*; **for ~** par exemple

excavate ['ekskəveıt] (*dig*) excaver; *of archeologist* fouiller; **excavation** excavation *f*; *archeological* fouille(s) *f(pl)*

exceed [ık'siːd] dépasser; *authority* outrepasser; **exceedingly** extrêmement

excel [ık'sel] **1** *v/i* exceller (**at** en) **2** *v/t:* **~ o.s.** se surpasser; **excellence** excellence *f*; **excellent** excellent

except [ık'sept] sauf; **~ for** à l'exception de; **exception** exception *f*; **exceptional** exceptionnel

excerpt ['eksɜːrpt] extrait *m*

excess [ık'ses] **1** *n* excès *m* **2** *adj:* **~ water** excédent *m* d'eau; **excessive** excessif

exchange [ıks'tʃeındʒ] **1** *n* échange *m* **2** *v/t* échanger; **exchange rate** FIN cours *m* du change

excite [ık'saıt] (*make enthusiastic*) enthousiasmer; **excited** excité; **get~** s'exciter; **excitement** excitation *f*; **exciting** passionnant

exclaim [ık'skleım] s'exclamer; **exclamation** exclamation *f*; **exclamation point** point *m* d'exclamation

exclude [ık'skluːd] exclure; **excluding** sauf; **exclusive** *hotel* huppé; *rights, interview* exclusif

excuse [ık'skjuːs] **1** *n* excuse *f* **2** *v/t* [ık'skjuːz] *(forgive)* pardonner; **~ me** excusez-moi

ex-directory *Br:* **be~** être sur liste rouge

execute ['eksıkjuːt] *criminal, plan* exécuter; **execution** *of criminal, plan* exécution *f*; **executive** cadre *m*

exempt [ıg'zempt] exempt

exercise ['eksərsaız] **1** *n* exercice *m* **2** *v/t muscle* exercer; *dog* promener; *caution, restraint* user de **3** *v/i* prendre de l'exercice

exhale [eks'heıl] exhaler

exhaust [ıg'zɔːst] **1** *n fumes* gaz *m* d'échappement; *pipe* tuyau *m* d'échappement **2** *v/t (tire, use up)* épuiser; **exhausted** *(tired)* épuisé; **exhausting** épuisant; **exhaustion** épuisement *m*; **exhaustive** exhaustif

exhibit [ıg'zıbıt] **1** *n in exhibition* objet *m* exposé **2** *v/t of artist* exposer; *(give evidence of)* montrer; **exhibition** exposition *f*; *of bad behavior* étalage *m*; *of skill* démonstration *f*

exhilarating [ıg'zıləreıtıŋ] *weather* vivifiant; *sensation* grisant

exile ['eksaıl] **1** *n* exil *m*; *per-*

son exilé(e) *m(f)* **2** *v/t* exiler

exist [ɪgˈzɪst] exister; **~ on** subsister avec; **existence** existence *f*; **be in ~** exister; **existing** existant

exit [ˈeksɪt] **1** *n* sortie *f* **2** *v/i* COMPUT sortir

exonerate [ɪgˈzɑːnəreɪt] (*clear*) disculper

exotic [ɪgˈzɑːtɪk] exotique

expand [ɪkˈspænd] **1** *v/t* étendre **2** *v/i of population* s'accroître; *of business, city* se développer; *of metal, gas* se dilater; **expanse** étendue *f*; **expansion** *of population* accroissement *m*; *of business, city* développement *m*; *of metal, gas* dilatation *f*

expect [ɪkˈspekt] **1** *v/t also baby* attendre; (*suppose*) penser; (*demand*) exiger **2** *v/i*: **be ~ing** attendre un bébé; **I ~ so** je pense que oui; **expectant mother** future maman *f*; **expectation** attente *f*, espérance *f*

expedition [ekspɪˈdɪʃn] expédition *f*

expel [ɪkˈspel] expulser

expendable [ɪkˈspendəbl] *person* pas indispensable

expenditure [ɪkˈspendɪtʃər] dépenses *fpl* (**on** de)

expense [ɪkˈspens] dépense *f*; **expenses** frais *mpl*; **expensive** cher

experience [ɪkˈspɪrɪəns] **1** *n* expérience *f* **2** *v/t pain, pleasure* éprouver; *difficulty* connaître; **experienced** expérimenté

experiment [ɪkˈsperɪmənt] **1** *n* expérience *f* **2** *v/i* faire des expériences; **experimental** expérimental

expert [ˈekspɜːrt] **1** *adj* expert **2** *n* expert(e) *m(f)*; **expertise** savoir-faire *m*

expiration date [ˈekspɪreɪʃn] date *f* d'expiration; **expire** expirer; **expiry** expiration *f*; **expiry date** *Br* date *f* d'expiration

explain [ɪkˈspleɪn] expliquer; **explanation** explication *f*; **explanatory** explicatif

explicit [ɪkˈsplɪsɪt] *instructions* explicite

explode [ɪkˈsploud] **1** *v/i of bomb, fig* exploser **2** *v/t bomb* faire exploser

exploit[1] [ˈeksplɔɪt] *n* exploit *m*

exploit[2] [ɪkˈsplɔɪt] *v/t person, resources* exploiter

exploitation [eksplɔɪˈteɪʃn] *of person* exploitation *f*

exploration [ekspləˈreɪʃn] exploration *f*; **explore** *country, possibility* explorer; **explorer** explorateur(-trice) *m(f)*

explosion [ɪkˈsplouʒn] *also in population* explosion *f*; **explosive** explosif *m*

export [ˈekspɔːrt] **1** *n* exportation *f* **2** *v/t also* COMPUT exporter; **exporter** exportateur(-trice) *m(f)*

expose [ɪkˈspouz] (*uncover*)

mettre à nu; *scandal* dévoiler; *person* démasquer; **~ X to Y** exposer X à Y; **exposure** exposition *f*; MED effets *mpl* du froid; *of dishonest behavior* dénonciation *f*; PHOT pose *f*; *in media* couverture *f*

express [ɪk'spres] **1** *adj* (*fast*) express; (*explicit*) explicite **2** *n train* express *m* **3** *v/t* exprimer; **expression** expression *f*; **expressive** expressif; **expressly** (*explicitly*) expressément; (*deliberately*) exprès; **expressway** voie *f* express

expulsion [ɪk'spʌlʃn] expulsion *f*

extend [ɪk'stend] **1** *v/t house, garden* agrandir; *search* étendre (**to** à); *runway, contract, visa* prolonger **2** *v/i of garden etc* s'étendre; **extension** *to house* agrandissement *m*; *of contract, visa* prolongation *f*; TELEC poste *m*; **extensive** *search, knowledge* vaste, étendu; *damage* considérable; **extent** étendue *f*, ampleur *f*; **to a certain ~** jusqu'à un certain point

exterior [ɪk'stɪrɪər] **1** *adj* extérieur **2** *n of building* extérieur *m*; *of person* dehors *mpl*

exterminate [ɪk'stɜːrmɪneɪt] exterminer

external [ɪk'stɜːrnl] extérieur

extinct [ɪk'stɪŋkt] *species* disparu; **extinction** *of species* extinction *f*; **extinguish** *fire,*

cigarette éteindre; **extinguisher** extincteur *m*

extortion [ɪk'stɔːrʃn] extortion *f*

extra ['ekstrə] **1** *n* extra *m* **2** *adj* (*spare*) de rechange; (*additional*) en plus; **be ~** (*cost more*) être en supplément **3** *adv* ultra-

extract¹ ['ekstrækt] *n* extrait *m*

extract² [ɪk'strækt] extraire; *tooth* also arracher; *information* arracher; **extraction** extraction *f*

extradite ['ekstrədaɪt] extrader; **extradition** extradition *f*

extramarital [ekstrə'mærɪtl] extraconjugal

extraordinary [ɪkstrə'ɔːrdɪnerɪ] extraordinaire

extra 'time *Br* SP prolongation(s) *f(pl)*

extravagance [ɪk'strævəgəns] dépenses *fpl* extravagantes; *single act* dépense *f* extravagante; **extravagant** *person* dépensier; *price* exorbitant; *claim* excessif

extreme [ɪk'striːm] **1** *n* extrême *m* **2** *adj* extrême; **extremely** extrêmement; **extremist** extrémiste *m/f*

extrovert ['ekstrəvɜːrt] **1** *n* extraverti(e) *m(f)* **2** *adj* extraverti

exuberant [ɪg'zuːbərənt] exubérant

familiar

eye [aɪ] **1** n œil m **2** v/t regarder; **eye-catching** accrocheur; **eyeglasses** lunettes fpl; **eyeliner** eye-liner m;

eyeshadow ombre f à paupières; **eyesight** vue f; **eyewitness** témoin m oculaire

F

fabric ['fæbrɪk] tissu m
fabulous ['fæbjʊləs] fabuleux
façade ['fəˈsɑːd] façade f
face [feɪs] **1** n visage m, figure f **2** v/t person, sea faire face à
◆ **face up to** bully affronter; responsibilities faire face à
'**facecloth** gant m de toilette;
facelift lifting m
facial ['feɪʃl] soin m du visage
facilitate [fəˈsɪlɪteɪt] faciliter;
facilities of school, town etc installations fpl; (equipment) équipements mpl
fact [fækt] fait m; in ~, as a matter of ~ en fait
faction ['fækʃn] faction f
factor ['fæktər] facteur m
faculty ['fækəltɪ] faculté f
fad [fæd] lubie f
fade [feɪd] of colors passer; faded color passé
fag [fæg] pej F (homosexual) pédé m F
fail [feɪl] **1** v/i échouer **2** v/t exam être refusé à; failing défaut m, faiblesse f; failure échec m
faint [feɪnt] **1** adj faible, léger **2** v/i s'évanouir; faintly légèrement
fair[1] [fer] (fun~), COM foire f

fair[2] [fer] hair blond; complexion blanc
fairly ['ferlɪ] treat équitablement; (quite) assez; fairness of treatment équité f
faith [feɪθ] also REL foi f; faithful fidèle; faithfully fidèlement
fake [feɪk] **1** n (article m) faux m **2** adj faux; suicide attempt simulé **3** v/t (forge) falsifier; (feign) feindre; suicide, kidnap simuler
fall[1] [fɔːl] n season automne m
fall[2] [fɔːl] **1** v/i tomber; of prices baisser **2** n chute f; in price, temperature baisse f
◆ **fall behind** prendre du retard
◆ **fall for** person tomber amoureux de; (be deceived by) se laisser prendre à
◆ **fall through** of plans tomber à l'eau
fallible ['fæləbl] faillible
false [fɔːls] faux; false start in race faux départ m; false teeth fausses dents fpl; falsify falsifier
fame [feɪm] célébrité f
familiar [fəˈmɪljər] familier; be ~ with sth bien connaître

qch; **familiarity** *with subject etc* connaissance *f* (**with** de); **familiarize:** ~ *o.s.* **with** se familiariser avec

family ['fæmǝlɪ] famille *f*; **family doctor** médecin *m* de famille; **family planning clinic** centre *m* de planning familial; **family tree** arbre *m* généalogique

famine ['fæmɪn] famine *f*

famous ['feɪmǝs] célèbre

fan¹ [fæn] *n in sport* fana *m/f* F; *of singer, band* fan *m/f*

fan² [fæn] **1** *n electric* ventilateur *m; handheld* éventail *m* **2** *v/t:* ~ *o.s.* s'éventer

fanatical [fǝ'nætɪkl] fanatique; **fanaticism** fanatisme *m*

fantasize ['fæntǝsaɪz] fantasmer (**about** sur); **fantastic** fantastique; **fantasy** *hopeful* rêve *m; unrealistic, sexual* fantasme *m*

fanzine ['fænziːn] fanzine *m*

far [fɑːr] loin; (*much*) bien; ~ **away** très loin; **as** ~ **as the corner** jusqu'au coin

farce [fɑːrs] farce *f*

fare [fer] *for ticket* prix *m* du billet; *for taxi* prix *m*

Far 'East Extrême-Orient *m*

farewell [fer'wel] adieu *m*

farfetched [fɑːr'fetʃ] tiré par les cheveux

farm [fɑːrm] ferme *f*; **farmer** fermier(-ière) *m(f)*; **farming** agriculture *f*; **farmworker** ouvrier(-ière) *m(f)* agricole; **farmyard** cour *f* de ferme

far-'off lointain, éloigné; **far-sighted** prévoyant; *visually* hypermétrope; **farther** plus loin; **farthest** le plus loin

fascinate ['fæsɪneɪt] fasciner; **fascinating** fascinant; **fascination** fascination *f*

fascism ['fæʃɪzm] fascisme *m*; **fascist 1** *n* fasciste *m/f* **2** *adj* fasciste

fashion ['fæʃn] mode *f*; (*manner*) manière *f*, façon *f*; **in** ~ à la mode; **out of** ~ démodé; **fashionable** à la mode; **fashionably** à la mode; **fashion-conscious** au courant de la mode; **fashion designer** créateur(-trice) *m(f)* de mode; **fashion show** défilé *m* de mode

fast¹ [fæst] **1** *adj* rapide; **be** ~ *of clock* avancer **2** *adv* vite; **be** ~ **asleep** dormir à poings fermés

fast² [fæst] *n* (*not eating*) jeûne *m*

fasten ['fæsn] **1** *v/t* attacher; *lid, window* fermer **2** *v/i of dress etc* s'attacher; **fastener** ['fæsnǝr] *for dress* agrafe *f*; *for lid* fermeture *f*

fast 'food fast-food *m*; **fast lane** voie *f* rapide; **fast train** train *m* rapide

fat [fæt] **1** *adj* gros **2** *n on meat* gras *m*; *for baking* graisse *f*

fatal ['feɪtl] *also error* fatal; **fatality** accident *m* mortel; **fatally** fatalement; ~ **injured** mortellement blessé

fate [feɪt] destin *m*

'fat free sans matières grasses; yoghurt etc 0%

father ['fɑ:ðər] père *m*; fatherhood paternité *f*; father-in-law beau-père *m*; fatherly paternel

fatigue [fə'ti:g] fatigue *f*

fatten [fætn] *animal* engraisser; fatty 1 *adj* adipeux 2 *n* F *person* gros(se) *m(f)*

faucet ['fɔ:sɪt] robinet *m*

fault [fɔ:lt] *(defect)* défaut *m*; it's your/my ~ c'est de ta/ma faute; faultless impeccable; faulty défectueux

favor ['feɪvər] 1 *n* faveur *f*; do s.o. a ~ rendre (un) service à qn 2 *v/t (prefer)* préférer; favorable favorable; favorite 1 *n person* préféré(e) *m(f)*; food plat *m* préféré; in race 2 *adj* préféré; favoritism favoritisme *m*

favour *Br* → favor

fax [fæks] 1 *n* fax *m* 2 *v/t* faxer

fear [fɪr] 1 *n* peur *f* 2 *v/t* avoir peur de; fearless sans peur; fearlessly sans peur

feasibility study [fi:zə'bɪlətɪ] étude *f* de faisabilité; feasible faisable

feast [fi:st] festin *m*

feat [fi:t] exploit *m*

feather ['feðər] plume *f*

feature ['fi:tʃər] on face trait *m*; of city, building, style caractéristique *f*; article in paper chronique *f*; feature film long métrage *m*

February ['februərɪ] février *m*

federal ['fedərəl] fédéral; federation fédération *f*

fed 'up I: be ~ with en avoir ras-le-bol de F

fee [fi:] of lawyer, doctor etc honoraires *mpl*; for membership frais *mpl*

feeble ['fi:bl] faible

feed [fi:d] nourrir; feedback réactions *fpl*

feel [fi:l] 1 *v/t (touch)* toucher; *(sense)* sentir; pain, pleasure ressentir; *(think)* penser 2 *v/i*: it ~s like silk on dirait de la soie; do you ~ like a drink? est-ce que tu as envie de boire quelque chose?
♦ feel up to se sentir capable de

feeler ['fi:lər] of insect antenne *f*; feeling sentiment *m*; *(sensation)* sensation *f*

fellow 'citizen concitoyen(ne) *m(f)*

felony ['felənɪ] crime *m*

felt [felt] feutre *m*; felt tip stylo *m* feutre

female ['fi:meɪl] 1 *adj* femelle; relating to people féminin 2 *n* femelle *f*; person femme *f*

feminine ['femɪnɪn] 1 *adj* féminin 2 *n* GRAM féminin *m*; feminism féminisme *m*; feminist 1 *n* féministe *m/f* 2 *adj* féministe

fence [fens] barrière *f*, clôture *f*

fender ['fendər] MOT aile *f*

fermentation [fɜːrmen'teɪʃn]

fermentation f

ferocious [fəˈrouʃəs] féroce
ferry [ˈferɪ] ferry m
fertile [ˈfɜːtl] fertile; **fertility**
fertilité f; **fertilize** féconder;
fertilizer for soil engrais m
fervent [ˈfɜːrvənt] fervent
fester [ˈfestər] of wound sup-
purer
festival [ˈfestɪvl] festival m;
festive de fête; **festivities**
festivités fpl
fetal [ˈfiːtl] fœtal
fetch [fetʃ] (go and ~) aller
chercher (**from** à); (come
and ~) venir chercher (**from**
à); price atteindre
fetus [ˈfiːtəs] fœtus m
feud [fjuːd] querelle f
fever [ˈfiːvər] fièvre f; **fever-**
ish also fig fiévreux
few [fjuː] **1** adj (not many) peu
de; **a ~ ...** quelques; **quite a**
~, a good ~ (a lot) beaucoup
de **2** pron (not many) peu; **a**
~ quelques-un(e)s m(f); **quite**
a ~, a good ~ beaucoup; **few-**
er moins de
fiancé [fɪˈɑːnseɪ] fiancé m; **fi-**
ancée fiancée f
fiber [ˈfaɪbər] fibre f; **fiber-**
glass n fibre f de verre; **fiber**
optics fibres fpl optiques
fibre Br → **fiber**
fickle [ˈfɪkl] inconstant
fiction [ˈfɪkʃn] romans mpl;
(made-up story) fiction f; **fic-**
tional de roman; **fictitious**
fictif
fiddle [ˈfɪdl] **1** n (violin) violon

m **2** v/i: **~ around with** tripoter **3** v/t accounts, results truquer
fidgety [ˈfɪdʒɪtɪ] remuant
field [fiːld] champ m; for sport
terrain m; (competitors in
race) concurrent(e)s m(f)pl;
fielder in baseball joueur m
de champ
fierce [fɪrs] animal féroce;
wind, storm violent; **fiercely**
avec férocité
fiery [ˈfaɪrɪ] ardent, fougueux
fifteen [fɪfˈtiːn] quinze; **fif-**
teenth quinzième; **fifth** cinquième; **fiftieth** cinquantième; **fifty** cinquante; **fifty-fifty**
moitié-moitié
fight [faɪt] **1** n combat m; (argument) dispute f; for surviv-
al etc lutte f **2** v/t enemy, person combattre; in boxing se
battre contre; injustice lutter
contre **3** v/i se battre; (argue)
se disputer; **fighter** combat-
tant(e) m(f); airplane avion
m de chasse; (boxer) boxeur
m; **fighting** physical combat
m; verbal dispute f
figure [ˈfɪgjər] **1** n (digit) chiffre m; of person ligne f;
(form, shape) figure f **2** v/t
F (think) compter
◆ **figure on** F (plan) compter
◆ **figure out** comprendre;
calculation calculer
file¹ [faɪl] **1** n of documents
dossier m; COMPUT fichier m
2 v/t documents classer
file² [faɪl] for wood etc lime f

'file cabinet classeur *m*
fill [fɪl] remplir; *tooth* plomber; *prescription* préparer
◆ **fill in** *form* remplir; *hole* boucher
◆ **fill out 1** *v/t form* remplir **2** *v/i (get fatter)* grossir
fillet ['fɪlɪt] filet *m*
filling ['fɪlɪŋ] **1** *n in sandwich* garniture *f*; *in tooth* plombage *m* **2** *adj food* nourrissant; **filling station** station-service *f*
film [fɪlm] **1** *n* pellicule *f*; *(movie)* film *m* **2** *v/t* filmer; **film-maker** réalisateur(-trice) *m(f)* de films; **film star** star *f* de cinéma
filter ['fɪltər] **1** *n* filtre *m* **2** *v/t* filtrer
filth [fɪlθ] saleté; **filthy** sale; *language etc* obscène
final ['faɪnl] **1** *adj* dernier; *decision* définitif, irrévocable **2** *n* SP finale *f*; **finale** apothéose *f*; **finalist** finaliste *m/f*; **finalize** finaliser, mettre au point; **finally** finalement, enfin
finance ['faɪnæns] **1** *n* finance *f*; *(funds)* financement *m* **2** *v/t* financer; **financial** financier; **financially** financièrement; **financier** financier (-ière) *m(f)*
find [faɪnd] trouver
◆ **find out** découvrir; *(enquire about)* se renseigner sur
findings ['faɪndɪŋz] *of report*

constatations *fpl*
fine¹ [faɪn] *day* beau; *(good)* bon, excellent; *distinction* subtil; *line* fin; **how's that? – that's ~** que dites-vous de ça? – c'est bien
fine² [faɪn] **1** *n* amende *f* **2** *v/t* condamner à une amende de $5.000
finger ['fɪŋgər] **1** *n* doigt *m* **2** *v/t* toucher; **fingerprint** empreinte *f* digitale
finicky ['fɪnɪkɪ] *person* tatillon; *design* alambiqué
finish ['fɪnɪʃ] **1** *v/t* finir, terminer **2** *n* finish *m* **3** *n of product* finition *f*; *of race* arrivée *f*
◆ **finish with** *boyfriend etc* en finir avec
fire ['faɪr] **1** *n* feu *m*; *(blaze)* incendie *m*; *(electric, gas)* radiateur *m*; **be on ~** être en feu; **set ~ to sth** mettre le feu à qch **2** *v/i (shoot)* tirer **3** *v/t F (dismiss)* virer F; **fire alarm** signal *m* d'incendie; **firearm** arme *f* à feu; **firecracker** pétard *m*; **fire department** sapeurs-pompiers *mpl*; **fire engine** *esp Br* voiture *f* de pompiers; **fire escape** *ladder* échelle *f* de secours; *stairs* escalier *m* de secours; **fire extinguisher** extincteur *m* d'incendie; **fire fighter** pompier *m*; **fireplace** cheminée *f*; **fire station** caserne *f* de pompiers; **fire truck** voiture *f* de pompiers; **firework** pièce *f* d'artifice; **~s**

(*display*) feu *m* d'artifice

firm[1] [fɜːrm] *adj* ferme

firm[2] [fɜːrm] *n* COM firme *f*

first [fɜːrst] **1** *adj* premier **2** *n*
premier(-ière) *m(f)* **3** *adv* arrive, finish le/la premier(-ière) *m(f)*; (*beforehand*)
d'abord; **at ~** au début; **first
aid** premiers secours *mpl*;
first class 1 *adj* ticket de première classe; (*very good*) de
première qualité **2** *adv* travel
en première classe; **first
floor** rez-de-chaussée *m*; *Br*
premier étage *m*; **First Lady**
première dame *f*; **firstly** premièrement; **first name** prénom *m*; **first night** première
f; **first-rate** de premier ordre

fiscal ['fɪskl] fiscal; **fiscal year**
année *f* fiscale

fish [fɪʃ] **1** *n* poisson *m* **2** *v/i*
pêcher; **fisherman** pêcheur
m; **fishing** pêche *f*; **fishing
boat** bateau *m* de pêche;
fish stick bâtonnet *m* de
poisson; **fishy** F (*suspicious*)
louche

fist [fɪst] poing *m*

fit[1] [fɪt] *n* MED crise *f*, attaque *f*

fit[2] [fɪt] *adj* physically en forme; *morally* digne

fit[3] [fɪt] **1** *v/t* of clothes aller à;
(*install, attach*) poser; *it
doesn't ~ me any more* je
ne rentre plus dedans **2** *v/i*
of clothes aller

fitness ['fɪtnɪs] physical (bonne) forme *f*; **fitting** approprié; **fittings** installations *fpl*

five [faɪv] cinq

fix [fɪks] **1** *n* (*solution*) solution
f **2** *v/t* (*attach*) attacher; (*repair*) réparer; *meeting etc* arranger; *lunch* préparer; *dishonestly: match etc* truquer;
fixed fixe; **fixings** garniture *f*

flab [flæb] *on body* graisse *f*;
flabby muscles etc mou

flag[1] [flæg] *n* drapeau *m*; NAUT
pavillon *m*

flag[2] [flæg] *v/i* (*tire*) faiblir

flagpole mât *m* (de drapeau)

flagrant ['fleɪgrənt] flagrant

flair [fler] (*talent*) flair *m*; **have
a natural ~ for** avoir un don
pour

flake [fleɪk] *n of snow* flocon *m*;
of plaster écaille *f*

flamboyant [flæm'bɔɪənt] extravagant; **flamboyantly**
avec extravagance

flame [fleɪm] flamme *f*

flammable ['flæməbl] inflammable

flank [flæŋk] **1** *n* flanc *m* **2** *v/t*:
be ~ed by être flanqué de

flap [flæp] **1** *n of envelope,
pocket* rabat *m* **2** *v/t* wings
battre **3** *v/i of flag etc* battre

◆ **flare up** [fler] *of violence,
rash* éclater; *of fire* s'enflammer; (*get very angry*) s'emporter

flash [flæʃ] **1** *n of light* éclair
m; PHOT flash *m*; *in a ~* F en
un rien de temps; *~ of lightning* éclair *m* **2** *v/i of light* clignoter; **flashback** *in movie*
flash-back *m*; **flashlight** lam-

flow

pe f de poche; PHOT flash m;
flashy pej voyant
flask [flæsk] (*hip* ~) fiole f
flat[1] [flæt] **1** *adj* plat; *beer*
éventé; *battery, tire* à plat;
bémol **2** *adv* MUS trop bas **3**
n pneu m crevé
flat[2] [flæt] *n* Br (*apartment*)
appartement m
flatly ['flætlɪ] *deny* catégoriquement; **flat rate** tarif m
unique; **flatten** *land, road*
aplanir; *by bombing, demolition* raser
flatter ['flætər] flatter; **flatterer** flatteur(-euse) m(f); **flattering** *comments* flatteur;
color, clothes avantageux;
flattery flatterie f
flavor ['fleɪvər] **1** *n* goût m; *of
ice cream* parfum m **2** *v/t
food* assaisonner; **flavoring**
arôme m
flavour Br → **flavor**
flaw [flɔː] défaut m; **flawless**
parfait
flee [fliː] s'enfuir
fleet [fliːt] NAUT flotte f; *of vehicles* parc m
fleeting ['fliːtɪŋ] *visit etc* très
court
flesh [fleʃ] *also of fruit* chair f
flex [fleks] *muscles* fléchir;
flexibility flexibilité f; **flexible** flexible; **flextime** horaire
m à la carte
flicker ['flɪkər] vaciller
flier ['flaɪr] (*circular*) prospectus m
flight [flaɪt] *in airplane* vol m;

(*fleeing*) fuite f; ~ (*of stairs*)
escalier m; **flight attendant**
male steward m; *female* hôtesse f de l'air; **flight path**
trajectoire f de vol; **flight recorder** enregistreur m de vol;
flight time *departure* heure f
de vol; *duration* durée f de
vol; **flighty** frivole
flimsy ['flɪmzɪ] *furniture* fragile; *dress, material* léger; *excuse* faible
flinch [flɪntʃ] tressaillir
flipper ['flɪpər] nageoire f
flirt [flɜːrt] **1** *v/i* flirter **2** *n* flir-
teur(-euse) m(f); **flirtatious**
flirteur
float [floʊt] *also* FIN flotter
flock [flɑːk] **1** *n of sheep* troupeau m **2** *v/i* venir en masse
flood [flʌd] **1** *n* inondation f **2**
v/t of river inonder; **flooding**
inondation(s) f(pl)
'**floodlight** projecteur m;
flood waters inondations fpl
floor [flɔːr] sol m; *wooden*
plancher m; (*story*) étage m
flop [flɑːp] **1** *v/i* s'écrouler; *F
(fail)* faire un bide F **2** *n* F
(*failure*) bide m F; **floppy**
(*disk*) disquette f
florist ['flɔːrɪst] fleuriste m/f
flour ['flaʊr] farine f
flourish ['flʌrɪʃ] *of plants*
fleurir; *fig* prospérer; **flourishing** *business* fleurissant,
prospère
flow [floʊ] **1** *v/i of river* couler;
of electric current passer; *of
traffic* circuler; *of work* se

dérouler **2** *n of river* cours *m*; *of information* circulation *f*; **flowchart** organigramme *m*

flower ['flaur] **1** *n* fleur *f* **2** *v/i* fleurir

flu [flu:] grippe *f*

fluctuate ['flʌktʃueɪt] fluctuer; **fluctuation** fluctuation *f*

fluency ['flu:ənsɪ] *in a language* maîtrise *f* (*in* de); **fluent** *person* qui s'exprime avec aisance; **he speaks ~ Spanish** il parle couramment l'espagnol; **fluently** couramment; *in own language* avec aisance

fluid ['flu:ɪd] fluide *m*

flunk [flʌŋk] F *subject* rater

flush [flʌʃ] **1** *v/t*: **~ the toilet** tirer la chasse d'eau **2** *v/i* (*go red*) rougir

flutter ['flʌtər] *of bird* voleter; *of wings* battre; *of flag* s'agiter; *of heart* palpiter

fly[1] [flaɪ] *n* (*insect*) mouche *f*

fly[2] [flaɪ] *n on pants* braguette *f*

fly[3] [flaɪ] **1** *v/i* voler; *in airplane* prendre l'avion; *of flag* flotter **2** *v/t airplane* piloter, voler; *airline* voyager par; (*transport by air*) envoyer par avion

◆ **fly past** *of time* filer

flying ['flaɪɪŋ]: **I hate ~** je déteste prendre l'avion

foam [foum] *on sea* écume *f*; *on drink* mousse *f*; **foam rubber** caoutchouc *m* mous-

se

focus ['foukəs] *of attention* centre *m*; PHOT mise *f* au point

◆ **focus on** se concentrer sur; PHOT mettre au point sur

fodder ['fɑːdər] fourrage *m*

fog [fɑːg] brouillard *m*; **foggy** brumeux

foil[1] [fɔɪl] *n silver* feuille *f* d'aluminium

foil[2] [fɔɪl] *v/t* (*thwart*) faire échouer

fold [fould] **1** *v/t paper etc* plier; **~ one's arms** croiser les bras **2** *v/i of business* fermer (ses portes) **3** *n in cloth etc* pli *m*

◆ **fold up 1** *v/t* plier **2** *v/i of chair, table* se (re)plier

folder ['fouldər] *for documents* chemise *f*; COMPUT dossier *m*; **folding** pliant

foliage ['foulɪdʒ] feuillage *m*

folk [fouk] (*people*) gens *mpl*; **folk music** folk *m*; **folk singer** chanteur(-euse) *m(f)* de folk

follow ['fɑːlou] **1** *v/t also* (*understand*) suivre **2** *v/i logically* s'ensuivre

◆ **follow up** *inquiry* donner suite à

follower ['fɑːlouər] *of politician etc* partisan(e) *m(f)*; *of football team* supporteur (-trice) *m(f)*; **following 1** *adj* suivant **2** *n people* partisans *mpl*

fond [fɑːnd] (*loving*) aimant;

memory agréable; *be ~ of* beaucoup aimer

fondle ['fɑːndl] caresser

fondness ['fɑːndnɪs] *for s.o.* tendresse *f*; *for sth* penchant *m*

font [fɑːnt] *for printing* police *f*; *in church* fonts *mpl* baptismaux

food [fuːd] nourriture *f*; *French* ~ la cuisine française; **food poisoning** intoxication *f* alimentaire

fool [fuːl] **1** *n* idiot(e) *m(f)* **2** *v/t* berner; **foolhardy** téméraire; **foolish** bête; **foolproof** à toute épreuve

foot [fʊt] *also measurement* pied *m*; *of animal* patte *f*; *put one's ~ in it* F mettre les pieds dans le plat; **footage** séquences *fpl*; **football** *football m américain*; football F; *(ball)* ballon *m* de football; **football player** joueur(-euse) *m(f)* de football américain; *soccer* joueur(-euse) *m(f)* de football; **foothills** contreforts *mpl*; **footnote** note *f* (de bas de page); **footpath** sentier *m*; **footprint** trace *f* de pas; **footstep** pas *m*

for [fər], [fɔːr] pour; *a train* ~ ... un train à destination de ...; *what is this* ~? pour quoi est-ce que c'est fait?; *what* ~? pourquoi?; ~ *three days* pendant trois jours; *it lasted* ~ *three days* ça a duré trois

jours; *I've been waiting* ~ *an hour* j'attends depuis une heure

forbid [fər'bɪd] interdire; **forbidden** interdit; **forbidding** menaçant

force [fɔːrs] **1** *n* force *f*; *come into* ~ *of law etc* entrer en vigueur **2** *v/t door, lock* forcer; ~ *s.o. to do sth* forcer qn à faire qch; **forced** forcé; **forced landing** atterrissage *m* forcé; **forceful** *argument, speaker* puissant; *character* énergique

forceps ['fɔːrseps] MED forceps *m*

forcibly ['fɔːrsəblɪ] *restrain* par force

foreboding [fər'boʊdɪŋ] pressentiment *m*; **forecast 1** *n of results* pronostic *m*; *of weather* prévisions *fpl* **2** *v/t result* pronostiquer; *future, weather* prévoir; **forefathers** ancêtres *mpl*; **forefinger** index *m*; **foreground** premier plan *m*; **forehead** front *m*

foreign ['fɔːrən] étranger; **foreign affairs** affaires *fpl* étrangères; **foreign body** corps *m* étranger; **foreign currency** devises *fpl* étrangères; **foreigner** étranger (-ère) *m(f)*; **foreign exchange** devises *fpl* étrangères

'foreman chef *m* d'équipe; **foremost 1** *adv* (*uppermost*) le plus important **2** *adj* (*lead-*

ing) premier

forensic 'medicine [fəˈrensɪk] médecine *f* légale; **forensic scientist** expert *m* légiste

'forerunner *person* prédécesseur *m*; *thing* ancêtre *m/f*; **foresee** prévoir; **foresight** prévoyance *f*

forest [ˈfɒrɪst] forêt *f*; **forestry** sylviculture *f*

fore'tell prédire

forever [fəˈrevər] toujours

'foreword avant-propos *m*

forfeit [ˈfɔːrfɪt] (*lose*) perdre; (*give up*) renoncer à

forge [fɔːrdʒ] contrefaire; **forgery** *bank bill* faux billet *m*; *document* faux *m*; *signature* contrefaçon *f*

forget [fərˈget] oublier; **forgetful: you're so ~** tu as vraiment mauvaise mémoire

forgive [fərˈgɪv] **1** *v/t*: **~ s.o. sth** pardonner qch à qn **2** *v/i* pardonner; **forgiveness** pardon *m*

fork [fɔːrk] fourchette *f*; *for gardening* fourche *f*; *in road* embranchement *m*

form [fɔːrm] **1** *n* (*shape*) forme *f*; *document* formulaire *m* **2** *v/t* former; *friendship* développer; *opinion* se faire **3** *v/i* (*take shape, develop*) se former; **formal** *language* soutenu; *dress* de soirée; *manner, reception* cérémonieux; *recognition etc* officiel; **formality** *of language*

caractère *m* soutenu; *of occasion* cérémonie *f*; **it's just a ~** c'est juste une formalité; **formally** *speak* cérémonieusement; *recognized* officiellement

format [ˈfɔːrmæt] **1** *v/t* formater **2** *n* format *m*

formation [fɔːrˈmeɪʃn] formation *f*

former [ˈfɔːrmər] ancien; **the ~** le premier, la première; **formerly** autrefois

formidable [ˈfɔːrmɪdəbl] redoutable

formula [ˈfɔːrmjʊlə] MATH, CHEM formule *f*; *fig* recette *f*

fort [fɔːrt] MIL fort *m*

forthcoming [ˈfɔːrθkʌmɪŋ] (*future*) futur; *personality* ouvert

'forthright franc

fortieth [ˈfɔːrtɪɪθ] quarantième

fortnight [ˈfɔːrtnaɪt] *Br* quinze jours *mpl*, quinzaine *f*

fortress [ˈfɔːrtrɪs] MIL forteresse *f*

fortunate [ˈfɔːrtʃənət] *decision* heureux; **be ~** avoir de la chance; **fortunately** heureusement; **fortune** (*fate*) destin *m*; (*luck*) chance *f*; (*lot of money*) fortune *f*

forty [ˈfɔːrtɪ] quarante

forward [ˈfɔːrwərd] **1** *adv* en avant **2** *adj pej*: *person* effronté **3** *n* SP avant *m* **4** *v/t* *letter* faire suivre; **forward-looking** moderne

363   freezer

fossil ['fɒsɪl] fossile *m*
foster ['fɒstər] *child* servir de
famille d'accueil à; *attitude,*
belief encourager
foul [faʊl] **1** *n* SP faute *f* **2** *adj*
smell infect; *weather* sale **3**
v/t SP commettre une faute
contre
found [faʊnd] *school etc* fonder; **foundation** *of theory*
etc fondement *m*; (*organiza-*
tion) fondation *f*; **founda-**
tions *of building* fondations
fpl; **founder** fondateur(-tri-
ce) *m(f)*
fountain ['faʊntɪn] fontaine *f*;
with vertical spout jet *m*
d'eau
four [fɔːr] quatre; **four-star**
quatre étoiles; **fourteen** quatorze; **fourteenth** quatorziè-
me; **fourth** quatrième; **four-**
wheel drive MOT quatre-qua-
tre *m*
fox [fɒks] **1** *n* renard *m* **2** *v/t*
(*puzzle*) mystifier
foyer ['fɔɪər] hall *m* d'entrée
fraction ['frækʃn] fraction *f*;
fractionally très légèrement
fracture ['fræktʃər] **1** *n* fracture *f* **2** *v/t* fracturer
fragile ['frædʒəl] fragile
fragment ['frægmənt] fragment *m*
fragrance ['freɪɡrəns] parfum
m; **fragrant** parfumé
frail [freɪl] frêle, fragile
frame [freɪm] **1** *n of picture,*
bicycle cadre *m*; *of window*
châssis *m*; *of eyeglasses* mon-

ture *f* **2** *v/t picture* encadrer;
F *person* monter un coup
contre; **framework** structure
f; **within the ~ of** dans le cadre de
France [frɑːns] France *f*
franchise ['fræntʃaɪz] *for*
business franchise *f*
frank [fræŋk] franc; **frankly**
franchement; **frankness**
franchise *f*
frantic ['fræntɪk] frénétique
fraternal [frə'tɜːrnl] fraternel
fraud [frɔːd] fraude *f*; *person*
imposteur *m*; **fraudulent**
frauduleux
frayed [freɪd] *cuffs* usé
freak [friːk] **1** *n* (*unusual*
event) phénomène *m* étran-
ge; (*two-headed animal etc*)
monstre *m*; F (*strange per-*
son) taré(e) *m(f)*F **2** *adj*
storm etc anormalement violent
free [friː] **1** *adj* libre; *no cost*
gratuit **2** *v/t prisoners* libérer;
freedom liberté *f*; **free en-**
terprise libre entreprise *f*;
free kick *in soccer* coup *m*
franc; **freelance** indépendant, free-lance *inv*; **freely**
admit volontiers; **free**
speech libre parole *f*; **free-**
way autoroute *f*
freeze [friːz] *v/t* congeler;
bank account bloquer; **~ a**
video faire un arrêt sur image **2** *v/i of water* geler;
freeze-dried lyophilisé;
freezer congélateur *m*;

freezing 1 *adj* glacial **2** *n*: **10 below** ~ 10 degrés au-dessous de zéro

freight [freɪt] fret *m*; **freighter** shipcargo *m*; airplane avion-cargo *m*

French [frentʃ] **1** *adj* français **2** *n* language français *m*; **the** ~ les Français *mpl*; **French fries** frites *fpl*; **Frenchman** Français *m*; **Frenchwoman** Française *f*

frenzied ['frenzɪd] attack, activity forcené; mob déchaîné; **frenzy** frénésie *f*

frequency ['friːkwənsɪ] also of radio fréquence *f*

frequent¹ adj fréquent

frequent² [frɪ'kwent] *v/t bar etc* fréquenter

frequently ['friːkwəntlɪ] fréquemment

fresh [freʃ] frais; start nouveau; sheets propre; (impertinent) insolent; **fresh air** air *m*
◆ **freshen up 1** *v/i* se rafraîchir **2** *v/t paintwork* rafraîchir
freshly ['freʃlɪ] fraîchement; **freshman** étudiant(e) *m(f)* de première année; **freshwater** d'eau douce

fret [fret] s'inquiéter

friction ['frɪkʃn] friction *f*

Friday ['fraɪdeɪ] vendredi *m*

fridge [frɪdʒ] frigo *m* F

friend [frend] ami(e) *m(f)*; **friendliness** amabilité *f*; **friendly** amical; hotel, city sympathique; argument entre amis; **friendship** amitié *f*

fries [fraɪz] frites *fpl*

fright [fraɪt] peur *f*; **frighten** faire peur à; **be ~ed** avoir peur (**of** de); **frightening** effrayant

frill [frɪl] on dress etc, (extra) falbala *m*

fringe [frɪndʒ] frange *f*; of city périphérie *f*; of society marge *f*; **fringe benefits** avantages *mpl* sociaux

frisk [frɪsk] fouiller
◆ **fritter away** ['frɪtər] time, fortune gaspiller

frivolity [frɪ'vɑːlətɪ] frivolité *f*; **frivolous** frivole

frizzy ['frɪzɪ] hair crépu

frog [frɑːg] grenouille *f*; **frogman** homme-grenouille *m*

from [frɑːm] ◊ de; ~ **9 to 5 (o'clock)** de 9 heures à 5 heures; ~ **the 18th century** à partir du XVIIIe siècle; ~ **today on** à partir d'aujourd'hui; ~ **here to there** d'ici à là(-bas); **I am** ~ **New Jersey** je viens du New Jersey; **tired** ~ **the journey** fatigué du voyage; **it's** ~ **overeating** c'est d'avoir trop mangé

front [frʌnt] **1** *n* of building façade *f*, devant *m*; of book devant *m*; (cover organization) façade *f*; MIL, of weather front *m*; **in** ~ devant; **in** ~ **in a race** en tête; **in** ~ **of** devant **2** *adj wheel, seat* avant **3** *v/t TV program* présenter; **front door** porte *f* d'entrée

frontier ['frʌntɪr] also fig

frontière *f*

'front line MIL front *m*; **front page** *of newspaper* une *f*; **front-wheel drive** traction *f* avant

frost [frɒst] gel *m*; **frostbite** gelure *f*; **frosting** *on cake* glaçage *m*; **frosty** *also fig* glacial

froth [frɒθ] écume *f*, mousse *f*

frown [fraʊn] froncer les sourcils

frozen ['frəʊzn] gelé; *food* surgelé

fruit [fruːt] fruit *m*; *collective* fruits *mpl*; *fruitful discussions etc* fructueux; **fruit juice** jus *m* de fruit; **fruit salad** salade *f* de fruits

frustrate ['frʌstreɪt] *person* frustrer; *plans* contrarier; **frustrating** frustrant; **frustration** frustration *f*

fry [fraɪ] (faire) frire; **frypan** poêle *f* (à frire)

fuck [fʌk] V baiser V; **~ you!** putain! V

fuel ['fjuːəl] **1** *n* carburant *m* **2** *v/t fig* entretenir

fugitive ['fjuːdʒətɪv] fugitif (-ive) *m(f)*

fulfill, *Br* **fulfil** [fʊl'fɪl] *dreams* réaliser; *task* accomplir; *contract* remplir; **fulfillment**, *Br* **fulfilment** *of contract etc* exécution *f*; *moral, spiritual* accomplissement *m*

full [fʊl] plein (**of** de); *hotel, account* complet; **pay in ~** tout payer; **full moon** pleine

lune *f*; **full stop** *Br* point *m*; **full-time** à plein temps; **fully** complètement; *describe* en détail

fumble ['fʌmbl] *catch* mal attraper

fumes [fjuːmz] *s* fumée *f*

fun [fʌn] **1** *n* amusement *m*; **it was great ~** on s'est bien amusé; **have ~!** amuse-toi bien! **2** *adj* F marrant F

function ['fʌŋkʃn] **1** *n* fonction *f*; *(reception etc)* réception *f* **2** *v/i* fonctionner; **~ as** faire fonction de; **functional** fonctionnel

fund [fʌnd] **1** *n* fonds *m* **2** *v/t project etc* financer

fundamental [fʌndə'mentl] fondamental; **fundamentalist** fondamentaliste *m/f*; **fundamentally** fondamentalement

funding ['fʌndɪŋ] *(money)* financement *m*

funeral ['fjuːnərəl] enterrement *m*; **funeral home** établissement *m* de pompes funèbres

fungus ['fʌŋgəs] champignon *m*; *mold* moisissure *f*

funnies ['fʌnɪz] *fpl* F pages *fpl* drôles; **funnily** *(oddly)* bizarrement; *(comically)* comiquement; **~ enough** chose curieuse; **funny** *(comical)* drôle; *(odd)* bizarre, curieux

fur [fɜːr] fourrure *f*

furious ['fjʊrɪəs] furieux

furnace ['fɜːrnɪs] four(neau)

furnish

366

m

furnish ['fɜːrnɪʃ] *room* meubler; *(supply)* fournir; **furniture** meubles *mpl; a piece of ~* un meuble

further ['fɜːrðər] **1** *adj* supplémentaire; *(more distant)* plus éloigné **2** *adv* walk, drive plus loin **3** *v/t* cause *etc* faire avancer, promouvoir; **furthermore** de plus, en outre

furtive ['fɜːrtɪv] furtif

fury ['fjʊrɪ] fureur *f*

fuse [fjuːz] **1** *n* ELEC fusible *m*, plomb *m* F **2** *v/i* ELEC: *the*

lights have ~d les plombs ont sauté **3** *v/t* ELEC faire sauter; **fusebox** boîte *f* à fusibles

fusion ['fjuːʒn] fusion *f*

fuss [fʌs] agitation *f;* **fussy** *person* difficile; *design etc* trop compliqué

futile ['fjuːtl] futile; **futility** futilité *f*

future ['fjuːtʃər] **1** *n* avenir *f;* GRAM futur *m* **2** *adj* futur; **futuristic** *design* futuriste

fuzzy ['fʌzɪ] *hair* crépu; *(out of focus)* flou

G

gadget ['gædʒɪt] gadget *m*

gag [gæg] **1** *n* bâillon *m; (joke)* gag *m* **2** *v/t also fig* bâillonner

gain [geɪn] acquérir; *victory* remporter; *advantage, sympathy* gagner

gala ['gælə] gala *m*

galaxy ['gæləksɪ] galaxie *f*

gale [geɪl] tempête *f*

gallery ['gælərɪ] *for art, in theater* galerie *f*

gallon ['gælən] gallon *m (0,785l, en GB 0,546l)*

gallop ['gæləp] galoper

gamble ['gæmbl] jouer; **gambler** joueur(-euse) *m(f);* **gambling** jeu *m*

game [geɪm] *also in tennis* jeu *m; have a ~ of tennis* faire une partie de tennis

gang [gæŋ] gang *m; of friends* bande *f;* **gangster** gangster *m;* **gangway** passerelle *f*

gap [gæp] trou *m; in time* intervalle *m; between personalities* fossé *m*

gape [geɪp] rester bouche bée; **gaping** *hole* béant

garage [gə'rɑːʒ] garage *m*

garbage ['gɑːrbɪdʒ] ordures *fpl, (fig : nonsense)* bêtises *fpl;* **garbage can** poubelle *f;* **garbage truck** benne *f* à ordures

garbled ['gɑːrbld] *message* confus

garden ['gɑːrdn] jardin *m;* **gardening** jardinage *m*

garish ['geriʃ] criard

garlic ['gɑːrlɪk] ail *m*

garment ['gɑːrmənt] vêtement *m*

garnish ['gɑːrnɪʃ] garnir (**with** de)

gas [gæs] gaz *m*; (*gasoline*) essence *f*

gash [gæʃ] entaille *f*

gasket ['gæskɪt] joint *m* d'étanchéité

gasoline ['gæsəliːn] essence *f*

gasp [gæsp] **1** *n in surprise* hoquet *m*; *with exhaustion* halètement *m* **2** *v/i with exhaustion* haleter; **with surprise** pousser une exclamation de surprise

'gas pedal accélérateur *m*; gas pump pompe *f* (à essence); gas station station-service *f*

gate [geɪt] *also at airport* porte *f*; **gateway** entrée *f*; *also fig* porte *f*

gather ['gæðər] **1** *v/t facts* recueillir; ~ **speed** prendre de la vitesse **2** *v/i of crowd* s'assembler; **gathering** (*group of people*) assemblée *f*

gaudy ['gɔːdɪ] voyant

gauge [geɪdʒ] **1** *n* jauge *f* **2** *v/t pressure* jauger; *opinion* mesurer

gaunt [gɒnt] émacié

gawky ['gɔːkɪ] gauche

gawp [gɒːp] F rester bouche bée (**at** devant)

gay [geɪ] gay

gaze [geɪz] **1** *n* regard *m* (fixe) **2** *v/i* regarder fixement

gear [gɪr] (*equipment*) équipement *m*; *in vehicles* vitesse *f*;

gearbox MOT boîte *f* de vitesses; gear shift MOT levier *m* de vitesse

gel [dʒel] *for hair, shower* gel *m*

gem [dʒem] pierre *f* précieuse; *fig* perle *f*

gender ['dʒendər] genre *m*

gene [dʒiːn] gène *m*

general ['dʒenrəl] **1** *n* MIL général(e) *m(f)* **2** *adj* général; generalization généralisation *f*; generalize généraliser; generally généralement; ~ **speaking** de manière générale

generate ['dʒenəreɪt] produire; generation génération *f*; generator générateur *m*

generosity [dʒenə'rɑːsətɪ] générosité *f*; generous généreux

genetic [dʒɪ'netɪk] génétique; genetically génétiquement; genetically engineered transgénique; genetically modified génétiquement modifié; genetic engineering génie *m* génétique; genetic fingerprint empreinte *f* génétique; genetics génétique *f*

genial ['dʒiːnjəl] agréable

genitals ['dʒenɪtlz] organes *mpl* génitaux

genius ['dʒiːnjəs] génie *m*

genocide ['dʒenəsaɪd] génocide *m*

gentle ['dʒentl] doux; *breeze* léger; **gentleman** monsieur m; **he's a real ~** c'est un vrai gentleman; **gentleness** douceur f; **gently** doucement; *blow* légèrement

genuine ['dʒenʊɪn] authentique; **genuinely** vraiment, sincèrement

geographical [dʒɪə'græfɪkl] géographique; **geography** géographie f

geological [dʒɪə'lɑːdʒɪkl] géologique; **geologist** géologue m/f; **geology** géologie f

geometric, **geometrical** [dʒɪə'metrɪk(l)] géométrique; **geometry** géométrie f

geriatric [dʒerɪ'ætrɪk] **1** adj gériatrique **2** n patient(e) m(f) gériatrique

germ [dʒɜːrm] also of idea etc germe m

German ['dʒɜːrmən] **1** adj allemand(e) m(f); **2** n person Allemand(e) m(f); language allemand m; **German shepherd** berger m allemand; **Germany** Allemagne f

gesture ['dʒestʃər] also fig geste m

get [get] (obtain) obtenir; (buy) acheter; (fetch) aller chercher; (receive: letter) recevoir; (receive: knowledge, respect etc) acquérir; (catch: bus, train etc) prendre; (understand) comprendre; (become) devenir; **when we ~ home** quand nous arrivons chez nous; **~ old/tired** vieil-

lir/se fatiguer; **~ sth done** (by s.o. else) faire faire qch;
~ s.o. to do sth faire faire qch à qn; **~ one's hair cut** se faire couper les cheveux; **~ sth ready** préparer qch; **have got** avoir; **have got to** devoir; **I have got to study** je dois étudier, il faut que j'étudie (subj); **~ to know** commencer à bien connaître

◆ **get at** (criticize) s'en prendre à; (imply, mean) vouloir dire

◆ **get by** (pass) passer; financially s'en sortir

◆ **get down 1** v/i from ladder etc descendre; (duck) se baisser **2** v/t (depress) déprimer

◆ **get in 1** v/i (of train, plane) arriver; (come home) rentrer; to car entrer **2** v/t to suitcase etc rentrer

◆ **get into** house entrer dans; car monter dans

◆ **get off 1** v/i from bus etc descendre; (finish work) finir; (not be punished) s'en tirer **2** v/t (remove) enlever

◆ **get on 1** v/i to bike, bus monter; (be friendly) s'entendre; (advance: of time) se faire tard; (become old) prendre de l'âge; (progress: of book) avancer **2** v/t: **get on the bus** monter dans le bus

◆ **get out 1** v/i of car, prison

etc sortir; **get out!** va-t-en! **2**
v/t nail, stain enlever; *gun,
pen* sortir
◆ **get through** *on telephone*
obtenir la communication
◆ **get up 1** *v/i* se lever **2** *v/t*
(*climb: hill*) monter
'getaway car voiture utilisée
pour s'enfuir; **get-together**
réunion *f*
ghastly ['gɑːstlɪ] horrible
ghetto ['getəu] ghetto *m*
ghost [gəust] fantôme *m*,
spectre *m*; **ghostly** spectral
ghoul [guːl] personne *f* morbide
giant ['dʒaɪənt] **1** *n* géant(e)
m(f) **2** *adj* géant
gibberish ['dʒɪbərɪʃ] F charabia *m*
gibe [dʒaɪb] moquerie *f*
giddiness ['gɪdɪnɪs] vertige
m; **giddy**: **feel ~** avoir le vertige
gift [gɪft] cadeau *m*; *talent* don
m; **gift card** carte *f* cadeau;
gifted doué·e; **giftwrap**: **~ sth**
faire un paquet-cadeau
gig [gɪg] F concert *m*
gigabyte ['gɪgəbaɪt] COMPUT
gigaoctet *m*
gigantic [dʒaɪ'gæntɪk] gigantesque
giggle ['gɪgl] **1** *v/i* glousser **2** *n*
gloussement *m*
gimmick ['gɪmɪk] truc F
gin [dʒɪn] gin *m*; **~ and tonic**
gin *m* tonic
gipsy ['dʒɪpsɪ] gitan·e *m(f)*
girder ['gɜːrdər] poutre *f*

girl [gɜːrl] (jeune) fille *f*; **girlfriend** *of boy* petite amie *f*;
younger also copine *f*; *of girl*
amie *f*, *younger also* copine
f; **girlish** de jeune fille
gist [dʒɪst] essence *f*
give [gɪv] donner; *present* offrir; (*supply: electricity etc*)
fournir; *talk, lecture* faire;
cry, groan pousser
◆ **give away** *as present* donner; (*betray*) trahir
◆ **give back** rendre
◆ **give in 1** (*surrender*) se
rendre **2** *v/t* (*hand in*) remettre
◆ **give onto** (*open onto*) donner sur
◆ **give out 1** *v/t leaflets etc*
distribuer **2** *v/i of supplies,
strength* s'épuiser
◆ **give up 1** *v/t smoking etc*
arrêter de **2** *v/i* (*stop making
effort*) abandonner
◆ **give way** *of bridge etc*
s'écrouler
give-and-'take concessions
fpl mutuelles
gizmo ['gɪzmou] F truc *m*
glad [glæd] heureux; **gladly**
volontiers, avec plaisir
glamor ['glæmər] éclat *m*, fascination *f*; **glamorize** donner
un aspect séduisant à; **glam-
orous** séduisant, fascinant;
job prestigieux; **glamour** *Br*
→ **glamor**
glance [glæns] **1** *n* regard *m* **2**
v/i jeter un regard, lancer un
coup d'œil

gland [glænd] glande f

glare [gler] **1** n of sun, lights éclat m (éblouissant) **2** v/i of sun, lights briller d'un éclat éblouissant

◆ **glare at** lancer un regard furieux à

glaring ['glerɪŋ] mistake flagrant

glass [glæs] material, for drink verre m; **glasses** lunettes fpl

glazed [gleɪzd] expression vitreux

gleam [gli:m] **1** n lueur f **2** v/i luire

glee [gli:] joie f; **gleeful** joyeux

glib [glɪb] désinvolte; **glibly** avec désinvolture

glide [glaɪd] glisser; of bird, plane planer; **glider** planeur m; **gliding** sport vol m à voile

glimpse [glɪmps] **1** n: catch a ~ of ... entrevoir **2** v/t entrevoir

glint [glɪnt] **1** n lueur f **2** v/i of light, eyes luire

glisten ['glɪsn] of light luire; of water miroiter; of silk chatoyer

glitter ['glɪtər] of light, jewels briller, scintiller

gloat [gloʊt] jubiler

◆ **gloat over** se réjouir de

global ['gloʊbl] (worldwide) mondial; (without exceptions) global; **globalization** mondialisation f; **global warming** réchauffement m

de la planète; **globe** globe m

gloom [glu:m] (darkness) obscurité f; mood tristesse f; **gloomy** sombre

glorious ['glɔːrɪəs] weather magnifique; victory glorieux; **glory** gloire f

gloss [glɑːs] (shine) brillant m; (general explanation) glose f; **glossary** glossaire m; **glossy 1** adj paper glacé **2** n magazine magazine m de luxe

glove [glʌv] gant m; **glove compartment** boîte f à gants

glow [gloʊ] **1** n of light lueur f; of fire rougeoiement m; in cheeks couleurs fpl **2** v/i of light luire; of fire rougeoyer; of cheeks être rouge; **glowing** description élogieux

glucose ['glu:koʊs] glucose m

glue [glu:] **1** n colle f **2** v/t coller

glum [glʌm] morose

glut [glʌt] surplus m

glutton ['glʌtən] glouton(ne) m(f)

gnaw [nɔː] bone ronger

go [goʊ] aller; (leave) partir; (work, function) marcher, fonctionner; (come out: of stain etc) s'en aller; (cease: of pain etc) partir, disparaître; (match: of colors etc) aller ensemble; **hamburger to ~** hamburger à emporter

◆ **go away** of person s'en aller, partir; of rain cesser; of

pain, clouds partir
◆ **go back** (return) retourner;
(date back) remonter (**to** à)
◆ **go by** of car, time passer
◆ **go down** descendre; of sun
se coucher
◆ **go in** to room, house entrer;
of sun se cacher; (fit: of part
etc) s'insérer
◆ **go off** (leave) partir; of
bomb exploser; of gun partir; of alarm se déclencher
◆ **go on** (continue) continuer;
(happen) se passer
◆ **go out** of person sortir; of
light, fire s'éteindre
◆ **go over** (check) revoir
◆ **go through** hard times traverser; illness subir; (check)
revoir; (read through) lire
en entier
◆ **go under** (sink) couler; of
company faire faillite
◆ **go up** (climb) monter; of
prices augmenter
◆ **go without 1** v/t food etc se
passer de **2** v/i s'en passer
'**go-ahead 1** n feu vert m **2** adj
(enterprising, dynamic) entreprenant, dynamique
goal [gəʊl] n in sport, (objective)
but m; **goalkeeper** gardien
m de but; **goal kick** remise
f en jeu; **goalpost** poteau
m de but
goat [gəʊt] chèvre m
gobble ['gɑːbl] dévorer
gobbledygook ['gɑːbldɪguːk]
F charabia m F
'**go-between** intermédiaire

m/f
god [gɑːd] dieu m; **thank
God!** Dieu merci!
'**godchild** filleul(e) m(f); **godfather** also in mafia parrain
m; **godmother** marraine m
gofer ['gəʊfər] F coursier(-iè-
re) m(f)
goggles ['gɑːglz] lunettes fpl
goings-on [gəʊɪnz'ɑːn] activités fpl
gold [gəʊld] **1** n or m **2** adj en
or; **ingot** d'or; **golden** sky
doré; **hair** also d'or; **golden
wedding** noces fpl d'or; **gold
medal** médaille f d'or; **gold
mine** fig mine f d'or
golf [gɑːlf] golf m; **golf ball**
balle f de golf; **golf club** organization, stick club m de
golf; **golf course** terrain m
de golf; **golfer** golfeur(-euse)
m(f)
good [gʊd] bon; weather
beau; child sage; **goodbye**
au revoir; **good-for-
nothing** n bon(ne) m(f) à rien; **Good
Friday** Vendredi m saint;
good-humored, Br **good-
humoured** jovial; **good-
looking** beau; **good-natured** bon, au bon naturel;
goodness moral bonté f;
of fruit etc bonnes choses
fpl; **goods** COM marchandises fpl; **goodwill** bonne volonté f
goof [guːf] F gaffer F
goose [guːs] oie f; **goose
bumps** chair f de poule

gorgeous ['gɔːrdʒəs] magnifique, superbe

gospel ['gɑːspl] évangile *m*

gossip ['gɑːsɪp] **1** *n* potins *mpl*; *malicious* commérages *mpl*; *person* commère *f* **2** *v/i* bavarder; *maliciously* faire des commérages; **gossip column** échos *mpl*

gourmet ['gʊrmeɪ] gourmet *m*

govern ['gʌvərn] gouverner; **government** gouvernement *m*; **governor** gouverneur *m*

gown [gaʊn] robe *f*; *wedding dress* robe *f* de mariée; *of academic, judge* toge *f*; *of surgeon* blouse *f*

grab [græb] saisir; *food* saisir

grace [greɪs] *of dancer etc* grâce *f*; *before meals* bénédicité *m*; **graceful** gracieux; **gracious** *person* bienveillant; *style* élégant

grade [greɪd] **1** *n* (*quality*) qualité *f*; EDU classe *f*; (*mark*) note *f* **2** *v/t* classer; *school work* noter; **grade crossing** passage *m* à niveau; **grade school** école *f* primaire

gradient ['greɪdɪənt] pente *f*

gradual ['grædʒʊəl] graduel; **gradually** peu à peu, progressivement

graduate 1 ['grædʒʊət] *n* diplômé(e) *m(f)* **2** ['grædʒʊeɪt] *v/i* obtenir son diplôme (*from* de); **graduation** obtention *f* du diplôme

graffiti [grə'fiːtiː] graffitis *mpl*; *single* graffiti *m*

graft [græft] **1** *n* BOT, MED greffe *f*; F (*corruption*) corruption *f* **2** *v/t* BOT, MED greffer

grain [greɪn] blé *m*; *of rice etc*, *in wood* grain *m*

gram [græm] gramme *m*

grammar ['græmər] grammaire *f*; **grammatical** grammatical

grand [grænd] **1** *adj* grandiose; F (*very good*) génial F **2** *n* F (*$1000*) mille dollars *mpl*; **grandchild** petit-fils *m*, petite-fille *f*; **granddaughter** petite-fille *f*; **grandeur** grandeur *f*; **grandfather** grand-père *m*; **grand jury** grand jury *m*; **grandmother** grand-mère *f*; **grandparents** grands-parents *mpl*; **grand piano** piano *m* à queue; **grandson** petit-fils *m*

granite ['grænɪt] granit *m*

grant [grænt] **1** *n money* subvention *f* **2** *v/t wish*, *visa* accorder

granule ['grænuːl] grain *m*

grape [greɪp] (grain *m* de) raisin *m*; *some ~s* du raisin; **grapefruit juice** jus *m* de pamplemousse

graph [græf] graphique *m*, courbe *f*; **graphic 1** *adj* (*vivid*) très réaliste **2** *n* COMPUT graphique *m*

♦ **grapple with** ['græpl] *attacker* en venir aux prises avec; *problem etc* s'attaquer à

grasp [græsp] **1** *n physical prise f; mental* compréhension *f* **2** *v/t physically* saisir; *(understand)* comprendre

grass [græs] herbe *f;* **grasshopper** sauterelle *f;* **grass roots** *people* base *f;* **grassy** ['græsɪ] herbeux, herbu

grate[1] [greɪt] *n metal* grille *f*

grate[2] [greɪt] **1** *v/t in cooking* râper **2** *v/i:* ~ **on the ear** faire mal aux oreilles

grateful ['greɪtfəl] reconnaissant; **gratefully** avec reconnaissance

gratify ['grætɪfaɪ] satisfaire

grating ['greɪtɪŋ] **1** *n* grille *f* **2** *adj sound, voice* grinçant

gratitude ['grætɪtuːd] gratitude *f,* reconnaissance *f*

grave[1] [greɪv] *n* tombe *f*

grave[2] [greɪv] *adj* grave

gravel ['grævl] gravier *m*

gravestone pierre *f* tombale; **graveyard** cimetière *m*

gravity ['grævətɪ] PHYS, *of situation* gravité *f*

gray [greɪ] gris; **gray-haired** aux cheveux gris

graze[1] [greɪz] *v/i of cow etc* paître

graze[2] [greɪz] **1** *v/t arm etc* écorcher **2** *n* écorchure *f*

grease [griːs] *for cooking* graisse *f; for car* lubrifiant *m;* **greasy** gras; *(covered in grease)* graisseux

great [greɪt] grand; *mistake, sum* gros; F *(very good)* su-

per F; **Great Britain** Grande-Bretagne *f;* **greatly** beaucoup; *not* ~ *different* pas très différent; **greatness** grandeur *f*

Greece [griːs] Grèce *f*

greed [griːd] *for money* avidité *f; for food also* gourmandise *f;* **greedily** avec avidité; *for food also* gourmand

Greek [griːk] **1** *n* Grec(que) *m(f); language* grec *m* **2** *adj* grec

green [griːn] vert; **green beans** haricots *mpl* verts; **green belt** ceinture *f* verte; **green card** *(work permit)* permis *m* de travail; **greenhouse effect** effet *m* de serre; **greens** légumes *mpl* verts

greet [griːt] saluer; *(welcome)* accueillir; **greeting** salut *m*

grenade [grɪˈneɪd] grenade *f*

grey [greɪ] Br → **gray**

grid [grɪd] grille *f;* **gridiron** SP terrain *m* de football; **gridlock** *in traffic* embouteillage *m*

grief [griːf] chagrin *m,* douleur *f;* **grief-stricken** affligé; **grievance** grief *m;* **grieve** être affligé; ~ *for s.o.* pleurer qn

grill [grɪl] **1** *n on window* grille *f* **2** *v/t (interrogate)* mettre sur la sellette

grille [grɪl] grille *f*

grim [grɪm] sinistre, sombre

grimace ['grɪməs] grimace f

grime [graɪm] crasse f; **grimy** crasseux

grin [grɪn] **1** n (large) sourire m **2** v/i sourire

grind [graɪnd] coffee moudre; meat hacher

grip [grɪp] saisir, serrer; **gripping** prenant, captivant

gristle ['grɪsl] cartilage m

grit [grɪt] **1** n for roads gravillon m **2** v/t: ~ one's teeth grincer des dents; **gritty** F réaliste

groan [groʊn] **1** n gémissement m **2** v/i gémir

groceries ['groʊsərɪz] provisions fpl; **grocery store** épicerie f l'épicerie f

groggy ['grɑːgɪ] F groggy F

groin [grɔɪn] ANAT aine f

groom [gruːm] **1** n for bride marié m; for horse palefrenier(-ère) m(f) **2** v/t horse panser; (train, prepare) préparer

groove [gruːv] rainure f; on record sillon m

grope [groʊp] **1** v/i in the dark tâtonner **2** v/t sexually peloter F

gross [groʊs] (coarse, vulgar) grossier; exaggeration gros; FIN brut

ground [graʊnd] **1** n sol m, terre f; for football etc, fig terrain; (reason) motif m; ELEC terre f **2** v/t ELEC mettre une prise de terre à; **grounding** in subject bases fpl;

groundless sans fondement; **ground meat** viande f hachée; **groundwork** travail m préparatoire

group [gruːp] **1** n groupe m **2** v/t grouper

groupie ['gruːpɪ] F groupie f F

grouse [graʊs] **1** n F rouspéter F **2** v/i F plainte f

grovel ['grɑːvl] fig ramper (**to** devant)

grow [groʊ] **1** v/i grandir; of plants, hair pousser; of number augmenter; of business se développer; (become) devenir **2** v/t flowers faire pousser

◆ **grow up** of person devenir adulte; of city se développer

growl [graʊl] **1** n grognement m **2** v/i grogner

grown-up n adulte m/f **2** adj adulte

growth [groʊθ] of person, company croissance f; (increase) augmentation f; MED tumeur f

grudge [grʌdʒ] rancune f; **grudging** accordé à contrecœur; person plein de ressentiment; **grudgingly** à contrecœur

grueling, Br **gruelling** ['gruːəlɪŋ] épuisant

gruff [grʌf] bourru, revêche

grumble ['grʌmbl] ronchonner; **grumbler** grognon(ne) m(f)

grunt [grʌnt] **1** n grognement m **2** v/i grogner

guarantee [gærən'tiː] **1** *n* garantie *f* **2** *v/t* garantir; **guarantor** garant(e) *m(f)*

guard [gɑːrd] **1** *n* gardien(ne) *m(f)*; MIL garde *f* **2** *v/t* garder; **guard dog** chien *m* de garde; **guarded** *reply* prudent; **guardian** LAW tuteur(-trice) *m(f)*

guerrilla [gə'rɪlə] guérillero *m*; **guerrilla warfare** guérilla *f*

guess [ges] **1** *n* conjecture *f* **2** *v/t* answer deviner **2** *v/i* deviner; **I ~ so** je crois; **guesswork** conjecture(s) *f(pl)*

guest [gest] invité(e) *m(f)*; *in hotel* hôte *m/f*; **guestroom** chambre *f* d'amis

guidance ['gaɪdəns] conseils *mpl*; **guide 1** *n person* guide *m/f*; *book* guide **m 2** *v/t* guider; **guidebook** guide *m*; **guided missile** missile *m* téléguidé; **guided tour** visite *f* guidée; **guidelines** directives *fpl*

guilt [gɪlt] culpabilité *f*; **guilty** *also* LAW coupable

guinea pig ['gɪnɪpɪg] *also fig* cobaye *m*

guitar [gɪ'tɑːr] guitare *f*; **guitarist** guitariste *m/f*

gulf [gʌlf] golfe *m*; *fig* gouffre *m*

gull [gʌl] mouette *f*; *bigger* goéland *m*

gullet ['gʌlɪt] ANAT gosier *m*

gullible ['gʌlɪbl] crédule

gulp [gʌlp] **1** *n of drink* gorgée *f* **2** *v/i in surprise* dire en s'étranglant

◆ **gulp down** *drink* avaler à grosses gorgées; *food* avaler à grosses bouchées

gum[1] [gʌm] *in mouth* gencive *f*

gum[2] [gʌm] *(glue)* colle *f*; *(chewing gum)* chewing-gum *m*

gun [gʌn] *arme* f à feu; *pistol* pistolet *m*; *revolver* revolver *m*; *rifle* fusil *m*; *cannon* canon *m*

◆ **gun down** abattre

'**gunfire** coups *mpl* de feu; **gunman** homme *m* armé; **gunshot** coup *m* de feu; **gunshot wound** blessure *f* par balle

gurgle ['gɜːrgl] *of baby* gazouiller; *of drain* gargouiller

guru ['guːruː] *fig* gourou *m*

gush [gʌʃ] *of liquid* jaillir

gust [gʌst] rafale *f*, coup *m* de vent

gusto ['gʌstoʊ]: **with ~** avec enthousiasme

gusty ['gʌstɪ] *weather* très venteux

gut [gʌt] **1** *n* intestin *m*; F *(stomach)* bide **m 2** *v/t (destroy)* ravager; **guts** F *(courage)* cran **m** F; **gutsy** F *(brave)* qui a du cran F

gutter ['gʌtər] *on sidewalk* caniveau *m*; *on roof* gouttière *f*

guy [gaɪ] F type *m* F

guzzle ['gʌzl] *food* engloutir; *drink* avaler

gym [dʒɪm] *sports club* club *m* de gym; *in school* gymnase *m*; *activity* gym(nastique) *f*; **gymnast** gymnaste *m/f*; **gymnastics** gymnastique *f*

gynecology, *Br* **gynaecology** [gaɪnɪˈkɑːlədʒɪ] gynécologie

gypsy [ˈdʒɪpsɪ] gitan(e) *m(f)*

H

habit [ˈhæbɪt] habitude *f*
habitable [ˈhæbɪtəbl] habitable; **habitat** habitat *m*
habitual [həˈbɪtʃʊəl] habituel; *smoker, drinker* invétéré
hacker [ˈhækər] COMPUT pirate *m* informatique
hackneyed [ˈhæknɪd] rebattu
haemorrhage *Br* → **hemorrhage**
haggard [ˈhægərd] hagard, égaré
haggle [ˈhægl] marchander
hail [heɪl] grêle *f*
hair [her] cheveux *mpl*; *single* cheveu *m*; *on body* poils *mpl*; *single* poil *m*; **hairbrush** brosse *f* à cheveux; **haircut** coupe *f* de cheveux; **have a ~** se faire couper les cheveux
'**hairdo** coiffure *f*; **hairdresser** coiffeur(-euse) *m(f)*; **hairdryer** sèche-cheveux *m*; **hairpin** épingle *f* à cheveux; **hairpin curve** virage *m* en épingle à cheveux; **hair-raising** horrifique; **hair remover** crème *f* épilatoire; **hair-splitting** ergotage *m*; **hairstyle** coiffure *f*; **hairstylist** coiffeur(-euse) *m(f)*; **hairy** *arm*,

animal poilu; F (*frightening*) effrayant
half [hæf] **1** *n* moitié *f*; **~ past ten** dix heures et demie; **~ an hour** une demi-heure **2** *adj* demi; **at ~ price** à moitié prix **3** *adv* à moitié; **half-hearted** tiède; **half time** SP mi-temps *f*; **halfway 1** *adj*: **reach the ~ point** être à la moitié **2** *adv* in space, distance à mi-chemin
hall [hɔːl] (*large room*) salle *f*; (*hallway in house*) vestibule *m*
Hallowe'en [hælouˈwiːn] halloween *f*
halo [ˈheɪlou] auréole *f*
halt [hɔːlt] **1** *v/i* faire halte, s'arrêter **2** *v/t* arrêter
halve [hæv] couper en deux; *input, costs* réduire de moitié
ham [hæm] jambon *m*; **hamburger** hamburger *m*
hammer [ˈhæmər] **1** *n* marteau *m* **2** *v/i* marteler; **~ at the door** frapper à la porte à coups redoublés
hammock [ˈhæmək] hamac *m*
hamper¹ [ˈhæmpər] *n for food* panier *m*
hamper² [ˈhæmpər] *v/t* (ob-

struct) entraver, gêner

hand [hænd] **1** *n* main *f; of clock* aiguille *f;* (*worker*) ouvrier(-ère) *m(f);* **at ~, to ~** *thing* sous la main; **at ~** *person* à disposition; **on the one ~ ..., on the other ~** d'une part ..., d'autre part; **on your right ~** sur votre droite; **give s.o. a ~** donner un coup de main à qn
♦ **hand down** transmettre
♦ **hand out** distribuer
♦ **hand over** donner; *to authorities* livrer

'**handbag** *Br* sac *m* à main; **hand baggage bagages** *mpl* à main; **handcuff** menotter; **handcuffs** menottes *fpl*

handicap ['hændikæp] handicap *m;* **handicapped** handicapé; **handiwork** *object* ouvrage *m*

handkerchief ['hæŋkətʃif] mouchoir *m*

handle ['hændl] **1** *n of door, suitcase* poignée *f; of knife, pan* manche *m* **2** *v/t goods* manier, manipuler; *case, deal* s'occuper de; **handle-bars** guidon *m*

handsome ['hænsəm] beau

'**handwriting** écriture *f;* **handwritten** écrit à la main;

handy *device* pratique

hang [hæŋ] **1** *v/t person* pendre **2** *v/i of dress, hair* tomber
♦ **hang on** (*wait*) attendre
♦ **hang up** TELEC raccrocher

hangar ['hæŋər] hangar *m*

hanger ['hæŋər] *for clothes* cintre *m*

'**hang glider** *person* libériste *m/f; device* deltaplane *m;* **hang gliding** deltaplane *m;* **hangover** gueule *f* de bois

hankie, hanky ['hæŋkı] F mouchoir *m*

haphazard [hæp'hæzərd] au hasard

happen ['hæpn] se passer, arriver

happily ['hæpılı] gaiement; *spend* volontiers; (*luckily*) heureusement; **happiness** bonheur *m;* **happy** heureux; **happy-go-lucky** insouciant

harass [hə'ræs] harceler; **harassed** surmené; **harassment** harcèlement *m*

harbor, *Br* **harbour** ['hɑːrbər] **1** *n* port *m* **2** *v/t criminal* héberger; *grudge* entretenir

hard [hɑːrd] **1** *adj* dur; *facts* brut; *evidence* concret **2** *adv work* dur; *rain, pull, push* fort; **try ~** faire tout son possible; **hardback** livre *m* cartonné; **hard-boiled egg** dur; **hard copy** copie *f* sur papier; **hard core** *pornography* (pornographie *f*) hard *m;* **hard currency** monnaie *f* forte; **hard disk** disque *m*

dur; **harden 1** v/t durcir **2** v/i
of glue, attitude se durcir;
hard hat casque m; *(construction worker)* ouvrier m
du bâtiment; **hardheaded**
réaliste; **hardhearted** au
cœur dur; **hard line** ligne f
dure; **hardliner** dur(e) m(f)
hardly ['haːrdlɪ] à peine; *see*
s.o. etc presque pas
hardness ['haːrdnɪs] dureté f;
(difficulty) difficulté f; **hardship** privation f; **hardware**
COMPUT hardware m, matériel m; **hardware store** quincaillerie f; **hard-working** travailleur; **hardy** robuste
harm [haːrm] **1** n mal m **2** v/t
faire du mal à; *non-physically*
nuire à; **harmful** *substance*
nocif; *influence* nuisible;
harmless inoffensif
harmonious [haːr'moʊnɪəs]
harmonieux; **harmonize**
s'harmoniser; **harmony** harmonie f
harsh [haːrʃ] *words* dur; *color*
criard; *light* cru; **harshly** durement
harvest ['haːrvɪst] moisson f
hash browns [hæʃ] pommes
de terre fpl sautées
hashtag ['hæʃtæg] COMPUT
hashtag m, mot-dièse m
haste [heɪst] hâte f; **hastily** à
la hâte; **hasty** hâtif, précipité
hat [hæt] chapeau m
hatch [hætʃ] *for serving* guichet m; *on ship* écoutille f
♦ **hatch out** éclore

hatchet ['hætʃɪt] hachette f;
bury the ~ enterrer la hache
de guerre
hate [heɪt] **1** n haine f **2** v/t détester, haïr; **hatred** haine f
haul [hɔːl] **1** n *of fish* coup m
de filet **2** v/t *(pull)* tirer, traîner
haunch [hɔːntʃ] *of person*
hanche f; *of animal* arrière-
-train m
haunt [hɔːnt] v/t hanter; *this*
place is ~ed ce lieu est hanté
have [hæv] **1** v/t *(own)* avoir;
breakfast, lunch prendre; *(got) to* devoir; **you don't ~**
to do it tu n'es pas obligé
de le faire; **do I ~ to pay?**
est-ce qu'il faut payer?; **I'll**
~ it sent to you je vous le ferai envoyer; **I had my hair**
cut je me suis fait couper
les cheveux **2** v/aux *(past*
tense): **~ you seen her?**
l'as-tu vue?; **they ~ arrived**
ils sont arrivés
♦ **have on** *(wear)* porter
haven ['heɪvn] *fig* havre m
hawk [hɔːk] *also fig* faucon m
hay [heɪ] foin m; **hay fever**
rhume m des foins
hazard ['hæzərd] danger m;
hazard lights MOT feux mpl
de détresse; **hazardous** dangereux
haze [heɪz] brume f; **hazy**
view brumeux; *image* flou;
memories vague
he [hiː] il; **there ~ is** le voilà
head [hed] **1** n tête f; *(boss,*

leader) chef *m/f*; *Br* : *of school* directeur(-trice) *m(f)*; *on beer* mousse *f* **2** *v/t* (*lead*) être à la tête de; *ball* jouer de la tête

◆ **head for** se diriger vers

'**headache** mal *m* de tête; **headband** bandeau *m*; **header** *in soccer* (coup *m* de) tête *f*; *in document* en-tête *m*; **headhunter** COM chasseur *m* de têtes; **heading** *in list* titre *m*; **headlamp** phare *m*; **headline** *in newspaper* (gros) titre *m*; **head office** *of company* bureau *m* central; **head-on 1** *adv crash* de front **2** *adj* frontal; **headphones** écouteurs *mpl*; **headquarters** quartier *m* général; **headrest** appui-tête *m*; **headroom** *under bridge* hauteur *f* limite; *in car* hauteur *f* au plafond; **headscarf** foulard *m*; **headstrong** entêté; **head waiter** maître *m* d'hôtel; **heady** *wine etc* capiteux

heal [hi:l] guérir

health [helθ] santé *f*; **health food store** magasin *m* d'aliments diététiques; **health insurance** assurance *f* maladie; **healthy** *person* en bonne santé; *food, lifestyle, economy* sain

heap [hi:p] tas *m*

hear [hɪr] entendre

◆ **hear from** (*have news from*) avoir des nouvelles de

hearing ['hɪrɪŋ] ouïe *f*; LAW audience *f*; **hearing aid** appareil *m* acoustique, audiophone *m*

hearse [hɜːrs] corbillard *m*

heart [hɑːrt] *also fig* cœur *m*; **know sth by ~** connaître qch par cœur; **heart attack** crise *f* cardiaque; **heartbreaking** navrant; **heartbroken**: **be ~** avoir le cœur brisé; **heartburn** brûlures *fpl* d'estomac; **heartfelt** sincère

hearth [hɑːrθ] foyer *m*, âtre *f*

heartless ['hɑːrtlɪs] insensible, cruel; **hearty** *appetite* gros; *meal* copieux; *person* jovial

heat [hi:t] chaleur *f*

◆ **heat up** réchauffer

heated ['hi:tɪd] *pool* chauffé; *discussion* passionné; **heater** radiateur *m*; *in car* chauffage *m*; **heating** chauffage *m*; **heatproof, heat-resistant** résistant à la chaleur; **heatwave** vague *f* de chaleur

heave [hi:v] (*lift*) soulever

heaven ['hevn] ciel *m*; **heavenly** F divin

heavy ['hevɪ] *also food, loss* lourd; *cold* grand; *rain, accent* fort; *traffic, smoker, bleeding* gros; **heavy-duty** très résistant; **heavyweight** SP poids lourd

hectic ['hektɪk] agité

hedge [hedʒ] haie *f*

heel [hi:l] talon *m*; **heel bar** talon-minute *m*

hefty ['heftɪ] gros; *person also*

costaud

height [haɪt] *of person* taille *f*; *of building* hauteur *f*; *of airplane* altitude *f*; **heighten** tension accroître

heir [er] héritier *m*; **heiress** héritière *f*

helicopter ['helikɑːptər] hélicoptère *m*

hell [hel] enfer *m*; **what the ~ are you doing?** F mais enfin qu'est-ce que tu fais?; **go to ~!** F va te faire foutre! P

hello [hə'loʊ] bonjour; TELEC allô

helmet ['helmɪt] casque *m*

help [help] **1** *n* aide *f* **2** *v/t* aider; **~ o.s. to food** se servir; **I can't ~ it** je ne peux pas m'en empêcher; **helper** aide *m/f*, assistant(e) *m(f)*; **helpful** *advice* utile; *person* serviable; **helping** *of food* portion *f*; **helpless** *(unable to cope)* sans défense; *(powerless)* impuissant; **helplessness** impuissance *f*

hem [hem] *of dress etc* ourlet *m*

hemisphere ['hemɪsfɪr] hémisphère *m*

'hemline ourlet *m*

hemorrhage ['hemərɪdʒ] **1** *n* hémorragie *f* **2** *v/i* faire une hémorragie

hen [hen] poule *f*; **hen party** soirée *f* entre femmes

hepatitis [hepə'taɪtɪs] hépatite *f*

her [hɜːr] **1** *adj* son, sa; *pl* ses **2**

pron *object* la; *before vowel* l'; *indirect object* lui, à elle; *with prep* elle; **I know ~** je la connais; **I gave ~ a dollar** je lui ai donné un dollar; **this is for ~** c'est pour elle; **who? ~ ~** qui? - elle

herb [ɜːrb] herbe *f*; **herb(al) tea** tisane *f*

herd [hɜːrd] troupeau *m*

here [hɪr] ici; **in ~, over ~** ici; **~'s to you!** as toast à votre santé!; **~ you are** *giving sth* voilà

hereditary [hə'redɪterɪ] héréditaire; **heredity** hérédité *f*; **heritage** héritage *m*

hero ['hɪroʊ] héros *m*; **heroic** héroïque; **heroically** héroïquement

heroin ['heroʊɪn] héroïne *f*

heroine ['heroʊɪn] héroïne *f*

heroism ['heroʊɪzm] héroïsme *f*

herpes ['hɜːrpiːz] herpès *m*

hers [hɜːrz] le sien, la sienne; *pl* les siens, les siennes; **it's ~** c'est à elle

herself [hɜːr'self] elle-même; *reflexive* se; *after prep* elle; **she hurt ~** elle s'est blessée

hesitant ['hezɪtənt] hésitant; **hesitantly** avec hésitation; **hesitate** hésiter; **hesitation** hésitation *f*

heterosexual [hetəroʊ-'sekʃʊəl] hétérosexuel

hi [haɪ] salut

hibernate ['haɪbərneɪt] hiberner

hiccup ['hɪkʌp] hoquet *m*; (*minor problem*) hic *m* F

hidden ['hɪdn] caché

hide¹ [haɪd] **1** *v/t* cacher **2** *v/i* se cacher

hide² [haɪd] *n of animal* peau *f*; *as product* cuir *m*

hide-and-seek cache-cache *m*; hideaway cachette *f*

hideous ['hɪdɪəs] affreux, horrible

hiding ['haɪdɪŋ] (*beating*) rossée *f*; hiding place cachette *f*

hierarchy ['haɪrɑːrkɪ] hiérarchie *f*

high [haɪ] **1** *adj* haut; *salary, price, rent, temperature* élevé; *wind* fort; *speed* grand; *on drugs* défoncé F **2** *n* MOT quatrième *f*; cinquième *f*; *in statistics* pointe *f*; EDU collège *m*, lycée *m*; highbrow intellectuel; highchair chaise *f* haute; high-class de première class; high-frequency de haute fréquence; high-grade *ore* à haute teneur; **gasoline** supercarburant *m*; high-handed arbitraire; high-heeled à hauts talons; high jump saut *m* en hauteur; high-level à haut niveau; highlight **1** *n* (*main event*) point *m* marquant; *in hair* reflets *mpl*, mèches *fpl* **2** *v/t with pen* surligner; COMPUT mettre en relief; highlighter *pen* surligneur *m*; highly *desirable, likely* fort, très; **think ~** *of s.o.* pen-

ser beaucoup de bien de qn; high performance *drill, battery* haute performance; high-pitched aigu; high point *of career* point *m* culminant; high-powered *engine* très puissant; *intellectual* très compétent; high pressure *weather* anticyclone *m*; high-pressure TECH à haute pression; *salesman* de choc; *job, lifestyle* dynamique; high school collège *m*, lycée *m*; high-strung nerveux, très sensible; high tech **1** *n* technologie *f* de pointe, high-tech *m* **2** *adj* de pointe, high-tech; highway grande route *f*

hijack ['haɪdʒæk] **1** *v/t* détourner **2** *n* détournement *m*; hijacker *of plane* pirate *m* de l'air; *of bus* pirate *m* de la route

hike¹ [haɪk] **1** *n* randonnée *f* à pied **2** *v/i* marcher à pied

hike² [haɪk] *n in prices* hausse *f*

hiker ['haɪkər] randonneur (-euse) *m(f)*; hiking randonnée *f* (pédestre)

hilarious [hɪ'leɪrɪəs] hilarant, désopilant

hill [hɪl] colline *f*; (*slope*) côte *f*; hilltop sommet *m* de la colline; hilly montagneux; *road* vallonné

hilt [hɪlt] poignée *f*

him [hɪm] *object* le; *before vowel* l'; *indirect object, with prep* lui; **I know ~** je le connais; **I gave ~ a dollar** je lui ai donné un dollar; **this is for~** c'est pour lui; **who? - him** qui? – lui; **himself** lui-même; *reflexive* se; *after prep* lui; **he hurt ~** il s'est blessé

hinder ['hɪndər] gêner, entraver; **~ s.o. from doing sth** empêcher qn de faire qch; **hindrance** obstacle *m*

hinge [hɪndʒ] charnière *f*

hint [hɪnt] (*clue*) indice *m*; (*piece of advice*) conseil *m*; (*suggestion*) allusion *f*; *of red, sadness etc* soupçon *m*

hip [hɪp] hanche *f*; **hip pocket** poche *f* revolver

hire ['haɪr] louer

his [hɪz] **1** *adj* son, sa; *pl* ses **2** *pron* le sien, la sienne; *pl* les siens, les siennes; **it's ~** c'est à lui

Hispanic [hɪ'spænɪk] **1** *n* Hispano-Américain(e) *m(f)* **2** *adj* hispano-américain

hiss [hɪs] siffler

historian [hɪ'stɔːrɪən] historien(ne) *m(f)*; **historic** historique; **historical** historique; **history** histoire *f*

hit [hɪt] **1** *v/t* frapper; (*collide with*) heurter; **he was ~ by a bullet** il a été touché par une balle **2** *n* (*blow*) coup *m*; MUS, (*success*) succès *m*; *on website* visiteur *m*

hitch [hɪtʃ] **1** *n* (*problem*) anicroche *f*, accroc *m* **2** *v/t* attacher; **hitchhike** faire du stop; **hitchhiker** auto-stoppeur (-euse) *m(f)*

hi-'tech 1 *n* technologie *f* de pointe, high-tech *m* **2** *adj* de pointe, high-tech

'hitman tueur *m* à gages; **hit-or-miss** aléatoire

HIV [eɪtʃaɪ'viː] (= *human immunodeficiency virus*) V.I.H. *m* (= Virus de l'Immunodéficience Humaine); **people with ~** les séropositifs

hive [haɪv] *for bees* ruche *f*

HIV-'positive séropositif

hoard [hɔːrd] **1** *n* réserves *fpl* **2** *v/t* amasser; *in times of shortage* faire des réserves de

hoarse [hɔːrs] rauque

hoax [hoʊks] canular *m*

hobble ['haːbl] boitiller

hobby ['haːbɪ] hobby *m*

hobo ['hoʊboʊ] F vagabond *m*

hockey ['haːkɪ] (*ice hockey*) hockey *m* (sur glace)

hog [haːg] (*pig*) cochon *m*

hoist [hɔɪst] **1** *n* palan *m* **2** *v/t* hisser

hold [hoʊld] **1** *v/t in hand* tenir; (*support, keep in place*) soutenir; *passport, license, prisoner* détenir; (*contain*) contenir; *job, post* occuper; **~ the line** TELEC ne quittez pas! **2** *n in ship* cale *f*; *in plane* soute *f*; **take ~ of sth** saisir qch

◆ **hold back** *crowds* contenir; *facts* retenir

◆ **hold out 1** *v/t* hand tendre;
prospect offrir **2** *v/i of supplies* durer; (*survive*) tenir
(bon)

◆ **hold up** hand lever; *bank
etc* attaquer; (*make late*) retenir

holder ['hǝʊldǝr] (*container*)
boîtier *m*; (*of passport, ticket,
record*) détenteur(-trice)
m(f); **holding company** holding *m*; **holdup** (*robbery*)
hold-up *m*; (*delay*) retard *m*

hole [hǝʊl] trou *m*

holiday ['hɒlǝdeɪ] jour *m* de
congé; *Br: period* vacances
fpl

hollow ['hɒlǝʊ] creux; *promise* faux

holocaust ['hɒlǝkɔːst] holo-
causte *m*

hologram ['hɒlǝgræm] holo-
gramme *m*

holster ['hǝʊlstǝr] holster *m*

holy ['hǝʊlɪ] saint; **Holy Spirit**
Saint-Esprit *m*

home [hǝʊm] **1** *n* maison *f*;
(*native country, town*) patrie
f; *for old people* maison *f* de
retraite; **at~** chez moi/lui *etc*;
(*in own country*) dans mon/
son *etc* pays; **sp à** domicile;
make o.s. at ~ faire comme
chez soi **2** *adv* à la maison,
chez soi; (*in own country*)
dans son pays; (*in own town*)
dans sa ville; **go** ~ rentrer;
home address adresse *f* per-
sonnelle; **home banking** services *mpl* télématiques (bancaires); **homecoming** retour
m (à la maison); **home computer** ordinateur *m* familial;
home game match *m* à domicile; **homeless 1** *adj* sans
abri **2** *npl*: **the** ~ les sans-abri
mpl, les S.D.F. *mpl* (sans domicile fixe); **homeloving** casanier; **homely** (*homelike*)
simple, comme à la maison;
(*not good-looking*) sans
beauté; **homemade** fait (à
la) maison; **home page** com-
PUT page *f* d'accueil; **homesick**: **be** ~ avoir le mal du
pays; **home town** ville *f* na-
tale; **homeward** *to own
house* vers la maison; *to
own country* vers son pays;
homework EDU devoirs *mpl*

homicide ['hɒmɪsaɪd] homicide *m*; *department* homi-
cides *mpl*

homophobia [hǝʊmǝ'fǝʊbɪǝ]
homophobie *f*

homosexual [hǝʊmǝ'sekʃʊ-
ǝl] **1** *adj* homosexuel **2** *n* ho-
mosexuel(le) *m(f)*

honest ['ɒnɪst] honnête;
honestly honnêtement; ~!
vraiment!; **honesty** honnêteté *f*

honey ['hʌnɪ] miel *m*; F (*darling*) chéri(e) *m(f)*; **honeymoon** lune *f* de miel

honk [hɒŋk] *horn* klaxonner

honor ['ɒnǝr] → **honour**

honour ['ɒnǝr] **1** *n* honneur *f* **2**
v/t honorer; **honorable** honorable; **honour** Br → **hon-
or**

hood [hʊd] *over head* capuche f; *over cooker* hotte f; MOT capot m

hook [hʊk] *to hang clothes on* patère f; *for fishing* hameçon m; **off the ~** TELEC décroché; **hooked** accro F; **be ~ on sth** être accro de qch; **hooker** F putain f P

hoot [huːt] **1** v/t *horn* donner un coup de **2** v/i *of car* klaxonner; *of owl* huer

hop [hɑːp] sauter, sautiller

hope [hoʊp] **1** n espoir m **2** v/i espérer; **I ~ so** je l'espère, j'espère que oui **2** v/t: **~ that** espérer que; **hopeful** plein d'espoir; *(promising)* prometteur; **hopefully** *say, wait* avec espoir; *(I/we hope)* avec un peu de chance; **hopeless** *position* sans espoir, désespéré; *(useless: person)* nul

horizon [həˈraɪzn] horizon m; **horizontal** horizontal

hormone [ˈhɔːrmoʊn] hormone f

horn [hɔːrn] *of animal* corne f; MOT klaxon m

hornet [ˈhɔːrnɪt] frelon m

horny [ˈhɔːrnɪ] F *sexually* excité

horrible [ˈhɑːrɪbl] horrible, affreux; **horrify** horrifier; **horrifying** horrifiant; **horror** horreur f

horse [hɔːrs] cheval m; **horse race** course f de chevaux; **horseshoe** fer m à cheval

horticulture horticulture f

hose [hoʊz] tuyau m

hospitable [ˈhɑːspɪtəbl] hospitalier

hospital [ˈhɑːspɪtl] hôpital m; **hospitality** hospitalité f

host [hoʊst] *at party* hôte m/f; *of TV program* présentateur(-trice) m(f)

hostage [ˈhɑːstɪdʒ] otage m; **hostage taker** preneur(-euse) m(f) d'otages

hostel [ˈhɑːstl] *for students* foyer m; *(youth ~)* auberge f de jeunesse

hostess [ˈhoʊstɪs] hôtesse f

hostile [ˈhɑːstl] hostile; **hostility** hostilité f; **hostilities** hostilités

hot [hɑːt] chaud; *(spicy)* épicé, fort; **I'm ~** j'ai chaud; **it's ~** *weather* il fait chaud; **hot dog** hot-dog m

hotel [hoʊˈtel] hôtel m

hot spot [ˈhɑːtspɑːt] *crise* point m chaud *ou* névralgique; *wireless ~, wifi ~* point m d'accès wifi (public)

hour [ˈaʊər] heure f

house [haʊs] maison f; **at your ~** chez vous; **housebreaking** cambriolage m; **household** ménage m; **household name** nom m connu de tous; **housekeeper** femme f de ménage; **House of Representatives** Chambre f des Représentants; **housewarming (party)** pendaison f de crémaillère; **housewife** femme f au foyer;

housework travaux *mpl* domestiques; **housing** logement *m*; TECH boîtier *m*

hovel ['hɑːvl] taudis *m*

hover ['hɑːvər] planer

how [haʊ] comment; ~ *are you?* comment allez-vous?; ~ *about a drink?* et si on allait prendre un pot?; ~ *much?* combien?; ~ *much is it?* *cost* combien ça coûte?; ~ *many?* combien?; ~ *often?* tous les combien?; ~ *sad!* comme c'est triste!; however cependant; ~ *big they are* quels qu'ils soient grands ou non

howl [haʊl] hurler

hub [hʌb] *of wheel* moyeu *m*; **hubcap** enjoliveur *m*

◆ **huddle together** ['hʌdl] se blottir les uns contre les autres

hug [hʌg] serrer dans ses bras

huge [hjuːdʒ] énorme

hull [hʌl] coque *f*

hum [hʌm] fredonner

human ['hjuːmən] 1 *n* être m humain 2 *adj* humain; **human being** être *m* humain

humane [hjuːˈmeɪn] humain, plein d'humanité

humanitarian [hjuːmænɪˈterɪən] humanitaire

humanity [hjuːˈmænɪtɪ] humanité *f*; **human race** race *f* humaine; **human resources** ressources *fpl* humaines

humble ['hʌmbl] modeste

humdrum ['hʌmdrʌm] monotone, banal

humid ['hjuːmɪd] humide; **humidifier** humidificateur *m*; **humidity** humidité *f*

humiliate [hjuːˈmɪlɪeɪt] humilier; **humiliating** humiliant; **humiliation** humiliation *f*; **humility** humilité *f*

humor ['hjuːmər] humour *m*; *(mood)* humeur *f*; *sense of* ~ sens m de l'humour; **humorous** drôle; **humour** Br → **humor**

hunch [hʌntʃ] *(idea)* intuition *f*, pressentiment *m*

hundred ['hʌndrəd] cent *m*; **hundredth** centième

hunger ['hʌŋgər] faim *f*

hung-over: *be* ~ avoir la gueule de bois F

hungry ['hʌŋgrɪ] affamé; *I'm* ~ j'ai faim

hunk [hʌŋk] gros morceau *m*; F *man* beau mec F

hunt [hʌnt] 1 *n* chasse *f* (*for* à); *for new leader, missing child etc* recherche *f* (*for* de) 2 *v/t* chasser; **hunter** chasseur (-euse) *m(f)*; **hunting** chasse *f*

hurdle ['hɜːrdl] SP haie *f*; *fig* obstacle *m*

hurl [hɜːrl] lancer, jeter

hurray [hʊˈreɪ] hourra

hurricane ['hʌrɪkən] ouragan *m*

hurried ['hʌrɪd] précipité; **hurry** 1 *n* hâte *f*; *be in a* ~ être pressé 2 *v/i* se dépêcher

◆ **hurry up 1** *v/i* se dépêcher; *hurry up!* dépêchez-vous! **2** *v/t* presser

hurt [hɜːrt] **1** *v/i* faire mal **2** *v/t* faire mal à; *emotionally* blesser

husband ['hʌzbənd] mari *m*

hush [hʌʃ] silence *m*

◆ **hush up** *scandal etc* étouffer

husky ['hʌskɪ] *voice* rauque

hut [hʌt] cabane *f*, hutte *f*

hybrid ['haɪbrɪd] hybride *m*

hydrant ['haɪdrənt] prise *f* d'eau; *(fire* ∿*)* bouche *f* d'incendie

hydraulic [haɪ'drɔːlɪk] hydraulique

hydroelectric [haɪdroʊɪ'lektrɪk] hydroélectrique

hydrogen ['haɪdrədʒən] hydrogène *m*

hygiene ['haɪdʒiːn] hygiène *f*;

hygienic hygiénique

hymn [hɪm] hymne *m*

hype [haɪp] battage *m* publicitaire

hyperactive [haɪpər'æktɪv] hyperactif; **hypersensitive** hypersensible; **hypertext** COMPUT hypertexte *m*

hypnosis [hɪp'noʊsɪs] hypnose *f*; **hypnotize** hypnotiser

hypocrisy [hɪ'pɑːkrəsɪ] hypocrisie *f*; **hypocrite** hypocrite *m/f*; **hypocritical** hypocrite

hypothesis [haɪ'pɑːθəsɪs] hypothèse *f*; **hypothetical** hypothétique

hysterectomy [hɪstə'rektəmɪ] hystérectomie *f*

hysteria [hɪ'stɪrɪə] hystérie *f*; **hysterical** hystérique; F *(very funny)* à mourir de rire F; **hysterics** crise *f* de nerfs; *laughter* fou rire *m*

I

I [aɪ] je; *before vowel* j'; *here* ∿ *am* me voici

ice [aɪs] glace *f*; *on road* verglas *m*; **icebox** glacière *f*; **ice cream** glace *f*; **ice cube** glaçon *m*; **iced** *drink* glacé; **ice hockey** hockey *m* sur glace; **ice rink** patinoire *f*; **ice skate** patin *m* (à glace); **ice skating** patinage *m* (sur glace)

icon ['aɪkɑːn] symbole *m*; COMPUT icône *f*

icy ['aɪsɪ] gelé; *welcome* glacial

ID [aɪdiː] (= *identity*) identité *f*; COMPUT identifiant *m*

idea [aɪ'diːə] idée *f*; **ideal** idéal; **idealistic** idéaliste

identical [aɪ'dentɪkl] identique; **identification** identification *f*; *(papers etc)* papiers *mpl* d'identité; **identify** identifier; **identity** identité *f*; ∿ *card* carte *f* d'identité

ideological [aɪdɪə'lɑːdʒɪkl]

idéologique; **ideology** idéologie *f*

idiomatic [ɪdɪə'mætɪk] (*natural*) idiomatique

idiot ['ɪdɪət] idiot(e) *m(f)*; **idiotic** idiot, bête

idle ['aɪdl] **1** *adj* (*not working*) inoccupé; (*lazy*) paresseux; *threat* oiseux; *machinery* non utilisé **2** *v/i of engine* tourner au ralenti

idol ['aɪdl] idole *f*; **idolize** idolâtrer

if [ɪf] si

ignite [ɪg'naɪt] mettre le feu à; **ignition** *in car* allumage *m*; ~ **key** clef *f* de contact

ignorance ['ɪgnərəns] ignorance *f*; **ignorant** ignorant; (*rude*) grossier; **ignore** ignorer

ill [ɪl] malade; *fall ~, be taken ~* tomber malade

illegal [ɪ'liːgl] illégal

illegible [ɪ'ledʒəbl] illisible

illegitimate [ɪlɪ'dʒɪtɪmət] *child* illégitime

illicit [ɪ'lɪsɪt] illicite

illiterate [ɪ'lɪtərət] illettré

illness ['ɪlnɪs] maladie *f*

illogical [ɪ'lɑːdʒɪkl] illogique

ill'treat maltraiter

illuminating [ɪ'luːmɪneɪtɪŋ] *remarks etc* éclairant

illusion [ɪ'luːʒn] illusion *f*

illustrate ['ɪləstreɪt] illustrer; **illustration** illustration *f*; **illustrator** illustrateur(-trice) *m(f)*

image ['ɪmɪdʒ] image *f*

imaginary [ɪ'mædʒɪnərɪ] imaginaire; **imagination** imagination *f*; **imaginative** imaginatif; **imagine** imaginer; *you're imagining things* tu te fais des idées

IMF [aɪem'ef] (= *International Monetary Fund*) F.M.I. *m* (= Fonds *m* Monétaire International)

imitate ['ɪmɪteɪt] imiter; **imitation** imitation *f*

immaculate [ɪ'mækjʊlət] impeccable

immature [ɪmə'tʊr] immature

immediate [ɪ'miːdɪət] immédiat; **immediately** immédiatement

immense [ɪ'mens] immense

immerse [ɪ'mɜːrs] immerger, plonger

immigrant ['ɪmɪgrənt] immigrant(e) *m(f)*; **immigrate** immigrer; **immigration** immigration *f*

imminent ['ɪmɪnənt] imminent

immobilize [ɪ'moʊbɪlaɪz] immobiliser

immoderate [ɪ'mɑːdərət] immodéré

immoral [ɪ'mɔːrəl] immoral; **immorality** immoralité *f*

immortal [ɪ'mɔːrtl] immortel; **immortality** immortalité *f*

immune [ɪ'mjuːn] *to illness* immunisé (*to* contre); *from ruling* exempt (*from* de); **immune system** MED système *m* immunitaire; **immunity**

immunité f; *from ruling exemption* f

impact ['ımpækt] impact *m*

impair [ım'per] affaiblir

impartial [ım'pɑ:rʃl] impartial

impassable [ım'pæsəbl] *road* impraticable

impassioned [ım'pæʃnd] *speech, plea* passionné

impatience [ım'peɪʃəns] impatience f; **impatient** impatient

impatiently impatiemment

impeccable [ım'pekəbl] impeccable

impede [ım'pi:d] gêner, empêcher; **impediment** *obstacle* obstacle *m*; **speech** ~ défaut *m* d'élocution

impending [ım'pendıŋ] imminent

imperative [ım'perətıv] **1** *adj* impératif **2** *n* GRAM impératif *m*

imperfect [ım'pɜ:rfekt] **1** *adj* imparfait **2** *n* GRAM imparfait *m*

impersonal [ım'pɜ:rsənl] impersonnel; **impersonate** *as a joke* imiter; *illegally* se faire passer pour

impertinence [ım'pɜ:rtınəns] impertinence f; **impertinent** impertinent

impervious [ım'pɜ:rvıəs]: ~ **to** insensible à

impetuous [ım'petʃuəs] impétueux

impetus ['ımpətəs] *of cam-*

paign etc force f, élan *m*

implement ['ımplımənt] **1** *n* instrument *m*, outil *m* **2** *v/t* ['ımplıment] appliquer

implicate ['ımplıkeıt] impliquer; **implication** implication f

implore [ım'plɔ:r] implorer

imply [ım'plaı] impliquer; *(suggest)* suggérer

impolite [ımpə'laıt] impoli

import ['ımpɔ:rt] **1** *n* importation f **2** *v/t* importer

importance [ım'pɔ:rtəns] importance f; **important** important

importer [ım'pɔ:rtər] importateur(-trice) *m(f)*

impose [ım'pouz] *tax* imposer; **imposing** imposant

impossibility [ımpɑ:sı'bılıtı] impossibilité f; **impossible** impossible

impotence ['ımpətəns] impuissance f; **impotent** impuissant

impractical [ım'præktıkəl] dénué de sens pratique

impress [ım'pres] impressionner; **impression** impression f; *(impersonation)* imitation f; **impressive** impressionnant

imprint ['ımprınt] *of credit card* empreinte f

imprison [ım'prızn] emprisonner; **imprisonment** emprisonnement *m*

improbable [ım'prɑ:bəbəl] improbable

income

improve [ɪmˈpruːv] **1** v/t améliorer **2** v/i s'améliorer; **improvement** amélioration f

improvise [ˈɪmprəvaɪz] improviser

impudent [ˈɪmpjʊdənt] impudent

impulse [ˈɪmpʌls] impulsion f; **impulsive** impulsif

in [ɪn] **1** prep dans; with time en; ~ **Rouen** à Rouen; ~ **1999** en 1999; ~ **the morning** le matin; ~ **the summer** l'été; ~ **August** en août, au mois d'août; ~ **two hours** from now dans deux heures; over period of en deux heures; ~ **English** en anglais; ~ **yellow** en jaune; ~ **crossing the road** en traversant la route **2** adv (at home, in the building etc) là; (arrived: train) arrivé; (in its position) dedans; ~ **here** ici **3** adj (fashionable, popular) à la mode

inability [ɪnəˈbɪlɪtɪ] incapacité f

inaccurate [ɪnˈækjʊrət] inexact

inadequate [ɪnˈædɪkwət] insuffisant, inadéquat

inadvisable [ɪnədˈvaɪzəbl] peu recommandé

inanimate [ɪnˈænɪmət] inanimé

inappropriate [ɪnəˈprəʊprɪət] peu approprié

inaudible [ɪnˈɔːdəbl] inaudible

inaugural [ɪˈnɔːgjʊrəl] speech

inaugural; **inaugurate** inaugurer

inborn [ˈɪnbɔːrn] inné

inc. (= **incorporated**) S.A. f (= Société f Anonyme)

incalculable [ɪnˈkælkjʊləbl] damage incalculable

incapable [ɪnˈkeɪpəbl] incapable

incentive [ɪnˈsentɪv] encouragement m, stimulation f

incessant [ɪnˈsesnt] incessant; **incessantly** sans arrêt

incest [ˈɪnsest] inceste m

inch [ɪntʃ] pouce m

incident [ˈɪnsɪdənt] incident m; **incidental** fortuit; ~ **expenses** frais mpl accessoires; **incidentally** soit dit en passant

incision [ɪnˈsɪʒn] incision f; **incisive** incisif

incite [ɪnˈsaɪt] inciter

inclination [ɪnklɪˈneɪʃn] (liking) penchant m; (tendency) tendance f

inclose, inclosure → **enclose, enclosure**

include [ɪnˈkluːd] inclure, comprendre; including y compris; ~ **service** service compris; **inclusive 1** adj price tout compris **2** prep: ~ **of** en incluant **3** adv tout compris; **from Monday to Thursday** du lundi au jeudi inclus

incoherent [ɪnkəʊˈhɪrənt] incohérent

income [ˈɪnkəm] revenu m;

income tax impôt *m* sur le revenu

incomparable [ɪnˈkɒmpərəbl] incomparable

incompatibility [ɪnkəmpætɪ-ˈbɪlɪtɪ] incompatibilité *f*; **incompatible** incompatible

incompetence [ɪnˈkɒmpɪtəns] incompétence *f*; **incompetent** incompétent

incomplete [ɪnkəmˈpliːt] incomplet

incomprehensible [ɪnkɒm-prɪˈhensɪbl] incompréhensible

inconceivable [ɪnkənˈsiːvəbl] inconcevable

inconsiderate [ɪnkənˈsɪd-ərət] *action* inconsidéré; *be ~ of person* manquer d'égards

inconsistent [ɪnkənˈsɪstənt] incohérent; *person* inconstant

inconspicuous [ɪnkənˈspɪk-juəs] discret

inconvenience [ɪnkənˈviːn-ɪəns] inconvénient *m*; **inconvenient** *time* inopportun; *place, arrangement* peu commode

incorporate [ɪnˈkɔːrpəreɪt] incorporer

incorrect [ɪnkəˈrekt] incorrect

increase 1 [ɪnˈkriːs] *v/t & v/i* augmenter **2** [ˈɪnkriːs] *n* augmentation *f*; **increasing** croissant; **increasingly** de plus en plus

incredible [ɪnˈkredɪbl] incroyable

incur [ɪnˈkɜːr] *costs* encourir; *debts* contracter; *s.o.'s anger* s'attirer

incurable [ɪnˈkjʊərəbl] *also fig* incurable

indecent [ɪnˈdiːsnt] indécent

indecisive [ɪndɪˈsaɪsɪv] *argument* peu concluant; *person* indécis; **indecisiveness** indécision *f*

indeed [ɪnˈdiːd] *(in fact)* vraiment; *(yes, agreeing)* en effet; *very much ~* beaucoup

indefinable [ɪndɪˈfaɪnəbl] indéfinissable

indefinite [ɪnˈdefɪnɪt] indéfini; **indefinitely** indéfiniment

indelicate [ɪnˈdelɪkət] indélicat

independence [ɪndɪˈpend-əns] indépendance *f*; **Independence Day** fête *f* de l'Indépendance; **independent** indépendant

indescribable [ɪndɪˈskraɪbə-bl] indescriptible; *(very bad)* inqualifiable

index [ˈɪndeks] *for book* index *m*

India [ˈɪndɪə] Inde *f*; **Indian 1** *adj* indien **2** *n also American* Indien(ne) *m(f)*

indicate [ˈɪndɪkeɪt] **1** *v/t* indiquer **2** *v/i when driving* mettre ses clignotants; **indication** indication *f*, signe *m*

indict [ɪnˈdaɪt] accuser

indifference [ɪnˈdɪfrəns] indifférence *f*; **indifferent** indifférent; (*mediocre*) médiocre

indigestion [ɪndɪ'dʒestʃn] indigestion *f*

indignant [ɪn'dɪɡnənt] indigné; **indignation** indignation *f*

indirect [ɪndɪ'rekt] indirect; **indirectly** indirectement

indiscreet [ɪndɪ'skriːt] indiscret

indiscriminate [ɪndɪ'skrɪmɪnət] aveugle; *accusations* à tort et à travers

indispensable [ɪndɪ'spensəbl] indispensable

indisposed [ɪndɪ'spəʊzd] (*not well*) indisposé

indisputable [ɪndɪ'spjuːtəbl] incontestable

indistinct [ɪndɪ'stɪŋkt] indistinct

indistinguishable [ɪndɪ'stɪŋwɪʃəbl] indifférenciable

individual [ɪndɪ'vɪdʒʊəl] **1** *n* individu *m* **2** *adj* (*separate*) particulier; (*personal*) individuel; **individually** individuellement

indoctrinate [ɪn'dɒːktrɪneɪt] endoctriner

Indonesia [ɪndə'niːʒə] Indonésie *f*; **Indonesian 1** *adj* indonésien **2** *n person* Indonésien(ne) *m(f)*

indoor ['ɪndɔːr] *activities, games* d'intérieur; *sport* en salle; *arena* couvert; **indoors** à l'intérieur; (*at home*) à la maison

indorse → **endorse**

indulgent [ɪn'dʌldʒənt] (*not strict enough*) indulgent

industrial [ɪn'dʌstriəl] industriel; **industrial dispute** conflit *m* social; **industrialist** industriel(le) *m(f)*; **industrious** travailleur; **industry** industrie *f*

ineffective [ɪnɪ'fektɪv] inefficace

inefficient [ɪnɪ'fɪʃənt] inefficace

inept [ɪ'nept] inepte

inequality [ɪnɪ'kwɒːlɪtɪ] inégalité *f*

inescapable [ɪnɪ'skeɪpəbl] inévitable

inevitable [ɪn'evɪtəbl] inévitable; **inevitably** inévitablement

inexcusable [ɪnɪk'skjuːzəbl] inexcusable

inexhaustible [ɪnɪɡ'zɒːstəbl] inépuisable

inexpensive [ɪnɪk'spensɪv] bon marché, pas cher

inexperienced [ɪnɪk'spɪriənst] inexpérimenté

inexplicable [ɪnɪk'splɪkəbl] inexplicable

infallible [ɪn'fælɪbl] infaillible

infamous ['ɪnfəməs] infâme

infancy ['ɪnfənsɪ] *of person* petite enfance *f*; *of state, institution* débuts *mpl*; **infant** petit(e) enfant *m(f)*; **infantile** *pej* infantile

infantry ['ɪnfəntrɪ] infanterie

f

infect [ɪnˈfekt] contaminer; **become ~ed** of wound s'infecter; Infection contamination f; (disease), of wound infection f; **infectious** disease infectieux; laughter contagieux

infer [ɪnˈfɜːr]: **~ X from Y** déduire X de Y

inferior [ɪnˈfɪərɪər] inférieur; **inferiority** infériorité f; **inferiority complex** complexe m d'infériorité

infertile [ɪnˈfɜːtl] stérile; **infertility** stérilité f

infidelity [ɪnfɪˈdelɪtɪ] infidélité f

infinite [ˈɪnfɪnət] infini; **infinitive** infinitif m

infinity [ɪnˈfɪnətɪ] infinité f; MATH infini m

inflammable [ɪnˈflæməbl] inflammable; **inflammation** MED inflammation f

inflatable [ɪnˈfleɪtəbl] dinghy gonflable; **inflate** tire, dinghy gonfler; **inflation** inflation f; **inflationary** inflationniste

inflexible [ɪnˈfleksɪbl] attitude, person inflexible

inflict [ɪnˈflɪkt] infliger (**on** à)

influence [ˈɪnfluəns] **1** n influence f **2** v/t influencer; **influential** influent

inform [ɪnˈfɔːrm] **1** v/t informer **2** v/i: **~ on** dénoncer

informal [ɪnˈfɔːrml] meeting, agreement non-officiel; form of address familier; conver-

sation, dress simple; **informality** of meeting, agreement caractère m non officiel; of form of address familiarité f; of conversation, dress simplicité f

informant [ɪnˈfɔːrmənt] informateur(-trice) m(f); **information** renseignements mpl; **information technology** informatique f; **informative** instructif; **informer** dénonciateur(-trice) m(f)

infra-red [ɪnfrəˈred] infrarouge

infrastructure [ˈɪnfrəstrʌktʃər] infrastructure f

infrequent [ɪnˈfriːkwənt] rare

infuriate [ɪnˈfjʊərɪeɪt] rendre furieux; **infuriating** exaspérant

ingenious [ɪnˈdʒiːnɪəs] ingénieux

ingot [ˈɪŋgət] lingot m

ingratitude [ɪnˈgrætɪtuːd] ingratitude f

ingredient [ɪnˈgriːdɪənt] for cooking ingrédient m; for success recette f

inhabit [ɪnˈhæbɪt] habiter; **inhabitant** habitant(e) m(f)

inhale [ɪnˈheɪl] **1** v/t inhaler **2** v/i when smoking avaler la fumée

inherit [ɪnˈherɪt] hériter; **inheritance** héritage m

inhibited [ɪnˈhɪbɪtɪd] inhibé; **inhibition** inhibition f

inhospitable [ɪnhɑˈspɪtəbl] inhospitalier

inhuman [ɪnˈhjuːmən] inhumain

initial [ɪˈnɪʃl] **1** adj initial **2** n initiale f **3** v/t (write initials on) parapher; **initially** au début; **initiate** procedure lancer; person initier; **initiation** lancement m; of person initiation f; **initiative** initiative f

inject [ɪnˈdʒekt] injecter; **injection** injection f

injure [ˈɪndʒər] blesser; **injury** blessure f

injustice [ɪnˈdʒʌstɪs] injustice f

ink [ɪŋk] encre f

inland [ˈɪnlənd] intérieur

in-laws [ˈɪnlɔːz] belle-famille f

inmate [ˈɪnmeɪt] of prison détenu(e) m(f); of mental hospital interné(e) m(f)

inn [ɪn] auberge f

innate [ɪˈneɪt] inné

inner [ˈɪnər] courtyard intérieur; thoughts intime; ear interne

innocence [ˈɪnəsəns] innocence f; **innocent** innocent

innocuous [ɪˈnɑːkjuəs] inoffensif

innovation [ɪnəˈveɪʃn] innovation f; **innovative** innovant; **innovator** innovateur(-trice) m(f)

inoculate [ɪˈnɑːkjuleɪt] inoculer; **inoculation** inoculation f

inoffensive [ɪnəˈfensɪv] inoffensif

'in-patient patient(e) hospitalisé(e) m(f)

input [ˈɪnput] **1** n into project etc apport m, contribution f; COMPUT entrée f **2** v/t into project apporter; COMPUT entrer

inquest [ˈɪnkwest] enquête f (into sur)

inquire [ɪnˈkwaɪr] se renseigner; **inquiry** demande f de renseignements; **government ~** enquête f officielle

inquisitive [ɪnˈkwɪzətɪv] curieux

insane [ɪnˈseɪn] fou

insanitary [ɪnˈsænɪterɪ] insalubre

insanity [ɪnˈsænɪtɪ] folie f

inscription [ɪnˈskrɪpʃn] inscription f

insect [ˈɪnsekt] insecte m; **insecticide** insecticide m

insecure [ɪnsɪˈkjur]: be ~ not safe ne pas se sentir en sécurité; not sure of self manquer d'assurance; **insecurity** psychological manque m d'assurance

insensitive [ɪnˈsensɪtɪv] insensible (to à)

insert [ˈɪnsɜːrt] n in magazine etc encart m **2** [ɪnˈsɜːrt] v/t insérer

inside [ɪnˈsaɪd] **1** n intérieur m; ~ out à l'envers **2** prep à l'intérieur de; ~ of 2 hours en moins de 2 heures **3** adv à l'intérieur **4** adj: ~ **information** informations fpl internes; **~ lane** SP couloir *m* intérieur

inside pocket poche *f* intérieure; **insider** initié(e) *m(f)*; **insider trading** FIN délit *m* d'initié; **insides** (*stomach*) ventre *m*

insignificant [ɪnsɪg'nɪfɪkənt] insignifiant

insincere [ɪnsɪn'sɪr] peu sincère; **insincerity** manque *f* de sincérité

insinuate [ɪn'sɪnjueɪt] insinuer

insist [ɪn'sɪst] insister (**on** sur); **insistent** insistant

insolent ['ɪnsələnt] insolent

insolvent [ɪn'sɑːlvənt] insolvable

insomnia [ɪn'sɑːmnɪə] insomnie *f*

inspect [ɪn'spekt] *work, tickets, baggage* contrôler; *factory, school* inspecter; **inspection** *of work, tickets, baggage* contrôle *m*; *of factory, school* inspection *f*; **inspector** *in factory* inspecteur(-trice) *m(f)*

inspiration [ɪnspə'reɪʃn] inspiration *f*; **inspire** inspirer

instability [ɪnstə'bɪlɪtɪ] instabilité *f*

install [ɪn'stɔːl] installer; **installation** installation *f*; **installment**, *Br* **instalment** *of story etc* épisode *m*; (*payment*) versement *m*; **installment plan** vente *f* à crédit

instance ['ɪnstəns] (*example*)

exemple *m*; **for ~** par exemple

instant ['ɪnstənt] **1** *adj* instantané **2** *n* instant *m*; **instantaneous** instantané; **instant coffee** café *m* soluble; **instantly** immédiatement

instead [ɪn'sted] à la place; **~ of me** à ma place; **~ of going home** au lieu de rentrer à la maison

instinct ['ɪnstɪŋkt] instinct *m*; **instinctive** instinctif

institute ['ɪnstɪtuːt] **1** *n* institut *m*; (*special home*) établissement *m* **2** *v/t new law, inquiry* instituer; **institution** institution *f*

instruct [ɪn'strʌkt] (*order*) ordonner; (*teach*) instruire; **instruction** instruction *f*; **~s for use** mode *m* d'emploi; **instructive** instructif; **instructor** moniteur(-trice) *m(f)*

instrument ['ɪnstrəmənt] instrument *m*

insubordinate [ɪnsə'bɔːrdɪneɪt] insubordonné

insufficient [ɪnsə'fɪʃnt] insuffisant

insulate ['ɪnsəleɪt] ELEC, *against cold* isoler; **insulation** isolation *f*; *material* isolement *m*

insulin ['ɪnsəlɪn] insuline *f*

insult 1 ['ɪnsʌlt] *n* insulte *f* **2** *v/t* insulter

insurance [ɪn'ʃurəns] assurance *f*; **insurance company**

compagnie f d'assurance; **insurance policy** police f d'assurance; **insurance premium** prime f d'assurance; **insure** assurer

insurmountable [ɪnsərˈmaʊntəbl] insurmontable

intact [ɪnˈtækt] (*not damaged*) intact

integrate [ˈɪntɪɡreɪt] intégrer; **integrity** (*honesty*) intégrité f

intellect [ˈɪntəlekt] intellect m; **intellectual 1** *adj* intellectuel **2** *n* intellectuel(le) m(f)

intelligence [ɪnˈtelɪdʒəns] intelligence f; (*information*) renseignements mpl; **intelligent** intelligent

intelligible [ɪnˈtelɪdʒəbl] intelligible

intend [ɪnˈtend] *v/i*: ~ **to do sth** avoir l'intention de

intense [ɪnˈtens] intense; *personality* passionné; **intensify 1** *v/t* intensifier **2** *v/i* *of pain, fighting* s'intensifier; **intensity** intensité f; **intensive** intensif; **intensive care** MED service m de soins intensifs

intention [ɪnˈtenʃn] intention f; **intentional** intentionnel; **intentionally** délibérément

interaction [ɪntərˈækʃn] interaction f; **interactive** interactif

intercept [ɪntərˈsept] intercepter

interchange [ˈɪntərtʃeɪndʒ] *of highways* échangeur m; **in-**

terchangeable interchangeable

intercom [ˈɪntərkɑːm] interphone m

intercourse [ˈɪntərkɔːrs] *sexual* rapports mpl

interdependent [ɪntərdɪˈpendənt] interdépendant

interest [ˈɪntrəst] **1** *n* intérêt m; *financial* intérêt(s) m(pl) **2** *v/t* intéresser; **interested** intéressé; **interesting** intéressant; **interest rate** taux m d'intérêt

interface [ˈɪntərfeɪs] **1** *n* interface f **2** *v/i* avoir une interface (**with** avec)

interfere [ɪntərˈfɪr] se mêler (**with** de); **interference** ingérence f; *on radio* interférence f

interior [ɪnˈtɪriər] **1** *adj* intérieur **2** *n* intérieur m; **interior design** design m d'intérieurs; **interior designer** designer m/f d'intérieurs

interlude [ˈɪntərluːd] intermède m

intermediary [ɪntərˈmiːdɪeri] intermédiaire m/f; **intermediate** *level* intermédiaire; *course* (de niveau) moyen

intermission [ɪntərˈmɪʃn] *in theater* entracte m

internal [ɪnˈtɜːrnl] interne; *trade* intérieur; **internally** *in organization* en interne; **not to be taken** ~ à usage externe; **Internal Revenue (Service)** direction f générale des) impôts *mpl*

international [ɪntərˈnæʃnl] international; **internationally** internationalement

Internet [ˈɪntərnet] Internet *m*; **on the ~** sur Internet

interpret [ɪnˈtɜːrprit] interpréter; **interpretation** interprétation *f*; **interpreter** interprète *m/f*

interrogate [ɪnˈterəgeit] interroger; **interrogation** interrogatoire *m*; **interrogator** interrogateur(-trice) *m(f)*

interrupt [ɪntəˈrʌpt] interrompre; **interruption** interruption *f*

intersect [ɪntərˈsekt] **1** *v/t* couper, croiser **2** *v/i* s'entre-couper, s'entrecroiser; **intersection** *of roads* carrefour *m*

interstate [ˈɪntərsteit] autoroute *f*

interval [ˈɪntərvl] intervalle *m*; *in theater* entracte *m*

intervene [ɪntərˈviːn] intervenir; **intervention** intervention *f*

interview [ˈɪntərvjuː] **1** *n* interview *f*; *for job* entretien *m* **2** *v/t* interviewer; *for job* faire passer un entretien à; **interviewer** interviewer (-euse) *m(f)*; *for job* personne *f* responsable d'un entretien

intimate [ˈɪntɪmət] intime

intimidate [ɪnˈtɪmɪdeit] intimider; **intimidation** intimidation *f*

into [ˈɪntʊ] dans; *translate ~ English* traduire en anglais; *be ~ sth* F *(like)* aimer qch; *politics etc* être engagé dans qch

intolerable [ɪnˈtɑːlərəbl] intolérable; **intolerant** intolérant

intoxicated [ɪnˈtɑːksɪkeitɪd] ivre

intravenous [ɪntrəˈviːnəs] intraveineux

intricate [ˈɪntrɪkət] compliqué, complexe

intrigue 1 [ˈɪntriːg] *n* intrigue *f* **2** [ɪnˈtriːg] *v/t* intriguer; **intriguing** intrigant

introduce [ɪntrəˈduːs] *new technique etc* introduire; *~ s.o. to s.o.* présenter qn à qn; **introduction** *to person* présentations *fpl*; *in book, of new techniques* introduction *f*

intrude [ɪnˈtruːd] déranger; **intruder** intrus(e) *m(f)*; **intrusion** intrusion *f*

intuition [ɪntuːˈɪʃn] intuition *f*

invade [ɪnˈveɪd] envahir

invalid[1] [ɪnˈvælɪd] *adj* non valable

invalid[2] [ˈɪnvəlɪd] *n* MED invalide *m/f*

invalidate [ɪnˈvælɪdeit] *claim, theory* invalider

invaluable [ɪnˈvæljubl] inestimable

invariably [ɪnˈveɪrɪəbli] *(always)* invariablement

invasion [ɪnˈveɪʒn] invasion *f*

invent [ɪnˈvent] inventer; **in-**

vention invention *f*; **inventive** inventif; **inventor** inventeur(-trice) *m(f)*

inventory ['ɪnvəntɔːrɪ] inventaire *m*

invert [ɪn'vɜːrt] inverser

invest [ɪn'vest] investir

investigate [ɪn'vestɪgeɪt] *crime* enquêter sur; *scientific phenomenon* étudier; **investigation** *of crime* enquête *f*; *in science* étude *f*

investment [ɪn'vestmənt] investissement *m*; **investor** investisseur *m*

invincible [ɪn'vɪnsəbl] invincible

invisible [ɪn'vɪzɪbl] invisible

invitation [ɪnvɪ'teɪʃn] invitation *f*; **invite** inviter

invoice ['ɪnvɔɪs] **1** *n* facture *f* **2** *v/t customer* facturer

involuntary [ɪn'vɑːləntərɪ] involontaire

involve [ɪn'vɑːlv] *work* nécessiter; *expense* entraîner; (*concern*) concerner; **what does it ..?** qu'est-ce que cela implique?; **involved** (*complex*) compliqué; **involvement** *in project, crime etc* participation *f*; *in politics* engagement *m*

invulnerable [ɪn'vʌlnərəbl] invulnérable

inward ['ɪnwərd] **1** *adj* intérieur **2** *adv* vers l'intérieur; **inwardly** vers l'intérieur

IQ [aɪ'kjuː] (= *intelligence quotient*) Q.I. *m* (= Quotient *m* intellectuel)

Iran [ɪ'rɑːn] Iran *m*; **Iranian 1** *adj* iranien **2** *n* Iranien(ne) *m(f)*

Iraq [ɪ'rɑːk] Iraq *m*; **Iraqi 1** *adj* irakien **2** *n* Irakien(ne) *m(f)*

Ireland ['aɪrlənd] Irlande *f*; **Irish 1** *adj* irlandais **2** *npl*: **the ~** les Irlandais

iron ['aɪərn] **1** *n* fer *m*; *for clothes* fer *m* à repasser **2** *v/t shirts etc* repasser

ironic(al) [aɪ'rɑːnɪk(l)] ironique

'ironing board planche *f* à repasser

irony ['aɪrənɪ] ironie *f*

irrational [ɪ'ræʃənl] irrationnel

irreconcilable [ɪrekən'saɪləbl] *people* irréconciliable; *positions* inconciliables

irregular [ɪ'regjʊlər] irrégulier

irrelevant [ɪ'reləvənt] hors de propos

irreplaceable [ɪrɪ'pleɪsəbl] irremplaçable

irrepressible [ɪrɪ'presəbl] *sense of humor* à toute épreuve; *person* qui ne se laisse pas abattre

irresistible [ɪrɪ'zɪstəbl] irrésistible

irresponsible [ɪrɪ'spɑːnsəbl] irresponsable

irreverent [ɪ'revərənt] irrévérencieux

irrevocable [ɪ'revəkəbl] irrévocable

irrigate ['ırıgeıt] irriguer; **irrigation** irrigation *f*

irritable ['ırıtəbl] irritable; **irritate** irriter; **irritating** irritant; **irritation** irritation *f*

Islam ['ızlɑːm] *religion* islam *m*; *peoples, civilization* Islam *m*; **Islamic** islamique

island ['aılənd] île *f*

isolate ['aısəleıt] isoler; **isolated** isolé; **isolation** isolement *m*

ISP [aıes'piː] (= *Internet service provider*) fournisseur *m* Internet

Israel ['ızreıl] Israël *m*; **Israeli** 1 *adj* israélien 2 *n person* Israélien(ne) *m(f)*

issue ['ıʃuː] 1 *n* (*matter*) question *f*, problème *m*; *of magazine* numéro *m* 2 *v/t supplies* distribuer; *coins, warning* émettre; *passport* délivrer

IT [aı'tiː] (= *information technology*) informatique *f*

it [ıt] *as subject* il, elle; *as object* le, la; *~'s through there*

c'est par là; *give ~ to him* donne-le lui; *on top of ~* dessus; *let's talk about ~* parlons-en; *~'s raining* il pleut; *~'s me/him* c'est moi/lui; *that's ~!* (*that's right*) c'est ça!; (*finished*) c'est fini!

Italian [ı'tæljən] 1 *adj* italien 2 *n person* Italien(ne) *m(f)*; *language* italien *m*

italics [ı'tælıks] italique *m*

Italy ['ıtəlı] Italie *f*

itch [ıtʃ] 1 *n* démangeaison *f* 2 *v/i: it ~es* ça me démange

item ['aıtəm] article *m*; *on agenda* point *m*; *~ of news* nouvelle *f*; **itemize** *invoice* détailler

itinerary [aı'tınərerı] itinéraire *m*

its [ıts] son, sa; *pl* ses

it's [ıts] → **it is, it has**

itself [ıt'self] *reflexive* se; *stressed* lui-même; elle-même; *by ~* (*automatically*) tout(e) seul(e)

J

jab [dʒæb]:*~ a stick into s.o.* donner un coup de bâton à qn

jack [dʒæk] MOT cric *m*; *in cards* valet *m*

jacket ['dʒækıt] veste *f*; *of book* couverture *f*

'jackpot jackpot *m*

jagged ['dʒægıd] découpé

jail [dʒeıl] prison *f*

jam¹ [dʒæm] *n for bread* confiture *f*

jam² [dʒæm] 1 *n* MOT embouteillage *m*; F (*difficulty*) pétrin *m* F 2 *v/t* (*ram*) fourrer; (*cause to stick*) bloquer; *broadcast* brouiller 3 *v/i* (*stick*) se bloquer

janitor ['dʒænɪtər] concierge m/f

January ['dʒænjʊərɪ] janvier m

Japan [dʒə'pæn] Japon m; **Japanese** [dʒæpə'niːz] **1** adj japonais **2** n person Japonais(e) m(f); language japonais m; **the ~** les Japonais mpl

jar [dʒɑːr] container pot m

jargon ['dʒɑːrɡən] jargon m

jaw [dʒɔː] mâchoire f

jaywalker ['dʒeɪwɔːkər] piéton(ne) m(f) imprudent(e)

jazz [dʒæz] jazz m

jealous ['dʒeləs] jaloux; **jealousy** jalousie f

jeans [dʒiːnz] jean m

jeep [dʒiːp] jeep f

jeer [dʒɪr] **1** n raillerie f; of crowd huée f **2** v/i of crowd huer

Jello® ['dʒeləʊ] gelée f

jelly ['dʒelɪ] jam confiture f; **jellyfish** méduse f

jeopardize ['dʒepərdaɪz] mettre en danger

jerk¹ [dʒɜːrk] **1** n saccade f **2** v/t tirer d'un coup sec

jerk² [dʒɜːrk] F couillon m

jerky ['dʒɜːrkɪ] movement saccadé

Jesus ['dʒiːzəs] Jésus

jet [dʒet] (airplane) avion m à réaction, jet m; of water jet m; (nozzle) bec m; **jetlag** (troubles mpl dus au) décalage m horaire

jettison ['dʒetɪsn] jeter par-dessus bord; fig abandonner

jetty ['dʒetɪ] jetée f

Jew [dʒuː] Juif(-ive) m(f)

jewel ['dʒuːəl] bijou m; fig : person perle f; **jeweler**, Br **jeweller** bijoutier(-ère) m(f); **jewelry**, Br **jewellery** bijoux mpl

Jewish ['dʒuːɪʃ] juif

jigsaw (puzzle) ['dʒɪɡsɔː] puzzle m

jilt [dʒɪlt] laisser tomber

jingle ['dʒɪŋɡl] **1** n song jingle m **2** v/i of keys, coins cliqueter

jinx [dʒɪŋks] person porte-malheur m/f; **there's a ~ on this project** ce projet porte malheur

jittery ['dʒɪtərɪ] F nerveux

job [dʒɑːb] travail m; **jobless** sans travail

jockey ['dʒɑːkɪ] jockey m

jog [dʒɑːɡ] as exercise faire du footing ou jogging; **jogger** person joggeur(-euse) m(f); **jogging** jogging m

john [dʒɑːn] F (toilet) petit coin m F

join [dʒɔɪn] **1** n joint m **2** v/i/t of roads, rivers se rejoindre; (become a member) devenir membre **3** v/t (connect) relier; person, of road rejoindre; club devenir membre de
♦ **join in** participer

joint [dʒɔɪnt] ANAT articulation f; in woodwork joint m; of meat rôti m; **joint account** compte m joint; **joint venture** entreprise f commune

joke [ʒəʊk] **1** *n* plaisanterie *f*, blague *f* F; (*practical ~*) tour *m* **2** *v/i* plaisanter; **joker** farceur(-euse) *m(f)*, blagueur (-euse) *m(f)* F; *in cards* joker *m*; **jokingly** en plaisantant

jostle ['dʒɒsl] bousculer

journal ['dʒɜːrnl] (*magazine*) revue *f*; (*diary*) journal *m*; **journalism** journalisme *m*; **journalist** journaliste *m/f*

journey ['dʒɜːrnɪ] voyage *m*; *across town etc* trajet *m*

joy [dʒɔɪ] joie *f*

jubilant ['dʒuːbɪlənt] débordant de joie; **jubilation** jubilation *f*

judge [dʒʌdʒ] **1** *n* juge *m/f* **2** *v/t* juger; *measurement, age* estimer **3** *v/i* juger; **judg(e)-ment** jugement *m*; (*opinion*) avis *m*; **Judg(e)ment Day** le Jugement dernier

judicial [dʒuː'dɪʃl] judiciaire

juggle ['dʒʌgl] *also fig* jongler avec

juice [dʒuːs] jus *m*; **juicy** juteux; *gossip* croustillant

July [dʒuː'laɪ] juillet *m*

jumbo (jet) ['dʒʌmbəʊ] jumbo-jet *m*; **jumbo-sized** F géant

jump [dʒʌmp] **1** *n* saut *m*; (*increase*) bond *m* **2** *v/i* sauter; *in surprise* sursauter; (*increase*) faire un bond **3** *v/t* *fence etc* sauter; F (*attack*) attaquer; *~ the lights* griller un feu (rouge)

♦ **jump at** *opportunity* sauter sur

jumper ['dʒʌmpər] *dress* robe-chasuble *f*; **jumpy** nerveux

June [dʒuːn] juin *m*

jungle ['dʒʌŋgl] jungle *f*

junior ['dʒuːnjər] **1** *adj* subalterne; (*younger*) plus jeune **2** *n in rank* subalterne *m/f*; **she is ten years my ~** elle est ma cadette de dix ans; **junior high** collège *m*

junk [dʒʌŋk] camelote *f* F; **junk food** cochonneries *fpl*; **junkie** F drogué(e) *m(f)*; **junk mail** prospectus *mpl*

jurisdiction [dʒʊrɪs'dɪkʃn] LAW juridiction *f*

juror ['dʒʊrər] juré(e) *m(f)*; **jury** jury *m*

just [dʒʌst] **1** *adj cause* juste **2** *adv* (*barely, only*) tout juste; *~ as intelligent* tout aussi intelligent; *I've ~ seen her* je viens de la voir; *~ about* (*almost*) presque; *I was ~ about to leave when ...* j'étais sur le point de partir quand ...; *~ now* (*a few moments ago*) tout à l'heure; (*at this moment*) en ce moment

justice ['dʒʌstɪs] justice *f*

justifiable [dʒʌstɪ'faɪəbl] justifiable; **justifiably** à juste titre; **justification** justification *f*; **justify** *also text* justifier

justly ['dʒʌstlɪ] (*fairly*) de manière juste; (*rightly*) à juste titre

◆ **jut out** [dʒʌt] être en saillie

juvenile ['dʒuːvənail] *crime* juvénile; *court* pour enfants; *pej* puéril; **juvenile delinquent** mineur(e) délinquant(e) *m(f)*

k [kei] (= *kilobyte*) Ko *m* (= kilo-octet *m*); (= *thousand*) mille

keel [kiːl] NAUT quille *f*

keen [kiːn] (*intense*) vif

keep [kiːp] **1** *v/t* garder; (*detain*) retenir; *in specific place* mettre; *family* entretenir; *dog etc* avoir; *bees, cattle* élever; *promise* tenir; **~ sth from s.o.** cacher qch à qn; **~ s.o. from doing sth** empêcher qn de faire qch; **~ trying!** essaie encore!; **don't ~ interrupting!** arrête de m'interrompre tout le temps! **2** *v/i* (*remain*) rester; *of food, milk* se conserver

◆ **keep back** (*hold in check*) retenir; *information* cacher

◆ **keep down** *costs etc* réduire; *food* garder

◆ **keep to** *path* rester sur; *rules* s'en tenir à

◆ **keep up 1** *v/i when walking, running etc* suivre; **keep up with** aller au même rythme que **2** *v/t pace, payments* continuer; *bridge, pants* soutenir

'**keepsake** souvenir *m*

kennel ['kenl] niche *f*; **kennels** chenil *m*

kerosene ['kerəsiːn] AVIA kérosène *m*; *for lamps* pétrole *m* (lampant)

ketchup ['ketʃʌp] ketchup *m*

kettle ['ketl] bouilloire *f*

key [kiː] **1** *n* clef *f*, clé *f*; COMPUT, MUS touche *f* **2** *adj* (*vital*) clef *inv*, clé *inv* **3** *v/t & v/i* COMPUT taper

◆ **key in** *data* taper

'**keyboard** COMPUT, MUS clavier *m*; **keyboarder** COMPUT claviste *m/f*; **keycard** carteclef *f*; **keyed-up** tendu; **keyring** porte-clefs *m*

kick [kik] **1** *n* coup *m* de pied **2** *v/t* donner un coup de pied dans **3** *v/i of horse* ruer

◆ **kick around** *ball* taper dans; F (*discuss*) débattre

◆ **kick off** donner le coup d'envoi; F (*start*) démarrer F

◆ **kick out** mettre à la porte; **be kicked out of the company** être mis à la porte de la société

'**kickback** F (*bribe*) dessous-de-table *m* F

'**kickoff** SP coup *m* d'envoi

kid [kid] **1** *n* F (*child*) gamin(e) *m(f)* **2** *v/t* F taquiner **3** *v/i* F plaisanter

kidnap ['kidnæp] kidnapper;

kidnap(p)er kidnappeur (-euse) *m(f)*; **kidnap(p)ing** kidnapping *m*

kidney [ˈkɪdnɪ] ANAT rein *m*; *in cooking* rognon *m*

kill [kɪl] *also time* tuer; **killer** (*murderer*) tueur (-euse) *m(f)*; **killing** meurtre *m*

kiln [kɪln] four *m*

kilo [ˈkiːləʊ] kilo *m*; **kilobyte** kilo-octet *m*; **kilogram** kilogramme *m*; **kilometer**, *Br* **kilometre** kilomètre *m*

kind¹ [kaɪnd] *adj* gentil

kind² [kaɪnd] *n* (*sort*) sorte *f*, genre *m*; (*make, brand*) marque *f*; **~ of sad/strange** F plutôt triste/bizarre

kind-hearted [kaɪndˈhɑːrtɪd] bienveillant, bon; **kindly** gentil, bon; **kindness** bonté *f*, gentillesse *f*

king [kɪŋ] roi *m*; **kingdom** royaume *m*

kinky [ˈkɪŋkɪ] F bizarre

kiosk [ˈkiːɑːsk] kiosque *m*

kiss [kɪs] **1** *n* baiser *m* **2** *v/t* embrasser **3** *v/i* s'embrasser

kit [kɪt] (*equipment*) trousse *f*; *for assembly* kit *m*

kitchen [ˈkɪtʃɪn] cuisine *f*

kitten [ˈkɪtn] chaton(ne) *m(f)*

kitty [ˈkɪtɪ] *money* cagnotte *f*

knack [næk]: **have the ~ of doing** avoir le chic pour faire; **there's a ~ to it** il y a un truc F

knee [niː] genou *m*; **kneecap** rotule *f*

kneel [niːl] s'agenouiller

'knee-length à la hauteur du genou

knife [naɪf] couteau *m*

knit [nɪt] tricoter; **knitwear** tricot *m*

knob [nɑːb] *on door* bouton *m*; *of butter* noix *f*

knock [nɑːk] **1** *n on door,* (*blow*) coup *m* **2** *v/t* (*hit*) frapper; *knee etc* se cogner; F (*criticize*) débiner F **3** *v/i on door* frapper

◆ **knock down** renverser; *wall, building* abattre; F (*reduce the price of*) solder

◆ **knock out** assommer; *boxer* mettre knock-out; *power lines etc* détruire; (*eliminate*) éliminer

◆ **knock over** renverser

'knockout *in boxing* knock-out *m*

knot [nɑːt] **1** *n* nœud *m* **2** *v/t* nouer

know [nəʊ] **1** *v/t* savoir; *person, place, language* connaître; (*recognize*) reconnaître **2** *v/i* savoir; **~ about sth** être au courant de qch; **know-how** F savoir-faire *m*; **knowing** *smile* entendu; **knowingly** (*wittingly*) sciemment; *smile etc* d'un air entendu; **know-it-all** F je-sais-tout *m/f*; **knowledge** savoir *m*; *of a subject* connaissance(s) *f(pl)*; **to the best of my ~** autant que je sache

knuckle [ˈnʌkl] articulation *f* du doigt

landslide victory

Koran [kə'ræn] Coran *m*

Korea [kə'ri:ə] Corée *f*; **Korean 1** *adj* coréen **2** *n* Coréen(ne) *m(f)*; *language* coréen *m*

kosher ['kouʃər] REL casher *inv*; F réglo *inv* F

kudos ['kju:dɑ:s] prestige *m*

L

lab [læb] labo *m*

label ['leɪbl] **1** *n* étiquette *f* **2** *v/t also fig* étiqueter

labor ['leɪbər] *also in pregnancy* travail *m*

laboratory ['læbrətɔ:rɪ] laboratoire *m*

labored ['leɪbərd] *style, speech* laborieux; **laborer** travailleur *m* manuel; **laborious** laborieux; **labor union** syndicat *m*

labour *Br* → **labor**

lace [leɪs] dentelle *f*; *for shoe* lacet *m*

lack [læk] **1** *n* manque *m* **2** *v/t* manquer de **3** *v/i*: **be ~ing** manquer

lacquer ['lækər] laque *f*

lactose ['læktəʊs] lactose *m*

ladder ['lædər] échelle *f*

laden ['leɪdn] chargé (**with** de)

ladies room ['leɪdi:z] toilettes *fpl* (pour dames)

lady ['leɪdɪ] dame *f*; **ladybug** coccinelle *f*; **ladylike** distingué

lager ['lɑ:gər] *Br* bière *f* blonde

laidback [leɪd'bæk] relax F

lake [leɪk] lac *m*

lamb [læm] agneau *m*

réen *m*

lame [leɪm] boiteux; *excuse* mauvais

laminated ['læmɪneɪtɪd] *flooring, paper* stratifié; *wood* contreplaqué; *with plastic* plastifié; **~ glass** verre *m* feuilleté

lamp [læmp] lampe *f*; **lamppost** réverbère *m*; **lampshade** abat-jour *m inv*

land [lænd] **1** *n* terre *f*; *(country)* pays *m*; **by ~** par (voie de) terre **2** *v/t airplane* faire atterrir; *job* décrocher F **3** *v/i of airplane* atterrir; *of ball* tomber; **landing** *of airplane* atterrissage *m*; *(top of staircase)* palier *m*; **landing strip** piste *f* d'atterrissage; **landlady** propriétaire *f*; *of rented room* logeuse *f*; *Br of bar* patronne *f*; **landlord** propriétaire *m*; *of rented room* logeur *m*; *Br of bar* patron *m*; **landmark** point *m* de repère; **be a ~ in** *fig* faire date dans; **land owner** propriétaire *m* foncier; **landscape 1** *n* paysage *m* **2** *adv print* en format paysage; **landslide** glissement *m* de terrain; **landslide victory** victoire *f* écrasante

lane [leɪn] *in country* petite route *f* (de campagne); *(alley)* ruelle *f*; мот usic *f*

language ['læŋgwɪdʒ] langue *f*; *(style, code etc)* langage *m*; **language lab** laboratoire *m* de langues

lap¹ [læp] *of track* tour *m*

lap² [læp] *of water* clapotis *m*

lap³ [læp] *of person* genoux *mpl*

lapel [lə'pel] revers *m*

lapse [læps] **1** *n (mistake)* erreur *f*; *in behavior* écart *m* (de conduite); *of time* intervalle *m* **2** *v/i* expirer

laptop ['læptɒp] comput portable *m*

larceny ['lɑ:rsənɪ] vol *m*

larder ['lɑ:rdər] garde-manger *m inv*

large [lɑ:rdʒ] grand; *sum of money, head* gros; **largely** *(mainly)* en grande partie

laryngitis [lærɪn'dʒaɪtɪs] laryngite *f*

laser ['leɪzər] laser *m*; **laser printer** imprimante *f* laser

lash¹ [læʃ] *v/t with whip* fouetter

lash² [læʃ] *n (eyelash)* cil *m*

last¹ [læst] **1** *adj* dernier; **~ night** hier soir **2** *adv* arrive, leave en dernier; **at ~** enfin

last² [læst] *v/i* durer; **lasting** durable; **lastly** pour finir

late [leɪt] **1** *adj (behind time)* en retard; *in day* tard; **it's getting ~** il se fait tard **2** *adv* arrive, leave tard; *lately* récemment; *later* plus tard; *latest* dernier

Latin A'merica Amérique *f* latine; **Latin American 1** *n* Latino-Américain *m* **2** *adj* latino-américain

latitude ['lætɪtu:d] *also (freedom)* latitude *f*

latter ['lætər] dernier

laugh [læf] **1** *n* rire **2** *v/i* rire
◆ **laugh at** rire de; *(mock)* se moquer de

laughter ['læftər] rires *mpl*

launch [lɒntʃ] **1** *n boat* vedette *f*; *of rocket, product* lancement *m*; *of ship* mise *f* à l'eau **2** *v/t rocket, product* lancer; *ship* mettre à l'eau

launder ['lɒndər] *clothes, money* blanchir; **laundromat** laverie *f* automatique; **laundry** *place* blanchisserie *f*; *clothes* lessive *f*

lavatory ['lævətərɪ] W.-C. *mpl*

lavish ['lævɪʃ] somptueux

law [lɒ:] *n*; *subject* droit *m*; **be against the ~** être contraire à la loi; **law-abiding** respecteurs des lois; **law court** tribunal *m*; **lawful** légal; *wife, child* légitime; **lawless** anarchique

lawn [lɒ:n] pelouse *f*; **lawn mower** tondeuse *f* (à gazon)

'lawsuit procès *m*; **lawyer** avocat *m*

lax [læks] laxiste; *security* relâché

laxative ['læksətɪv] laxatif *m*

lay [leɪ] (*put down*) poser; *eggs* pondre; V *sexually* s'envoyer V

◆ **lay off** *workers* licencier; *temporarily* mettre au chômage technique

◆ **lay out** *objects* disposer; *page* mise en page de

layer ['leɪr] couche *f*

'layman REL laïc *m*; *fig* profane *ne m*

'lay-out agencement *m*; *of page* mise *f* en page de

lazy ['leɪzɪ] *person* paresseux; *day* tranquille

lb (= *pound*) livre *f*

lead[1] [liːd] 1 *v/t* mener; *company* être à la tête de 2 *v/i in race, competition* mener; (*provide leadership*) diriger

lead[2] [liːd] *for dog* laisse *f*

lead[3] [led] *substance* plomb *m*; **leaded** *gas* au plomb

leader ['liːdər] *of state* dirigeant *m*; *in race* leader *m*; *of group* chef *m*; **leadership** *of party etc* direction *f*

lead-free ['ledfriː] *gas* sans plomb

leading ['liːdɪŋ] *runner* en tête (de la course); *company, product* premier; **leading-edge** *company, technology* de pointe

leaf [liːf] feuille *f*

◆ **leaf through** feuilleter

leaflet ['liːflət] dépliant *m*

league [liːg] ligue *f*

leak [liːk] 1 *n also of informa-* tion fuite *f* 2 *v/i of pipe* fuir; *of boat* faire eau 3 *v/t information* divulguer

lean[1] [liːn] 1 *v/i* (*be at an angle*) pencher; **~ against** *sth* s'appuyer contre qch 2 *v/t* appuyer

lean[2] [liːn] *adj meat* maigre

leap [liːp] 1 *n* saut *m* 2 *v/i* sauter; **leap year** année *f* bissextile

learn [lɜːrn] apprendre; **learner** apprenant(e) *m(f)*; **learning** (*knowledge*) savoir *m*; *act* apprentissage *m*

lease [liːs] 1 *n for apartment* bail *m*; *for equipment* location *f* 2 *v/t* louer

◆ **lease out** louer

leash [liːʃ] *for dog* laisse *f*

least [liːst] 1 *adj* (*slightest*) (le ou la) moindre; *smallest quantity of* le moins de 2 *adv* (le) moins 3 *n* le moins; **at ~** au moins

leather ['leðər] 1 *n* cuir *m* 2 *adj* de cuir

leave [liːv] 1 *n* (*vacation*) congé *m* 2 *v/t* quitter; *food, scar, memory* laisser; (*forget, leave behind*) oublier; **~ sth alone** ne pas toucher à qch; **~ s.o. alone** laisser qn tranquille; **be left** rester 2 *v/i of person, plane etc* partir

◆ **leave behind** *intentionally* laisser; (*forget*) oublier

◆ **leave out** omettre; (*not put away*) ne pas ranger

leaving party ['liːvɪŋ] soirée *f*

d'adieu

lecture ['lektʃər] *n* conférence *f*; *at university* cours *m* **2** *v/i at university* donner des cours; **lecturer** conférencier *m*; *at university* maître *m* de conférences

ledge [ledʒ] *of window* rebord *m*; *on rock face* saillie *f*; **ledger** COM registre *m* de comptes

left [left] **1** *adj* gauche **2** *n also* POL gauche *f*; *on/to the ~* à gauche **3** *adv* turn, look à gauche; **left-hand** gauche; **left-handed** gaucher; **left luggage (office)** *Br* consigne *f*; **left-overs** food restes *mpl*; **left-wing** POL de gauche

leg [leg] jambe *f*; *of animal* patte *f*; *of table* pied *m*

legacy ['legəsɪ] héritage *m*, legs *m*

legal ['liːgl] (*allowed*) légal; *relating to the law* juridique; **legal adviser** conseiller (-ère) *m(f)* juridique; **legality** légalité *f*; **legalize** légaliser

legend ['ledʒənd] légende *f*; **legendary** légendaire

legible ['ledʒəbl] lisible

legislate ['ledʒɪsleɪt] légiférer; **legislation** (*laws*) législation *f*; **legislative** législatif; **legislature** POL corps *m* législatif

legitimate [lɪ'dʒɪtɪmət] légitime

'**leg room** place *f* pour les jambes

leisure ['liːʒər] loisir *m*; (*free time*) temps *m* libre; **leisurely** tranquille

lemon ['lemən] citron *m*; **lemonade** citronnade *f*; *carbonated* limonade *f*

lend [lend] prêter

length [leŋθ] longueur *f*; (*piece: of material*) pièce *f*; *of piping, road* tronçon *m*; *at ~ describe, explain* en détail; (*eventually*) finalement; **lengthen** *sleeve etc* allonger; *contract* prolonger; **lengthy** long

lenient ['liːnɪənt] indulgent

lens [lenz] *of microscope etc* lentille *f*; *of eyeglasses* verre *m*; *of camera* objectif *m*; *of eye* cristallin *m*

Lent [lent] REL Carême *m*

leotard ['liːoʊtɑːrd] justaucorps *m*

lesbian ['lezbɪən] **1** *n* lesbienne *f* **2** *adj* lesbien

less [les] **1** *adv* moins; *~ than $200* moins de 200 dollars **2** *adj money, salt* moins de; **lessen 1** *v/t* réduire **2** *v/i* diminuer

lesson ['lesn] leçon *f*; *at school* cours *m*

let [let] (*allow*) laisser; *Br house* louer; *~'s stay here* restons ici; *~ go of sth* lâcher qch

◆ **let down** *hair* détacher; *blinds* baisser; (*disappoint*) décevoir

◆ **let in** *to house* laisser entrer
◆ **let out** *from room, building* laisser sortir; *jacket etc* agrandir; *groan,yell* laisser échapper; *Br (rent)* louer
◆ **let up** *(stop)* s'arrêter
lethal ['li:θl] mortel
lethargic [lɪ'θɑ:rdʒɪk] léthargique; **lethargy** léthargie *f*
letter ['letər] *of alphabet, in mail* lettre *f*; **letterbox** *Br* boîte *f* aux lettres; **letterhead** *(heading)* en-tête *m*; *(headed paper)* papier *m* à en-tête
lettuce ['letɪs] laitue *f*
leukemia [lu:'ki:mɪə] leucémie *f*
level ['levl] **1** *adj surface* plat; *in competition* à égalité **2** *n on scale, in hierarchy* échelon *m*; **on the ~** F *(honest)* réglo F; **level-headed** pondéré
lever ['levər] levier *m*; **leverage** effet *m* de levier; *(influence)* poids *m*
levy ['levɪ] *taxes* lever
liability [laɪə'bɪlətɪ] *(responsibility)* responsabilité *f*; *(likeliness)* disposition *f* (**to** à); **liable** responsable (**for** de); **~ to** *(likely)* être susceptible de
◆ **liaise with** [lɪ'eɪz] assurer la liaison avec
liaison [lɪ'eɪzɑ:n] *(contacts)* communication(s) *f*
liar [laɪr] menteur(-euse) *m(f)*
libel ['laɪbl] **1** *n* diffamation *f* **2** *v/t* diffamer

liberal ['lɪbərəl] large d'esprit; *portion etc* généreux; POL libéral
liberate ['lɪbəreɪt] libérer; **liberated** libéré; **liberation** libération *f*; **liberty** liberté *f*
librarian [laɪ'breərɪən] bibliothécaire *m/f*; **library** bibliothèque *f*
Libya ['lɪbɪə] Libye *f*; **Libyan 1** *adj* libyen **2** *n* Libyen(ne) *m(f)*
lice [laɪs] *pl* → **louse**
licence ['laɪsns] *Br* → **license 1** *n*
license ['laɪsns] **1** *n* permis *m* **2** *v/t company* accorder une licence à (**to do** pour faire); **be ~d** *equipment* être autorisé; **license number** numéro *m* d'immatriculation; **license plate** *of car* plaque *f* d'immatriculation
lick [lɪk] lécher
lid [lɪd] couvercle *m*
lie¹ [laɪ] **1** *n (untruth)* mensonge *m* **2** *v/i* mentir
lie² [laɪ] *v/i of person (lie down)* s'allonger; *(be lying down)* être allongé; *of object* être; *(be situated)* être, se trouver
◆ **lie down** se coucher
lieutenant [lu:'tenənt] lieutenant *m*
life [laɪf] vie *f*; **life expectancy** espérance *f* de vie; **lifeguard** maître nageur *m*; **life imprisonment** emprisonnement *m* à vie; **life insurance** assuran-

ce-vie *f*; **life jacket** gilet *m* de sauvetage; **lifeless** *body* inanimé; *personality* mou; *town* mort; **lifelike** réaliste; **lifelong** de toute sa vie; **life-sized** grandeur nature; **life support** (équipement *m* de) maintien *m* artificiel; **life-threatening** *illness* extrêmement grave; **lifetime** vie *f*; **in my ~** de mon vivant

lift [lɪft] **1** *v/t* soulever **2** *v/i* of fog se lever **3** *n Br* (*elevator*) ascenseur *m*; **give s.o. a ~ in car** emmener qn en voiture; **lift-off** of rocket décollage *m*

ligament ['lɪgəmənt] ligament *m*

light[1] [laɪt] **1** *n* lumière *f*; **do you have a ~?** vous avez du feu? **2** *v/t* fire, cigarette allumer; (*illuminate*) éclairer **3** *adj* (*not dark*) clair

light[2] [laɪt] *adj* (*not heavy*) léger

◆ **light up 1** *v/t* éclairer **2** *v/i* (*start to smoke*) s'allumer une cigarette

'light bulb ampoule *f*

lighten[1] ['laɪtn] *color* éclaircir

lighten[2] ['laɪtn] *load* alléger

lighter ['laɪtər] *for cigarettes* briquet *m*; **light-headed** étourdi; **lighting** éclairage *m*; **lightness** of room, color clarté *f*; in weight légèreté *f*; **lightning** éclair *m*, foudre *f*; **lightweight** in boxing poids *m* léger; **light year** année-lumière *f*

like[1] [laɪk] **1** *prep* comme; **be ~ s.o./sth** ressembler à qn/ qch; **what is she ~?** comment est-elle? **it's not ~ him** not his character ça ne lui ressemble pas **2** *conj* F (*as*) comme; ~ **I said** comme je l'ai dit

like[2] [laɪk] *v/t* aimer; **I ~ it** ça me plaît (bien); **I ~ Susie** j'aime bien Susie; *romantically* Susie me plaît (bien); **I would ~ ...** je voudrais, j'aimerais ...; **I would ~ to leave** je voudrais *or* j'aimerais partir; **would you ~ ...?** voulez-vous...?; **would you ~ to ...?** as-tu envie de ...?; **~ to do sth** aimer faire qch; **if you ~** si vous voulez; **likeable** agréable, plaisant; **likelihood** probabilité *f*; **likely** probable; **likeness** ressemblance *f*; **likewise** de même, aussi; **liking** for person affection *f*; for sth penchant *m*

limb [lɪm] membre *m*

lime[1] [laɪm] *fruit* citron *m* vert; *tree* limettier *m*

lime[2] [laɪm] *substance* chaux *f*

limit ['lɪmɪt] **1** *n* limite *f* **2** *v/t* limiter; **limitation** limitation *f*; **limited company** *Br* société *f* à responsabilité limitée

limousine ['lɪməziːn] limousine *f*

limp[1] [lɪmp] *adj* mou

limp[2] [lɪmp] **1** *n* claudication *f*; **he has a ~** il boite **2** *v/i* boiter

line¹ [laɪn] *n* ligne *f*; RAIL voie *f*; *of people* file *f*; *of trees* rangée *f*; *of poem* vers *m*; **stand in ~** faire la queue

line² [laɪn] *v/t with material* recouvrir, garnir; *clothes* doubler

linear ['lɪnɪər] linéaire

linen ['lɪnɪn] *material* lin *m*; *(sheets etc)* linge *m*

liner ['laɪnər] *ship* paquebot *m* de grande ligne

linesman ['laɪnzmən] SP *juge m* de touche; *tennis* juge *m* de ligne

linger ['lɪŋgər] *of person* s'attarder; *of pain* persister

lingerie ['lænʒərɪ] lingerie *f*

linguist ['lɪŋgwɪst] linguiste *m*; *linguistic* linguistique

lining ['laɪnɪŋ] *of clothes* doublure *f*; *of brakes, pipes* garniture *f*

link [lɪŋk] **1** *n* lien *m*; *in chain* maillon *m* **2** *v/t* lier, relier

lion ['laɪən] lion *m*

lip [lɪp] lèvre *f*

liposuction ['lɪpousʌkʃən] liposuccion *f*

'lipread lire sur les lèvres; **lipstick** rouge *m* à lèvres

liqueur [lɪ'kjʊr] liqueur *f*

liquid ['lɪkwɪd] **1** *n* liquide *m* **2** *adj* liquide; **liquidate** liquider; **liquidation** liquidation *f*; **go into ~** entrer en liquidation; **liquidity** FIN liquidité *f*; **liquidize** passer au mixeur; **liquidizer** mixeur *m*

liquor ['lɪkər] alcool *m*; **liquor**

store magasin *m* de vins et spiritueux

lisp [lɪsp] **1** *n* zézaiement *m* **2** *v/i* zézayer

list [lɪst] **1** *n* liste *f* **2** *v/t* faire la liste de; *(enumerate)* énumérer

♦ **listen** ['lɪsn] écouter

♦ **listen to** écouter

listener ['lɪsnər] *to radio* auditeur(-trice) *m(f)*

listless ['lɪstlɪs] amorphe

liter ['liːtər] litre *m*

literal ['lɪtərəl] littéral; **literally** littéralement

literary ['lɪtərerɪ] littéraire; **literature** littérature *f*; *about a product* documentation *f*

litre ['liːtər] *Br* → **liter**

litter ['lɪtər] détritus *mpl*, ordures *fpl*; *of animal* portée *f*

little ['lɪtl] **1** *adj* petit **2** *n* peu *m*; **a ~ wine** un peu de vin **3** *adv* peu; **a ~ bigger** un peu plus gros

live¹ [lɪv] *v/i* vivre

live² [laɪv] *adj broadcast* en direct; *bomb* non désamorcé

♦ **live up to** être à la hauteur de

livelihood ['laɪvlɪhʊd] gagne-pain *m*/*inv*; **liveliness** vivacité *f*; **lively** *person, city* plein de vie; *party* animé; *music* entraînant

liver ['lɪvər] foie *m*

livestock ['laɪvstɑːk] bétail *m*

livid ['lɪvɪd] *(angry)* furieux

living ['lɪvɪŋ] **1** *adj* vivant **2** *n* vie *f*; **living room** salle *f* de séjour

lizard ['lɪzəd] lézard *m*

load [ləʊd] **1** *n* charge *f* **2** *v/t* charger

loaf [ləʊf]: *a ~ of bread* un pain

◆ **loaf around** F traîner

loafer ['ləʊfər] *shoe* mocassin *m*

loan [ləʊn] **1** *n* prêt *m* **2** *v/t*: *~ s.o. sth* prêter qch à qn

loathe [ləʊð] détester; **loathing** dégoût *m*

lobby ['lɒbɪ] *in hotel* hall *m*; *in theater* vestibule *m*; POL lobby *m*

lobe [ləʊb] *of ear* lobe *m*

lobster ['lɒbstər] homard *m*

local ['ləʊkl] **1** *adj* local **2** *n* habitant *m* de la région/du quartier; **local call** TELEC appel *m* local; **local elections** élections *fpl* locales; **local government** autorités *f* locales; **locality** endroit *m*; **localize** localiser; **locally** *live, work* dans le quartier, dans la région; **local time** heure *f* locale

locate [ləʊ'keɪt] *new factory etc* établir; *(identify position of)* localiser; *be ~d* se trouver; **location** *m*; *(siting)* emplacement *m*; *(identifying position of)* localisation *f*; *on ~ movie* en extérieur

lock¹ [lɒk] *n of hair* mèche *f*

lock² [lɒk] **1** *n on door* serrure *f* **2** *v/t door* fermer à clef

◆ **lock up** *in prison* mettre

sous les verrous

locker ['lɒkər] casier *m*; **locker room** vestiaire *m*

locust ['ləʊkəst] locuste *f*, sauterelle *f*

lodge [lɒdʒ] **1** *v/t complaint* déposer **2** *v/i of bullet* se loger

lofty ['lɒftɪ] *heights* haut; *ideals* élevé

log [lɒg] bûche *f*; *(written record)* journal *m* de bord

◆ **log in** se connecter (*to* à)

◆ **log off** se déconnecter

◆ **log on** se connecter (*to* à)

◆ **log out** se déconnecter

log 'cabin cabane *f* en rondins

logic ['lɒdʒɪk] logique *f*; **logical** logique; **logically** logiquement

logistics [lə'dʒɪstɪks] logistique *f*

logo ['ləʊgəʊ] logo *m*, sigle *m*

loiter ['lɔɪtər] traîner

lollipop ['lɒlɪpɒp] sucette *f*

London ['lʌndən] Londres

loneliness ['ləʊnlɪnɪs] *of person* solitude *f*; *of place* isolement *m*; **lonely** *person* seul, solitaire; *place* isolé; **loner** solitaire *m/f*

long¹ [lɒŋ] **1** *adj* long; *it's a ~ way* c'est loin **2** *adv* longtemps; *how ~ will it take?* combien de temps cela va-t-il prendre?; *he no ~er works here* il ne travaille plus ici; *so ~ as (provided)* pourvu que; *so ~!* à bientôt!

long² [lɒŋ] *v/i*: *~ for sth* avoir

très envie de qch; **be ~ing to do sth** avoir très envie de faire qch

long-'distance *phonecall* longue distance; *race* de fond; *flight* long-courrier; **longevity** longévité *f*; **longing** désir *m*, envie *f*; **longitude** longitude *f*; **long jump** saut *m* en longueur; **long-range missile** à longue portée; *forecast* à long terme; **long-sleeved** à manches longues; **long-standing** de longue date; **long-term** à long terme; *unemployment* de longue durée

loo [luː] *Br F* toilettes *fpl*

look [luk] **1** *n* (*appearance*) air *m*; (*glance*) coup *m* d'œil, regard *m*; **~s** (*beauty*) beauté *f* **2** *v/i* regarder; (*search*) chercher, regarder; (*seem*) avoir l'air

◆ **look after** s'occuper de

◆ **look ahead** *fig* regarder en avant

◆ **look around** jeter un coup d'œil

◆ **look at** regarder; (*examine*) examiner; (*consider*) envisager

◆ **look back** regarder derrière soi

◆ **look down on** mépriser

◆ **look for** chercher

◆ **look into** (*investigate*) examiner

◆ **look onto** *garden etc* donner sur

◆ **look out** *of window etc* regarder dehors; (*pay attention*) faire attention

◆ **look over** *house, translation* examiner

◆ **look through** *magazine, notes* parcourir, feuilleter

◆ **look up 1** *v/i from paper etc* lever les yeux; (*improve*) s'améliorer **2** *v/t word, phone number* chercher; (*visit*) passer voir

◆ **look up to** (*respect*) respecter

'lookout *person* sentinelle *f*; **be on the ~ for** être à l'affût de

loop [luːp] boucle *f*; **loophole** *in law etc* lacune *f*

loose [luːs] *knot* lâche; *connection, screw* desserré; *clothes* ample; *morals* relâché; *wording* vague; **~ change** petite monnaie *f*; **loosely** *worded* de manière approximative; **loosen** desserrer

loot [luːt] **1** *n* butin *m* **2** *v/i* se livrer au pillage; **looter** pilleur(-euse) *m(f)*

lop-sided [lɒpˈsaɪdɪd] déséquilibré, disproportionné

Lord [lɔːrd] (*god*) Seigneur *m*

lorry [ˈlɒrɪ] *Br* camion *m*

lose [luːz] **1** *v/t* perdre **2** *v/i sp* perdre; *of clock* retarder; **loser** perdant(e) *m(f)*

loss [lɒs] perte *f*

lost [lɒst] perdu; **lost-and-found**, *Br* **lost property (of-**

fice) (bureau *m* des) objets
mpl trouvés

lot [lɑːt]: **a ~ (of)**, **~s (of)** beaucoup (de)

lotion ['ləʊʃn] lotion *f*

lottery ['lɒtərɪ] loterie *f*

loud [laʊd] *music, voice* fort; *noise* grand; *color* criard; **loudspeaker** haut-parleur *m*

louse [laʊs] pou *m*; **lousy** F minable F, mauvais

lout [laʊt] rustre *m*

lovable ['lʌvəbl] sympathique, adorable; **love** **1** *n* amour *m*; *in tennis* zéro *m*; **fall in ~** tomber amoureux (**with** de); **make ~** faire l'amour (**to** avec) **2** *v/t* aimer; *wine, music* adorer; **love affair** aventure *f*; **lovely** beau; *house, wife* ravissant; *character* charmant; *meal* délicieux; **lover** *man* amant *m*; *woman* maîtresse *f*; *person in love* amoureux(-euse) *m(f)*; **loving** affectueux; **lovingly** avec amour

low [ləʊ] **1** *adj* bas; *quality* mauvais **2** *n in weather* dépression *f*; *in statistics* niveau *m* bas; **lowbrow** peu intellectuel; **low-calorie** hypocalorique; **low-cut** *dress* décolleté; **lower** baisser; *to the ground* faire descendre; **low-fat** allégé; **lowkey** discret, mesuré; **loyal** ['lɔɪəl] fidèle, loyal; **loyally** fidèlement; **loyalty** loyauté *f*

lozenge ['lɒzɪndʒ] *shape* lo-

sange *m*; *tablet* pastille *f*

Ltd (= *limited*) *company* à responsabilité limitée

lubricant ['luːbrɪkənt] lubrifiant *m*; **lubricate** lubrifier; **lubrication** lubrification *f*

lucid ['luːsɪd] *(clear)* clair; *(sane)* lucide

luck [lʌk] chance *f*; **good ~!** bonne chance!; **luckily** heureusement; **lucky** *person* chanceux; *number* porte-bonheur *inv*; *coincidence* heureux; **you were ~** tu as eu de la chance

lucrative ['luːkrətɪv] lucratif

ludicrous ['luːdɪkrəs] ridicule

lug [lʌg] F traîner

luggage ['lʌgɪdʒ] bagages *mpl*

lukewarm ['luːkwɔːrm] *also fig* tiède

lull [lʌl] *in storm, fighting* accalmie *f*; *in conversation* pause *f*

lumber ['lʌmbər] *(timber)* bois *m* de construction

luminous ['luːmɪnəs] lumineux

lump [lʌmp] *of sugar* morceau *m*; *(swelling)* grosseur *f*; **lump sum** forfait *m*; **lumpy** *liquid, sauce* grumeleux; *mattress* défoncé

lunacy ['luːnəsɪ] folie *f*

lunar ['luːnər] lunaire

lunatic ['luːnətɪk] fou *m*, folle *f*

lunch [lʌntʃ] déjeuner *m*; **have ~** déjeuner; **lunch**

box panier-repas *m*; **lunch break** pause-déjeuner *f*; **lunchtime** heure *f* du déjeuner, midi *m*

lung [lʌŋ] poumon *m*

lurch [lɜːrtʃ] *of person* tituber; *of ship* tanguer

lure [lʊr] **1** *n* appât *m* **2** *v/t* attirer

lurid ['lʊrɪd] *color* cru; *details* choquant

lurk [lɜːrk] *of person* se cacher

lush [lʌʃ] *vegetation* luxuriant

lust [lʌst] désir *m*

luxurious [lʌg'ʒʊrɪəs] luxueux; **luxuriously** luxueusement; **luxury 1** *n* luxe *m* **2** *adj* de luxe

lynch [lɪntʃ] lyncher

lyrics ['lɪrɪks] paroles *fpl*

M

ma'am [mæm] madame

machine [mə'ʃiːn] machine *f*; **machine gun** mitrailleuse *f*; **machinery** machines *fpl*

machismo [mə'kɪzmoʊ] machisme *m*

macho ['mætʃoʊ] macho *inv*; **~ type** macho *m*

macro ['mækroʊ] COMPUT macro *f*

mad [mæd] (*insane*) fou; F (*angry*) furieux; **madden** (*infuriate*) exaspérer; **maddening** exaspérant; **madhouse** *fig* maison *f* de fous; **madman** fou *m*; **madness** folie *f*

Madonna [mə'dɑːnə] Madone *f*

Mafia ['mɑːfiə]: **the ~** la Mafia

magazine [mægə'ziːn] *printed* magazine *m*

Magi ['meɪdʒaɪ] REL: **the ~** les Rois *mpl* mages

magic ['mædʒɪk] **1** *adj* magique **2** *n* magie *f*; **magical** magique; **magician** *performer*

prestidigitateur(-trice) *m(f)*

magnanimous [mæg'nænɪməs] magnanime

magnet ['mægnɪt] aimant *m*; **magnetic** *also fig* magnétique; **magnetism** *also fig* magnétisme *m*

magnificence [mæg'nɪfɪsəns] magnificence *f*; **magnificent** magnifique

magnify ['mægnɪfaɪ] grossir; *difficulties* exagérer; **magnifying glass** loupe *f*

magnitude ['mægnɪtuːd] ampleur *f*

maid [meɪd] *servant* domestique *f*; *in hotel* femme *f* de chambre

maiden name ['meɪdn] nom *m* de jeune fille

mail [meɪl] **1** *n* courrier *m*, poste *f* **2** *v/t letter* poster; **mailbox** boîte *f* aux lettres; **mailing list** fichier *m* d'adresses; **mailman** facteur *m*; **mailshot** mailing *m*, publipostage *m*

maim [meɪm] estropier, mutiler

main [meɪn] principal; **main course** plat *m* principal; **mainframe** ordinateur *m* central; **mainly** principalement; **main road** route *f* principale; **main street** rue *f* principale

maintain [meɪn'teɪn] *peace, law and order* maintenir; *speed* soutenir; *relationship, machine, building* entretenir; *innocence, guilt* affirmer; **maintenance** of *machine, building* entretien *m*; *Br money* pension *f* alimentaire; *of law and order* maintien *m*

majestic [mə'dʒestɪk] majestueux

major ['meɪdʒər] **1** *adj* (*significant*) important, majeur **2** *n* MIL commandant *m*

◆ **major in** se spécialiser en

majority [mə'dʒɑːrətɪ] *also* POL majorité *f*

make [meɪk] **1** *n* (*brand*) marque *f* **2** *v/t* faire; (*manufacture*) fabriquer; (*earn*) gagner; *decision* prendre; *3 and 3 = 6* 3 et 3 font 6; ~ *it* (*catch bus, train*) arriver à temps; (*come*) venir; (*succeed*) réussir; (*survive*) s'en sortir; *what time do you ~ it?* quelle heure est-tu?; ~ *believe* prétendre; ~ *do with* se contenter de, faire avec;

what do you ~ of it? qu'en dis-tu?; ~ *s.o. do sth* (*force to*) forcer qn à faire qch; (*cause to*) obliger qn à faire qch; ~ *s.o. happy/angry* rendre qn heureux/furieux

◆ **make out** *list, check* faire; (*see*) distinguer; (*imply*) prétendre

◆ **make up 1** *v/i of woman, actor* se maquiller; *after quarrel* se réconcilier **2** *v/t story* inventer; *face* maquiller; (*constitute*) constituer

◆ **make up for** compenser

'make-believe: it's just ~ c'est juste pour faire semblant

maker ['meɪkər] (*manufacturer*) fabricant *m*; **makeshift** de fortune; **make-up** (*cosmetics*) maquillage *m*

maladjusted [mælə'dʒʌstɪd] inadapté

male [meɪl] **1** *adj* masculin; *animal* mâle **2** *n* (*man*) homme *m*; *animal, bird* mâle *m*; **male chauvinism** machisme *m*; **male chauvinist pig** macho *m*

malevolent [mə'levələnt] malveillant

malfunction [mæl'fʌŋkʃn] **1** *n* mauvais fonctionnement *m*, défaillance *f* **2** *v/i* mal fonctionner

malice ['mælɪs] méchanceté *f*, malveillance *f*; **malicious** méchant, malveillant

malignant [mə'lɪɡnənt] *tumor* malin

manuscript

mall [mɔːl] (*shopping ~*) centre *m* commercial

malnutrition [mælnuːˈtrɪʃn] malnutrition *f*

maltreat [mælˈtriːt] maltraiter; **maltreatment** mauvais traitement *m*

mammal [ˈmæml] mammifère *m*

man [mæn] **1** *n* (*pl* **men** [men]) homme *m*; (*humanity*) l'homme *m*; *in checkers* pion *m* **2** *v/t* telephones être de permanence à; *front desk* être de service à

manage [ˈmænɪdʒ] **1** *v/t business* diriger; *money* gérer; *bags* porter; **~ to ...** réussir à ... **2** *v/i* (*cope*) se débrouiller; **manageable** gérable; *vehicle* maniable; *task* faisable; **management** (*managing*) gestion *f*, direction *f*; (*managers*) direction *f*; **management consultant** conseiller(-ère) *m(f)* en gestion; **manager** directeur(-trice) *m(f)*; *of store, restaurant, hotel* gérant(e) *m(f)*; *of department* responsable *m/f*; *of singer, band, team* manageur(-euse) *m(f)*; **managerial** de directeur, de gestionnaire; **managing director** directeur(-trice) *m(f)* général(e)

mandate [ˈmændeɪt] mandat *m*; **mandatory** obligatoire

maneuver [məˈnuːvər] **1** *n* manœuvre *f* **2** *v/t* manœuvrer

mangle [ˈmæŋgl] (*crush*) broyer

manhandle [ˈmænhændl] *person* malmener; *object* déplacer manuellement

manhood [ˈmænhʊd] (*maturity*) âge *m* d'homme; (*virility*) virilité *f*; **manhunt** chasse *f* à l'homme

mania [ˈmeɪnɪə] (*craze*) manie *f*; **maniac** F fou *m*, folle *f*

manicure [ˈmænɪkjʊr] manucure *f*

manifest [ˈmænɪfest] **1** *adj* manifeste **2** *v/t* manifester

manipulate [məˈnɪpjəleɪt] manipuler; **manipulation** manipulation *f*; **manipulative** manipulateur

mankind humanité *f*; **manly** viril; **man-made** synthétique

manner [ˈmænər] *of doing sth* manière *f*, façon *f*; (*attitude*) comportement *m*; **manners** manières *fpl*

manoeuvre [məˈnuːvər] *Br* → **maneuver**

'manpower main-d'œuvre *f*

manual [ˈmænjʊəl] **1** *adj* manuel **2** *n* manuel *m*; **manually** manuellement

manufacture [mænjʊˈfæktʃər] **1** *n* fabrication *f* **2** *v/t equipment* fabriquer; **manufacturer** fabricant *m*; **manufacturing industry** industrie *f*

manure [məˈnʊr] fumier *m*

manuscript [ˈmænjʊskrɪpt] manuscrit *m*

many ['menɪ] **1** adj beaucoup de; **~ times** bien des fois; **too ~ problems** trop de problèmes; **as ~ as possible** autant que possible **2** pron beaucoup; **a great ~, a good ~** un bon nombre; **how ~ do you need?** combien en veux-tu?

map [mæp] carte f; of town plan m

maple ['meɪpl] érable m

mar [mɑːr] gâcher

marathon ['mærəθɑːn] race marathon m

marble ['mɑːrbl] material marbre m

March [mɑːrtʃ] mars m

march [mɑːrtʃ] **1** n also (demonstration) marche f **2** v/i marcher au pas; in protest défiler; **marcher** manifestant(e) m(f)

Mardi Gras ['mɑːrdɪgrɑː] mardi m gras

margin ['mɑːrdʒɪn] of page, COM marge f; **marginal** (slight) **marginally** (slightly) légèrement

marihuana, marijuana [mærɪ'hwɑːnə] marijuana f

marina [mə'riːnə] port m de plaisance

marine [mə'riːn] **1** adj marin **2** n MIL marine m

marital ['mærɪtl] conjugal; **marital status** situation f de famille

maritime ['mærɪtaɪm] maritime

mark [mɑːrk] **1** n marque f; (stain) tache f; (sign, token) signe m; (trace) trace f; Br EDU note f **2** v/t marquer; (stain) tacher; Br EDU noter **3** v/i of fabric se tacher; **marked** (definite) marqué; **marker** (highlighter) marqueur m

market ['mɑːrkɪt] **1** n marché m **2** v/t commercialiser; **marketable** commercialisable; **market economy** économie f de marché; **marketing** marketing m; **market leader** product produit m vedette; company leader m du marché; **market place** in town place f du marché; for commodities marché m; **market research** étude f de marché; **market share** part f du marché

mark-up ['mɑːrkʌp] majoration f

marriage ['mærɪdʒ] mariage m; **marriage certificate** acte m de mariage; **married** marié; **be ~ to** être marié à; **married life** vie f conjugale; **marry** épouser, se marier avec; of priest marier; **get married** se marier

marsh [mɑːrʃ] Br marais m

marshal ['mɑːrʃl] in police chef m de la police; in security service membre m du service d'ordre

martial 'law loi f martiale

martyr ['mɑːrtər] also fig martyr(e) *m(f)*

márvel ['mɑːrvl] merveille *f*;
marvelous, *Br* **marvellous**
merveilleux

Marxism ['mɑːrksɪzm]
marxisme *m*; **Marxist** 1 *adj*
marxiste 2 *n* marxiste *m/f*

mascara [mæ'skærə] mascara
m

mascot ['mæskət] mascotte *f*

masculine ['mæskjulɪn] *also*
GRAM masculin; **masculinity**
masculinité *f*

mash [mæʃ] réduire en purée

mask [mæsk] 1 *n* masque *m* 2
v/t feelings masquer

masochism ['mæsəkɪzm]
masochisme *m*; **masochist**
masochiste *m/f*

mass[1] [mæs] *n* (*great
amount*) masse *f*; **~es of** F
des tas de F 2 *v/i* se masser

mass[2] [mæs] *n* REL messe *f*

massacre ['mæsəkr] 1 *n* (*fabric*) tissu *m* ; (*substance*) matériau *m*, matière *f* 2 *adj* matériel; **materialism** matérialisme *m*; **materialist** matérialiste *m/f*; **materialize**
(*appear*) apparaître ; (*happen*) se concrétiser

massage ['mæsɑːʒ] 1 *n* massage *m* 2 *v/t* masser; *figures*
manipuler

massive ['mæsɪv] énorme;
heart attack grave

mass 'media médias *mpl*;
mass-produce fabriquer en
série; **mass production** fabrication *f* en série

mast [mæst] *of ship* mât *m*;
for radio signal pylône *m*

master ['mæstr] 1 *n* *of dog*
maître *m*; *of ship* capitaine
m 2 *v/t* maîtriser; **master**

bedroom chambre *f* principale; **master key** passe-partout *m inv*; **masterly** magistral; **mastermind** 1 *n* cerveau
m 2 *v/t* organiser; **masterpiece** chef-d'œuvre *m*; **master's (degree)** UNIV master
m; **mastery** maîtrise *f*

mat [mæt] *for floor* tapis *m*;
for table napperon *m*

match[1] [mæʃ] *n for cigarette*
allumette *f*

match[2] [mæʃ] 1 *n* (*competition*) match *m*, partie *f* 2 *v/t*
(*be the same as*) être assorti
à; (*equal*) égaler 3 *v/i of colors, patterns* aller ensemble;
matching assorti; **match
stick** allumette *f*

mate [meɪt] 1 *n of animal* mâle *m*, femelle *f*; NAUT second
m 2 *v/i* s'accoupler

material [mə'tɪrɪəl] 1 *n* (*fabric*) tissu *m* ; (*substance*) matériau *m*, matière *f* 2 *adj* matériel; **materialism** matérialisme *m*; **materialist** matérialiste *m/f*; **materialize**
(*appear*) apparaître ; (*happen*) se concrétiser

maternal [mə'tɜːrnl] maternel; **maternity** maternité *f*;
maternity leave congé *m*
de maternité

math [mæθ] maths *fpl*; **mathematical** mathématique; **mathematician** mathématicien(ne) *m(f)*; **maths** *Br* →
math

matinée ['mætineɪ] matinée *f*

matriarch ['meɪtrɪɑːrk] femme *f* chef de famille

matrimony ['mætrəmoʊnɪ] mariage *m*

matt [mæt] mat

matter ['mætər] **1** *n (affair)* affaire *f*, question *f*; PHYS matière *f*; **what's the ~?** qu'est-ce qu'il y a? **2** *v/i* importer; **it doesn't ~** cela ne fait rien; **matter-of-fact** impassible

mattress ['mætrɪs] matelas *m*

mature [mə'tʃʊr] **1** *adj* mûr **2** *v/i of person* mûrir; *of insurance policy* arriver à échéance; **maturity** maturité *f*

maximize ['mæksɪmaɪz] maximiser; **maximum 1** *adj* maximal, **maximum 2** *n* maximum *m*

May [meɪ] mai *m*

may [meɪ] ◇ *possibility:* **it ~ rain** il va peut-être pleuvoir; **it ~ not happen** cela n'arrive peut-être pas
◇ *permission:* pouvoir; **~ I help?** puis-je aider?

maybe ['meɪbiː] peut-être

mayo, mayonnaise ['meɪoʊ, meɪə'neɪz] mayonnaise *f*

mayor ['meɪər] maire *m*

maze [meɪz] labyrinthe *m*

MB (= **megabyte**) Mo (= mégaoctet)

MBA [embiː'eɪ] (= **master of business administration**) MBA *m*

MD [em'diː] (= **Doctor of Med-**

icine) docteur *m* en médecine; (= **managing director**) DG *m* (= directeur général)

me [miː]: *before vowel* m'; *after prep* moi; **he knows ~** il me connaît; **she gave ~ a dollar** elle m'a donné un dollar; **it's for ~** c'est pour moi; **it's ~** c'est moi

meadow ['medoʊ] pré *m*

meager, *Br* **meagre** ['miːgər] maigre

meal [miːl] repas *m*; **enjoy your ~!** bon appétit!

mean¹ [miːn] *adj with money* avare; *(nasty)* mesquin

mean² [miːn] *v/t (signify)* signifier, vouloir dire; **be ~t for** être destiné à; *of remark* être adressé à; **meaning** *of word* sens *m*; **meaningful** *(comprehensible)* compréhensible; *(constructive)* significatif; *glance* éloquent; **meaningless** *sentence etc* dénué de sens; *gesture* insignifiant

means [miːnz] *financial* moyens *mpl*; *(way)* moyen *m*; **by all ~** *(certainly)* bien sûr; **by ~ of** au moyen de

meantime ['miːntaɪm] entre-temps

measles ['miːzlz] rougeole *f*

measure ['meʒər] **1** *n (step)* mesure *f* **2** *v/t & v/i* mesurer
♦ **measure up to** être à la hauteur de

measurement ['meʒərmənt] *action* mesure *f*; *(dimension)*

419

melt

dimension *f*; **measuring tape** mètre *m* ruban

meat [miːt] viande *f*; **meatball** boulette *f* de viande

mechanic [mɪˈkænɪk] mécanicien(ne) *m(f)*; **mechanical device** mécanique; *gesture etc also* machinal; **mechanical engineer** ingénieur *m* mécanicien; **mechanically** mécaniquement; *do sth* machinalement; **mechanism** mécanisme *m*; **mechanize** mécaniser

medal [ˈmedl] médaille *f*; **medalist**, *Br* **medallist** médaillé *m*

meddle [ˈmedl] se mêler (*in* de)

media [ˈmiːdɪə]: **the** ~ les médias *mpl*; **media coverage** couverture *f* médiatique

median strip [miːdɪənˈstrɪp] terre-plein *m* central

'media studies études *fpl* de communication

mediate [ˈmiːdɪeɪt] arbitrer; **mediation** médiation *f*; **mediator** médiateur(-trice) *m(f)*

medical [ˈmedɪkl] **1** *adj* médical **2** *n* visite *f* médicale; **medicated** pharmaceutique, traitant; **medication** médicaments *mpl*; **medicinal** médicinal

medicine *science* médecine *f*; *(medication)* médicament *m*

medieval [medɪˈiːvl] médiéval

mediocre [miːdɪˈoʊkər] médiocre; **mediocrity** *of work etc* médiocrité *f*; *person* médiocre *m/f*

meditate [ˈmedɪteɪt] méditer; **meditation** méditation *f*

Mediterranean [medɪtəˈreɪnɪən] **1** *adj* méditerranéen **2** *n*: **the** ~ la Méditerranée

medium [ˈmiːdɪəm] **1** *adj (average)* moyen; *steak* à point **2** *n in size* taille *f* moyenne; *(vehicle)* moyen *m*; *(spiritualist)* médium *m*

medley [ˈmedlɪ] *(assortment)* mélange *m*

meet [miːt] **1** *v/t* rencontrer; *(be introduced to)* faire la connaissance de; *(collect)* (aller/venir) chercher; *in competition* affronter; *of eyes* croiser; *(satisfy)* satisfaire **2** *v/i* se rencontrer; *by appointment* se retrouver; *of committee etc* se réunir **3** *n* SP rencontre *f*; **meeting** *by accident* rencontre *f*; *in business, of committee* réunion *f*; **he's in a** ~ il est en réunion

megabyte [ˈmegəbaɪt] COMPUT méga-octet *m*

mellow [ˈmeloʊ] **1** *adj* doux **2** *v/i of person* s'adoucir

melodious [mɪˈloʊdɪəs] mélodieux

melodramatic [melədrəˈmætɪk] mélodramatique

melody [ˈmelədɪ] mélodie *f*

melon [ˈmelən] melon *m*

melt [melt] **1** *v/i* fondre **2** *v/t*

faire fondre; **melting pot** *fig* creuset *m*

member ['membər] membre *m*; **Member of Congress** membre *m* du Congrès; **membership** adhésion *f*; *number of members* membres *mpl*

membrane ['membreɪn] membrane *f*

memento [me'mentou] souvenir *m*

memo ['memou] note *f* (de service)

memoirs ['memwɑːrz] mémoires *fpl*

memorable ['memərəbl] mémorable

memorial [mɪ'mɔːrɪəl] **1** *adj* commémoratif **2** *n* mémorial *m*; **Memorial Day** jour commémoration des soldats américains morts à la guerre

memorize ['meməraɪz] apprendre par cœur; **memory** mémoire *f*; *sth remembered* souvenir *m*

men [men] *pl* → **man**

menace ['menɪs] **1** *n* menace *f*; *person* danger *m* **2** *v/t* menacer; **menacing** menaçant

mend [mend] réparer; *clothes* raccommoder

menial ['miːnɪəl] subalterne

menopause ['menoupɔːz] ménopause *f*

'men's room toilettes *fpl* pour hommes

menstruate ['menstrʊeɪt] avoir ses règles

mental ['mentl] mental; *ability, powers* intellectuel; *health, suffering* moral; F *(crazy)* malade F; **mental hospital** hôpital *m* psychiatrique; **mental illness** maladie *f* mentale; **mentality** mentalité *f*; **mentally** *(inwardly)* intérieurement; *calculate etc* mentalement

mention ['menʃn] **1** *n* mention *f* **2** *v/t* mentionner; *don't ~ it (you're welcome)* il n'y a pas de quoi!

mentor ['mentɔːr] mentor *m*

menu ['menjuː] *also* COMPUT menu *m*

mercenary ['mɜːrsɪnerɪ] **1** *adj* intéressé **2** *n* MIL mercenaire *m*

merchandise ['mɜːrtʃəndaɪz] marchandises *fpl*

merchant ['mɜːrtʃənt] négociant *m*, commerçant *m*

merciful ['mɜːrsɪfl] clément; *God* miséricordieux; **mercifully** *(thankfully)* heureusement; **merciless** impitoyable; **mercy** clémence *f*, pitié *f*

mere [mɪr] simple; **merely** simplement, seulement

merge [mɜːrdʒ] *of two lines etc* se rejoindre; *of companies* fusionner; **merger** COM fusion *f*

merit ['merɪt] **1** *n* mérite *m* **2** *v/t* mériter

mesh [meʃ] *of net* maille(s) *f(pl)*; *of grid* grillage *m*

mess [mes] (*untidiness*) désordre *m*, pagaille *f*; (*trouble*) gâchis *m*

message ['mesɪdʒ] *also of movie etc* message *m*

messenger ['mesɪndʒər] (*courier*) messager *m*

messy ['mesɪ] *room* en désordre; *person* désordonné; *job* salissant; *divorce* pénible

metabolism [mə'tæbəlɪzm] métabolisme *m*

metal [metl] **1** *adj* en métal **2** *n* métal *m*; **metallic** métallique; *paint* métallisé

metaphor ['metəfər] métaphore *f*

meteor ['miːtɪɔːr] météore *m*; **meteoric** *fig* fulgurant; **meteorite** météorite *m* or *f*

meteorological [miːtɪərə-'lɑːdʒɪkl] météorologique; **meteorologist** météorologiste *m/f*; **meteorology** météorologie *f*

meter[1] ['miːtər] *for gas, electricity* compteur *m*; (*parking* ∼) parcmètre *m*

meter[2] ['miːtər] *unit of length* mètre *m*

method ['meθəd] méthode *f*; **methodical** méthodique

meticulous [mə'tɪkjələs] méticuleux

metre ['miːtə(r)] *Br* → **meter**[2]

metropolis [mə'trɑːpəlɪs] métropole *f*; **metropolitan** citadin; *area* urbain

mew [mjuː] → **miaow**

Mexican ['meksɪkən] **1** *adj* mexicain **2** *n* Mexicain(e) *m(f)*; **Mexico** Mexique *m*

miaow [mɪau] **1** *n* miaou *m* **2** *v/i* miauler

mice [maɪs] *pl* → **mouse**

microchip puce *f*; **microclimate** microclimat *m*; **microcosm** microcosme *m*; **microorganism** micro-organisme *m*; **microphone** microphone *m*; **microprocessor** microprocesseur *m*; **microscope** microscope *m*; **microscopic** microscopique; **microwave oven** micro-ondes *m inv*

midday [mɪd'deɪ] midi *m*

middle ['mɪdl] **1** *adj* du milieu **2** *n* milieu *m*; **be in the ∼ of doing sth** être en train de faire qch; **middle-aged** entre deux âges; **middle-class** bourgeois; **middle class(es)** classe(s) moyenne(s) *f(pl)*; **Middle East** Moyen-Orient *m*; **middleman** intermédiaire *m*; **middle name** deuxième prénom *m*; **middleweight** boxer poids moyen *m*

midfielder [mɪd'fiːldər] *in soccer* milieu *m* de terrain

midget ['mɪdʒɪt] miniature

midnight ['mɪdnaɪt] minuit *m*; **midsummer** milieu *m* de l'été; **midweek** en milieu de semaine; **Midwest** Middle West *m*; **midwife** sage-femme *f*; **midwinter** milieu *m* de l'hiver

might[1] [maɪt] *v/aux*: **I ∼ be late** je serai peut-être en retard; **you ∼ have told me!**

might 422

vous auriez pu m'avertir!

might² [maɪt] *n (power)* puissance *f*

mighty ['maɪtɪ] **1** *adj* puissant **2** *adv* F *(extremely)* vachement F, très

migraine ['miːɡreɪn] migraine *f*

migrant worker ['maɪɡrənt] travailleur *m* itinérant; **migrate** migrer; **migration** migration *f*

mike [maɪk] F micro *m*

mild [maɪld] **1** *adj* doux; *taste* léger; **mildly** doucement; *spicy* légèrement; **mildness** douceur *f*; *of taste* légèreté *f*

mile [maɪl] mile *m*; **milestone** *fig* événement *m* marquant, jalon *m*

militant ['mɪlɪtənt] **1** *adj* militant **2** *n* militant(e) *m(f)*

military ['mɪlɪtərɪ] **1** *adj* militaire **2** *n*: **the ~** l'armée *f*

militia [mɪˈlɪʃə] milice *f*

milk [mɪlk] **1** *n* lait *m* **2** *v/t* traire; **milk chocolate** chocolat *m* au lait; **milkshake** milk-shake *m*

mill [mɪl] *for grain* moulin *m*; *for textiles* usine *f*

millennium [mɪˈlenɪəm] millénaire *m*

milligram ['mɪlɪɡræm] milligramme *m*

millimeter, *Br* **millimetre** ['mɪlɪmiːtər] millimètre *m*

million ['mɪljən] million *m*

millionaire [mɪljəˈner] millionnaire *m/f*

mime [maɪm] mimer

mimic ['mɪmɪk] **1** *n* imitateur(-trice) *m(f)* **2** *v/t* imiter

mince [mɪns] hacher

mind [maɪnd] **1** *n* esprit *m*; **bear** *or* **keep sth in ~** ne pas oublier qch; **change one's ~** changer d'avis; **make up one's ~** se décider; **have sth on one's ~** être préoccupé par qch; **keep one's ~ on sth** se concentrer sur qch **2** *v/t (look after)* surveiller; *(heed)* faire attention à; **I don't ~ what he thinks** il peut penser ce qu'il veut, cela m'est égal; **do you ~ if I smoke?** cela ne vous dérange pas si je fume?; **~ the step!** attention à la marche! **3** *v/i*: **~!** *(be careful)* fais attention!; **never ~!** peu importe!; **I don't ~** cela m'est égal; **mind-boggling** ahurissant; **mindless** *violence* gratuit

mine¹ [maɪn] *pron* le mien *m*, la mienne *f*; *pl* les miens, les miennes; **it's ~** c'est à moi

mine² [maɪn] *n for coal etc* mine *f*

mine³ [maɪn] **1** *n* explosive mine *f* **2** *v/t* miner; **minefield** MIL champ *m* de mines; *fig* poudrière *f*; **miner** mineur *m*

mineral ['mɪnərəl] minéral *m*; **mineral water** eau *f* minérale

'minesweeper NAUT dragueur *m* de mines

mingle ['mɪŋɡl] *of sounds* se

423

miserly

mélanger; *at party* se mêler
(aux gens)
mini ['mɪnɪ] *skirt* minijupe f
miniature ['mɪnɪtʃər] miniature
minimal ['mɪnɪməl] minime;
minimalism minimalisme
m; minimize réduire au minimum; (*downplay*) minimiser; minimum 1 *adj* minimal,
minimum 2 n minimum m
mining ['maɪnɪŋ] exploitation
f minière
'miniskirt minijupe f
minister ['mɪnɪstər] POL, REL
ministre m; ministerial mi-
nistériel
mink [mɪŋk] vison m
minor ['maɪnər] 1 *adj* mineur;
pain léger 2 n LAW mineur(e)
m(f); minority minorité f
mint [mɪnt] *herb* menthe f;
chocolate chocolat m à la
menthe; *hard candy* bonbon
m à la menthe
minus ['maɪnəs] 1 n (~ *sign*)
moins m 2 *prep* moins
minuscule ['mɪnəskjuːl] minuscule
minute¹ ['mɪnɪt] n *of time* minute f
minute² [maɪ'nuːt] *adj* (*tiny*)
minuscule; (*detailed*) minutieux
minute hand ['mɪnɪt] grande
aiguille f
minutely [maɪ'nuːtlɪ] (*in detail*) minutieusement; (*very
slightly*) très légèrement
minutes ['mɪnɪts] *of meeting*

procès-verbal m
miracle ['mɪrəkl] miracle m;
miraculous miraculeux; mi-
raculously par miracle
mirror ['mɪrər] 1 n miroir m;
MOT rétroviseur m 2 *v/t* refléter
misanthropist [mɪ'zænθrə-
pɪst] misanthrope m/f
misbehave [mɪsbə'heɪv] se
conduire mal
misbehavior, *Br* misbehav-
iour mauvaise conduite f
miscalculate [mɪs'kælkju-
leɪt] mal calculer; miscalculation erreur f de calcul; *fig*
mauvais calcul m
miscarriage ['mɪskærɪdʒ]
MED fausse couche f
miscellaneous [mɪsə'leɪnɪəs]
divers; *collection* varié
mischief ['mɪstʃɪf] (*naughti-
ness*) bêtises *fpl*; (*mischievous* (*naughty*) espiègle;
(*malicious*) malveillant
misconception [mɪs-
kən'sepʃn] idée f fausse
misconduct [mɪs'kɑːndʌkt]
mauvaise conduite f
misconstrue [mɪskən'struː]
mal interpréter
misdemeanor, *Br* misde-
meanour [mɪsdə'miːnər] délit m
miser ['maɪzər] avare m
miserable ['mɪzrəbl] (*unhappy*) malheureux; *weather,
performance* épouvantable
miserly ['maɪzərlɪ] avare; *sum*
dérisoire

misery ['mɪzərɪ] (*unhappiness*) tristesse f; (*wretchedness*) misère f

misfire [mɪs'faɪr] *of scheme* rater; *of joke* tomber à plat

misfit ['mɪsfɪt] *in society* marginal(e) *m(f)*

misfortune [mɪs'fɔːrtʃən] malheur *m*, malchance f

misguided [mɪs'gaɪdɪd] malavisé, imprudent

mishandle [mɪs'hændl] *situation* mal gérer

misinform [mɪsɪn'fɔːrm] mal informer

misinterpret [mɪsɪn'tɜːrprɪt] mal interpréter; **misinterpretation** mauvaise interprétation f

misjudge [mɪs'dʒʌdʒ] mal juger

mislay [mɪs'leɪ] égarer

mislead [mɪs'liːd] induire en erreur, tromper; **misleading** trompeur

mismanage [mɪs'mænɪdʒ] mal gérer; **mismanagement** mauvaise gestion f

misprint ['mɪsprɪnt] faute f typographique

mispronounce [mɪsprə'naʊns] mal prononcer; **mispronunciation** mauvaise prononciation f

misread [mɪs'riːd] *word, figures* mal lire; *situation* mal interpréter

misrepresent [mɪsreprɪ'zent] présenter sous un faux jour

miss[1] [mɪs]: **Miss Smith** Ma-

demoiselle Smith; **~!** mademoiselle!

miss[2] [mɪs] **1** *n* SP coup *m* manqué **2** *v/t* manquer, rater; *bus, train etc*, (*not notice*) rater; **I ~ you** tu me manques **3** *v/i* rater son coup

misshapen [mɪs'ʃeɪpən] déformé; *person, limb* difforme

missile ['mɪsəl] *mil* missile *m*; *stone etc* projectile *m*

missing ['mɪsɪŋ]: **be ~** have disappeared avoir disparu; *member of school party, one of a set etc* ne pas être là

mission ['mɪʃn] mission f

misspell [mɪs'spel] mal orthographier

mist [mɪst] brume f

mistake [mɪ'steɪk] **1** *n* erreur f, faute f; **make a ~** faire une erreur, se tromper **2** *v/t* se tromper de; **~ s.o./sth for s.o./sth** prendre qn/qch pour qn/qch d'autre; **mistaken** erroné, faux; **be ~** faire erreur, se tromper

mister ['mɪstər] → **Mr**

mistress ['mɪstrɪs] maîtresse f

mistrust [mɪs'trʌst] **1** *n* méfiance f **2** *v/t* se méfier de

misunderstand [mɪsʌndər'stænd] mal comprendre; **misunderstanding** malentendu *m*

misuse 1 [mɪs'juːs] *n* mauvais usage *m* **2** [mɪs'juːz] *v/t* faire mauvais usage de; *word* employer à tort mitigating circumstances ['mɪtɪgeɪtɪŋ] circonstances *fpl* atténuantes

mitt [mɪt] *in baseball* gant *m*; mitten moufle *f*

mix [mɪks] **1** *n* mélange *m*; *in cooking: ready to use* préparation *f* **2** *v/t* mélanger; *cement* malaxer **3** *v/i socially* être sociable

♦ **mix up** confondre; *get out of order* mélanger; **be mixed up in** être mêlé à; mixed economy, school, races mixte; reactions mitigé; mixer *for food* mixeur *m*; drink boisson non-alcoolisée que l'on mélange avec certains alcools; mixture mélange *m*; medicine mixture *f*; mix-up confusion *f*

moan [moʊn] **1** *n of pain* gémissement *m* **2** *v/i in pain* gémir

mob [mɑːb] **1** *n* foule *f* **2** *v/t* assaillir

mobile ['moʊbəl] **1** *adj* mobile; **be ~** *have car* être motorisé **2** *n for decoration* mobile *m*; *Br phone* portable *m*; **mobile home** mobile home *m*; **mobile phone** *Br* téléphone *m* portable; **mobility** mobilité *f*

mobster ['mɑːbstər] gangster *m*

mock [mɑːk] **1** *adj* faux, feint **2** *v/t* se moquer de; **mockery** *(derision)* moquerie *f*; *(travesty)* parodie *f*

mode [moʊd] mode *m*

model ['mɑːdl] **1** *adj employee, husband* modèle; *boat, plane* modèle réduit *inv* **2** *n (miniature)* maquette *f*; *(pattern)* modèle *m*; *(fashion ~)* mannequin *m* **3** *v/i for designer* être mannequin; *for artist, photographer* poser

modem ['moʊdem] modem *m*

moderate **1** ['mɑːdərət] *adj also POL* modéré **2** ['mɑːdərət] *n POL* modéré *m* **3** ['mɑːdəreɪt] *v/t* modérer; **moderately** modérément; **moderation** *(restraint)* modération *f*

modern ['mɑːdərn] moderne; modernization modernisation *f*; modernize **1** *v/t* moderniser **2** *v/i* se moderniser

modest ['mɑːdɪst] modeste; wage, amount modique; modesty *of apartment* simplicité *f*; *of wage* modicité *f*; *(lack of conceit)* modestie *f*

modification [mɑːdɪfɪ'keɪʃn] modification *f*; modify modifier

module ['mɑːdʒuːl] module *m*

moist [mɔɪst] humide; moisten humidifier; moisture humidité *f*; moisturizer *for skin* produit *m* hydratant

molasses [mə'læsɪz] mélasse *f*

mold¹ [moʊld] *n on food* moisi *m*, moisissure(s) *f(pl)*

mold² [moʊld] **1** *n* moule *m* **2**

v/t clay modeler; *character* façonner

moldy ['məʊldɪ] *food* moisi

molecule ['mɒlɪkjuːl] molécule *f*

molest [mə'lest] *child, woman* agresser (sexuellement)

mollycoddle ['mɒlɪkɒdl] F dorloter

molten ['məʊltən] en fusion

mom [mɑːm] F maman *f*

moment ['məʊmənt] instant *m*, moment *m*; *at the ~* en ce moment; **momentarily** (*for a moment*) momentanément; (*in a moment*) dans un instant; **momentary** momentané; **momentous** capital

momentum [mə'mentəm] élan *m*

monarch ['mɒnərk] monarque *m*

monastery ['mɒnəstrɪ] monastère *m*; **monastic** monastique

Monday ['mʌndeɪ] lundi *m*

monetary ['mʌnətərɪ] monétaire

money ['mʌnɪ] argent *m*; **money belt** sac *m* banane; **money market** marché *m* monétaire; **money order** mandat *m* postal

mongrel ['mʌŋɡrəl] bâtard *m*

monitor ['mɒnɪtər] **1** *n* COMPUT moniteur *m* **2** *v/t* surveiller, contrôler

monk [mʌŋk] moine *m*

monkey ['mʌŋkɪ] singe *m*; F

child polisson *m*; **monkey wrench** clef *f* anglaise

monolog, *Br* **monologue** ['mɒnəlɒɡ] monologue *m*

monopolize [mə'nɒpəlaɪz] exercer un monopole sur; *fig* monopoliser; **monopoly** monopole *m*

monotonous [mə'nɒtənəs] monotone; **monotony** monotonie *f*

monster ['mɒnstər] monstre *m*; **monstrosity** horreur *f*

month [mʌnθ] mois *m*; **monthly 1** *adj* mensuel **2** *adv* mensuellement **3** *n* *magazine* mensuel *m*

monument ['mɒnjʊmənt] monument *m*

mood [muːd] (*frame of mind*) humeur *f*; (*bad ~*) mauvaise humeur *f*; *of meeting, country* état *m* d'esprit; **moody** changing moods lunatique; (*bad-tempered*) maussade

moon [muːn] lune *f*; **moonlight** clair *m* de lune; **moonlit** éclairé par la lune

moor [mʊr] *boat* amarrer

moose [muːs] orignal *m*

mop [mɒp] **1** *n for floor* balai *m* lave-sol; *for dishes* éponge *f* à manche **2** *v/t floor* laver; *eyes, face* éponger, essuyer ◆ **mop up** éponger; MIL balayer

moral ['mɒrəl] **1** *adj* moral **2** *n of story* morale *f*; **~s** moralité *f*

morale [mə'ræl] moral *m*

morality [məˈrælətɪ] moralité f

morbid [ˈmɔːrbɪd] morbide

more [mɔːr] 1 *adj* plus de; **some ~ tea?** encore un peu de thé?; **there's no ~ coffee** il n'y a plus de café; **~ and ~ students** de plus en plus d'étudiants 2 *adv* plus; **~ important** plus important; **~ and ~** de plus en plus; **~ or less** plus ou moins; **once ~** une fois de plus; **I don't live there any ~** je n'habite plus là-bas 3 *pron* plus; **do you want some ~?** est-ce que tu en veux encore *or* davantage?; **a little ~** un peu plus; **moreover** de plus

morgue [mɔːrg] morgue f

morning [ˈmɔːrnɪŋ] matin m; **in the ~** le matin; (*tomorrow*) demain matin; **tomorrow ~** demain matin; **good ~** bonjour

moron [ˈmɔːrɑːn] F crétin m

morphine [ˈmɔːrfiːn] morphine f

mortal [ˈmɔːrtl] 1 *adj* mortel 2 *n* mortel m; **mortality** condition f mortelle; (*death rate*) mortalité f

mortar [ˈmɔːrtər] MIL, *cement* mortier m

mortgage [ˈmɔːrgɪdʒ] 1 *n* prêt m immobilier; *on own property* hypothèque f 2 *v/t* hypothéquer

mosaic [mouˈzeɪk] mosaïque f

Moscow [ˈmɑːskau] Moscou

Moslem [ˈmʊzlɪm] 1 *adj* musulman 2 *n* Musulman(e) m(f)

mosque [mɒsk] mosquée f

mosquito [mɒˈskiːtou] moustique m

moss [mɑːs] mousse f

most [moust] 1 *adj* la plupart de 2 *adv* (*very*) extrêmement, très; *play, swim, eat etc* le plus; **the ~ beautiful** le plus beau; **~ of all** surtout 3 *pron*: **~ of** la plupart de; **at (the) ~** au maximum; **make the ~ of** profiter au maximum de; **mostly** surtout

motel [mouˈtel] motel m

moth [mɑːθ] papillon m de nuit

mother [ˈmʌðər] 1 *n* mère f 2 *v/t* materner; **motherhood** maternité f; **Mothering Sunday** → *Mother's Day*; **mother-in-law** belle-mère f; **motherly** maternel; **Mother's Day** la fête des Mères; **mother tongue** langue f maternelle

motif [mouˈtiːf] motif m

motion [ˈmouʃn] 1 *n* (*movement*) mouvement m; (*proposal*) motion f; **motionless** immobile

motivate [ˈmoutɪveɪt] motiver; **motivation** motivation f; **motive** *for crime* mobile m

motor [ˈmoutər] moteur m; **motorbike** moto f; **motorcycle** moto f; **motorcyclist** motocycliste *m/f*; **motor home** camping-car *m*; **motor mechanic** mécanicien(ne) *m(f)*; **motor racing** course *f* automobile; **motor vehicle** véhicule *m* à moteur

motto ['mɑːtəʊ] devise *f*

mould *etc Br* → **mold** *etc*

mound [maʊnd] *(hillock)* monticule *m*; *(pile)* tas *m*

mount [maʊnt] **1** *n (mountain)* mont *m*; *(horse)* monture *f* **2** *v/t steps, photo* monter; *horse, bicycle* monter sur; *campaign* organiser **3** *v/i* monter

♦ **mount up** s'accumuler

mountain ['maʊntɪn] montagne *f*; **mountaineer** alpiniste *m/f*; **mountaineering** alpinisme *m*; **mountainous** montagneux

mourn [mɔːrn] pleurer; **mourner** parent/ami *m* du défunt; **mournful** triste, mélancolique

mouse [maʊs] *(pl mice* [maɪs] *) also* COMPUT souris *f*; **mouse mat** tapis *m* de souris

moustache *Br* → **mustache**

mouth [maʊθ] bouche *f*; *of animal* gueule *f*; *of river* embouchure *f*; **mouthful** *of food* bouchée *f*; *of drink* gorgée *f*; **mouthpiece** *of instrument* embouchure *f*; *(spokesperson)* porte-parole *m inv*; **mouthwash** bain *m* de bouche; **mouthwatering** allé-

chant

move [muːv] **1** *n* mouvement *m*; *in chess etc* coup *m*; *(step, action)* action *f*; *(change of house)* déménagement *m* **2** *v/t object* déplacer; *limbs* bouger; *(transfer)* transférer; *emotionally* émouvoir; **~ house** déménager **3** *v/i* bouger; *(transfer)* être transféré

♦ **move around** bouger, remuer; *from place to place* bouger, déménager

♦ **move in** emménager

movement ['muːvmənt] *also organization*, MUS mouvement *m*; **movers** déménageurs *mpl*

movie ['muːvɪ] film *m*; **go to a/the ~s** aller au cinéma; **moviegoer** amateur *m* de cinéma, cinéphile *m/f*; **movie theater** cinéma *m*

moving ['muːvɪŋ] *parts* mobile; *emotionally* émouvant

mow [məʊ] *grass* tondre; **mower** tondeuse *f* (à gazon)

mph [empiː'eɪtʃ] (= **miles per hour**) miles à l'heure

Mr ['mɪstər] Monsieur, M.

Mrs ['mɪsɪz] Madame, Mme

Ms [mɪz] Madame, Mme

much [mʌtʃ] **1** *adj* beaucoup de; **so ~ money** tant d'argent; **as ~ ... as ...** autant (de)... que... **2** *adv* beaucoup; **very ~** beaucoup; **too ~** trop **3** *pron* beaucoup; **nothing ~** pas grand-chose; **as ~ as ...** autant que...

mud [mʌd] boue f

muddle ['mʌdl] **1** n (mess) désordre m; (confusion) confusion f **2** v/t embrouiller

muddy ['mʌdɪ] boueux

muffin ['mʌfɪn] muffin m

muffle ['mʌfl] étouffer; **muffler** MOT silencieux m

mug¹ [mʌg] n for coffee chope f; F (face) gueule f F

mug² v/t (attack) agresser

mugger ['mʌgər] agresseur m; **mugging** agression f; **muggy** lourd, moite

mule [mjuːl] animal mulet m, mule f; slipper mule f

multicultural [mʌltɪ'kʌltʃərəl] multiculturel; **multilateral** POL multilatéral; **multimedia 2** adj multimédia **2** n multimédia m; **multinational 1** adj multinational **2** n COM multinationale f

multiple ['mʌltɪpl] multiple; **multiple sclerosis** sclérose f en plaques

multiplex ['mʌltɪpleks] (cinéma m) multiplex m

multiplication [mʌltɪplɪ-'keɪʃn] multiplication f; **multiply** ['mʌltɪplaɪ] **1** v/t multiplier **2** v/i se multiplier

multitasking [mʌltɪ'tæskɪŋ] multitâche m; for persons multiplicité f des tâches

mumble ['mʌmbl] **1** n marmonnement m **2** v/t & v/i marmonner

munch [mʌntʃ] mâcher

municipal [mjuː'nɪsɪpl] municipal

mural ['mjʊrəl] peinture f murale

murder ['mɜːrdər] **1** n meurtre m **2** v/t person assassiner; song massacrer; **murderer** meurtrier(-ière) m(f)

murky ['mɜːrkɪ] also fig trouble

murmur ['mɜːrmər] **1** n murmure m **2** v/t murmurer

muscle ['mʌsl] muscle m; **muscular** pain musculaire; person musclé

museum [mjuː'zɪəm] musée m

mushroom ['mʌʃrʊm] **1** n champignon m **2** v/i fig proliférer

music ['mjuːzɪk] musique f; in written form partition f; **musical 1** adj musical; person musicien **2** n comédie f musicale; **musician** musicien(ne) m(f)

mussel ['mʌsl] moule f

must [mʌst] **1** v/aux ◇ necessity devoir; **I ~ be on time** je dois être à l'heure, il faut que je sois (subj) à l'heure; **I ~n't be late** je ne dois pas être en retard, il ne faut pas que je sois en retard

◇ probability devoir; **it ~ be about 6 o'clock** il doit être environ six heures

mustache [məˈstæʃ] moustache f

mustard ['mʌstərd] moutarde f

musty ['mʌstɪ] *room* qui sent le renfermé; *smell* de renfermé

mutilate ['mjuːtɪleɪt] mutiler

mutiny ['mjuːtɪnɪ] **1** *n* mutinerie *f* **2** *v/i* se mutiner

mutter ['mʌtər] marmonner

mutual ['mjuːtʃʊəl] (*reciprocal*) mutuel; (*common*) commun

muzzle ['mʌzl] **1** *n of animal* museau *m*; *for dog* muselière *f* **2** *v/t*: **~ the press** bâillonner

la presse

my [maɪ] mon *m*, ma *f*; *pl* mes; **myself** moi-même; *reflexive* me; *before vowel* m'; *after prep* moi; **I hurt ~** je me suis blessé

mysterious [mɪ'stɪrɪəs] mystérieux; **mysteriously** mystérieusement; **mystery** mystère *m*; **mystify** rendre perplexe; *of tricks* mystifier

myth [mɪθ] *also fig* mythe *m*; **mythical** mythique

N

nag [næg] **1** *v/i of person* faire des remarques continuelles **2** *v/t* harceler; **nagging** *pain* obsédant; **I have this ~ doubt that ...** je n'arrive pas à m'empêcher de penser que ...

nail [neɪl] *for wood* clou *m*; *on finger, toe* ongle *m*; **nail polish** vernis *m* à ongles; **nail polish remover** dissolvant *m*

naive [naɪ'iːv] naïf

naked ['neɪkɪd] nu

name [neɪm] **1** *n* nom *m*; **what's your ~?** comment vous appelez-vous? **2** *v/t* appeler; **namely** à savoir; **namesake** homonyme *m/f*

nanny ['nænɪ] nurse *f*

nap [næp] sieste *f*

napkin ['næpkɪn] (*table ~*) serviette *f* (de table); (*sanitary~*) serviette *f* hygiénique

narcotic [nɑːr'kɑːtɪk] stupéfiant *m*

narrate ['næreɪt] raconter; **narrative** **1** *adj poem, style* narratif **2** *n* (*story*) récit *m*; **narrator** narrateur(-trice) *m(f)*

narrow ['næroʊ] étroit; *victory* serré; **narrowly** *win* de justesse; *escape* de peu; **narrow-minded** étroit d'esprit

nasty ['næstɪ] *person, thing to say* méchant; *smell* nauséabond; *weather, cut, wound, disease* mauvais

nation ['neɪʃn] nation *f*; **national** **1** *adj* national **2** *n* national *m*, ressortissant *m*; **national anthem** hymne *m* national; **national debt** dette *f* publique; **nationalism** nationalisme *m*; **nationality** nationalité *f*; **nationalize** in-

dustry etc nationaliser

native ['neɪtɪv] **1** *adj* natal **2** *n* natif(-ive) *m(f)*; *(tribesman)* indigène *m*; **Native American 1** *adj* amérindien **2** *n* Amérindien(ne) *m(f)*

NATO ['neɪtəʊ] (= *North Atlantic Treaty Organization*) OTAN *f* (= Organisation du traité de l'Atlantique Nord)

natural ['næʧrəl] naturel; **naturalist** naturaliste *m(f)*; **naturalize**: *become ~d* se faire naturaliser; **naturally** *(of course)* bien entendu; *behave, speak* naturellement, avec naturel; *(by nature)* de nature; **nature** nature *f*; **nature reserve** réserve *f* naturelle

naughty ['nɔːtɪ] vilain; *photograph, word etc* coquin

nausea ['nɔːzɪə] nausée *f*; **nauseate** *fig* écœurer; **nauseating** écœurant; **nauseous**: *feel ~* avoir la nausée

nautical ['nɔːtɪkl] nautique, marin

naval ['neɪvl] naval, maritime; *history* de la marine

navel ['neɪvl] nombril *m*

navigate ['nævɪgeɪt] *also* COMPUT naviguer; *in car* diriger; **navigation** navigation *f*; *in car* indications *fpl*; **navigator** navigateur *m*

navy ['neɪvɪ] marine *f*; **navy blue 1** *adj* bleu marine *inv* **2** *n* bleu *m* marine

near [nɪr] **1** *adv* près; *come ~er* approche-toi **2** *prep* près de **3** *adj* proche; *in the ~ future* dans un proche avenir; **nearby** tout près; **nearly** presque; *I ~ lost it* j'ai failli le perdre; **near-sighted** myope

neat [niːt] *room, desk* bien rangé; *person* ordonné; *in appearance* soigné; *whiskey etc* sec; *solution* ingénieux; F *(terrific)* super *inv* F

necessarily ['nesəserɪlɪ] nécessairement, forcément; **necessary** nécessaire; *it is ~ to …* il faut …; **necessity** nécessité *f*

neck [nek] cou *m*; *of clothing* col *m*; **necklace** collier *m*; **neckline** *of dress* encolure *f*; **necktie** cravate *f*

née [neɪ] née

need [niːd] **1** *n* besoin *m*; *if ~ be* si besoin est; *in ~* dans le besoin **2** *v/t* avoir besoin de; *you don't ~ to wait* vous n'êtes pas obligés d'attendre; *I ~ to talk to you* il faut que je te parle

needle ['niːdl] aiguille *f*; **needlework** travaux *mpl* d'aiguille

needy ['niːdɪ] nécessiteux

negative ['negətɪv] négatif

neglect [nɪ'glekt] **1** *n* négligence *f*; *state* abandon *m* **2** *v/t* négliger; **neglected** négligé

negligence ['neglɪdʒəns] négligence *f*; **negligent** négligent; **negligible** *quantity* négligeable

negotiable [nɪˈɡəʊʃəbl] négociable; **negotiate 1** *v/i* négocier **2** *v/t deal* négocier; *obstacles* franchir; *bend in road* négocier, prendre; **negotiation** négociation *f*; **negotiator** négociateur(-trice) *m(f)*

neighbor [ˈneɪbər] voisin(e) *m(f)*; **neighborhood** *in town* quartier *m*; **neighboring** *house, state* voisin; **neighborly** aimable

neighbour *etc Br* → **neighbor** *etc*

neither [ˈniːðər] **1** *adj*: ~ **player** aucun(e) des deux joueurs **2** *pron* ni l'un ni l'autre **3** *adv*: ~ **... nor ...** ni ... ni ... **4** *conj*: ~ **do/can I** moi non plus

neon light [ˈniːɑːn] néon *m*

nephew [ˈnefjuː] neveu *m*

nerve [nɜːrv] nerf *m*; (*courage*) courage *m*; (*impudence*) culot *m* F; **nerve-racking** angoissant, éprouvant; **nervous** nerveux; **nervous breakdown** dépression *f* nerveuse; **nervousness** nervosité *f*; **nervy** (*fresh*) effronté, culotté F

nest [nest] nid *m*

net[1] [net] *n for fishing, tennis etc* filet *m*; *Internet* Net *m*

net[2] [net] *adj price etc* net

nettle [ˈnetl] ortie *f*

'**network** *also* COMPUT réseau *m*; **social** ~ réseau *m* social

neurologist [nʊˈrɑːlədʒɪst] neurologue *m/f*

neurosis [nʊˈrəʊsɪs] névrose *f*; **neurotic** névrosé, obsédé

neuter [ˈnuːtər] *animal* castrer; **neutral 1** *adj* neutre **2** *n gear* point *m* mort; **neutrality** neutralité *f*; **neutralize** neutraliser

never [ˈnevər] jamais; *I've ~ been to New York* je ne suis jamais allé à New York; **nevertheless** néanmoins

new [nuː] nouveau; (*not used*) neuf; **newborn** nouveau-né; **newcomer** nouveau venu *m*, nouvelle venue *f*; **newly** (*recently*) récemment, nouvellement; **newly-weds** jeunes mariés *mpl*

news [nuːz] nouvelle(s) *f(pl)*; *on TV, radio* informations *fpl*; **newscast** TV journal *m* télévisé; **newscaster** TV présentateur(-trice) *m(f)*; **news flash** flash *m* d'information; **newspaper** journal *m*; **newsreader** TV *etc* présentateur(-trice) *m(f)*; **news report** reportage *m*; **newsstand** kiosque *m* à journaux; **newsvendor** vendeur(-euse) *m(f)* de journaux

'**New Year** nouvel an *m*; *Happy ~!* Bonne année!; **New Year's Day** jour *m* de l'an; **New Year's Eve** la Saint-Sylvestre

next [nekst] **1** *adj* prochain; *the ~ month* le mois suivant

2 adv (after) ensuite, après; **~ to** à côté de; **next-door 1** adj neighbor d'à côté **2** adv live à côté; **next of kin** parent m le plus proche

nibble ['nɪbl] cheese grignoter; ear mordiller

nice [naɪs] agréable; person also sympathique; house, hair beau; **that's very ~ of you** c'est très gentil de votre part; **nicely** written, presented bien; (pleasantly) agréablement

niche [niːʃ] in market créneau m; (special position) place f

nick [nɪk] (cut) coupure f

nickel ['nɪkl] MIN nickel m; coin pièce f de cinq cents

'nickname surnom n

niece [niːs] nièce f

night [naɪt] nuit f; (evening) soir m; **11 o'clock at ~** onze heures du soir; **during the ~** pendant la nuit; **good~** going to bed bonne nuit; leaving office, friends' house etc bonsoir; **nightcap** drink boisson f du soir; **nightclub** boîte f de nuit; **nightdress** chemise f de nuit; **night flight** vol m de nuit; **nightlife** vie f nocturne; **nightly 1** adj de toutes les nuits; in evening de tous les soirs **2** adv tous les nuits; in evening tous les soirs; **nightmare** also fig cauchemar m; **night porter** gardien m de nuit; **night school** cours mpl du soir; **night shift**

équipe f de nuit; **nightshirt** chemise f de nuit (d'homme); **nightspot** boîte f (de nuit); **nighttime: at ~, in the ~** la nuit

nimble ['nɪmbl] agile; mind vif

nine [naɪn] neuf; **nineteen** dix-neuf; **nineteenth** dix-neuvième; **ninetieth** quatre-vingt-dixième; **ninety** quatre-vingt-dix; **ninth** neuvième

nip [nɪp] (pinch) pincement m; (bite) morsure f

nipple ['nɪpl] mamelon m

nitrogen ['naɪtrədʒn] azote m

no [noʊ] **1** adj non **2** adj aucun, pas de; **there's ~ coffee left** il ne reste plus de café; **I have ~ money** je n'ai pas d'argent; **~ smoking** défense de fumer

noble ['noʊbl] noble

nobody ['noʊbədɪ] personne; **~ knows** personne ne le sait; **there was ~ at home** il n'y avait personne

no-brainer [noʊ'breɪnər] jeu m d'enfant; **the math test was a ~** le devoir de maths était super facile

nod [nɑːd] **1** n signe m de tête **2** v/i faire un signe de tête

noise [nɔɪz] bruit m; **noisy** bruyant; **be ~** of person faire du bruit

nominal ['nɑːmɪnl] nominal; (token) symbolique

nominate ['nɑːmɪneɪt] (ap-

point) nommer; **nomination** (*appointment*) nomination *f*; (*person proposed*) candidat *m*; **nominee** candidat *m*

nonalco'holic non alcoolisé

noncommissioned 'officer ['nɑːnkəmɪʃnd] sous-officier *m*

noncommittal [nɑːnkə'mɪtl] évasif

nondescript ['nɑːndɪskrɪpt] quelconque; *color* indéfinissable

none [nʌn] aucun(e); **there is/ are ~ left** il n'en reste plus

nonentity [nɑː'nentɪtɪ] être *m* insignifiant

none'xistent inexistant

non'fiction ouvrages *mpl* non littéraires

noninter'ference non-ingérence *f*

noninter'vention non-intervention *f*

no-'nonsense *approach* pragmatique

non'payment non-paiement *m*

nonpol'luting non polluant

non'resident non-résident *m*; *in hotel* client *m* de passage

nonre'turnable non remboursable

nonsense ['nɑːnsəns] absurdité(s) *f(pl)*; **don't talk ~** ne raconte pas n'importe quoi

non'smoker non-fumeur (-euse) *m(f)*

non'standard non standard *inv*; *use of word* impropre

non'stop 1 *adj flight, train* direct; *chatter* incessant **2** *adv fly, travel* sans escale; *chatter, argue* sans arrêt

non'union non syndiqué

non'violence non-violence *f*; **nonviolent** non-violent

noodles ['nuːdlz] nouilles *fpl*

noon [nuːn] midi *m*

no-one → *nobody*

noose [nuːs] nœud *m* coulant

nor [nɔːr] ni; **~ do I** moi non plus

norm [nɔːrm] norme *f*; **normal** normal; **normality** normalité *f*; **normally** normalement

north [nɔːrθ] **1** *n* nord *m* **2** *adj* nord *inv*; *wind* du nord **3** *adv travel* vers le nord; **North America** Amérique *f* du Nord; **North American 1** *adj* nord-américain **2** *n* Nord-Américain(e) *m(f)*; **northeast** nord-est *m*; **northerly** *wind* du nord; *direction* vers le nord; **northern** du nord; **northerner** habitant *m* du Nord; **North Korea** Corée *f* du Nord; **North Korean 1** *adj* nord-coréen **2** *n* Nord-Coréen(ne) *m(f)*; **North Pole** pôle *m* Nord; **northward** *travel* vers le nord; **northwest** nord-ouest *m*

nose [nouz] nez *m*

◆ **nose around** F fouiner

nostalgia [nɑː'stældʒə] nostalgie *f*; **nostalgic** nostalgique

nostril ['nɑ:strəl] narine f

nosy ['nouzı] F curieux

not [nɑ:t] pas; *~ now* pas maintenant; *~ there* pas là; *~ a lot* pas beaucoup *with verbs* ne … pas; *it's ~ allowed* ce n'est pas permis; *he didn't help* il n'a pas aidé

notable ['noutəbl] notable

notch [nɑ:tʃ] entaille f

note [nout] MUS, *written* note f; (*short letter*) mot m; **notebook** carnet m; COMPUT ordinateur m bloc-notes; **noted** célèbre; **notepad** bloc-notes m; **notepaper** papier m à lettres

nothing ['nʌθıŋ] rien; *she said ~* elle n'a rien dit; *~ but* rien que; *~ much* pas grand-chose; *for ~* (*for free*) gratuitement; (*for no reason*) pour un rien

notice ['noutıs] 1 n *on bulletin board, in street* affiche f; (*advance warning*) préavis m; *in newspaper* avis m; *to leave job* démission f; *to leave house* préavis m; *at short ~* dans un délai très court; *until further ~* jusqu'à nouvel ordre; *hand in one's ~ to employer* donner sa démission; *take no ~ of* ne pas faire attention à 2 *v/t* remarquer; **noticeable** visible

notify ['noutıfaı] *~ s.o. of sth* signaler qch à qn

notion ['nouʃn] idée f

notorious [nou'tɔ:rıəs] notoire

noun [naun] substantif m, nom m

nourishing ['nʌrıʃıŋ] nourrissant; **nourishment** nourriture f

novel ['nɑ:vl] roman m; **novelist** romancier(-ière) m(f); **novelty** nouveauté f

November [nou'vembər] novembre m

novice ['nɑ:vıs] (*beginner*) novice m, débutant m

now [nau] maintenant; *~ and again*, *~ and then* de temps à autre; *by ~* maintenant; **nowadays** aujourd'hui, de nos jours

nowhere ['nouwer] nulle part; *it's ~ near finished* c'est loin d'être fini

nuclear ['nu:klıər] nucléaire; **nuclear energy** énergie f nucléaire; **nuclear power** énergie f nucléaire; POL puissance f nucléaire; **nuclear power station** centrale f nucléaire; **nuclear reactor** réacteur m nucléaire; **nude** [nu:d] 1 *adj* nu 2 *n painting* nu m; *in the ~* tout nu

nudge [nʌdʒ] *person* donner un coup de coude à; *parked car* pousser (un peu)

nudist ['nu:dıst] nudiste m/f

nuisance ['nu:sns] peste f, plaie f F; *event, task* ennui m; *make a ~ of o.s.* être embêtant F null and 'void [nʌl] nul et non avenu

numb [nʌm] engourdi; *emotionally* insensible

number ['nʌmbər] **1** *n* nombre *m*; *symbol* chiffre *m*; *of hotel room, phone* ~ *etc* numéro *m* **2** *v/t* (*put a* ~ *on*) numéroter

numeral ['nuːmərəl] chiffre *m*

numerous ['nuːmərəs] nombreux

nun [nʌn] religieuse *f*

nurse [nɜːrs] infirmier(-ière) *m(f)*; **nursery** maternelle *f*; *for plants* pépinière *f*; **nurs-**ery rhyme comptine *f*; **nurs-ery school** école *f* maternelle; **nursing** profession *f* d'infirmier; **nursing home** *for old people* maison *f* de retraite

nut [nʌt] (*walnut*) noix *f*; (*Brazil*) noix *f* du Brésil; (*hazelnut*) noisette *f*; (*peanut*) cacahuète *f*; *for bolt* écrou *m*; **nutcrackers** casse-noisettes *m inv*

nutrient ['nuːtrɪənt] élément *m* nutritif; **nutrition** nutrition *f*; **nutritious** nutritif

nuts [nʌts] F (*crazy*) fou

O

oar [ɔːr] aviron *m*, rame *f*

oasis [ouˈeɪsɪs] *also fig* oasis *f*

oath [ouθ] LAW serment *m*; (*swearword*) juron *m*

oats [outs] *npl* avoine *f*

obedience [ouˈbiːdɪəns] obéissance *f*; **obedient** obéissant; **obediently** docilement

obese [ouˈbiːs] obèse; **obesi-ty** obésité *f*

obey [ouˈbeɪ] obéir à

obituary [ouˈbɪtʃuərɪ] nécrologie *f*

object¹ ['ɑːbdʒɪkt] *n* (*thing*) objet *m*; (*aim*) objectif *m*; GRAM complément *m* d'objet

object² [əbˈdʒekt] *v/i* protester; *if nobody* ~*s* si personne n'y voit d'objection

objection [əbˈdʒekʃn] objection *f*; **objectionable** (*unpleasant*) désagréable; **objective 1** *adj* objectif **2** *n* objectif *m*; **objectively** objectivement; **objectivity** objectivité *f*

obligation [ɑːblɪˈɡeɪʃn] obligation *f*; **obligatory** obligatoire; **obliging** serviable, obligeant

oblique [əˈbliːk] **1** *adj* *reference* indirect; *line* oblique **2** *n* *in punctuation* barre *f* oblique

obliterate [əˈblɪtəreɪt] *city* détruire; *memory* effacer

oblivion [əˈblɪvɪən] oubli *m*

oblong [ˈɑːblɑːŋ] **1** *adj* oblong **2** *n* rectangle *m* obscene [əb'siːn] obscène; *salary, poverty* scandaleux; **obscenity** obscénité *f*

obscure [əb'skjʊr] obscur; *village* inconnu; **obscurity** obscurité *f*

observant [əb'zɜːrvnt] observateur; **observation** observation *f*; **observe** observer; **observer** observateur(-trice) *m(f)*

obsess [əb'ses]: **be ~ed with** être obsédé par; **obsession** obsession *f* (**with** de)

obsoiete ['ɑːbsəliːt] obsolète

obstacle ['ɑːbstəkl] *also fig* obstacle *m*

obstetrician [ɑːbstə'trɪʃn] obstétricien(ne) *m(f)*; **obstetrics** obstétrique *f*

obstinacy ['ɑːbstɪnəsɪ] entêtement *m*, obstination *f*; **obstinate** obstiné

obstruct [əb'strʌkt] *road* bloquer, obstruer; *investigation* entraver; *police* gêner; **obstruction** *on road etc* obstacle *m*; **obstructive** *behavior* qui met des bâtons dans les roues; *tactics* obstructionniste

obtain [əb'teɪn] obtenir; **obtainable** *products* disponible

obtuse [əb'tuːs] *fig* obtus

obvious ['ɑːbvɪəs] évident, manifeste; **obviously** manifestement; **~!** évidemment!

occasion [ə'keɪʒn] occasion *f*; **occasional** occasionnel; **occasionally** de temps en temps, occasionnellement

occupant ['ɑːkjʊpənt] occupant(e) *m(f)*; **occupation** (*job*) métier *m*; *of country* occupation *f*; **occupy** occuper

occur [ə'kɜːr] avoir lieu, se produire; (*event*) fait *m*; **occurrence** *event* fait *m*

ocean ['oʊʃn] océan *m*

o'clock [ə'klɑːk]: **at five ~** à cinq heures

October [ɑːk'toʊbər] octobre *m*

odd [ɑːd] (*strange*) bizarre; (*not even*) impair; **oddball** F original *m*; **odds and ends** petites choses *fpl*, bricoles *fpl*; **odds-on: the ~ favorite** le grand favori

odometer [oʊ'dɑːmətər] odomètre *m*

odor, *Br* odour ['oʊdər] odeur *f*

of [ɑːv] de; *the name ~ the street/hotel* le nom de la rue/de l'hôtel; *the color ~ the paper* la couleur du papier; *five minutes ~ ten* dix heures moins cinq; *~ cancer* mourir du cancer; *love ~ money* l'amour de l'argent

off [ɑːf] **1** *prep:* **~ the main road** away from en retrait de la route principale; *near* près de la route principale; *$20 ~ the price* 20 dollars de réduction **2** *adv:* **be ~ of** *light, TV, machine* être éteint; *of brake* être desserré; *of lid* ne pas être mis; *not at work* ne pas être là; *canceled* être annulé; **we're ~ tomorrow** *leaving* nous partons demain; **take a day ~** prendre un jour de congé; **it's 3 miles ~** c'est à 3 miles; **it's a long way ~** c'est loin **3** *adj:* **the ~ switch** le bouton d'arrêt

offence *Br* → **offense**

offend [ə'fend] (*insult*) offenser; **offender** LAW délinquant(e) *m(f)*; **offense** LAW *minor* infraction *f*; *serious* délit *m*; **take ~ at sth** s'offenser de qch; **offensive 1** *adj behavior, remark* offensant; *smell* repoussant **2** *n* MIL offensive *f*

offer ['ɒːfər] **1** *n* offre *f* **2** *v/t* offrir

off'hand *attitude* désinvolte

office ['ɒːfɪs] bureau *m*; (*position*) fonction *f*; **officer** MIL officier *m*; *in police* agent *m* de police; **official 1** *adj* officiel **2** *n* civil servant etc fonctionnaire *m/f*; **officially** officiellement; (*strictly speaking*) en théorie; **officious** trop zélé

'off-line *work* hors connexion; **go ~** se déconnecter

'off-peak *rates* en période creuse

'off-season basse saison *f*

'offset *losses* compenser

'offshore offshore

'offside SP hors jeu

'offspring progéniture *f*

'off-the-record officieux

often ['ɒːfn] souvent; **how ~ do you go there?** vous y allez tous les combien?

oil [ɔɪl] **1** *n* huile *f*; *petroleum* pétrole *m* **2** *v/t* lubrifier, huiler; **oil change** vidange *f*; **oil company** compagnie *f* pétrolière; **oilfield** champ *m* pétrolifère; **oil painting** peinture *f* à l'huile; **oil refinery** raffinerie *f* de pétrole; **oil rig** *at sea* plate-forme *f* de forage; *on land* tour *f* de forage; **oil slick** marée *f* noire; **oil tanker** *ship* pétrolier *m*; **oil well** puits *m* de pétrole; **oily** graisseux

ointment ['ɔɪntmənt] pommade *f*

ok [oʊ'keɪ]: **can I? – ~** je peux? – d'accord; **is it ~ with you if ...?** ça te dérange si ...?; **does that look ~?** est-ce que ça va?; **that's ~ by me** ça me va; **are you ~?** (*well, not hurt*) ça va?

old [oʊld] vieux; (*previous*) ancien; **how ~ is he?** quel âge a-t-il?; **old age** vieillesse *f*; **old-fashioned** démodé

olive ['ɑːlɪv] olive *f*; **olive oil** huile *f* d'olive

Olympic Games [ə'lɪmpɪk] Jeux *mpl* Olympiques

omelet, *Br* **omelette** ['ɑːmlət] omelette *f*

ominous ['ɑːmɪnəs] inquiétant

omission [ou'mɪʃn] omission *f*; **omit** [ou'mɪt] omettre

on [ɑːn] **1** *prep* sur; ~ **the table** sur la table; ~ **the bus** dans le bus; ~ **the third floor** au deuxième étage; ~ **TV** à la télé; ~ **Sunday** dimanche; ~ **Sundays** le dimanche; ~ **the 1st of …** le premier...; **this is ~ me** (*I'm paying*) c'est moi qui paie; **have you any money ~ you?** as-tu de l'argent sur toi?; ~ **his arrival** à son arrivée; ~ **his departure** au moment de son départ; ~ **hearing this** en entendant ceci **2** *adv*: **be ~ of** *light, TV, computer etc* être allumé; *of brake* être serré; *of lid* être mis; *of program: being broadcast* passer; *of meeting etc: be scheduled to happen* avoir lieu; **what's ~ tonight?** *on TV etc* qu'est-ce qu'il y a ce soir?; (*what's planned?*) qu'est-ce qu'on fait ce soir?; **you're ~** (*I accept*) c'est d'accord; ~ **you go** (*go ahead*) vas-y; **talk ~** continuer à parler; **and so ~** et ainsi de suite; **~ and talk etc** pendant des heures **3** *adj*: **the ~ switch** le bouton marche

once [wʌns] **1** *adv* (*one time*) une fois; (*formerly*) autrefois; ~ **again**, ~ **more** encore une fois; **at ~** (*immediately*) tout de suite **2** *conj* une fois que; ~ **you have finished**

une fois que tu auras terminé

one [wʌn] **1** *n number* un *m* **2** *adj* un(e); ~ **day** un jour **3** *pron*: ~ **is bigger than the other** l'un(e) est plus grand(e) que l'autre; **which ~?** lequel/laquelle?; ~ **by ~** *enter, deal with* un(e) à la fois; **the little ~s** les petits *mpl*; **I for ~** pour ma part; **what can ~ say?** qu'est-ce qu'on peut dire?; **one-parent family** famille *f* monoparentale; **oneself: hurt ~** se faire mal; **for ~** pour soi *or* soi-même; **do sth by ~** faire qch tout seul; **one-way street** rue *f* à sens unique; **one--way ticket** aller *m* simple

onion ['ʌnjən] oignon *m*

'on-line en ligne; **go ~ to** se connecter à; **on-line banking** (*services mpl de*) banque *f* en ligne; **on-line dating** rencontres *fpl* en ligne; **on--line shopping** shopping *m* en ligne

onlooker ['ɑːnlukər] spectateur(-trice) *m(f)*

only ['ounlɪ] **1** *adv* seulement; **he's ~ six** il n'a que six ans **2** *adj* unique

'onset début *m*

on-the-job 'training formation *f* sur le tas

opaque [ou'peɪk] *glass* opaque

open ['oupən] **1** *adj* ouvert; **in the ~ air** en plein air **2** *v/t* ouvrir **3** *v/i of shop, flower* s'ouvrir; **open-air** *meeting, concert* en plein air; *pool* découvert; **open day** journée *f* portes ouvertes; **open-ended** *contract etc* flexible; **opening** *in wall etc* ouverture *f*; *of film, novel etc* début *m*; *(job)* poste *m* (vacant); **openly** *(honestly, frankly)* ouvertement; **open-minded** à l'esprit ouvert, ouvert; **open ticket** billet *m* open

opera ['ɑːpərə] opéra *m*; **opera house** opéra *m*; **opera singer** chanteur(-euse) *m(f)* d'opéra

operate ['ɑːpəreɪt] **1** *v/i of company* opérer; *of airline, bus service* circuler; *of machine* fonctionner; MED opérer **2** *v/t machine* faire marcher

♦ **operate on** MED opérer

'operate room MED salle *f* d'opération; **operating system** COMPUT système *m* d'exploitation; **operation** MED opération *f* (chirurgicale); *of machine* fonctionnement *m*; **have an ~** MED se faire opérer; **operator** *of machine* opérateur(-trice) *m(f)*; *(tour ~)* tour-opérateur *m*, voyagiste *m*; TELEC standardiste *m/f*

opinion [ə'pɪnjən] opinion *f*; **opinion poll** sondage *m* d'opinion

opponent [ə'poʊnənt] adversaire *m/f*

opportunist [ɑːpər'tuːnɪst] opportuniste *m/f*; **opportunity** occasion *f*

oppose [ə'poʊz] s'opposer à; **be ~d to** être opposé à

opposite ['ɑːpəzɪt] **1** *adj* opposé; *meaning* contraire **2** *adv* en face; **the house ~** la maison d'en face **3** *prep* en face de; **opposite 'number** homologue *m/f*

opposition [ɑːpə'zɪʃn] opposition *f*

oppress [ə'pres] *people* opprimer; **oppressive** *rule* oppressif; *weather* oppressant

optician [ɑːp'tɪʃn] opticien (-ne) *m(f)*

optimism ['ɑːptɪmɪzəm] optimisme *m*; **optimist** optimiste *m/f*; **optimistic** optimiste; **optimistically** avec optimisme

optimum ['ɑːptɪməm] optimal

option ['ɑːpʃn] option *f*; **optional** facultatif

or [ɔːr] ou; **~ else!** sinon ...

oral ['ɔːrəl] *exam* oral; *hygiene* dentaire

orange ['ɔːrɪndʒ] **1** *adj color* orange *inv* **2** *n fruit* orange *f*; *color* orange *m*; **orange juice** jus *m* d'orange

orator ['ɔːrətər] orateur(-trice) *m(f)*

orbit ['ɔːrbɪt] **1** *n of earth* orbite *f* **2** *v/t the earth* décrire une orbite autour de

orchard ['ɔːrtʃərd] verger *m*

orchestra ['ɔ:rkəstrə] orchestre *m*

orchid ['ɔ:rkɪd] orchidée *f*

ordain [ɔ:r'deɪn] ordonner

ordeal [ɔ:r'di:l] épreuve *f*

order ['ɔ:rdər] **1** *n* ordre *m*; *for goods, in restaurant* commande *f*; *an* ∼ *of fries* une portion de frites; *in* ∼ to pour; *out of* ∼ (*not functioning*) hors service; *in* ∼ (*not in sequence*) pas dans l'ordre **2** *v/t* (*put in sequence, proper layout*) ranger; *goods, meal* commander; ∼ *s.o. to do sth* ordonner à qn de faire qch **3** *v/i in restaurant* commander; **ordered 1** *adj lifestyle* bien réglé **2** *n in hospital* aide-soignant *m*

ordinarily [ɔ:rdɪ'nerɪlɪ] (*as a rule*) d'habitude; **ordinary** ordinaire

ore [ɔ:r] minerai *m*

organ ['ɔ:rgən] ANAT organe *m*; MUS orgue *m*; **organic** *food, fertilizer* biologique; **organically** *grown* biologiquement; **organism** organisme *m*

organization [ɔ:rgənaɪ'zeɪʃn] organisation *f*; **organize** organiser; **organizer** *person* organisateur(-trice) *m(f)*

Orient ['ɔ:rɪənt] Orient *m*; **Oriental** oriental

origin ['ɑ:rɪdʒɪn] origine *f*; **original 1** *adj* (*not copied*) original; (*first*) d'origine, initial **2** *n painting etc* original

m; **originality** originalité *f*; **originally** à l'origine; (*at first*) au départ; **originate 1** *v/t idea* être à l'origine de **2** *v/i of idea, belief* émaner (*from* de); *of family* être originaire (*from* de)

ornamental [ɔ:rnə'mentl] décoratif

ornate [ɔ:r'neɪt] *architecture* chargé; *prose style* fleuri

orphan ['ɔ:rfn] orphelin(e) *m(f)*

orthodox ['ɔ:rθədɑ:ks] orthodoxe

orthopedic [ɔ:rθə'pi:dɪk] orthopédique

ostensibly [ɑ:'stensəblɪ] en apparence

ostentatious [ɑ:sten'teɪʃəs] prétentieux, tape-à-l'œil *inv*

ostracize ['ɑ:strəsaɪz] frapper d'ostracisme

other ['ʌðər] **1** *adj* autre; *the* ∼ *day* (*recently*) l'autre jour; *every* ∼ *day* un jour sur deux; ∼ *people* d'autres **2** *n:* *the* ∼ l'autre *m/f*

otherwise ['ʌðərwaɪz] **1** *conj* sinon **2** *adv* (*differently*) autrement

ought [ɔ:t]: *I/you* ∼ *to know* je/tu devrais le savoir; *you* ∼ *to have done it* tu aurais dû le faire

ounce [aʊns] once *f*

our ['aʊər] notre; *pl* nos; **ours** le nôtre, la nôtre; *pl* les nôtres; *it's* ∼ c'est à nous; **ourselves** nous-mêmes; *reflex-*

ive nous; *after prep* nous; **we enjoyed** nous nous sommes amusé(e)s

oust [aʊst] *from office* évincer

out [aʊt]: **be~** *of light, fire* être éteint; *of flower* être en fleur; *of sun* briller; (*not at home, not in building*) être sorti; *of calculations* être faux; (*be published*) être sorti; *of secret* être connu; (*no longer in competition*) être éliminé; (*no longer in fashion*) être passé de mode; ~ **here in Dallas** ici à Dallas; (**get**) ~! dehors!; (**get**) ~ **of my room!** sors de ma chambre!; **that's ~!** (*~ of the question*) hors de question!; **he's ~ to win** (*fully intends to*) il est bien décidé à gagner; **outbreak** *of war* déclenchement *m*; *of violence* éruption *f*

'**outcast** exclu(e) *m(f)*
'**outcome** résultat *m*
'**outcry** tollé *m*
out'**dated** démodé
out'**do** surpasser
'**outdoor** *activities* de plein air; *life* au grand air; *toilet* extérieur; **outdoors** dehors
'**outer** [ˈaʊtər] *wall etc* extérieur
'**outfit** (*clothes*) tenue *f*, ensemble *m*; (*company, organization*) boîte *f* F
out'**last** durer plus longtemps que
'**outlet** *of pipe* sortie *f*; for

sales point *m* de vente; ELEC prise *f* de courant
'**outline 1** *n* silhouette *f*; *of plan, novel* esquisse *f* **2** *v/t plans* ébaucher
out'**live** survivre à
'**outlook** (*prospects*) perspective *f*
out'**number** être plus nombreux que
out of ◇ *motion* de, hors de; **run ~ the house** sortir de la maison en courant ◇ *position*: **20 miles ~ Detroit** à 32 kilomètres de Détroit ◇ *cause* par; ~ **jealousy** par jalousie ◇ *without*: **we're ~ gas** nous n'avons plus d'essence ◇ *from a group* sur; **5 ~ 10** 5 sur 10
out-of-'date dépassé; (*expired*) périmé
'**output 1** *n of factory* production *f*, rendement *m*; COMPUT sortie *f* **2** *v/t* (*produce*) produire
'**outrage 1** *n feeling* indignation *f*; *act* outrage *m* **2** *v/t* faire outrage à; **outrageous** *acts* révoltant; *prices* scandaleux
'**outright 1** *adj winner* incontesté **2** *adv kill* sur le coup; *refuse* catégoriquement
'**outset** début *m*
out'**shine** éclipser
'**outside 1** *adj* extérieur **2** *adv* dehors, à l'extérieur **3** *prep* à

l'extérieur de; *(apart from)*
en dehors de **4** *n of building,
case etc* extérieur *m*
'outsize *clothing* grande taille
'outskirts *of town* banlieue *f*
out'smart → **outwit**
'outsource externaliser
out'standing exceptionnel,
remarquable; FIN impayé
outstretched [ˈaʊtstretʃt]
hands tendu
outward [ˈaʊtwəd] *appearance* extérieur; *~ journey*
voyage *m* aller; **outwardly**
en apparence
out'weigh l'emporter sur
out'wit se montrer plus malin
que
oval [ˈəʊvl] ovale
oven [ˈʌvn] four *m*
over [ˈəʊvə] **1** *prep (above)*
au-dessus de; *(across)* de
l'autre côté de; *(more than)*
plus de; *(during)* pendant;
she walked ~ the street elle
traversa la rue; *travel all ~
Brazil* voyager à travers le
Brésil; *we're ~ the worst* le
pire est passé; *~ and above*
en plus de **2** *adv*: *be ~ (finished)* être fini; *(left)* rester;
there were just 6 ~ il n'en
restait que 6; *~ in Japan* au
Japon; *~ here* ici; *~ there*
là-bas; *it hurts all ~* ça fait
mal partout; *painted white
all ~* peint tout en blanc;
it's all ~ c'est fini; *~ and ~
again* maintes et maintes
fois; *do sth ~ (again)* refaire

qch; *overall* mesure en tout;
(in general) dans l'ensemble;
overalls bleu *m* de travail
over'awe impressionner, intimider
over'balance *of person* perdre l'équilibre
over'bearing dominateur
'overcast *sky* couvert
over'charge faire payer trop
cher à
'overcoat pardessus *m*
over'come *difficulties* surmonter
over'crowded *city* surpeuplé;
train bondé
over'do *(exaggerate)* exagérer;
in cooking trop cuire; **over-
'done** *meat* trop cuit
'overdose overdose *f*
'overdraft découvert *m*; *have
an ~* être à découvert; **over-
'draw** *account* mettre à découvert
overdressed trop habillé
over'estimate surestimer
overex'pose surexposer
'overflow[1] *n pipe* trop-plein *m
inv*
over'flow[2] *v/i of water* déborder
over'haul *engine etc* remettre
à neuf; *plans* remanier
'overhead **1** *adj* au-dessus *m* **2**
n FIN frais *mpl* généraux
over'hear entendre (par hasard)
over'heated *room* surchauffé;
engine qui chauffe
overjoyed [əʊvəˈdʒɔɪd] ravi,

enchanté

'**overland 1** adj transport par terre **2** adv travel par voie de terre

over'**lap** of tiles, periods etc se chevaucher; of theories se recouper

over'**load** surcharger

over'**look** of tall building etc surplomber, dominer; of window donner sur; (not see) laisser passer

overly ['ouvərlı] trop

'**overnight** travel la nuit; fig: change etc du jour au lendemain

'**overpass** pont m

over'**power** physically maîtriser

overpriced [ouvər'praıst] trop cher

overrated [ouvə'reıtıd] surfait

over'**ride** decision etc annuler; technically forcer; overriding concern principal

over'**rule** decision annuler

over'**seas** à l'étranger

over'**see** superviser

over'**shadow** fig éclipser

'**oversight** omission f

over'**sleep** se réveiller en retard

over'**state** exagérer; overstatement exagération f

over'**take** also Br мот dépasser

over'**throw**[1] v/t government renverser

'**overthrow**[2] n of government renversement m

'**overtime 1** n sp temps m supplémentaire **2** adv: work ~ faire des heures supplémentaires

over'**turn 1** v/t also government renverser **2** v/i of vehicle se retourner

'**overview** vue f d'ensemble

overwhelming [ouvər'welmıŋ] feeling irrépressible; relief énorme; majority écrasant

over'**work 1** n surmenage m **2** v/i se surmener

owe [ou] devoir (s.o. à qn); owing to à cause de

owl [aul] hibou m, chouette f

own[1] [oun] v/t posséder

own[2] [oun] pron: **an apartment of my ~** un appartement à moi; **on my/his ~** tout seul

♦ **own up** avouer

owner ['ounər] propriétaire m/f; ownership possession f, propriété f

oxygen ['ɑːksıdʒən] oxygène m

oyster ['ɔıstər] huître f

ozone ['ouzoun] ozone m; ozone layer couche f d'ozone

P

PA [piːˈeɪ] (= *personal assistant*) secrétaire *m/f*

pace [peɪs] (*step*) pas *m*; (*speed*) allure *f*; **pacemaker** MED stimulateur *m* cardiaque, pacemaker *m*; SP lièvre *m*

Pacific [pəˈsɪfɪk]: **the ~ (Ocean)** le Pacifique, l'océan *m* Pacifique

pacifier [ˈpæsɪfaɪər] *for baby* sucette *f*; **pacifism** pacifisme *m*; **pacifist** pacifiste *m/f*; **pacify** calmer, apaiser

pack [pæk] **1** *n* (*back~*) sac *m* à dos; *of cereal, cigarettes etc* paquet *m*; *of cards* jeu *m* **2** *v/t item of clothing etc* mettre dans ses bagages; *goods* emballer; **~ one's bag** faire sa valise **3** *v/i* faire ses bagages; **package 1** *n* (*parcel*) paquet *m*; *of offers etc* forfait *m* **2** *v/t in packs* conditionner; *idea, project* présenter; **packaging** *of product* conditionnement *m*; *material* emballage *m*; *of idea* présentation *f*; **packet** paquet *m*

pact [pækt] pacte *m*

pad¹ [pæd] *n protective* tampon *m* de protection; *over wound* tampon *m*; *for writing* bloc *m* **2** *v/t with material* rembourrer; *speech, report* délayer

pad² [pæd] *v/i* (*move quietly*) marcher à pas feutrés

padding [ˈpædɪŋ] *material* rembourrage *m*; *in speech etc* remplissage *m*

paddle [ˈpædl] **1** *n for canoe* pagaie *f* **2** *v/i in canoe* pagayer

paddock [ˈpædək] paddock *m*

padlock [ˈpædlɑːk] cadenas *m*

page¹ [peɪdʒ] *n of book etc* page *f*

page² [peɪdʒ] (*call*) (faire) appeler

pager [ˈpeɪdʒər] pager *m*, radiomessageur *m*; *for doctor* bip *m*

paid em'ployment travail *m* rémunéré

pain [peɪn] douleur *f*; **be in ~** souffrir; *painful arm, leg etc* douloureux; (*distressing*) pénible; (*laborious*) difficile; *idea, project* présenter; **painfully** (*extremely, acutely*) terriblement; **painkiller** analgésique *m*; **painstaking** minutieux

paint [peɪnt] **1** *n* peinture *f* **2** *v/t* peindre; **paintbrush** pinceau *m*; **painter** peintre *m*; **painting** *activity* peinture *f*; *picture* tableau *m*; **paintwork** peinture *f*

pair [per] paire *f*; *of people, animals* couple *m*; **a ~ of pants** un pantalon

pajamas [pə'dʒɑːməz] pyjama *m*

Pakistan [pækɪ'stɑːn] Pakistan *m*; **Pakistani 1** *adj* pakistanais **2** *n* Pakistanais(e) *m(f)*

pal [pæl] F *(friend)* copain *m*, copine *f*

palace ['pælɪs] palais *m*

palate ['pælət] ANAT, *fig* palais *m*

palatial [pə'leɪʃl] somptueux

pale [peɪl] pâle; *go ~* pâlir

Palestine ['pæləstaɪn] Palestine *f*; **Palestinian 1** *adj* palestinien **2** *n* Palestinien(ne) *m(f)*

pallet ['pælɪt] palette *f*

pallor ['pælər] pâleur *f*

palm [pɑːm] *of hand* paume *f*

palm tree palmier *m*

paltry ['pɔːltrɪ] dérisoire

pamper ['pæmpər] gâter

pamphlet ['pæmflɪt] *for information* brochure *f*; *political* tract *m*

pan [pæn] casserole *f*; *for frying* poêle *f*

pancake ['pænkeɪk] crêpe *f*

pandemonium [pændɪ'moʊnɪəm] désordre *m*

pane [peɪn]: *a ~ of glass* un carreau

panel ['pænl] panneau *m*; *people* comité *m*; *on TV program* invités *mpl*

paneling ['pænəlɪŋ], *Br* **panelling** lambris *m*

panic ['pænɪk] **1** *n* panique *f* **2** *v/i* paniquer; **panic-stricken**

affolé, pris de panique

panorama [pænə'rɑːmə] panorama *m*; **panoramic** panoramique

pant [pænt] *of person* haleter

panties ['pæntɪz] culotte *f*

pantihose → pantyhose

pants [pænts] pantalon *m*

pantyhose ['pæntɪhoʊz] collant *m*

papal ['peɪpəl] papal

paparazzi [pæpə'rætsiː] paparazzi *m/f*

paper ['peɪpər] **1** *n* papier *m*; *(news~)* journal *m*; *(wall~)* papier *m* peint; *academic* article *m*, exposé *m*; *(examination ~)* épreuve *f*; *~s (documents)* documents *mpl*; *(identity ~s)* papiers *mpl* **2** *adj (made of ~)* en papier **3** *v/t room* tapisser; **paperback** livre *m* de poche; **paper clip** trombone *m*; **paperwork** tâches *fpl* administratives

parachute ['pærəʃuːt] **1** *n* parachute *m* **2** *v/i* sauter en parachute **3** *v/t troops, supplies* parachuter

parade [pə'reɪd] **1** *n* *(procession)* défilé *m* **2** *v/i of soldiers* défiler; *showing off* parader

paradise ['pærədaɪs] REL, *fig* paradis *m*

paradox ['pærədɑːks] paradoxe *m*; **paradoxical** paradoxal; **paradoxically** paradoxalement

paragraph ['pærəgræf] paragraphe *m*

parallel ['pærəlel] **1** *n* parallèle *f*; GEOG, *fig* parallèle *m* **2** *adj* also *fig* parallèle **3** *v/t* (*match*) égaler

paralysis [pə'rælɪsɪs] *also fig* paralysie *f*; **paralyze** paralyser

paramedic [pærə'medɪk] auxiliaire *m/f* médical(e)

parameter [pə'ræmɪtər] paramètre *m*

paramilitary [pærə'mɪlɪteri] **1** *adj* paramilitaire **2** *n* membre *m* d'une organisation paramilitaire

paranoia [pærə'nɔɪə] paranoïa *f*; **paranoid** paranoïaque

paraphrase ['pærəfreɪz] paraphraser

parasite ['pærəsaɪt] *also fig* parasite *m*

parasol ['pærəsɔːl] parasol *m*

paratrooper ['pærətruːpər] parachutiste *m*, para *m* F

parcel ['pɑːrsl] colis *m*, paquet *m*

pardon ['pɑːrdn] **1** *n* LAW grâce *f*; **I beg your ~?** (*what did you say?*) comment?; (*I'm sorry*) je vous demande pardon **2** *v/t* pardonner; LAW gracier; **~ me?** pardon?

parent ['perənt] père *m*; mère *f*; **my ~s** mes parents; **parental** parental; **parent company** société *f* mère

parent-'teacher association association *f* de parents

d'élèves

parish ['pærɪʃ] paroisse *f*

park[1] [pɑːrk] *n* parc *m*

park[2] [pɑːrk] MOT **1** *v/t* garer **2** *v/i* stationner, se garer; **parking** MOT stationnement *m*; **parking brake** frein *m* à main; **parking garage** parking *m* couvert; **parking lot** parking *m*; **parking meter** parcmètre *m*; **parking ticket** contravention *f*

parliament ['pɑːrləmənt] parlement *m*

parole [pə'roʊl] **1** *n* libération *f* conditionnelle **2** *v/t* mettre en liberté conditionnelle

parrot ['pærət] perroquet *m*

part [pɑːrt] **1** *n* partie *f*; *of machine* pièce *f*; *in movie* rôle *m*; *in hair* raie *f*; **take ~ in** participer à, prendre part à **2** *adv* (*partly*) en partie **3** *v/i of two people* se quitter, se séparer; **partial** (*incomplete*) partiel; **partially** partiellement

participant [pɑːr'tɪsɪpənt] participant(e) *m(f)*; **participate** participer (*in* à); **participation** participation *f*

particular [pər'tɪkjələr] particulier; (*fussy*) à cheval (*about* sur), exigeant; **particularly** particulièrement

partition [pɑːr'tɪʃn] (*screen*) cloison *f*; *of country* partage *m*, division *f*

partly ['pɑːrtlɪ] en partie

partner ['pɑːrtnər] partenaire

m; COM associé *m*; *in relationship* compagnon(ne) *m(f)*; **partnership** COM, *in relationship* association *f*; *in particular activity* partenariat *m*

'**part-time** à temps partiel

party ['pɑːrtɪ] **1** *n* (*celebration*) fête *f*; *for adults in the evening also* soirée *f*; POL parti *m*; (*group of people*) groupe *m* **2** *v/i* F faire la fête

pass [pæs] **1** *n for entry* laissez-passer *m inv*; SP passe *f*; *in mountains* col *m* **2** *v/t* (*go past*) passer devant; *another car* doubler, dépasser; *competitor* dépasser; (*go beyond*); (*approve*) approuver; **~ an exam** réussir (à) un examen **3** *v/i of time* passer; *in exam* être reçu; SP faire une passe; (*go away*) passer

◆ **pass away** (*euph*: *die*) s'éteindre

◆ **pass on 1** *v/t information, book* passer **2** *v/i* (*euph*: *die*) s'éteindre

◆ **pass out** (*faint*) s'évanouir

◆ **pass up** *opportunity* laisser passer

passable ['pæsəbl] *road* praticable; (*acceptable*) passable

passage ['pæsɪdʒ] (*corridor*) couloir *m*; *from book, of time* passage *m*

passenger ['pæsɪndʒər] passager(-ère) *m(f)*

passer-by [pæsər'baɪ] passant(e) *m(f)*

passion ['pæʃn] passion *f*;

passionate *lover* passionné; (*fervent*) fervent, véhément

passive ['pæsɪv] *adj* passif **2** *n* GRAM passif *m*; **passive smoking** tabagisme *m* passif

'**passport** passeport *m*; **passport control** contrôle *m* des passeport; **password** mot *m* de passe

past [pæst] **1** *adj* (*former*) passé; *the* **~** *few days* ces derniers jours **2** *n* passé *m*; *in the* **~** autrefois **3** *prep* après; *it's* **~** *7 o'clock* il est plus de 7 heures; *it's half* **~** *two* il est deux heures et demie **4** *adv*: *run* **~** passer en courant

pasta ['pæstə] pâtes *fpl*

paste [peɪst] **1** *n* (*adhesive*) colle *f* **2** *v/t* (*stick*) coller

pastime ['pæstaɪm] passe-temps *m inv*

past par'ticiple GRAM participe *m* passé

pastry ['peɪstrɪ] *for pie* pâte *f*; *small cake* pâtisserie *f*

'**past tense** GRAM passé *m*

pasty ['peɪstɪ] *complexion* blafard

pat [pæt] **1** *n* petite tape *f* **2** *v/t* tapoter

patch [pætʃ] **1** *n on clothing* pièce *f*; (*period of time*) période *f*; (*area*) tache *f*; *go through a bad* **~** traverser une mauvaise passe **2** *v/t clothing* rapiécer

◆ **patch up** (*repair*) rafistoler F; *quarrel* régler

patchy ['pætʃɪ] inégal

patent ['peɪtnt] **1** adj (obvious) manifeste **2** n for invention brevet m **3** v/t invention breveter

paternal [pə'tɜːrnl] paternel; **paternalism** paternalisme m; **paternalistic** paternaliste; **paternity** paternité f

path [pæθ] chemin m; surfaced allée f; fig voie f

pathetic [pə'θetɪk] touchant; F (very bad) pathétique

pathological [pæθə'lɑːdʒɪk] pathologique

patience ['peɪʃns] patience f; **patient 1** adj patient **2** n patient m; **patiently** patiemment

patio ['pætɪoʊ] Br patio m

patriot ['peɪtrɪət] patriote m/f; **patriotic** person patriote; song patriotique; **patriotism** patriotisme m

patrol [pə'troʊl] **1** n patrouille f **2** v/t streets, border patrouiller dans/à; **patrol car** voiture f de police; **patrolman** agent m de police; **patrol wagon** fourgon m cellulaire

patron ['peɪtrən] of store, movie theater client(e) m(f); of artist, charity etc protecteur(-trice) m(f); **patronize** person traiter avec condescendance; **patronizing** condescendant; **patron saint** patron(ne) m(f)

pattern ['pætərn] on fabric motif m; for sewing patron m; (model) modèle m; in events scénario m

paunch [pɔːntʃ] ventre m

pause [pɔːz] **1** n pause f **2** v/i faire une pause **3** v/t tape mettre en mode pause

pave [peɪv] paver; pavement (roadway) chaussée f; Br (sidewalk) trottoir m

paw [pɔː] **1** n patte f **2** v/t F tripoter

pawn [pɔːn] in chess, fig pion m

pay [peɪ] **1** n paye f, salaire m **2** v/t payer; ~ attention faire attention **3** v/i payer; (be profitable) être rentable; ~ for purchase payer

♦ **pay back** rembourser; (get revenge on) faire payer à

♦ **pay off 1** v/t debt rembourser; corrupt official acheter **2** v/i (be profitable) être rentable

♦ **pay up** payer

payable ['peɪəbl] payable; **pay check**, Br **pay cheque** chèque m de paie; **payday** jour m de paie; **payee** bénéficiaire m/f; **payment** paiement m; **pay phone** téléphone m public

PC [piː'siː] (= **personal computer**) P.C. m; (= **politically correct**) politiquement correct

pea [piː] petit pois m

peace [piːs] paix f; **peaceful** paisible, tranquille; demonstration pacifique; **peace-**

fully paisiblement
peach [piːtʃ] pêche f
peak [piːk] **1** n of mountain pic m; fig apogée f **2** v/i culminer; **peak hours** of electricity consumption heures fpl pleines; of traffic heures fpl de pointe
peanut ['piːnʌt] cacahuète f; **get paid ~s** être payé trois fois rien; **peanut butter** beurre m de cacahuètes
pear [per] poire f
pearl [pɜːrl] perle f
pecan ['piːkən] pécan m
peck [pek] **1** n (bite) coup m de bec; (kiss) bise f (rapide) **2** v/t (bite) donner un coup de bec à; (kiss) embrasser rapidement
peculiar [pɪ'kjuːljər] (strange) bizarre; **peculiarity** bizarrerie f; (special feature) particularité f
pedal ['pedl] **1** n of bike pédale f **2** v/i pédaler; **he ~ed off home** il est rentré chez lui à vélo
peddle ['pedl] drugs faire du trafic de
pedestrian [pɪ'destrɪən] piéton(ne) m(f)
pediatric [piːdɪ'ætrɪk] pédiatrique; **pediatrician** pédiatre m/f; **pediatrics** pédiatrie f
pedicure ['pedɪkjʊr] soins mpl des pieds
pedigree ['pedɪgriː] **1** adj avec pedigree **2** n of dog, racehorse pedigree m; of person

arbre m généalogique
pee [piː] F faire pipi F
peek [piːk] **1** n coup m d'œil (furtif) **2** v/i jeter un coup d'œil, regarder furtivement
peel [piːl] **1** n peau f **2** v/t fruit, vegetables éplucher, peler **3** v/i of nose, shoulders peler; of paint s'écailler
peep [piːp] v/i → **peek**
'peephole judas m
peer[1] [pɪr] n (equal) pair m; of same age group personne f du même âge
peer[2] [pɪr] v/i regarder
peg [peg] for hat, coat patère f; for tent piquet m; **off the ~** de confection
pejorative [pɪ'dʒɔːrətɪv] péjoratif
pellet ['pelɪt] boulette f; for gun plomb m
pen[1] [pen] stylo m
pen[2] [pen] (enclosure) enclos m
pen[3] [pen] → **penitentiary**
penalize ['piːnəlaɪz] pénaliser
penalty ['penltɪ] sanction f; JUR peine f; fine amende f; SP pénalisation f; soccer penalty m; **penalty area** soccer surface f de réparation; **penalty clause** LAW clause f pénale; **penalty kick** soccer penalty m
pencil ['pensl] crayon m (de bois); **pencil sharpener** taille-crayon m inv
pendant ['pendənt] necklace pendentif m

penetrate ['penɪtreɪt] pénétrer; **penetration** pénétration f

penguin ['peŋgwɪn] manchot m

penicillin [penɪ'sɪlɪn] pénicilline f

peninsula [pə'nɪnsʊlə] presqu'île f

penitence ['penɪtəns] pénitence f, repentir m; **penitentiary** pénitencier m

'pen name nom m de plume

pennant ['penənt] fanion m

penniless ['penɪlɪs] sans le sou

'pen pal correspondant(e) m(f)

pension ['penʃən] retraite f, pension f
◆ **pension off** mettre à la retraite

pensive ['pensɪv] pensif

Pentagon ['pentəgɑːn]: **the ~** le Pentagone

pentathlon [pen'tæθlən] pentathlon m

penthouse ['penthaʊs] penthouse m, appartement m luxueux (édifié sur le toit d'un immeuble)

pent-up ['pentʌp] refoulé

penultimate [pe'nʌltɪmət] avant-dernier

people ['piːpl] gens mpl; (race, tribe) peuple m; **10 ~** 10 personnes; **the ~** le peuple; **~ say ...** on dit...

pepper ['pepər] spice poivre m; vegetable poivron m; **pep-**permint candy bonbon m à la menthe; flavoring menthe f poivrée

per [pɜːr] par; **~ annum** par an

perceive [pər'siːv] percevoir

percent [pər'sent] pour cent; **percentage** pourcentage m

perceptible [pər'septəbl] perceptible; **perceptibly** sensiblement; **perception** perception f; (insight) perspicacité f; **perceptive** perspicace

percolate ['pɜːrkəleɪt] of coffee passer; **percolator** cafetière f à pression

perfect 1 ['pɜːrfɪkt] adj parfait 2 ['pɜːrfɪkt] n GRAM passé m composé 3 [pər'fekt] v/t perfectionner; **perfection** perfection f; **perfectionist** perfectionniste m/f; **perfectly** parfaitement; (totally) tout à fait

perforated ['pɜːrfəreɪtɪd] perforé; **~ line** pointillé m

perform [pər'fɔːrm] 1 v/t (carry out) exécuter; of actor etc jouer 2 v/i of actor, musician, dancer jouer; of machine fonctionner; **performance** by actor, musician etc interprétation f; (event) représentation f; of employee, company etc résultats mpl; of machine performances fpl, rendement m; **performer** interprète m/f

perfume ['pɜːrfjuːm] parfum m

perfunctory [pər'fʌŋktərɪ]

sommaire

perhaps [pə'hæps] peut-être

peril ['perəl] péril *m*

perimeter [pə'rɪmɪtər] périmètre *m*

period ['pɪərɪəd] période *f*; *(menstruation)* règles *fpl*; *punctuation mark* point *m*; **periodic** périodique; **periodical** périodique *m*

peripheral [pə'rɪfərəl] **1** *adj (not crucial)* secondaire **2** *n* COMPUT périphérique *m*; **periphery** périphérie *f*

perish ['perɪʃ] *of rubber* se détériorer; *of person* périr; **perishable** *food* périssable

perjure ['pɜːrdʒər]: ~ *o.s.* faire un faux témoignage; **perjury** faux témoignage *m*

perm [pɜːrm] **1** *n* permanente *f* **2** *v/t:* **have one's hair ~ed** se faire faire une permanente

permanent ['pɜːrmənənt] permanent; *address* fixe; **permanently** en permanence

permeate ['pɜːrmɪeɪt] *also fig* imprégner

permissible [pər'mɪsəbl] permis; **permission** permission *f*; **permissive** permissif; **permit 1** *n* permis *m* **2** *v/t* permettre **(s.o. to do** à qn de faire)

perpendicular [pɜːrpən'dɪkjʊlər] perpendiculaire

perpetual [pər'petʃʊəl] perpétuel; **perpetually** perpétuellement

perplex [pər'pleks] laisser perplexe; **perplexity** perplexité *f*

persecute ['pɜːrsɪkjuːt] persécuter; **persecution** persécution *f*; **persecutor** persécuteur(-trice) *m(f)*

perseverance [pɜːrsɪ'vɪrəns] persévérance *f*; **persevere** persévérer

persist [pər'sɪst] persister; **persistent** *person* tenace, têtu; *questions* incessant; *rain, unemployment etc* persistant; **persistently** *(continually)* continuellement

person ['pɜːrsn] personne *f*; **personal** personnel; **personal computer** ordinateur *m* individuel; **personality** personnalité *f*; **personally** personnellement; *come, intervene* en personne; **personal organizer** organiseur *m*, agenda *m* électronique; *in book form* agenda *m*; **personal stereo** baladeur *m*; **personify** *of person* personnifier

personnel [pɜːrsə'nel] *(employees)* personnel *m*; *department* service *m* du personnel

perspective [pər'spektɪv] *in art* perspective *f*; **get sth into** ~ relativiser qch

perspiration [pɜːrspɪ'reɪʃn] transpiration *f*; **perspire** transpirer

persuade [pər'sweɪd] *person*

persuader; **persuasion** persuasion *f*; **persuasive** *person* persuasif; *argument* convaincant

perturb [pər'tɜːrb] perturber; **perturbing** perturbant

pervasive [pər'veɪsɪv] *influence, ideas* envahissant

perversion [pər'vɜːrʃn] *sexual* perversion *f*; **pervert** *sexual* pervers(e) *m(f)*

pessimism ['pesɪmɪzm] pessimisme *m*; **pessimist** pessimiste *m/f*; **pessimistic** pessimiste

pest [pest] parasite *m*; F *person* peste *f*

pester ['pestər] harceler

pesticide ['pestɪsaɪd] pesticide *m*

pet [pet] **1** *n animal* animal *m* domestique; (*favorite*) chouchou *m* F **2** *adj* préféré, favori **3** *v/t animal* caresser **4** *v/i of couple* se peloter F

petite [pə'tiːt] menu

petition [pə'tɪʃn] pétition *f*

petrify ['petrɪfaɪ] pétrifier

petrochemical [petrou'kemɪkl] pétrochimique

petrol ['petrl] *Br* essence *f*

petroleum [pɪ'trouliəm] pétrole *m*

petting ['petɪŋ] pelotage *m* F

petty ['peti] *person, behavior* mesquin; *details* insignifiant

pew [pjuː] banc *m* d'église

pharmaceutical [faːrmə'suːtɪkl] pharmaceutique; **pharmaceuticals** produits *mpl*

pharmaceutiques

pharmacist ['faːrmsɪst] pharmacien(ne) *m(f)*; **pharmacy** *store* pharmacie *f*

phase [feɪz] phase *f*

phenomenal [fə'naːmɪnl] phénoménal; **phenomenon** phénomène *m*

philanthropic [fɪlən'θrɑːpɪk] *person* philanthrope; *action* philanthropique; **philanthropist** philanthrope *m/f*; **philanthropy** philanthropie *f*

Philippines ['fɪlɪpiːnz]: *the ~* les Philippines *fpl*

philosopher [fɪ'lɑːsəfər] philosophe *m/f*; **philosophical** philosophique; *attitude etc* philosophe; **philosophy** philosophie *f*

phobia ['foubɪə] phobie *f* (*about* de)

phone [foun] **1** *n* téléphone *m* **2** *v/t* téléphoner à **3** *v/i* téléphoner; **phone book** annuaire *m*; **phone booth** cabine *f* téléphonique; **phonecall** coup *m* de fil *or* de téléphone; **phone card** télécarte *f*; **phone number** numéro *m* de téléphone

phon(e)y ['founɪ] F faux

photo ['foutou] photo *f*; **photocopier** photocopieuse *f*; **photocopy 1** *n* photocopie *f* **2** *v/t* photocopier; **photogenic** photogénique; **photograph 1** *n* photographie *f* **2** *v/t* photographier; **photog-**

rapher photographe *m/f*;
photography photographie
f

phrase [freɪz] **1** *n* expression
f; *in grammar* syntagme *m*
2 *v/t* formuler

physical ['fɪzɪkl] **1** *adj* physique **2** *n* MED visite *f* médicale; **physically** physiquement

physician [fɪ'zɪʃn] médecin *m*

physicist ['fɪzɪsɪst] physicien(ne) *m(f)*; **physics** physique *f*

physiotherapist [fɪzɪou'θerəpɪst] kinésithérapeute *m/f*;
physiotherapy kinésithérapie *f*

physique [fɪ'ziːk] physique *m*

pianist ['pɪənɪst] pianiste *m/f*;
piano piano *m*

pick [pɪk] (*choose*) choisir;
flowers, fruit cueillir

◆ **pick up 1** *v/t* prendre;
phone décrocher; *from ground* ramasser; (*collect*) passer prendre; *information* recueilli(e); *in car* prendre; *in sexual sense* lever F; *language, skill* apprendre; *illness* attraper; (*buy*) acheter **2** *v/i of business, economy* reprendre; *of weather* s'améliorer

picket ['pɪkɪt] **1** *n of strikers* piquet *m* de grève **2** *v/t*: **~ a factory** faire le piquet de grève devant une usine

'**pickpocket** voleur *m* à la tire,

pickpocket *m*

pick-up (truck) ['pɪkʌp] pick-up *m*, camionnette *f*

picky ['pɪkɪ] F difficile

picnic ['pɪknɪk] **1** *n* pique-nique *m* **2** *v/i* pique-niquer

picture ['pɪktʃər] **1** *n* (*photo*) photo *f*; (*painting*) tableau *m*; (*illustration*) image *f*; (*movie*) film *m* **2** *v/t* imaginer

picturesque [pɪktʃə'resk] pittoresque

pie [paɪ] tarte *f*; *with top* tourte *f*

piece [piːs] morceau *m*; (*component*) pièce *f*; *in board game* pion *m*; **a ~ of advice** un conseil; **take to ~s** démonter

◆ **piece together** *broken plate* recoller; *evidence* regrouper

piecemeal ['piːsmiːl] petit à petit

pier [pɪr] *Br at seaside* jetée *f*

pierce [pɪrs] (*penetrate*) transpercer; *ears* percer; **piercing** *noise, eyes* perçant; *wind* pénétrant

pig [pɪg] cochon *m*, porc *m*; (*unpleasant person*) porc *m*

pigeon ['pɪdʒɪn] pigeon *m*; **pigeonhole** casier *m*

pigheaded ['pɪghedɪd] obstiné; **pigpen** *also fig* porcherie *f*

pile [paɪl] *of books, plates etc* pile *f*; *of sand etc* tas *m*; **a ~ of work** F un tas de boulot F

◆ **pile up 1** *v/i of work, bills*

s'accumuler **2** v/t empiler

'pile-up MOT carambolage m

pilfering ['pɪlfərɪŋ] chapardage m F

pill [pɪl] pilule f

pillar ['pɪlər] pilier m

pillow ['pɪləʊ] oreiller m; **pillowcase** taie f d'oreiller

pilot ['paɪlət] **1** n AVIA, NAUT pilote m **2** v/t airplane piloter

pimp [pɪmp] maquereau m, proxénète m

pimple ['pɪmpl] bouton m

PIN [pɪn] (= **personal identification number**) code m confidentiel

pin [pɪn] **1** n for sewing épingle f; in bowling quille f; (badge) badge m; fiche f **2** v/t (hold down) clouer; (attach) épingler

♦ **pin up** notice accrocher

pincers ['pɪnsərz] of crab pinces fpl; tool tenailles fpl

pinch [pɪntʃ] **1** n pincement m; of salt etc pincée f **2** v/t pincer **3** v/i of shoes serrer

pine [paɪn] tree, wood pin m; **pineapple** ananas m

pink [pɪŋk] rose

pinnacle ['pɪnəkl] fig apogée f

'pinpoint indiquer précisément; find identifier; **pins and needles** fourmillements mpl; **pin-up (girl)** pin-up f inv

pioneer [paɪə'nɪr] **1** n fig pionnier(-ière) m(f) **2** v/t lancer; **pioneering** work innovateur

pious ['paɪəs] pieux

pip [pɪp] Br of fruit pépin m

pipe [paɪp] **1** n tuyau m; for smoking pipe f **2** v/t transporter par tuyau; **pipeline** for oil oléoduc m; for gas gazoduc m

pirate ['paɪrət] **1** n pirate m **2** v/t software pirater

pissed [pɪst] P (annoyed) en rogne F; Br P (drunk) bourré

pistol ['pɪstl] pistolet m

piston ['pɪstən] piston m

pit [pɪt] (hole) fosse f; (coalmine) mine f

pitch¹ [pɪtʃ] n ton m

pitch² [pɪtʃ] **1** v/i in baseball lancer **2** v/t tent planter; ball lancer

pitcher¹ ['pɪtʃər] in baseball lanceur m

pitcher² ['pɪtʃər] container pichet m

pitfall ['pɪtfɔːl] piège m

pitiful ['pɪtɪfl] pitoyable; **pitiless** impitoyable

pittance ['pɪtns] somme f dérisoire

pity ['pɪtɪ] **1** n pitié f; **what a ~!** quel dommage! **2** v/t person avoir pitié de

pizza ['piːtsə] pizza f

placard ['plækɑːrd] pancarte f

place [pleɪs] **1** n endroit m; in race, competition place f; (seat) place f; **at my/his ~** chez moi/lui; **in ~ of** à la place de; **take ~** avoir lieu **2** v/t (put) mettre, poser; order passer

placid ['plæsɪd] placide
plagiarism ['pleɪdʒərɪzm]
plagiat *m*; **plagiarize** plagier
plain¹ [pleɪn] *n* plaine *f*
plain² [pleɪn] **1** *adj* (*clear, obvious*) clair, évident; (*not ornate*) simple; (*not patterned*) uni; (*not pretty*) ordinaire; (*blunt*) franc **2** *adv* tout simplement; **plainly** (*clearly*) manifestement; (*bluntly*) franchement; (*simply*) simplement; **plain-spoken** direct
plaintive ['pleɪntɪv] plaintif
plan [plæn] **1** *n* plan *m*, projet *m*; (*drawing*) plan *m* **2** *v/t* (*prepare*) organiser, planifier; (*design*) concevoir **3** *v/i* faire des projets
plane¹ [pleɪn] AVIA avion *m*
plane² [pleɪn] *tool* rabot *m*
planet ['plænɪt] planète *f*
plank [plæŋk] *of wood* planche *f*; *fig: of policy* point *m*
planning ['plænɪŋ] organisation *f*, planification *f*
plant¹ [plænt] **1** *n* BOT plante *f* **2** *v/t* planter
plant² [plænt] (*factory*) usine *f*; (*equipment*) installation *f*, matériel *m*
plantation [plæn'teɪʃn] plantation *f*
plaque [plæk] *on wall* plaque *f*; *on teeth* plaque *f* dentaire
plaster ['plæstər] **1** *n* plâtre *m* **2** *v/t wall, ceiling* plâtrer
plastic ['plæstɪk] **1** *adj* en plastique **2** *n* plastique *m*;

plastic money cartes *fpl* de crédit; **plastic surgeon** spécialiste *m* en chirurgie esthétique; **plastic surgery** chirurgie *f* esthétique
plate [pleɪt] *for food* assiette *f*; (*sheet of metal*) plaque *f*
plateau ['plætoʊ] plateau *m*
platform ['plætfɔːrm] (*stage*) estrade *f*; *of railroad station* quai *m*; *fig: political* plate-forme *f*
platinum ['plætɪnəm] **1** *adj* en platine **2** *n* platine *m*
platonic [plə'tɒnɪk] platonique
platoon [plə'tuːn] *of soldiers* section *f*
plausible ['plɔːzəbl] plausible
play [pleɪ] **1** *n* jeu *m*; *in theater, on TV* pièce *f* **2** *v/i* jouer **3** *v/t musical instrument* jouer de; *piece of music* jouer; *game* jouer à; *opponent* jouer contre; (*perform: Macbeth etc*) jouer
◆ **play around** F (*be unfaithful*) coucher à droite et à gauche
◆ **play down** minimiser
player ['pleɪr] SP joueur(-euse) *m(f)*; (*musician*) musicien (-ne) *m(f)*; (*actor*) acteur (-trice) *m(f)*; **playful** enjoué; **playground** aire *f* de jeu; **playing card** carte *f* à jouer; **playwright** dramaturge *m/f*
plaza ['plɑːzə] *for shopping* centre *m* commercial
plc [piːel'siː] *Br* (= *public lim-*

ited company) S.A. *f* (= société anonyme)

plea [pliː] *n* appel

plead [pliːd]: ~ *guilty/not guilty* plaider coupable/non coupable; ~ *with* supplier

pleasant ['pleznt] agréable

please [pliːz] **1** *adv* s'il vous plaît, il te plaît; ~ *do* je vous en prie **2** *v/t* plaire à; ~ *yourself* comme tu veux; **pleased** content, heureux; ~ *to meet you* enchanté; **pleasing** agréable; **pleasure** plaisir *m*; **with** ~ avec plaisir

pleat [pliːt] *in skirt* pli *m*

pledge [pledʒ] **1** *n* (*promise*) promesse *f*; *as guarantee* gage *m*; *Pledge of Allegiance* serment *m* d'allégeance **2** *v/t* (*promise*) promettre; *money* mettre en gage

plentiful ['plentɪfl] abondant; *be* ~ abonder; **plenty** (*abundance*) abondance *f*; ~ *of* beaucoup de

pliable ['plaɪəbl] flexible

pliers ['plaɪərz] pinces *fpl*

plight [plaɪt] détresse *f*

plod [plɒːd] (*walk*) marcher d'un pas lourd

plot¹ [plɒːt] *of land* parcelle *f*

plot² [plɒːt] **1** *n* (*conspiracy*) complot *m*; *of novel* intrigue *f* **2** *v/t & v/i* comploter

plotter ['plɒːtər] conspirateur(-trice) *m(f)*; COMPUT traceur *m*

plow, *Br* **plough** [plaʊ] **1** *n* charrue *f* **2** *v/t & v/i* labourer

♦ **plow back** *profits* réinvestir

pluck [plʌk] *chicken* plumer; ~ *one's eyebrows* s'épiler les sourcils

plug [plʌg] **1** *n for sink, bath* bouchon *m*; *electrical* prise *f*; (*spark* ~) bougie *f* **2** *v/t hole* boucher; *new book etc* faire de la pub pour F

♦ **plug in** brancher

plumage ['pluːmɪdʒ] plumage *m*

plumber ['plʌmər] plombier *m*; **plumbing** plomberie *f*

plummet ['plʌmɪt] *of airplane* plonger; *of share prices* dégringoler

plump [plʌmp] *person, chicken* dodu; *hands, feet* potelé; *face, cheek* rond

plunge [plʌndʒ] **1** *n* plongeon *m*; *in prices* chute *f* **2** *v/i* tomber; *of prices* chuter **3** *v/t* plonger; *knife* enfoncer; **plunging** *neckline* plongeant

plural ['plʊrəl] pluriel *m*

plus [plʌs] **1** *prep* plus **2** *adj* plus de **3** *n sign* signe *m* plus; (*advantage*) plus *m* **4** *conj* (*moreover, in addition*) en plus

plush [plʌʃ] luxueux

plywood ['plaɪwʊd] contreplaqué *m*

PM [piː'em] *Br* (= *Prime Minister*) Premier ministre

p.m. [piː'em] (= *post meridiem*) *afternoon* de l'après-midi; *evening* du soir

pneumonia [nuːˈməʊnɪə] pneumonie *f*

poach[1] [pəʊtʃ] *cook* pocher

poach[2] [pəʊtʃ] *salmon etc* braconner

poached egg [pəʊtʃˈteg] œuf *m* poché

P.O. Box [piːˈəʊbɑːks] boîte *f* postale, B. P. *f*

pocket [ˈpɑːkɪt] **1** *n* poche *f* **2** *adj* (*miniature*) de poche **3** *v/t* empocher; **pocketbook** *purse* pochette *f*; (*billfold*) portefeuille *m*; *book* livre *m* de poche; **pocket calculator** calculatrice *f* de poche

podium [ˈpəʊdɪəm] estrade *f*; *for winner* podium *m*

poem [ˈpəʊɪm] poème *m*; **poet** poète *m*, poétesse *f*; **poetic** poétique; **poetry** poésie *f*

poignant [ˈpɔɪnjənt] poignant

point [pɔɪnt] **1** *n of pencil, knife* pointe *f*; *in competition, exam* point *m*; (*purpose*) objet *m*; (*moment*) moment *m*; *in argument, discussion* point *m*; *in decimals* virgule *f*; *that's beside the* ~ là n'est pas la question; *be on the* ~ *of doing sth* être sur le point de faire qch; *get to the* ~ en venir au fait; *the* ~ *is ...* le fait est (que)...; *there's no* ~ *in waiting* ça ne sert à rien d'attendre **2** *v/i* montrer (du doigt)

◆ **point out** *sights* montrer; *advantages etc* faire remarquer

◆ **point to** *with finger* montrer du doig; *fig* (*indicate*) indiquer

pointed [ˈpɔɪntɪd] *remark* acerbe, mordant; **pointer** *for teacher* baguette *f*; (*hint*) conseil *m*; (*sign, indication*) indice *m*; **pointless** inutile; **point of view** point *m* de vue

poise [pɔɪz] assurance *f*, aplomb *m*; **poised** *person* posé

poison [ˈpɔɪzn] **1** *n* poison *m* **2** *v/t* empoisonner; **poisonous** *snake, spider* venimeux; *plant* vénéneux

poke [pəʊk] **1** *n* coup *m* **2** *v/t* (*prod*) pousser; (*stick*) enfoncer

◆ **poke around** F fouiner F

poker [ˈpəʊkər] *card game* poker *m*

polar [ˈpəʊlər] polaire

pole[1] [pəʊl] *of wood, metal* perche *f*

pole[2] [pəʊl] *of earth* pôle *m*

police [pəˈliːs] police *f*; **police car** voiture *f* de police; **policeman** gendarme *m*; *criminal* policier *m*; **police state** État *m* policier; **police station** gendarmerie *f*; *for criminal matters* commissariat *m*; **policewoman** femme *f* gendarme; *criminal* femme *f* policier

policy[1] [ˈpɑːləsɪ] politique *f*

policy[2] [ˈpɑːləsɪ] (*insurance* ~) police *f* (d'assurance)

polio [ˈpəʊlɪəʊ] polio *f*

polish ['pɒlɪʃ] **1** *n for furniture* cire *f*; *for shoes* cirage *m*; *for metal* produit *m* lustrant; (*nail* ~) vernis *m* (à ongles) **2** *v/t* faire briller, lustrer; *shoes* cirer; *speech* parfaire; **polished** *performance* impeccable

polite [pə'laɪt] poli; **politely** poliment; **politeness** politesse *f*

political [pə'lɪtɪkl] politique; **politically correct** politiquement correct; **politician** politicien *m*, homme *m*/femme *f* politique; **politics** politique *f*

poll [pəʊl] **1** *n* (*survey*) sondage *m*; **go to the ~s** (*vote*) aller aux urnes **2** *v/t people* faire un sondage auprès de; *votes* obtenir

pollen ['pɒlən] pollen *m*

pollster ['pəʊlstər] sondeur *m*

pollutant [pə'luːtənt] polluant *m*; **pollute** polluer; **pollution** pollution *f*

'polo shirt polo *m*

polyester [pɒlɪ'estər] polyester *m*

polystyrene [pɒlɪ'staɪriːn] polystyrène *m*

polyunsaturated [pɒlɪʌn-'sætʃəreɪtɪd] polyinsaturé

pond [pɒnd] étang *m*; *artificial* bassin *m*

pontiff ['pɒntɪf] pontife *m*

pony ['pəʊnɪ] poney *m*; **ponytail** queue *f* de cheval

pool¹ [puːl] (*swimming* ~) piscine *f*; *of water, blood* flaque

f

pool² [puːl] *game* billard *m* américain

pool³ [puːl] **1** *n* (*common fund*) caisse *f* commune **2** *v/t resources* mettre en commun

'pool hall salle *f* de billard; **pool table** table *f* de billard

poop [puːp] F caca *m* F

pooped [puːpt] F crevé F

poor [pʊr] **1** *adj* pauvre; *quality etc* médiocre, mauvais **2** *npl* **the ~** les pauvres *mpl*; **poorly 1** *adj* (*unwell*) malade **2** *adv* mal

pop¹ [pɒp] MUS pop *f*

pop² [pɒp] F (*father*) papa *m*

'popcorn pop-corn *m*

pope [pəʊp] pape *m*

Popsicle® ['pɒpsɪkl] glace *f* à l'eau

popular ['pɒpjələr] populaire; **popularity** popularité *f*

populate ['pɒpjəleɪt] peupler; **population** population *f*

porch [pɔːrtʃ] porche *m*

pork [pɔːrk] porc *m*

porn [pɔːrn] F porno F; **pornographic** pornographique; **pornography** pornographie *f*

port¹ [pɔːrt] *n port m*

port² [pɔːrt] *adj* (*left-hand*) de bâbord

portable ['pɔːrtəbl] **1** *adj* portable, portatif **2** *n* COMPUT portable *m*; *TV* téléviseur *m* portable *or* portatif

porter ['pɔːrtər] (*doorman*) portier *m*

portion ['pɔːrʃn] partie *f*, part *f*; *of food* portion *f*

portrait ['pɔːrtreɪt] **1** *n* portrait *m* **2** *adv* print en mode portrait, à la française; **por-tray** *of artist* représenter; *of actor* interpréter; *of author* décrire

Portugal ['pɔːrtʃəgl] le Portugal; **Portuguese 1** *adj* portugais **2** *n person* Portugais(e) *m(f)*; *language* portugais *m*

pose [pouz] **1** *n* attitude *f* **2** *v/i for artist* poser; **~ as** se faire passer pour **3** *v/t problem* poser; *threat* constituer

position [pə'zɪʃn] **1** *n* position *f* **2** *v/t* placer

positive ['pɑːzətɪv] positif; **be ~** (*sure*) être sûr; **posi-tively** vraiment

possess [pə'zes] posséder; **possession** possession *f*; **possessive** possessif

possibility [pɑːsə'bɪlətɪ] possibilité *f*; **possible** possible; **possibly** (*perhaps*) peut-être

post¹ [poust] **1** *n of wood, metal* poteau *m* **2** *v/t notice* afficher; *profits* enregistrer

post² [poust] **1** *n* (*place of duty*) poste *m* **2** *v/t soldier, employee* affecter; *guards* poster

post³ [poust] *Br* **1** *n* (*mail*) courrier *m* **2** *v/t letter* poster

postage ['poustɪdʒ] affran-

chissement *m*; **postage stamp** *fml* timbre *m*; **postal** postal; **postcard** carte *f* postale; **postdate** postdater

poster ['poustər] poster *m*, affiche *f*

postgraduate ['poustgrædʒu-ət] étudiant(e) *m(f)* de troisième cycle

posthumous ['pɑːstʃəməs] posthume

posting ['poustɪŋ] (*assignment*) affectation *f*

postmark cachet *m* de la poste

post-mortem [poust'mɔːr-təm] autopsie *f*

post office poste *f*

postpone [poust'poun] remettre (à plus tard), reporter; **postponement** report *m*

pot¹ [pɑːt] *for cooking* casserole *f*; *for coffee* cafetière *f*; *for tea* théière *f*; *for plant* pot *m*

pot² [pɑːt] F (*marijuana*) herbe *f*

potato [pə'teɪtou] pomme *f* de terre; **potato chips**, *Br* **potato crisps** chips *fpl*

potent ['poutənt] puissant

potential [pə'tenʃl] **1** *adj* potentiel **2** *n* potentiel *m*; **po-tentially** potentiellement

pothole *in road* nid-de-poule *m*

potter ['pɑːtər] potier(-ière) *m(f)*; **pottery** poterie *f*; *items* poteries *fpl*

pouch [pautʃ] *bag* petit sac *m*

poultry ['poʊltrɪ] volaille f
pound[1] [paʊnd] *weight* livre f (0,453kg)
pound[2] [paʊnd] n *for strays, cars* fourrière f
pound[3] [paʊnd] v/i *of heart* battre (la chamade)
pour [pɔːr] 1 v/t *liquid* verser 2 v/i: **it's ~ing (with rain)** il pleut à verse
♦ **pour out** *liquid* verser; *troubles* déballer F
poverty ['pɒvərtɪ] pauvreté f
powder ['paʊdər] 1 n poudre f 2 v/t: **~ one's face** se poudrer le visage
power ['paʊər] 1 n *(strength)* puissance f, force f; *(authority)* pouvoir m; *(energy)* énergie f; *(electricity)* courant m; **power drill** perceuse f; **power failure** panne f d'électricité; **powerful** puissant; **powerless** impuissant; **power line** ligne f électrique; **power outage** coupure f de courant; **power station** centrale f électrique; **power steering** direction f assistée
PR [piːˈɑːr] (= **public relations**) relations fpl publiques
practical ['præktɪkl] pratique; **practically** *in a manner* pratique; *(almost)* pratiquement
practice ['præktɪs] 1 n pratique f; *training also* entraînement m; *(rehearsal)* répétition f; *(custom)* coutume f 2 v/i s'entraîner 3 v/t travail-

ler; *law, medicine* exercer
practise Br → **practice** v/i & v/t
prairie ['prerɪ] prairie f
praise [preɪz] 1 n louange f, éloge m 2 v/t louer; **praiseworthy** méritoire, louable
pray [preɪ] prier; **prayer** prière f
preach [priːtʃ] prêcher; **preacher** pasteur m
precaution [prɪˈkɔːʃn] précaution f; **precautionary measure** préventif, de précaution
precede [prɪˈsiːd] précéder; **precedent** précédent m; **preceding** précédent
precious ['preʃəs] précieux
precise [prɪˈsaɪs] précis; **precisely** précisément; **precision** précision f
preconceived ['priːkənsiːvd] *idea* préconçu
precondition [priːkənˈdɪʃn] condition f requise
predator ['predətər] prédateur m; **predatory** prédateur
predecessor ['priːdɪsesər] prédécesseur m
predicament [prɪˈdɪkəmənt] situation f délicate
predict [prɪˈdɪkt] prédire, prévoir; **prediction** prédiction f
predominant [prɪˈdɑːmɪnənt] prédominant; **predominantly** principalement
prefabricated [priːˈfæbrɪkeɪtɪd] préfabriqué
preface ['prefɪs] préface f

prefer

prefer [prɪˈfɜːr] préférer; **preferable** préférable; **preferably** de préférence; **preference** préférence f; **preferential** préférentiel

pregnancy [ˈpregnənsɪ] grossesse f; **pregnant** enceinte; *animal* pleine

prehistoric [priːhɪˈstɒrɪk] *also fig* préhistorique

prejudice [ˈpredʒʊdɪs] **1** n (*bias*) préjugé m **2** v/t *person* influencer; *chances* compromettre; **prejudiced** partial

preliminary [prɪˈlɪmɪnərɪ] préliminaire

premarital [priːˈmærɪtl] *sex* avant le mariage

premature [prɪməˈtʊər] prématuré

premier [ˈpremɪr] POL Premier ministre m

première [ˈpremɪər] première f

premises [ˈpremɪsɪz] locaux mpl

premium [ˈpriːmɪəm] *in insurance* prime f

prenatal [priːˈneɪtl] prénatal

preoccupied [prɪˈɒkjupaɪd] préoccupé

preparation [prepəˈreɪʃn] préparation f; **~s** préparatifs mpl; **prepare** [prɪˈper] **1** v/t préparer; **be ~d to do sth** *willing, ready* être prêt à faire qch **2** v/i se préparer

preposition [prepəˈzɪʃn] préposition f

prerequisite [priːˈrekwɪzɪt]

---

condition f préalable

prescribe [prɪˈskraɪb] *of doctor* prescrire; **prescription** MED ordonnance f

presence [ˈprezns] présence f; *in the ~ of* en présence de

present¹ [ˈpreznt] **1** *adj* (*current*) actuel; *be ~* être présent **2** n: *the ~* also GRAM le présent

present² [ˈpreznt] n (*gift*) cadeau m

present³ [prɪˈzent] v/t *award, bouquet* remettre; *program* présenter

presentation [preznˈteɪʃn] présentation f; **present-day** actuel; **presenter** présentateur(-trice) m(f); **presently** (*at the moment*) à présent; (*soon*) bientôt

preservative [prɪˈzɜːrvətɪv] conservateur m; **preserve 1** n (*domain*) domaine m **2** v/t *standards, peace etc* maintenir; *wood etc* préserver; *food* conserver

preside [prɪˈzaɪd] *at meeting* présider; **presidency** présidence f; **president** POL président(e) m(f); *of company* président-directeur m général, PDG m; **presidential** présidentiel

press [pres] **1** n: *the ~* la presse **2** v/t *button* appuyer sur; *hand* serrer; *grapes, olives* presser; *clothes* repasser; **pressing** pressant; **pressure 1** n pression f **2** v/t faire pression sur

prestige [pre'sti:ʒ] prestige *m*; **prestigious** prestigieux

presumably [prɪ'zu:məblɪ] sans doute; **presume** présumer; **presumption** *of innocence, guilt* présomption *f*

presuppose [pri:sə'pouz] présupposer

pre-tax ['pri:tæks] avant impôts

pretence *Br* → **pretense**

pretend [prɪ'tend] **1** *v/t* prétendre **2** *v/i* faire semblant; **pretense** semblant *m*; **under the ~ of cooperation** sous prétexte de coopération; **pretentious** prétentieux

pretext ['pri:tekst] prétexte *m*

pretty ['prɪtɪ] **1** *adj* joli **2** *adv* (*quite*) assez

prevail [prɪ'veɪl] (*triumph*) prévaloir, l'emporter; **prevailing** *wind* dominant; *opinion* prédominant; (*current*) actuel

prevent [prɪ'vent] empêcher; *disease* prévenir; **~ s.o. (from) doing sth** empêcher qn de faire qch; **prevention** prévention *f*; **preventive** préventif

preview ['pri:vju:] **1** *n* avant-première **2** *v/t* voir en avant-première

previous ['pri:vɪəs] (*earlier*) antérieur; (*the one before*) précédent; **previously** auparavant, avant

prey [preɪ] proie *f*

price [praɪs] **1** *n* prix *m* **2** *v/t* COM fixer le prix de; **priceless** sans prix

prick¹ [prɪk] **1** *n* pain piqûre *f* **2** *v/t* (*jab*) piquer

prick² [prɪk] V (*penis*) bite *f* V; *person* con *m* F

prickle ['prɪkl] *on plant* épine *f*, piquant *m*; **prickly** *beard, plant* piquant; (*irritable*) irritable

pride [praɪd] fierté *f*; (*self-respect*) amour-propre *m*, orgueil *m*

priest [pri:st] prêtre *m*

primarily [praɪ'merɪlɪ] principalement; **primary 1** *adj* principal **2** *n* POL (*élection f*) primaire *f*

prime 'minister Premier ministre *m*

primitive ['prɪmɪtɪv] primitif; *conditions* rudimentaire

prince [prɪns] prince *m*; **princess** princesse *f*

principal ['prɪnsəpl] **1** *adj* principal **2** *n of school* directeur(-trice) *m(f)*; **principally** principalement

principle ['prɪnsəpl] principe *m*; **on ~** par principe; **in ~** en principe

print [prɪnt] **1** *n* in book etc texte *m*; (*photograph*) épreuve *f*; **out of ~** épuisé **2** *v/t* imprimer; (*use block capitals*) écrire en majuscules; **printer** ['prɪntər] *person* imprimeur *m*; *machine* imprimante *f*; **printout** impression *f*

prior ['praɪr] **1** adj préalable, antérieur **2** prep: ~ **to** avant

prioritize (put in order of priority) donner un ordre de priorité à; (give priority to) donner la priorité à; **priority** priorité f

prison ['prɪzn] prison f; **prisoner** prisonnier(-ière) m(f); **take s.o.** ~ faire qn prisonnier; **prisoner of war** prisonnier(-ière) m(f) de guerre

privacy ['praɪvsɪ] intimité f; **private 1** adj privé; letter personnel; secretary particulier **2** n MIL simple soldat m; **privately** talk to s.o. en privé; (inwardly) intérieurement; ~ **owned** privé

privilege ['prɪvəlɪdʒ] privilège m; **privileged** privilégié

prize [praɪz] **1** n prix m **2** v/t priser, faire (grand) cas de; **prizewinner** gagnant m; **prizewinning** gagnant

probability [prɑːbə'bɪlətɪ] probabilité f; **probable** probable; **probably** probablement

probation [prə'beɪʃn] in job période f d'essai; LAW probation f

probe [proub] **1** n (investigation) enquête f; scientific sonde f **2** v/t sonder; (investigate) enquêter sur

problem ['prɑːbləm] problème m; **no** ~ pas de problème; it doesn't worry me c'est pas grave

procedure [prə'siːdʒər] procédure f; **proceed** (go: of people) se rendre; (of work etc) avancer, se dérouler; **proceedings** (events) événements mpl; **proceeds** bénéfices mpl

process ['prɑːses] **1** n processus m **2** v/t food, raw materials transformer; data, application traiter; **procession** procession f; **processor** processeur m

prod [prɑːd] **1** n (petit) coup m **2** v/t donner un (petit) coup à, pousser

prodigy ['prɑːdɪdʒɪ]: prodige m; (child) ~ enfant m/f prodige

produce¹ ['prɑːduːs] n produits mpl (agricoles)

produce² [prə'duːs] v/t produire; (bring about) provoquer; (bring out) sortir

producer [prə'duːsər] producteur m; of play, movie, TV program producteur m; **product** produit m; **production** production f; **productive** productif; **productivity** productivité f

profess [prə'fes] prétendre; **profession** profession f; **professional 1** adj professionnel **2** n (doctor, lawyer etc) personne f qui exerce une profession libérale; not amateur professionnel(le) m(f); **professionally** play sport professionnellement;

(*well, skillfully*) de manière professionnelle

professor [prəˈfesər] professeur *m*

proficient [prəˈfɪʃnt] excellent, compétent

profile [ˈprəʊfaɪl] profil *m*

profit [ˈprɑːfɪt] **1** *n* bénéfice *m*, profit *m* **2** *v/i*: ~ *from* profiter de; **profitability** rentabilité *f*; **profitable** rentable

profound [prəˈfaʊnd] profond

prognosis [prɑːgˈnəʊsɪs] MED pronostic *m*

program [ˈprəʊgræm] **1** *n* programme *m*; *on radio, TV* émission *f* **2** *v/t* programmer; **programme** *Br* → **program**; **programmer** programmeur(-euse) *m(f)*

progress [ˈprɑːgres] *n* progrès *m(pl)* **2** [prəˈgres] *v/i (in time)* avancer; *(move on)* passer à; *(make* ~*)* faire des progrès, progresser; **progressive** *(enlightened)* progressiste; *(which progresses)* progressif; **progressively** progressivement

prohibit [prəˈhɪbɪt] défendre, interdire; **prohibitive** *prices* prohibitif

project[1] [ˈprɑːdʒekt] *n* projet *m*; EDU étude *f*; *(housing area)* cité *f* (H.L.M.)

project[2] [prəˈdʒekt] **1** *v/t figures, sales* prévoir; *movie* projeter **2** *v/i (stick out)* faire saillie

projection [prəˈdʒekʃn] *(forecast)* projection *f*, prévision *f*; **projector** *for slides* projecteur *m*

prolog, *Br* **prologue** [ˈprəʊlɑːg] prologue *m*

prolong [prəˈlɒːŋ] prolonger

prominent [ˈprɑːmɪnənt] *nose, chin* proéminent; *visually* voyant; *(significant)* important

promiscuity [prɑːmɪˈskjuːətɪ] promiscuité *f*; **promiscuous** dévergondé

promise [ˈprɑːmɪs] **1** *n* promesse *f* **2** *v/t & v/i* promettre; **promising** prometteur

promote [prəˈməʊt] *employee, idea* promouvoir; COM *also* faire la promotion de; **promoter** *of sports event* organisateur *m*; **promotion** promotion *f*

prompt [prɑːmpt] **1** *adj (on time)* ponctuel; *(speedy)* prompt **2** *v/t (cause)* provoquer; *actor* souffler à; **promptly** *(on time)* ponctuellement; *(immediately)* immédiatement

prone [prəʊn]: *be ~ to* être sujet à

pronoun [ˈprəʊnaʊn] pronom *m*

pronounce [prəˈnaʊns] prononcer

pronto [ˈprɑːntəʊ] F illico (presto) F

pronunciation [prənʌnsɪˈeɪʃn] prononciation *f*

proof [pruːf] preuve f; of book épreuve f

prop [prɒp] THEA accessoire m

◆ **prop up** soutenir

propaganda [prɒpəˈɡændə] propagande f

propel [prəˈpel] propulser; **propeller** hélice f

proper [ˈprɒpər] (real) vrai; (correct) bon, correct; (fitting) convenable; **properly** (correctly) correctement; (fittingly also) convenablement; **property** propriété f

proportion [prəˈpɔːrʃn] proportion f; **proportional** proportionnel

proposal [prəˈpəʊzl] proposition f; of marriage demande f en mariage; **propose** v/t (suggest) proposer; **~ to do sth** (plan) se proposer de faire qch **2** v/i (make offer of marriage) faire sa demande en mariage (**to** à); **proposition 1** n proposition f **2** v/t woman faire des avances à

proprietor [prəˈpraɪətər] propriétaire m

prosecute [ˈprɒsɪkjuːt] LAW poursuivre (en justice); **prosecution** LAW poursuites fpl (judiciaires); lawyers accusation f

prospect [ˈprɒspekt] (chance, likelihood) chance(s) f(pl); (thought of something in the future) perspective f; **~s** perspectives fpl

(d'avenir); **prospective** potentiel

prosper [ˈprɒspər] prospérer; **prosperity** prospérité f; **prosperous** prospère

prostitute [ˈprɒstɪtuːt] prostituée f; **male ~** prostitué m; **prostitution** prostitution f

protect [prəˈtekt] protéger; **protection** protection f; **protective** protecteur; **protector** protecteur(-trice) m(f)

protein [ˈprəʊtiːn] protéine f

protest [ˈprəʊtest] **1** [ˈprəʊtest] n protestation f; (demonstration) manifestation f **2** [prəˈtest] v/t (object to) protester contre **3** [prəˈtest] v/i protester; (demonstrate) manifester

Protestant [ˈprɒtɪstənt] **1** adj protestant **2** n protestant(e) m(f)

protester [prəˈtestər] manifestant(e) m(f)

prototype [ˈprəʊtətaɪp] prototype m

protrude [prəˈtruːd] of eyes, ear être saillant; from pocket etc sortir; **protruding** saillant; ears décollé; chin avancé; teeth en avant

proud [praʊd] fier; **proudly** fièrement, avec fierté

prove [pruːv] prouver

proverb [ˈprɒvɜːrb] proverbe m

provide [prəˈvaɪd] fournir; **~d that** (on condition that) pourvu que (+*subj*), à condition que (+*subj*)

province ['prɒvɪns] province *f*; **provincial** *also pej* provincial; *city* de province

provision [prə'vɪʒn] *of food* fourniture *f*; *of services* prestation *f*; *in a law, contract* disposition *f*; **provisional** provisoire

provocation [prɒvə'keɪʃn] provocation *f*; **provocative** provocant; **provoke** provoquer

prowl [praʊl] *of tiger etc* chasser; *of burglar* rôder; **prowler** rôdeur(-euse) *m(f)*

proximity [prɒk'sɪmɪtɪ] proximité *f*

proxy ['prɒksɪ] (*authority*) procuration *f*; *person* mandataire *m/f*

prudence ['pruːdns] prudence *f*; **prudent** prudent

pry [praɪ] être indiscret

PS ['piːes] (= *postscript*) P.-S. *m*

pseudonym ['suːdənɪm] pseudonyme *m*

psychiatric [saɪkɪ'ætrɪk] psychiatrique; **psychiatrist** psychiatre *m/f*; **psychiatry** psychiatrie *f*

psychoanalysis [saɪkəʊən'ælɪsɪs] psychanalyse *f*; **psychoanalyst** psychanalyste *m/f*; **psychoanalyze** psychanalyser

psychological [saɪkə'lɒdʒɪkl] psychologique; **psychol-**

ogist psychologue *m/f*

psychology psychologie *f*

psychopath ['saɪkoʊpæθ] psychopathe *m/f*

psychosomatic [saɪkoʊsə'mætɪk] psychosomatique

pub [pʌb] *Br* pub *m*

public ['pʌblɪk] **1** *adj* public **2** *n*: **the ~** le public

publication [pʌblɪ'keɪʃn] publication *f*

public 'holiday jour *m* férié

publicity [pʌb'lɪsətɪ] publicité *f*; **publicize** (*make known*) faire connaître, rendre public; COM faire de la publicité pour

publicly ['pʌblɪklɪ] en public, publiquement

'**public school** école *f* publique; *Br* école privée (du secondaire)

publish ['pʌblɪʃ] publier; **publisher** éditeur(-trice) *m(f)*; maison *f* d'édition; **publishing** édition *f*; **publishing company** maison *f* d'édition

puff [pʌf] **1** *n* *of wind* bourrasque *f*; *of smoke* bouffée *f* **2** *v/i* (*pant*) souffler, haleter; **puffy** *eyes, face* bouffi

pull [pʊl] **1** *n on rope* coup *m*; F (*appeal*) attrait *m*; F (*influence*) influence *f* **2** *v/t* tirer; *tooth* arracher; *muscle* se déchirer **3** *v/i* tirer

♦ **pull ahead** *in race, competition* prendre la tête

◆ **pull down** (*lower*) baisser; (*demolish*) démolir
◆ **pull in** *of bus, train* arriver
◆ **pull up 1** *v/t* (*raise*) remonter; *plant* arracher **2** *v/i of car etc* s'arrêter
pulley ['pʊlɪ] poulie *f*
pulsate ['pʌlseɪt] *of heart, blood* battre; *of rhythm* vibrer
pulse [pʌls] pouls *m*
pulverize ['pʌlvəraɪz] pulvériser
pump [pʌmp] **1** *n* pompe *f* **2** *v/t* pomper
pumpkin ['pʌmpkɪn] potiron *m*
pun [pʌn] jeu de mots
punch [pʌntʃ] **1** *n blow* coup *m* de poing; *implement* perforeuse *f* **2** *v/t with fist* donner un coup de poing à; *hole* percer; *ticket* composter
punctual ['pʌŋktʃʊəl] ponctuel; **punctuality** ponctualité *f*
punctuation [pʌŋktʃʊ'eɪʃn] ponctuation *f*
puncture ['pʌŋktʃər] **1** *n* piqûre *f* **2** *v/t* percer, perforer
punish ['pʌnɪʃ] punir; **punishing** *pace, schedule* éprouvant, épuisant; **punishment** punition *f*
puny ['pju:nɪ] *person* chétif
pup [pʌp] chiot *m*
pupil[1] ['pju:pl] *of eye* pupille *f*
pupil[2] ['pju:pl] (*student*) élève *m/f*
puppet ['pʌpɪt] *also fig* marionnette *f*
purchase[1] ['pɜ:rtʃəs] **1** *n* achat *m* **2** *v/t* acheter
purchase[2] ['pɜ:rtʃəs] *n* (*grip*) prise *f*
purchaser ['pɜ:rtʃəsər] acheteur(-euse) *m(f)*
pure [pjʊr] pur; *white* immaculé; **purely** purement
purge [pɜ:rdʒ] **1** *n* POL purge *f* **2** *v/t* POL épurer
purify ['pjʊrɪfaɪ] *water* épurer
puritan ['pjʊrɪtən] puritain(e) *m(f)*
purity ['pjʊrɪtɪ] pureté *f*
purpose ['pɜ:rpəs] (*aim, object*) but *m*; **on ~** exprès; **purposely** exprès
purr [pɜ:r] *of cat* ronronner
purse [pɜ:rs] (*pocketbook*) sac *m* à main; *Br for money* porte-monnaie *m inv*
pursue [pər'su:] poursuivre; **pursuer** poursuivant(e) *m(f)*; **pursuit** poursuite *f*; (*activity*) activité *f*
push [pʊʃ] **1** *n* (*shove*) poussée *f* **2** *v/t* (*shove, pressure*) pousser; *button* appuyer sur; F *drugs* revendre, trafiquer **3** *v/i* pousser; **pusher** F *of drugs* dealer(-euse) *m(f)*; **push-up:** *do* **~s** faire des pompes; **pushy** F qui se met en avant
puss, pussy (*cat*) [pus, 'pusɪ (kæt)] F minou *m*
put [put] mettre; *question* poser; **~ the cost at** estimer le prix à

♦ **put across** *idea etc* faire comprendre
♦ **put aside** *money, work* mettre de côté
♦ **put away** *in closet etc* ranger; *in institution* enfermer; *in prison* emprisonner; F *(consume)* s'enfiler F; *animal* faire piquer
♦ **put back** *(replace)* remettre
♦ **put down** poser; *deposit* verser; *rebellion* réprimer; *(belittle)* rabaisser
♦ **put forward** *idea etc* soumettre, suggérer
♦ **put in for** *(apply for)* demander
♦ **put off** *light, TV* éteindre; *(postpone)* repousser; *(deter)* dissuader; *(repel)* dégoûter
♦ **put on** *light, TV* allumer; *music, jacket etc* mettre; *(perform)* monter; *accent*

etc prendre
♦ **put out** *hand* tendre; *fire, light* éteindre
♦ **put together** *(assemble)* monter; *(organize)* organiser
♦ **put up** *hand* lever; *person* héberger; *(erect)* ériger; *prices* augmenter; *poster* accrocher; *money* fournir
♦ **put up with** supporter, tolérer

putty ['pʌtɪ] mastic *m*
puzzle ['pʌzl] **1** *n (mystery)* énigme *f*, mystère *m*; *game* jeu *m*, casse-tête *m*; *(jigsaw ~)* puzzle *m* **2** *v/t* laisser perplexe; **puzzling** curieux
PVC [piːviːˈsiː] (= *polyvinyl chloride*) P.V.C. *m* (= polychlorure de vinyle)
pyjamas *Br* → *pajamas*
pylon ['paɪlən] pylône *m*

Q

quadrangle ['kwɑːdræŋgl] *figure* quadrilatère *m*; *courtyard* cour *f*
quadruped ['kwɑːdruped] quadrupède *m*
quail [kweɪl] flancher
quaint [kweɪnt] *cottage* pittoresque; *(eccentric: ideas etc)* curieux
quake [kweɪk] **1** *n (earthquake)* tremblement *m* de terre **2** *v/i of earth, with fear* trembler

qualification [kwɑːlɪfɪˈkeɪʃn] *from university etc* diplôme *m*; *qualified doctor, engineer etc* qualifié; *(restricted)* restreint; **qualify 1** *v/t of degree, course etc* qualifier; *remark etc* nuancer **2** *v/i (get degree etc)* obtenir son diplôme; *in competition* se qualifier
quality ['kwɑːlɪtɪ] qualité *f*; **quality control** contrôle *m* de qualité
quandary ['kwɑːndərɪ] di-

lemme *m*

quantify ['kwɒntɪfaɪ] quantifier

quantity ['kwɒntɪtɪ] quantité *f*

quarantine ['kwɒrəntiːn] quarantaine *f*

quarrel ['kwɒrəl] **1** *n* dispute *f*, querelle *f* **2** *v/i* se disputer

quarry¹ ['kwɒrɪ] *in hunt* gibier *m*

quarry² ['kwɒrɪ] *for mining* carrière *f*

quart [kwɔːt] quart *m* de gallon *(0,946 litre)*

quarter ['kwɔːtər] quart *m*; *25 cents* vingt-cinq cents *mpl*; *part of town* quartier *m*; *a ~ of an hour* un quart d'heure; *a ~ of 5* cinq heures moins le quart; *a ~ after 5* cinq heures et quart; **quarterfinal** quart *m* de finale; **quarterfinalist** quart de finaliste *m*, quart-finaliste *m*; **quarterly** *adj* trimestriel **2** *adv* trimestriellement; **quarters** MIL quartiers *mpl*; **quartet** MUS quatuor *m*

quartz [kwɔːts] quartz *m*

quash [kwɒʃ] *rebellion* réprimer, écraser; *court decision* casser, annuler

quaver ['kweɪvər] **1** *n in voice* tremblement *m* **2** *v/i of voice* trembler

queasy ['kwiːzɪ] nauséeux; *feel ~* avoir la nausée

queen [kwiːn] reine *f*

queer [kwɪr] *(peculiar)* bizarre

quell [kwel] réprimer

quench [kwentʃ] *thirst* étancher, assouvir; *flames* éteindre

query ['kwɪrɪ] **1** *n* question *f* **2** *v/t* *(express doubt about)* mettre en doute; *(check)* vérifier

quest [kwest] quête *f*

question ['kwestʃn] **1** *n* question *f* **2** *v/t* *person* questionner, interroger; *(doubt)* mettre en question; **questionable** contestable; **questioning 1** *adj look* interrogateur **2** *n* interrogatoire *m*; **question mark** point *m* d'interrogation; **questionnaire** questionnaire *m*

queue [kjuː] *Br* **1** *n* queue *f* **2** *v/i* faire la queue

quibble ['kwɪbl] chipoter, chercher la petite bête

quick [kwɪk] rapide; *be ~!* fais vite!; **quickly** vite, rapidement; **quickwitted** à l'esprit vif

quiet ['kwaɪət] *street, life* tranquille; *music* doux; *engine* silencieux; *voice* bas; *~!* silence!; **quietly** doucement, sans bruit; *(unassumingly, peacefully)* tranquillement; **quietness** calme *m*, tranquillité *f*

quilt [kwɪlt] *on bed* couette *f*

quinine ['kwɪniːn] quinine *f*

quip [kwɪp] **1** *n* trait *m* d'esprit **2** *v/i* plaisanter

quirk [kwɜːrk] manie *f*, lubie *f*

f; **quirky** bizarre, excentrique

quit [kwɪt] **1** v/t job quitter; v/i (leave job) démissionner; COMPUT quitter

quite [kwaɪt] (fairly) assez; (completely) tout à fait; **~ a lot** pas mal, beaucoup

quiver [ˈkwɪvər] trembler

quiz [kwɪz] **1** n on TV jeu m télévisé; on radio jeu m radiophonique; at school interrogation f **2** v/t interroger

quota [ˈkwoʊtə] quota m

quotation [kwoʊˈteɪʃn] from author citation f; price devis m; **quotation marks** guillemets mpl; **quote 1** n from author citation f; price devis m; (quotation mark) guillemet m; **in ~s** entre guillemets **2** v/t text citer; price proposer

R

rabbit [ˈræbɪt] lapin m

rabble [ˈræbl] cohue f, foule f; **rabble-rouser** agitateur(-trice) m(f)

rabies [ˈreɪbiːz] rage f

raccoon [rəˈkuːn] raton m laveur

race[1] [reɪs] n of people race f

race[2] [reɪs] **1** n an event course f **2** v/i (run fast) courir à toute vitesse **3** v/t: **I'll ~ you** je suis le premier arrivé a gagné

ˈ**racecourse** champ m de courses, hippodrome m; ˈ**racehorse** cheval m de course; **race riot** émeute f raciale; ˈ**racetrack** for cars circuit m, piste f; for horses hippodrome m

racial [ˈreɪʃl] racial

racing [ˈreɪsɪŋ] course f

racism [ˈreɪsɪzm] racisme m; **racist 1** adj raciste **2** n raciste m/f

rack [ræk] **1** n for bags on train porte-bagages m inv; for CDs range-CD m inv **2** v/t: **~ one's brains** se creuser la tête

racket[1] [ˈrækɪt] SP raquette f

racket[2] [ˈrækɪt] (noise) vacarme m; criminal activity escroquerie f

radar [ˈreɪdɑːr] radar m

radiance [ˈreɪdɪəns] éclat m; **radiant** smile radieux; **radiate** of heat, light irradier, rayonner; **radiation** nuclear radiation f; **radiator** radiateur m

radical [ˈrædɪkl] **1** adj radical **2** n POL radical(e) m(f); **radicalism** POL radicalisme m; **radically** radicalement

radio [ˈreɪdɪoʊ] radio f; **radioactive** radioactif; **radioactivity** radioactivité f; **radio alarm** radio-réveil m; **radiographer** radiologue m/f; **radiography** radiographie f;

radio station station f de radio

radius ['reidiəs] rayon m

raft [ræft] radeau m

rafter [ræftər] chevron m

rag [ræg] for cleaning etc chiffon m

rage [reidʒ] **1** n colère f, rage f **2** v/i of storm faire rage

ragged ['rægid] edge irrégulier; appearance négligé; clothes en loques

raid [reid] **1** n by troops, FIN raid m; by police descente f; by robbers hold-up m **2** v/t of troops attaquer; of police faire une descente dans; of robbers attaquer; fridge faire une razzia dans; **raider** (robber) voleur m

rail [reil] on track rail m; (hand~) rampe f; for towel porte-serviettes m inv; **by ~** en train; **railings** around park etc grille f; **railroad** chemin m de fer; **track** voie f ferrée; **railroad station** gare f; **railway** Br chemin m de fer; **track** voie f ferrée

rain [rein] **1** n pluie f **2** v/i pleuvoir; **it's ~ing** il pleut; **rainbow** arc-en-ciel m; **raincheck**: **can I take a ~ on that?** F peut-on remettre cela à plus tard?; **raincoat** imperméable m; **raindrop** goutte f de pluie; **rainfall** précipitations fpl; **rain forest** forêt f tropicale (humide); **rainproof** fabric imperméa-

ble; **rainstorm** pluie f torrentielle; **rainy** pluvieux

raise [reiz] **1** n in salary augmentation f (de salaire) **2** v/t shelf etc surélever; offer augmenter; children élever; question soulever; money rassembler

rake [reik] for garden râteau m

rally ['ræli] (meeting, reunion) rassemblement m; MOT rallye m; in tennis échange m

RAM [ræm] COMPUT (= **random access memory**) RAM f, mémoire f vive

ram [ræm] **1** n bélier m **2** v/t ship, car heurter, percuter

ramble ['ræmbl] **1** n walk randonnée f **2** v/i walk faire de la randonnée; when speaking discourir; (talk incoherently) divaguer; **rambling 1** adj speech décousu **2** n walking randonnée f; in speech digression f

ramp [ræmp] rampe f (d'accès), passerelle f; for raising vehicle pont m élévateur

rampant ['ræmpənt] inflation galopant

rampart ['ræmpɑːrt] rempart m

ramshackle ['ræmʃækl] délabré

ranch [ræntʃ] ranch m; **rancher** propriétaire m/f de ranch; **ranchhand** employé m de ranch

rancid ['rænsid] rance

rancor, *Br* **rancour** ['ræŋkər] rancœur *f*

R & D [ɑːrənˈdiː] *(= research and development)* R&D *f* (= recherche et développement)

random ['rændəm] **1** *adj* aléatoire, au hasard; ~ *sample* échantillon *m* pris au hasard **2** *n*: *at* ~ au hasard

range [reɪndʒ] **1** *n of products* gamme *f*; *of gun* portée *f*; *of airplane* autonomie *f*; *of voice, instrument* registre *m*; *of mountains* chaîne *f*; *at close* ~ de très près **2** *v/i*: ~ *from X to Y* aller de X à Y; **ranger garde** *m* forestier

rank [ræŋk] **1** *n* MIL grade *m*; *in society* rang *m* **2** *v/t* classer
♦ **rank among** compter parmi

ransack ['rænsæk] *searching* fouiller; *plundering* saccager

ransom ['rænsəm] *money* rançon *f*

rap [ræp] **1** *n at door etc* petit coup *m* sec; MUS rap *m* **2** *v/t table etc* taper sur

rape[1] [reɪp] **1** *n* viol *m* **2** *v/t* violer

rape[2] [reɪp] *n* BOT colza *m*

rapid ['ræpɪd] rapide; **rapidity** rapidité *f*; **rapidly** rapidement; **rapids** rapides *mpl*

rapist ['reɪpɪst] violeur *m*

rare [rer] rare; *steak* saignant, bleu; **rarely** rarement; **rarity** rareté *f*

rash[1] [ræʃ] *n* MED éruption *f* (cutanée)

rash[2] [ræʃ] *adj action*, imprudent, impétueux; **rashly** sans réfléchir

rat [ræt] rat *m*

rate [reɪt] taux *m*; *(price)* tarif *m*; *(speed)* rythme *m*; *at this* ~ *(at this speed)* à ce rythme; *(carrying on like this)* si ça continue comme ça; *at any* ~ en tout cas

rather ['ræðər] *(fairly, quite)* plutôt; *I would* ~ *stay here* je préférerais rester ici

ratification [rætɪfɪˈkeɪʃn] *of treaty* ratification *f*; **ratify** ratifier

ratings ['reɪtɪŋz] indice *m* d'écoute

ratio ['reɪʃɪou] rapport *m*, proportion *f*

ration ['ræʃn] **1** *n* ration *f* **2** *v/t supplies* rationner

rational ['ræʃənl] rationnel; **rationality** rationalité *f*; **rationalization** rationalisation *f*; **rationalize 1** *v/t* rationaliser **2** *v/i* (se) chercher des excuses; **rationally** rationnellement

rattle ['rætl] **1** *n of bottles, chains* cliquetis *m*; *in engine* bruit *m* de ferraille; *toy* hochet *m* **2** *v/t chains etc* entrechoquer **3** *v/i* faire du bruit; *of engine* faire un bruit de ferraille; *of crates* s'entrechoquer; *of chains* cliqueter; **rattlesnake** serpent *m* à sonnette

raucous ['rɔːkəs] bruyant

rave [reɪv] **1** n party rave f, rave-party f **2** v/i délirer; ~ **about sth** (be very enthusiastic) s'emballer pour qch

ravenous ['rævənəs] affamé

ravine [rə'viːn] ravin m

raw [rɔː] meat, vegetable cru; sugar, iron brut; **raw materials** matières fpl premières

ray [reɪ] rayon m

razor ['reɪzər] rasoir m; **razor blade** lame f de rasoir

re [riː] com en référence à

reach [riːtʃ] **1** n: **within** ~ à portée; **out of** ~ hors de portée **2** v/t atteindre; destination arriver à; decision parvenir à

react [rɪ'ækt] réagir; **reaction** réaction f; **reactionary 1** adj POL réactionnaire **2** n POL réactionnaire m/f; **reactor** nuclear réacteur m

read [riːd] lire

◆ **read out** aloud lire à haute voix

readable ['riːdəbl] lisible; **reader** person lecteur(-trice) m(f)

readily ['redɪlɪ] admit, agree volontiers, de bon cœur

reading ['riːdɪŋ] activity lecture f; from meter etc relevé m

readjust [riːə'dʒʌst] **1** v/t régler (de nouveau) **2** v/i to conditions se réadapter (**to** à)

ready ['redɪ] (prepared, willing) prêt; **get sth** ~ préparer qch; **ready cash** (argent m)

liquide m; **ready-made** stew etc cuisiné; solution tout trouvé; **ready-to-wear** de confection; ~ **clothing** prêt-à-porter m

real [riːl] not imaginary réel; not fake vrai; **real estate** immobilier m, biens mpl immobiliers; **real estate agent** agent m immobilier; **realism** réalisme m; **realist** réaliste m/f; **realistic** réaliste; **realistically** de façon réaliste; **reality** réalité f; **realize** se rendre compte de; FIN réaliser; **really** vraiment; **real time** COMPUT temps m réel; **real-time** COMPUT en temps réel

realtor ['riːltər] agent m immobilier; **realty** immobilier m

reappear [riːə'pɪr] réapparaître

reappearance réapparition f

rear [rɪr] **1** adj arrière inv, de derrière **2** n arrière m

rearm [riː'ɑːrm] réarmer

rearrange [riːə'reɪndʒ] flowers réarranger; furniture déplacer; schedule, meetings réorganiser

rear-view 'mirror rétroviseur m, rétro m F

reason ['riːzn] n (cause), faculty raison f; **reasonable** raisonnable; **reasonably** act, behave raisonnablement; (quite) relativement; **reasoning** raisonnement m

reassure [riːə'ʃur] rassurer;

reassuring rassurant

rebate ['riːbeɪt] (*refund*) remboursement *m*

rebel 1 ['rebl] *n* rebelle *m/f* **2** [rɪ'bel] *v/i* se rebeller; **rebellion** rébellion *f*; **rebellious** rebelle; **rebelliousness** esprit *m* de rébellion

rebound [rɪ'baʊnd] *of ball etc* rebondir

rebuild [riː'bɪld] reconstruire

recall [rɪ'kɔːl] *goods, ambassador* rappeler; (*remember*) se rappeler

recap ['riːkæp] récapituler

recapture [riː'kæptʃər] reprendre

recede [rɪ'siːd] *of flood waters* baisser

receipt [rɪ'siːt] *for purchase* reçu *m* (**for**); ticket *m* de caisse; **~s** FIN recette(s) *f(pl)*; **receive** recevoir; **receiver** TELEC combiné *m*; *for radio* (poste *m*) récepteur *m*; **receivership**: *be in* **~** être en liquidation judiciaire

recent ['riːsnt] récent; **recently** récemment

reception [rɪ'sepʃn] réception *f*; (*welcome*) accueil *m*; **reception desk** réception *f*; **receptionist** réceptionniste *m/f*; **receptive**: *be* **~** *to sth* être réceptif à qch

recess ['riːses] *in wall etc* renfoncement *m*, recoin *m*; EDU récréation *f*; *of legislature* vacances *fpl* judiciaires; **recession** *economic* récession *f*

recharge [riː'tʃɑːrdʒ] *battery* recharger

recipe ['resəpɪ] recette *f*

recipient [rɪ'sɪpɪənt] *of parcel etc* destinataire *m/f*; *of payment* bénéficiaire *m/f*

reciprocal [rɪ'sɪprəkl] réciproque

recite [rɪ'saɪt] *poem* réciter; *details, facts* énumérer

reckless ['rekləs] imprudent; **recklessly** imprudemment

reckon ['rekən] (*think, consider*) penser

◆ **reckon on** compter sur

reclaim [rɪ'kleɪm] *land from sea* gagner sur la mer; *lost property* récupérer

recline [rɪ'klaɪn] s'allonger; **recliner** *chair* chaise *f* longue, relax *m*

recluse [rɪ'kluːs] reclus *m*

recognition [rekəg'nɪʃn] reconnaissance *f*; **recognizable** reconnaissable; **recognize** reconnaître

recoil [rɪ'kɔɪl] reculer

recollect [rekə'lekt] se souvenir de; **recollection** souvenir *m*

recommend [rekə'mend] recommander; **recommendation** recommandation *f*

recompense ['rekəmpens] compensation *f*, dédommagement *m*

reconcile ['rekənsaɪl] réconcilier; *differences* concilier; *facts* faire concorder; **reconciliation** réconciliation *f*; *of* *differences, facts* conciliation *f*

recondition [riːkən'dɪʃn] refaire, remettre à neuf

reconnaissance [rɪ'kɒnɪsəns] MIL reconnaissance *f*

reconsider [riːkən'sɪdər] **1** *v/t* reconsidérer **2** *v/i* reconsidérer la question

reconstruct [riːkən'strʌkt] reconstruire; *crime* reconstituer

record[1] ['rekɔːd] *n* MUS disque *m*; SP *etc* record *m*; *written document etc* rapport *m*; *in database* article *m*, enregistrement *m*; **~s** *(archives)* archives *fpl*, dossiers *mpl*; *have a criminal ~* avoir un casier judiciaire

record[2] [rɪ'kɔːd] *v/t electronically* enregistrer; *in writing* consigner

'record-breaking qui bat tous les records; **record holder** recordman *m*, recordwoman *f*

recording [rɪ'kɔːdɪŋ] enregistrement *m*

recount [rɪ'kaʊnt] *(tell)* raconter

re-count [riː'kaʊnt] **1** *n of votes* recompte *m* **2** *v/t* recompter

recoup [rɪ'kuːp] *financial losses* récupérer

recover [rɪ'kʌvər] **1** *v/t* retrouver **2** *v/i from illness* se remettre; *of business* reprendre; **recovery** *of sth lost* ré-

cupération *f*; *from illness* rétablissement *m*

recreation [rekrɪ'eɪʃn] récréation *f*; **recreational** *done for pleasure* de loisirs

recruit [rɪ'kruːt] **1** *n* recrue *f* **2** *v/t* recruter; **recruitment** recrutement *m*

rectangle ['rektæŋgl] rectangle *m*; **rectangular** rectangulaire

rectify ['rektɪfaɪ] rectifier

recuperate [rɪ'kuːpəreɪt] récupérer

recur [rɪ'kɜːr] *of error, event* se reproduire; *of symptoms* réapparaître; **recurrent** récurrent

recycle [riː'saɪkl] recycler; **recycling** recyclage *m*

red [red] **1** *adj* rouge **2** *n: in the ~* FIN dans le rouge; **Red Cross** Croix-Rouge *f*

redecorate [riː'dekəreɪt] refaire

redeem [rɪ'diːm] *debt* rembourser; *sinners* racheter

redevelop [riːdɪ'veləp] *part of town* réaménager

'redhead roux *m*, rousse *f*; **red light** *for traffic* feu *m* rouge; **red light district** quartier *m* chaud; **red meat** viande *f* rouge; **redneck** F plouc *m* F; **red tape** F paperasserie *f*

reduce [rɪ'duːs] réduire; **reduction** réduction *f*

reek [riːk] empester *(of sth* qch)

reel [riːl] *of film, thread* bobine f

re-e'lect réélire; **re-election** réélection f

re-'entry of spacecraft rentrée f

ref [ref] F arbitre m

♦ **refer to** faire allusion à; *dictionary etc* se reporter à

referee [refə'riː] SP arbitre m; *for job:* personne qui fournit des références; **reference** (*allusion*) allusion f; *for job* référence f; (~ *number*) (numéro m de) référence f; **reference book** ouvrage m de référence; **reference number** numéro m de référence

referendum [refə'rendəm] référendum m

refill ['riːfɪl] remplir

refine [rɪ'faɪn] *oil, sugar* raffiner; *technique* affiner; **refinement** *to process, machine* perfectionnement m; **refinery** raffinerie f

reflect [rɪ'flekt] **1** v/t refléter **2** v/i (*think*) réfléchir; **reflection** *also fig* reflet m; (*consideration*) réflexion f

reflex ['riːfleks] *in body* réflexe m

reform [rɪ'fɔːrm] **1** n réforme f **2** v/t réformer; **reformer** réformateur(-trice) m(f)

refresh [rɪ'freʃ] rafraîchir; *of sleep, rest* reposer; *of meal* redonner des forces à; **refreshing** *drink* rafraîchissant; *experience* agréable; **refreshments** rafraîchisse-

ments mpl

refrigerate [rɪ'frɪdʒəreɪt] réfrigérer; **refrigerator** réfrigérateur m

refuel [riː'fjuːəl] **1** v/t *airplane* ravitailler **2** v/i *of airplane* se ravitailler (en carburant)

refuge ['refjuːdʒ] refuge m; *take ~ from storm etc* se réfugier; **refugee** réfugié(e) m(f)

refund 1 ['riːfʌnd] n remboursement m **2** [rɪ'fʌnd] v/t rembourser

refusal [rɪ'fjuːzl] refus m; **refuse** refuser; ~ *to do sth* refuser de faire qch

regain [rɪ'geɪn] *control, territory, the lead* reprendre; *composure* retrouver

regard [rɪ'ɡɑːrd] **1** n: *with ~ to* en ce qui concerne; (*kind*) ~s cordialement; *with no ~ for* sans égard pour **2** v/t: ~ *as* considérer comme; **regarding** en ce qui concerne; **regardless** quand même; ~ *of* sans se soucier de

regime [reɪ'ʒiːm] (*government*) régime m

regiment ['redʒɪmənt] régiment m

region ['riːdʒən] région f; **regional** régional

register ['redʒɪstər] **1** n registre m **2** v/t *birth, death* déclarer; *vehicle* immatriculer; *letter* recommander; *emotion* exprimer **3** v/i *for a course* s'inscrire; *with police* se déclarer (*with* à); regis-

tered letter lettre *f* recommandée; **registration** *of birth, death* déclaration *f*; *of vehicle* immatriculation *f*; *for a course* inscription *f*

regret [rɪ'gret] **1** *v/t* regretter **2** *n* regret *m*; **regretful** plein de regrets; **regrettable** regrettable

regular ['regjʊlər] **1** *adj* régulier; *(normal)* normal **2** *n at bar etc* habitué(e) *m(f)*; **regularity** régularité *f*; **regularly** régulièrement

regulate ['regjʊleɪt] régler; *expenditure* contrôler; **regulation** *(rule)* règlement *m*

rehabilitate [ri:hə'bɪlɪteɪt] *ex--criminal* réinsérer; *disabled person* rééduquer

rehearsal [rɪ'hɜːsl] répétition *f*; **rehearse** répéter

reign [reɪn] **1** *n* règne *m* **2** *v/i* régner

reimburse [ri:ɪm'bɜːrs] rembourser

reinforce [ri:ɪn'fɔːrs] renforcer; *argument* étayer; **reinforced concrete** béton *m* armé; **reinforcements** MIL renforts *mpl*

reinstate [ri:ɪn'steɪt] *person in office* réintégrer, rétablir dans ses fonctions; *paragraph etc* réintroduire

reject [rɪ'dʒekt] rejeter; **rejection** rejet *m*

relapse ['ri:læps] MED rechute *f*

related [rɪ'leɪtɪd] *by family*

apparenté; *events, ideas etc* associé; **relation** *in family* parent(e) *m(f)*; *(connection)* rapport *m*, relation *f*; **relationship** relation *f*; *sexual* liaison *f*; **relative** **1** *adj* relatif **2** *n* parent(e) *m(f)*; **relatively** relativement

relax [rɪ'læks] **1** *v/i* se détendre; *..! du calme!* **2** *v/t muscle* relâcher; **relaxation** détente *f*, relaxation *f*; **relaxed** détendu, décontracté; **relaxing** reposant, relaxant

relay 1 *v/t* [rɪ'leɪ] *message* transmettre; *radio, TV signals* relayer, retransmettre **2** *n* ['ri:leɪ]: ~ *(race)* (course *f* de) relais *m*

release [rɪ'li:s] **1** *n from prison* libération *f*; *of CD, movie etc* sortie *f*; *CD, record* nouveauté *f* **2** *v/t prisoner* libérer; *CD, record, movie* sortir; *parking brake* desserrer; *information* communiquer

relegate ['relɪgeɪt] reléguer

relent [rɪ'lent] se calmer; *of person* s'adoucir; **relentless** *(determined)* acharné; *rain etc* incessant

relevance ['relʌvəns] pertinence *f*; **relevant** pertinent

reliability [rɪlaɪə'bɪlɪtɪ] fiabilité *f*; **reliable** fiable; **reliance** [rɪ'laɪəns] confiance *f* *(on* en); *on equipment* dépendance *f* *(on* vis-à-vis de)

relic ['relɪk] relique *f*

relief [rɪ'li:f] soulagement *m*;

relieve *pain* soulager; (*take over from*) relayer, relever

religion [rɪ'lɪdʒən] religion *f*; **religious** [rɪ'lɪdʒəs] religieux; *person* croyant

relinquish [rɪ'lɪŋkwɪʃ] abandonner

relish ['relɪʃ] **1** *n sauce* relish *f*; (*enjoyment*) délectation *f* **2** *v/t idea, prospect* se réjouir de

relive [riː'lɪv] *event* revivre

relocate [riːləʊ'keɪt] *of business* se réimplanter; *of employee* être muté

reluctance [rɪ'lʌktəns] réticence *f*; **reluctant** réticent; **be ~ to do sth** hésiter à faire qch

♦ **rely on** [rɪ'laɪ] compter sur; **rely on s.o. to do sth** compter sur qn pour faire qch

remain [rɪ'meɪn] rester; **~ silent** garder le silence; **remainder** *also* MATH reste *m*; **remaining** restant; **the ~ refugees** le reste des réfugiés; **remains** *of body* restes *mpl*

remake ['riːmeɪk] *of movie* remake *m*, nouvelle version *f*

remark [rɪ'mɑːrk] **1** *n* remarque *f* **2** *v/t* (*comment*) faire remarquer; **remarkable** remarquable; **remarkably** remarquablement

remarry [riː'mærɪ] se remarier

remedy ['remədɪ] MED, *fig* remède *m*

remember [rɪ'membər] **1** *v/t* se souvenir de, se rappeler

2 *v/i* se souvenir

remind [rɪ'maɪnd]: **~ s.o. to do sth** rappeler à qn de faire qch; **~ X of Y** rappeler Y à X; **~ s.o. of sth** (*bring to their attention*) rappeler qch à qn; **reminder** rappel *m*

reminisce [remɪ'nɪs] évoquer le passé

remission [rɪ'mɪʃn] MED rémission *f*; **go into ~** *of patient* être en sursis

remnant ['remnənt] vestige *m*, reste *m*

remorse [rɪ'mɔːrs] remords *m*; **remorseless** impitoyable; *demands* incessant

remote [rɪ'məʊt] *village* isolé; *possibility* vague; *ancestor* lointain; **remote control** télécommande *f*; **remotely** *related, connected* vaguement

removable [rɪ'muːvəbl] amovible; **removal** enlèvement *m*; *of demonstrators* expulsion *f*; *of doubt* dissipation *f*; **remove** enlever; *demonstrators* expulser; *doubt* dissiper

rename [riː'neɪm] rebaptiser; *file* renommer

rendez-vous ['rɑːndeɪvuː] rendez-vous *m*

renew [rɪ'nuː] *contract* renouveler; *discussion* reprendre; **renewal** *of contract etc* renouvellement *m*; *of discussion* reprise *f*

renounce [rɪ'naʊns] renoncer à

renovate ['renəveɪt] rénover; **renovation** rénovation *f*

rent [rent] **1** *n* loyer *m*; **for ~** à louer **2** *v/t* louer; **rental** *for apartment* loyer *m*; *for TV, car* location *f*; **rental car** voiture *f* de location; **rent-free** sans payer de loyer

reopen [riː'əʊpn] **1** *v/t* rouvrir; *negotiations* reprendre **2** *v/i* of store etc rouvrir

reorganization [riːɔːgənaɪ-'zeɪʃn] réorganisation *f*; **reorganize** réorganiser

repaint [riː'peɪnt] repeindre

repair [rɪ'per] **1** *v/t* réparer **2** *n* réparation *f*; **repairman** réparateur *m*

repatriate [riː'pætrɪeɪt] rapatrier; **repatriation** rapatriement *m*

repay [riː'peɪ] rembourser; **repayment** remboursement *m*

repeal [rɪ'piːl] *law* abroger

repeat [rɪ'piːt] **1** *v/t* répéter **2** *n TV program etc* rediffusion *f*; **repeatedly** à plusieurs reprises

repel [rɪ'pel] repousser; *(disgust)* dégoûter; **repellent 1** *adj* repoussant, répugnant **2** *n* (*insect ~*) répulsif *m*

repercussions [riːpə'kʌʃnz] répercussions *fpl*

repertoire ['repərtwɑːr] répertoire *m*

repetition [repɪ'tɪʃn] répétition *f*; **repetitive** répétitif

replace [rɪ'pleɪs] (*put back*)

remettre; (*take the place of*) remplacer; **replacement** *person* remplaçant *m*; *product* produit *m* de remplacement; **replacement part** pièce *f* de rechange

replay ['riːpleɪ] **1** *n recording* relecture *f*, replay *m*; *match* nouvelle rencontre *f*, replay *m* **2** *v/t match* rejouer

replenish [rɪ'plenɪʃ] *container* remplir (de nouveau); *supplies* refaire

replica ['replɪkə] réplique *f*

reply [rɪ'plaɪ] **1** *n* réponse *f* **2** *v/t & v/i* répondre

report [rɪ'pɔːrt] **1** *n* (*account*) rapport *m*, compte-rendu *m*; *in newspaper* bulletin *m* **2** *v/t facts* rapporter; *to authorities* déclarer **3** *v/i* (*present o.s.*) se présenter; **reporter** reporter *m/f*

repossess [riːpə'zes] COM reprendre possession de

represent [reprɪ'zent] représenter; **representative 1** *adj* (*typical*) représentatif **2** *n* représentant(e) *m(f)*

repress [rɪ'pres] réprimer; **repression** POL répression *f*; **repressive** POL répressif

reprieve [rɪ'priːv] **1** *n* LAW sursis *m*; *fig also* répit *m* **2** *v/t prisoner* accorder un sursis à

reprimand ['reprɪmænd] réprimander

reprint ['riːprɪnt] **1** *n* réimpression *f* **2** *v/t* réimprimer

reprisal [rɪ'praɪzl] représailles

fpl

reproach [rɪ'prəʊtʃ] **1** *n* reproche *m* **2** *v/t*: **~ s.o. for sth** reprocher qch à qn; **reproachful** réprobateur

reproduce [riːprə'djuːs] **1** *v/t* reproduire **2** *v/i* BIO se reproduire; **reproduction** reproduction *f*

reproductive reproducteur

reptile ['reptaɪl] reptile *m*

republic [rɪ'pʌblɪk] république *f*; **Republican 1** *adj* républicain **2** *n* Républicain(e) *m(f)*

repulsive [rɪ'pʌlsɪv] repoussant

reputable ['repjʊtəbl] de bonne réputation; **reputation** réputation *f*

request [rɪ'kwest] **1** *n* demande *f*; **on ~** sur demande **2** *v/t* demander

require [rɪ'kwaɪr] (*need*) avoir besoin de; **required** (*necessary*) requis; **requirement** (*need*) besoin *m*, exigence *f*; (*condition*) condition *f* (requise)

requisition [rekwɪ'zɪʃn] réquisitionner

re-route [riː'ruːt] *airplane etc* dérouter

rerun ['riːrʌn] **1** *n* of TV program rediffusion *f* **2** *v/t* tape repasser

reschedule [riː'skedjuːl] changer l'heure/la date de

rescue ['reskjuː] **1** *n* sauvetage *m* **2** *v/t* sauver, secourir

research [rɪ'sɜːtʃ] recherche *f*; **research and development** recherche *f* et développement; **researcher** chercheur(-euse) *m(f)*

resemblance [rɪ'zembləns] ressemblance *f*; **resemble** ressembler à

resent [rɪ'zent] ne pas aimer; *person also* en vouloir à; **resentful** plein de ressentiment; **resentment** ressentiment *m* (*of* par rapport à)

reservation [rezər'veɪʃn] réservation *f*; *mental, (special area)* réserve *f*

reserve [rɪ'zɜːv] **1** *n* (*store, aloofness*) réserve *f*; SP remplaçant(e) *m(f)* **2** *v/t seat, judgment* réserver; **reserved** *table, manner* réservé

reservoir ['rezərvwɑːr] *for water* réservoir *m*

residence ['rezɪdəns] *fml: house etc* résidence *f*; (*stay*) séjour *m*; **resident** résident(e) *m(f)*; *on street* riverain(e) *m(f)*; *in hotel* client(e) *m(f)*; **residential** résidentiel

residue ['rezɪduː] résidu *m*

resign [rɪ'zaɪn] *v/t position* démissionner de; **~ o.s. to** se résigner à **2** *v/i from job* démissionner; **resignation** *from job* démission *f*; *mental* résignation *f*

resilient [rɪ'zɪliənt] *personality* fort; *material* résistant

resist [rɪ'zɪst] **1** *v/t* résister à; *new measures* s'opposer à **2** *v/i* résister; **resistance** résistance f; **resistant** *material* résistant

resolution [rezə'luːʃn] résolution f

resort [rɪ'zɔːrt] *place* lieu m de vacances; *at seaside station* f balnéaire; *for health cures* station f thermale; **as a last ~** en dernier ressort

◆ **resort to** avoir recours à, recourir à

◆ **resound with** [rɪ'zaʊnd] résonner de

resounding [rɪ'zaʊndɪŋ] *success, victory* retentissant

resource [rɪ'sɔːrs] ressource f; **resourceful** ingénieux

respect [rɪ'spekt] **1** n respect m; **in this/that ~** à cet égard; **in many ~s** à bien des égards **2** v/t respecter; **respectability** respectabilité f; **respectable** respectable; **respectful** respectueux; **respective** respectif; **respectively** respectivement

respiration [respɪ'reɪʃn] respiration f; **respirator** MED respirateur m

respond [rɪ'spɑːnd] répondre; (*react also*) réagir; **response** réponse f; (*reaction also*) réaction f,

responsibility [rɪspɑːnsɪ'bɪl-ətɪ] responsabilité f; **responsible** responsable (**for** de); **a ~ job** un poste à responsabilités

rest[1] [rest] **1** n repos m; *during walk, work* pause f **2** v/i

se reposer **3** v/t (*lean, balance*) poser

rest[2] [rest]: **the ~** *objects* le reste; *people* les autres

restaurant ['restərɑːnt] restaurant m

restful ['restfl] reposant; **rest home** maison f de retraite; **restless** agité; **restlessly** nerveusement

restoration [restə'reɪʃn] *of building* restauration f; **restore** *building etc* restaurer; (*bring back*) restituer; *confidence* redonner

restrain [rɪ'streɪn] retenir; **restraint** (*moderation*) retenue f

restrict [rɪ'strɪkt] restreindre; **I'll ~ myself to …** je me limiterai à …; **restriction** restriction f

'rest room toilettes fpl

result [rɪ'zʌlt] résultat m; **as a ~ of this** par conséquent

resume [rɪ'zuːm] reprendre

résumé ['rezʊmeɪ] *of career* curriculum vitæ m inv, C.V. m inv

resumption [rɪ'zʌmpʃn] reprise f

resurface [riː'sɜːrfɪs] **1** v/t *roads* refaire (le revêtement de) **2** v/i (*reappear*) refaire surface

Resurrection [rezə'rekʃn] REL Résurrection f

retail ['riːteɪl] **1** adv: **sell sth ~** vendre qch au détail **2** v/i: **~ at** se vendre à; **retailer** détaillant(e) *m(f)*

retain [rɪ'teɪn] conserver; **re-tainer** FIN provision *f*

retaliate [rɪ'tælieɪt] riposter, se venger; **retaliation** riposte *f*

rethink [riː'θɪŋk] repenser

reticence ['retɪsns] réserve *f*; **reticent** réservé

retire [rɪ'taɪr] *from work* prendre sa retraite; **retired** à la retraite; **retirement** retraite *f*; **retiring** réservé

retort [rɪ'tɔːrt] **1** *n* réplique *f* **2** *v/t* répliquer

retract [rɪ'trækt] *claws, undercarriage* rentrer; *statement* retirer

're-train se recycler

retreat [rɪ'triːt] **1** *v/i also* MIL battre en retraite **2** *n* MIL, *place* retraite *f*

retrieve [rɪ'triːv] récupérer

retroactive [retroʊ'æktɪv] *law etc* rétroactif; **retroactively** rétroactivement, par rétroaction

retrograde ['retrəgreɪd] rétrograde

retrospective [retrə'spektɪv] rétrospective *f*

return [rɪ'tɜːrn] **1** *n* retour *m*; *(profit)* bénéfice *m*; **~ (ticket)** Br aller *m* retour; **many happy ~s (of the day)** bon anniversaire; **in ~ for** en échange de; *(contre* 2 *v/t (give back)* rendre; *(send back)* renvoyer; *(put back)* remettre **3** *v/i (go back)* retourner;

(come back) revenir

reunification [riːjuːnɪfɪ-'keɪʃn] réunification *f*

reunion [riː'juːnjən] réunion *f*; **reunite** réunir; *country* réunifier

reusable [riː'juːzəbl] réutilisable; **reuse** réutiliser

♦ **rev up** [rev] *engine* emballer

revaluation [riːvæljuˈeɪʃn] réévaluation *f*

reveal [rɪ'viːl] révéler; *(make visible)* dévoiler; **revealing** *remark* révélateur; *dress* suggestif; **revelation** révélation *f*

revenge [rɪ'vendʒ] vengeance *f*; **take one's ~** se venger

revenue ['revənuː] revenu *m*

reverberate [rɪ'vɜːrbəreɪt] *of sound* retentir, résonner

revere [rɪ'vɪr] révérer; **reverence** déférence *f*, respect *m*; **reverent** respectueux

reverse [rɪ'vɜːrs] **1** *adj sequence* inverse **2** *n (opposite)* contraire *m*; *(back)* verso *m*; MOT *gear* marche *f* arrière **3** *v/i* MOT faire marche arrière

review [rɪ'vjuː] **1** *n* of book, movie critique *f*; of troops revue *f*; of situation etc bilan *m* **2** *v/t book, movie* faire la critique de; *troops* passer en revue; *situation etc* faire le bilan de; EDU réviser; **reviewer** of book, movie critique *m*

revise [rɪ'vaɪz] *opinion* revenir sur; *text* réviser; **revision**

of text révision f

revival [rɪ'vaɪvl] *of custom, old style* renouveau m; *of patient* rétablissement m; **revive 1** v/t *custom, old style* faire renaître; *patient* ranimer **2** v/i *of business* reprendre

revoke [rɪ'vouk] *law* abroger; *license* retirer

revolt [rɪ'voult] **1** n révolte f **2** v/i se révolter; **revolting** répugnant; **revolution** révolution f; **revolutionary 1** adj révolutionnaire **2** n révolutionnaire m/f; **revolutionize** révolutionner

revolve [rɪ'vɑːlv] tourner (**around** autour de); **revolver** revolver m

revulsion [rɪ'vʌlʃn] répugnance f

reward [rɪ'wɔːrd] **1** n *financial* récompense f; (*benefit derived*) gratification f **2** v/t *financially* récompenser; **rewarding** *experience* gratifiant, valorisant

rewind [riː'waɪnd] *film, tape* rembobiner

rewrite [riː'raɪt] réécrire

rhetoric ['retərɪk] rhétorique f

rhyme [raɪm] **1** n rime f **2** v/i rimer (**with** avec)

rhythm ['rɪðm] rythme m

rib [rɪb] ANAT côte f

ribbon ['rɪbən] ruban m

rice [raɪs] riz m

rich [rɪtʃ] **1** adj *person, food* ri-

che **2** npl: **the~** les riches mpl

ricochet ['rɪkəʃeɪ] ricocher (**off** sur)

rid [rɪd]: **get ~ of** se débarrasser de

ride [raɪd] **1** n *on horse* promenade f (à cheval); *excursion in vehicle* tour m; (*journey*) trajet m; **do you want a ~ into town?** est-ce que tu veux que je t'emmène en ville? **2** v/t *horse* monter; *bike* se déplacer en; **can I ~ your bike?** est-ce que je peux monter sur ton vélo? **3** v/i *on horse* monter à cheval; *on bike* rouler (à vélo); **rider** *on horse* cavalier(-ière) m(f); *on bike* cycliste m/f

ridge [rɪdʒ] (*raised strip*) arête f (saillante); *of mountain* crête f; *of roof* arête f

ridicule ['rɪdɪkjuːl] **1** n ridicule m **2** v/t ridiculiser; **ridiculous** ridicule; **ridiculously** ridiculement

riding ['raɪdɪŋ] *on horseback* équitation f

rifle ['raɪfl] fusil m, carabine f

rift [rɪft] *in earth* fissure f; *in party etc* scission f

rig [rɪg] **1** n (*oil ~*) tour f de forage; *at sea* plateforme f de forage; (*truck*) semi-remorque m **2** v/t *elections* truquer

right [raɪt] **1** adj bon; (*not left*) droit; **be~** *of answer* être juste; *of person* avoir raison; *of clock* être à l'heure; **it's not~ to ...** ce n'est pas bien de ...;

put things ~ arranger les choses; **that's ~!** c'est ça!; **that's all ~** *(doesn't matter)* ce n'est pas grave; *when s.o. says thank you* je vous en prie; **it's all ~** *(is acceptable)* ça me va; **I'm all ~ not hurt** je vais bien; **have enough ~** ça ira pour moi **2** *adv (directly)* directement, juste; *(correctly)* correctement, bien; *(not left)* à droite; **~ now** *(immediately)* tout de suite; *(at the moment)* en ce moment; **it's ~ here** c'est juste là **3** *n civil, legal* droit *m*; *(not left)*, POL droite *f*; **be in the ~** avoir raison; **right-angle** angle *m* droit; **rightful** *owner etc* légitime; **right-handed** *person* droitier; **right-hand man** bras *m* droit; **right of way** *in traffic* priorité *f*; *across land* droit *m* de passage; **right wing** POL droite *f*; SP ailier *m* droit; **right-wing** POL de droite

rigid ['rɪdʒɪd] *also fig* rigide

rigor ['rɪgər] *of discipline* rigueur *f*; **rigorous** rigoureux; **rigorously** *check* rigoureusement

rigour *Br* → **rigor**

rile [raɪl] F agacer

rim [rɪm] *of wheel* jante *f*; *of cup* bord *m*; *of eyeglasses* monture *f*

ring[1] [rɪŋ] *n (circle)* cercle *m*; *on finger* anneau *m*; *in box-*

ing ring *m*; *at circus* piste *f*

ring[2] [rɪŋ] **1** *n of bell* sonnerie *f*; *of voice* son *m* **2** *v/t Br* TELEC téléphoner à **3** *v/i of bell* sonner, retentir

'ringleader meneur(-euse) *m(f)*; **ring-pull** anneau *m* (d'ouverture)

rink [rɪŋk] patinoire *f*

rinse [rɪns] **1** *n for hair color* rinçage *m* **2** *v/t* rincer

riot ['raɪət] **1** *n* émeute *f* **2** *v/i* participer à une émeute; **start to ~** créer une émeute; **rioter** émeutier(-ière) *m(f)*; **riot police** police *f* anti-émeute

rip [rɪp] **1** *n in cloth etc* accroc *m* **2** *v/t in cloth etc* déchirer

◆ **rip-off** F *customers* arnaquer F

ripe [raɪp] *fruit* mûr; **ripen** *of fruit* mûrir; **ripeness** *of fruit* maturité *f*

'rip-off F arnaque *f* F

ripple ['rɪpl] *on water* ride *f*

rise [raɪz] **1** *v/i from chair, bed, of sun* se lever; *of rocket, price, temperature* monter **2** *n in price, temperature* hausse *f*; *in water level* élévation *f*; *Br: in salary* augmentation *f*

risk [rɪsk] **1** *n* risque *m*; **take a ~** prendre un risque **2** *v/t* risquer; **risky** risqué

ritual ['rɪtʊəl] **1** *adj* rituel **2** *n* rituel *m*

rival ['raɪvl] **1** *n* rival(e) *m(f)* **2**

v/t (match) égaler; *(compete with)* rivaliser avec; **rivalry** rivalité *f*

river ['rɪvər] rivière *f*; *bigger* fleuve *m*; **riverbank** rive *f*; **riverbed** lit *m* de la rivière/ du fleuve; **riverside 1** *adj* en bord de rivière **2** *n* berge *f*, bord *m* de l'eau

riveting ['rɪvɪtɪŋ] fascinant

road [rəʊd] route *f*; *in city* rue *f*; **roadblock** barrage *m* routier; **road-holding** of vehicle tenue *f* de route; **road map** carte *f* routière; **road safety** sécurité *f* routière; **roadsign** panneau *m* (de signalisation); **roadway** chaussée *f*; **roadworthy** en état de marche

roam [rəʊm] errer

roar [rɔːr] **1** *n* rugissement *m*; *of traffic* grondement *m*; *of engine* vrombissement *m* **2** *v/i* rugir; *of traffic* gronder; *of engine* vrombir

roast [rəʊst] **1** *n of beef etc* rôti *m* **2** *v/t* rôtir **3** *v/i of food* rôtir; **roast beef** rosbif *m*

rob [rɑːb] *person* voler, dévaliser; *bank* cambrioler, dévaliser; **robber** voleur(-euse) *m(f)*; **robbery** vol *m*

robe [rəʊb] *of judge, priest* robe *f*; *(bath~)* peignoir *m*; *(dressing gown)* robe *f* de chambre

robot ['rəʊbɑːt] robot *m*

robust [rəʊ'bʌst] robuste

rock [rɑːk] **1** *n* rocher *m*; MUS

rock *m* **2** *v/t baby* bercer; *cradle* balancer; *(surprise)* secouer **3** *v/i on chair, of boat* se balancer; **rock-bottom** *price* le plus bas possible; **rock climber** varappeur(-euse) *m(f)*; **rock climbing** varappe *f*

rocket ['rɑːkɪt] **1** *n* fusée *f* **2** *v/i of prices etc* monter en flèche

rocking chair ['rɑːkɪŋ] rocking-chair *m*; **rock 'n' roll** rock-and-roll *m inv*; **rocky** *beach* rocheux

rod [rɑːd] baguette *f*; *for fishing* canne *f* à pêche

rodent ['rəʊdnt] rongeur *m*

rogue [rəʊg] vaurien *m*

role [rəʊl] rôle *m*; **role model** modèle *m*

roll [rəʊl] **1** *n (bread ~)* petit pain *m*; *of film* pellicule *f*; *(list, register)* liste *f* **2** *v/i of ball, boat* rouler

♦ **roll over 1** *v/i* se retourner **2** *v/t person, object* tourner; *(renew)* renouveler; *(extend)* prolonger

'roll call appel *m*; **roller** *for hair* rouleau *m*; **roller blade®** roller *m* (en ligne); **roller coaster** montagnes *fpl* russes; **roller skate** patin *m* à roulettes

ROM [rɑːm] COMPUT *(= read only memory)* ROM *f*, mémoire *f* morte

Roman 'Catholic 1 *adj* REL catholique **2** *n* catholique *m/f*

romance ['rəʊmæns] *(affair)*

idylle f; *novel, movie* histoire f d'amour; **romantic** romantique

roof [ru:f] toit m; **roof-rack** MOT galerie f

rookie ['rʊkɪ] F bleu m F

room [ru:m] pièce f, salle f; (bed∼) chambre f; (space) place f; **room clerk** réceptionniste m/f; **roommate** in apartment colocataire m/f; in room camarade m/f de chambre; **room service** service m en chambre; **room temperature** température f ambiante; **roomy** spacieux; clothes ample

root [ru:t] racine f

rope [roʊp] corde f

rosary ['roʊzərɪ] REL rosaire m, chapelet m

rose [roʊz] BOT rose f

roster ['rɑːstər] tableau m de service

rostrum ['rɑːstrəm] estrade f

rosy ['roʊzɪ] also fig rose

rot [rɑːt] **1** n pourriture f **2** v/i pourrir

rotate [roʊ'teɪt] **1** v/i tourner **2** v/t (turn) (faire) tourner; crops alterner; **rotation** rotation f

rotten ['rɑːtn] also F weather, luck pourri

rough [rʌf] **1** adj surface rugueux; hands, skin rêche; voice rude; (violent) brutal; crossing, seas agité; (approximate) approximatif; ∼ **draft** brouillon m **2** n in golf rough

m; **roughage** in food fibres fpl; **roughly** (approximately) environ; (harshly) brutalement

roulette [ru:'let] roulette f

round [raʊnd] **1** adj rond **2** n of mailman, doctor, drinks tournée f; of competition manche f; tour m; in boxing round m **3** v/t corner tourner **4** adv & prep → **around**

♦ **round up** figure arrondir; suspects ramasser

roundabout ['raʊndəbaʊt] **1** adj détourné, indirect **2** n Br: on road rond-point m; **round-the-world** autour du monde; **round trip** aller-retour m; **round-up** of cattle rassemblement m; of suspects rafle f; of news résumé m

rouse [raʊz] from sleep réveiller; emotions soulever; **rousing** exaltant

route [raʊt] itinéraire m

routine [ru:'ti:n] **1** adj de routine; behavior routinier **2** n routine f

row¹ [roʊ] n (line) rangée f; of troops rang m; **5 days in a ∼** 5 jours de suite

row² [roʊ] v/i in boat ramer

rowboat ['roʊboʊt] bateau m à rames

rowdy ['raʊdɪ] tapageur, bruyant

royal ['rɔɪəl] royal; **royalty** (membres mpl de) la famille royale; on book, recording droits *mpl* d'auteur

rub [rʌb] frotter

rubber ['rʌbər] **1** *n material* caoutchouc *m* **2** *adj* en caoutchouc; **rubber band** élastique *m*

rubble ['rʌbl] *from building* gravats *mpl*, décombres *mpl*

ruby ['ru:bɪ] *jewel* rubis *m*

rudder ['rʌdər] gouvernail *m*

ruddy ['rʌdɪ] *complexion* coloré

rude [ru:d] impoli; *language, gesture* grossier; **rudely** (*impolitely*) impoliment; **rudeness** impolitesse *f*

rudimentary [ru:dɪ'mentərɪ] rudimentaire; **rudiments** rudiments *mpl*

rueful ['ru:fl] *n* contrit, résigné; **ruefully** *we regret; smile* d'un air contrit

ruffian ['rʌfɪən] voyou *m*, brute *f*

ruffle ['rʌfl] *n on dress* ruche *f* **2** *v/t hair* ébouriffer; *person* énerver

rug [rʌg] tapis *m; blanket* couverture *f*

rugby ['rʌgbɪ] rugby *m*

rugged ['rʌgɪd] *scenery, cliffs* escarpé; *face* aux traits rudes; *resistance* acharné

ruin ['ru:ɪn] **1** *n* ruine *f* **2** *v/t* ruiner; *party, plans* gâcher

rule [ru:l] **1** *n* règle *f; of monarch* règne *m; **as a ~*** en règle générale **2** *v/t country* gouverner **3** *v/i of monarch* régner; **ruler** *for measuring* rè-

gle *f; of state* dirigeant(e) *m(f);* **ruling 1** *n* décision *f* **2** *adj party* dirigeant, au pouvoir

rum [rʌm] *drink* rhum *m*

rumble ['rʌmbl] *of stomach* gargouiller; *of thunder* gronder

rumor, *Br* **rumour** ['ru:mər] **1** *n* bruit *m*, rumeur *f* **2** *v/t: it is ~ed that ...* le bruit court que ...

rump [rʌmp] *of animal* croupe *f*

rumple ['rʌmpl] *clothes, paper* froisser

'rumpsteak rumsteck *m*

run [rʌn] **1** *n on foot course f; in pantyhose* échelle *f; **go for a ~*** *for exercise* aller courir; **in the short/long ~** à court/ long terme **2** *v/i* courir; *of river, paint, makeup* couler; *of trains, buses* passer, circuler; *of play* être à l'affiche; *of engine, machine* marcher, tourner; *of software* fonctionner; *in election* se présenter; **~ for President** être candidat à la présidence **3** *v/t race* courir; *business, hotel etc* diriger; *software* exécuter, faire tourner; *car* entretenir

◆ **run away** s'enfuir; *from home for a while* faire une fugue; *for good* s'enfuir de chez soi

◆ **run down 1** *v/t* (*knock down*) renverser; (*criticize*)

critiquer; *stocks* diminuer **2** *v/i of battery* se décharger
◆ **run off 1** *v/i* s'enfuir **2** *v/t (print off)* tirer
◆ **run out** *of contract* expirer; *of time* s'écouler; *of supplies* s'épuiser
◆ **run out of** ne plus avoir de
◆ **run over 1** *v/t (knock down)* renverser **2** *v/i of water etc* déborder
◆ **run up** *debts* accumuler
runaway fugueur(-euse) *m(f)*; **run-down** *person* épuisé; *area* délabré
rung [rʌŋ] *of ladder* barreau *m*
runner ['rʌnər] *athlete* coureur(-euse) *m(f)*; **runner beans** haricots *mpl* d'Espagne; **runner-up** second(e) *m(f)*; **running 1** *n* SP course *f*; *of business* gestion *f* **2** *adj*: *for two days* ~ pendant deux jours de suite; **running water** eau *f* courante; **runny** *substance* liquide; *nose qui* coule; **run-up** SP élan *m*; *in the* ~ *to* pendant la période

qui précède; **runway** AVIA piste *f*
rupture ['rʌptʃər] **1** *n also fig* rupture *f* **2** *v/i of pipe* éclater
rural ['rʊərəl] rural
ruse [ruːz] ruse *f*
rush [rʌʃ] **1** *n* ruée *f*; *do sth in a* ~ faire qch à la hâte; *be in a* ~ être pressé **2** *v/t person* presser; *meal* avaler (à toute vitesse) **3** *v/i* se presser; **rush hour** heures *fpl* de pointe
Russia ['rʌʃə] Russie *f*; **Russian** ['rʌʃən] **1** *adj* russe **2** *n* Russe *m/f*; *language* russe *m*
rust [rʌst] **1** *n* rouille *f* **2** *v/i* se rouiller; **rust-proof** anti-rouille *inv*; **rusty** *also fig* rouillé
rut [rʌt] *in road* ornière *f*; *be in a* ~ *fig* être tombé dans la routine
ruthless ['ruːθlɪs] impitoyable, sans pitié; **ruthlessly** impitoyablement; **ruthlessness** dureté *f* (impitoyable)
rye [raɪ] seigle *m*; **rye bread** pain *m* de seigle

S

sabotage ['sæbətɑːʒ] **1** *n* sabotage *m* **2** *v/t* saboter; **saboteur** saboteur(-euse) *m(f)*
sachet ['sæʃeɪ] sachet *m*
sack [sæk] **1** *n* bag sac *m* **2** *v/t* F virer F
sacred ['seɪkrɪd] sacré

sacrifice ['sækrɪfaɪs] **1** *n* sacrifice *m* **2** *v/t also fig* sacrifier
sacrilege ['sækrɪlɪdʒ] REL, *fig* sacrilège *m*
sad [sæd] triste
saddle ['sædl] **1** *n* selle *f* **2** *v/t*

horse seller

sadism ['seɪdɪzm] sadisme *m*;
sadist sadique *m/f*; **sadistic**
sadique

sadly ['sædlɪ] tristement; (*regrettably*) malheureusement;
sadness tristesse *f*

safe [seɪf] **1** *adj* (*not dangerous*) pas dangereux; *driver*
prudent; (*not in danger*) en
sécurité **2** *n* coffre-fort *m*;
safeguard 1 *n*: **as a ~
against** par mesure de protection contre **2** *v/t* protéger;
safely *arrive, drive, assume*
sans risque; **safety** sécurité
f; *of investment, prediction*
sûreté *f*; **safety pin** épingle
f de nourrice

sag [sæg] *of ceiling* s'affaisser;
of rope se détendre; *fig: of
output* fléchir

saga ['sɑːgə] saga *f*

sage [seɪdʒ] *herb* sauge *f*

sail [seɪl] **1** *n of boat* voile *f*;
trip voyage *m* (en mer) **2**
v/i faire de la voile; (*depart*)
partir; **sailboard 1** *n* planche
f à voile **2** *v/i* faire de la planche à voile; **sailboarding**
planche *f* à voile; **sailboat**
bateau *m* à voiles; **sailing**
SP voile *f*; **sailor** marin *m*

saint [seɪnt] saint(e) *m(f)*

sake [seɪk]: **for my ~** pour moi

salad ['sæləd] salade *f*

salary ['sælərɪ] salaire *m*

sale [seɪl] vente *f*; *reduced
prices* soldes *mpl*; **for ~** *sign*
à vendre; **be on ~** être en

vente; *at reduced prices* être
en solde; **sales** *department*
vente *f*; **sales clerk** *in store*
vendeur(-euse) *m(f)*; **sales
figures** chiffre *m* d'affaires;
salesman vendeur *m*; (*rep*)
représentant *m*; **saleswoman** vendeuse *f*

salient ['seɪlɪənt] marquant

saliva [sə'laɪvə] salive *f*

salmon ['sæmən] saumon *m*

saloon [sə'luːn] (*bar*) bar *m*
Br мот berline *f*

salt [sɒlt] sel *m*; **salty** salé

salute [sə'luːt] **1** *n* MIL salut *m*
2 *v/t* MIL saluer **3** *v/i* MIL faire
un salut

salvage ['sælvɪdʒ] *from
wreck* sauver

salvation [sæl'veɪʃn] *also fig*
salut *m*

same [seɪm] **1** *adj* même **2**
pron: **the ~** le/la même; *pl*
the ~ les mêmes; **Happy
New Year – the ~ to you**
Bonne année – à vous aussi;
all the ~ (*even so*) quand même **3** *adv:* **look/sound the ~**
se ressembler, être pareil

sample ['sæmpl] *of work,
cloth* échantillon *m*; *of blood*
prélèvement *m*

sanction ['sæŋkʃn] **1** *n* (*approval*) approbation *f*; (*penalty*) sanction *f* **2** *v/t* (*approve*)
approuver

sand [sænd] **1** *n* sable *m* **2** *v/t
with sandpaper* poncer au
papier de verre

sandal ['sændl] sandale *f*

'sandbag sac *m* de sable; **sand dune** dune *f*; **sander** *tool* ponceuse *f*; **sandpaper 1** *n* papier *m* de verre **2** *v/t* poncer au papier de verre

sandwich ['sænwɪtʃ] sandwich *m*

sandy ['sændɪ] *beach* de sable; *soil* sablonneux; *feet, towel* plein de sable; *hair* blond roux

sane [seɪn] sain (d'esprit)

sanitarium [sænɪ'terɪəm] sanatorium *m*

sanitary ['sænɪterɪ] sanitaire; *(clean)* hygiénique; **sanitary napkin** serviette *f* hygiénique; **sanitation** installations *fpl* sanitaires; *(removal of waste)* système *m* sanitaire

sanity ['sænətɪ] santé *f* mentale

Santa Claus ['sæntəklɔːz] le Père Noël

sap [sæp] **1** *n* *in tree* sève *f* **2** *v/t s.o.'s energy* saper

sapphire ['sæfaɪr] saphir *m*

sarcasm ['saːrkæzm] sarcasme *m*; **sarcastic** sarcastique; **sarcastically** sarcastiquement

sardine [saːr'diːn] sardine *f*

sardonic [saːr'daːnɪk] sardonique

satellite ['sætəlaɪt] satellite *m*; **satellite dish** antenne *f* parabolique; **satellite TV** télévision *f* par satellite

satin ['sætɪn] satin *m*

satire ['sætaɪr] satire *f*; **satiri-**

cal satirique; **satirize** satiriser

satisfaction [sætɪs'fækʃn] satisfaction *f*; **satisfactory** satisfaisant; *(just good enough)* convenable; **satisfy** satisfaire; *conditions* remplir

Saturday ['sætərdeɪ] samedi *m*

sauce [sɔːs] sauce *f*; **saucepan** casserole *f*; **saucer** soucoupe *f*

Saudi Arabia [saʊdɪə'reɪbɪə] Arabie *f* saoudite; **Saudi Arabian 1** *adj* saoudien **2** *n* Saoudien(ne) *m(f)*

sausage ['sɔːsɪdʒ] saucisse *f*; *dried* saucisson *m*

savage ['sævɪdʒ] **1** *adj* féroce **2** *n* sauvage *m/f*; **savagery** férocité *f*

save [seɪv] **1** *v/t (rescue)*, SP sauver; *(economize, put aside)* économiser; *(collect)* faire collection de; COMPUT sauvegarder **2** *v/i (put money aside)* économiser; SP arrêter le ballon **3** *n* SP arrêt *m*; **saver** *person* épargneur(-euse) *m(f)*; **savings** économies *fpl*; **savings account** compte *m* d'épargne; **savings and loan** caisse *f* d'épargne-logement; **savings bank** caisse *f* d'épargne

savior, *Br* **saviour** ['seɪvjər] REL sauveur *m*

savor ['seɪvər] savourer; **savory** *not sweet* salé

savour *etc Br* → **savor** *etc*

saw [sɔː] **1** n tool scie f **2** v/t
scier; **sawdust** sciure f
saxophone ['sæksəfoʊn]
saxophone m
say [seɪ] dire; *that is to ~*
c'est-à-dire; **saying** dicton m
scab [skæb] on wound croûte
f
scaffolding ['skæfəldɪŋ]
échafaudage m
scald [skɔːld] ébouillanter
scale[1] [skeɪl] n on fish écaille
f
scale[2] [skeɪl] **1** n of project,
map etc, on thermometer
échelle f; MUS gamme f **2**
v/t cliffs etc escalader
scales [skeɪlz] for weighing
balance f
scallop ['skæləp] shellfish coquille f Saint-Jacques
scalp [skælp] cuir m chevelu
scalpel ['skælpl] scalpel m
scam [skæm] F arnaque m F
scampi ['skæmpɪ] scampi m
scan [skæn] **1** n MED scanner
m; during pregnancy écho-
graphie f **2** v/t horizon, page
parcourir du regard; MED faire un scanner de; COMPUT
scanner
♦ **scan in** COMPUT scanner
scandal ['skændl] scandale
m; **scandalize** scandaliser;
scandalous scandaleux
scanner ['skænər] MED, COM-
PUT scanner m
scanty ['skæntɪ] dress réduit
au minimum
scapegoat ['skeɪpɡoʊt] bouc

m émissaire
scar [skɑːr] **1** n cicatrice f **2** v/t
marquer d'une cicatrice
scarce [skers] rare; **scarcely**
['skersli] à peine; *~ anything*
presque rien; **scarcity** manque m
scare [sker] **1** v/t faire peur à;
be ~d of avoir peur de **2** n
(panic, alarm) rumeurs fpl
alarmantes; **scaremonger**
alarmiste m/f
scarf [skɑːrf] around neck
écharpe f; over head foulard
m
scarlet ['skɑːrlət] écarlate
scary ['skerɪ] effrayant
scathing ['skeɪðɪŋ] cinglant
scatter ['skætər] **1** v/t leaflets,
seed éparpiller **2** v/i of people
se disperser; **scattered**
showers intermittent; vil-
lages éparpillé
scavenge ['skævɪndʒ]: *~ for
sth* fouiller pour trouver
qch; **scavenger** charognard
m; person fouilleur(euse)
m(f)
scenario [sɪ'nɑːrɪoʊ] scénario
m
scene [siːn] scène f; of accident, crime etc lieu m; *make
a ~* faire une scène; *behind
the ~s* dans les coulisses;
scenery paysage m; THEA dé-
cor(s) m(pl)
scent [sent] odeur f; Br (perfume) parfum m
sceptic etc Br → **skeptic** etc
schedule ['skedjuːl] **1** n of

events calendrier *m*; *for trains* horaire *m*; *of lessons, work* programme *m*; **be on ~ of work**, workers être dans les temps; *of train* être à l'heure; **be behind ~** être en retard **2** *v/t (put on ~)* prévoir; **scheduled flight** vol *m* régulier

scheme [skiːm] **1** *n* plan *m* **2** *v/i (plot)* comploter; **scheming** intrigant

schizophrenia [skɪtsəˈfriːnɪə] schizophrénie *f*; **schizophrenic 1** *adj* schizophrène **2** *n* schizophrène *m/f*

scholar [ˈskɑːlər] érudit(e) *m(f)*; **scholarly** savant, érudit; **scholarship** *(learning)* érudition *f*; *financial award* bourse *f*

school [skuːl] école *f*; *(university)* université *f*; **school bag** cartable *m*; **schoolchildren** écoliers *mpl*

science [ˈsaɪəns] science *f*; **scientific** scientifique; **scientist** scientifique *m/f*

scissors [ˈsɪzərz] ciseaux *mpl*

scoff¹ [skɑːf] *food* engloutir

scoff² [skɑːf] *(mock)* se moquer

scold [skoʊld] réprimander

scoop [skuːp] *for ice-cream* cuiller *f* à glace; *of ice cream* boule *f*; *story* scoop *m*

scooter [ˈskuːtər] *with motor* scooter *m*; *child's* trottinette *f*

scope [skoʊp] ampleur *f*;

(freedom, opportunity) possibilités *fpl*

scorch [skɔːrtʃ] brûler; **scorching** très chaud

score [skɔːr] **1** *n* SP score *m*; *(written music)* partition *f*; *of movie etc* musique *f* **2** *v/t goal, point* marquer; *(cut: line)* rayer **3** *v/i* SP marquer; *(keep the ~)* marquer les points; **scoreboard** tableau *m* des scores; **scorer** marqueur(-euse) *m(f)*

scorn [skɔːrn] **1** *n* mépris *m* **2** *v/t idea* mépriser; **scornful** méprisant; **scornfully** avec mépris

Scot [skɑːt] Écossais(e) *m(f)*; **Scotch** *whiskey* scotch *m*; **Scotch tape®** scotch *m*; **Scotland** Écosse *f*; **Scottish** écossais

scoundrel [ˈskaʊndrəl] gredin *m*

scour [ˈskaʊər] *(search)* fouiller

scowl [skaʊl] **1** *n* air *m* renfrogné **2** *v/i* se renfrogner

scramble [ˈskræmbl] **1** *n (rush)* course *f* folle **2** *v/t message* brouiller **3** *v/i*: **he ~d to his feet** il se releva d'un bond; **scrambled eggs** œufs *mpl* brouillés

scrap [skræp] **1** *n metal* ferraille *f*; *(fight)* bagarre *f*; *of food, paper* bout *m* **2** *v/t idea, plan* abandonner

scrape [skreɪp] **1** *n on paint, skin* éraflure *f* **2** *v/t paint-*

work, arm etc érafler

'**scrap metal** ferraille *f*

'**scrappy** ['skræpɪ] *work, essay* décousu

scratch [skrætʃ] **1** *n mark* égratignure *f*; *start from ~* partir de zéro; *not up to ~* pas à la hauteur de **2** *v/t (mark: skin, paint)* égratigner; *of cat* griffer; *because of itch* se gratter **3** *v/i of cat* griffer

scrawl [skrɔːl] **1** *n* gribouillis *m* **2** *v/t* gribouiller

scrawny ['skrɔːnɪ] décharné

scream [skriːm] **1** *n* cri *m* **2** *v/i* pousser un cri

screech [skriːtʃ] **1** *n of tires* crissement *m*; *(scream)* cri *m* strident **2** *v/i of tires* crisser; *(scream)* pousser un cri strident

screen [skriːn] **1** *n in room, hospital* paravent *m; in movie theater, of TV, computer* écran *m* **2** *v/t (protect, hide)* cacher; *movie* projeter; *for security reasons* passer au crible; *screenplay* scénario *m*; **screen saver** COMPUT économiseur *m* d'écran; **screen test** *for movie* bout *m* d'essai

screw [skruː] **1** *n vis f* **2** *v/t attach* visser (*to* à); F *(cheat)* rouler F; V *(have sex with)* baiser V; **screwdriver** tournevis *m*; **screwed up** F *psychologically* paumé F; **screwy** F déjanté F

scribble ['skrɪbl] **1** *n* griffonnage *m* **2** *v/t (write quickly)*

griffonner **3** *v/i* gribouiller

script [skrɪpt] *for movie* scénario *m; for play* texte *m; form of writing* script *m*; **Scripture:** *the (Holy) ~s* les Saintes Écritures *fpl*; **scriptwriter** scénariste *m/f*

◆ **scroll down** [skroul] COMPUT faire défiler vers le bas

◆ **scroll up** COMPUT faire défiler vers le haut

scrounge [skraundʒ] se faire offrir; **scrounger** profiteur(-euse) *m(f)*

scrub [skrʌb] *floor* laver à la brosse

scruples ['skruːplz] scrupules *mpl*; **scrupulous** *morally, (thorough)* scrupuleux; **scrupulously** *(meticulously)* scrupuleusement

scrutinize ['skruːtɪnaɪz] *(examine closely)* scruter; **scrutiny** examen *m* minutieux

scuba diving ['skuːbə] plongée *f* sous-marine autonome

scuffle ['skʌfl] bagarre *f*

sculptor ['skʌlptər] sculpteur(-trice) *m(f)*; **sculpture** sculpture *f*

scum [skʌm] *on liquid* écume *f; pej: people* bande *f* d'ordures F

sea [siː] mer *f*; **seabird** oiseau *m* de mer; **seafood** fruits *mpl* de mer; **seagull** mouette *f*

seal¹ [siːl] *n animal* phoque *m*

seal² [siːl] **1** *n on document* sceau *m*; TECH étanchéité *f*

2 v/t container sceller

'**sea level: above/below ~** au-dessus/au-dessous du niveau de la mer

seam [si:m] on garment couture f; of ore veine f

'**seaman** marin m; **seaport** port m maritime

search [sɜːrtʃ] **1** n recherche f (**for** de) **2** v/t chercher dans ◆ **search for** chercher

searching ['sɜːrtʃɪŋ] look, question pénétrant; **searchlight** projecteur m

'**seashore** plage f; **seasick: get ~** avoir le mal de mer; **seaside: at the ~** au bord de la mer

season ['si:zn] saison f; **seasonal** vegetables, employment saisonnier; **seasoned** wood sec; traveler, campaigner expérimenté; **seasoning** assaisonnement m; **season ticket** carte f d'abonnement

seat [si:t] place f; chair siège m; of pants fond m; **please take a ~** veuillez vous asseoir; **seat belt** ceinture f de sécurité

'**seaweed** algues fpl

secluded [sɪ'klu:dɪd] retiré

second ['sekənd] **1** n of time seconde f **2** adj deuxième **3** adv come in deuxième **4** v/t motion appuyer; **secondary** secondaire; **second floor** premier étage m, Br deuxième étage m; **second-hand**

d'occasion;   **secondly** deuxièmement;   **second-rate** de second ordre

secrecy ['si:krəsɪ] secret m; **secret 1** n secret m **2** adj secret

secretarial [sekrə'terɪəl] job de secrétariat; **secretary** secrétaire m/f; POL ministre m/f; **Secretary of State** secrétaire m/f d'État

secretive ['si:krətɪv] secret; **secretly** en secret

sect [sekt] secte f

section ['sekʃn] section f

sector ['sektər] secteur m

secular ['sekjələr] séculier

secure [sɪ'kjʊr] **1** adj shelf etc bien fixé; job, contract sûr **2** v/t shelf etc fixer; s.o.'s help, finances se procurer; **securities market** FIN marché m des valeurs; **security** sécurité f; for investment garantie f; **security alert** alerte f de sécurité; **security forces** forces fpl de sécurité; **security guard** garde m de sécurité; **security risk** menace potentielle à la sécurité de l'État ou d'une organisation

sedan [sɪ'dæn] MOT berline f

sedate [sɪ'deɪt] donner un calmant à; **sedative** calmant m

sedentary ['sedənterɪ] job sédentaire

sediment ['sedɪmənt] sédiment m

seduce [sɪ'du:s] séduire; **se-**

duction séduction f; **seductive** *dress, offer* séduisant

see [si:] *with eyes*, *(understand)* voir; **~ you!** F à plus! F
♦ **see off** *at airport etc* raccompagner; *(chase away)* chasser

seed [si:d] *single* graine f; *collective* graines fpl; *of fruit* pépin m; *in tennis* tête f de série; **seedy** miteux

seeing '**eye dog** chien m d'aveugle; **seeing (that)** étant donné que

seek [si:k] chercher

seem [si:m] sembler; **seemingly** apparemment

seesaw ['si:sɔ:] bascule f

'**see-through** transparent

segment ['segmənt] segment m; *of orange* morceau m

segregate ['segrɪgeɪt] séparer; **segregation** ségrégation f; *of sexes* séparation f

seismology [saɪz'mɑ:lədʒɪ] sismologie f

seize [si:z] *opportunity, arm, of police etc* saisir; *power* s'emparer de; **seizure** MED crise f; *of drugs etc* saisie f

seldom ['seldəm] rarement

select [sɪ'lekt] **1** *v/t* sélectionner **2** *adj group of people* choisi; *hotel etc* chic *inv*; **selection** sélection f; **selective** sélectif

self [self] moi m; **self-assurance** confiance f en soi; **self-assured** sûr de soi; **self-centered**, Br **self-cen-**

tred égocentrique; **self-confidence** confiance en soi; **self-confident** sûr de soi; **self-conscious** intimidé; *about sth* gêné (**about** par); **self-consciousness** timidité f; *about sth* gêne f (**about** par rapport à); **self-control** contrôle m de soi; **self-defense**, Br **self-defence** autodéfense f; LAW légitime défense f; **self-employed** indépendant; **self-evident** évident; **self-expression** expression f

selfie ['selfi] selfie m, autoportrait m

self-interest intérêt m (personnel); **selfish** égoïste; **selfless** désintéressé; **self-made man** self made man m; **self-pity** apitoiement m sur soi-même; **self-portrait** autoportrait m; **self-reliant** autonome; **self-respect** respect m de soi; **self-satisfied** pej suffisant; **self-service** libre-service; **self-service restaurant** self m

sell [sel] **1** *v/t* vendre **2** *v/i of products* se vendre; **sell-by date** date f limite de vente; **seller** vendeur(-euse) m(f); **selling** COM vente f; **selling point** COM point m fort

Sellotape® ['seləteɪp] Br scotch m

semester [sɪ'mestər] semestre m

semi ['semɪ] *truck* semi-remorque *f*; **semicircle** demi-cercle *m*; **semiconductor** ELEC semi-conducteur *m*; **semifinal** demi-finale *f*; **semifinalist** demi-finaliste *m/f*

seminar ['semɪnɑːr] séminaire *m*

semi-skilled *worker* spécialisé

senate ['senət] Sénat *m*; **senator** sénateur(-trice) *m(f)*

send [send] envoyer (*to a*)
◆ **send back** renvoyer
◆ **send for** *doctor* faire venir; *help* envoyer chercher

sender ['sendər] *of letter* expéditeur(-trice) *m(f)*

senile ['siːnaɪl] sénile; **senility** sénilité *f*

senior ['siːnjər] (*older*) plus âgé; *in rank* supérieur; **senior citizen** personne *f* âgée; **seniority** *in job* ancienneté *f*

sensation [sen'seɪʃn] sensation *f*; **sensational** sensationnel

sense [sens] **1** *n* sens *m*; (*common ~*) bon sens *m*; (*feeling*) sentiment *m*; **come to one's ~s** revenir à la raison; **it doesn't make ~** cela n'a pas de sens **2** *v/t* sentir; **senseless** (*pointless*) stupide

sensible ['sensəbl] sensé; *clothes, shoes* pratique; **sensibly** raisonnablement

sensitive ['sensɪtɪv] sensible; **sensitivity** sensibilité *f*

sensor ['sensər] détecteur *m*

sensual ['senʃʊəl] sensuel; **sensuality** sensualité *f*

sensuous ['senʃʊəs] voluptueux

sentence ['sentəns] **1** *n* GRAM phrase *f*; LAW peine *f* **2** *v/t* LAW condamner

sentiment ['sentɪmənt] (*sentimentality*) sentimentalité *f*; (*opinion*) sentiment *m*; **sentimental** sentimental; **sentimentality** sentimentalité *f*

sentry ['sentrɪ] sentinelle *f*

separate **1** ['sepərət] *adj* séparé **2** ['sepəreɪt] *v/t* séparer (*from* de) **3** *v/i* of couple se séparer; **separated** *couple* séparé; **separately** séparément; **separation** séparation *f*

September [sep'tembər] septembre *m*

septic ['septɪk] septique

sequel ['siːkwəl] suite *f*

sequence ['siːkwəns] ordre *m*

serene [sɪ'riːn] serein

sergeant ['sɑːrdʒənt] sergent *m*

serial ['sɪrɪəl] feuilleton *m*; **serialize** *novel on TV* adapter en feuilleton; **serial number** *of product* numéro *m* de série

series ['sɪriːz] série *f*

serious ['sɪrɪəs] *person, company* sérieux; *illness, situation, damage* grave; **seriously injured** gravement; *under-*

staffed sérieusement; **take s.o. ~** prendre qn au sérieux; **seriousness** *of person, situation, illness etc* gravité *f*

sermon ['sɜːmən] sermon *m*

servant ['sɜːrvənt] domestique *m/f*

serve [sɜːrv] **1** *n in tennis* service *m* **2** *v/t & v/i* servir; **server** *in tennis* serveur(-euse) *m(f)*; COMPUT serveur *m*; **service 1** *n also in tennis* service *m*; *for vehicle, machine* entretien *m*; **~s** services *mpl* **2** *v/t vehicle, machine* entretenir; **service charge** service *m*; **serviceman** MIL militaire *m*; **service station** station-service *f*; **serving** *of food* portion *f*

session ['seʃn] session *f*; *meeting, talk* discussion *f*

set [set] **1** *n* (*collection*) série *f*; (*group of people*) groupe *m*; MATH ensemble *m*; THEA (*scenery*) décor *m*; *for movie* plateau *m*; *in tennis* set *m* **2** *v/t* (*place*) *movie, novel etc* situer; *date, time, limit* fixer; *alarm* mettre; *broken limb* remettre en place; *jewel* sertir; **~ the table** mettre la table **3** *v/i of sun* se coucher; *of glue* durcir **4** *adj ideas* arrêté; (*ready*) prêt

◆ **set off 1** *v/i on journey* partir **2** *v/t alarm etc* déclencher

◆ **set out 1** *v/i on journey* partir **2** *v/t ideas, goods* exposer

◆ **set up 1** *v/t company,* *equipment, machine* monter; *market stall* installer; *meeting* arranger; F (*frame*) faire un coup à **2** *v/i in business* s'établir

'setback revers *m*

settee [se'tiː] *Br* (*couch, sofa*) canapé *m*

setting ['setɪŋ] *of novel, play, house* cadre *m*

settle ['setl] **1** *v/i of bird* se poser; *of dust* se déposer; *of building* se tasser; *to live* s'installer **2** *v/t dispute, issue, debts* régler; *nerves, stomach* calmer; **that ~s it!** ça règle la question!

◆ **settle down** (*stop being noisy*) se calmer; (*stop wild living*) se ranger; *in an area* s'installer

◆ **settle for** (*accept*) accepter

settled ['setld] *weather* stable; **settlement** *of claim, debt, dispute,* (*payment*) règlement *m*; *of building* tassement *m*; **settler** *in new country* colon *m*

'set-up (*structure*) organisation *f*; (*relationship*) relation *f*; F (*frame-up*) coup *m* monté

seven ['sevn] sept; **seventeen** dix-sept; **seventeenth** dix-septième; **seventh** septième; **seventieth** soixante-dixième; **seventy** soixante-dix

sever ['sevər] sectionner; *relations* rompre

several ['sevrl] plusieurs

severe [sɪ'vɪr] *illness* grave; *penalty* lourd; *winter, weather* rigoureux; *teacher* sévère; **severely** *punish, speak* sévèrement; *injured* grièvement; *disrupted* fortement; **severity** of *illness* gravité f; of *penalty* lourdeur f; of *winter* rigueur f; of *teacher* sévérité f

sew [soʊ] coudre

sewage ['suːɪdʒ] eaux fpl d'égouts; **sewer** égout m

sewing ['soʊɪŋ] *skill* couture f; (*that being sewn*) ouvrage m

sex [seks] sexe m; **have ~ with** coucher avec; **sexist** 1 *adj* sexiste 2 *n* sexiste m/f; **sexual** sexuel; **sexuality** sexualité f; **sexually** sexuellement; **sexy** sexy *inv*

shabbily ['ʃæbɪlɪ] *dressed* pauvrement; *treat* mesquinement; **shabby** *coat etc* usé; *treatment* mesquin

shack [ʃæk] cabane f

shade [ʃeɪd] 1 *n* for *lamp* abat-jour m; of *color* nuance f; on *window* store m; **in the ~** à l'ombre 2 *v/t* from *sun* protéger du soleil; from *light* protéger de la lumière

shadow ['ʃædoʊ] ombre f

shady ['ʃeɪdɪ] *spot* ombragé; *character* louche

shaft [ʃæft] of *axle* arbre m; of *mine* puits m

shake [ʃeɪk] 1 *n*: **give sth a good ~** bien agiter qch 2

v/t bottle agiter; *emotionally* bouleverser; **~ one's head** *in refusal* dire non de la tête; **~ hands with s.o.** serrer la main à qn 3 *v/i* of *hands, voice, building* trembler; **shaken** *emotionally* bouleversé; **shake-up** remaniement m; **shaky** *table etc* branlant; *after illness, shock* faible; *voice, hand* tremblant; *grasp of sth, grammar etc* incertain

shall [ʃæl] ◇ *future*: **I ~ do my best** je ferai de mon mieux ◇ *suggesting*: **~ we go now?** si nous y allions maintenant?

shallow ['ʃæloʊ] *water* peu profond; *person* superficiel

shame [ʃeɪm] 1 *n* honte f; **what a ~!** quel dommage! 2 *v/t* faire honte à; **shameful** honteux; **shameless** effronté

shampoo [ʃæm'puː] shampo(o)ing m

shape [ʃeɪp] 1 *n* forme f 2 *v/t clay, character* façonner; *the future* influencer; **shapeless** *dress etc* informe; **shapely** *figure* bien fait

share [ʃer] 1 *n* part f; FIN action f 2 *v/t & v/i* partager; **shareholder** actionnaire m/f

shark [ʃɑːrk] requin m

sharp [ʃɑːrp] 1 *adj knife* tranchant; *mind, pain* vif; *taste* piquant 2 *adv* MUS trop haut; **at 3 o'clock ~** à 3 heures pile; **sharpen** *knife, skills* aiguiser

shatter ['ʃætər] **1** v/t glass, illusions briser **2** v/i of glass se briser; **shattered** ['ʃætərd] F (exhausted) crevé F; F (very upset) bouleversé; **shattering** news bouleversant

shave [ʃeɪv] **1** v/t raser **2** v/i se raser **3** n: **have a ~** se raser; **shaven** head rasé; **shaver** rasoir m électrique

shawl [ʃɔːl] châle m

she [ʃiː] elle; **there ~ is** la voilà

sheath [ʃiːθ] for knife étui m; contraceptive préservatif m

shed[1] [ʃed] v/t blood, tears verser; leaves perdre

shed[2] [ʃed] n abri m

sheep [ʃiːp] mouton m; **sheepdog** chien m de berger; **sheepish** penaud

sheer [ʃɪr] pur; cliffs abrupt

sheet [ʃiːt] drap m; of paper, metal, glass feuille f

shelf [ʃelf] étagère f; **shelves** set of shelves étagère(s) f(pl)

shell [ʃel] **1** n of mussel, egg coquille f; of tortoise carapace f; MIL obus m **2** v/t peas écosser; MIL bombarder; **shellfire** bombardements mpl; **shellfish** fruits mpl de mer

shelter ['ʃeltər] **1** n abri m **2** v/i s'abriter (from de) **3** v/t (protect) protéger; **sheltered** place protégé; **lead a ~ life** mener une vie protégée

shelve [ʃelv] fig mettre en suspens

shepherd ['ʃepərd] berger (-ère) m(f)

sheriff ['ʃerɪf] shérif m

shield [ʃiːld] **1** n MIL bouclier m; sports trophy plaque f; badge: of policeman plaque f **2** v/t (protect) protéger

shift [ʃɪft] **1** n (change) changement m; (move, switchover) passage m (**to** à); at work poste m; people équipe f **2** v/t (move) déplacer; production, employee transférer; stains etc faire partir **3** v/i (move) se déplacer; in attitude virer; **shifty** F person louche; eyes fuyant

shin [ʃɪn] tibia m

shine [ʃaɪn] **1** v/i briller; fig: of student etc être brillant (**at**, **in** en) **2** n on shoes etc brillant m; **shiny** brillant

ship [ʃɪp] **1** n bateau m, navire m **2** v/t (send) expédier **3** v/i of new product être lancé (sur le marché); **shipment** envoi m; **shipowner** armateur m; **shipping** (sea traffic) navigation f; (sending) expédition f; **shipwreck** naufrage m; **shipyard** chantier m naval

shirt [ʃɜːrt] chemise f

shit [ʃɪt] **1** n P merde f P **2** v/i P chier P **3** int P merde P; **shitty** F dégueulasse F

shiver ['ʃɪvər] trembler

shock [ʃaːk] **1** n choc m; ELEC décharge f; **be in ~** MED être en état de choc **2** v/t choquer;

shock absorber MOT amortisseur *m*; **shocking** choquant; F (*very bad*) épouvantable

shoddy ['ʃɑːdɪ] *goods* de mauvaise qualité; *behavior* mesquin

shoe [ʃuː] chaussure *f*, soulier *m*; **shoelace** lacet *m*; **shoemaker** cordonnier(-ière) *m(f)*; **shoe mender** cordonnier(-ière) *m(f)*; **shoestore** magasin *m* de chaussures

shoot [ʃuːt] **1** BOT pousse *f* **2** *v/t* tirer sur; *and kill* tuer d'un coup de feu; *movie* tourner **3** *v/i* tirer

◆ **shoot down** *airplane* abattre; *fig: suggestion* descendre

◆ **shoot up** *of prices* monter en flèche; *of children, new buildings etc* pousser

shooting star ['ʃuːtɪŋ] étoile *f* filante

shop [ʃɑːp] **1** *n* magasin *m* **2** *v/i* faire ses courses; **go ~ping** faire les courses; **shopkeeper** commerçant *m*,-ante *f*; **shoplifter** voleur(-euse) *m(f)* à l'étalage; **shoplifting** vol *m* à l'étalage

shopping *items* courses *fpl*; **go ~** faire des courses; **shopping bag** sac *m* à provisions; **shopping list** liste *f* de commissions; **shopping mall** centre *m* commercial

shore [ʃɔːr] rivage *m*; **on ~** *not at sea* à terre

short [ʃɔːrt] **1** *adj* court; *in*

height petit; **be ~ of** manquer de **2** *adv*: **cut ~** abréger; **go ~ of** se priver de; **in ~** bref; **shortage** manque *m*; **shortcoming** défaut *m*; **shortcut** raccourci *m*; **shorten** raccourcir; **shortfall** déficit *m*; **short-lived** de courte durée; **shortly** (*soon*) bientôt; **~ before/after** peu avant/après; **shortness** *of visit* brièveté *f*; *in height* petite taille *f*; **shorts** short *m*; *underwear* caleçon *m*; **shortsighted** myope; *fig* peu perspicace; **short-sleeved** à manches courtes; **short-tempered** *by nature* d'un caractère emporté; *at a particular time* de mauvaise humeur; **short-term** à court terme

shot [ʃɑːt] *from gun* coup *m* de feu; (*photograph*) photo *f*; (*injection*) piqûre *f*; **shotgun** fusil *m* de chasse

should [ʃud]: **what ~ I do?** que dois-je faire?; **you ~n't do that** tu ne devrais pas faire ça; **you ~ have heard him** tu aurais dû l'entendre

shoulder ['ʃouldər] épaule *f*

shout [ʃaut] **1** *n* cri *m* **2** *v/t* & *v/i* crier; **shouting** cris *mpl*

shove [ʃʌv] **1** *n*: **give s.o. a ~** pousser qn **2** *v/t* & *v/i* pousser

shovel ['ʃʌvl] pelle *f*

show [ʃou] **1** *n* THEA, TV spectacle *m*; (*display*) démonstration *f* **2** *v/t* montrer; *at exhibition* présenter; *movie* pro-

1# show in

502

jeter **3** v/i (be visible) se voir;
of movie passer

◆ **show in** faire entrer

◆ **show off 1** v/t skills faire
étalage de **2** v/i pej crâner

◆ **show up 1** v/t shortcomings
etc faire ressortir **2** v/i (arrive, turn up) se pointer F;
(be visible) se voir

'**show business** monde m du
spectacle; **showcase** also fig
vitrine f; **showdown** confrontation f

shower ['ʃaʊər] **1** n of rain
averse f; to wash douche f;
party: petite fête avant un mariage ou un accouchement à
laquelle tout le monde ap-
porte un cadeau; **take a ~**
prendre une douche **2** v/i
prendre une douche

'**show-off** pej prétentieux
(-euse) m(f); **showroom** salle f d'exposition; **showy**
voyant

shred [ʃred] **1** n of paper etc
lambeau m; of meat etc morceau m **2** v/t documents déchiqueter; in cooking râper;
shredder for documents dé-
chiqueteuse f

shrewd [ʃruːd] perspicace;
shrewdness perspicacité f

shriek [ʃriːk] **1** n cri m aigu **2**
v/i pousser un cri aigu

shrill [ʃrɪl] perçant

shrimp [ʃrɪmp] crevette f

shrine [ʃraɪn] lieu m saint

shrink¹ [ʃrɪŋk] v/i of material
rétrécir; of support diminuer

shrink² [ʃrɪŋk] n F (psychiatrist) psy m F

shrivel ['ʃrɪvl] se flétrir

shrub [ʃrʌb] arbuste m;
shrubbery massif m d'ar-
bustes

shrug [ʃrʌg]: **~ (one's
shoulders)** hausser les épaules

shudder ['ʃʌdər] **1** n of fear,
disgust frisson m; of earth vibration f **2** v/i with fear, disgust frissonner; of earth vibrer

shuffle ['ʃʌfl] v/t cards battre

shun [ʃʌn] fuir

shut [ʃʌt] **1** v/t fermer **2** v/i of
door, box se fermer; of store
fermer

◆ **shut down 1** v/t business
fermer; computer éteindre
2 v/i of business fermer ses
portes; of computer s'éteindre

◆ **shut up** F (be quiet) se taire; **shut up!** tais-toi!

shutter ['ʃʌtər] on window
volet m; PHOT obturateur m

shuttle bus ['ʃʌtl] at airport
navette f

shy [ʃaɪ] timide; **shyness** timidité f

sick [sɪk] malade; sense of humor noir; **be~** Br (vomit) vomir; **sicken 1** v/t (disgust)
écœurer; (make ill) rendre
malade **2** v/i: **be~ing for** couver; **sickening** écœurant;
sick leave congé m de mala-

die; **sickness** maladie f;
(*vomiting*) vomissements
mpl
side [saɪd] côté m; SP équipe f;
take **~s** (*favor one* ~) prendre parti; ~ **by** ~ côte à côte;
side effect effet m secondaire; **sidestep** éviter; *fig also*
contourner; **side street** rue
f transversale; **sidewalk** trottoir m; **sideways** de côté
siege [siːdʒ] siège m
sieve [sɪv] *for flour* tamis m
sift [sɪft] tamiser; *data* passer
en revue
sigh [saɪ] **1** n soupir m **2** v/i
soupirer
sight [saɪt] spectacle m; (*power of seeing*) vue f; ~**s** *of city
monuments* mpl; **know by** ~
connaître de vue; **sightseeing: go** ~ faire du tourisme;
sightseer touriste m/f
sign [saɪn] **1** n signe m;
(*road-*) panneau m; *outside
shop* enseigne f **2** v/t & v/i signer
signal ['sɪɡnl] **1** n signal m **2**
v/i *of driver* mettre son clignotant
signatory ['sɪɡnətɔːri] signataire m/f
signature ['sɪɡnətʃər] signature f
significance [sɪɡ'nɪfɪkəns]
importance f; **significant
event, sum of money, improvement** *etc* important;
significantly *larger, more expensive* nettement

signify ['sɪɡnɪfaɪ] signifier
'**sign language** langage m des
signes; **signpost** poteau m
indicateur
silence ['saɪləns] **1** n silence
m **2** v/t faire taire; **silent** silencieux
silhouette [sɪluː'et] silhouette
f
silicon ['sɪlɪkən] silicium m
silk [sɪlk] **1** *adj shirt etc* en soie
2 n soie f; **silky** soyeux
silliness ['sɪlɪnɪs] stupidité f;
silly bête
silo ['saɪloʊ] silo m
silver ['sɪlvər] **1** *adj ring* en argent; *hair* argenté **2** n argent
m; **silverware** argenterie f
similar ['sɪmɪlər] semblable
(**to** à); **similarity** ressemblance f; **similarly** de la même façon
simple ['sɪmpl] simple; **simple-minded** *pej* simple, simplet; **simplicity** simplicité f;
simplify simplifier; **simplistic** simpliste; **simply** (*absolutely*) absolument; (*in a simple way*) simplement
simultaneous [saɪməl'teɪnɪəs] simultané; **simultaneously** simultanément
sin [sɪn] **1** n péché m **2** v/i pécher
since [sɪns] **1** *prep & adv* depuis; **I've been here** ~ *last
week* je suis là depuis la semaine dernière **2** *conj in expressions of time* depuis que;
(*seeing that*) puisque

sincere [sɪn'sɪr] sincère; sincerely sincèrement; **Sincerely yours** Je vous prie d'agréer, Madame/Monsieur, l'expression de mes sentiments les meilleurs; sincerity sincérité f

sinful ['sɪnfʊl] *deeds* honteux; **~ person** pécheur *m*, pécheresse f

sing [sɪŋ] chanter

singe [sɪndʒ] brûler légèrement

singer ['sɪŋər] chanteur(-euse) m(f)

single ['sɪŋgl] **1** *adj* (*sole*) seul; (*not double*) simple; *bed* à une place; (*not married*) célibataire **2** *n* MUS single *m*; (*~ room*) chambre f à un lit; *person* personne f seule; **~s** *in tennis* simple *m*; **single-handed** tout seul; **single-minded** résolu; **single parent** mère/père qui élève ses enfants tout seul; **single parent family** famille f monoparentale; **single room** chambre f à un lit

singular ['sɪŋgjʊlər] GRAM **1** *adj* au singulier **2** *n* singulier *m*

sinister ['sɪnɪstər] sinistre

sink [sɪŋk] **1** *n* évier *m* **2** *v/i* of *ship, object* couler; *of sun* descendre; *of interest rates etc* baisser **3** *v/t* *of ship* couler; *money* investir

sinner ['sɪnər] pécheur *m*, pécheresse f

sip [sɪp] **1** *n* petite gorgée f **2** *v/t* boire à petites gorgées

sir [sɜːr] monsieur *m*

siren ['saɪrən] sirène f

sirloin ['sɜːrlɔɪn] aloyau *m*

sister ['sɪstər] sœur f; **sister-in-law** belle-sœur f

sit [sɪt] (**~ down**) s'asseoir; *she was sitting* elle était assise

◆ **sit down** s'asseoir

sitcom ['sɪtkɑːm] sitcom *m*

site [saɪt] **1** *n* emplacement *m*; *of battle* site *m* **2** *v/t* *new offices etc* situer

sitting ['sɪtɪŋ] *of committee, court, for artist* séance f; *for meals* service *m*; **sitting room** salon *m*

situated ['sɪtʊeɪtɪd] situé; situation situation f; *of building etc* emplacement *m*

six [sɪks] six; **sixteen** seize; **sixteenth** seizième; **sixth** sixième; **sixtieth** soixantième; **sixty** soixante

size [saɪz] *of room, jacket* taille f; *of project* envergure f; *of loan* montant *m*; *of shoes* pointure f; **sizeable** *meal, house* assez grand; *order, amount* assez important

skate [skeɪt] **1** *n* patin *m* **2** *v/i* patiner; **skateboard** skateboard *m*; **skateboarding** skateboard *m*; **skater** patineur(-euse) m(f); **skating** patinage f; **skating rink** patinoire f

skeleton ['skelɪtn] squelette

m

skeptic ['skeptɪk] sceptique *m/f*; **skeptical** sceptique; **skepticism** scepticisme *m*

sketch [sketʃ] **1** *n* croquis *m*; THEA sketch *m* **2** *v/t* esquisser; **sketchy** *knowledge etc* sommaire

ski [skiː] **1** *n* ski *m* **2** *v/i* faire du ski

skid [skɪd] **1** *n* dérapage *m* **2** *v/i* déraper

skier ['skiːər] skieur(-euse) *m(f)*; **skiing** ski *m*

skilful *etc* Br → **skillful**

skill [skɪl] technique *f*; **~s** compétences *fpl*; **skilled** habile; **skillful** habile; **skillfully** habilement

skim [skɪm] *surface* effleurer

skimpy ['skɪmpɪ] *account etc* sommaire; *dress* étriqué

skin [skɪn] **1** *n* peau *f* **2** *v/t animal* écorcher; *tomato* peler; **skin diving** plongée *f* sous--marine autonome; **skinny** maigre; **skin-tight** moulant

skip [skɪp] **1** *n* (*little jump*) saut *m* **2** *v/i* sautiller **3** *v/t* (*omit*) sauter; **skipper** capitaine *m/f*

skirt [skɜːrt] jupe *f*

skull [skʌl] crâne *m*

skunk [skʌŋk] mouffette *f*

sky [skaɪ] ciel *m*; **skylight** lucarne *f*; **skyline** silhouette *f*; **skyscraper** gratte-ciel *m inv*

slab [slæb] *of stone, butter* plaque *f*; *of cake* grosse tranche *f*

slack [slæk] *rope* mal tendu; *work* négligé; *period* creux; **slacken** *rope* détendre; *pace* ralentir; **slacks** pantalon *m*

slam [slæm] claquer

slander ['slændər] **1** *n* calomnie *f* **2** *v/t* calomnier; **slanderous** calomnieux

slang [slæŋ] *also of a specific group* argot *m*

slant [slænt] **1** *v/i* pencher **2** *n* inclinaison *f*; *given to a story* perspective *f*; **slanting** *roof* en pente; *eyes* bridé

slap [slæp] **1** *n* (*blow*) claque *f* **2** *v/t* donner une claque à

slash [slæʃ] **1** *n* *cut* entaille *f*; *in punctuation* barre *f* oblique **2** *v/t* *painting, skin* entailler; *prices* réduire radicalement

slaughter ['slɔːtər] **1** *n* *of animals* abattage *m*; *of people, troops* massacre *m* **2** *v/t animals* abattre; *people, troops* massacrer; **slaughterhouse** abattoir *m*

slave [sleɪv] esclave *m/f*

slay [sleɪ] tuer; **slaying** (*murder*) meurtre *m*

sleaze [sliːz] POL corruption *f*; **sleazy** *bar, character* louche

sleep [sliːp] **1** *n* sommeil *m*; **go to ~** s'endormir **2** *v/i* dormir

◆ **sleep with** (*have sex with*) coucher avec

'sleeping bag sac *m* de couchage; **sleeping car** RAIL wagon-lit *m*; **sleeping pill** somnifère m; **sleepwalker** somnambule m/f; **sleepwalking** somnambulisme m; **sleepy person** qui a envie de dormir; _yawn, town_ endormi; **I'm ~** j'ai sommeil

sleet [sli:t] neige f fondue

sleeve [sli:v] _of jacket etc_ manche f; **sleeveless** sans manches

slender ['slendər] mince; _chance, margin_ faible

slice [slais] **1** n _of bread, pie_ tranche f; _fig: of profits_ part f **2** v/t _loaf etc_ couper en tranches

slick [slik] **1** adj _performance_ habile; _pej (cunning)_ rusé **2** n _of oil_ marée f noire

slide [slaid] **1** n _for kids_ toboggan m; PHOT diapositive f **2** v/i glisser; _of exchange rate etc_ baisser **3** v/t _item of furniture_ faire glisser

slight [slait] _person, figure_ frêle; _(small)_ léger; **no, not in the ~est** non, pas le moins du monde; **slightly** légèrement

slim [slim] _person_ mince; _chance_ faible

slime [slaim] _(mud)_ vase f; _of slug etc_ bave f; **slimy** _liquid etc_ vaseux

sling [sliŋ] **1** n _for arm_ écharpe f **2** v/t F _(throw)_ lancer

slip [slip] **1** n _(mistake)_ erreur f **2** v/i glisser; _in quality, quantity_ baisser

◆ **slip up** _(make a mistake)_

faire une gaffe

slipped 'disc [slipt] hernie f discale

slipper ['slipər] chausson m

slippery ['slipəri] glissant

'slip-up _(mistake)_ gaffe f

slit [slit] **1** n _(tear)_ déchirure f; _(hole), in skirt_ fente f **2** v/t ouvrir, fendre

sliver ['slivər] petit morceau m; _of wood, glass_ éclat m

slob [slɑ:b] _pej_ rustaud(e) m(f)

slog [slɑ:g] _long walk_ trajet m pénible; _hard work_ corvée f

slogan ['slougən] slogan m

slop [slɑ:p] _(spill)_ renverser

slope [sloup] **1** n _inclinaison f; of mountain_ côté m **2** v/i être incliné

sloppy ['slɑ:pi] F _work, in dress_ négligé; _(too sentimental)_ gnangnan F

slot [slɑ:t] fente f; _in schedule_ créneau m; **slot machine** _for vending_ distributeur m _(automataku);_ _for gambling_ machine f à sous

slovenly ['slʌvnli] négligé

slow [slou] lent; **be ~** _of clock_ retarder

◆ **slow down 1** v/t ralentir **2** v/i ralentir; _in life_ faire moins de choses

'slowdown _in production_ ralentissement m; **slowly** lentement; **slowness** lenteur f

sluggish ['slʌgɪʃ] lent; _river_ à cours lent

slum [slʌm] _area_ quartier m

pauvre; *house* taudis *m*

slump [slʌmp] **1** *n in trade* effondrement *m* **2** *v/i of economy* s'effondrer; *of person* s'affaisser

slur [slɜːr] **1** *n on character* tache *f* **2** *v/t words* mal articuler

slush [slʌʃ] neige *f* fondue; **slush fund** caisse *f* noire

slut [slʌt] *pej* pute *f* F

sly [slaɪ] *(furtive)* sournois; *(crafty)* rusé

small [smɔːl] petit

smart¹ [smɑːrt] *adj* élégant; *(intelligent)* intelligent; *pace* vif

smart² [smɑːrt] *v/i (hurt)* brûler

'smart card carte *f* à puce

smartphone [ˈsmɑːtfəʊn] smartphone *m*

smartly *dressed* avec élégance

smash [smæʃ] **1** *n noise* fracas *m*; *(car crash)* accident *m*; *in tennis* smash *m* **2** *v/t break* fracasser; *(hit hard)* frapper **3** *v/i break* se fracasser

smattering [ˈsmætərɪŋ]: **have a ~ of Chinese** savoir un peu de chinois

smear [smɪr] **1** *n of ink etc* tache *f*; *Br* MED frottis *m*; *on character* diffamation *f* **2** *v/t character* entacher

smell [smel] **1** *n* odeur *f*; **sense of ~** sens *m* de l'odorat **2** *v/t* sentir **3** *v/i unpleasantly* sentir mauvais; *(sniff)* renifler; **smelly** qui sent mauvais

smile [smaɪl] **1** *n* sourire *m* **2**

v/i sourire

smirk [smɜːrk] petit sourire *m* narquois

smoke [sməʊk] **1** *n* fumée *f* **2** *v/t also food* fumer **3** *v/i of person* fumer; **smoker** fumeur(-euse) *m(f)*; **smoke-free** non-fumeur *inv*; **smoking: no ~** défense de fumer; **smoky** enfumé

smolder [ˈsməʊldər] *of fire* couver

smooth [smuːð] **1** *adj surface, skin, sea* lisse; *ride, flight, crossing* bon; *pej: person* mielleux **2** *v/t hair* lisser; **smoothly** *without any problems* sans problème

smother [ˈsmʌðər] *person, flames* étouffer

smoulder *Br* → **smolder**

smudge [smʌdʒ] **1** *n* tache *f* **2** *v/t paint* faire des traces sur; *ink, mascara* étaler

smug [smʌg] suffisant

smuggle [ˈsmʌgl] passer en contrebande; **smuggler** contrebandier(-ière) *m(f)*; **smuggling** contrebande *f*

smutty [ˈsmʌtɪ] *joke* grossier

snack [snæk] en-cas *m*

snag [snæg] *(problem)* hic *m* F

snake [sneɪk] serpent *m*

snap [snæp] **1** *n sound* bruit *m* sec; PHOT instantané *m* **2** *v/t break* casser **3** *v/i break* se casser net **4** *adj decision, judgement* rapide, subit; **snappy** *person, mood* cas-

sant; *decision* prompt; **be a ~ dresser** s'habiller chic;
snapshot photo *f*

snarl [snɑːrl] **1** *n of dog* grondement **2** *v/i of dog* gronder en montrant les dents

snatch [snætʃ] (*grab*) saisir; F (*steal*) voler; F (*kidnap*) enlever

snazzy ['snæzı] F *necktie etc* qui tape F

sneakers ['sniːkərz] *tennis mpl*

sneaky ['sniːkı] F (*underhanded*) sournois

sneer [snıːr] **1** *n* ricanement *m* **2** *v/i* ricaner

sneeze [sniːz] **1** *n* éternuement *m* **2** *v/i* éternuer

snicker ['snıkər] pouffer de rire

sniff [snıf] renifler

sniper ['snaıpər] tireur *m* embusqué

snitch [snıtʃ] **1** *n* (*telltale*) mouchard(e) *m(f)* F **2** *v/i* (*tell tales*) vendre la mèche

snivel ['snıvl] pleurnicher

snob [snɑːb] snob *m/f*; **snobbery** snobisme *m*; **snobbish** snob *inv*

◆ **snoop around** [snuːp] fourrer le nez partout

snooty ['snuːtı] arrogant

snooze [snuːz] **1** *n* petit somme *m* **2** *v/i* roupiller F

snore [snɔːr] ronfler; **snoring** ronflement *m*

snorkel ['snɔːrkl] tuba *m*

snort [snɔːrt] *of bull, horse*

s'ébrouer; *of person* grogner

snow [snou] **1** *n* neige *f* **2** *v/i* neiger; **snowball** boule *f* de neige; **snowdrift** amoncellement *m* de neige; **snowman** bonhomme *m* de neige; **snowplow** chasse-neige *m inv*; **snowstorm** tempête *f* de neige; **snowy** *weather* neigeux; *roads, hills* enneigé

snub [snʌb] **1** *n* rebuffade *f* **2** *v/t* snober; **snub-nosed** au nez retroussé

snug [snʌg] bien au chaud; (*tight-fitting*) bien ajusté

so [sou] **1** *adv* si, tellement; **~ kind** tellement gentil; **not ~ much for me** pas autant pour moi; **~ much easier** tellement plus facile; **drink ~ much** tellement boire; **~ many people** tellement de gens; **I miss you ~** tu me manques tellement; **~ am/do I** moi aussi; **~ is/does she** le aussi; **and ~ on** et ainsi de suite **2** *pron*: **I hope ~** je l'espère bien; **I think ~** je pense que oui; **50 or ~** une cinquantaine, à peu près cinquante **3** *conj* (*for that reason*) donc; (*in order that*) pour que (+*subj*); **~ (that) I could come too** pour que je puisse moi aussi venir; **~ what?** F et alors?

soak [souk] (*steep*) faire tremper; *of water* tremper; **soaked** trempé

soap [soup] *for washing* savon

m; **soap (opera)** feuilleton *m*; **soapy** savonneux

soar [sɔːr] *of rocket, prices etc* monter en flèche

sob [sɑːb] **1** *n* sanglot *m* **2** *v/i* sangloter

sober ['soubər] en état de sobriété; *(serious)* sérieux

so-'called *(referred to as)* comme on le/la/les appelle; *(incorrectly referred to as)* soi-disant *inv*

soccer ['sɑːkər] football *m*

sociable ['souʃəbl] sociable

social ['souʃl] social; *(recreational)* mondain; **social democrat** social-démocrate *m/f*; **socialism** socialisme *m*; **socialist 1** *adj* socialiste **2** *n* socialiste *m/f*; **socialize** fréquenter des gens; **social worker** assistant sociale *m*, assistante sociale *f*

society [sə'saɪətɪ] société *f*

sociologist [sousɪ'ɑːlədʒɪst] sociologue *m/f*; **sociology** sociologie *f*

sock[1] [sɑːk] *n for wearing* chaussette *f*

sock[2] [sɑːk] *v/t (punch)* donner un coup de poing à

socket ['sɑːkɪt] ELEC *for light bulb* douille *f*; *Br (wall ~)* prise *f* de courant; *of eye* orbite *f*

soda ['soudə] *(~ water)* eau *f* gazeuse; *(soft drink)* soda *m*; *(ice-cream ~)* soda *m* à la crème glacée

sofa ['soufə] canapé *m*

soft [sɑːft] doux; *(lenient)* gentil; **soften** position assouplir; *impact, blow* adoucir; **softly** doucement; **software** logiciel *m*

soggy ['sɑːgɪ] *soil* détrempé; *pastry* pâteux

soil [sɔɪl] **1** *n (earth)* terre *f* **2** *v/t* salir

solar energy ['soulər] énergie *f* solaire

soldier ['souldʒər] soldat *m*

sole[1] [soul] *n of foot* plante *f*; *of shoe* semelle *f*

sole[2] [soul] *adj* seul; *responsibility* exclusif

solely ['soulɪ] exclusivement

solemn ['sɑːləm] solennel; **solemnity** solennité *f*; **solemnly** solennellement

solid ['sɑːlɪd] *(hard)* dur; *(without holes)* compact; *gold, silver etc, support* massif; **solidarity** solidarité *f*; **solidify** se solidifier; **solidly** *built* solidement; *in favor of* massivement

solitaire [sɑːlɪ'ter] *card game* réussite *f*

solitary ['sɑːlɪterɪ] *life, activity* solitaire; *(single)* isolé; **solitude** solitude *f*

solo ['soulou] **1** *adj* en solo **2** *n* MUS solo *m*; **soloist** soliste *m/f*

soluble ['sɑːljubl] *substance, problem* soluble; **solution** *also mixture* solution *f*

solve [sɑːlv] résoudre; **solvent** *financially* solvable

somber, *Br* sombre ['sɒmbər] sombre

some [sʌm] **1** *adj:* ~ *cream/ chocolate/cookies* de la crè-me/du chocolat/des biscuits; ~ *people say that* ... certains disent que ... **2** *pron:* ~ *of the money* une partie de l'argent; ~ *of the group* certaines personnes du groupe, certains du groupe; *would you like* ~? est-ce que vous en voulez?; *give me* ~ donnez-m'en **3** *adv* (*a bit*) un peu; **somebody** quelqu'un; **someday** un jour; **somehow** (*by one means or another*) d'une manière ou d'une autre; (*for some unknown reason*) sans savoir pourquoi; **someone** → **somebody**; **someplace** → **somewhere**

somersault ['sʌmərsɔːlt] **1** *n* roulade *f*; *by vehicle* tonneau *m* **2** *v/i of vehicle* faire un tonneau

'**something** quelque chose; **sometime** un de ces jours; ~ *last year* dans le courant de l'année dernière; **sometimes** parfois; **somewhat** quelque peu; **somewhere 1** *adv* quelque part **2** *pron:* *let's go* ~ *quiet* allons dans un endroit calme; ~ *to park* un endroit où se garer

son [sʌn] fils *m*

song [sɒŋ] chanson *f*

'**son-in-law** beau-fils *m*; **son of a bitch** V fils *m* de pute V

soon [suːn] (*in a short while*) bientôt; (*quickly*) vite; (*early*) tôt; *how* ~? dans combien de temps?; *as* ~ *as* dès que; *as* ~ *as possible* le plus tôt possible; *sooner or later* tôt ou tard; *the* ~*er the better* le plus tôt sera le mieux

soothe [suːð] calmer

sophisticated [səˈfɪstɪkeɪtɪd] sophistiqué; **sophistication** sophistication *f*

sophomore [ˈsɑːfəmɔːr] étudiant(e) *m(f)* de deuxième année

soprano [səˈprɑːnoʊ] soprano *m/f*

sordid [ˈsɔːrdɪd] sordide

sore [sɔːr] **1** *adj* F (*angry*) fâché; (*painful*): *is it* ~? ça vous fait mal? **2** *n* plaie *f*

sorrow [ˈsɑːroʊ] chagrin *m*

sorry [ˈsɑːrɪ] *day* triste; *sight* misérable; (*I'm*) ~! (*apologizing*) pardon!; *be* ~ être désolé

sort [sɔːrt] **1** *n* sorte *f*; ~ *of* ... F plutôt **2** *v/t also* COMPUT trier

SOS [esoʊˈes] S.O.S. *m*; *fig*: *plea for help* appel *m* à l'aide

so-so F comme ci comme ça F

soul [soʊl] *also fig* âme *f*

sound[1] [saʊnd] **1** *adj* (*sensible*) judicieux; *structure* solide; (*healthy*) en bonne santé; *sleep* profond **2** *adv:* *be* ~ *asleep* être profondément endormi

sound[2] [saʊnd] **1** *n* son *m*;

(noise) bruit *m* **2** *v/i: that ~s interesting* ça a l'air intéressant

soundly ['saʊndlɪ] *sleep* profondément; *beaten* à plates coutures; **soundproof** insonorisé; **soundtrack** bande *f* sonore

soup [suːp] soupe *f*

sour ['saʊər] *apple, milk* aigre; *comment* désobligeant

source [sɔːrs] *of river, information etc* source *f*

south [saʊθ] **1** *n* sud *m*; *the South of France* le Midi *m* **2** *adj* sud *inv*; *wind* du sud **3** *adv travel* vers le sud; **South Africa** Afrique *f* du sud; **South African 1** *adj* sud-africain **2** *n* Sud-Africain *m*, Sud-Africaine *f*; **South America** Amérique *f* du sud; **South American 1** *adj* sud-américain **2** *n* Sud-Américain(e) *m(f)*; **southeast 1** *n* sud-est *m* **2** *adj* sud-est *inv* **3** *adv travel* vers le sud-est; **southeastern** sud-est *inv*; **southerly** *wind* du sud; *direction* vers le sud; **southern** du Sud; **southerner** habitant(e) *m(f)* du Sud; **southernmost** le plus au sud; **South Pole** pôle *m* Sud; **southward** vers le sud; **southwest 1** *n* sud-ouest *m* **2** *adj* sud-ouest *inv* **3** *adv* vers le sud-ouest; **southwestern** sud-ouest *inv*

souvenir [suːvəˈnɪr] souvenir *m*

sovereign ['sɑːvrɪn] *state* souverain

sow[1] [saʊ] *n (female pig)* truie *f*

sow[2] [soʊ] *v/t seeds* semer

soya ['sɔɪə], *US* **soy** [sɔɪ] soja *m*; **soy(a) milk** lait *m* de soja

spa [spɑː] *(resort)* station *f* thermale; *(day spa)* spa *m*

space [speɪs] espace *m*; *(room)* place *f*; **space shuttle** navette *f* spatiale; **space station** station *f* spatiale; **spacious** spacieux

spade [speɪd] *for digging* bêche *f*; *~s in card game* pique *m*

spaghetti [spəˈgetɪ] spaghetti *mpl*

Spain [speɪn] Espagne *f*

spam (mail) [spæm] spam *m*

span [spæn] *(cover)* recouvrir; *of bridge* traverser

Spaniard ['spænjərd] Espagnol *m*, Espagnole *f*; **Spanish 1** *adj* espagnol **2** *n language* espagnol *m*; *the ~* les Espagnols

spanner ['spænər] *Br* clef *f*

spare [sper] **1** *v/t time* accorder; *(lend: money)* prêter; *(do without)* se passer de; *can you ~ the time?* est-ce que vous pouvez trouver un moment? **2** *adj (extra) cash* en trop; *pair of glasses, clothes* de rechange **3** *n* pièce *f* de rechange; **spare part** pièce *f* de rechange; **spare**

spare ribs

512

ribs côtelette f de porc dans
l'échine; **spare room** chambre f d'ami; **spare time**
temps m libre; **spare wheel**
roue f de secours

sparing: *be ~ with* économiser; **sparingly** en petite
quantité

spark [spɑːrk] étincelle f

sparkle ['spɑːrkl] étinceler;
sparkling wine vin m mousseux

'spark plug bougie f

sparse [spɑːrs] *vegetation*
épars

spartan ['spɑːrtn] *room* spartiate

spasm [spæzm] crampe f

spate [speɪt] *fig* série f, avalanche f

spatial ['speɪʃl] spatial

speak [spiːk] **1** *v/i* parler (*to*,
with à); *~ing* TELEC lui-même, elle-même **2** *v/t foreign
language* parler; **speaker** *at
conference* intervenant(e)
m(f); (*orator*) orateur(-trice)
m(f); *of sound system* haut-parleur m; *French/Spanish
~* francophone m/f / hispanophone m/f

special ['speʃl] spécial; *effort,
day etc* exceptionnel; **specialist** spécialiste m/f; **specialize** se spécialiser (*in* en,
dans); **specially** → **especially**; **specialty** spécialité f

species ['spiːʃiːz] espèce f

specific [spə'sɪfɪk] spécifique; **specifically** spécifique-

ment; **specifications** *of machine etc* spécifications fpl;
specify préciser

specimen ['spesɪmən] *of
work* spécimen m; *of blood,
urine* prélèvement m

spectacular [spek'tækjʊlər]
spectaculaire

spectator [spek'teɪtər] spectateur(-trice) m(f)

spectrum ['spektrəm] *fig*
éventail m

speculate ['spekjʊleɪt] *also*
FIN spéculer; **speculation**
spéculations fpl; FIN spéculation f; **speculator** FIN spéculateur(-trice) m(f)

speech [spiːtʃ] *discours* m;
(*ability to speak*) parole f;
(*way of speaking*) élocution
f; **speechless** *with shock,
surprise* sans voix

speed [spiːd] **1** *n* vitesse f **2** *v/i*
(*go quickly*) se précipiter; *of
vehicle* foncer; *drive too
quickly* faire de la vitesse;
speedboat vedette f; *with
outboard motor* hors-bord
m *inv*; **speed bump** dos
d'âne m, ralentisseur m;
speed-dial button bouton
m de numérotation abrégée;
speedily rapidement;
speeding *when driving* excès m de vitesse; **speed limit**
limitation f de vitesse;
speedometer compteur m
de vitesse; **speedy** rapide

spell[1] [spel] **1** *v/t word* écrire,
épeler; *how do you ~ it?*

513

split

comment ça s'écrit? **2** v/i: **he
can/can't ~** il a une bonne/
mauvaise orthographe

spell² n of time période f

spelling ['spelɪŋ] orthographe
f

spend [spend] money dépenser; time passer; **spendthrift**
pej dépensier(-ière) m(f)

sperm [spɜːrm] spermatozoïde m; (semen) sperme m

sphere [sfɪr] also fig sphère f

spice [spaɪs] (seasoning) épice f; **spicy** food épicé

spider ['spaɪdər] araignée f;
spiderweb toile f d'araignée

spike [spaɪk] pointe f; on
plant, animal piquant m

spill [spɪl] **1** v/t renverser **2** v/i
se répandre **3** n of oil déver-
sement m accidentel

spin¹ [spɪn] **1** n (turn) tour m **2**
v/t faire tourner **3** v/i of wheel
tourner

spin² v/t wool etc filer; web
tisser

spinach ['spɪnɪdʒ] épinards
mpl

spinal ['spaɪnl] de vertèbres;
spinal column colonne f
vertébrale; **spinal cord**
moelle f épinière; **spine** colonne f vertébrale; of book
dos m; on plant, hedgehog
épine f; **spineless** (cowardly) lâche

'spin-off retombée f

spiny ['spaɪnɪ] épineux

spiral ['spaɪrəl] **1** n spirale f **2**
v/i rise quickly monter en

spirale

spire ['spaɪr] of church flèche
f

spirit ['spɪrɪt] esprit m; (courage) courage m; **spirited** (energetic) énergique; **spirits**
(alcohol) spiritueux mpl;
(morale) moral m; **be in
good/poor ~** avoir/ne pas
avoir le moral; **spiritual** spirituel

spit [spɪt] of person cracher

spite [spaɪt] malveillance f; **in
~ of** en dépit de; **spiteful**
malveillant; **spitefully** avec
malveillance

splash [splæʃ] **1** n noise plouf
m; small amount of liquid
goutte f; of color tache f **2**
v/t person éclabousser; water,
mud asperger **3** v/i of person
patauger; **~ against sth** of
waves s'écraser contre qch;
splashdown amerrissage m

splendid ['splendɪd] magnifique; **splendor,** Br **splendour** splendeur f

splint [splɪnt] MED attelle f

splinter ['splɪntər] **1** n of
wood, glass éclat m; in finger
écharde f **2** v/i se briser

split [splɪt] **1** n damage fente
f; (disagreement) division f;
(of profits etc) partage m;
(share) part f **2** v/t wood fendre; log fendre en deux;
(cause disagreement in, divide) diviser **3** v/i of wood
etc se fendre; (disagree) se diviser

◆ **split up** *of couple* se séparer

spoil [spɔɪl] *child* gâter; *surprise, party* gâcher; **spoilsport** F rabat-joie *m/f*; **spoilt** *child* gâté

spoke [spəʊk] *of wheel* rayon *m*

spokesperson ['spəʊkspɜːrsən] porte-parole *m/f*

sponge [spʌndʒ] éponge *f*; **sponger** F parasite *m/f*

sponsor ['spɒnsər] **1** *n for club membership* parrain *m*, marraine *f*, RAD, TV, SP sponsor *m/f* **2** *v/t for club membership* parrainer; RAD, TV, SP sponsoriser; **sponsorship** RAD, TV, SP sponsorisation *f*

spontaneous [spɑːnˈteɪnɪəs] spontané; **spontaneously** spontanément

spool [spuːl] bobine *f*

spoon [spuːn] cuillère *f*; **spoonful** cuillerée *f*

sporadic [spəˈrædɪk] intermittent

sport [spɔːrt] sport *m*; **sporting** *event* sportif; *(fair, generous)* chic *inv*; **sports car** voiture *f* de sport; **sportsman** sportif *m*; **sportswoman** sportive *f*; **sporty** *person* sportif

spot¹ [spɑːt] *n on skin* bouton *m*; *in pattern* pois *m*

spot² *n (place)* endroit *m*

spot³ *v/t (notice, identify)* repérer

'spot check contrôle *m* au hasard; **spotless** impeccable; **spotlight** *beam* feu *m* de projecteur; *device* projecteur *m*; **spotty** *with pimples* boutonneux

spouse [spaʊs] *fml* époux *m*, épouse *f*

spout [spaʊt] **1** *n* bec *m* **2** *v/i of liquid* jaillir **3** *v/t* F débiter

sprain [spreɪn] **1** *n* foulure *f*; *serious* entorse *f* **2** *v/t ankle, wrist* se fouler; *seriously* se faire une entorse

sprawl [sprɔːl] s'affaler; *of city* s'étendre; **sprawling** tentaculaire

spray [spreɪ] **1** *n of sea water* embruns *mpl*; *from fountain* gouttes *fpl* d'eau; *for hair* laque *f*; *container* atomiseur *m* **2** *v/t perfume, lacquer* vaporiser; *paint, weed-killer etc* pulvériser; **~ graffiti on sth** peindre des graffitis à la bombe sur qch; **spraygun** pulvérisateur *m*

spread [spred] **1** *n of disease, religion etc* propagation *f*; F *(big meal)* festin *m* **2** *v/t (lay), butter* étaler; *news, rumor, disease* répandre; *arms, legs* étendre **3** *v/i* se répandre; **spreadsheet** COMPUT feuille *f* de calcul; *program* tableur *m*

sprightly ['spraɪtlɪ] alerte

spring¹ [sprɪŋ] *n season* printemps *m*

spring² [sprɪŋ] *n* device ressort *m*

spring³ [sprɪŋ] **1** *n* (*jump*) bond *m*; (*stream*) source *f* **2** *v/i* bondir

'springboard tremplin *m*; **springtime** printemps *m*

sprinkle ['sprɪŋkl] saupoudrer; **sprinkler** *for garden* arroseur *m*; *in ceiling* extincteur *m*

sprint [sprɪnt] **1** *n* sprint *m* **2** *v/i* sprinter; *fig* risquer un sprint **f**; **sprinter** SP sprinteur(-euse) *m*(*f*)

spy [spaɪ] **1** *n* espion(ne) *m*(*f*) **2** *v/i* faire de l'espionnage **3** *v/t* (*see*) apercevoir

♦ **spy on** espionner

squabble ['skwɒbl] **1** *n* querelle *f* **2** *v/i* se quereller

squalid ['skwɒlɪd] sordide; **squalor** misère *f*

squander ['skwɒndər] gaspiller

square [skwer] **1** *adj in shape* carré; **~ mile** mile carré **2** *n shape*, MATH carré *m*; *in town* place *f*; *in board game* case *f*

squash¹ [skwɒʃ] *n vegetable* courge *f*

squash² [skwɒʃ] *n game* squash *m*

squash³ [skwɒʃ] *v/t* (*crush*) écraser

squat [skwɒt] **1** *adj in shape* ramassé **2** *v/i sit* s'accroupir; *illegally* squatter

squeak [skwiːk] **1** *n of mouse* couinement *m*; *of hinge* grin-

cement *m* **2** *v/i of mouse* couiner; *of hinge* grincer

squeal [skwiːl] **1** *n* cri *m* aigu; *of brakes* grincement *m* **2** *v/i* pousser des cris aigus; *of brakes* grincer

squeamish ['skwiːmɪʃ] trop sensible

squeeze [skwiːz] *hand* serrer; *shoulder*, (*remove juice from*) presser; *fruit*, *parcel* palper

squid [skwɪd] calmar *m*

squirm [skwɜːrm] se tortiller

St (= *saint*) St(e) (= saint(e)); (= *street*) rue

stab [stæb] poignarder

stability [stəˈbɪlətɪ] stabilité *f*; **stabilize 1** *v/t* stabiliser **2** *v/i* se stabiliser; **stable 1** *adj* stable **2** *n for horses* écurie *f*

stack [stæk] **1** *n* (*pile*) pile *f* **2** *v/t* empiler

stadium ['steɪdɪəm] stade *m*

staff [stæf] (*employees*) personnel *m*; (*teachers*) personnel *m* enseignant

stage¹ [steɪdʒ] *n in project etc* étape *f*

stage² [steɪdʒ] **1** *n* THEA scène *f* **2** *v/t play* mettre en scène; *demonstration* organiser

stagger ['stægər] **1** *v/i* tituber **2** *v/t* (*amaze*) ébahir; *coffee breaks etc* échelonner; **staggering** stupéfiant

stagnant ['stægnənt] *water*, *economy* stagnant; **stagnate** *fig* stagner

'stag party enterrement *m* de

vie de garçon

stain [steɪn] **1** *n* (*dirty mark*) tache *f*; *for wood* teinture *f* **2** *v/t* (*dirty*) tacher; *wood* teindre; **stained-glass window** vitrail *m*; **stainless steel** acier *m* inoxydable

stair [ster] marche *f*; **the ~s** l'escalier *m*; **staircase** escalier *m*

stake [steɪk] **1** *n of wood* pieu *m*; *when gambling* enjeu *m*; (*investment*) investissements *mpl*; **be at ~** être en jeu **2** *v/t tree* soutenir avec un pieu; *money* jouer; *person* financer

stale [steɪl] *bread* rassis; *air* empesté; *fig: news* plus très frais

stalk¹ [stɔːk] *n of fruit, plant* tige *f*

stalk² [stɔːk] *v/t animal, person* traquer

stall¹ [stɔːl] *n at market* étalage *m*; *for cow, horse* stalle *f*

stall² [stɔːl] **1** *v/i of vehicle, engine* caler; (*play for time*) chercher à gagner du temps **2** *v/t engine* caler; *person* faire attendre

stalls [stɔːlz] THEA orchestre *m*

stalwart ['stɔːlwərt] *supporter* fidèle

stamina ['stæmɪnə] endurance *f*

stammer ['stæmər] **1** *n* bégaiement *m* **2** *v/i* bégayer

stamp¹ [stæmp] **1** *n for letter*

timbre *m*; *device, mark* tampon *m* **2** *v/t letter* timbrer; *passport* tamponner

stamp² [stæmp] *v/t*: **~ one's foot** taper du pied

stance [stæns] position *f*

stand [stænd] **1** *n at exhibition* stand *m*; (*witness ~*) barre *f* des témoins; (*support, base*) support *m*; **take the ~** LAW venir à la barre **2** *v/i* (*be situated*) se trouver; *as opposed to sit* rester debout; (*rise*) se lever **3** *v/t* (*tolerate*) supporter; (*put*) mettre

◆ **stand by 1** *v/i* (*not take action*) rester là sans rien faire; (*be ready*) se tenir prêt **2** *v/t person* soutenir; *decision* s'en tenir à

◆ **stand down** (*withdraw*) se retirer

◆ **stand for** (*tolerate*) supporter; (*represent*) représenter

◆ **stand out** *be visible* ressortir

◆ **stand up 1** *v/i* se lever **2** *v/t* F poser un lapin à

◆ **stand up for** défendre

◆ **stand up to** (*face*) tenir tête à

standard ['stændərd] **1** *adj procedure etc* normal; **~ practice** pratique *f* courante **2** *n* (*level*) niveau *m*; *moral* critère *m*; TECH norme *f*; **standardize** normaliser; **standard of living** niveau *m* de vie

'standby *fly* en stand-by;

standing *in society* position *f* sociale; (*repute*) réputation *f*;

standoffish distant;

standpoint point *m* de vue; **standstill:** *be at a* ~ être paralysé; *bring to a* ~ paralyser

staple[1] ['steɪpl] *n foodstuff* aliment *m* de base

staple[2] ['steɪpl] **1** *n fastener* agrafe *f* **2** *v/t* agrafer

stapler ['steɪplər] agrafeuse *f*

star [stɑːr] **1** *n in sky* étoile *f*; *fig also* vedette *f* **2** *v/t of movie* avoir comme vedette(s); **starboard** de tribord

stare [ster]: ~ *into space* regarder dans le vide; *it's rude to* ~ ce n'est pas poli de fixer les gens

stark [stɑːrk] **1** *adj landscape, color* austère; *reminder, contrast etc* brutal **2** *adv:* ~ *naked* complètement nu

starry ['stɑːrɪ] *night* étoilé; **Stars and Stripes** bannière *f* étoilée

start [stɑːrt] **1** *n* début *m* **2** *v/i* commencer; *of engine, car* démarrer; ~*ing from tomorrow* à partir de demain **3** *v/t* commencer; *engine, car* mettre en marche; *business* monter; **starter** *of meal* entrée *f*; *of car* démarreur *m*

startle ['stɑːrtl] effrayer; **startling** surprenant

starvation [stɑːr'veɪʃn] inanition *f*; **starve** souffrir de la faim; *I'm starving* F je meurs de faim F

state[1] [steɪt] **1** *n* (*condition, country, part of country*) état *m*; **the States** les États-Unis *mpl* **2** *adj* capital, police etc d'état; *banquet, occasion etc* officiel

state[2] [steɪt] *v/t* déclarer; *name and address* décliner

'State Department Département *m* d'État (américain); **statement** *to police* déclaration *f*; (*announcement*) communiqué *m*; (*bank* ~) relevé *m* de compte; **state of emergency** état *m* d'urgence; **state-of-the-art** de pointe; **statesman** homme *m* d'État

static (**electricity**) ['stætɪk] électricité *f* statique

station ['steɪʃn] **1** *n* RAIL gare *f*; *of subway,* RAD station *f*; TV chaîne *f* **2** *v/t guard etc* placer; **stationary** immobile

stationery ['steɪʃənrɪ] papeterie *f*

'station wagon break *m*

statistical [stə'tɪstɪkl] statistique; **statistically** statistiquement; **statistician** statisticien(ne) *m(f)*; **statistics** *science* statistique *f figures* statistiques *fpl*

statue ['stætʃuː] statue *f*; **Statue of Liberty** Statue *f* de la Liberté

status ['steɪtəs] statut *m*; (*prestige*) prestige *m*; **status symbol** signe *m* extérieur de richesse

statute ['stætʃuːt] loi *f*

staunch [stɔːntʃ] *supporter* fervent

stay [steɪ] **1** *n* séjour *m* **2** *v/i* rester; ~ *in a hotel* descendre dans un hôtel; ~ *right there!* tenez-vous là!

♦ **stay behind** rester; *in school* rester après la classe

♦ **stay up** (*not go to bed*) rester debout

steadily ['stedɪlɪ] *improve etc* de façon régulière; **steady 1** *adj* hand ferme; *voice* posé; (*regular*) régulier; (*continuous*) continu **2** *adv*: *be going ~ of couple* sortir ensemble **3** *v/t person* soutenir; *voice* raffermir

steak [steɪk] bifteck *m*

steal [stiːl] **1** *v/t* voler **2** (*be a thief*) voler; ~ *in/out* entrer/sortir à pas feutrés

stealthy ['stelθɪ] furtif

steam [stiːm] **1** *n* vapeur *f* **2** *v/t food* cuire à la vapeur; **steamed up** F fou de rage; **steamer** *for cooking* cuiseur *m* à vapeur

steel [stiːl] **1** *adj* (*made of* ~) en acier **2** *n* acier *m*; **steelworker** ouvrier(-ière) *m(f)* de l'industrie sidérurgique

steep¹ [stiːp] *adj hill etc* raide; F *prices* excessif

steep² [stiːp] *v/t* (*soak*) faire tremper

steer¹ [stɪr] *n animal* bœuf *m*

steer² [stɪr] *v/t* diriger

steering ['stɪrɪŋ] MOT direction *f*; **steering wheel** volant

stem¹ [stem] *n* of plant tige *f*; of glass pied *m*; of word racine *f*

stem² [stem] *v/t* (*block*) enrayer

stench [stentʃ] odeur *f* nauséabonde

stencil ['stensɪl] **1** *n* pochoir *m*; *pattern* peinture *f* au pochoir **2** *v/t pattern* peindre au pochoir

step [step] **1** *n* (*pace*) pas *m*; (*stair*) marche *f*; (*measure*) mesure *f* **2** *v/i*: ~ *forward/back* faire un pas en avant/en arrière

♦ **step down** *from post etc* se retirer

♦ **step up** (*increase*) augmenter

'stepbrother demi-frère *m*; **stepdaughter** belle-fille *f*; **stepfather** beau-père *m*; **stepladder** escabeau *m*; **stepmother** belle-mère *f*; **stepsister** demi-sœur *f*; **stepson** beau-fils *m*

stereo ['sterɪoʊ] (*sound system*) chaîne *f* stéréo; **stereotype** stéréotype *m*

sterile ['steraɪl] stérile; **sterilize** stériliser

sterling ['stɜːrlɪŋ] FIN sterling *m*

stern¹ [stɜːrn] *adj* sévère

stern² [stɜːrn] *n* NAUT arrière *m*

sternly ['stɜːrnlɪ] sévèrement

steroids ['sterɔɪdz] stéroïdes

mpl

stew [stu:] ragoût *m*

steward ['stjuəd] *on plane, ship* steward *m*; *at demonstration, meeting* membre *m* du service d'ordre; **stewardess** *on plane, ship* hôtesse *f*

stick¹ [stɪk] *n* morceau *m* de bois; *of policeman* bâton *m*; (*walking* ~) canne *f*

stick² [stɪk] **1** *v/t with adhesive* coller (**to** à); F (*put*) mettre **2** *v/i* (*jam*) se coincer; (*adhere*) adhérer

◆ **stick by** F ne pas abandonner

◆ **stick to** (*adhere to*) coller à; F (*keep to*) s'en tenir à; F (*follow*) suivre

◆ **stick up for** F défendre

sticker ['stɪkər] autocollant *m*; **stick-in-the-mud** F encroûté(e) *m(f)*; **sticky** gluant; *label* collant

stiff [stɪf] brush, cardboard, mixture etc dur; muscle, body raide; in manner guindé; drink bien tassé; competition acharné; fine sévère; **stiffness** *of muscles* raideur *f*; *in manner* aspect *m* guindé

stifle ['staɪfl] étouffer; **stifling** étouffant

stigma ['stɪgmə] honte *f*

still¹ [stɪl] **1** *adj* calme **2** *adv*: **keep ~!** reste tranquille!; **stand ~!** ne bouge pas!

still² [stɪl] *adv* (*yet*) encore, toujours; (*nevertheless*) quand même

'stillborn: **be ~** être mort à la naissance; **still life** nature *f* morte

stilted ['stɪltɪd] guindé

stimulant ['stɪmjulənt] stimulant *m*; **stimulate** stimuler; **stimulating** stimulant; **stimulation** stimulation *f*; **stimulus** (*incentive*) stimulation *f*

sting [stɪŋ] **1** *n from bee, jellyfish* piqûre *f* **2** *v/t & v/i* piquer; **stinging** *criticism* blessant

stink [stɪŋk] **1** *n* (*bad smell*) puanteur *f*; F (*fuss*) grabuge *m* F **2** *v/i* (*smell bad*) puer; F (*be very bad*) être nul

stipulate ['stɪpjuleɪt] stipuler; **stipulation** condition *f*; *of will, contract* stipulation *f*

stir [stɜːr] **1** *v/t* remuer **2** *v/i of sleeping person* bouger; **stirring** music, speech émouvant

stitch [stɪtʃ] **1** *n* point *m*; **~es** MED points *mpl* de suture **2** *v/t* (*sew*) coudre; **stitching** (*stitches*) couture *f*

stock [stɑːk] **1** *n* (*reserve*) réserves *fpl*; COM *of store* stock *m*; *animals* bétail *m*; FIN actions *fpl*; *for soup etc* bouillon *m*; **be in/out of ~** être en stock/épuisé **2** *v/t* COM avoir (en stock)

'stockbreeder éleveur *m*; **stockbroker** agent *m* de change; **stock exchange** bourse *f*; **stockholder** actionnaire *m/f*; **stockist** revendeur *m*; **stock market**

marché *m* boursier; **stock-pile 1** *n of food, weapons* stocks *mpl* de réserve **2** *v/t* faire des stocks de

stocky ['stɒkɪ] trapu

stodgy ['stɒdʒɪ] *food* bourratif

stoical ['stəʊɪkl] stoïque; **stoicism** stoïcisme *m*

stomach ['stʌmək] **1** *n* (*insides*) estomac *m*; (*abdomen*) ventre *m* **2** *v/t* (*tolerate*) supporter

stone [stəʊn] pierre *f*; (*pebble*) caillou *m*; **stoned** F *on drugs* défoncé F

stool [stuːl] *seat* tabouret *m*

stoop¹ [stuːp] *v/i* (*bend down*) se pencher

stoop² [stuːp] *n* (*porch*) perron *m*

stop [stɒp] **1** *n for train, bus* arrêt *m* **2** *v/t* arrêter; (*prevent*) empêcher; *check* faire opposition à; **~ doing sth** arrêter de faire qch **3** *v/i* s'arrêter

♦ **stop over** faire escale

'stopgap bouche-trou *m*; **'stoplight** (*traffic light*) feu *m* rouge; (*brake light*) stop *m*; **stopover** étape *f*; **stopper** *for bottle* bouchon *m*; **stop sign** stop *m*; **stopwatch** chronomètre *m*

storage ['stɔːrɪdʒ] COM emmagasinage *m*; *in house* rangement *m*; **store 1** *n* magasin *m*; (*stock*) provision *f*; (*~house*) entrepôt *m* **2** *v/t* en

treposer; COMPUT stocker; **storefront** devanture *f* de magasin; **storekeeper** commerçant(e) *m(f)*

storey *Br* → **story²**

storm [stɔːrm] *with rain, wind* tempête *f*; (*thunder~*) orage *m*; **stormy** orageux

story¹ ['stɔːrɪ] (*tale, account*, F: *lie*) histoire *f*; (*newspaper article*) article *m*

story² ['stɔːrɪ] *of building* étage *m*

stout [staʊt] *person* corpulent, costaud

stove [stəʊv] *for cooking* cuisinière *f*; *for heating* poêle *m*

stow [stəʊ] ranger

♦ **stow away** s'embarquer clandestinement

'stowaway passager clandestin *m*, passagère clandestine *f*

straight [streɪt] **1** *adj line, back, knees* droit; *hair* raide; (*honest, direct*) franc; (*not criminal*) honnête; *whiskey etc* sec; (*tidy*) en ordre; (*conservative*) sérieux; (*not homosexual*) hétéro F **2** *adv* (*in a straight line*) droit; (*directly, immediately*) directement; **go ~** F *of criminal* revenir dans le droit chemin; **~ ahead** tout droit; **~ away**, **~ off** tout de suite; **~ out** très clairement; **~ up** *without ice* sans glace; **straighten** redresser; **straightforward** (*honest, direct*) direct; (*sim *ple*) simple

strain¹ [streɪn] **1** *n* on rope, engine tension *f*; on heart pression *f*; **suffer from ~** souffrir de tension nerveuse **2** *v/t* back se fouler; eyes s'abîmer; finances grever

strain² [streɪn] *v/t* vegetables faire égoutter; oil, fat etc filtrer

strained [streɪnd] *relations* tendu; **strainer** for vegetables etc passoire *f*

strait [streɪt] détroit *m*; **straitlaced** collet monté *inv*

strange [streɪndʒ] (*odd, curious*) étrange, bizarre; (*unknown, foreign*) inconnu; **strangely** (*oddly*) bizarrement; **~ enough, ...** c'est bizarre, mais ...; **stranger** étranger(-ère) *m* (*f*); **he's a ~ complete** je ne le connais pas du tout; **I'm a ~ here myself** moi non plus je ne suis pas d'ici

strangle ['stræŋgl] étrangler

strap [stræp] *of purse, shoe* lanière *f*; *of brassiere, dress* bretelle *f*; *of watch* bracelet *m*; **strapless** sans bretelles

strategic [strə'tiːdʒɪk] stratégique; **strategy** stratégie *f*

straw [strɔː] *material, for drink* paille *f*; **strawberry** fraise *f*

stray [streɪ] **1** *adj animal, bullet* perdu **2** *n* animal *m* errant **3** *v/i of animal* vagabonder; *of child* s'égarer; *fig: of eyes,*

thoughts errer (**to** vers)

streak [striːk] **1** *n of dirt, paint* traînée *f*; *in hair* mèche *f*; *fig: of nastiness etc* pointe *f* **2** *v/i move quickly* filer

stream [striːm] ruisseau *m*; *fig: of people* flot *m*; **streamline** *fig* rationaliser; **streamlined** *car, plane* caréné; *organization* rationalisé

street [striːt] rue *f*; **streetcar** tramway *m*; **streetlight** réverbère *m*; **street people** sans-abri *mpl*; **street value** of drugs prix *m* à la revente;

strength [streŋθ] force *f*; (*strong point*) point *m* fort; **strengthen 1** *v/t body* fortifier; *bridge, currency, bonds etc* consolider **2** *v/i* se consolider

strenuous ['strenjʊəs] fatigant; **strenuously** *deny* vigoureusement

stress [stres] **1** *n* (*emphasis*) accent *m*; (*tension*) stress *m* **2** *v/t syllable* accentuer; *importance etc* souligner; **stressed out** F stressé *f*; **stressful** stressant

stretch [stretʃ] **1** *n of land, water* étendue *f*; *of road* partie *f* **2** *adj fabric* extensible **3** *v/t material* tendre; *small income* tirer le maximum de; F *rules* assouplir **4** *v/i to relax muscles, to reach sth* s'étirer; (*spread*) s'étendre; **stretcher** brancard *m*

strict [strɪkt] strict; **strictly**

strictement; *it is ~ forbidden*
c'est strictement défendu
stride [straɪd] **1** *n* (grand) pas
m **2** *v/i* marcher à grandes en-
jambées
strident ['straɪdnt] strident;
demands véhément
strike [straɪk] **1** *n* of workers
grève *f; in baseball* balle *f*
manquée *f; of oil* découverte
f; **be on ~** être en grève **2**
v/i of workers faire grève;
(attack: of wild animal) attaquer; *of killer* frapper; *of disaster* arriver; *of clock* sonner
3 *v/t* (hit) frapper; *match*
allumer; *oil* découvrir
◆ **strike out** *delete* rayer
strikebreaker ['straɪkbreɪk-
ər] briseur(-euse) *m(f)* de
grève; **striker** *(person on
strike)* gréviste *m/f; in soccer*
buteur *m;* **striking** *(marked,
eye-catching)* frappant
string [strɪŋ] ficelle *f; of violin, tennis racket* corde *f;*
stringed instrument instrument *m* à cordes
stringent ['strɪndʒnt] rigoureux
strip [strɪp] **1** *n* bande *f; (comic ~)* bande *f* dessinée **2** *v/t
(remove)* enlever; *(undress)*
déshabiller **3** *v/i (undress)*
se déshabiller; *of stripper* faire du strip-tease; **strip club**
boîte *f* de strip-tease
stripe [straɪp] rayure *f;* MIL galon *m;* **striped** rayé
stripper ['strɪpər] strip-tea-

seuse *f; male ~* strip-teaseur
m; **striptease** strip-tease *m*
stroke [strouk] **1** *n* MED attaque *f; when painting* coup
m de pinceau; *style of swimming* nage *f* **2** *v/t* caresser
stroll [stroul] **1** *n* balade *f* **2** *v/i*
flâner; **stroller** *for baby*
poussette *f*
strong [strɔŋ] fort; *structure*
solide; *candidate* sérieux;
support, supporter vigoureux; **strongly** fortement;
strong-minded: **be ~** avoir
de la volonté; **strong point**
point *m* fort; **strongroom**
chambre *f* forte; **strong-
willed** qui sait ce qu'il/elle
veut
structural ['strʌktʃərl] *damage* de structure; *fault, problems* de construction; **structure 1** *n (something built)*
construction *f; of novel, po-
em etc* structure *f* **2** *v/t* struc-
turer
struggle ['strʌgl] **1** *n* lutte *f* **2**
v/i with a person se battre; *~
to do sth* avoir du mal à faire
qch
strut [strʌt] se pavaner
stub [stʌb] *of cigarette* mégot
m; of check, ticket souche
f
stubborn ['stʌbərn] *person,
refusal etc* entêté; *defense* farouche
stubby ['stʌbɪ] boudiné
stuck [stʌk] F: **be ~ on s.o.**
être fou de qn

student ['stu:dnt] *at high school* élève *m/f*; *at college, university* étudiant(e) *m(f)*

studio ['stu:dɪəʊ] studio *m*; *of artist* atelier *m*

studious ['stu:dɪəs] studieux; study 1 *n room* bureau *m*; (*learning*) études *fpl*; (*investigation*) étude *f* 2 *v/t* & *v/i* étudier

stuff [stʌf] 1 *n* (*things*) trucs *mpl*; *substance*, *powder etc* truc *m*; (*belongings*) affaires *fpl* 2 *v/t* turkey farcir; **~ sth into sth** fourrer qch dans qch; **stuffing** *for turkey* farce *f*; *in chair*, *toy* rembourrage *m*; **stuffy** *room* mal aéré; *person* vieux jeu *inv*

stumble ['stʌmbl] trébucher; **stumbling block** pierre *f* d'achoppement

stump [stʌmp] 1 *n of tree* souche *f* 2 *v/t*: **I'm ~ed** je colle F

stun [stʌn] étourdir; *animal* assommer; *fig* (*shock*) abasourdir; **stunning** (*amazing*) stupéfiant; (*very beautiful*) épatant

stunt [stʌnt] *for publicity* coup *m* de publicité; *in movie* cascade *f*; **stuntman** *in movie* cascadeur *m*

stupefy ['stu:pɪfaɪ] stupéfier

stupendous [stu:'pendəs] prodigieux

stupid ['stu:pɪd] stupide; **stupidity** stupidité *f*

sturdy ['stɜ:rdɪ] robuste

stutter ['stʌtər] bégayer

style [staɪl] (*method, manner*) style *m*; (*fashion*) mode *f*; (*fashionable elegance*) classe *f*; **stylish** qui a de la classe; **stylist** (*hair ~*) styliste *m/f*

subcommittee ['sʌbkəmɪtɪ] sous-comité *m*

subconscious [sʌb'kɑ:nʃəs] subconscient; **subconsciously** subconsciemment

subcontract [sʌbkən'trakt] sous-traiter; **subcontractor** sous-traitant *m*

subdivide [sʌbdɪ'vaɪd] sous-diviser

subdue [səb'du:] contenir

subheading ['sʌbhedɪŋ] sous-titre *m*

subhuman [sʌb'hju:mən] sous-humain

subject 1 ['sʌbdʒɪkt] *n of country*, GRAM, (*topic*) sujet *m*; (*branch of learning*) matière *f* 2 ['sʌbdʒɪkt] *adj*: **be ~ to** être sujet à 3 [səb'dʒekt] *v/t* soumettre (*to* à); **subjective** subjectif

sublet ['sʌblet] sous-louer

submachine gun [sʌbmə-'ʃi:ngʌn] mitraillette *f*

submarine ['sʌbməri:n] sous-marin *m*

submission [səb'mɪʃn] (*surrender*), *to committee etc* soumission *f*; **submissive** soumis; **submit 1** *v/t plan* soumettre **2** *v/i* se soumettre

subordinate [sə'bɔ:rdɪnət] 1 *adj position* subalterne 2 *n* subordonné(e) *m(f)*

subpoena [sə'piːnə] LAW **1** n
assignation f **2** v/t person assigner à comparaître

◆ **subscribe to** [səb'skraɪb]
magazine etc s'abonner à;
theory souscrire à

subscriber [səb'skraɪbər] *to
magazine* abonné(e) m(f);
subscription abonnement
m

subsequent ['sʌbsɪkwənt]
ultérieur

subside [səb'saɪd] *of waters*
baisser; *of winds* se calmer;
of building s'affaisser; *of
fears* s'apaiser

subsidiary [səb'sɪdɪrɪ] filiale
f

subsidize ['sʌbsɪdaɪz] subventionner; **subsidy** subvention f

substance ['sʌbstəns] substance f

substandard [sʌb'stændərd]
de qualité inférieure

substantial [səb'stænʃl] considérable; *meal* consistant;
substantially (*considerably*)
considérablement; (*in essence*) de manière générale

substantive [səb'stæntɪv]
réel

substitute ['sʌbstɪtuːt] **1** n
substitut m (*for* de); SP rem-
plaçant(e) m(f) (*for* de) **2**
v/t remplacer; **~ X for Y** remplacer Y par X; **substitution**
remplacement m

subtitle ['sʌbtaɪtl] sous-titre
m

subtle ['sʌtl] subtil

subtract [səb'trækt] soustraire

suburb ['sʌbɜːrb] banlieue f;
the ~s la banlieue; **suburban** typique de la banlieue;
attitudes etc de banlieusards

subversive [səb'vɜːrsɪv] **1**
adj subversif **2** n personne f
subversive

subway ['sʌbweɪ] métro m

succeed [sək'siːd] **1** v/i réussir; *to throne* succéder à; **~ in
doing sth** réussir à faire qch
2 v/t (*come after*) succéder à;
success réussite f; **be a ~**
avoir du succès; **successful**
person qui a réussi; *talks, operation* réussi; **be ~ in doing
sth** réussir à faire qch; **suc-
cessfully** avec succès; **suc-
cessive** successif; **on three
~ days** trois jours de suite;
successor successeur m

succinct [sək'sɪŋkt] succinct

succumb [sə'kʌm] (*give in*)
succomber

such [sʌtʃ] **1** adj: **~ a** (*so much
of a*) un tel, une telle; **it was
~ a surprise** c'était une telle
surprise; (*of that kind*): **~ as**
tel/telle que; **there is no ~
word as ...** le mot ... n'existe
pas **2** adv tellement; **~ an
easy question** une question
tellement facile

suck [sʌk] **1** v/t *candy etc* sucer **2** v/i P: **it ~s** c'est merdi-
que P; **sucker** F *person*
niais(e) m(f); F (*lollipop*) su-

cette *f*; **suction** succion *f*

sudden ['sʌdn] soudain; **suddenly** tout à coup, soudain

sue [suː] poursuivre en justice

suede [sweɪd] daim *m*

suffer ['sʌfər] **1** *v/i* souffrir **2** *v/t experience* subir; **suffering** souffrance *f*

sufficient [sə'fɪʃnt] suffisant; **not ~ funds** pas assez d'argent; **sufficiently** suffisamment

suffocate ['sʌfəkeɪt] **1** *v/i* s'étouffer **2** *v/t* étouffer; **suffocation** étouffement *m*

sugar ['ʃʊgər] **1** *n* sucre *m* **2** *v/t* sucrer

suggest [sə'dʒest] suggérer; **suggestion** suggestion *f*

suicide ['suːɪsaɪd] suicide *m*

suit [suːt] **1** *n for man* costume *m*; *for woman* tailleur *m*; *in cards* couleur *f* **2** *v/t of clothes, color* aller à; **suitable** approprié, convenable; **suitably** convenablement; **suitcase** valise *f*

suite [swiːt] *of rooms* suite *f*; *furniture* salon *m* trois pièces; MUS suite *f*

sulk [sʌlk] bouder; **sulky** boudeur

sullen ['sʌlən] maussade

sultry ['sʌltrɪ] *climate* lourd; *sexually* sulfureux

sum [sʌm] *(total, amount)* somme *f*; *in arithmetic* calcul *m*

◆ **sum up 1** *v/t (summarize)* résumer; *(assess)* se faire

une idée de **2** *v/i* LAW résumer les débats

summarize ['sʌməraɪz] résumer; **summary** résumé *m*

summer ['sʌmər] été *f*

summit ['sʌmɪt] *also* POL sommet *m*

summon ['sʌmən] *staff, meeting* convoquer; **summons** LAW assignation *f* (à comparaître)

sun [sʌn] soleil *m*; **sunbathe** prendre un bain de soleil; **sunbed** lit *m* à ultraviolets; **sunblock** écran *m* solaire; **sunburn** coup *m* de soleil; **sunburnt: be ~** avoir des coups de soleil; **Sunday** dimanche *m*; **sunglasses** lunettes *fpl* de soleil; **sunny day** ensoleillé; *disposition* gai; **it's ~** il y a du soleil; **sunrise** lever *m* du soleil; **sunset** coucher *m* du soleil; **sunshade** *handheld* ombrelle *f*; *over table* parasol *m*; **sunshine** soleil *m*; **sunstroke** insolation *f*; **suntan** bronzage *m*; **get a ~** bronzer

super ['suːpər] **1** *adj* F super *inv* F **2** *n (janitor)* concierge *m/f*

superb [sʊ'pɜːrb] excellent

superficial [suːpər'fɪʃl] superficiel

superfluous [sʊ'pɜːrfluəs] superflu

superintendent [suːpərɪn'tendənt] *of apartment block* concierge *m/f*

superior [suːˈpɪərɪər] **1** *adj* supérieur **2** *n in organization* supérieur *m*

superlative [suːˈpɜːrlətɪv] **1** *adj* (*superb*) excellent **2** *n* GRAM superlatif *m*

'supermarket supermarché *m*

'superpower POL superpuissance *f*

supersonic [suːpərˈsɑːnɪk] supersonique

superstition [suːpərˈstɪʃn] superstition *f*; **superstitious** superstitieux

supervise ['suːpərvaɪz] *children activities etc* surveiller; *workers* superviser; **supervisor** *at work* superviseur *m*

supper ['sʌpər] dîner *m*

supplement ['sʌplɪmənt] (*extra payment*) supplément *m*

supplier [səˈplaɪr] COM fournisseur(-euse) *m(f)*; **supply 1** *n of electricity, water etc* alimentation *f* (**of** en); **~ and demand** l'offre et la demande; **supplies** *of food* provisions *fpl* **2** *v/t goods* fournir

support [səˈpɔːrt] **1** *n for structure* support *m*; (*backing*) soutien *m* **2** *v/t structure* supporter; *financially* entretenir; (*back*) soutenir; **supporter** *of politician, football etc team* supporteur(-trice) *m(f)*; *of theory* partisan(e) *m(f)*; **supportive** *attitude* de soutien; **be very ~ of s.o.** beaucoup soutenir qn

suppose [səˈpouz] (*imagine*)

supposer; **be ~d to do sth** (*be meant to, said to*) être censé faire qch; **supposing ...** (et) si ...; **supposedly** apparemment

suppress [səˈpres] réprimer; **suppression** répression *f*

supremacy [suːˈpreməsɪ] suprématie *f*; **supreme** suprême; **Supreme Court** Cour *f* suprême

surcharge ['sɜːrtʃɑːrdʒ] surcharge *f*

sure [ʃʊr] **1** *adj* sûr; **make ~ that ...** s'assurer que ... **2** *adv*: **~ enough** en effet; **it is hot today** F il fait vraiment chaud aujourd'hui; **~!** F mais oui, bien sûr!; **surety** *for loan* garant(e) *m(f)*

surf [sɜːrf] **1** *n on sea* écume *f* **2** *v/t the Net* surfer sur

surface ['sɜːrfɪs] **1** *n surface f* **2** *v/i from water* faire surface; (*appear*) refaire surface; **surface mail** courrier *m* par voie terrestre ou maritime

'surfboard planche *f* de surf; **surfer** surfeur(-euse) *m(f)*; **surfing** surf *m*; **go ~** aller faire du surf

surge [sɜːrdʒ] *in electric current* surtension *f*; *in demand etc* poussée *f*

surgeon ['sɜːrdʒən] chirurgien *m(f)*; **surgery** chirurgie *f*; **surgical** chirurgical; **surgically** *remove* par opération chirurgicale

surly ['sɜːrlɪ] revêche

surmount [sərˈmaʊnt] *difficulties* surmonter

surname [ˈsɜːrneɪm] nom *m* de famille

surpass [sərˈpæs] dépasser

surplus [ˈsɜːrpləs] **1** *n* surplus *m* **2** *adj* en surplus

surprise [sərˈpraɪz] **1** *n* surprise *f* **2** *v/t* étonner; *be/look ~d* être/avoir l'air surpris; **surprising** étonnant; **surprisingly** étonnamment

surrender [səˈrendər] **1** *v/i of army* se rendre **2** *v/t weapons etc* rendre **3** *n* capitulation *f*; (*handing in*) reddition *f*

surrogate mother [ˈsʌrəgət] mère *f* porteuse

surround [səˈraʊnd] **1** *v/t* entourer **2** *n of picture etc* bordure *f*; **surrounding** environnant; **surroundings** environs *mpl*; *setting* cadre *m*

survey [ˈsɜːrveɪ] *n of modern literature etc* étude *f*; *Br of building* inspection *f*; (*poll*) sondage *m* **2** [sərˈveɪ] *v/t* (*look at*) contempler; *Br building* inspecter; **surveyor** *Br* expert *m*

survival [sərˈvaɪvl] survie *f*; **survive 1** *v/i* survivre **2** *v/t accident*, (*outlive*) survivre à; **survivor** survivant(e) *m(f)*

suspect [ˈsʌspekt] *n* suspect(e) *m(f)* **2** [səˈspekt] *v/t person* soupçonner; (*suppose*) croire; **suspected** *murderer* soupçonné; *cause*, *heart attack etc* présumé

suspend [səˈspend] (*hang*), *from office* suspendre; **suspenders** *for pants* bretelles *fpl*; *Br* porte-jarretelles *m*

suspense [səˈspens] suspense *m*; **suspension** *in vehicle*, *from duty* suspension *f*

suspicion [səˈspɪʃn] soupçon *m*; **suspicious** (*causing suspicion*) suspect; (*feeling suspicion*) méfiant; *be ~ of s.o.* se méfier de qn; **suspiciously** *behave* de manière suspecte; *ask* avec méfiance

sustain [səˈsteɪn] soutenir; **sustainable** durable

SUV [esjuːˈviː] (= *sports utility vehicle*) véhicule *m* utilitaire sport

swab [swɑːb] tampon *m*

swallow[1] [ˈswɑːloʊ] *v/t & v/i* avaler

swallow[2] [ˈswɑːloʊ] *n bird* hirondelle *f*

swamp [swɑːmp] **1** *n* marécage *m* **2** *v/t be ~ed with* submergé de; **swampy** marécageux

swap [swɑːp] échanger (*for* contre)

swarm [swɔːrm] **1** *n of bees* essaim *m* **2** *v/i: the town was ~ing with ...* la ville grouillait de ...

swarthy [ˈswɔːrðɪ] basané

swat [swɑːt] *insect* écraser

sway [sweɪ] **1** *n* (*influence*, *power*) emprise *f* **2** *v/i in wind* se balancer; *because drunk*, *ill* tituber

swear [swer] **1** v/i (*use swear-word*) jurer; **~ at s.o.** injurier qn **2** v/t LAW, (*promise*) jurer
◆ **swear in** witnesses etc faire prêter serment à
'swearword juron m

sweat [swet] **1** n sueur f **2** v/i transpirer, suer; **sweat band** bandeau m en éponge; **sweater** pull m; **sweatshirt** sweat(-shirt) m; **sweaty** plein de sueur

sweep [swi:p] **1** v/t floor, leaves balayer **2** n (*long curve*) courbe f; **sweeping** statement hâtif; changes radical

sweet [swi:t] taste, tea sucré; F (*kind*) gentil; F (*cute*) mignon; **sweetcorn** maïs m; **sweeten** sucrer; **sweetheart** amoureux(-euse) m(f)

swell [swel] **1** v/i of wound, limb enfler **2** adj F (*good*) super F inv **3** n of the sea houle f; **swelling** MED enflure f

swerve [sw3:rv] of driver, car s'écarter brusquement

swift [swift] rapide

swim [swim] **1** v/i nager **2** n baignade f; **go for a ~** aller se baigner; **swimmer** nageur(-euse) m(f); **swimming** natation f; **swimming pool** piscine f; **swimsuit** maillot m de bain

swindle ['swindl] **1** n escroquerie f **2** v/t escroquer; **~ s.o. out of sth** escroquer qch à qn

swing [swiŋ] **1** n oscillation f; for child balançoire f; **~ to the Democrats** revirement m d'opinion en faveur des démocrates **2** v/t object in hand, hips balancer **3** v/i se balancer; (*turn*) tourner; of public opinion etc virer

Swiss [swis] **1** adj suisse **2** n person Suisse m/f; **the ~** les Suisses mpl

switch [switʃ] **1** n for light bouton m; (*change*) changement m **2** v/t (*change*) changer de **3** v/i (*change*) passer
◆ **switch off** lights, engine, PC éteindre; engine arrêter
◆ **switch on** lights, engine, PC allumer; engine démarrer

Switzerland ['switsərlənd] Suisse f

swivel ['swivl] pivoter

swollen ['swoulən] stomach ballonné; ankles, face enflé

syllabus ['siləbəs] programme m

symbol ['simbəl] symbole m; **symbolic** symbolique; **symbolism** symbolisme m; **symbolist** symboliste m/f; **symbolize** symboliser

symmetrical [si'metrikl] symétrique; **symmetry** symétrie

sympathetic [simpə'θetik] (*showing pity*) compatissant; (*understanding*) compréhensif
◆ **sympathize with** ['simpə-

θaiz] *person* compatir avec; *views* avoir des sympathies pour

sympathizer ['simpəθaizər] POL sympathisant(e) *m(f)*; **sympathy** (*pity*) compassion *f*; (*understanding*) compréhension (**for** de)

symphony ['simfəni] symphonie *f*

symptom ['simptəm] MED, *fig* symptôme *m*

synchronize ['siŋkrənaiz] synchroniser

synonym ['sinənim] synonyme *m*; **synonymous** synonyme

synthesizer   ['sinθəsaizər]

MUS synthétiseur *m*; **synthetic** synthétique

syphilis ['sifilis] syphilis *f*

Syria ['siriə] Syrie *f*; **Syrian 1** *adj* syrien **2** *n* Syrien(ne) *m(f)*

syringe [si'rindʒ] seringue *f*

syrup ['sirəp] sirop *m*

system ['sistəm] système *m*; (*orderliness*) ordre *m*; (*computer*) ordinateur *m*; **systematic** systématique; **systematically** systématiquement

systems analyst COMPUT analyste-programmeur(-euse) *m(f)*

T

table ['teibl] table *f*; *of figures* tableau *m*; **tablecloth** nappe *f*; **table lamp** petite lampe *f*; **table of contents** table *f* des matières; **tablespoon** cuillère *f* à soupe

tablet ['tæblit] MED comprimé *m*; COMPUT tablette *f*

tabloid ['tæbloid] *newspaper* journal *m* à sensation

taboo [tə'bu:] tabou *inv in feminine*

tacit ['tæsit] tacite

tack [tæk] **1** *n* nail clou *m* **2** *v/t in sewing* bâtir **3** *v/i of yacht* louvoyer

tackle ['tækl] **1** *n* (*equipment*) attirail *m*; SP tacle *m*; *in rug-*

by plaquage *m* **2** *v/t* SP tacler; *in rugby* plaquer; *problem* s'attaquer à; (*confront*) confronter; *physically* s'opposer à

tacky ['tæki] *paint, glue* collant; F (*cheap, poor quality*) minable F

tact [tækt] tact *m*; **tactful** diplomate; **tactfully** avec tact

tactical ['tæktikl] tactique; **tactics** tactique *f* a

tactless ['tæktlis] qui manque de tact, peu délicat

tag [tæg] (*label*) étiquette *f*

tail [teil] queue *f*; **tail light** feu *m* arrière

tailor ['teilər] tailleur *m*; **tai-**

lor-made *also fig* fait sur mesure

'**tail pipe** *of car* tuyau *m*
d'échappement

take [teɪk] prendre; (*transport,
accompany*) amener; *subject
at school, photograph, photocopy, stroll* faire; *exam* passer; (*endure*) supporter; (*require: courage etc*) demander; **how long will it ~ you
to ...?** combien de temps
est-ce que tu vas mettre pour
...?

◆ **take after** ressembler à
◆ **take away** *object* enlever;
pain faire disparaître; MATH
soustraire (**from** de)
◆ **take back** *object* rapporter;
person to a place ramener;
she wouldn't take him back
husband elle ne voulait pas
qu'il revienne
◆ **take down** *from shelf* enlever; *scaffolding* démonter;
pants baisser; (*write down*)
noter
◆ **take in** (*take indoors*) rentrer; (*give accommodation
to*) héberger; (*make nar-
rower*) reprendre; (*deceive*)
duper; (*include*) inclure
◆ **take off** *v/t clothes, hat*
enlever; *10% etc* faire une
réduction de; (*mimic*) imiter
2 *v/i of airplane* décoller; (*become popular*) réussir
◆ **take on** *job* accepter; *staff*
embaucher
◆ **take out** *from bag, pocket*

sortir (**from** de); *tooth, word
from text* enlever; *money
from bank* retirer; *to dinner,
theater etc* emmener; *insurance policy* souscrire à

◆ **take over 1** *v/t company etc*
reprendre **2** *v/i* POL arriver au
pouvoir; *of new director*
prendre ses fonctions; (*do
sth in s.o.'s place*) prendre
la relève
◆ **take up** *carpet etc* enlever;
(*carry up*) monter; *dress etc*
raccourcir; *judo, Spanish
etc* se mettre à; *new job* commencer; *space, time* prendre;
offer accepter

'**takeoff** *of airplane* décollage
m; (*impersonation*) imitation
f; **takeover** COM rachat *m*;
takeover bid *offre f* publique
d'achat, OPA *f*; **takings** recette *f*

tale [teɪl] histoire *f*

talent ['tælənt] talent *m*; **talented** doué; **talent scout** dé-
nicheur(-euse) *m(f)* de ta-
lents

talk [tɔːk] **1** *v/t & v/i* parler; **~
business** parler affaires **2** *n*
(*conversation*) conversation
f; (*lecture*) exposé *m*; **~s**
pourparlers *mpl*
◆ **talk back** répondre
talkative ['tɔːkətɪv] bavard;
talk show talk-show *m*

tall [tɔːl] grand

tally ['tælɪ] **1** *n* compte *m* **2** *v/i*
correspondre; *of stories* con-
corder

tame [teɪm] apprivoisé; *not wild* pas sauvage; *joke etc* fade

◆ **tamper with** ['tæmpər] toucher à

tampon ['tæmpɑːn] tampon *m*

tan [tæn] **1** *n from sun* bronzage; *color* marron clair **2** *v/i in sun* bronzer **3** *v/t leather* tanner

tangent ['tændʒənt] MATH tangente *f*

tangible ['tændʒɪbl] tangible

tangle ['tæŋgl] enchevêtrement *m*

tango ['tæŋgoʊ] tango *m*

tank [tæŋk] MOT, *for water* réservoir *m*; *for fish* aquarium *m*; MIL char *m*; *for skin diver* bonbonne *f* d'oxygène; **tanker** (*oil* ~) pétrolier *m*; *truck* camion-citerne *m*

tanned [tænd] bronzé

tantalizing ['tæntəlaɪzɪŋ] alléchant

tantrum ['tæntrəm] caprice *m*

tap [tæp] **1** *n Br* (*faucet*) robinet *m* **2** *v/t* (*knock*) taper; *phone* mettre sur écoute

tape [teɪp] **1** *n for recording* bande *f*; *recording* cassette *f*; *sticky* ruban *m* adhésif **2** *v/t conversation etc* enregistrer; *with sticky tape* scotcher; **tape deck** platine *f* cassettes; **tape drive** COMPUT lecteur *m* de bandes; **tape measure** mètre *m* ruban

taper ['teɪpər] *of stick* s'effi-

ler; *of column, pant legs* se rétrécir

'**tape recorder** magnétophone *m*; **tape recording** enregistrement *m*

tar [tɑːr] goudron *m*

tardy ['tɑːrdɪ] tardif

target ['tɑːrgɪt] **1** *n in shooting* cible *f*; *fig* objectif *m* **2** *v/t market* cibler

'**target audience** public *m* cible; **target date** date *f* visée; **target market** marché *m* cible

tariff ['tærɪf] (*customs* ~) taxe *f*; (*prices*) tarif *m*

tarmac ['tɑːrmæk] *at airport* tarmac *m*

tarnish ['tɑːrnɪʃ] ternir

tarpaulin [tɑːr'pɔːlɪn] bâche *f*

tart [tɑːrt] tarte *f*

task [tæsk] tâche *f*; **task force** commission *f*; MIL corps *m* expéditionnaire

taste [teɪst] **1** *n* goût *m* **2** *v/t* goûter; (*perceive taste of*) sentir; *try, fig* goûter à **3** *v/i: it ~s like ...* ça a (un) goût de ...; *tasteful* de bon goût; *tastefully* avec goût; **tasteless** *food* fade; *remark, décor* de mauvais goût; **tasting** *of wine* dégustation *f*; **tasty** délicieux

tattered ['tætərd] en lambeaux

tattoo [tə'tuː] tatouage *m*

taunt [tɔːnt] **1** *n* raillerie *f* **2** *v/t* se moquer de

taut [tɒt] tendu

tax [tæks] **1** *n* on income impôt *m*; on goods, services taxe *f* **2** *v/t* income imposer; goods, services taxer; **taxable income** revenu *m* imposable; **taxation** *act* imposition *f*; (*taxes*) charges *fpl* fiscales; **tax bracket** fourchette *f* d'impôts; **tax-deductible** déductible des impôts; **tax evasion** fraude *f* fiscale; **tax-free** hors taxe; **tax haven** paradis *m* fiscal

taxi ['tæksı] taxi *m*; **taxi driver** chauffeur *m* de taxi

taxing ['tæksıŋ] exténuant

'taxi stand, *Br* **'taxi rank** station *f* de taxis

'taxpayer contribuable *m/f*; **tax return** déclaration *f* d'impôts; **tax year** année *f* fiscale

TB [tiː'biː] (= *tuberculosis*) tuberculose *f*

tea [tiː] *drink* thé *m*; **teabag** sachet *m* de thé

teach [tiːtʃ] enseigner; *person* enseigner à; **teacher** professeur *m/f*; *in elementary school* instituteur(-trice) *m(f)*; **teaching** *profession* enseignement *m*

'teacup tasse *f* à thé

teak [tiːk] tek *m*

team [tiːm] équipe *f*; **team spirit** esprit *m* d'équipe; **teamster** camionneur(-euse) *m(f)*; **teamwork** travail *m* d'équipe

teapot ['tiːpɒt] théière *f*

tear¹ [ter] **1** *n* in cloth etc dé-

chirure *f* **2** *v/t paper, cloth* déchirer **3** *v/i* (*run fast, drive fast*): **she tore down the street** elle a descendu la rue en trombe

◆ **tear down** *poster* arracher; *building* démolir

◆ **tear out** *page* arracher

◆ **tear up** déchirer; *contract etc* annuler

tear² [tır] *n* in eye larme *f*; **be in ~s** être en larmes; **tearful** *look* plein de larmes; **tear gas** gaz *m* lacrymogène

tease [tiːz] taquiner

'teaspoon cuillère *f* à café

technical ['teknıkl] technique; **technically** (*strictly speaking*) en théorie; **technician** technicien(ne) *m(f)*; **technique** technique *f*

technological [teknə'lɒdʒɪkl] technologique; **technology** technologie *f*; **technophobia** technophobie *f*

teddy bear ['tedıber] ours *m* en peluche

tedious ['tiːdıəs] ennuyeux

tee [tiː] *in golf* tee *m*

teenage ['tiːneɪdʒ] *fashion* pour adolescents; **teenager** adolescent(e) *m(f)*

teens [tiːnz] adolescence *f*

teeny ['tiːnı] F tout petit

teeth [tiːθ] *pl* → **tooth**

teethe [tiːð] faire ses dents

telecommunications [telıkəmjuːnı'keɪʃnz] télécommunications *fpl*

telegraph pole ['telıgræfpool] *Br* poteau *m* télégraphique

telepathic [telɪˈpæθɪk] télépathique; **telepathy** télépathie *f*

telephone [ˈtelɪfoun] **1** *n* téléphone *m* **2** *v/t person* téléphoner à **3** *v/i* téléphoner; **telephone book** annuaire *m*; **telephone booth** cabine *f* téléphonique; **telephone call** appel *m* téléphonique; **telephone conversation** conversation *f* téléphonique; **telephone directory** annuaire *m*; **telephone number** numéro *m* de téléphone

telephoto lens [telɪˈfoutoulenz] téléobjectif *m*

telesales [ˈtelɪseɪlz] télévente *f*

telescope [ˈtelɪskoup] télescope *m*

televise [ˈtelɪvaɪz] téléviser

television [ˈtelɪvɪʒn] *also set* télévision *f*; **on ~** à la télévision; **television program**, *Br* **television programme** émission *f* télévisée; **television studio** studio *m* de télévision

tell [tel] **1** *v/t story* raconter; *lie* dire; *I can't ~ the difference* je n'arrive pas à faire la différence; **~ s.o. sth** dire qch à qn; **on ~ s.o. to do sth** dire à qn de faire qch **2** *v/i* (*have effect*) se faire sentir; **teller** *in bank* guichetier(-ière) *m(f)*; **telling off**: **get a ~** se faire re-

monter les bretelles F; **telltale 1** *adj signs* révélateur **2** *n* rapporteur(-euse) *m(f)*

temp [temp] **1** *n employee* intérimaire *m/f* **2** *v/i* faire de l'intérim

temper [ˈtempər] (*bad ~*) mauvaise humeur *f*; **lose one's ~** se mettre en colère

temperament [ˈtempərmənt] tempérament *m*; **temperamental** (*moody*) capricieux

temperate [ˈtempərət] tempéré

temperature [ˈtemprətʃər] température *f*

temple¹ [ˈtempl] REL temple *m*

temple² [ˈtempl] ANAT tempe *f*

tempo [ˈtempou] MUS tempo *m*

temporarily [tempəˈrerɪlɪ] temporairement; **temporary** temporaire

tempt [tempt] tenter; **temptation** tentation *f*; **tempting** tentant

ten [ten] dix

tenacious [tɪˈneɪʃəs] tenace; **tenacity** ténacité *f*

tenant [ˈtenənt] locataire *m/f*

tend¹ [tend] *v/t lawn* entretenir; *sheep* garder; *the sick* soigner

tend² [tend] *v/i*: **~ to do sth** avoir tendance à faire qch

tendency [ˈtendənsɪ] tendance *f*

tender¹ [ˈtendər] *adj* (*sore*) sensible; (*affectionate*), *steak* tendre *f* tendre

tender² ['tendər] n COM offre f

tenderness ['tendənɪs] of kiss etc tendresse f; of steak tendreté f

tendon ['tendən] tendon m

tennis ['tenɪs] tennis m; **tennis ball** balle f de tennis; **tennis court** court m de tennis; **tennis player** joueur(-euse) m(f) de tennis

tenor ['tenər] MUS ténor m

tense¹ [tens] n GRAM temps m

tense² [tens] adj tendu

tension ['tenʃn] tension f

tent [tent] tente f

tentative ['tentətɪv] smile, steps hésitant; conclusion, offer provisoire

tenth [tenθ] dixième

tepid ['tepɪd] also fig tiède

term [tɜːrm] n (period, word) terme m; Br EDU trimestre m; (condition) condition f; be on good/bad ~s with s.o. être en bons/mauvais termes avec qn; in the long/short~ à long/court terme

terminal ['tɜːrmɪnl] 1 n at airport aérogare m; for buses terminus m; for containers, COMPUT terminal m; ELEC borne f 2 adj illness incurable; **terminally**: ~ ill en phase terminale; **terminate 1** v/t mettre fin à; pregnancy interrompre 2 v/i se terminer; **termination** of contract résiliation f; in pregnancy interrup-

tion f volontaire de grossesse

terminus ['tɜːrmɪnəs] terminus m

terrace ['terəs] terrasse f

terrain [te'reɪn] terrain m

terrible ['terəbl] horrible, affreux; **terribly** (very) très

terrific [tə'rɪfɪk] génial; **terrifically** (very) extrêmement, vachement F

terrify ['terɪfaɪ] terrifier; **terrifying** terrifiant

territorial [terə'tɔːrɪəl] territorial; **territory** territoire m; fig domaine m

terror ['terər] terreur f; **terrorism** terrorisme m; **terrorist** terroriste m/f; **terrorist attack** attentat m terroriste; **terrorize** terroriser

terse [tɜːrs] laconique

test [test] 1 n scientific, technical test m; academic, for driving examen m 2 v/t tester, mettre à l'épreuve; **test-drive** car essayer

testicle ['testɪkl] testicule m

testify ['testɪfaɪ] LAW témoigner

testimony ['testɪmənɪ] LAW témoignage m

testy ['testɪ] irritable

tetanus ['tetənəs] tétanos m

text [tekst] 1 n texte m; message texto m 2 v/t envoyer un texto à; **textbook** manuel m; **text-message** texto m, SMS m

textile ['tekstaɪl] textile m

texture ['tekstʃər] texture f

than [ðæn] que; *with numbers* de; *faster ~ me* plus rapide que moi

thank [θæŋk] remercier; *~ you* merci; *no ~ you* (non) merci; *thankful* reconnaissant; *thankfully* (luckily) heureusement; *thankless task* ingrat; *thanks* remerciements *mpl*; *~!* merci!; *~ to* grâce à; **Thanksgiving** (**Day**) jour *m* de l'action de grâces, Thanksgiving *m*

that [ðæt] **1** *adj* ce, cette; *masculine before vowel* cet; *~ one* celui-là, celle-là **2** *pron* cela, ça; *give me ~* donne-moi ça; *~'s tea* c'est du thé; *what is ~?* qu'est-ce que c'est que ça?; *who is ~?* qui est-ce? **3** *rel pron* que; *the car ~ you see* la voiture que vous voyez **4** *adv* (so) aussi; *~ expensive* aussi cher **5** *conj* que; *I think ~ ...* je pense que ...

thaw [θɔː] *of snow* fondre; *of frozen food* se décongeler

the [ðə] le, la; *pl* les; *to the station/theater* à la gare/au théâtre; *~ more I try* plus j'essaie

theater, *Br* **theatre** [ˈθɪətər] théâtre *m*; *theatrical also fig* théâtral

theft [θeft] vol *m*

their [ðer] leur; *pl* leurs; (*his or her*) son, sa; *pl* ses; **theirs** le leur, la leurs; *it's ~* c'est à eux/elles

them [ðem] *object* les; *indirect object* leur; *with prep* eux, elles; *I know ~* je les connais; *I gave ~ a dollar* je leur ai donné un dollar; *this is for ~* c'est pour eux/elles; *who? ~ ~* qui? - eux/elles

theme [θiːm] thème *m*; *theme park* parc *m* à thème

themselves [ðemˈselvz] eux-mêmes, elles-mêmes; *reflexive* se; *after prep* eux, elles; *they gave ~ a holiday* ils se sont offerts des vacances

then [ðen] (at that time) à l'époque; (after that) ensuite; deducing alors; *by ~* alors

theoretical [θɪəˈretɪkl] théorique; *theoretically* en théorie; *theory* théorie *f*

therapeutic [θerəˈpjuːtɪk] thérapeutique; *therapist* thérapeute *m/f*; *therapy* thérapie *f*

there [ðer] là; *over ~/down ~* là-bas; *~ is/are ...* il y a ...; *is/are ~ ...?* est-ce qu'il y a ...?, y a-t-il ...?; *~ is/are not ...* il n'y a pas ...; *~ you are* voilà; *~ and back* aller et retour; *~ he is!* le voilà!; *~, ~!* allons, allons; *we went ~ yesterday* nous y sommes allés hier; *thereabouts: $500 or ~* environ 500 $; *therefore* donc

thermometer [θərˈmɑːmɪtər] thermomètre *m*

thermos flask [ˈθɜːrməsflæsk] thermos *m*

these [ðiːz] **1** *adj* ces **2** *pron* ceux-ci, celles-ci

thesis ['θiːsɪs] thèse *f*

they [ðeɪ] ils, elles; *(he or she)* il; *there ~ are* les voilà; *~ say that ...* on dit que ...

thick [θɪk] *adj*: F *(stupid)* lourd; *it's 3 cm ~* ça fait 3 cm d'épaisseur; **thicken** *sauce* épaissir; **thick--skinned** *fig* qui a la peau dure

thief [θiːf] voleur(-euse) *m(f)*

thigh [θaɪ] cuisse *f*

thin [θɪn] *material* léger, fin; *layer* mince; *person* maigre; *line* fin; *soup* liquide

thing [θɪŋ] chose *f*; *~s (belongings)* affaires *fpl*

think [θɪŋk] penser; *I ~ so* je pense que oui; *I don't ~ so* je ne pense pas; *I'll ~ about it* offer je vais y réfléchir

◆ **think over** réfléchir à

◆ **think through** bien examiner

◆ **think up** *plan* concevoir

'**think tank** comité *m* d'experts

thin-skinned ['θɪnskɪnd] *fig* susceptible

third [θɜːrd] **1** *adj* troisième **2** *n* troisième *m/f*; **thirdly** troisièmement; **third-party** tiers *m*; **third-party insurance** *Br* assurance *f* au tiers; **Third World** Tiers-Monde *m*

thirst [θɜːrst] soif *f*; **thirsty** assoiffé; *be ~* avoir soif

thirteen [θɜːr'tiːn] treize; **thir-teenth** treizième; **thirtieth** trentième; **thirty** trente

this [ðɪs] **1** *adj* ce, cette; *masculine before vowel* cet; *~ one* celui-ci, celle-ci **2** *pron* cela, ça; *~ is good* c'est bien; *~ is ...* c'est ...; *introducing s.o.* je vous présente ... **3** *adv*: *~ high* haut comme ça

thorn [θɔːrn] épine *f*; **thorny** *also fig* épineux

thorough ['θʌroʊ] *search, knowledge* approfondi; *person* méticuleux; **thorough-bred** *horse* pur-sang *m*; **thoroughly** complètement; *clean, search for, know* à fond

those [ðoʊz] **1** *adj* ces **2** *pron* ceux-là, celles-là

though [ðoʊ] **1** *conj* (*although*) bien que (+subj), quoique (+subj); *as ~* comme si **2** *adv* pourtant

thought [θɔːt] pensée *f*; **thoughtful** pensif; *book* profond; *(considerate)* attentionné; **thoughtless** inconsidéré

thousand ['θaʊznd] mille *m*; *~s of* des milliers *mpl* de; **thousandth 1** *adj* millième **2** *n* millième *m/f*

thrash [θræʃ] rouer de coups; *sp* battre à plates coutures

◆ **thrash out** *solution* parvenir à

thrashing volée *f* de coups; *get a ~* *sp* se faire battre à plates coutures

thread [θred] **1** *n* fil *m*; *of screw* filetage *m* **2** *v/t needle, beads* enfiler; **threadbare** usé jusqu'à la corde

threat [θret] menace *f*; **threaten** menacer; **threatening** menaçant

three [θri:] trois; **three-quarters** les trois-quarts *mpl*

threshold ['θreʃhəʊld] *of house, new era* seuil *m*

thrifty ['θrɪftɪ] économe

thrill [θrɪl] **1** *n* frisson *m* **2** *v/t*: **be ~ed** être ravi; **thriller** thriller *m*; **thrilling** palpitant

thrive [θraɪv] *of plants* bien pousser; *of business* prospérer

throat [θrəʊt] gorge *f*; **throat lozenge** pastille *f* pour la gorge

throb [θrɒb] **1** *n of heart* pulsation *f*; *of music* vibration *f* **2** *v/i of heart* battre fort; *of music* vibrer

throne [θrəʊn] trône *m*

throttle ['θrɒtl] **1** *n on motorbike, boat* papillon *m* des gaz **2** *v/t* (*strangle*) étrangler

through [θruː] **1** *prep*
◇ (*across*) à travers; **go ~ the city** traverser la ville
◇ (*during*) pendant; **all ~ the night** toute la nuit; **Monday ~ Friday** du lundi au vendredi (inclus)
◇ (*by means of*) par **2** *adv*: **wet ~** mouillé jusqu'aux os **3** *adj*: **be ~** (*have arrived: of news etc*) être parvenu; **we're**

~ of couple c'est fini entre nous; **be ~ with s.o./sth** en avoir fini avec qn/qch; **throughout 1** *prep* tout au long de; pendant tout(e) **2** *adv* (*in all parts*) partout

throw [θrəʊ] **1** *v/t* jeter, lancer; *of horse* désarçonner; (*disconcert*) déconcerter; *party* organiser **2** *n* jet *m*; **it's your ~** c'est à toi de lancer

◆ **throw away** jeter

◆ **throw out** *old things* jeter; *from bar, home* jeter dehors, mettre à la porte; *from country* expulser; *plan* rejeter

◆ **throw up 1** *v/t ball* jeter en l'air **2** *v/i* (*vomit*) vomir

throw-away ['θrəʊəweɪ] (*disposable*) jetable; *remark* en l'air; **throw-in** SP remise *f* en jeu

thru [θruː] → **through**

thrust [θrʌst] (*push hard*) enfoncer

thud [θʌd] bruit *m* sourd

thug [θʌg] brute *f*

thumb [θʌm] **1** *n* pouce *m* **2** *v/t*: **~ a ride** faire de l'auto-stop; **thumbtack** punaise *f*

thunder ['θʌndər] tonnerre *m*; **thunderous** *applause* tonitruant; **thunderstorm** orage *m*; **thunderstruck** abasourdi; **thundery** *weather* orageux

Thursday ['θɜːrzdeɪ] jeudi *m*

thus [ðʌs] ainsi

thwart [θwɔːrt] contrarier

tick [tɪk] **1** *n of clock* tic-tac *m*

Br (checkmark) coche *f* **2** *v/i* faire tic-tac

ticket ['tɪkɪt] *for bus, museum* ticket *m*; *for train, airplane, theater, concert, lottery* billet *m*; *for speeding, illegal parking* P.V. *m*; **ticket machine** distributeur *m* de billets; **ticket office** billetterie *f*

ticking ['tɪkɪŋ] *noise* tic-tac *m*

tickle ['tɪkl] chatouiller

tidal wave ['taɪdlweɪv] raz-de-marée *m*

tide [taɪd] marée *f*

tidiness ['taɪdɪnɪs] ordre *m*; **tidy** *person, habits* ordonné; *room, house, desk* en ordre
♦ **tidy up 1** *v/t room, shelves* ranger; **tidy o.s. up** remettre de l'ordre dans sa tenue **2** *v/i* ranger

tie [taɪ] **1** *n (necktie)* cravate *f*; SP *(even result)* match *m* à égalité; **he doesn't have any ~s** il n'a aucune attache **2** *v/t laces* nouer; *knot* faire; *hands* lier **3** *v/i* SP *of teams* faire match nul; *of runner* finir ex æquo
♦ **tie down** attacher; *fig (restrict)* restreindre
♦ **tie up** *hair* attacher; *person* ligoter; *boat* amarrer

tier [tɪr] *of hierarchy* niveau *m*; *of seats* gradin *m*

tight [taɪt] **1** *adj clothes, knot, screw* serré; *shoes* trop petit; *(properly shut)* bien fermé; *not leaving much time* juste; *security* strict; F *(drunk)*

bourré F **2** *adv* hold fort; *shut* bien; **tighten** *control, security* renforcer; *screw* serrer; *(make tighter)* resserrer; **tight-fisted** radin; **tightly** *adv* → **tight** *adv*; **tightrope** corde *f* raide; **tights** *Br* collant *m*

tile [taɪl] *on floor, wall* carreau *m*; *on roof* tuile *f*

till¹ [tɪl] → **until**

till² [tɪl] *(cash register)* caisse *f*

tilt [tɪlt] pencher

timber ['tɪmbər] bois *m*

time [taɪm] **1** *n* temps *m*; *(occasion)* fois *f*; **have a good ~** bien s'amuser; **what's the ~?** quelle heure est-il?; **the first ~** la première fois; **all the ~** pendant tout ce temps; **at the same ~** speak, reply etc, *(however)* en même temps; **in ~** à temps; **on ~** à l'heure **2** *v/t* chronométrer; **time bomb** bombe *f* à retardement; **time difference** décalage *m* horaire; **time-lag** laps *m* de temps; **time limit** limite *f* dans le temps; **timely** opportun; **time out** SP temps *m* mort; **time** *device* minuteur *m*; **timesaving** économie *f* de temps; **timescale** *of project* durée *f*; **time switch** minuterie *f*; **time zone** fuseau *m* horaire

timid ['tɪmɪd] timide

tin [tɪn] *metal* étain *m*; **tinfoil** papier *m* aluminium

tinge [tɪndʒ] soupçon *m*

tingle ['tɪŋgl] picoter

tinkle ['tɪŋkl] *of bell* tintement *m*

tinsel ['tɪnsl] guirlandes *fpl* de Noël

tint [tɪnt] **1** *n of color* teinte *f*; *for hair* couleur *f* **2** *v/t*: ~ **one's hair** se faire une coloration; **tinted** *glasses* teinté; *paper* de couleur pastel

tiny ['taɪnɪ] minuscule

tip¹ [tɪp] *n (end)* bout *m*

tip² [tɪp] **1** *n advice* conseil *m*; *money* pourboire *m* **2** *v/t waiter etc* donner un pourboire à

◆ **tip off** informer

'**tip-off** renseignement *m*, tuyau *m* F

tipped [tɪpt] *cigarettes* à bout filtre

tippy-toe ['tɪpɪtoʊ]: *on* ~ sur la pointe des pieds

tipsy ['tɪpsɪ] éméché

tire¹ ['taɪr] *n* pneu *m*

tire² ['taɪr] **1** *v/t* fatiguer **2** *v/i* se fatiguer

tired ['taɪrd] fatigué; **tiredness** fatigue *f*; **tireless** *efforts* infatigable; **tiresome** *(annoying)* fatigant; **tiring** fatigant

tissue ['tɪʃuː] ANAT tissu *m*; *handkerchief* mouchoir *m* en papier; **tissue paper** papier *m* de soie

title ['taɪtl] *of novel, person etc* titre *m*; LAW titre *m* de propriét é *(to* de); **titleholder** SP tenant(e) *m(f)* du titre

to [tuː] **1** *prep* à; ~ *Japan* au Japon; ~ *Chicago* à Chicago; ~ *my place* chez moi; ~ *the north of* au nord de; *give sth* ~ *s.o.* donner qch à qn **2** *with verbs*: ~ *speak*, ~ *shout* parler, crier; *learn* ~ *drive* apprendre à conduire; *too heavy* ~ *carry* trop lourd à porter **3** *adv*: ~ *and fro walk, pace* de long en large

toast [toʊst] **1** *n for eating* pain *m* grillé; *when drinking* toast *m*; *propose a* ~ *to s.o.* porter un toast à qn **2** *v/t when drinking* porter un toast à

toaster grille-pain *m inv*

tobacco [təˈbækoʊ] tabac *m*

today [təˈdeɪ] aujourd'hui

toddler ['tɑːdlər] jeune enfant *m*

to-do [təˈduː] F remue-ménage *m*

toe [toʊ] orteil *m*; *of sock, shoe* bout *m*; **toenail** ongle *m* de pied

together [təˈgeðər] ensemble; *(at the same time)* en même temps

toilet ['tɔɪlət] toilettes *fpl*; **toilet paper** papier *m* hygiénique; **toiletries** articles *mpl* de toilette

token ['toʊkən] *sign* témoignage *m*; *Br (gift* ~) bon *m* d'achat; *instead of coin* jeton *m*

tolerable ['tɑːlərəbl] *pain etc* tolérable; *(quite good)* acceptable; **tolerance** tolérance *f*; **tolerant** tolérant; **tolerate** tolérer

toll¹ [tʊl] *v/i* of bell sonner

toll² [tʊl] *n* (deaths) bilan *m*

toll³ [tʊl] *n* for bridge, road péage *m*

'toll booth poste *m* de péage; **toll-free** TELEC gratuit; ~ **number** numéro *m* vert

tomato [təˈmeɪtoʊ] tomate *f*; **tomato ketchup** ketchup *m*

tomb [tuːm] tombe *f*; **tombstone** pierre *f* tombale

tomcat [ˈtɑːmkæt] matou *m*

tomorrow [təˈmɑːroʊ] demain; *the day after* ~ après-demain; ~ *morning* demain matin

ton [tʌn] tonne *f* courte (=*907 kg*)

tone [toʊn] of color, conversation ton *m*; of musical instrument timbre *m*; of neighborhood classe *f*; ~ *of voice* ton *m*; **toner** toner *m*

tongue [tʌŋ] langue *f*

tonic [ˈtɑːnɪk] MED fortifiant *m*; **tonic (water)** Schweppes® *m*, tonic *m*

tonight [təˈnaɪt] ce soir; *sleep* cette nuit

too [tuː] (also) aussi; (excessively) trop; *me* ~ moi aussi; ~ *much rice* trop de riz

tool [tuːl] outil *m*

tooth [tuːθ] dent *f*; **toothache** mal *m* de dents; **toothbrush** brosse *f* à dents; **toothpaste** dentifrice *m*; **toothpick** cure-

-dents *m*

top [tɑːp] **1** *n* also clothing haut *m*; (lid: of bottle etc) bouchon *m*; of pen capuchon *m*; of the class, league premier(-ère) *m(f)*; MOT: gear quatrième *f*; *cinquième f*; *on*~ *of* sur; *be at the* ~ *of* être en haut de; *be at the* ~ *of league* être premier de; *get to the* ~ *of* company, mountain être arriver au sommet **2** *adj* branches du haut; *floor* dernier; *player etc* meilleur; *speed* maximum; *note* le plus élevé; ~ *official* haut fonctionnaire *m*

topic [ˈtɑːpɪk] sujet *m*; **topical** d'actualité

topless [ˈtɑːplɪs] aux seins nus; **topmost** branch le plus haut; *floor* dernier; **topping** *on pizza* garniture *f*

topple [ˈtɑːpl] **1** *v/i* s'écrouler **2** *v/t* government renverser

top 'secret top secret *inv*

topsy-turvy [tɑːpsɪˈtɜːrvɪ] sens dessus dessous

torment 1 [ˈtɔːrment] *n* tourment *m* **2** [tɔːrˈment] *v/t* person, animal harceler

tornado [tɔːrˈneɪdoʊ] tornade *f*

torpedo [tɔːrˈpiːdoʊ] **1** *n* torpille *f* **2** *v/t* also fig torpiller

torrent [ˈtɑːrənt] also fig torrent *m*

torture [ˈtɔːrtʃər] **1** *n* torture *f* **2** *v/t* torturer

toss [tɑːs] **1** *v/t* ball lancer;

rider désarçonner; *salad remuer*

total ['təʊtl] **1** *adj* total; *disaster* complet; *idiot* fini; **he's a
~ stranger** c'est un parfait inconnu **2** *n* total *m*; **totalitarian** totalitaire; **totally** totalement

totter ['tɒtər] tituber

touch [tʌʃ] **1** *n* sense toucher
m; **lose ~ with s.o.** perdre
contact avec qn; **in ~** sp en
touche **2** *v/t also emotionally*
toucher; *exhibits etc* toucher
à **3** *v/i of two things* se toucher

◆ **touch down** *of airplane* atterrir; sp faire un touché-en-
-but

'touchdown *of airplane* atterrissage *m*; sp touché-en-but;
touching touchant; **touchline** sp ligne *f* de touche;
touch screen écran *m* tactile; **touchy** *person* susceptible

tough [tʌf] *person, material*
résistant; *meat, question, exam, punishment* dur

tour [tʊr] **1** *n* visite *f*; *as part of
package* circuit *m* (**of** dans);
of band etc tournée *f* **2** *v/t area* visiter **3** *v/i of tourist* faire
du tourisme; *of band* être en
tournée; **tour guide** accom-
pagnateur(-trice) *m(f)*; **tourism** tourisme; **tourist** touriste *m/f*; **tourist industry** industrie *f* touristique; **tourist
information office** office *m*

de tourisme

tournament ['tʊrnəmənt]
tournoi *m*

'tour operator tour-opérateur
m, voyagiste *m*

tow [toʊ] remorquer

◆ **tow away** *car* emmener à la
fourrière

toward [tɔːrd] vers; *with attitude, feelings etc* envers

towel ['taʊəl] serviette *f*

tower ['taʊər] tour *f*

town [taʊn] ville *f*; **town center**, *Br* **town centre** centre-
-ville *m*; **town council** conseil
m municipal; **town hall** hôtel
m de ville

toxic ['tɒksɪk] toxique; **toxin**
toxine *f*

toy [tɔɪ] jouet *m*

trace [treɪs] **1** *n of substance*
trace *f* **2** *v/t (find)* retrouver;
draw tracer

track [træk] *path*, *(racecourse)*
piste *f*; *motor racing* circuit
m; *on record, CD* morceau
m; RAIL voie *f* (ferrée); **~ 10**
RAIL voie 10; **keep ~ of sth**
suivre qch

◆ **track down** *person* retrouver; *criminal* dépister; *object*
dénicher

tracksuit *Br* survêtement *m*

tractor ['træktər] tracteur *m*

trade [treɪd] **1** *n* commerce *m*;
(profession, craft) métier *m* **2**
v/i (do business) faire du
commerce **3** *v/t (exchange)*
échanger (**for** contre); **trade
fair** foire *f* commerciale;

trademark marque *f* de commerce; **trade mission** mission *f* commerciale; **trader** commerçant(e) *m(f)*

tradition [trə'dıʃn] tradition *f*; **traditional** traditionnel; **traditionally** traditionnellement

traffic ['træfık] circulation *f*; *at airport, in drugs* trafic *m*
♦ **traffic in** *drugs* faire du trafic de

'traffic circle rond-point *m*; **traffic cop** F agent *m* de la circulation; **traffic jam** embouteillage *m*; **traffic light** feux *mpl* de signalisation; **traffic sign** panneau *m* de signalisation

tragedy ['trædʒədı] tragédie *f*; **tragic** tragique

trail [treıl] **1** *n* (*path*) sentier *m*; *of blood* traînée *f* **2** *v/t* (*follow*) suivre à la trace; (*tow*) remorquer **3** *v/i* (*lag behind*) traîner; **trailer** *pulled by vehicle* remorque *f*; (*mobile home*) caravane *f*; *of movie* bande-annonce *f*

train¹ [treın] *n* train *m*

train² [treın] **1** *v/t* entraîner; *dog* dresser; *employee* former **2** *v/i* *of team, athlete* s'entraîner; *of teacher etc* faire sa formation

trainee stagiaire *m/f*; **trainer** SP entraîneur(-euse) *m(f)*; *of dog* dresseur(-euse) *m(f)*; **~s** *Br: shoes* tennis *mpl*; **training** *of new staff* for-

mation *f*; SP entraînement *m*

'train station gare *f*

traitor ['treıtər] traître *m*, traîtresse *f*

♦ **trample on** piétiner

trampoline ['træmpəliːn] trampoline *m*

tranquil ['træŋkwıl] tranquille; **tranquility**, *Br* **tranquillity** tranquillité *f*; **tranquilizer**, *Br* **tranquillizer** tranquillisant *m*

transaction [træn'zækʃn] *of business* conduite *f*; *piece of business* transaction *f*

transatlantic [trænzət'læntık] transatlantique

transcript ['trænskrıpt] transcription *f*

transfer 1 [træns'fɜːr] *v/t* transférer **2** [træns'fɜːr] *v/i when traveling* changer; *in job* être muté (**to** à) **3** ['trænsfɜːr] *n* transfert *m*; **transferable** *ticket* transférable; **transfer fee** *for sportsman* prix *m* de transfert

transform [træns'fɔːrm] transformer; **transformation** transformation *f*; **transformer** ELEC transformateur *m*

transfusion [træns'fjuːʒn] transfusion *f*

transit ['trænzıt]: *in* **~** en transit; **transition** transition *f*; **transitional** de transition; **transit lounge** *at airport* salle *f* de transit; **transit pas-**

senger passager(-ère) *m(f)* en transit

translate [træns'leɪt] traduire; **translation** traduction *f*; **translator** traducteur(-trice) *m(f)*

transmission [trænz'mɪʃn] TV, AUT transmission *f*; **transmit** *news, program* diffuser; *disease* transmettre; **transmitter** RAD, TV émetteur *m*

transparency [træns'pærənsɪ] PHOT diapositive *f*; **transparent** transparent; (*obvious*) évident

transplant MED 1 ['trænsplænt] transplantation *n f*; *organ transplanted* transplant *m* 2 [træns'plænt] *v/t* transplanter

transport 1 ['trænspɔːrt] *n* transport *m* 2 [træns'pɔːrt] *v/t* transporter; **transportation** *of goods, people* transport *m*

transvestite [træns'vestaɪt] travesti *m*

trap [træp] 1 *n also fig* piège *m* 2 *v/t also fig* piéger; **trappings** *of power* signes extérieurs *mpl*

trash [træʃ] (*garbage*) ordures *fpl*; F *goods etc* camelote *f* F; *fig: person* vermine *f*; **trash can** poubelle *f*; **trashy** *goods* de pacotille; *novel* de bas étage

traumatic [trɔː'mætɪk] traumatisant; **traumatize** traumatiser

travel ['trævl] 1 *n* voyages *mpl* 2 *v/i* voyager 3 *v/t miles* parcourir; **travel agency** agence *f* de voyages; **travel agent** agent *m* de voyages; **traveler**, Br **traveller** voyageur(-euse) *m(f)*; **traveler's check**, Br **traveller's cheque** chèque-voyage *m*; **travel expenses** frais *mpl* de déplacement; **travel insurance** assurance-voyage *f*

trawler ['trɔːlər] chalutier *m*

tray [treɪ] *for food, photocopier* plateau *m*; *to go in oven* plaque *f*

treacherous ['tretʃərəs] traître; **treachery** traîtrise *f*

tread [tred] 1 *n* pas *m*; *of stair-case* dessus *m* des marches; *of tire* bande *f* de roulement 2 *v/i* marcher

treason ['triːzn] trahison *f*

treasure [treʒər] 1 *n* trésor *m* 2 *v/t gift etc* chérir; **treasurer** trésorier(-ière) *m(f)*; **Treasury Department** ministère *m* des Finances

treat [triːt] 1 *n* plaisir *m*; *it's my ~* (*I'm paying*) c'est moi qui paie *f*; *treat s.o. to sth* offrir qch à qn; **treatment** traitement *m*

treaty ['triːtɪ] traité *m*

treble ['trebl] 1 *adv*: *~ the price* le triple du prix 2 *v/i* tripler

tree [triː] arbre *m*

tremble ['trembl] trembler

tremendous [trɪ'mendəs]

(very good) formidable; *(enormous)* énorme; **tremendously** *(very)* extrêmement; *(a lot)* énormément

tremor ['tremər] *of earth* secousse *f* (sismique)

trench [trentʃ] tranchée *f*

trend [trend] tendance *f*; *(fashion)* mode *f*; **trendy** branché

trespass ['trespæs] entrer sans autorisation; **no ~ing** défense d'entrer; **trespasser** personne qui viole la propriété d'une autre

trial ['traɪəl] LAW procès *m*; *of equipment* essai *m*; **be on ~** LAW passer en justice

triangle ['traɪæŋgl] triangle *m*; **triangular** triangulaire

tribe [traɪb] tribu *f*

tribunal [traɪ'bju:nl] tribunal *m*

tributary ['trɪbjətərɪ] *of river* affluent *m*

trick [trɪk] **1** *n to deceive* tour *m*; *(knack)* truc *m* **2** *v/t* rouler; **trickery** tromperie *f*

trickle ['trɪkl] **1** *n* filet *m*; *fig* tout petit peu *m* **2** *v/i* couler goutte à goutte

tricky ['trɪkɪ] *(difficult)* délicat

trifling ['traɪflɪŋ] insignifiant

trigger ['trɪgər] *on gun* détente *f*

◆ **trigger off** déclencher

trim [trɪm] **1** *adj (neat)* bien entretenu; *figure* svelte **2** *v/t hair* couper un peu; *hedge* tailler; *costs* réduire; *(deco-rate: dress)* garnir **3** *n cut* taille *f*

trinket ['trɪŋkɪt] babiole *f*

trip [trɪp] **1** *n (journey)* voyage *m*; *(outing)* excursion *f* **2** *v/i (stumble)* trébucher **3** *v/t (make fall)* faire un croche-pied à

◆ **trip up 1** *v/t (make fall)* faire un croche-pied à; *(cause to go wrong)* faire trébucher **2** *v/i (stumble)* trébucher; *(make a mistake)* faire une erreur

triple ['trɪpl] → **treble**

trite [traɪt] banal

triumph ['traɪʌmf] triomphe *m*

trivial ['trɪvɪəl] insignifiant; **triviality** banalité *f*

trolley ['trɑːlɪ] *(streetcar)* tramway *m*

troops [tru:ps] troupes *fpl*

trophy ['troʊfɪ] trophée *m*

tropic ['trɑːpɪk] GEOG tropique *m*; **tropical** tropical; **tropics** tropiques *mpl*

trot [trɑːt] trotter

trouble ['trʌbl] **1** *n (difficulties)* problèmes *mpl*; *(inconvenience)* dérangement *m*; *(disturbance)* affrontements *mpl*; **get into ~** s'attirer des ennuis **2** *v/t (worry)* inquiéter; *(bother, disturb)* déranger; *of back, liver etc* faire souffrir; **troublemaker** fauteur(-trice) *m(f)* de troubles; **troubleshooting** dépannage *m*; **troublesome** pénible

trousers ['traʊzərz] *Br* pantalon *m*

trout [traʊt] truite *f*

truant ['truːənt]: **play ~** faire l'école buissonnière

truce [truːs] trêve *f*

truck [trʌk] camion *m*; **truck driver** camionneur(-euse) *m(f)*; **truck stop** routier *m*

trudge [trʌdʒ] **1** *v/i* se traîner **2** *n* marche *f* pénible

true [truː] vrai; *friend, American* véritable; **come ~** *of hopes, dream* se réaliser; *truly* vraiment; *Yours ~* je vous prie d'agréer mes sentiments distingués

trumpet ['trʌmpɪt] trompette *f*

trunk [trʌŋk] *of tree, body* tronc *m*; *of elephant* trompe *f*; *(large suitcase)* malle *f*; *of car* coffre *m*

trust [trʌst] **1** *n* confiance *f*; *FIN* fidéicommis *m* **2** *v/t* faire confiance à; *trusted* éprouvé; *trustee* fidéicommissaire *m/f*; *trustful, trusting* confiant; *trustworthy* fiable

truth [truːθ] vérité *f*; *truthful* honnête

try [traɪ] **1** *v/t & v/i* essayer; *LAW* juger; **~ to do sth** essayer de faire qch; **you must ~ harder** tu dois faire plus d'efforts **2** *n* *rugby* essai *m*; **trying** *(annoying)* éprouvant

T-shirt ['tiːʃɜːrt] tee-shirt *m*

tub [tʌb] *(bath)* baignoire *f* *for liquid* bac *m*; *for yoghurt* pot

m; **tubby** boulot

tube [tuːb] *(pipe)* tuyau *m*; *of toothpaste* tube *m*; **tubeless** *tire* sans chambre à air

Tuesday ['tuːzdeɪ] mardi *m*

tuft [tʌft] touffe *f*

tug [tʌg] **1** *n* *NAUT* remorqueur *m* **2** *v/t* tirer

tuition [tuːˈɪʃn] cours *mpl*

tumble ['tʌmbl] tomber; **tumbledown** qui tombe en ruines; **tumbler** *for drink* verre *m*; *in circus* acrobate *m/f*

tummy ['tʌmɪ] *F* ventre *m*; **tummy ache** mal *m* de ventre

tumor, *Br* **tumour** tumeur *f*

tumult ['tuːmʌlt] tumulte *m*; **tumultuous** tumultueux

tuna ['tuːnə] thon *m*

tune [tuːn] **1** *n* air *m* **2** *v/t instrument* accorder

♦ **tune up** *v/i of orchestra* s'accorder **2** *v/t engine* régler

tuneful ['tuːnfl] harmonieux; **tune-up** *of engine* règlement *m*

tunnel ['tʌnl] tunnel *m*

turbine ['tɜːrbaɪn] turbine *f*

turbulence ['tɜːrbjələns] *in air travel* turbulences *fpl*; **turbulent** agité

turf [tɜːrf] gazon *m*; *piece* motte *f* de gazon

turkey ['tɜːrkɪ] dinde *f*

turmoil ['tɜːrmɔɪl] confusion *f*

turn [tɜːrn] **1** *n* *(rotation)* tour *m*; *in road* virage *m*; *in vaudeville* numéro *m*; **take ~s doing sth** faire qch à tour de rôle; *it's my ~* c'est à moi **2** *v/t wheel* tourner; *~ the corner* tourner au coin de la rue **3** *v/i of driver, car, wheel* tourner; *of person* se retourner; *it has ~ed cold* le temps s'est refroidi

◆ **turn around 1** *v/t object* tourner; *company* remettre sur pied; COM *order* traiter **2** *v/i* se retourner; *with a car* faire demi-tour

◆ **turn away 1** *v/t (send away)* renvoyer **2** *v/i (walk away)* s'en aller; *(look away)* détourner le regard

◆ **turn back 1** *v/t edges, sheets* replier **2** *v/i of walkers, in course of action* faire demi-tour

◆ **turn down** *v/t offer* rejeter; *volume, heating* baisser; *edge* replier

◆ **turn off 1** *v/t TV, heater* éteindre; *faucet* fermer; *engine* arrêter **2** *v/i of car, driver* tourner; *of machine* s'éteindre

◆ **turn on 1** *v/t TV, heater* allumer; *faucet* ouvrir; *engine* mettre en marche; F *sexually* exciter **2** *v/i of machine* s'allumer

◆ **turn over 1** *v/i in bed* se retourner; *of vehicle* se renverser **2** *v/t (put upside down)* renverser; *page* tourner; FIN avoir un chiffre d'affaires de

◆ **turn up 1** *v/t collar* remonter; *volume* augmenter; *heat-*

ing monter **2** *v/i (arrive)* arriver, se pointer F

turning ['tɜːrnɪŋ] *in road* virage; **turning point** tournant *m*; **turnout** *at game etc* nombre *m* de spectateurs; **turnover** FIN chiffre *m* d'affaires

turnpike autoroute *f* payante; **turn signal** MOT clignotant *m*

turquoise ['tɜːrkwɔɪz] turquoise

turtle ['tɜːrtl] tortue *f* de mer; **turtleneck sweater** pull *m* à col cheminée

tusk [tʌsk] défense *f*

tutor ['tuːtər] *Br: at university* professeur *m/f*; **(private)** ~ professeur *m* particulier

tuxedo [tʌk'siːdəʊ] smoking *m*

TV [tiː'viː] télé *f*; *on* ~ à la télé; **TV dinner** plateau-repas *m*; **TV guide** guide *m* de télé; **TV program**, *Br* **TV programme** programme *m* télé

twang [twæŋ] **1** *n in voice* accent *m* nasillard **2** *v/t guitar string* pincer

tweezers ['twiːzərz] pince *f* à épiler

twelfth [twelfθ] douzième; **twelve** douze

twentieth ['twentɪɪθ] vingtième; **twenty** vingt

twice [twaɪs] deux fois; *~ as much* deux fois plus

twig [twɪg] brindille *f*

twilight ['twaɪlaɪt] crépuscule *m*

twin [twɪn] jumeau m, jumelle f; **twin beds** lits mpl jumeaux

twinge [twɪndʒ] of pain élancement m

twinkle ['twɪŋkl] scintiller

'**twin room** chambre f à lits jumeaux

twirl [twɜːrl] **1** v/t faire tourbillonner; mustache tortiller **2** n of cream etc spirale f

twist [twɪst] **1** v/t tordre; **~ one's ankle** se tordre la cheville **2** v/i of road faire des méandres; of river faire des lacets **3** n in rope entortillement m; in road lacet m; in plot dénouement m inattendu; **twisty** road qui fait des lacets

twitch [twɪtʃ] nervous tic m

twitter ['twɪtər] of birds gazouiller

two [tuː] deux; **the ~ of them** les deux

tycoon [taɪ'kuːn] magnat m

type [taɪp] **1** n (sort) type m **2** v/i (use a keyboard) taper **3** v/t with a typewriter taper à la machine

typhoon [taɪ'fuːn] typhon m

typhus ['taɪfəs] typhus m

typical ['tɪpɪkl] typique; **that's ~ of you!** c'est bien de vous!; **typically** typiquement

typist ['taɪpɪst] dactylo m/f

tyrannical [tɪ'rænɪkl] tyrannique; **tyrannize** tyranniser; **tyranny** tyrannie f; **tyrant** tyran m

tyre Br → **tire**[1]

U

ugly ['ʌɡlɪ] laid

UK [juː'keɪ] (= **United Kingdom**) R.-U. m (= Royaume-Uni)

ulcer ['ʌlsər] ulcère m

ultimate ['ʌltɪmət] (best, definitive) meilleur possible; (final) final; (fundamental) fondamental; **ultimately** (in the end) en fin de compte

ultimatum [ʌltɪ'meɪtəm] ultimatum m

ultrasound ['ʌltrəsaʊnd] MED ultrason m

ultraviolet [ʌltrə'vaɪələt] ul-

traviolet

umbrella [ʌm'brelə] parapluie m

umpire ['ʌmpaɪr] arbitre m/f

UN [juː'en] (= **United Nations**) O.N.U. f (= Organisation des Nations unies)

unable [ʌn'eɪbl]: **be ~ to do sth** not know how to ne pas savoir faire qch; not be in a position to ne pas pouvoir faire qch

unacceptable [ʌnək'septəbl] inacceptable

unaccountable [ʌnə-

'kaʊntəbl] inexplicable

un-American [ʌnə'merɪkən] (*not fitting*) antiaméricain

unanimous [juː'nænɪməs] *verdict* unanime; **unanimously** à l'unanimité

unapproachable [ʌnə-'prəʊtʃəbl] *person* d'un abord difficile

unarmed [ʌn'ɑːrmd] *person* non armé

unassuming [ʌnə'suːmɪŋ] modeste

unattached [ʌnə'tætʃt] *without a partner* sans attaches

unattended [ʌnə'tendɪd] laissé sans surveillance

unauthorized [ʌn'ɒːθəraɪzd] non autorisé

unavoidable [ʌnə'vɔɪdəbl] inévitable

unbalanced [ʌn'bælənst] *also* PSYCH déséquilibré

unbearable [ʌn'berəbl] insupportable

unbeatable [ʌn'biːtəbl] imbattable

unbeaten [ʌn'biːtn] *team* invaincu

unbelievable [ʌnbɪ'liːvəbl] *also* F incroyable

unbias(s)ed [ʌn'baɪəst] impartial

unblock [ʌn'blɑːk] *pipe* déboucher

unbreakable [ʌn'breɪkəbl] incassable

unbutton [ʌn'bʌtn] déboutonner

uncanny [ʌn'kænɪ] étrange,

mystérieux

unceasing [ʌn'siːsɪŋ] incessant

uncertain [ʌn'sɜːrtn] incertain; **uncertainty** *of the future* caractère *m* incertain; **there is still ~ about** des incertitudes demeurent quant à …

uncle [ʌŋkl] oncle *m*

uncomfortable [ʌn'kʌmftəbl] inconfortable

uncommon [ʌn'kɑːmən] inhabituel

uncompromising [ʌn'kɑːmprəmaɪzɪŋ] intransigeant

unconditional [ʌnkən'dɪʃnl] sans conditions

unconscious [ʌn'kɑːnʃəs] MED, PSYCH inconscient

uncontrollable [ʌnkən'trəʊləbl] incontrôlable

unconventional [ʌnkən-'venʃnl] non conventionnel

uncooperative [ʌnkoʊ-'ɑːpərətɪv] peu coopératif

uncover [ʌn'kʌvər] découvrir

undamaged [ʌn'dæmɪdʒd] intact

undecided [ʌndɪ'saɪdɪd] *question* laissé en suspens; **be ~ about** être indécis à propos de

undeniable [ʌndɪ'naɪəbl] indéniable

under ['ʌndər] sous; (*less than*) moins de; **it is ~ investigation** cela fait l'objet d'une enquête 'under**carriage** train *m* d'atterrissage

'under**cover** clandestin; ~ **agent** agent *m* secret

under'**cut** COM: ~ *the competition* vendre moins cher que la concurrence

under'**done** *meat* pas trop cuit; *pej* pas assez cuit

under'**estimate** sous-estimer

under'**fed** mal nourri

under'**go** subir

under'**graduate** *Br* étudiant(e) (de D.E.U.G. ou de licence)

'under**ground 1** *adj* souterrain; POL clandestin **2** *adv* *work* sous terre

under'**hand** (*devious*) sournois

under'**line** *text* souligner

under'**lying** sous-jacent

under'**mine** saper

under**neath** [ʌndər'niːθ] **1** *prep* sous **2** *adv* dessous

'under**pants** slip *m*

'under**pass** *for pedestrians* passage *m* souterrain

under**privileged** [ʌndər'prɪvɪlɪdʒd] défavorisé

under'**rate** sous-estimer

under**staffed** [ʌndər'stæft] en manque de personnel

under'**stand** comprendre; **understandable** compréhensible; **understandably** naturellement; **understanding 1** *adj person* compréhensif **2** *n* compréhension *f*;

(*agreement*) accord *m*

under'**take** *task* entreprendre; ~ *to do sth* (*agree to*) s'engager à faire qch; **undertaking** (*enterprise*) entreprise *f*; (*promise*) engagement *m*

under'**value** sous-estimer

'under**wear** sous-vêtements *mpl*

'under**world** *criminal* monde *m* du crime organisé

under'**write** FIN souscrire

unde**served** [ʌndɪ'zɜːrvd] non mérité

unde**sirable** [ʌndɪ'zaɪrəbl] indésirable

undis**puted** [ʌndɪ'spjuːtɪd] *champion* incontestable

un**do** [ʌn'duː] défaire

un**doubtedly** [ʌn'daʊtɪdlɪ] à n'en pas douter

un**dress** [ʌn'dres] **1** *v/t* déshabiller; *get ~ed* se déshabiller **2** *v/i* se déshabiller

un**due** [ʌn'duː] excessif; **unduly** (*excessively*) excessivement

un**earth** [ʌn'ɜːrθ] *also fig* déterrer

un**easy** [ʌn'iːzɪ] *relationship, peace* incertain vouloir signer cela

un**eatable** [ʌn'iːtəbl] immangeable

un**economic** [ʌniːkə'nɑːmɪk] pas rentable

un**educated** [ʌn'edʒəkeɪtɪd] sans instruction

un**employed** [ʌnɪm'plɔɪd] **1** *adj* au chômage **2** *npl*: **the**

~ les chômeurs(-euses); **un-employment** chômage *m*

unequal [ʌnˈiːkwəl] inégal

unerring [ʌnˈɜːrɪŋ] *judgment, instinct* infaillible

uneven [ʌnˈiːvn] *surface, ground* irrégulier

uneventful [ʌnɪˈventfl] *day, journey* sans événement

unexpected [ʌnɪkˈspektɪd] inattendu; **unexpectedly** inopinément

unfair [ʌnˈfer] injuste

unfaithful [ʌnˈfeɪθfl] *husband, wife* infidèle; **be ~ to s.o.** tromper qn

unfamiliar [ʌnfəˈmɪljər] peu familier

unfasten [ʌnˈfæsn] *belt* défaire

unfavorable [ʌnˈfeɪvərəbl] défavorable

unfinished [ʌnˈfɪnɪʃt] inachevé

unfold [ʌnˈfoʊld] **1** *v/t letter* déplier; *arms* ouvrir **2** *v/i of story etc* se dérouler; *of view* se déployer

unforeseen [ʌnfɔːrˈsiːn] imprévu

unforgettable [ʌnfərˈgetəbl] inoubliable

unforgivable [ʌnfərˈgɪvəbl] impardonnable

unfortunate [ʌnˈfɔːrtʃənət] malheureux; **unfortunately** malheureusement

unfounded [ʌnˈfaʊndɪd] non fondé

unfriendly [ʌnˈfrendli] *per-*

son, welcome, hotel froid

ungrateful [ʌnˈgreɪtfl] ingrat

unhappiness [ʌnˈhæpɪnɪs] chagrin *m*; **unhappy** malheureux; *customers etc* mécontent (**with** de)

unharmed [ʌnˈhɑːrmd] indemne

unhealthy [ʌnˈhelθɪ] *person* en mauvaise santé; *food, atmosphere* malsain; *economy* qui se porte mal

unheard-of [ʌnˈhɜːrdəv]: **be ~** ne s'être jamais vu

unhygienic [ʌnhaɪˈdʒiːnɪk] insalubre

unification [juːnɪfɪˈkeɪʃn] unification *f*

uniform [ˈjuːnɪfɔːrm] **1** *n* uniforme *m* **2** *adj* uniforme

unify [ˈjuːnɪfaɪ] unifier

unilateral [juːnɪˈlætərəl] unilatéral

unimaginable [ʌnɪˈmædʒɪnəbl] inimaginable

unimaginative [ʌnɪˈmædʒɪnətɪv] qui manque d'imagination

unimportant [ʌnɪmˈpɔːrtənt] sans importance

uninhabitable [ʌnɪnˈhæbɪtəbl] inhabitable; **uninhabited** inhabitée

unintentional [ʌnɪnˈtenʃnl] non intentionnel; **unintentionally** sans le vouloir

uninteresting [ʌnˈɪntrəstɪŋ] inintéressant

uninterrupted [ʌnɪntəˈrʌptɪd] ininterrompu

union ['juːnjən] POL union *f*; (*labor* ~) syndicat *m*

unique [juːniːk] unique

unit ['juːnɪt] unité *f*

unite [juːnaɪt] **1** *v/t* unir **2** *v/i* s'unir; **united** uni; *efforts* conjoint; **United Kingdom** Royaume-Uni *m*; **United Nations** *fpl* Unies

United States (of A'merica) États-Unis *mpl* (d'Amérique)

unity ['juːnətɪ] unité *f*

universal [juːnɪ'vɜːrsl] universel; **universe** univers *m*

university [juːnɪ'vɜːrsətɪ] université *f*

unjust [ʌn'dʒʌst] injuste

unkind [ʌn'kaɪnd] méchant, désagréable

unknown [ʌn'noun] inconnu

unleaded [ʌn'ledɪd] *gas* sans plomb

unless [ən'les] à moins que (+*subj*)

unlikely [ʌn'laɪklɪ] improbable

unlimited [ʌn'lɪmɪtɪd] illimité

unload [ʌn'loud] décharger

unlock [ʌn'lɑːk] ouvrir

unluckily [ʌn'lʌkɪlɪ] malheureusement; **unlucky** *day* de malchance; *choice* malheureux; *person* malchanceux; **that was so ~ for you!** tu n'as vraiment pas eu de chance!

unmanned [ʌn'mænd] *spacecraft* sans équipage

unmarried [ʌn'mærɪd] non

marié

unmistakable [ʌnmɪ'steɪkəbl] reconnaissable entre mille

unnatural [ʌn'nætʃrəl] contrenature

unnecessary [ʌn'nesəserɪ] non nécessaire

unnerving [ʌn'nɜːrvɪŋ] déstabilisant

unobtainable [ʌnəb'teɪnəbl] *goods* qu'on ne peut se procurer; TELEC hors service

unobtrusive [ʌnəb'truːsɪv] discret

unoccupied [ʌn'ɑːkjʊpaɪd] (*empty*) vide; *position* vacant; *person* désœuvré

unofficial [ʌnə'fɪʃl] non officiel; **unofficially** non officiellement

unorthodox [ʌn'ɔːrθədɑːks] peu orthodoxe

unpack [ʌn'pæk] **1** *v/t case* défaire **2** *v/i* défaire sa valise

unpaid [ʌn'peɪd] *work* non rémunéré

unpleasant [ʌn'pleznt] désagréable

unplug [ʌn'plʌg] *TV, computer* débrancher

unpopular [ʌn'pɑːpjələr] impopulaire

unprecedented [ʌn'presɪdentɪd] sans précédent

unpredictable [ʌnprɪ'dɪktəbl] imprévisible

unpretentious [ʌnprɪ'tenʃəs] modeste

unproductive [ʌnprə'dʌktɪv]

unprofessional

meeting, discussion, land improductif

unprofessional [ʌnprəˈfeʃnl] non professionnel; *workmanship* peu professionnel

unprofitable [ʌnˈprɒfɪtəbl] non profitable

unprovoked [ʌnprəˈvoʊkt] *attack* non provoqué

unqualified [ʌnˈkwɒlɪfaɪd] non qualifié

unquestionably [ʌnˈkwestʃnəblɪ] sans aucun doute; **unquestioning** *attitude* aveugle

unreadable [ʌnˈriːdəbl] *book* illisible

unrealistic [ʌnrɪəˈlɪstɪk] irréaliste

unreasonable [ʌnˈriːznəbl] déraisonnable

unrelated [ʌnrɪˈleɪtɪd] sans relation (**to** avec)

unrelenting [ʌnrɪˈlentɪŋ] incessant

unreliable [ʌnrɪˈlaɪəbl] pas fiable

unrest [ʌnˈrest] agitation *f*

unrestrained [ʌnrɪˈstreɪnd] *emotions* non contenu

unroll [ʌnˈroʊl] *carpet* dérouler

unruly [ʌnˈruːlɪ] indiscipliné

unsanitary [ʌnˈsænɪterɪ] *conditions, drains* insalubre

unsatisfactory [ʌnsætɪsˈfæktərɪ] insatisfaisant; (*unacceptable*) inacceptable

unscathed [ʌnˈskeɪðd] (*not injured*) indemne; (*not dam-*

aged) intact

unscrew [ʌnˈskruː] *sth screwed on* dévisser; *top* décapsuler

unscrupulous [ʌnˈskruːpjələs] peu scrupuleux

unselfish [ʌnˈselfɪʃ] désintéressé

unsettled [ʌnˈsetld] incertain; *lifestyle* instable; *bills* non réglé; *issue* non décidé

unshaven [ʌnˈʃeɪvn] mal rasé

unskilled [ʌnˈskɪld] *worker* non qualifié

unsophisticated [ʌnsəˈfɪstɪkeɪtɪd] peu sophistiqué

unstable [ʌnˈsteɪbl] instable

unsteady [ʌnˈstedɪ] *on feet* chancelant; *ladder* branlant

unsuccessful [ʌnsəkˈsesfl] *attempt* infructueux; *writer* qui n'a pas de succès; *candidate, marriage* malheureux; **unsuccessfully** sans succès

unsuitable [ʌnˈsuːtəbl] inapproprié

unswerving [ʌnˈswɜːrvɪŋ] *loyalty* inébranlable

unthinkable [ʌnˈθɪŋkəbl] impensable

untidy [ʌnˈtaɪdɪ] en désordre

untie [ʌnˈtaɪ] *knot* défaire; *prisoner, hands* détacher

until [ənˈtɪl] **1** *prep* jusqu'à; **from Monday ~ Friday** de lundi à vendredi; **not ~ Friday** pas avant vendredi **2** *conj* jusqu'à ce que; **can you wait ~ I'm ready?** est-ce que vous pouvez attendre que je sois prêt?

untiring [ʌnˈtaɪrɪŋ] *efforts* infatigable

untold [ʌnˈtoʊld] *riches, suffering* inouï; *story* inédit

untrue [ʌnˈtruː] faux

unused [ʌnˈjuːzd] *goods* non utilisé

unusual [ʌnˈjuːʒl] inhabituel; (*strange*) bizarre; **unusually** anormalement, exceptionnellement

unveil [ʌnˈveɪl] *statue etc* dévoiler

unwell [ʌnˈwel] malade

unwilling [ʌnˈwɪlɪŋ]: **be ~ to do** refuser de faire; **unwillingly** à contre-cœur

unwind [ʌnˈwaɪnd] **1** *v/t tape* dérouler **2** *v/i of tape, story* se dérouler; (*relax*) se détendre

unwise [ʌnˈwaɪz] malavisé

unwrap [ʌnˈræp] déballer

unzip [ʌnˈzɪp] *dress etc* descendre la fermeture-éclair de; COMPUT décompresser

up [ʌp] **1** *adv:* **~ in the sky/on the roof** dans le ciel/sur le toit; **~ here** ici; **~ there** là-haut; **be ~** (*out of bed*) être debout; *of sun* être levé; *of temperature* avoir augmenté; (*have expired*) être expiré; **what's ~?** F qu'est-ce qu'il y a?; **~ to 1989** jusqu'à 1989; **he came ~ to me** il s'est approché de moi; **what are you ~ to these days?** qu'est-ce que tu fais en ce moment?; **be ~ to something** (*bad*) être sur un mauvais coup; **I don't feel ~ to it** je ne m'en sens pas le courage; **it's ~ to you** c'est toi qui décides; **it's ~ to them to solve it** c'est à eux de le résoudre **2** *prep:* **further ~ the mountain** un peu plus haut sur la montagne; **they ran ~ the street** ils ont remonté la rue en courant; **we traveled ~ to Paris** nous sommes montés à Paris **3** *n:* **~s and downs** hauts *mpl* et bas

'upbringing éducation *f*

up'date *file* mettre à jour

up'grade moderniser; *ticket* surclasser

upheaval [ʌpˈhiːvl] bouleversement *m*

up'hold *rights* maintenir

'upkeep maintien *m*

'upload COMPUT transférer

'upmarket *Br restaurant, hotel* chic; *product* haut de gamme

upon [əˈpɑːn] → **on**

upper [ˈʌpər] supérieur

'upright 1 *adj citizen* droit **2** *adv sit* (bien) droit; **upright piano** piano *f* droit

'uprising soulèvement *m*

'uproar vacarme *m*; *fig* protestations *fpl*

up'set 1 *v/t* renverser; *emotionally* contrarier **2** *adj emotionally* contrarié, vexé; **upsetting** contrariant

upside 'down à l'envers; *car* renversé

up'stairs 1 *adv* en haut; ~ **from us** au-dessus de chez nous 2 *adj room* d'en haut

up'stream en remontant le courant

up'tight F (*nervous*) tendu; (*inhibited*) coincé

up-to-'date à jour

'upturn in economy reprise *f*

upward ['ʌpwəd]: **move sth ~** élever qch; **~ of 100** au-delà de 100

uranium [ju'reɪnɪəm] uranium *m*

urban ['ɜːrbən] urbain

urge [ɜːrdʒ] 1 *n* (forte) envie *f* 2 *v/t*: ~ *s.o.* **to do sth** encourager qn à faire qch; **urgency** urgence *f*; **urgent** urgent

urinate ['jʊrəneɪt] uriner; **urine** urine *f*

US [juːes] (= *United States*) USA *mpl*

us [ʌs] nous

USA [juːeseɪ] (= *United States of America*) USA *mpl*

usage ['juːzɪdʒ] usage *m*

use 1 [juːz] *v/t also pej*: *person* utiliser *2* [juːs] *n* utilisation *f*; **it's no ~ waiting** ce n'est pas la peine d'attendre

◆ use up épuiser

used[1] [juːzd] *car etc* d'occasion

used[2] [juːst]: **be ~ to** être habitué à; **get ~ to** s'habituer à

used[3] [juːst]: **I ~ to work there** je travaillais là-bas avant; **I ~ to know him well** je l'ai bien connu autrefois

useful ['juːsfʊl] utile; **usefulness** utilité *f*; **useless** inutile; F (*no good*) nul F; **user** of *product* utilisateur(-trice) *m(f)*; **user-friendly** facile à utiliser; COMPUT convivial

usual ['juːʒl] habituel; **as ~** comme d'habitude; **usually** d'habitude

utensil [juː'tensl] ustensile *m*

utilize ['juːtɪlaɪz] utiliser

utter ['ʌtər] 1 *adj* total 2 *v/t sound* prononcer; **utterly** totalement

V

vacant ['veɪkənt] *building* inoccupé; *look* vide, absent; *Br: position* vacant; **vacantly** *stare* d'un air absent; **vacate** *room* libérer

vacation [ver'keɪʃn] vacances *fpl*; **be on ~** être en vacances

vaccinate ['væksɪneɪt] vacci-

ner; **vaccination** vaccination *f*; **vaccine** vaccin *m*

vacuum ['vækjʊəm] 1 *n* vide *m* 2 *v/t floors* passer l'aspirateur sur

vague [veɪg] vague; **vaguely** vaguement

vain [veɪn] 1 *adj person* vaniteux; *hope* vain **2** *n*: *in* ~ en vain

valiant ['væljənt] vaillant

valid ['vælɪd] valable; **validate** *with official stamp* valider; *theory* confirmer; **validity** validité *f*; *of argument* justesse *f*; *of claim* bien-fondé *m*

valley ['vælɪ] vallée *f*

valuable ['væljʊbl] **1** *adj* de valeur; *colleague, help, advice* précieux **2** *npl*: ~**s** objets *mpl* de valeur; **valuation** estimation *f*, expertise *f*; **value 1** *n* valeur *f* **2** *v/t* tenir à, attacher un grand prix à

valve [vælv] soupape *f*, valve *f*; *in heart* valvule *f*

van [væn] *small* camionnette *f*; *large* fourgon *m*

vandal ['vændl] vandale *m*; **vandalism** vandalisme *m*; **vandalize** vandaliser

vanilla [vəˈnɪlə] **1** *n* vanille *f* **2** *adj* à la vanille

vanish ['vænɪʃ] disparaître; *of clouds, sadness* se dissiper

vanity ['vænətɪ] *of person* vanité *f*

vapor ['veɪpər] vapeur *f*; **vaporize** *of atomic bomb, explosion* pulvériser; **vapour** *Br* → **vapor**

variable ['verɪəbl] **1** *adj* variable; *moods* changeant **2** *n* MATH, COMPUT variable *f*; **variant** variante *f*; **variation** variation *f*; **varied** varié; **variety** variété *f*; **various** (*several*)

divers, plusieurs; (*different*) divers, différent

varnish ['vɑːrnɪʃ] **1** *n* vernis *m* **2** *v/t* vernir

vary ['verɪ] varier; *it varies* ça dépend

vase [veɪz] vase *m*

vast [væst] vaste; *improvement* considérable; **vastly** *improve etc* considérablement; *different* complètement

Vatican ['vætɪkən]: *the* ~ le Vatican

vault[1] [vɔːlt] *n in roof* voûte *f*; ~**s** *of bank* salle *f* des coffres

vault[2] [vɔːlt] **1** *n* sp saut *m* **2** *v/t* beam etc sauter

VCR [viːsiːˈɑːr] (= *video cassette recorder*) magnétoscope *m*

veal [viːl] veau *m*

veer [vɪr] virer; *of wind* tourner

vegan ['viːgən] (*food, person*) végétalien, végan

vegetable ['vedʒtəbl] légume *m*; **vegetarian 1** *n* végétarien(ne) *m(f)* **2** *adj* végétarien; **vegetation** végétation *f*

vehement ['viːəmənt] véhément

vehicle ['viːɪkl] véhicule *m*

veil [veɪl] voile *m*

vein [veɪn] ANAT veine *f*

velocity [vɪˈlɑːsətɪ] vélocité *f*

velvet ['velvɪt] velours *m*

vendetta [venˈdetə] vendetta *f*

vending machine ['vendɪŋ]

distributeur *m* automatique;
vendor LAW vendeur(-euse)
m(f)

veneer [vəˈnɪr] placage *m*; *of
politeness* vernis *m*

venerable [ˈvenərəbl] vénérable; **veneration** vénération *f*

venereal disease [vəˈnɪrɪəl]
M.S.T. *f*, maladie *f* sexuellement transmissible

venetian blind [vəˈniːʃn] store *m* vénitien

venom [ˈvenəm] venin *m*

ventilate [ˈventɪleɪt] ventiler;
ventilation ventilation *f*;
ventilator ventilateur *m*;
MED respirateur *m*

venture [ˈventʃər] **1** *n* (*undertaking*) entreprise *f*; COM tentative *f* **2** *v/i* s'aventurer

venue [ˈvenjuː] *for meeting,
concert* lieu *m*; *hall also*
salle *f*

veranda [vəˈrændə] véranda *f*

verb [vɜːrb] verbe *m*; **verbal**
(*spoken*) oral, verbal; **verbally** oralement, verbalement

verdict [ˈvɜːrdɪkt] LAW verdict
m; (*opinion, judgment*) avis
m, jugement *m*

verge [vɜːrdʒ] *of road* accotement *m*, bas-côté *m*; **be on
the ~ of …** être au bord de …

verification [verɪfɪˈkeɪʃn]
(*check*) vérification *f*; **verify**
(*check*) vérifier, contrôler;
(*confirm*) confirmer

vermin [ˈvɜːrmɪn] (*insects*)
vermine *f*, parasites *mpl*;
(*rats etc*) animaux *mpl* nuisi-
bles

vermouth [vərˈmuːθ] vermouth *m*

versatile [ˈvɜːrsətəl] *person*
plein de ressources, polyvalent; *piece of equipment* multiusages; **versatility** *of person* adaptabilité *f*, polyvalence *f*; *of piece of equipment*
souplesse *f* d'emploi

verse [vɜːrs] (*poetry*) vers
mpl, poésie *f*; *of poem* strophe *f*; *of song* couplet *m*

version [ˈvɜːrʃn] version *f*

versus [ˈvɜːrsəs] contre

vertical [ˈvɜːrtɪkl] vertical

vertigo [ˈvɜːrtɪgəʊ] vertige *m*

very [ˈverɪ] **1** *adv* très; *was it
cold? – not* – faisait-il froid?
– non, pas tellement; *the ~
best* le meilleur *f* de même;
at that ~ moment à cet instant même, à ce moment
précis; *that's the ~ thing I
need* c'est exactement ce
dont j'ai besoin

vessel [ˈvesl] NAUT bateau *m*,
navire *m*

vest [vest] gilet *m* Br: *undershirt* maillot *m* (de corps)

vestige [ˈvestɪdʒ] vestige *m*;
fig once *f*

vet¹ [vet] *n* (*veterinarian*) vétérinaire *m/f*, véto *m/f* F

vet² [vet] *v/t applicants etc*
examiner

vet³ [vet] *n* MIL F ancien combattant *m*

veteran [ˈvetərən] **1** *n* vétéran
m **2** *adj* (*old*) antique; (*old*

and experienced) aguerri, chevronné

veterinarian [vetərə'neriən] vétérinaire *m/f*

veto ['vi:təu] **1** *n* veto *m inv* **2** *v/t* opposer son veto à

via ['vaiə] par

viable ['vaiəbl] viable

vibrate [vai'breit] vibrer; **vibration** vibration *f*

vice[1] [vais] *n* vice *m*

vice[2] [vais] *Br* → **vise**

vice 'president vice-président *m*

vice versa [vais'vɜ:rsə] vice versa

vicious ['vɪʃəs] vicieux; *dog* méchant; *person, temper* cruel; *attack* brutal; **viciously** brutalement

victim ['vɪktɪm] victime *f*; **victimize** persécuter

victorious [vik'tɔ:riəs] victorieux; **victory** victoire *f*

video ['vɪdɪəu] **1** *n* vidéo *f*; *actual object* cassette *f* vidéo **2** *v/t* filmer; *tape off TV* enregistrer; **video camera** caméra *f* vidéo; **video cassette** cassette *f* vidéo; **video recorder** magnétoscope *m*; **videotape** bande *f* vidéo

vie [vai] rivaliser

Vietnam [vɪet'næm] Vietnam *m*; **Vietnamese 1** *adj* vietnamien **2** *n* Vietnamien(ne) *m(f)*; *language* vietnamien *m*

view [vju:] **1** *n* vue *f*; *(assessment, opinion)* opinion *f*, avis

m; **in ~ of** compte tenu de, étant donné **2** *v/t* considérer, envisager **3** *v/i* (*watch TV*) regarder la télévision; **viewer** TV téléspectateur(-trice) *m(f)*; **viewpoint** point *m* de vue

vigor ['vɪgər] vigueur *f*; **vigorous** vigoureux; **vigorously** vigoureusement; **vigour** *Br* → **vigor**

village ['vɪlɪdʒ] village *m*; **villager** villageois(e) *m(f)*

villain ['vɪlən] escroc *m*; *in drama* méchant *m*

vindicate ['vɪndɪkeɪt] (*prove correct*) confirmer, justifier; (*prove innocent*) innocenter

vindictive [vɪn'dɪktɪv] vindicatif

vine [vain] vigne *f*

vinegar ['vɪnɪgər] vinaigre *m*

vineyard ['vɪnjɑ:rd] vignoble *m*

vintage ['vɪntɪdʒ] **1** *n of wine* millésime *m* **2** *adj* (*classic*) classique

violate ['vaɪəleɪt] violer; **violation** violation *f*; (*traffic ~*) infraction *f* au code de la route

violence ['vaɪələns] violence *f*; **violent** violent

violin [vaɪə'lɪn] violon *m*; **violinist** violoniste *m/f*

VIP [vi:aɪ'pi:] (= **very important person**) V.I.P. *m*

viral ['vaɪrəl] viral

virgin ['vɜ:rdʒɪn] vierge *f*;

male puceau m F; **virginity** virginité f

virile ['vɪraɪl] viril; **virility** virilité f

virtual ['vɜːrtʃuəl] quasi-; **virtually** (*almost*) pratiquement, presque

virtue ['vɜːtʃuː] vertu f; **virtuous** vertueux

virus ['vaɪrəs] virus m

visa ['viːzə] visa m

vise [vaɪz] étau m

visibility [vɪzə'bɪlətɪ] visibilité f; **visible** visible

vision ['vɪʒn] (*eyesight*) vue f; REL vision f

visit ['vɪzɪt] **1** n visite f; (*stay*) séjour m **2** v/t rendre visite à; *doctor, dentist* aller voir; *city, country* aller à/en; *castle, museum* visiter; *website* consulter; **visitor** (*guest*) invité m; (*tourist*) visiteur m

visor ['vaɪzər] visière f

visual ['vɪʒuəl] visuel; **visualize** (*imagine*) (s')imaginer; (*foresee*) envisager, prévoir; **visually** visuellement

vital ['vaɪtl] (*essential*) vital, essentiel; **vitality** vitalité f; **vitally**: ~ **important** d'une importance capitale

vitamin ['vaɪtəmɪn] vitamine f; **vitamin pill** comprimé m de vitamines

vivacious [vɪ'veɪʃəs] plein de vivacité, vif; **vivacity** vivacité f

vivid ['vɪvɪd] vif; *description* vivant; **vividly** vivement; re-

member clairement; *describe* de façon vivante

V-neck ['viːnek] col m en V

vocabulary [voʊ'kæbjʊlərɪ] vocabulaire m; (*list of words*) glossaire m

vocal ['voʊkl] vocal; **vocalist** MUS chanteur(-euse) m(f)

vocation [və'keɪʃn] vocation f; **vocational** *guidance* professionnel

vodka ['vɑːdkə] vodka f

vogue [voʊg] vogue f; **be in ~** être en vogue

voice [vɔɪs] **1** n voix f **2** v/t *opinions* exprimer; **voicemail** messagerie f vocale

volcano [vɑːl'keɪnoʊ] volcan m

volley ['vɑːlɪ] volée f

volt [voʊlt] volt m; **voltage** tension f

volume ['vɑːljəm] volume m

voluntarily [vɑːlən'terɪlɪ] de son plein gré, volontairement; **voluntary** volontaire; *work* bénévole; **volunteer 1** n volontaire m/f; (*unpaid worker*) bénévole m/f **2** v/i se porter volontaire

vomit ['vɑːmɪt] **1** n vomi m, vomissure f **2** v/i vomir

voracious [və'reɪʃəs] vorace; *reader* avide

vote [voʊt] **1** n vote m **2** v/i voter (*for* pour; *against* contre); **voter** POL électeur m; **voting** POL vote m

◆ **vouch for** [vaʊtʃ] *truth, person* se porter garant de

vow [vaʊ] **1** n vœu m, serment m **2** v/t: **~ to do** jurer de faire
vowel ['vaʊl] voyelle f
voyage ['vɔɪdʒ] voyage m

vulgar ['vʌlgər] vulgaire
vulnerable ['vʌlnərəbl] vulnérable
vulture ['vʌltʃər] vautour m

W

waddle ['wɑːdl] se dandiner
wade [weɪd] patauger
wafer ['weɪfər] cookie gaufrette f; REL hostie f
waffle ['wɑːfl] to eat gaufre f
wag [wæg] remuer
wages ['weɪdʒɪz] salaire m
waggle ['wægl] remuer
wail [weɪl] hurler
waist [weɪst] taille f
wait [weɪt] **1** n attente f **2** v/i attendre
◆ **wait for** attendre
◆ **wait on** (serve) servir
◆ **wait up**: **don't wait up (for me)** ne m'attends pas pour aller te coucher
waiter ['weɪtər] serveur m; **~!** garçon!; **waiting list** liste f d'attente; **waiting room** salle f d'attente; **waitress** serveuse f
waive [weɪv] renoncer à
wake [weɪk] **1** v/i: **~ (up)** se réveiller **2** v/t person réveiller
walk [wɔːk] **1** n marche f; (path) allée f; **go for a ~** se promener **2** v/i marcher; as opposed to driving aller à pied; (hike) faire de la marche **3** v/t dog promener
◆ **walk out** of spouse prendre

la porte; from theater etc partir; (go on strike) se mettre en grève
walker ['wɔːkər] (hiker) randonneur(-euse) m(f); for baby trotte-bébé m; for old person déambulateur m; **walking** (hiking) randonnée f; **walkout** (strike) grève f; **walkover** (easy win) victoire f facile
wall [wɔːl] mur m
wallet ['wɑːlɪt] (billfold) portefeuille m
'wallpaper 1 n also COMPUT papier m peint **2** v/t tapisser; **wall-to-wall carpet** moquette f
waltz [wɔːlts] valse f
wan [wɑːn] face pâlot
wander ['wɑːndər] (roam) errer; (stray) s'égarer
wangle ['wæŋgl] F réussir à obtenir (par une combine)
want [wɑːnt] **1** n: **for ~ of** par manque de, faute de **2** v/t vouloir; (need) avoir besoin de; **~ to do sth** vouloir faire qch; **I ~ to stay here** je veux rester ici; **she ~ you to go back** elle veut que tu reviennes (subj) **3** v/i: **~ for nothing**

ne manquer de rien; **wanted by police** recherché

war [wɔːr] guerre f; *fig* lutte f

ward [wɔːrd] *Br: in hospital* salle f; *child* pupille m/f

♦ **ward off** éviter

warden ['wɔːrdn] *of prison* gardien (ne) m(f); *Br: of hostel* directeur (-trice) m (f)

'**wardrobe** *for clothes* armoire f; (*clothes*) garde-robe f

warehouse ['werhaʊs] entrepôt m

'**warfare** guerre f; **warhead** ogive f

warily ['werɪlɪ] avec méfiance

warm [wɔːrm] chaud; *welcome, smile* chaleureux

♦ **warm up** 1 v/t réchauffer 2 v/i se réchauffer; *of athlete etc* s'échauffer

warmly ['wɔːrmlɪ] chaudement; *welcome, smile* chaleureusement; **warmth** *also fig* chaleur f; **warm-up** SP échauffement m

warn [wɔːrn] prévenir; **warning** avertissement m

warp [wɔːrp] *of wood* gauchir; **warped** *fig* tordu

warrant ['wɔːrənt] 1 n mandat m 2 v/t justifier; **warranty** garantie f

warrior ['wɔːrɪər] guerrier (-ière) m (f)

wart [wɔːrt] verrue f

wary ['werɪ] méfiant; **be ~ of** se méfier de

wash [wɑː∫] 1 n: **have a ~** se laver 2 v/t *clothes, dishes* la-

ver 3 v/i se laver

♦ **wash up** (*wash one's hands and face*) se débarbouiller

washable ['wɑ:∫əbl] lavable; **washbasin, washbowl** lavabo m; **washcloth** gant m de toilette; **washed out** (*tired*) usé; **washer** *for faucet etc* rondelle f; **washing** lessive f; **do the ~** faire la lessive; **washing machine** machine f à laver; **washroom** toilettes fpl

wasp [wɑːsp] guêpe f

waste [weɪst] 1 n gaspillage m; *from industrial process* déchets mpl; **it's a ~ of time/money** c'est une perte de temps/d'argent 2 adj non utilisé 3 v/t gaspiller; **waste basket** corbeille f à papier; **waste disposal (unit)** broyeur m d'ordures; **wasteful** gaspilleur; **wasteland** désert m; **wastepaper** papier(s) m(pl) (jeté(s) à la poubelle)

watch [wɑː∫] 1 n *timepiece* montre f; **keep ~** monter la garde 2 v/t regarder; (*look after*) surveiller 3 v/i regarder; **watchful** vigilant

water ['wɔːtər] 1 n eau f 2 v/t *plant* arroser 3 v/i: **my mouth is ~ing** j'ai l'eau à la bouche; **watercolor,** *Br* **watercolour** aquarelle f; **watered down** *fig* atténué; **waterfall** chute f d'eau; **waterline** ligne f de flottaison; **waterlogged** dé-

wedge

trempé; *boat* plein d'eau; **watermelon** pastèque *f*; **waterproof** imperméable; **waterside** bord *m* de l'eau; **waterskiing** ski *m* nautique; **watertight** *compartment* étanche; *fig:* alibi parfait; **waterway** voie *f* d'eau; **watery** *soup* trop clair; *coffee* trop léger

watt [wɔːt] watt *m*

wave¹ [weɪv] *n in sea* vague *f*

wave² [weɪv] **1** *n of hand* signe *m* **2** *v/i with hand* saluer; *of flag* flotter **3** *v/t flag etc* agiter

'wavelength RAD longueur *f* d'onde; *be on the same ~ fig* être sur la même longueur d'onde

waver ['weɪvər] hésiter

wavy ['weɪvɪ] ondulé

wax [wæks] cire *f*

way [weɪ] *(method, manner)* façon *f*; *(route)* chemin *m* *(to* de); *this ~ (like this)* comme ça; *(in this direction)* par ici; *by the ~ (incidentally)* au fait; *in a ~ (in certain respects)* d'une certaine façon; *lose one's ~* se perdre; *be in the ~ (be an obstruction)* gêner le passage; *(disturb)* gêner; *no ~!* pas question!; **way in** entrée *f*; **way of life** mode *m* de vie; **way out** sortie *f*; *fig* issue *f*

we [wiː] nous

weak [wiːk] faible; *tea, coffee* léger; **weaken 1** *v/t* affaiblir

2 *v/i* s'affaiblir; *in negotiation etc* faiblir; **weakness** faiblesse *f*

wealth [welθ] richesse *f*; **wealthy** riche

weapon ['wepən] arme *f*

wear [wer] **1** *n:* **~ (and tear)** usure *f* **2** *v/t (have on)* porter; *(damage)* user **3** *v/i (wear out)* s'user; **~ well** *(last)* faire bon usage

◆ **wear down** user

◆ **wear off** *of effect* se dissiper

◆ **wear out 1** *v/t (tire)* épuiser; *shoes, carpet* user **2** *v/i of shoes, carpet* s'user

wearily ['wɪrɪlɪ] avec lassitude; **weary** las

weather ['weðər] **1** *n* temps *m* **2** *v/t crisis* survivre à; **weather-beaten** hâlé; **weather forecast** prévisions météorologiques *fpl*, météo *f*; **weatherman** présentateur *m* météo

weave [wiːv] **1** *v/t cloth* tisser **2** *v/i of cyclist* se faufiler

web [web] *of spider* toile *f*: *the ~* COMPUT le Web; **web page** page *f* de Web; **web site** site *m* Web

wedding ['wedɪŋ] mariage *m*; **wedding anniversary** anniversaire *m* de mariage; **wedding day** jour *m* de mariage; **wedding dress** robe *f* de mariée; **wedding ring** alliance *f*

wedge [wedʒ] *to hold sth in*

place cale *f*; *of cheese etc* morceau *m*

Wednesday ['wenzdeɪ] mercredi *m*

weed [wiːd] **1** *n* mauvaise herbe *f* **2** *v/t* désherber; **weedkiller** herbicide *f*; **weedy** F chétif

week [wiːk] semaine *f*; **a ~ to-morrow** demain en huit; **weekday** *jour m* de la semaine; **weekend** week-end *m*; **on the ~** this one ce week-end; *every one* le week-end; **weekly 1** *adj* hebdomadaire **2** *n magazine* hebdomadaire *m* **3** *adv* **be published** toutes les semaines; **be paid** à la semaine

weep [wiːp] pleurer

wee-wee ['wiːwiː] F pipi *m* F; **do a ~** faire pipi

weigh [weɪ] peser

♦ **weigh up** (*assess*) juger

weight [weɪt] poids *m*; **weightlessness** apesanteur *f*; **weightlifter** haltérophile *m/f*; **weightlifting** haltérophilie *f*; **weighty** *fig* (*important*) sérieux

weir [wɪr] barrage *m*

weird [wɪrd] bizarre; **weirdo** F cinglé(e) *m(f)* F

welcome ['welkəm] **1** *adj* bienvenu; **you're ~!** je vous en prie! **2** *n* accueil *m* **3** *v/t* accueillir; *fig*: *news, announcement* se réjouir de; *opportunity* saisir

weld [weld] souder

welfare ['welfer] bien-être *m*; *financial assistance* sécurité *f* sociale; **be on ~** toucher les allocations; **welfare check** chèque *m* d'allocations; **welfare state** État *m* providence; **welfare worker** assistant social *m*, assistante sociale *f*

well¹ [wel] *for water, oil* puits *m*

well² [wel] **1** *adv* bien; **~ done!** bien!; **as ~** (*too*) aussi; **as ~ as** (*in addition to*) en plus de; **very** acknowledging order entendu; *reluctantly agreeing* très bien; **~, ~!** surprise tiens, tiens!; **~ ...** uncertainty, thinking eh bien ... **2** *adj*: **be ~** aller bien; **well-balanced** équilibré; **well-behaved** bien élevé; **well-being** bien-être *m*; **well-done** *meat* bien cuit; **well-dressed** bien habillé; **well-earned** bien mérité; **well-heeled** F cossu; **well-informed** bien informé; **well-known** connu; **well-meaning** plein de bonnes intentions; **well-off** riche; **well-timed** bien calculé; **well-wisher** personne *f* apportant son soutien

west [west] **1** *n* ouest *m* **2** *adj* ouest *inv*; *wind* d'ouest **3** *adv* *travel* vers l'ouest; **westerly** *wind* d'ouest; *direction* vers l'ouest; **western 1** *adj* de l'Ouest **2** *n movie* western *m*; **Westerner** occidental(e); **westernized** occidentalisé;

West Indian 1 adj antillais **2** n Antillais(e) m(f); **West Indies: the ~** les Antilles fpl; **westward** vers l'ouest

wet [wet] mouillé; (rainy) humide; **wet suit** for diving combinaison f de plongée

whack [wæk] F (blow) coup m

whale [weɪl] baleine f

what [wɑːt] **1** pron ◇ : **~?** quoi?; **~ for?** (why?) pourquoi?; **so ~?** et alors?
◇ as object: **~ did he say?** qu'est-ce qu'il a dit?, **~ is that?** qu'est-ce que c'est?; **~ is it?** (what do you want?) qu'est-ce qu'il y a?
◇ as subject qu'est-ce qui; **~ just fell off?** qu'est-ce qui vient de tomber?
◇ relative as object ce que; **I did ~ I could** j'ai fait ce que j'ai pu
◇ relative as subject ce qui; **I didn't see ~ happened** je n'ai pas vu ce qui s'est passé
◇ suggestions: **~ about heading home?** et si nous rentrions? **2** adj quel, quelle; pl quels, quelles; **~ color is the car?** de quelle couleur est la voiture?

whatever [wɑːt'evər]: **~ the season** quelle que soit la saison; **~ you do** quoi que tu fasses; **ok, ~** F ok, si vous le dites

wheat [wiːt] blé m

wheel [wiːl] roue f; (steering ~) volant m; **wheelchair** fau-

teuil m roulant; **wheel clamp** Br sabot m de Denver

wheeze [wiːz] respirer péniblement

when [wen] quand; **on the day ~** le jour où; **whenever** each time chaque fois que; regardless of when n'importe quand

where [wer] où; **~ from? d'où?; ~ I used to live** c'est là que j'habitais; whereas tandis que; **wherever 1** conj partout où; **sit ~ you like** assieds-toi où tu veux **2** adv où (donc); **~ can it be?** où peut-il bien être?

whet [wet] appetite aiguiser

whether ['weðər] (if) si; **~ you approve or not** que tu sois (subj) d'accord ou pas

which [wɪtʃ] **1** adj quel, quelle; pl quels, quelles **2** pron ◇ interrogative lequel, laquelle; pl lesquels, lesquelles; **~ are your favorites?** lesquels préférez-vous?
◇ relative: subject qui; object que; after prep lequel, laquelle; pl lesquels, lesquelles

whiff [wɪf]: **catch a ~ of** sentir

while [waɪl] **1** conj pendant que; (although) bien que (+subj) **2** n: **a long ~** longtemps; **for a ~** pendant un moment

whim [wɪm] caprice m

whimper ['wɪmpər] pleurnicher; of animal geindre

whine [waɪn] *of dog etc* gémir; F (*complain*) pleurnicher

whip [wɪp] **1** *n* fouet **m 2** *v/t* (*beat*) fouetter; *cream* battre; F (*defeat*) battre à plates coutures

whirlpool ['wɜːrlpuːl] *in river* tourbillon *m*; *for relaxation* bain *m* à remous

whisk [wɪsk] **1** *n* fouet **m 2** *v/t eggs* battre

whiskey ['wɪskɪ] whisky *m*

whisper ['wɪspər] chuchoter

whistle ['wɪsl] **1** *n sound* sifflement *m*; *device* sifflet *m* **2** *v/t* & *v/i* siffler

white [waɪt] **1** *n color, of egg* blanc *m*; *person* Blanc *m*, Blanche *f* **2** *adj* blanc; **white-collar worker** col *m* blanc; **White House** Maison *f* Blanche; **white lie** pieux mensonge *m*; **whitewash 1** *n* blanc *m* de chaux; *fig* maquillage *m* de la vérité **2** *v/t* blanchir à la chaux; **white wine** vin *m* blanc

whittle ['wɪtl] *wood* tailler au couteau

◆ **whittle down** réduire

whizzkid ['wɪzkɪd] F prodige *m*

who [huː] *interrogative* qui; *relative: subject* qui; *object* que; **the woman ~ you saw** la femme que tu as vue; **whoever** qui que ce soit; ~ **gets the right answer** celui/celle qui trouve la bonne réponse

whole [houl] **1** *adj* entier; **the ~ town** toute la ville **2** *n* tout *m*, ensemble *m*; **on the ~** dans l'ensemble); **whole-hearted** inconditionnel; **wholesale** de gros; *fig* en masse; **wholesaler** grossiste *m/f*; **wholesome** sain; **wholly** totalement

whom [huːm] *fml* qui

whore [hɔːr] putain *f*

whose [huːz] *interrogative* à qui; *relative* dont; ~ **is this?** à qui c'est?; **a country's economy is booming** un pays dont l'économie prospère

why [waɪ] pourquoi

wicked ['wɪkɪd] méchant

wicker ['wɪkər] osier *m*

wicket ['wɪkɪt] *in station, bank etc* guichet *m*

wide [waɪd] *street, field* large; *experience* vaste; **be 12 foot ~** faire 3 mètres et demi de large; **widely** largement; ~ **known** très connu; **widen 1** *v/t* élargir **2** *v/i* s'élargir; **wide-open** grand ouvert; **wide-ranging** de vaste portée; **widespread** répandu

widow ['wɪdou] veuve *f*; **widower** veuf *m*

width [wɪdθ] largeur *f*

wield [wiːld] *weapon* manier; *power* exercer

wife [waɪf] femme *f*

wig [wɪg] perruque *f*

wiggle ['wɪgl] *tooth etc* remuer; *hips* tortiller

winter sports

wild [waɪld] **1** *adj animal, flowers* sauvage; *teenager* rebelle; *party* fou; *scheme* délirant; *applause* frénétique

wilderness ['wɪldərnɪs] désert *m*

wildlife faune *f* et flore *f*

wilful *Br* → **willful**

will¹ [wɪl] *n* LAW testament *m*

will² [wɪl] *n* (*willpower*) volonté *f*

will³ [wɪl] *v/aux:* **I ~ let you know tomorrow** je vous le dirai demain; **the car won't start** la voiture ne veut pas démarrer; **~ you tell her that ...?** est-ce que tu pourrais lui dire que ...?; **~ you stop that!** veux-tu arrêter!

willful ['wɪlfl] *person, refusal* volontaire; **willing** *helper* de bonne volonté; **be ~ to do sth** être prêt à faire qch; **willingly** (*with pleasure*) volontiers; **willingness** empressement *m*; **willpower** volonté *f*

willy-nilly [wɪlɪ'nɪlɪ] (*at random*) au petit bonheur la chance

wilt [wɪlt] *of plant* se faner

wily ['waɪlɪ] rusé

wimp [wɪmp] F poule *f* mouillée

win [wɪn] **1** *n* victoire *f* **2** *v/t & v/i* gagner; *prize* remporter

wince [wɪns] tressaillir

wind¹ [wɪnd] *n* vent *m*; (*flatulence*) gaz *m*

wind² [waɪnd] **1** *v/i of path,*

river serpenter **2** *v/t* enrouler

◆ **wind up** **1** *v/t clock, car window* remonter; *speech* terminer; *affairs* conclure; *company* liquider **2** *v/i* (*finish*) finir

wind-bag F moulin *m* à paroles F; **windfall** *fig* aubaine *f*

winding ['waɪndɪŋ] *path* qui serpente

window ['wɪndoʊ] *also* COMPUTER fenêtre *f*; *of airplane, boat* hublot *m*; *of store* vitrine *f*; **in the ~** *of store* dans la vitrine; **window seat** *on train* place *f* côté fenêtre; *on airplane* place côté hublot; **window-shop**: **go ~ping** faire du lèche-vitrines; **windowsill** rebord *m* de fenêtre; **windshield**, *Br* **windscreen** pare-brise *m*; **windshield wiper** essuie-glace *m*; **windsurfer** véliplanchiste *m/f*; **windsurfing** planche *f* à voile; **windy** venteux; **it's so ~** il y a tellement de vent

wine [waɪn] vin *m*; **wine cellar** cave *f* (à vin); **wine list** carte *f* des vins; **winery** établissement *m* viticole

wing [wɪŋ] *of bird, airplane*, SP aile *f*; **wingspan** envergure *f*

wink [wɪŋk] *of person* cligner des yeux

winner ['wɪnər] gagnant(e) *m(f)*; **winning** gagnant; **winning post** poteau *m* d'arrivée; **winnings** gains *mpl*

winter ['wɪntər] hiver *m*; **win-**

ter sports sports *mpl* d'hiver; **wintry** d'hiver

wipe [waɪp] essuyer; *tape* effacer; **wiper** ['waɪpər] → **windshield wiper**

wire [waɪr] fil *m* de fer; *electrical* fil *m* électrique; **wireless phone** téléphone *m* sans fil; **wiring** ELEC installation *f* électrique; **wiry** *person* nerveux

wisdom ['wɪzdəm] sagesse *f*

wise [waɪz] sage; **wisecrack** F vanne *f* F; **wisely** *act* sagement

wish [wɪʃ] **1** *n* vœu *m*; *best* **~es** cordialement; *for birthday, Christmas* meilleurs vœux **2** *v/t* souhaiter

◆ **wish for** vouloir

wisp [wɪsp] *of hair* mèche *f*; *of smoke* traînée *f*

wistful ['wɪstfl] nostalgique; **wistfully** avec nostalgie

wit [wɪt] (*humor*) esprit *m*; *person* homme *m*/femme *f* d'esprit

witch [wɪtʃ] sorcière *f*; **witch-hunt** *fig* chasse *f* aux sorcières

with [wɪð] avec; **~ no money** sans argent; *tired* **~ waiting** fatigué d'attendre; *the woman* **~ blue eyes** la femme aux yeux bleus; *I live* **~ my aunt** je vis chez ma tante; *are you* **~ me?** (*do you understand*) est-ce que vous me suivez?

withdraw [wɪð'drɔː] **1** *v/t* reti-

rer **2** *v/i* se retire; **withdrawal** retrait *m*; **withdrawal symptoms** (symptômes *mpl* de) manque *m*; **withdrawn** *person* renfermé

wither ['wɪðər] se faner

withhold *information, name, payment* retenir; *consent* refuser

within (*inside*) dans; *in expressions of time* en moins de; *in expressions of distance* à moins de

without sans

withstand résister à

witness ['wɪtnɪs] **1** *n* témoin *m* **2** *v/t* être témoin de

witticism ['wɪtɪsɪzm] mot *m* d'esprit; **witty** plein d'esprit

wobble ['wɑːbl] osciller; **wobbly** bancal

wolf [wʊlf] **1** *n* loup *m* **2** *v/t*: **~ (down)** engloutir

woman ['wʊmən] femme *f*; **womanizer** coureur *m* de femmes; **womanly** féminin

womb [wuːm] utérus *m*

women ['wɪmɪn] *pl* → **woman**; **women's lib** libération *f* des femmes

wonder ['wʌndər] **1** *n* (*amazement*) émerveillement *m*; *no* **~!** pas étonnant! **2** *v/i* se poser des questions; *I* **~ if you could help** je me demandais si vous pouviez m'aider; **wonderful** merveilleux; **wonderfully** (*extremely*) merveilleusement

won't [woʊnt] → **will not**

wood [wʊd] bois *m*; **wooded** boisé; **wooden** *(made of wood)* en bois; **woodpecker** pic *m*; **woodwork** *parts made of wood* charpente *f*; *activity* menuiserie *f*

wool [wʊl] laine *f*; **woolen,** *Br* **woollen 1** *adj* en laine **2** *n* lainage *m*

word [wɜːrd] **1** *n* mot *m*; *of song,* *(promise)* parole *f* **2** *v/t* *article, letter* formuler; **word processor** traitement *m* de texte

work [wɜːrk] **1** *n* travail *m*; **out of ~** au chômage **2** *v/i of person* travailler; *of machine,* *(succeed)* marcher

◆ **work out 1** *v/t solution,* *(find out)* trouver; *problem* résoudre **2** *v/i at gym* s'entraîner; *of relationship etc* bien marcher

workable ['wɜːrkəbl] *solution* possible; **workaholic** F bourreau *m* de travail; **workday** *(hours of work)* journée *f* de travail; *(not weekend)* jour *m* de travail; **worker** travailleur(-euse) *m(f)*; **workforce** main-d'œuvre *f*; **work hours** heures *fpl* de travail; **working class** classe *f* ouvrière; **working-class** *adj* ouvrier; **working hours = work hours**; **workload** quantité *f* de travail; **workman** ouvrier *m*; **workmanlike** *adj* professionnel; **workmanship** fabrication *f*; **work**

of art œuvre *f* d'art; **workout** séance *f* d'entraînement; **work permit** permis *m* de travail; **workshop** *also seminar* atelier *m*

world [wɜːrld] monde *m*; **world-class** de niveau mondial; **World Cup** *in soccer* Coupe *f* du monde; **world-famous** mondialement connu; **worldly** du monde; *person* qui a l'expérience du monde; **world record** record *m* mondial; **world war** guerre *f* mondiale; **worldwide 1** *adj* mondial **2** *adv* dans le monde entier

worn-out *shoes, carpet* trop usé; *person* éreinté

worried ['wʌrɪd] inquiet; **worry 1** *n* souci *m* **2** *v/t* inquiéter **3** *v/i* s'inquiéter; **worrying** inquiétant

worse [wɜːrs] **1** *adj* pire **2** *adv play, perform, feel* plus mal; **worsen** empirer

worship ['wɜːrʃɪp] **1** *n* culte *m* **2** *v/t God* honorer; *fig: person, money* vénérer

worst [wɜːrst] **1** *adj* pire **2** *adv:* **the areas ~ affected** les régions les plus (gravement) touchées

worth [wɜːrθ]: **be ~ ...** valoir; **be ~ it** valoir la peine; **worthwhile**: **it's not ~ waiting** cela ne vaut pas la peine d'attendre

worthy ['wɜːrðɪ] *person, cause* digne

would [wʊd]: *I ~ help if I could* je vous aiderais si je pouvais; *~ you like to go to the movies?* est-ce que tu voudrais aller au cinéma?; *~ you tell her ...?* pourriez--vous lui dire que ...?
wound [wuːnd] **1** *n* blessure *f* **2** *v/t* with weapon, words blesser
wow [waʊ] *int* oh là là!
wrap [ræp] gift envelopper; scarf etc enrouler; **wrapping paper** papier *m* d'emballage
wrath [ræθ] colère *f*
wreath [riːθ] couronne *f*
wreck [rek] **1** *n* of ship navire *m* naufragé; of car épave *f* **2** *v/t* détruire; **wreckage** of ship épave *m*; of airplane débris *mpl*; of marriage, career restes *mpl*; **wrecker** truck dépanneuse *f*
wrench [rentʃ] **1** *n* tool clef *f* **2** *v/t* (pull) arracher
wrestle ['resl] lutter; **wrestler** lutteur(-euse) *m(f)*; **wrestling** lutte *f*
wriggle ['rɪgl] (squirm) se tortiller

wrinkle ['rɪŋkl] in skin ride *f*; in clothes pli *m*
wrist [rɪst] poignet *m*; **wristwatch** montre *f*
write [raɪt] écrire; check faire
◆ **write off** debt amortir; car bousiller *f*
writer ['raɪtər] of letter, book, song auteur *m/f*; of book écrivain *m/f*; **write-up** critique *f*
writhe [raɪð] se tordre
writing ['raɪtɪŋ] (handwriting, script) écriture *f*; (words) inscription *f*; *in ~* par écrit; **writing paper** papier *m* à lettres
wrong [rɒŋ] **1** *adj* information, decision, side, number mauvais; answer also faux; *be ~* of person avoir tort; of answer être mauvais; morally être mal; *get the ~ train* se tromper de train; *what's ~?* qu'est-ce qu'il y a? **2** *adv* mal; *go ~* of person se tromper; of marriage, plan etc mal tourner **3** *n* mal *m*; injustice injustice *f*; **wrongful** injuste; **wrongly** à tort
wry [raɪ] ironique

X, Y

xenophobia [zenəʊ'fəʊbɪə] xénophobie *f*
X-ray ['eksreɪ] **1** *n* radio *f* **2** *v/t* radiographier
yacht [jɒt] yacht *m*; **yachting**

voile *f*
Yank [jæŋk] F Ricain(e) *m(f)* F
yank [jæŋk] *v/t* tirer violemment

yard¹ [jɑːrd] *of prison etc* cour f; *behind house* jardin m; *for storage* dépôt m

yard² [jɑːrd] *measurement* yard m

'yardstick point m de référence

yarn [jɑːrn] *(thread)* fil m; F *(story)* (longue) histoire f

yawn [jɔːn] **1** n bâillement m **2** v/i bâiller

year [jɪr] année f; *be six ~s old* avoir six ans; **yearly 1** adj annuel **2** adv tous les ans

yeast [jiːst] levure f

yell [jel] **1** n hurlement m **2** v/t & v/i hurler

yellow ['jeloʊ] jaune

yelp [jelp] **1** n *of animal* jappement m; *of person* glapissement m **2** v/i *of animal* japper; *of person* glapir

yes [jes] oui; *after negative question* si; **yes man** pej béni-oui-oui m F

yesterday ['jestərdeɪ] hier; *the day before ~* avant-hier

yet [jet] **1** adv: *the best ~* le meilleur jusqu'ici; *as ~* pour le moment; *have you finished ~?* as-tu (déjà) fini?; *he hasn't arrived ~* il n'est pas encore arrivé; *~ bigger* encore plus grand **2** conj *(however)* néanmoins

yield [jiːld] **1** n *from crops, investment etc* rendement m **2** v/t *fruit, good harvest* produire; *interest* rapporter **3** v/i *(give way)* céder; AUT céder

la priorité

yoga ['joʊgə] yoga m

yoghurt ['joʊgərt] yaourt m

yolk [joʊk] jaune m (d'œuf)

you [juː] ◊ *familiar singular: subject* tu; *object* te; *before vowel* t'; *after prep* toi; *he knows ~* il te connaît; *for ~* pour toi

◊ *polite singular, familiar plural and polite plural, all uses* vous

◊ *indefinite* on: *~ never know* on ne sait jamais

young [jʌŋ] jeune; **youngster** jeune m/f; *child* petit(e) m(f)

your [jʊr] *familiar* ton, ta; *pl* tes; *polite* votre; *pl familiar and polite* vos

yours [jʊrz] *familiar* le tien, la tienne; *pl* les tiens, les tiennes; *polite* le/la vôtre; *pl* les vôtres; *a friend of ~* un(e) de tes ami(e)s; un(e) de vos ami(e)s; *~ at end of letter* bien amicalement

your'self *familiar* toi-même; *polite* vous-même; *reflexive* te; *polite* se; *after prep* toi; *polite* vous; *did you hurt ~?* est-ce que tu t'es fait mal/ est-ce que vous vous êtes fait mal?

your'selves vous-mêmes; *reflexive* vous; *after prep* vous; *did you hurt ~?* est-ce que vous vous êtes fait mal?

youth [juːθ] jeunesse f; *(young man)* jeune homme m; *(young people)* jeunes

mpl; **youth club** centre *m* pour les jeunes; **youthful ju**-

vénile
yuppie ['jʌpɪ] F yuppie *m/f*

Z

zap [zæp] F COMPUT (*delete*) effacer; (*kill*) éliminer; (*hit*) donner un coup à; (*send*) envoyer vite fait
zeal [ziːl] zèle *m*
zero ['zɪrou] zéro *m*
zest [zest] *enjoyment* enthousiasme *m*
zigzag ['zɪgzæg] **1** *n* zigzag *m* **2** *v/i* zigzaguer
zilch [zɪltʃ] F que dalle F
zip ['zɪp] *Br* fermeture *f* éclair
◆ **zip up** *dress, jacket* remonter la fermeture éclair de;

COMPUT compresser
'zip code code *m* postal; **zipper** fermeture *f* éclair
zit [zɪt] F *on face* bouton *m*
zone [zoun] zone *f*
zonked [zɑːŋkt] P (*exhausted*) crevé F
zoo [zuː] jardin *m* zoologique
zoology [zuːˈɑːlədʒɪ] zoologie *f*
'zoom lens zoom *m*
zucchini [zuːˈkiːnɪ] courgette *f*

Verbes irréguliers anglais

Vous trouverez ci-après les trois formes principales de chaque verbe : l'infinitif, le prétérit et le participe passé.

arise - arose - arisen

awake - awoke - awoken, awaked

be (am, is, are) - was (were) - been

bear - bore - borne

beat - beat - beaten

become - became - become

begin - began - begun

bend - bent - bent

bet - bet, betted - bet, betted

bid - bid - bid

bind - bound - bound

bite - bit - bitten

bleed - bled - bled

blow - blew - blown

break - broke - broken

breed - bred - bred

bring - brought - brought

broadcast - broadcast - broadcast

build - built - built

burn - burnt, burned - burnt, burned

burst - burst - burst

buy - bought - bought

cast - cast - cast

catch - caught - caught

choose - chose - chosen

cling - clung - clung

come - came - come

cost (*v/i*) - cost - cost

creep - crept - crept

cut - cut - cut

deal - dealt - dealt

dig - dug - dug

dive - dived, dove [dʊv] (1) - dived

do - did - done

draw - drew - drawn

dream - dreamt, dreamed - dreamt, dreamed

drink - drank - drunk

drive - drove - driven

eat - ate - eaten

fall - fell - fallen

feed - fed - fed

feel - felt - felt

fight - fought - fought

find - found - found

flee - fled - fled

fling - flung - flung

fly - flew - flown

forbid - forbad(e) - forbidden

forecast - forecast(ed) - forecast(ed)

forget - forgot - forgotten

forgive - forgave - forgiven

freeze - froze - frozen

get - got - got, gotten (2)

give - gave - given

go - went - gone
grind - ground - ground
grow - grew - grown
hang - hung, hanged - hung, hanged (3)
have - had - had
hear - heard - heard
hide - hid - hidden
hit - hit - hit
hold - held - held
hurt - hurt - hurt
keep - kept - kept
kneel - knelt, kneeled - knelt, kneeled
know - knew - known
lay - laid - laid
lead - led - led
lean - leaned, leant - leaned, leant (4)
leap - leaped, leapt - leaped, leapt (4)
learn - learned, learnt - learned, learnt (4)
leave - left - left
lend - lent - lent
let - let - let
lie - lay - lain
light - lighted, lit - lighted, lit
lose - lost - lost
make - made - made
mean - meant - meant
meet - met - met
mow - mowed - mowed, mown

pay - paid - paid
plead - pleaded, pled - pleaded, pled (5)
prove - proved - proved, proven
put - put - put
quit - quit(ted) - quit(ted)
read - read [red] - read [red]
ride - rode - ridden
ring - rang - rung
rise - rose - risen
run - ran - run
saw - sawed - sawn, sawed
say - said - said
see - saw - seen
seek - sought - sought
sell - sold - sold
send - sent - sent
set - set - set
sew - sewed - sewed, sewn
shake - shook - shaken
shed - shed - shed
shine - shone - shone
shit - shit(ted), shat - shit(ted), shat
shoot - shot - shot
show - showed - shown
shrink - shrank - shrunk
shut - shut - shut
sing - sang - sung
sink - sank - sunk
sit - sat - sat
slay - slew - slain
sleep - slept - slept
slide - slid - slid

573

sling - slung - slung
slit - slit - slit
smell - smelt, smelled - smelt, smelled
sow - sowed - sown, sowed
speak - spoke - spoken
speed - sped, speeded - sped, speeded
spell - spelt, spelled - spelt, spelled (4)
spend - spent - spent
spill - spilt, spilled - spilt, spilled
spin - spun - spun
spit - spat - spat
split - split - split
spoil - spoiled, spoilt - spoiled, spoilt
spread - spread - spread
spring - sprang, sprung - sprung
stand - stood - stood
steal - stole - stolen
stick - stuck - stuck
sting - stung - stung
stink - stunk, stank - stunk

stride - strode - stridden
strike - struck - struck
swear - swore - sworn
sweep - swept - swept
swell - swelled - swollen
swim - swam - swum
swing - swung - swung
take - took - taken
teach - taught - taught
tear - tore - torn
tell - told - told
think - thought - thought
thrive - throve - thriven, thrived (6)
throw - threw - thrown
thrust - thrust - thrust
tread - trod - trodden
wake - woke, waked - woken, waked
wear - wore - worn
weave - wove - woven (7)
weep - wept - wept
win - won - won
wind - wound - wound
write - wrote - written

(1) **dove** n'est pas utilisé en anglais britannique
(2) **gotten** n'est pas utilisé en anglais britannique
(3) **hung** pour les tableaux mais **hanged** pour les meurtriers
(4) l'anglais américain n'emploie normalement que la forme en **-ed**
(5) **pled** s'emploie en anglais américain ou écossais
(6) la forme **thrived** est plus courante
(7) mais **weaved** au sens de *se faufiler*

Numbers / Les nombres

Cardinal Numbers / Les nombres cardinaux

0	nought *zero*; *BrE also* zero, *BrE* zéro	14	fourteen *quatorze*
1	one *un*	15	fifteen *quinze*
2	two *deux*	16	sixteen *seize*
3	three *trois*	17	seventeen *dix-sept*
4	four *quatre*	18	eighteen *dix-huit*
5	five *cinq*	19	nineteen *dix-neuf*
6	six *six*	20	twenty *vingt*
7	seven *sept*	21	twenty-one *vingt et un*
8	eight *huit*	22	twenty-two *vingt-deux*
9	nine *neuf*	30	thirty *trente*
10	ten *dix*	31	thirty-one *trente et un*
11	eleven *onze*	40	forty *quarante*
12	twelve *douze*	50	fifty *cinquante*
13	thirteen *treize*	60	sixty *soixante*
		70	seventy *soixante-dix*

71	seventy-one *soixante et onze*
72	seventy-two *soixante-douze*
79	seventy-nine *soixante-dix-neuf*
80	eighty *quatre-vingts*
81	eighty-one *quatre-vingt-un*
90	ninety *quatre-vingt-dix*
91	ninety-one *quatre-vingt-onze*
100	a hundred *cent*
101	a hundred and one *cent un*
200	two hundred *deux cents*
300	three hundred *trois cents*
324	three hundred and twenty-four *trois cent vingt-quatre*
1000	a thousand, one thousand *mille*
2000	two thousand *deux mille*

1959	one thousand nine hundred and fifty-nine	*mille neuf cent cinquante-neuf*
2000	two thousand	*deux mille*
1 000 000	a million, one million	*un million*
2 000 000	two million	*deux millions*
1 000 000 000	a billion, one billion	*un milliard*

Notes / Remarques:

(i) **vingt** and **cent** take an **-s** when preceded by another number, except if there is another number following.

(ii) **un** If **un** is used with a following noun, then it is the only number to agree
(one man **un homme**; one woman **une femme**).

(iii) 1.25 (one point two five) = 1,25 (un virgule vingt-cinq)

(iv) 1,000,000 (en anglais) = 1 000 000 = 1.000.000 (in French)

Ordinal Numbers / Les nombres ordinaux

1st first	1er/1ère	*premier / première*	
2nd second	2e	*deuxième*	
3rd third	3e	*troisième*	
4th fourth	4e	*quatrième*	
5th fifth	5e	*cinquième*	
6th sixth	6e	*sixième*	
7th seventh	7e	*septième*	
8th eighth	8e	*huitième*	
9th ninth	9e	*neuvième*	
10th tenth	10e	*dixième*	
11th eleventh	11e	*onzième*	
12th twelfth	12e	*douzième*	
13th thirteenth	13e	*treizième*	
14th fourteenth	14e	*quatorzième*	
15th fifteenth	15e	*quinzième*	

16th sixteenth	seizième	16e
17th seventeenth	dix-septième	17e
18th eighteenth	dix-huitième	18e
19th nineteenth	dix-neuvième	19e
20th twentieth	vingtième	20e
21st twenty-first	vingt et unième	21e
22nd twenty-second	vingt-deuxième	22e
30th thirtieth	trentième	30e
31st thirty-first	trente et unième	31e
40th fortieth	quarantième	40e
50th fiftieth	cinquantième	50e
60th sixtieth	soixantième	60e
70th seventieth	soixante-dixième	70e
71st seventy-first	soixante et onzième	71e
80th eightieth	quatre-vingtième	80e
90th ninetieth	quatre-vingt-dixième	90e
100th hundredth	centième	100e
101st hundred and first	cent unième	101e
10000th thousandth	millième	1000e
200000th two thousandth	deux millième	2000e
1,000,000th millionth	millionième	1 000 000e

Dates / Les dates

1996 nineteen ninety-six	mille neuf cent quatre-vingt-seize	
2005 two thousand (and) five	deux mille cinq	

November 10/11 (ten, eleven), *Br* the 10th/11th of November
le dix-onze novembre

March 1 (first), *Br* the 1st of March
le premier mars

French Pronunciation

Vowel			
a	[a]	valise, déjà	a short sound as in cat, and
	[ɑ]	bas	as in car, mask
		pâte	slightly more closed and drawn out as in pasture, vase
ai	[ɛ]	j'ai	as in make, day
	[e]	bébé, exprès	as in plenty, pest
au	[o]	faux, chaud	as in potato
	[ɔ]	Paul	similar to the vowel sound in hot, short
e	[e]	été, arriver	a slightly softer version of day, short
	[ə]	rendez-vous cher, après	like the vowel sound in pet, send say
	[ə]	le, que fenêtre, mère	as in the, a
ei	[ɛ]	peine	like the vowel sound in pet, send
ei	[ɛ]	éteindre	as in hand
eil	[ɛj]	bouteille, pareil	as in day, say
eau	[o]	bateau	as in tomato, potato
eu	[ø]	feu	similar to the articles the, a but slightly more drawn out
	[œ]	fleur	as in curtain, bird
i	[i]	cri	as in me, see
		dire	as in pier, clear
o	[o]	pot, hôtel	as in tomato, potato
	[ɔ]	fort	as in law, paw
eu	[ø]	nœud	similar to the articles the, a but slightly more drawn out
œu	[œ]	œuf	more drawn out when followed by a consonant as in turn

Semi vowels

ieu	[jø]	adieu	like the byeu sound in beautiful
oi	[wa]	choisir	pronounced wa as in wagon
oui	[wi]	oui	as in we
ui	[ɥi]	suite, fuir	no real equivalent in English – the closest would be we with the w pronounced with pursed lips

Nasal vowels

In the nasal sound, the air escapes through the nose as well as the mouth, like the **ng** sound in English:

an	[ɑ̃]	chambre, chanter, membre, entente
in	[ɛ̃]	cinq, timbre, train, éteindre, nymphe
on	[ɔ̃]	bombe, fond
un	[œ̃]	un, humble

Consonant

c	[k]	calcul	a hard vowel sound as in coffee, cat
	[s]	citron	like the s in sing
ç	[s]	façon	like the s in pasta
ch	[ʃ]	chercher	depending on the word, this is normally pronounced sh as in sugar, shoe

ou	[u]	goût, soupe	as in to
u	[y]	sûr, mur	no real equivalent in English – the closest would be the blue, menu. To make the sound, purse your lips tightly and try saying 'ee', keeping your lips pursed.